Hand-Dyeing
TISSUE PAPER

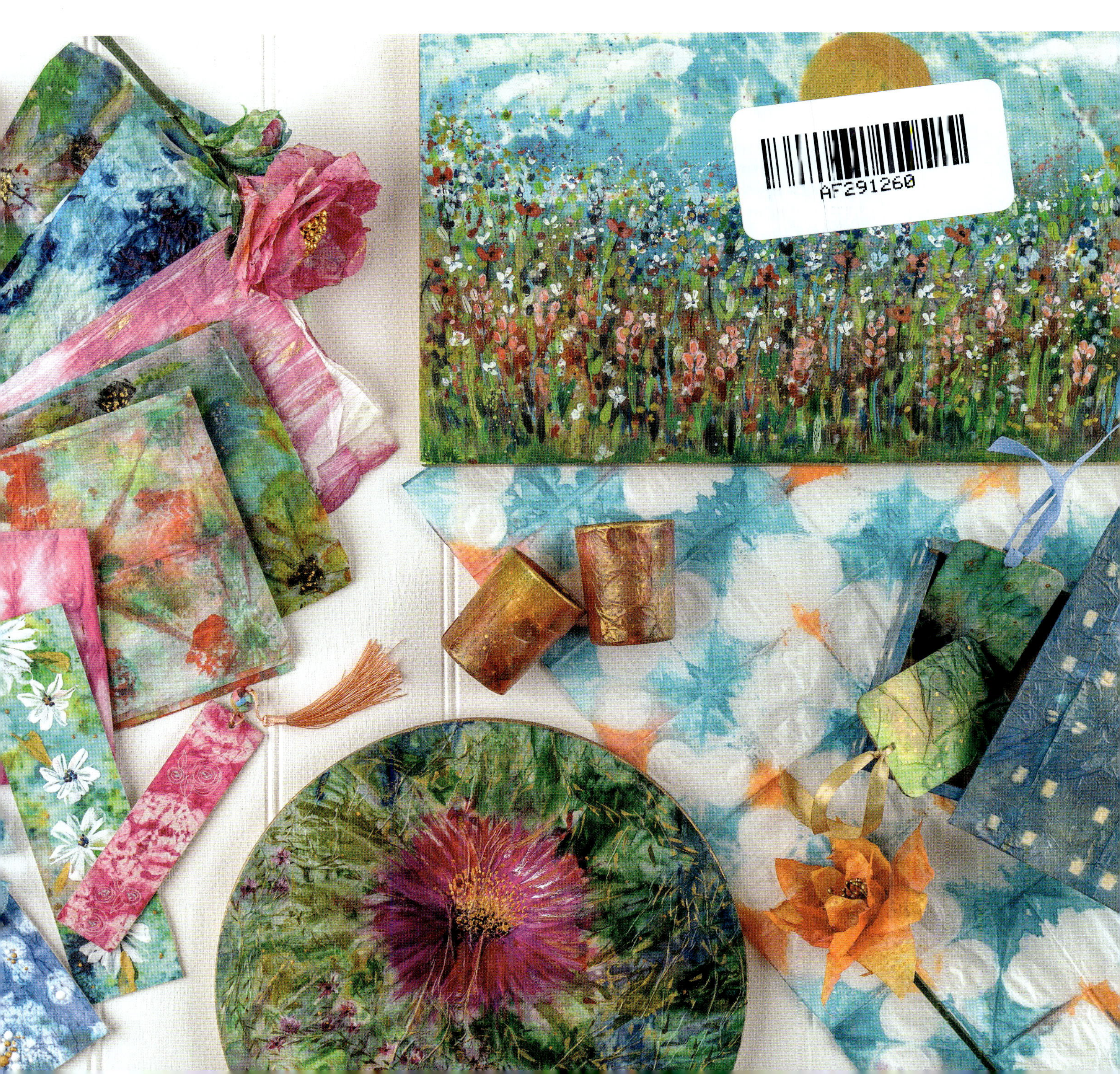

First published in 2026
Search Press Limited
Wellwood, North Farm Road,
Tunbridge Wells, Kent TN2 3DR

1 2 3 4 5 6 7 8 9 10

Text copyright © Search Press Ltd. 2026
Photographs on pages 1, 4–7, 10 (left),
66–67, 69, 77, 84–85, 93, 97, 99, 103, 111
(top right), 113, 121, 127, 133, 138–141
by Mark Davison at Search Press Studios.
All other photographs by the author.
Photographs and design copyright ©
Search Press Ltd. 2026

ISBN: 978-1-80092-325-6
ebook ISBN: 978-1-80093-312-5

Bookmarked Hub
An extra project is available to download
free from the Bookmarked Hub. Search for
this book by title or ISBN: the files can be
found under 'Book Extras'. Membership of
the Bookmarked online community is free:
www.bookmarkedhub.com

Publishers' notes
Metric measurements are used in this book;
the imperial conversions are rounded to the
nearest ¼in. Always use either metric or
imperial measurements, not a combination
of both.

The Publishers and author can accept no
responsibility for any consequences arising
from the information, advice or instructions
given in this publication.

For errata, please visit our website
(www.searchpress.com) or the Bookmarked
Hub (www.bookmarkedhub.com).

GPSR information can be found at
www.searchpress.com
Printed in China, AP012026

You are invited to visit the author's:

Website www.gillbarrettart.co.uk
Facebook @Gillian Barrett
Instagram @gillieb60
Please share your projects using
#gbhanddyedprojects

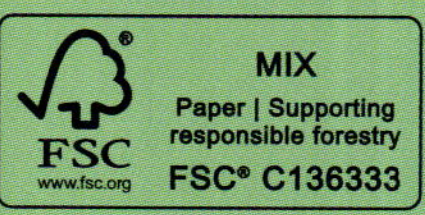

ACKNOWLEDGEMENTS

Many thanks to the amazing Search Press team, including Sam,
Lyndsey, Emma and Becky, who have been a dedicated and
inspirational publishing team to work with, guiding me through the
whole process of producing my first book. They understood my
vision from the first planning meeting and helped me to achieve
exactly the style and layout of the book I had imagined. I really
enjoyed the whole process, and I will be forever grateful for this
exciting opportunity.

To my readers, I really hope you fall in love with dyeing tissue paper
and enjoy this part of your creative journey. Who knows where it
might take you?

My thanks to Niki at Carnival Papers who has kindly provided some
wet-strength tissue paper for me to use for projects in this book.
This excellent product is available through their website at:
www.carnivalpapers.com

Many thanks to Tracey at J&T Blackman Ltd for kindly providing
some Zest-It® Brushable wax resist paste for me to use in my
projects. This excellent product is available through these stockists:
www.zest-it.com/stockist.htm

To my Instagram followers: thank you for your positive words and
encouragement which have helped me to push the boundaries
of my creativity. The Instagram community has been a source of
endless inspiration, friendship and connection.

Hand-Dyeing
TISSUE PAPER

10 techniques and 10 creative projects

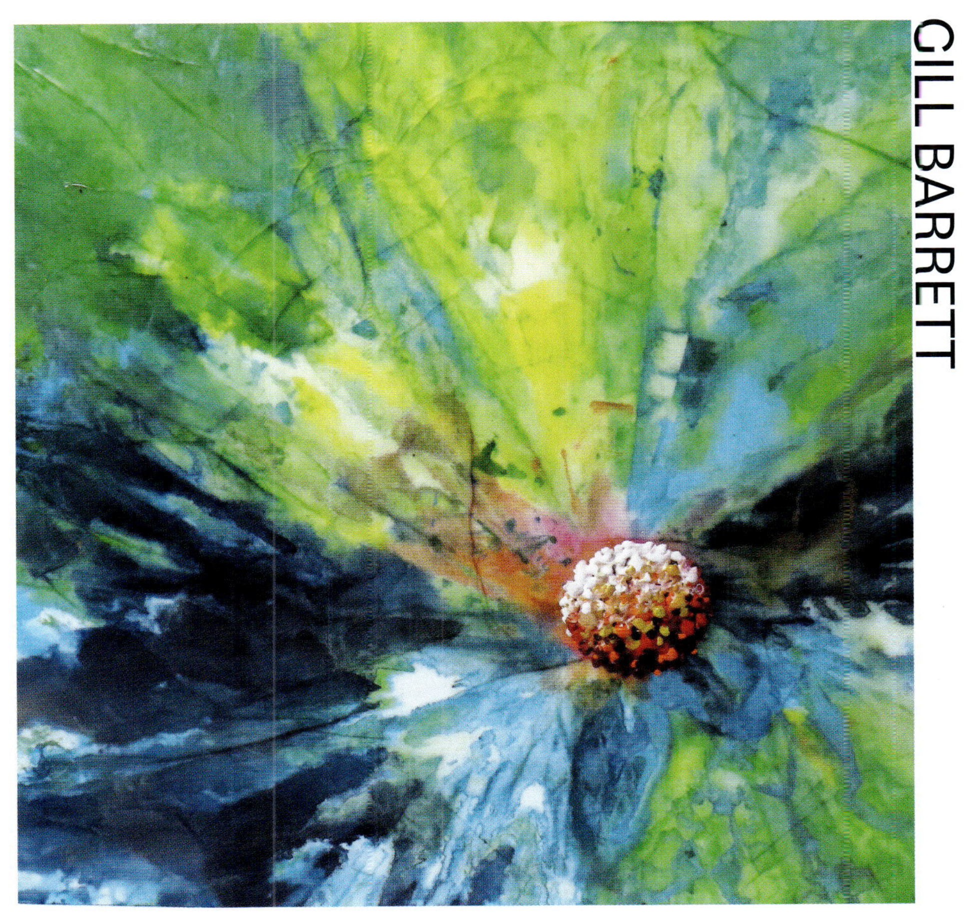

GILL BARRETT

SEARCH PRESS

Contents

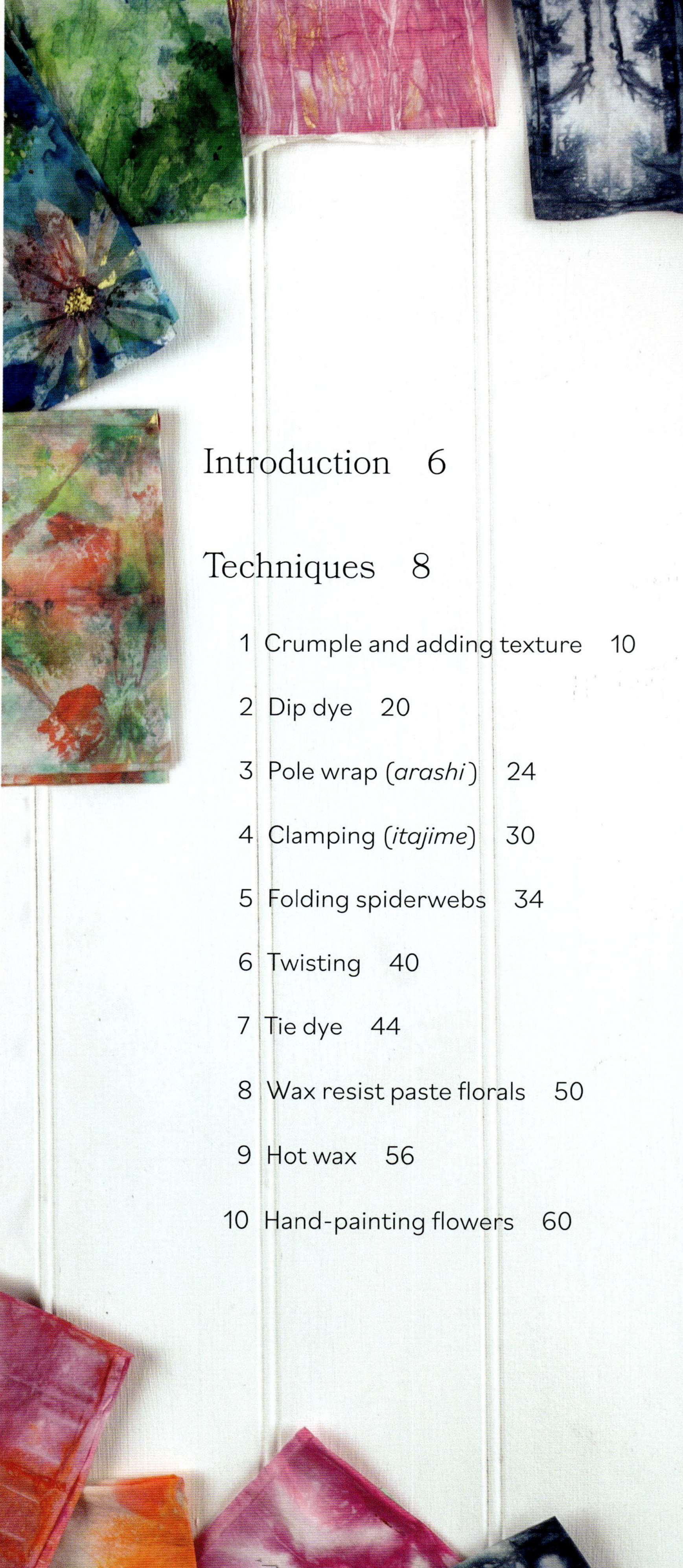

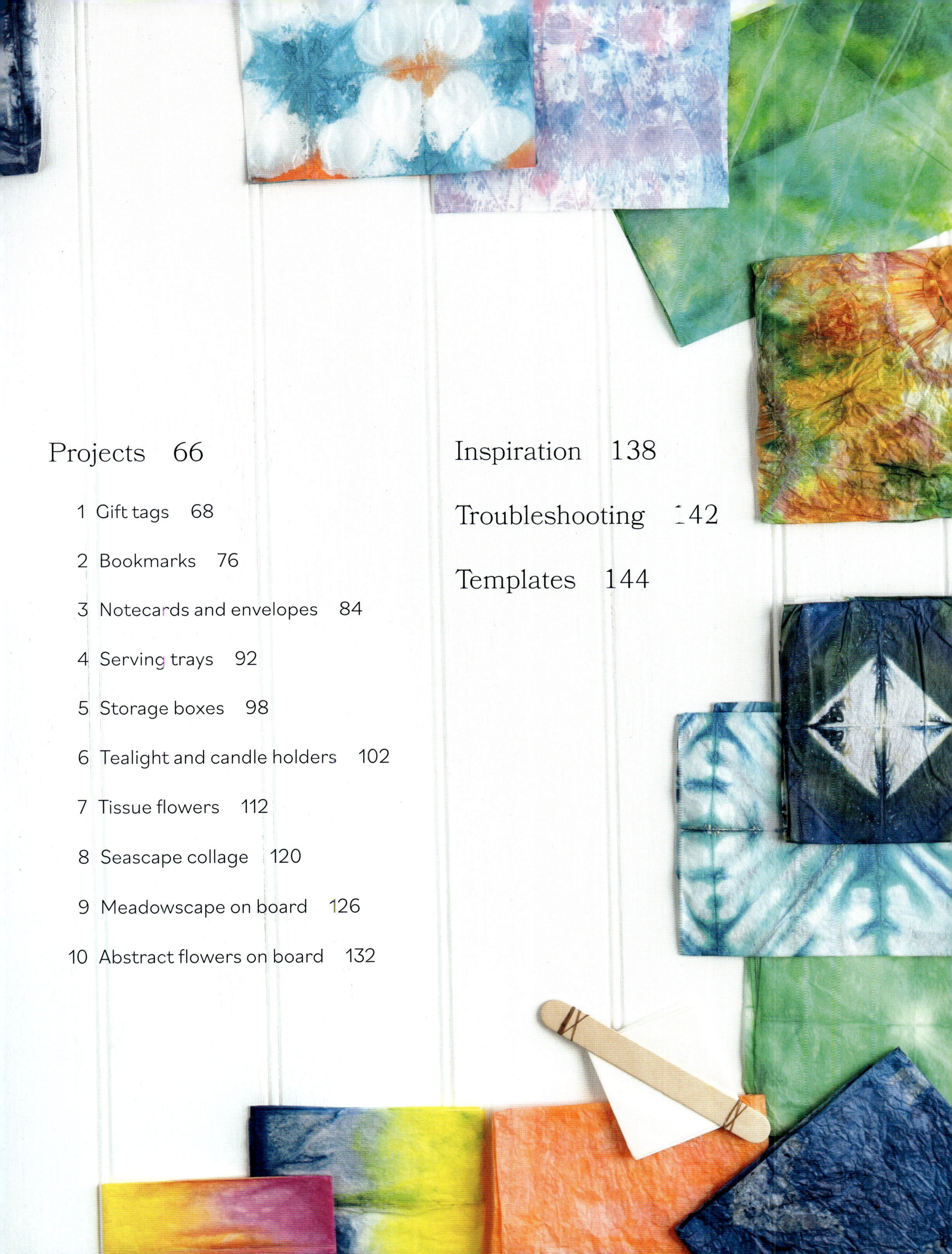

Introduction

Welcome to my vibrant world of hand-dyeing tissue paper.

I have always loved creating vibrant floral artwork and when I realized that something as simple as white tissue paper could easily be transformed into beautiful textures and incredible, organic designs to incorporate into my art, I was intrigued by the possibilities this offered.

I have been able to successfully transfer traditional Japanese *shibori* clamping, folding, wrapping and tie-dye techniques, usually used on fabric, for use on wet-strength tissue paper. I have also applied other techniques such as wax resist and direct painting to create a wide variety of incredible designs on tissue paper.

Having discovered the versatility of tissue paper in art and craft projects, I wanted to share my passion and expertise with others, by writing this comprehensive step-by-step guide to inspire you to explore this creative process.

I want to share with you the delight of carefully unfolding specially prepared and dyed tissue paper to reveal the organic blooms of merged inks, the unique splatters of dripped ink, the symmetry of undulating lines and the variable inky washes of resist patterns.

Experiment with different colours, techniques and patterns to create your own unique hand-dyed tissue paper that you can use for many projects. Enjoy the process of hand-dyeing your tissue paper and adding a personalized touch to your projects! Be warned: creating your own hand-dyed tissue paper is very addictive, because the design options are endless!

Whether you are a beginner or a more experienced crafter or artist, I will guide you through the processes involved in dyeing your tissue paper, explain the materials and equipment needed, as well as provide inspiration for applying the tissue paper in many creative projects including tealight holders, bookmarks, notecards or for use directly in your artwork.

On this journey, I encourage you to embrace *wabi-sabi* principles and celebrate the beauty of imperfection – become confident in incorporating unexpected designs into your creations. Enjoy the process and the intriguing results!

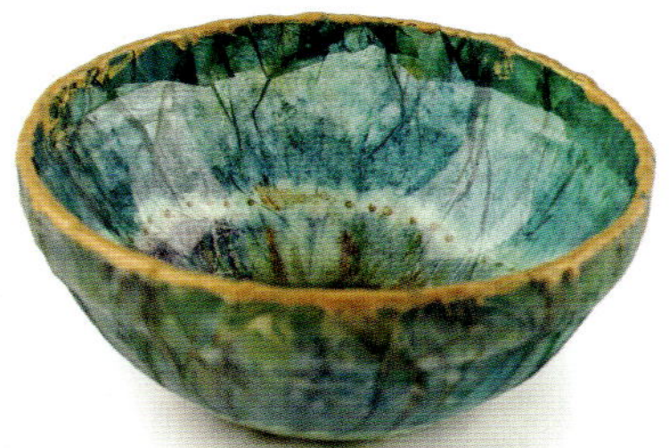

Come with me now on an extraordinary
and colourful adventure...

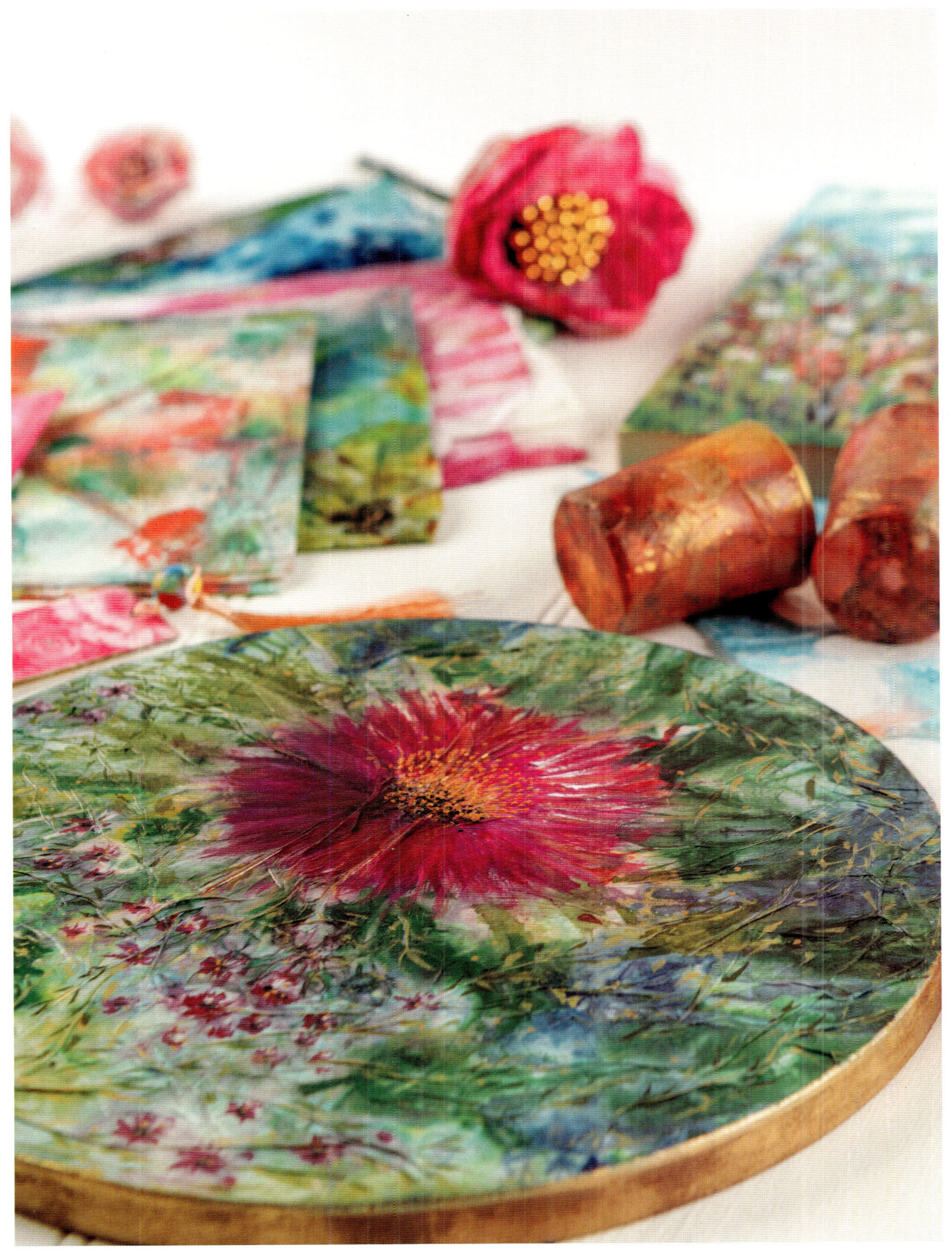

Techniques

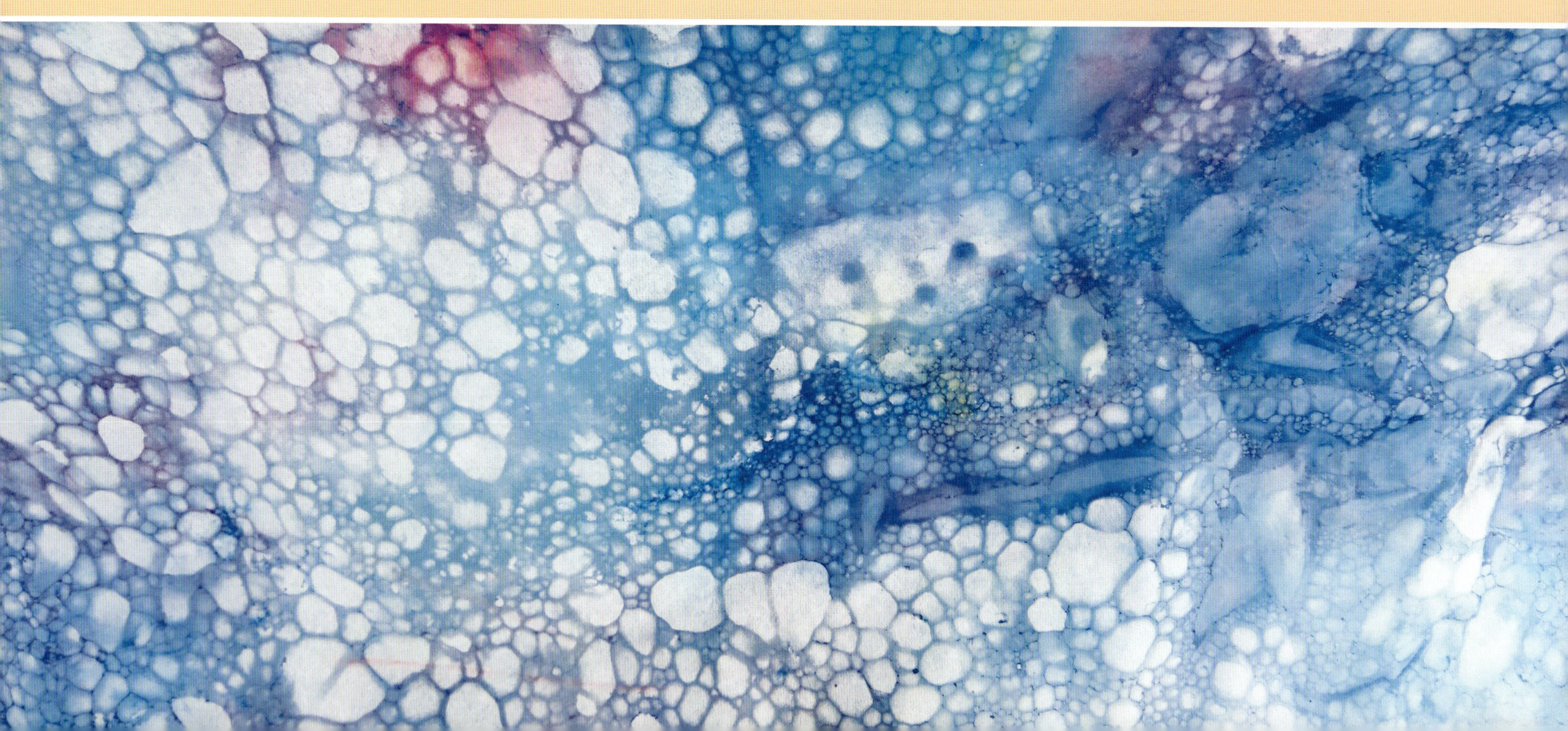

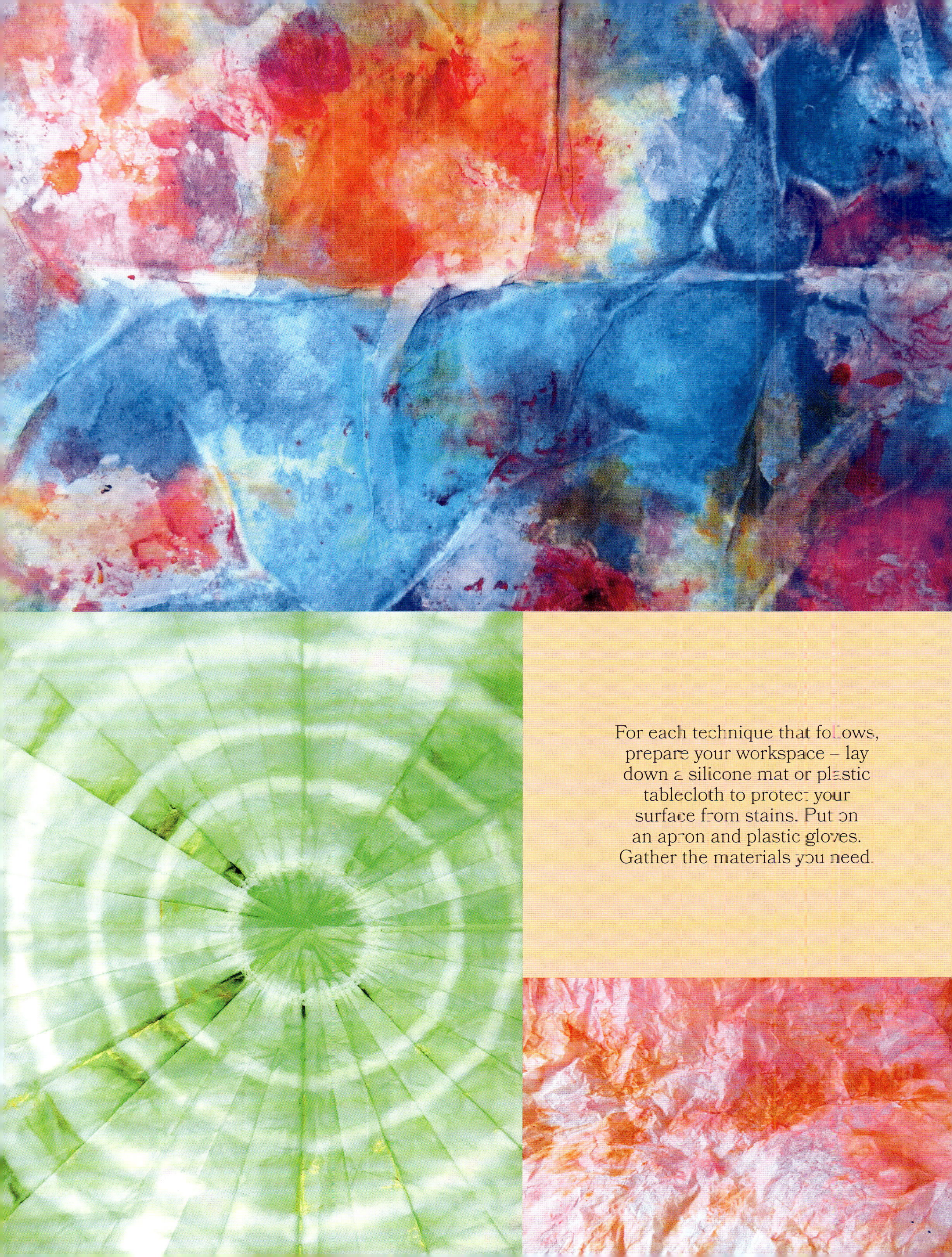

For each technique that follows,
prepare your workspace – lay
down a silicone mat or plastic
tablecloth to protect your
surface from stains. Put on
an apron and plastic gloves.
Gather the materials you need.

Technique 1:
crumple and adding texture

The crumple technique is the basic method of hand-dyeing wet-strength tissue paper. Once you have mastered this, I encourage you to try the variations on pages 16–19 before moving on to the other exciting techniques that follow.

MATERIALS

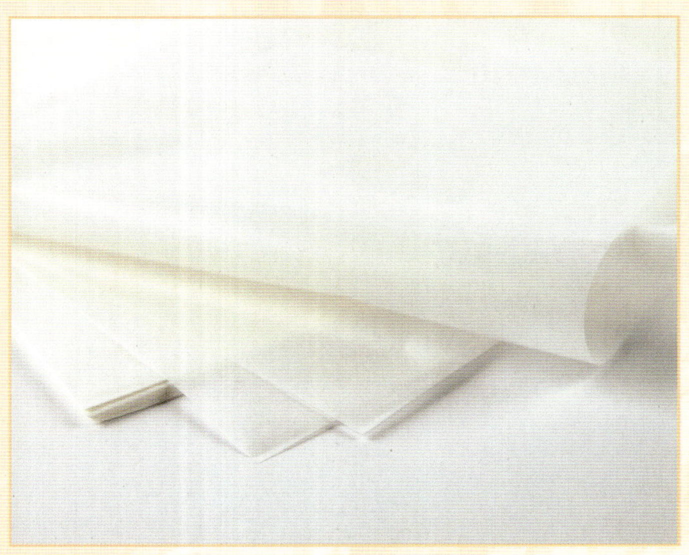

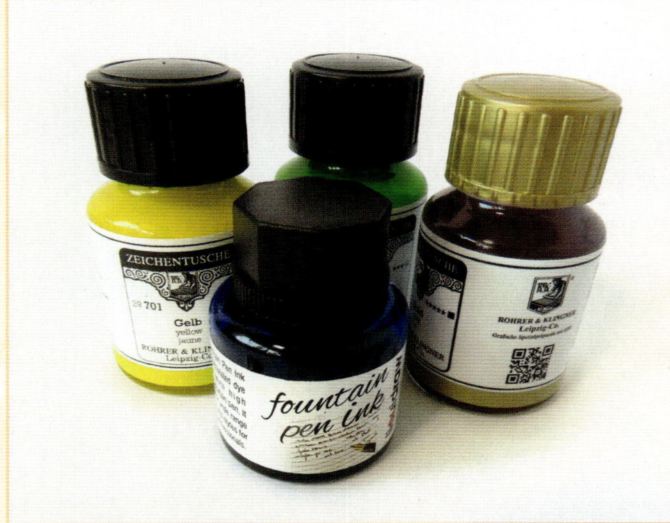

Wet-strength white tissue paper sheets

These paper sheets are excellent to use. They retain the water and ink very well, while maintaining their strength. The paper can still tear, especially if it is very wet. It has two sides, a matt, rougher side and a smoother, shinier side. I prefer to apply the inks to the matt side, however the ink will penetrate through the fibres of the paper. If you have added gold or another shimmer colour to your design, it is useful to know which is your top side.

Watercolour ink

Watercolour and calligraphy ink is a versatile medium that can be used on wet-strength tissue paper to create beautiful translucent effects. You can apply it directly onto the tissue paper or dilute it with water for a more subtle look. Use a brush, dropper, or spray bottle to apply the watercolour ink onto the tissue paper. Explore different techniques like blending colours, creating gradients, or adding splatters for extra interest.

Watercolour fixative

Spray on lightly to inked tissue to minimize colour bleed and fade. Use in a well-ventilated environment.

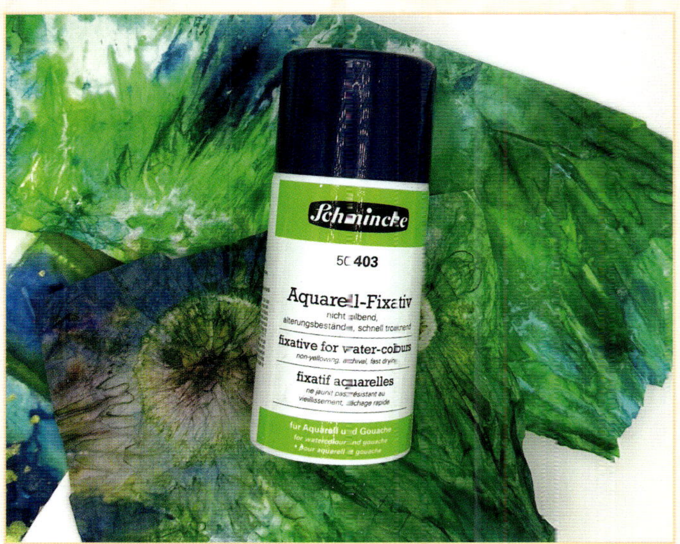

Tip

Store unused dyed tissue paper in a dry, flat place to prevent colour from fading. To minimize fading, spray the tissue paper with a watercolour fixative before using the dyed tissue paper in painting or collage projects.

Acrylic ink

This is a vibrant and permanent medium that can be used on wet-strength tissue paper. It provides bold and opaque colours, perfect for creating vibrant designs. Apply the acrylic ink onto the tissue paper using a brush, dropper, or dip pen. You can experiment with layering different colours or using masking techniques to create unique effects. Dilute to give the required colour strength.

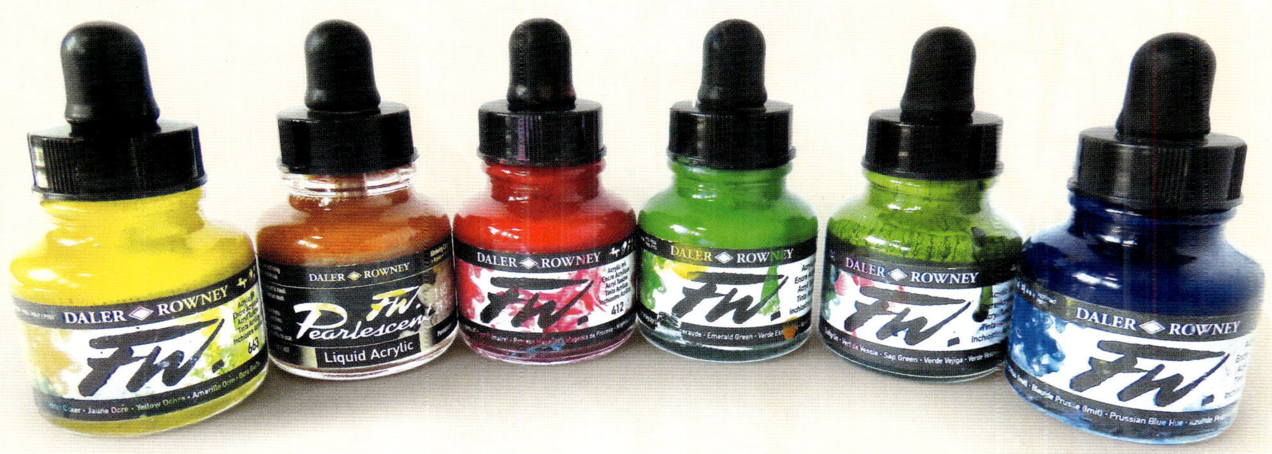

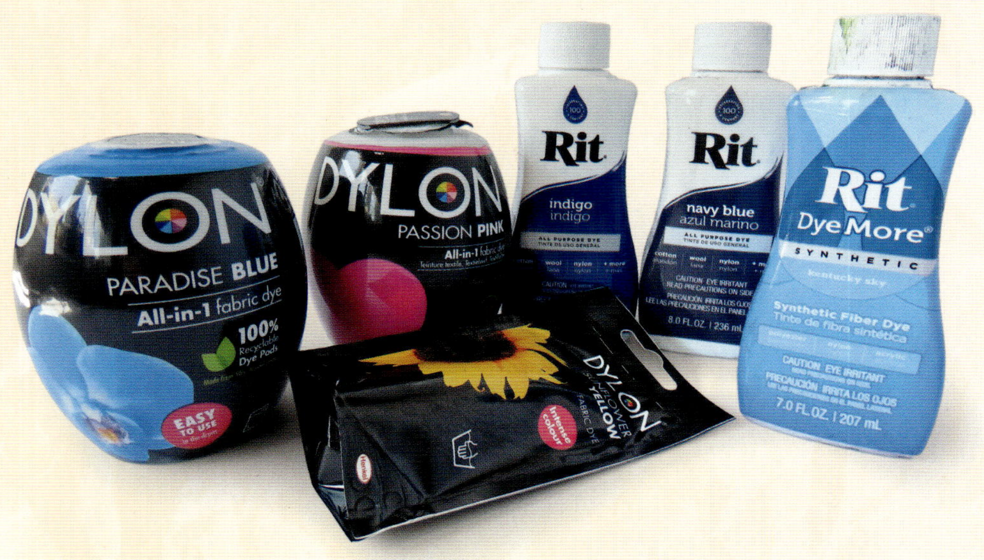

Fabric dyes

Fabric dyes work very well when used with wet-strength tissue paper. Use clip-top plastic tubs, glass jars or even rice pots to mix and store diluted fabric dye in. It is good to have a couple of pots with wide openings to allow you to fully submerge a large piece of tissue paper.

Once made up, these dyes will retain their colour and dyeing properties for several weeks. The fabric dyes can be in liquid form or dried powder; just dilute with water according to the manufacturer's specifications, or to the desired colour intensity.

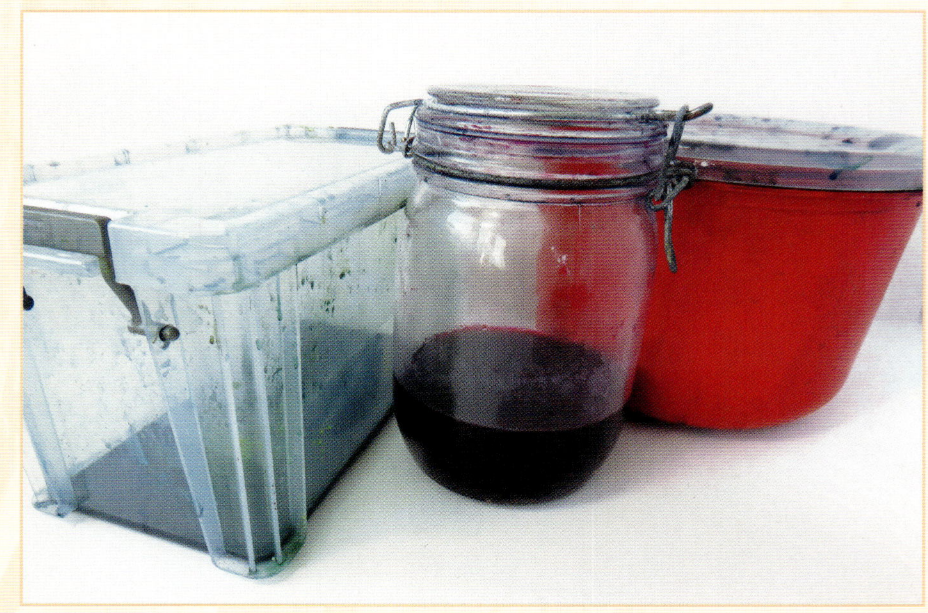

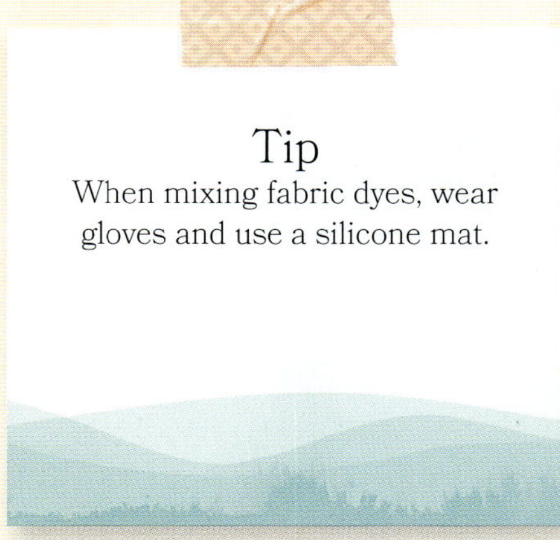

Tip
When mixing fabric dyes, wear gloves and use a silicone mat.

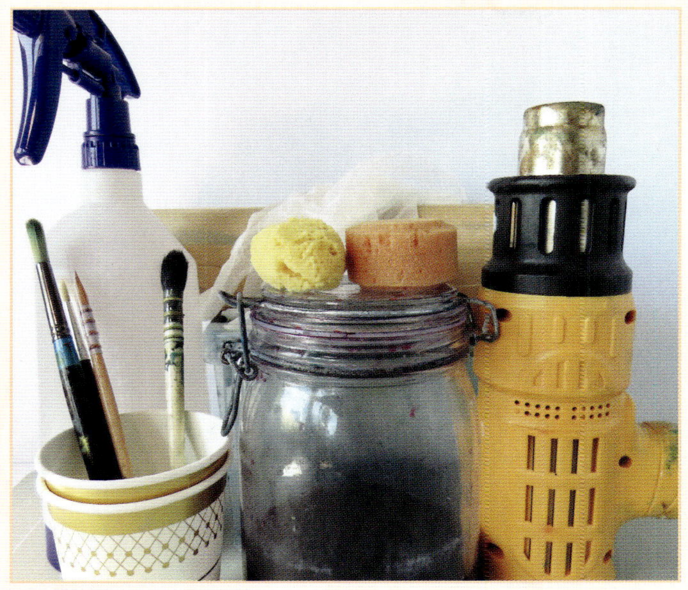 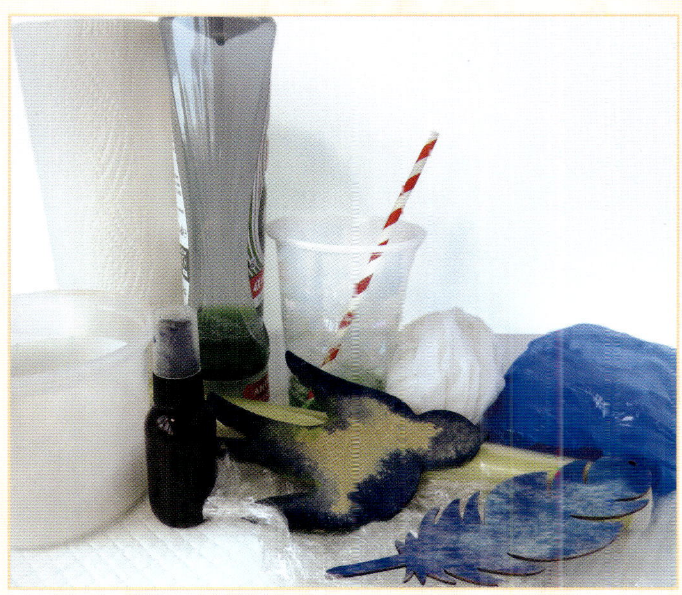

Equipment

- spray bottle of water
- disposable plastic gloves
- large silicone mat or plastic tablecloth (to protect your workspace)
- parchment paper
- small art sponges
- small paintbrush
- paper or plastic cups
- plastic or glass containers for fabric dye
- heat gun
- apron

Optional tools

- plastic food wrap offcuts or recycled plastic bags
- salt flakes
- wooden shapes, for example: flowers, leaves, feathers, or birds
- paper straw
- dish soap
- kitchen paper

METHOD 1: DYEING TISSUE PAPER

Here is my step-by-step guide to creating bespoke hand-dyed tissue paper.

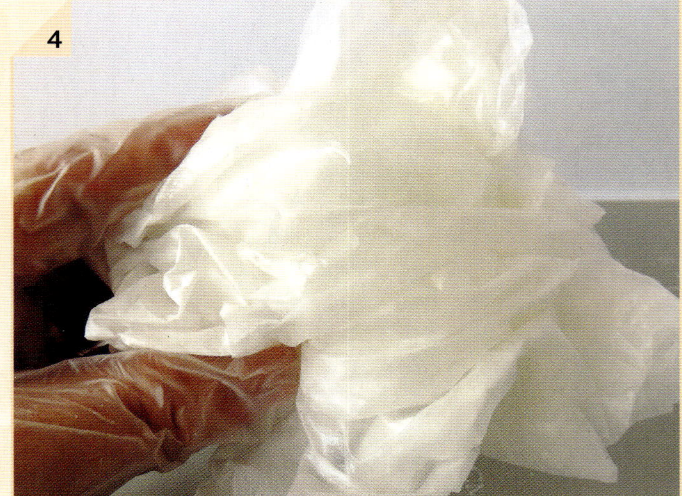

1 Mix your fabric dye: follow the instructions on the dye package to mix the solution. If you are using watercolour inks, dilute them in paper cups with water according to your desired colour intensity. For stronger hues, use watercolour or acrylic inks straight from the bottle.

2 Place the tissue paper on the protected surface.

3 Spray the tissue paper all over with water in a spray bottle.

4 Crumple the damp tissue paper in your hands – lightly for a subtle texture or more firmly for a pronounced wrinkled effect, being careful not to tear it.

5 Spread the paper out on your silicone mat.

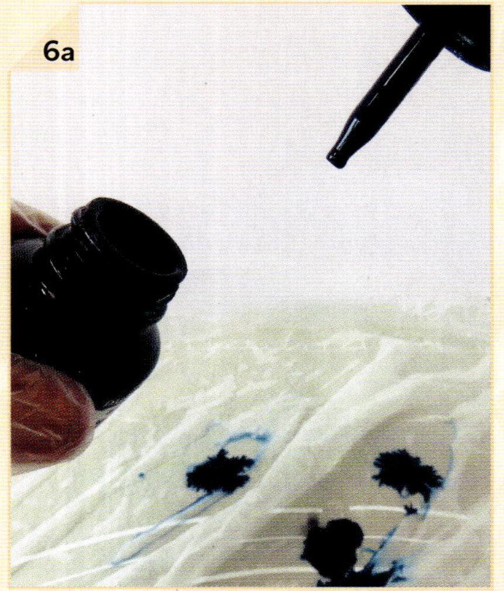

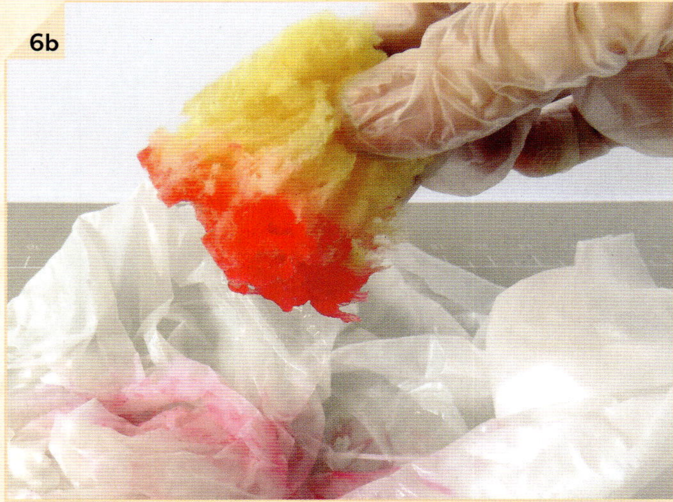

6 Apply the dye or inks onto the tissue paper with ink droppers or a small paintbrush (a). You can create patterns or splatters, or blend colours together. Applying the inks with a small piece of sponge will give a softer, more muted effect (b).

7 Add more water with the spray bottle, if needed, to encourage the colours to mix and be absorbed by the tissue paper. Always keep the paper damp.

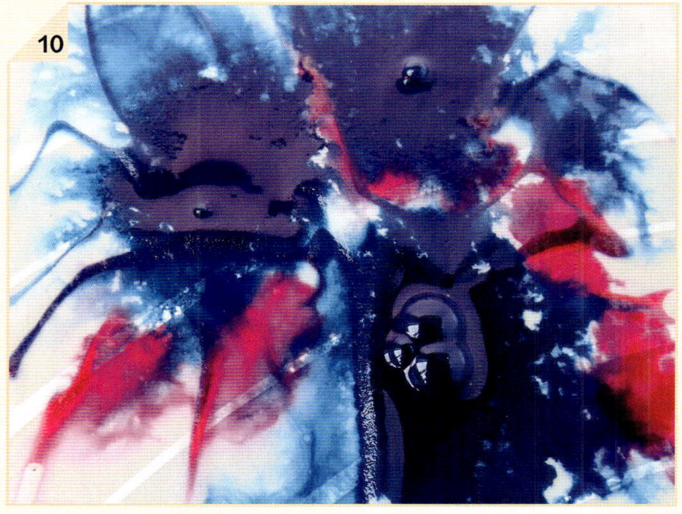

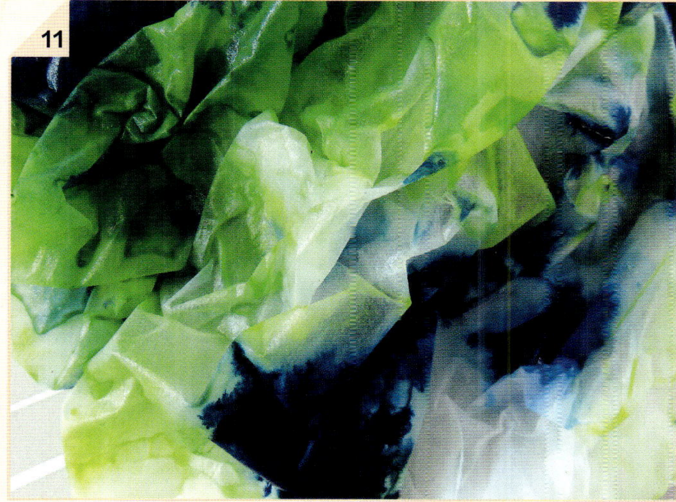

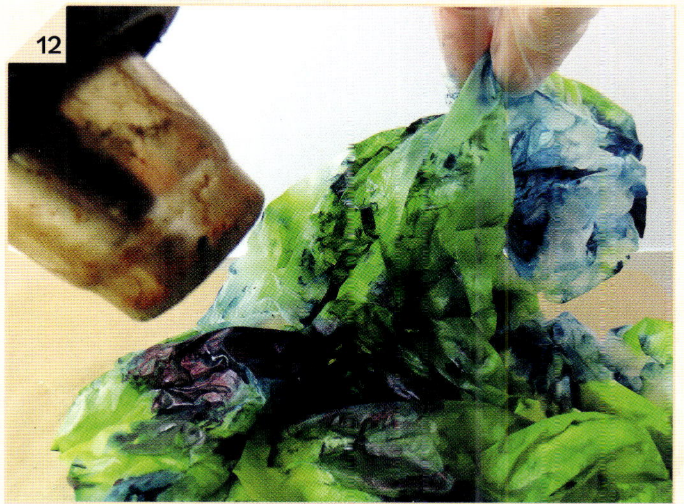

8 As the tissue paper comes into contact with the inks, the colours will start to blend and flow. Use a brush or your fingers to gently manipulate the inks, encouraging the colours to mix and create interesting patterns. You can tilt the surface to allow the colours to move and blend in different directions.

9 The tissue paper may start to crease and form intricate patterns against the silicone mat, which will add interest and texture.

10 By adding more water to the tissue paper, you can intensify the blending and bleeding effects of the inks.

11 Gather the tissue paper in a rough ball or twist and transfer it to a parchment sheet. Ideally, leave it to dry overnight.

12 If you can't wait to see your design, you can dry the dyed tissue with a heat gun on a low setting. Once it is nearly dry, you can then hang the sheet up to dry fully.

13 Clean your brushes and sponges in clean water and wipe any ink from your silicone mat.

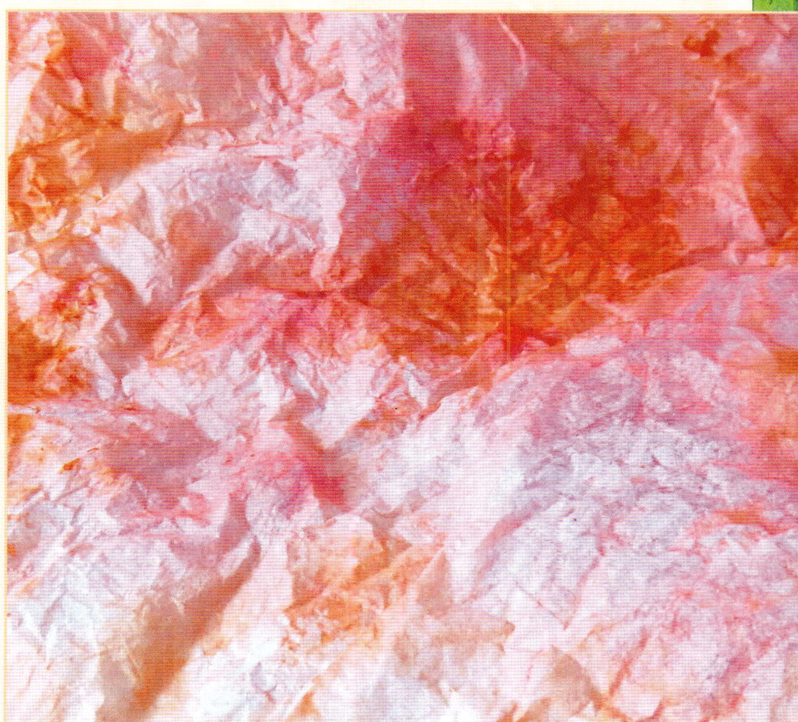

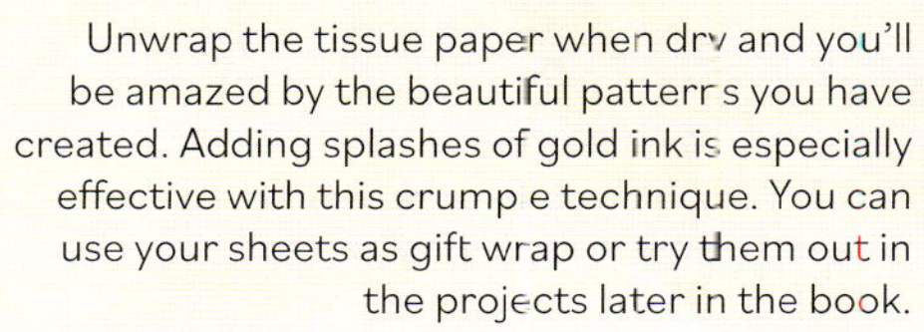

Unwrap the tissue paper when dry and you'll be amazed by the beautiful patterns you have created. Adding splashes of gold ink is especially effective with this crumple technique. You can use your sheets as gift wrap or try them out in the projects later in the book.

METHOD 2: OTHER WAYS TO ADD TEXTURE

Here are some variations to the crumple technique that will give extra texture to
your designs.

Full immersion

Crumple the damp tissue paper in your hands, then fully
immerse the whole sheet in a container of dye. Leave for a
few minutes and then squeeze out the excess dye.

   While the tissue is still damp you can add other colours
by hand with a paintbrush, for example, splashes of a
contrasting or complementary colour.

Tip

Be sure to wear disposable gloves for this method.

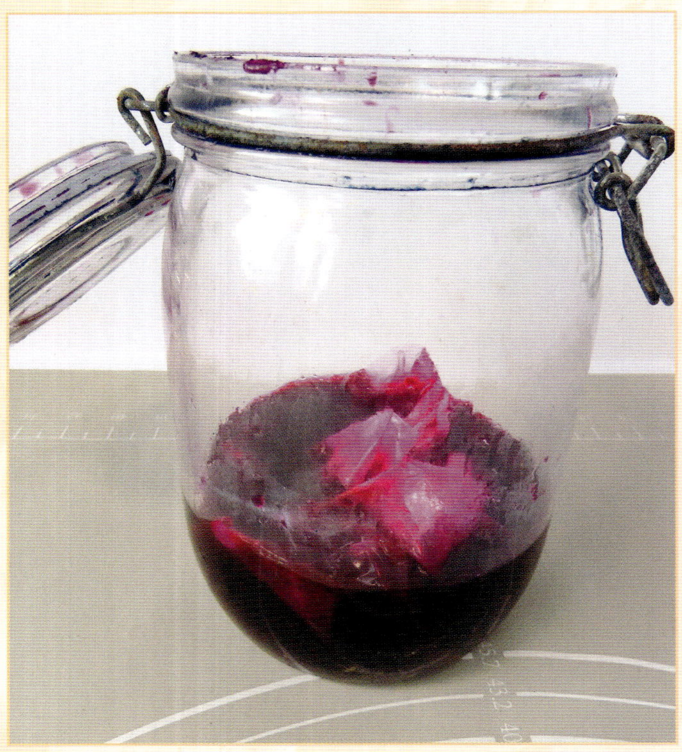

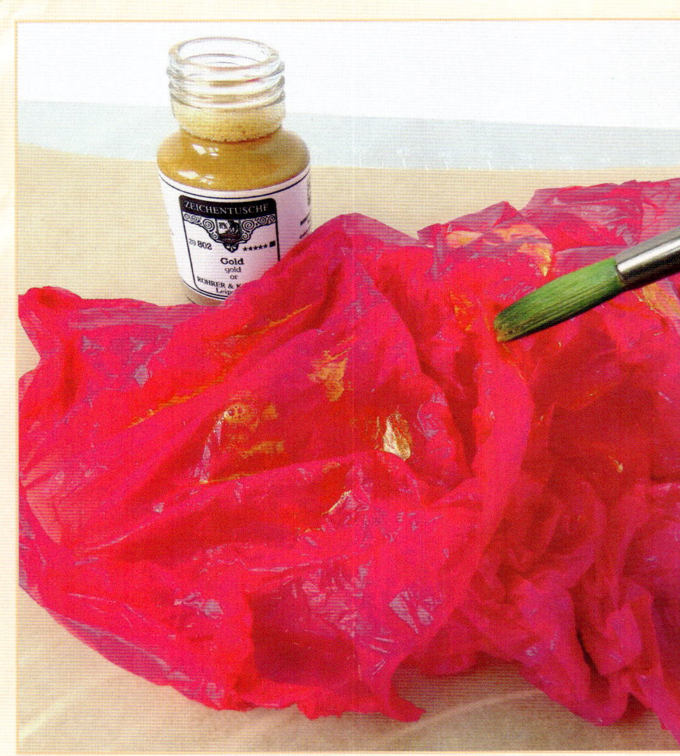

Plastic food wrap offcuts

This technique can give impressions of branches against a dappled sky – the perfect background for a painting. Spray the tissue paper so it is damp then add splashes of acrylic or watercolour ink. Lay a piece of plastic food wrap over it and leave to dry. Carefully peel off the plastic food wrap to reveal beautiful patterns (below left).

Crumple the plastic for a more textured appearance or pull it tight into lines to achieve a rippled, watery effect. Experiment with different thicknesses of plastic bags (below right) or recycled wrapping materials. You can also place the plastic behind the tissue paper, add inks and leave to dry to achieve unexpected organic results.

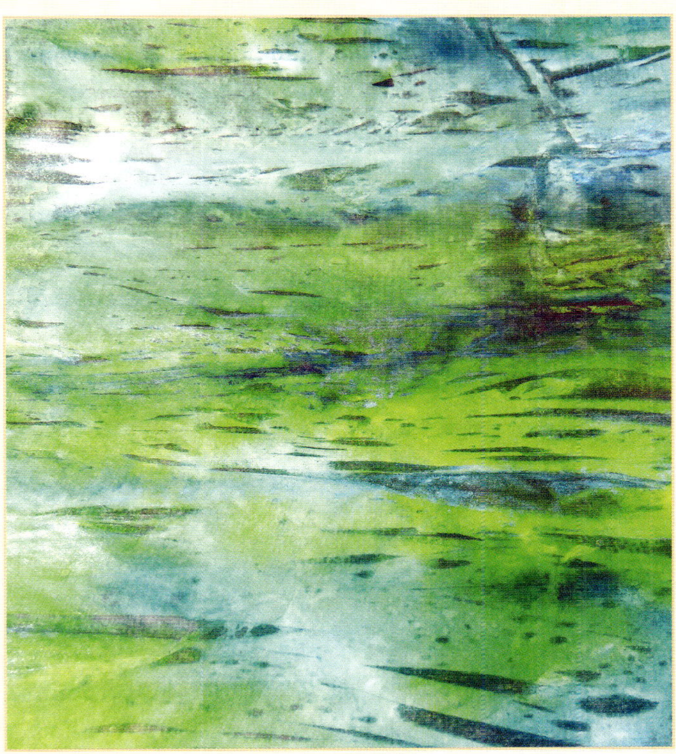

Dried plastic food wrap.

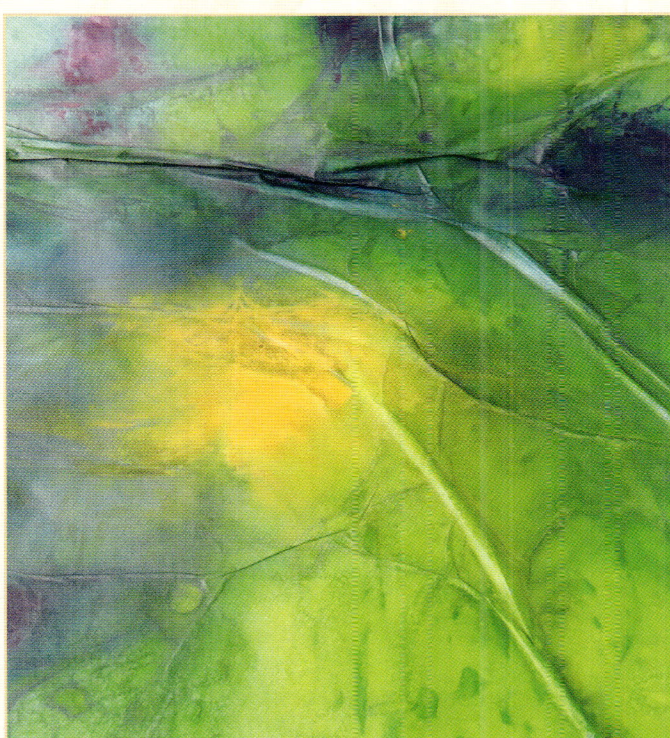

Dried bin liner.

Tip

Do not heat plastic food wrap to dry it, otherwise the plastic will melt!

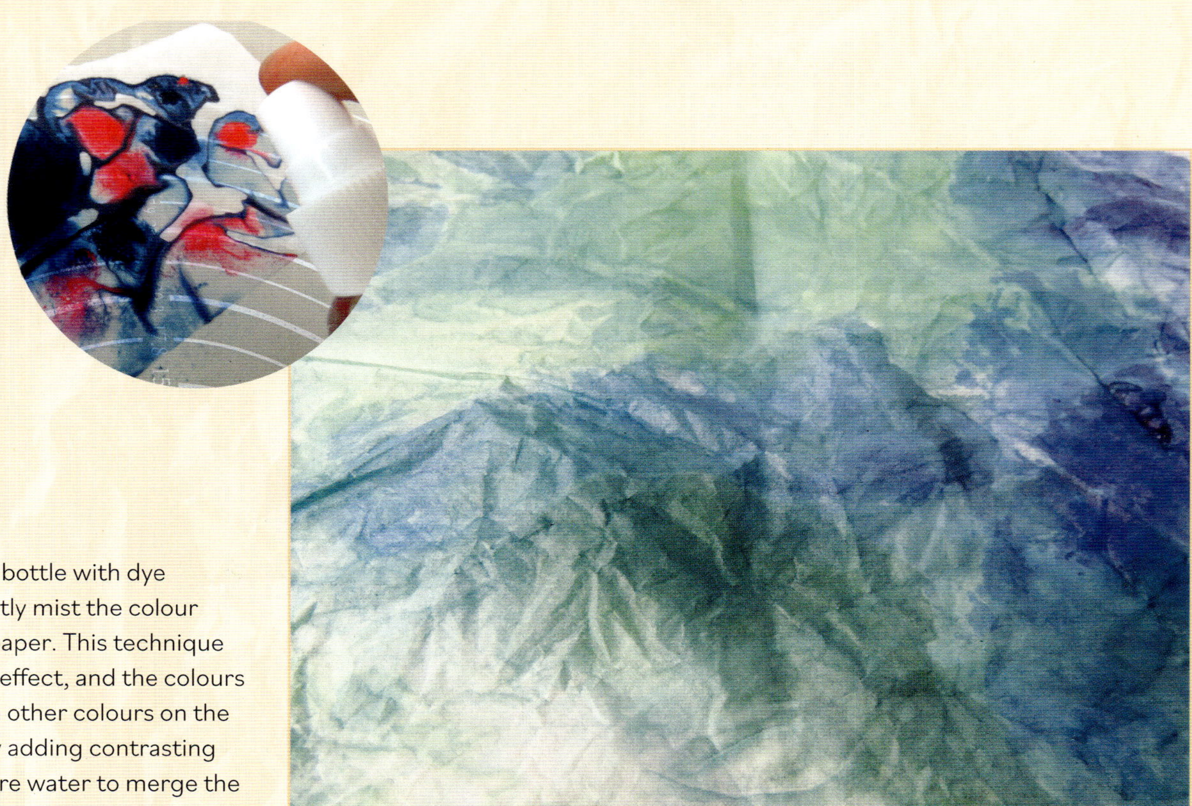

Spritzing

Fill a small spray bottle with dye solution and lightly mist the colour over the tissue paper. This technique creates a subtle effect, and the colours blend easily with other colours on the tissue paper. Try adding contrasting colours. Add more water to merge the inks if needed.

Wooden shape resists

Place a wooden shape, for example a feather or a flower shape, on *dry* tissue paper. Spray diluted ink from a small bottle over the area. After spraying, remove the wooden shape to reveal the outline below. Leave the sheet to dry, then you can add other colours if you want, taking care not to interfere with the pattern you have created.

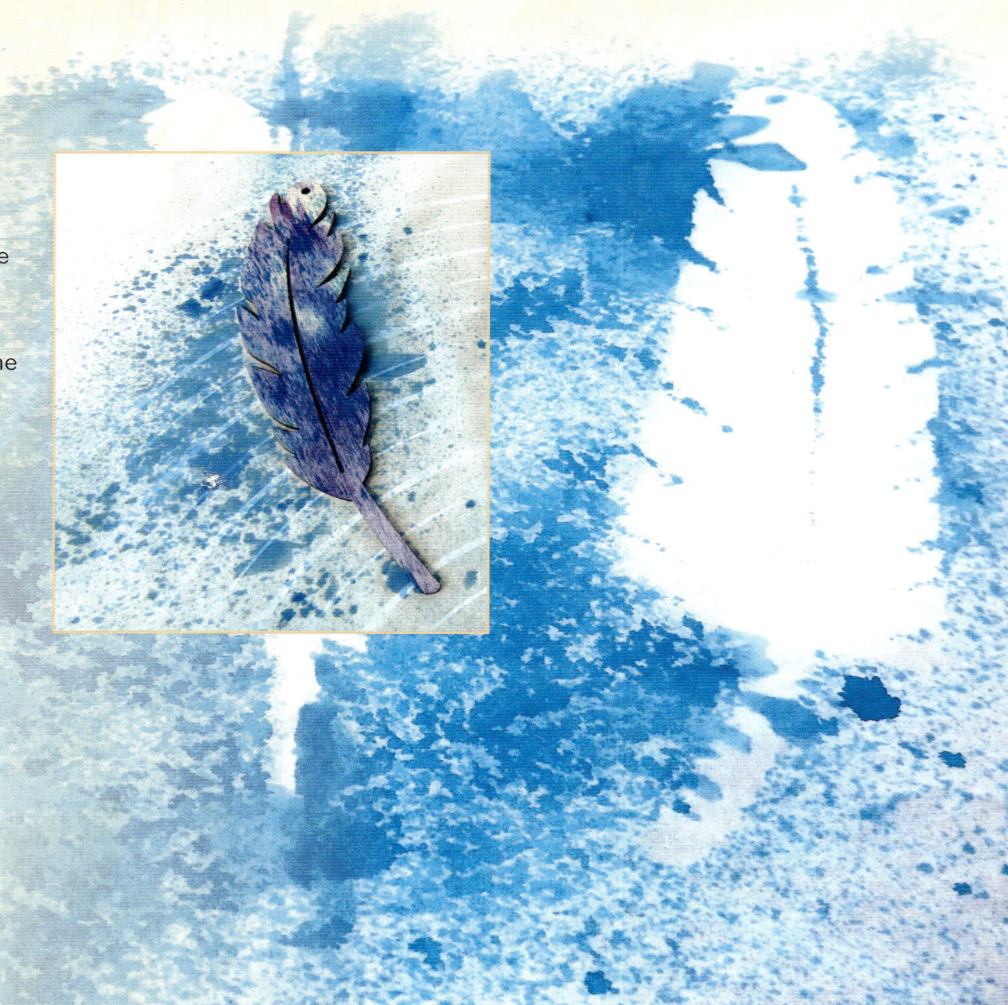

Salt flakes

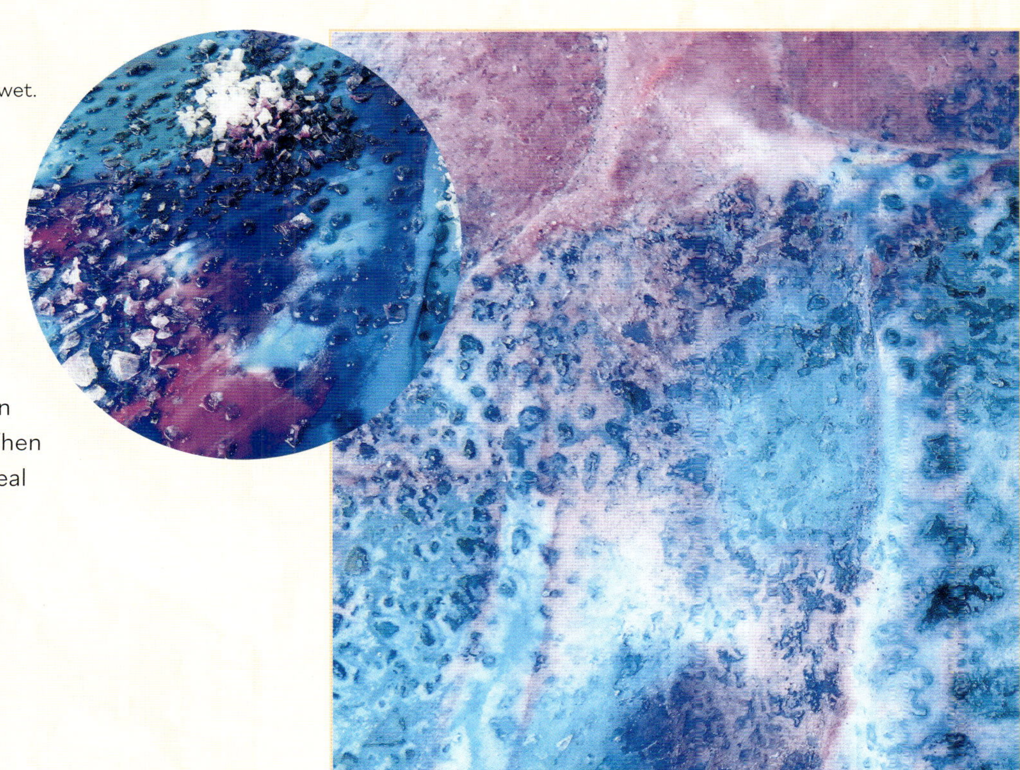

Adding salt flakes when wet.

Scatter lots of large, flaked sea salt over areas of tissue paper that have ink and water on them, on a silicone mat. Spray on more water. Leave to dry flat. When dry, rub the salt flakes off to reveal interesting organic patterns.

Dried salt flakes.

Bubble patterns

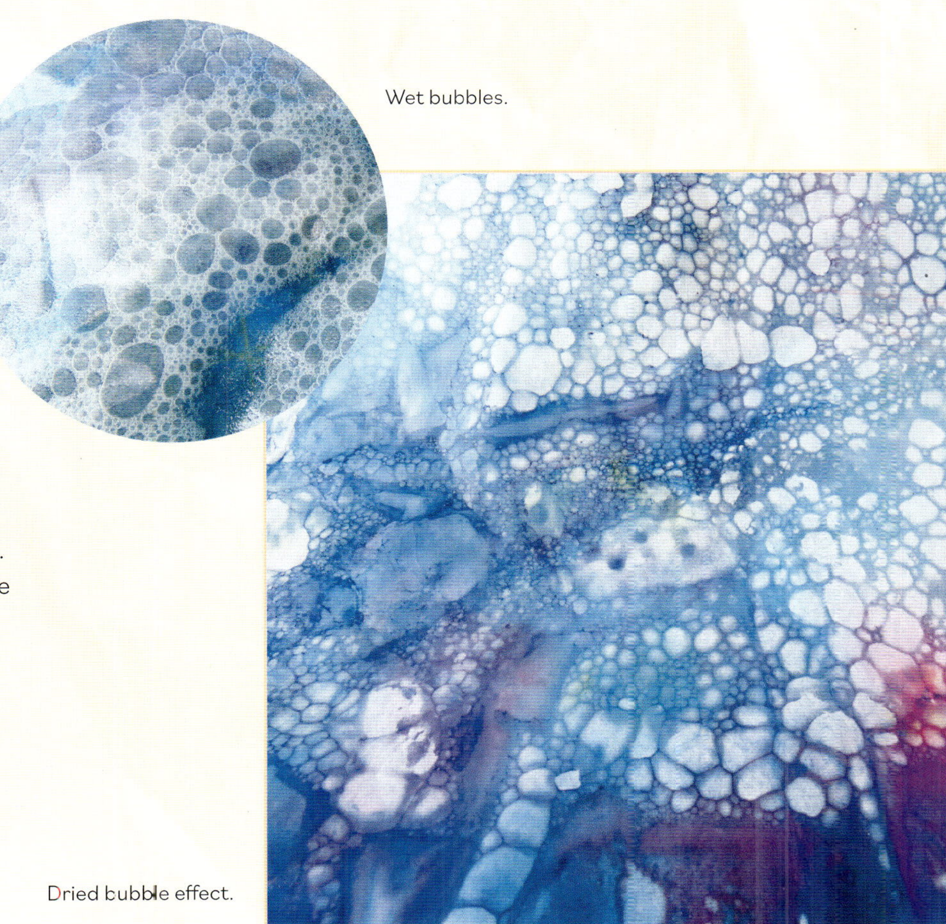

Wet bubbles.

Put two teaspoons of dish soap in a paper cup and add a little water so it is a thick mixture. Blow through a paper straw into the mixture to create bubbles. Tip the bubbles gently onto a piece of wet tissue paper with ink on it. Place another piece of damp tissue paper the same size on top. This soap suds sandwich will preserve the bubbles on the top later to create a subtle bubbly effect. Have kitchen paper to hand in case inky water leaks. Leave to dry fully on a silicone mat. The bubbles show up better when used with darker inks.

Dried bubble effect.

Technique 2:
dip dye

This technique involves submerging part of the tissue paper into your container of dye, giving a gradient effect as the dye penetrates the paper. Experiment with the strength of the dye to water ratio to achieve different intensities of colour. The fabric dye will always look darker when wet and will become lighter as it dries.
Remember any imperfections are part of the beauty of hand-dyeing. Explore ideas in the project section of this book to try out various ways you can use your dip-dyed tissue paper.

You will need

Materials

- wet-strength white tissue paper sheets
- fabric dye in a selection of colours, watercolour inks or acrylic inks

Equipment

- spray bottle of water
- disposable plastic gloves
- large silicone mat or plastic tablecloth (to protect your workspace)
- parchment paper
- kitchen paper
- small fold-back or bulldog clips
- plastic or glass containers for fabric dye
- small cups for diluted inks
- heat gun
- paintbrush
- scissors
- apron

METHOD:

1 Follow the instructions on the dye package to mix the dye solution(s), or dilute your watercolour or acrylic inks in a small cup.

2 Fold the tissue paper into a narrow rectangle so that the short side will fit into the aperture of your dyeing pot.

3 Spray the paper all over with water, using the spray bottle.

4 Carefully lower the end of the damp tissue paper into the container of dye to the desired depth, allowing the dye to saturate upwards through the paper. The folds in the tissue mean that the ink pattern will be replicated across the sheet.

5 Slowly lift the tissue paper up and allow ink to dribble from the end. Dab the end on some clean kitchen paper to remove excess ink.

6 Partially dry the inked area gently with a heat gun or a low setting so it is no longer saturated. This will allow you to manipulate the tissue paper so you can dye other sections easily.

7 Repeat with a further dip dye on the other end of the tissue paper.

8 Dry this new section with the heat gun on low.

9 You can use just one colour or dip the tissue into another colour. It is best not to mix colours before dyeing; instead dip one fold into just one colour, use another colour on another fold and let the colours bleed together. You can also dip dye the centre folds or other folds in your tissue paper.

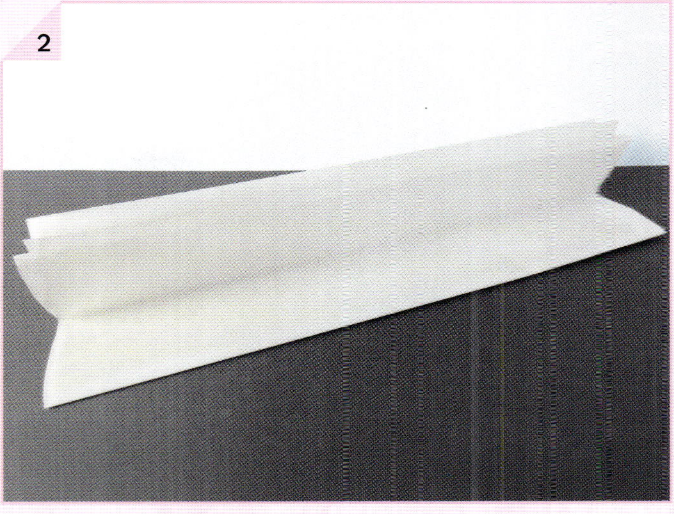

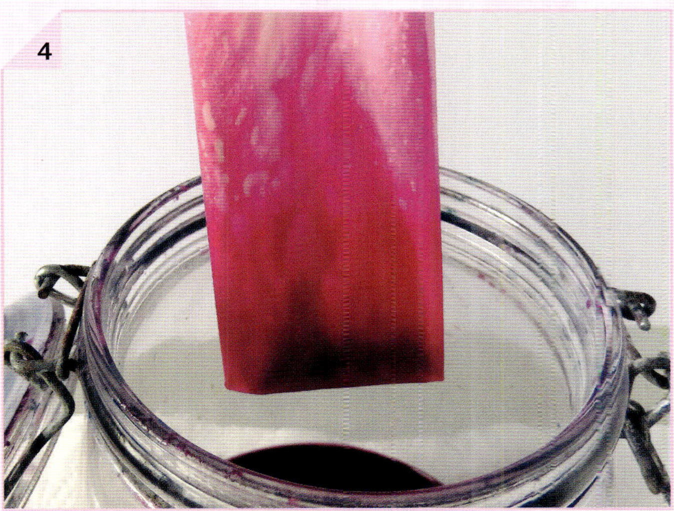

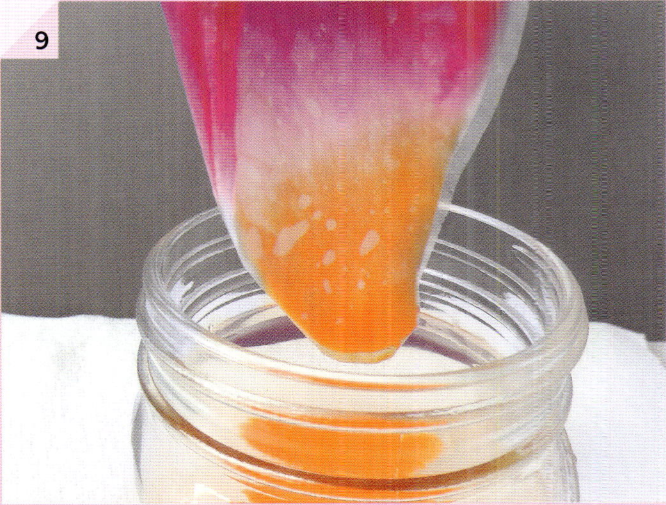

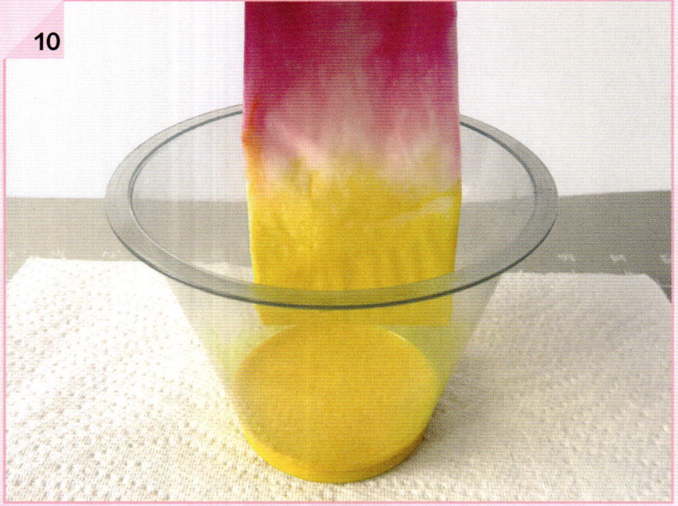

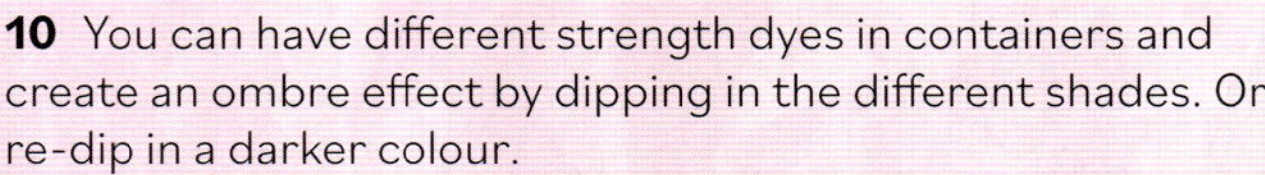

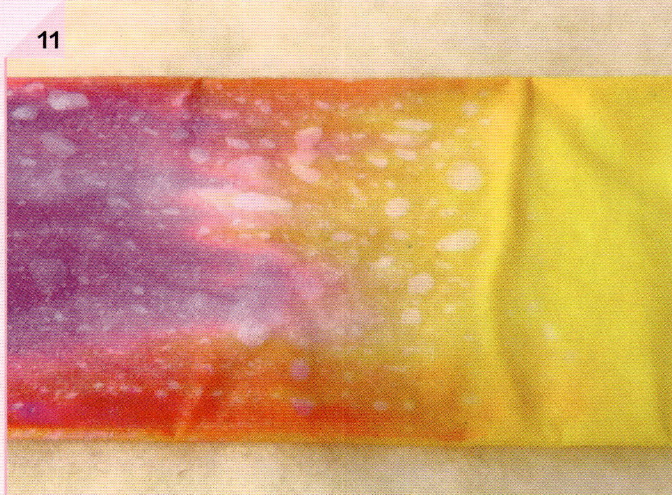

10 You can have different strength dyes in containers and create an ombre effect by dipping in the different shades. Or re-dip in a darker colour.

11 Watch the colours merge and create more colour mixes. You can encourage this spread by spraying the tissue paper with more water.

12 Leave the paper to dry overnight by laying it on parchment paper, or dry it gently with a heat gun on a low setting.

13 Unwrap carefully to see the beautiful, symmetrical, inky patterns you have created.

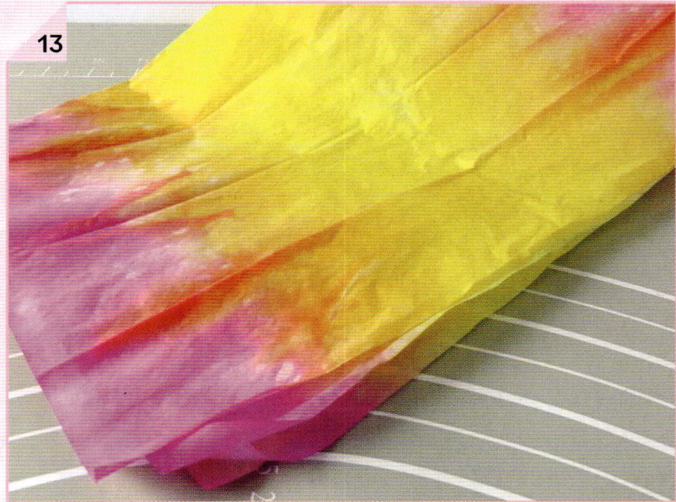

Tip

If you have large white areas on your finished piece of tissue paper, you can fold along these areas and re-dip into the dye on the creases.

VARIATIONS:
DIP DYE PETALS

To create a selection of beautiful petals for the tissue flowers demonstrated in project 7 on pages 112–119, cut out multiple petal shapes from white wet-strength tissue paper and spray them with water (a). See page 144 for petal and leaf templates. Use a small clip to hold a bunch of the same shaped petals together (b) and dip the ends of the petals in one colour of dye to let the colour slowly seep upwards (c). Carefully turn the petals up the other way and dip in another colour, allowing the ink to seep up (d). Or soak the petals in one colour only and with a fine paintbrush, add a little ink in another colour to the very edges of the petals to allow a little ink to fade downwards. Lay the petals out and leave to dry fully.

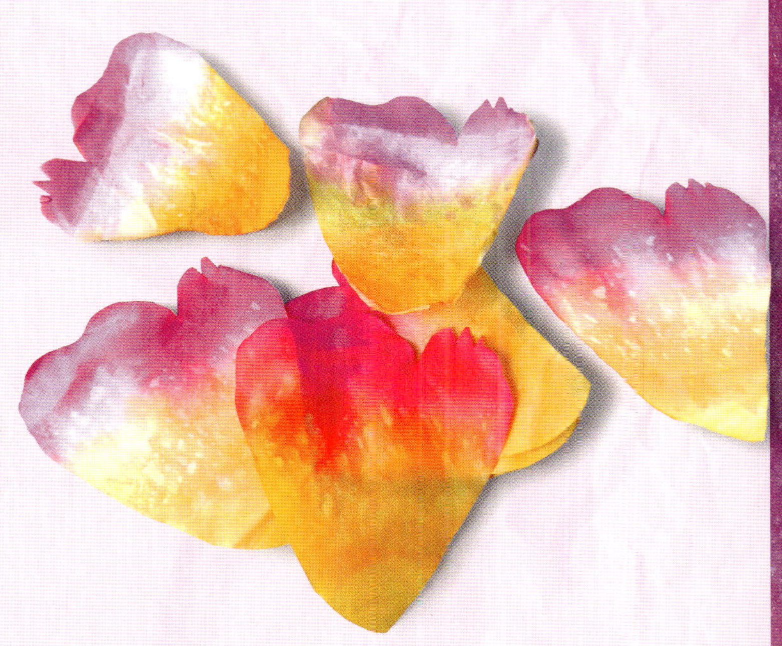

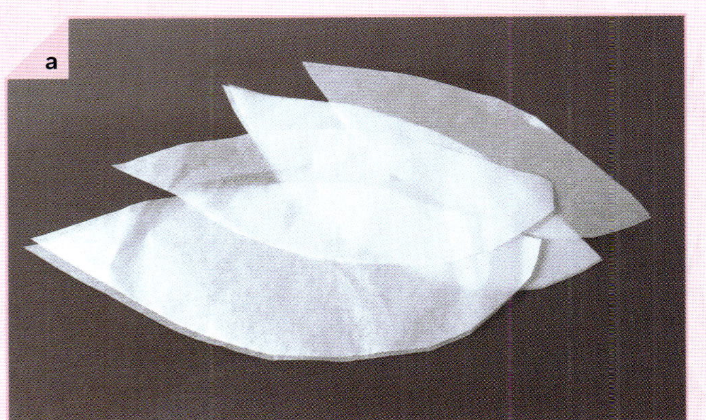

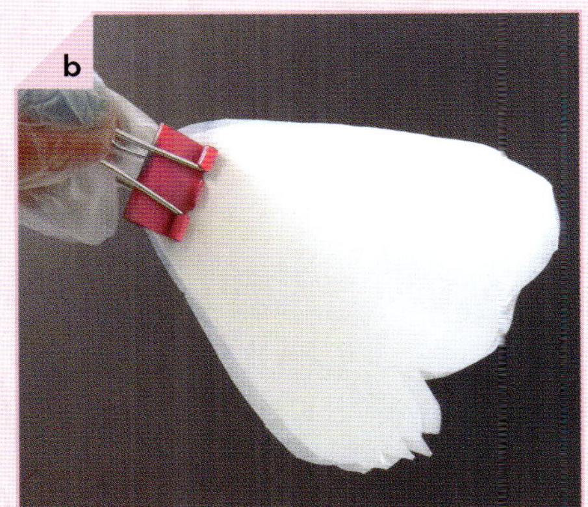

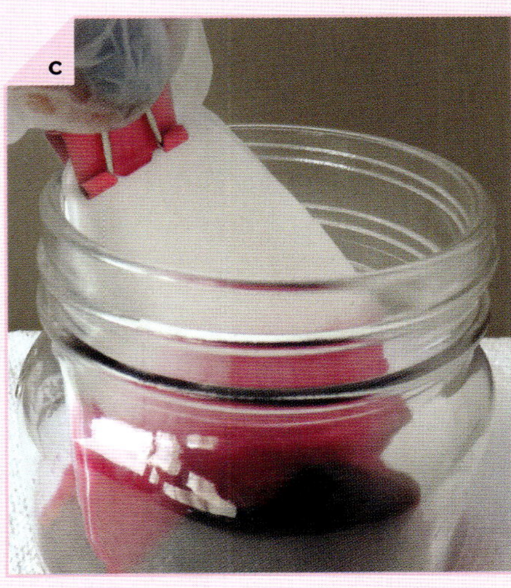

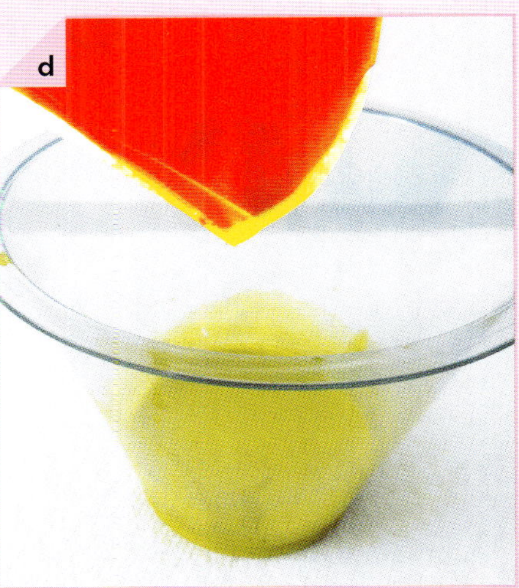

Technique 3:
pole wrap (*arashi*)

Arashi shibori is an ancient Japanese dyeing technique of wrapping fabric diagonally round a pole or hollow tube, compressed and tied with elastic bands. This creates a fluid, abstract rippled design which resembles water or driving rain: *arashi* means 'storm' in Japanese.
I use elastic bands or hair ties, however you can use varying thicknesses of thread or cord to achieve different effects.
This technique is also really effective on tissue paper. Note that the dye can only penetrate the outer layers of the tissue paper on the pole, so the tissue nearer the pole will have a fainter pattern and that closer to the outside will have a darker pattern. If the inside layer of the dried tissue paper is too white, you can rewrap the paper around the pole with the dyed section inside and the whiter section outside. Repeat the steps to give a fuller coverage of the dyed pattern.

You will need

Materials

- wet-strength white tissue paper sheets
- fabric dye and watercolour inks in a selection of colours including gold

Equipment

- hollow plastic tube, length 70cm (27½in), diameter 3.5cm (1⅜in); e. g. drainpipe from a DIY or plumber's store
- spray bottle of water
- disposable plastic gloves
- large silicone mat or plastic tablecloth (to protect your workspace)
- parchment paper
- kitchen paper
- plastic or glass containers for fabric dye
- elastic bands or hair ties
- small and medium paintbrushes
- small art sponges
- small scissors
- apron
- large glass cylindrical vase (optional)

METHOD:

1 Follow the instructions on the dye package to mix the dye solution(s).

2 Fold your tissue paper into a long rectangle and wrap it round the pole, lengthwise, overlapping as you go round. Add an elastic band to secure both ends snugly to the pole. Position your paper towards one end of the pole. This wrapping method gives horizontal lines of ripples.

3 Add elastics across the length of the tissue paper. The areas covered by these will act as resists to the dye, so will remain white or pale, especially if a darker colour is used over them. Try putting elastics on at an angle to give a more abstract rippled effect. Also experiment with different widths of elastic band for a variety of resist patterns.

4 Spray the paper all over with water, using the spray bottle.

5 Push the tissue paper down the tube towards an end by hand, to form folds. Repeat for the other end of the tissue paper. It can be quite hard to push the tissue down. Continue until all the tissue paper is tightly bunched. These folds also act as dye resists.

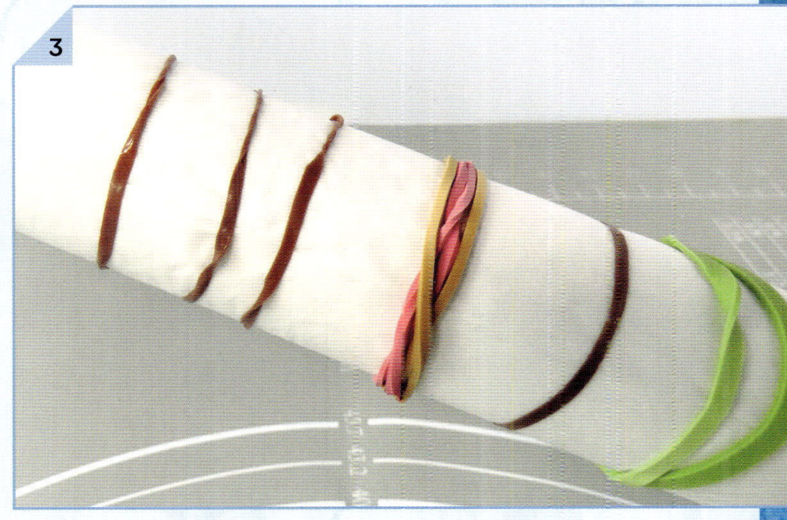

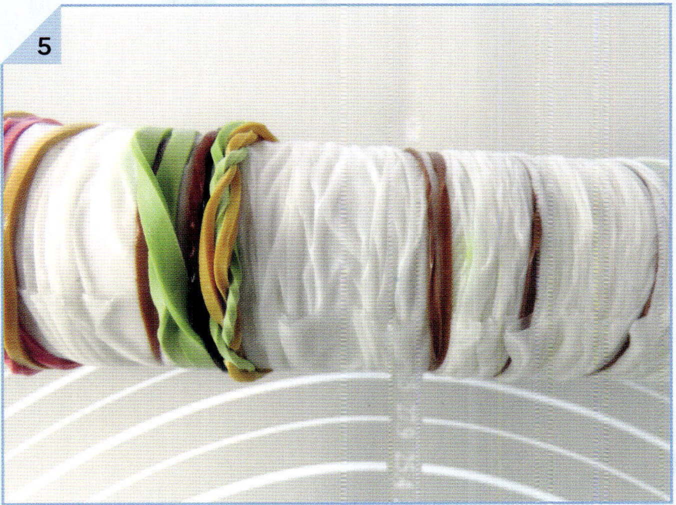

Tip
Follow the instructions and precautions provided by the dye manufacturer. Adhere to environmental regulations when disposing of leftover dye.

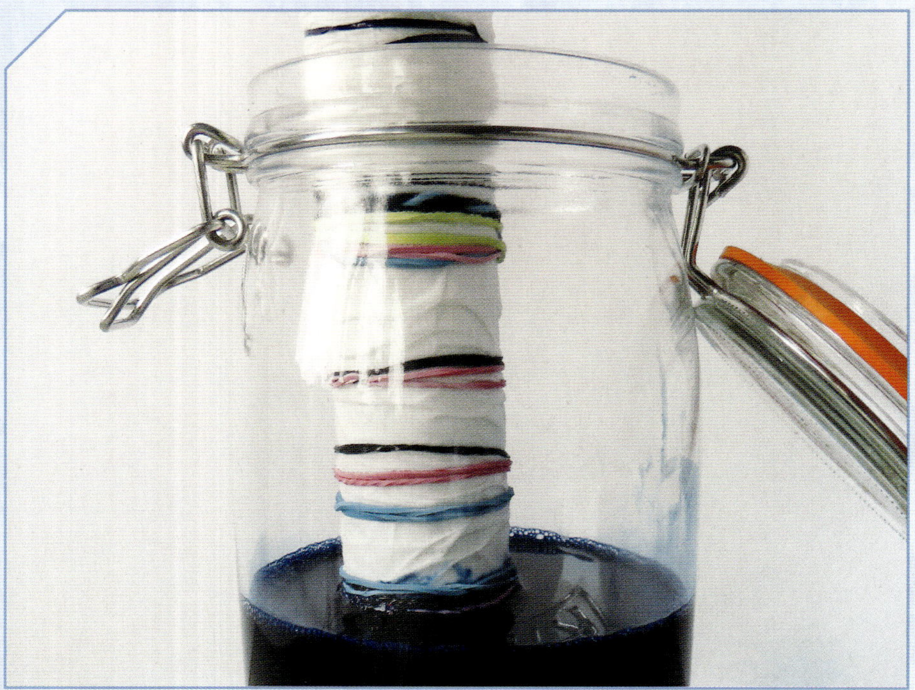

6 Carefully lower the end of the scrunched tissue-covered tube into the container of dye to the desired depth, allowing the dye to saturate upwards through the paper.

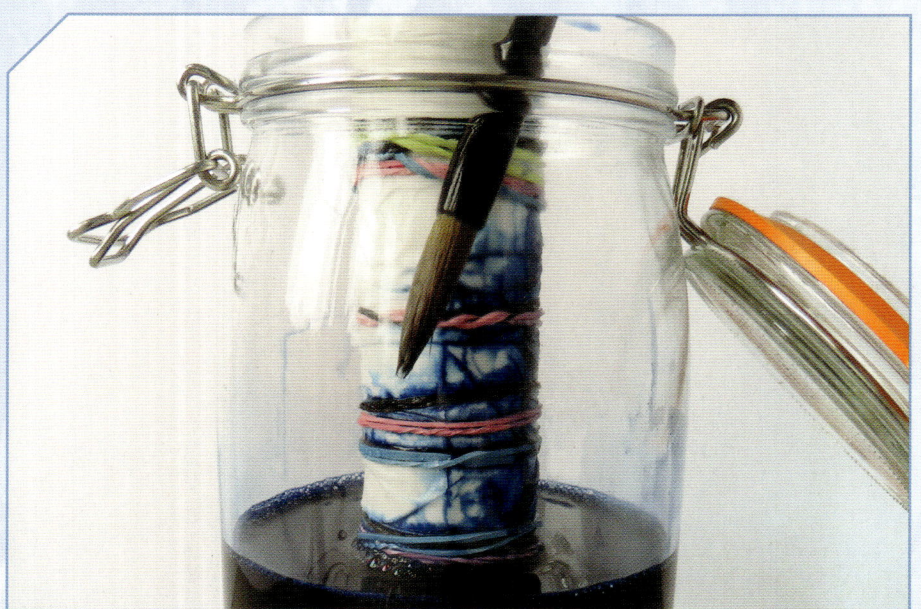

7 Use a medium paintbrush to lift ink from the dye pot up onto the wrapped tissue. Hold the tube over your pot so that any excess ink falls back into the pot.

Tip

Ensure the folds are consistent if you want to produce a regular pattern with even ink penetration. Irregular wrapping can result in a more uneven pattern.
If your scrunched tissue can't go in your dye pot, just paint the colours on with a medium-sized paintbrush, with your wrapped tube lying on the silicone mat.

8 Carefully remove the pole-wrapped tissue paper from the dye, allowing any excess dye to drip off onto kitchen paper.

9 Use a clean paintbrush to add splashes of gold or other ink colours across the length of the tissue paper on the tube. Spray with water if needed to encourage bleeding. My favourite colour combination is indigo, turquoise and green with a splash of gold.

10 Leave the wrapped pole to dry overnight by laying it on parchment paper or your silicone mat.

11 Once dry, unwrap the tissue by carefully cutting the elastics with scissors to see the abstract inky pattern you have created. Try to avoid cutting the tissue paper.

12 Unfold the paper very carefully.

Tip

Do not dry the tissue with a heat gun since this will burst the elastic bands.

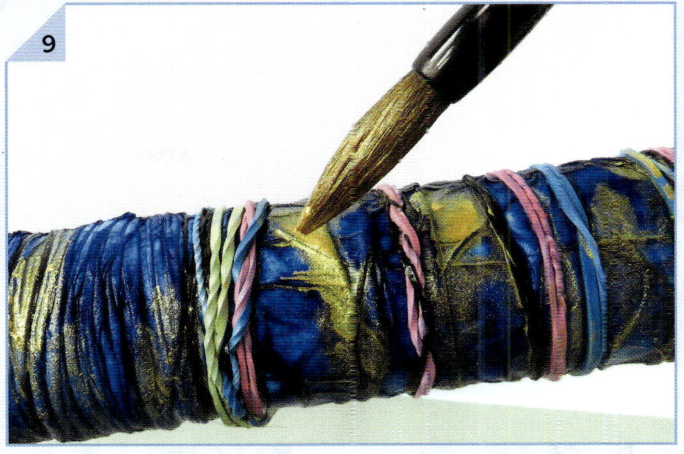

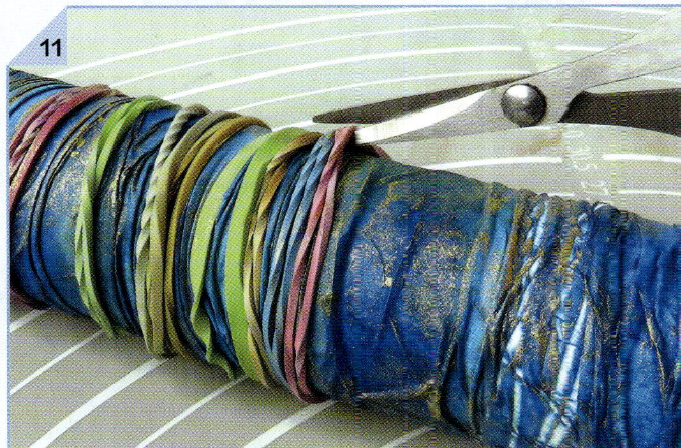

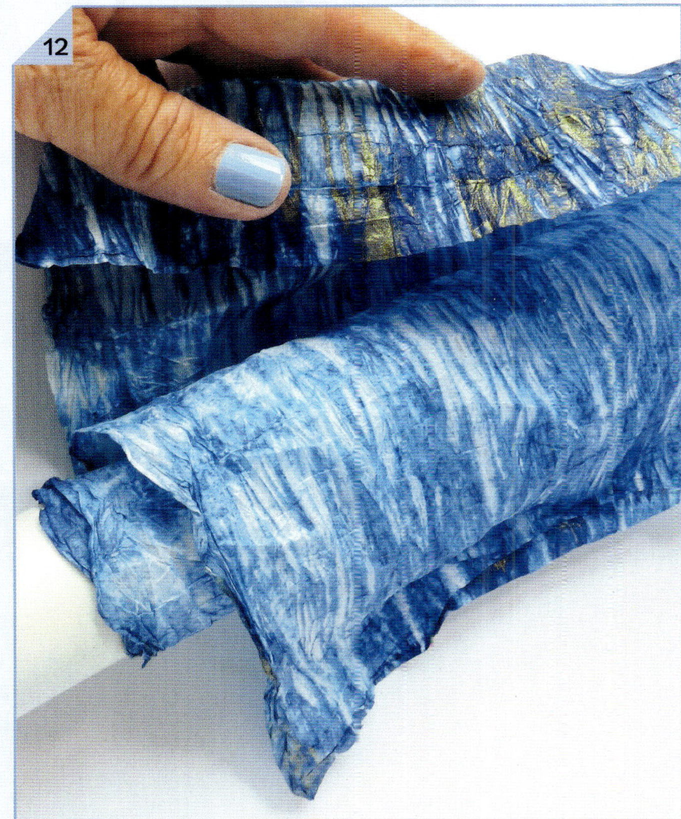

VARIATIONS:

Feel free to experiment and explore new ways of manipulating wet-strength tissue paper on the pole to create unique textures and effects in your artwork. Once the tissue paper is dry, you can use it for various crafts and decorations, such as gift wrap, paper flowers, or collage projects.

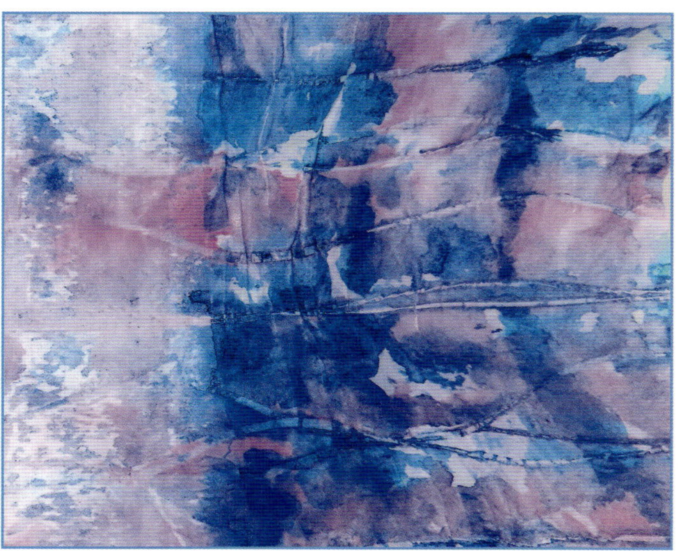

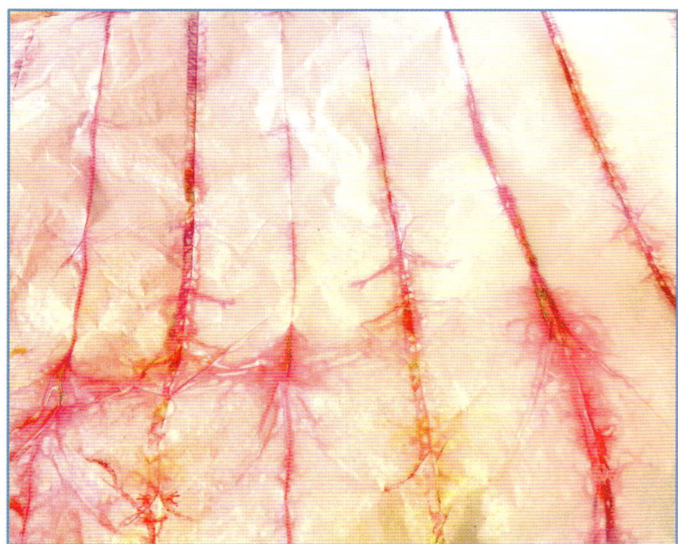

Hand painting

Rather than dipping the tissue, hand paint patterns with watercolour ink or dye using a paintbrush or sponge, while the tissue is wrapped on the pole, rather than dip dyeing. This enables the inks to mix and blend and allows you to create, for example, a beautiful watery effect when you use shades of blue, green and silver. Spray with more water to encourage further bleeding of colours, if needed.

Accordion folds

Fold the tissue paper into accordion pleats lengthwise before wrapping around the pole and securing with bands. Then wet and dye. Leave to dry overnight and remove the bands.
  This method can create defined stripes rather than ripples. The accordion folds give vertical lines and the elastic wraps give horizontal lines.

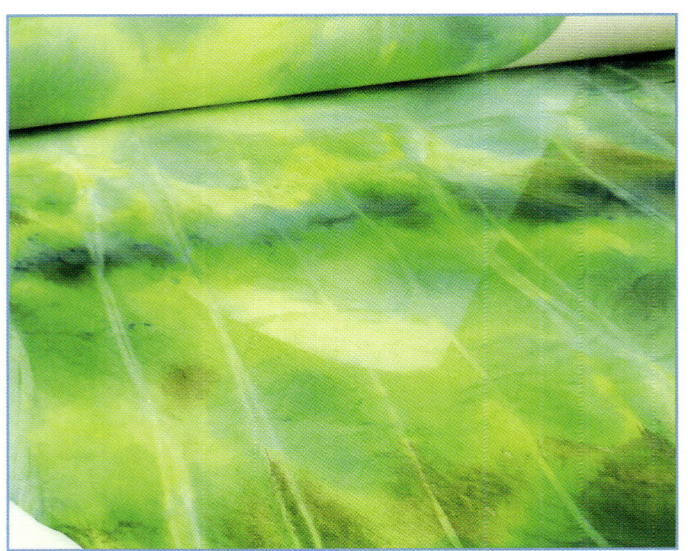

Diagonal ripples

Fold your tissue paper into a square or rectangle and turn it to a 45-degree angle across the pole. Wrap it round the pole in this diagonal way, overlapping as you go. Add an elastic band to secure both ends snugly to the pole. Add further elastic bands down the length to create more resist areas. Wet and dye, then leave to dry before snipping the elastic bands. Do not bunch the tissue paper (as in step 5 on page 25) when using this method.

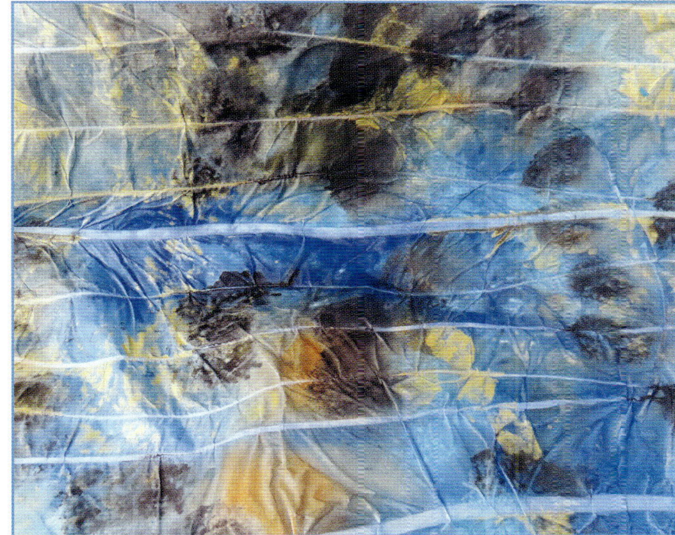

Tall glass jar shibori

Instead of a tube, reuse a large cylindrical vase (the type orchids are sold in) to wrap the tissue round, and add the elastics. I used a vase which was 35cm (13¾in) tall with a diameter of 11cm (4¼in). I folded a large sheet in half to fit over the jar. You will need larger elastic bands for this method. Add as many as you want. Then add ink using a sponge or paintbrush and leave to dry overnight. This technique gives a more open lined effect. Do not bunch the tissue paper when using this method.

Technique 4:
clamping (*itajime*)

Itajime is the name given to the ancient Japanese shibori tie-dye shape resist method, which involves folding fabric in triangles or squares then clamping it between wooden boards before dyeing. The wooden boards act as a resist to the dye, leaving undyed fabric beneath them.

This technique can easily be applied to wet-strength tissue paper. Choosing larger wooden shapes gives a less dense pattern than using smaller wooden resists. You can also fold the paper in a concertina and apply wooden pegs to act as a resist to the dye. Using this clamping method produces stunning repeating geometric patterns. You can use the dip-dye method on corners or sections, direct painting or full immersion into a dye bath.

You will need

Materials

- wet-strength white tissue paper sheets
- fabric dye in a selection of colours
- watercolour inks in a range of colours

Equipment

- selection of items to use as resists, e.g. wooden pegs, lollipop sticks, metal clips of different sizes, wooden chopsticks, coins or circular curtain weights (pairs of each shape are needed)
- spray bottle of water
- disposable plastic gloves
- large silicone mat or plastic tablecloth (to protect your workspace)
- parchment paper
- kitchen paper
- plastic or glass containers for fabric dye
- small and medium paintbrushes to apply ink
- plastic pipette
- elastic bands or hair ties
- heat gun
- scissors
- apron

METHOD:

1 Follow the instructions on the dye package to mix the dye solution(s).

2 Spread your tissue paper out on the silicone mat. Fold it in half lengthwise, matching the edges carefully.

3 Then fold the paper in half across the width.

4 Accordion fold the tissue paper until it is all folded into a triangle or square to suit the size of your shape. For neater patterns, be precise with your folds.

5 Place the folded tissue paper between two matching wooden shapes and add clips or elastic bands. Line up the shapes with each other. Ensure the binding is tight to minimize ink penetration. Alternatively, clip pairs of lollipop sticks or wooden shapes over the tissue paper, binding the ends with elastics.

6 It is easier to fold the paper when dry, then spray the paper all over with water, using the spray bottle.

7 Carefully submerge the damp, clamped tissue paper into the container of dye, allowing the dye to saturate through the paper.

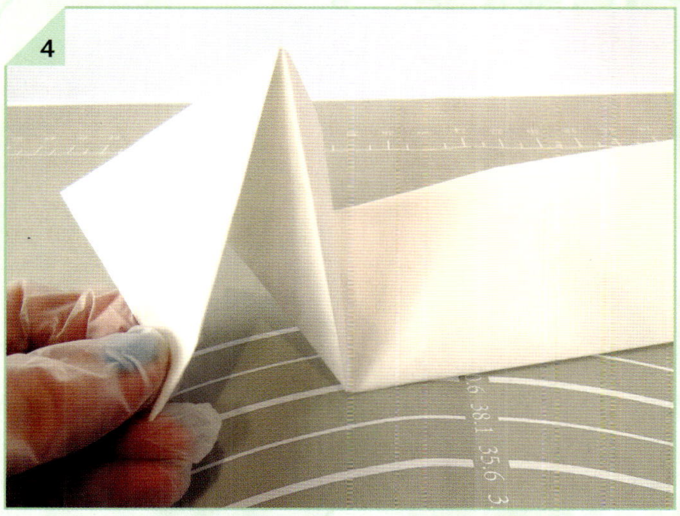

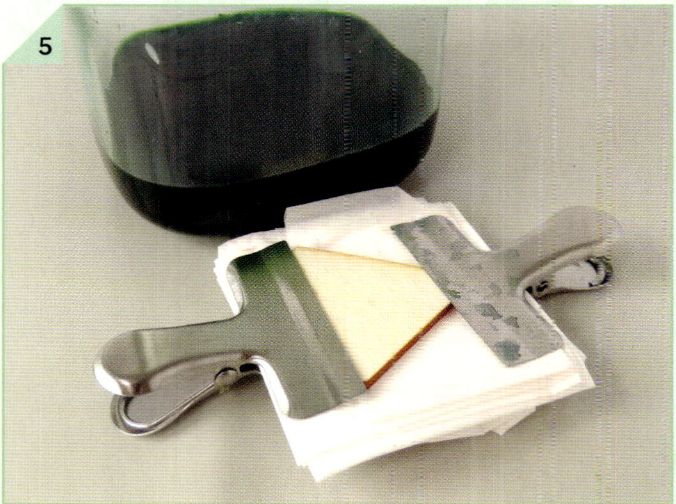

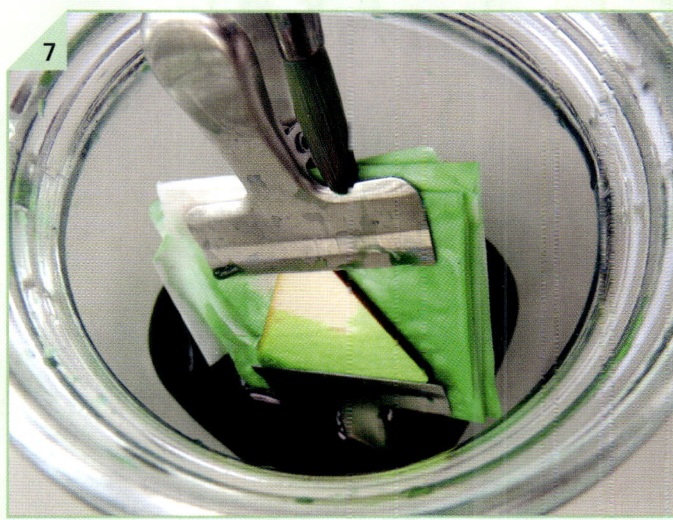

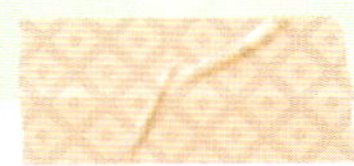

Tip

Wooden resist shapes or pegs absorb ink when used, so if you plan to reuse them, be aware that some of the previous dye may come off on your new project. To minimize this, keep certain shapes for certain dye colours.

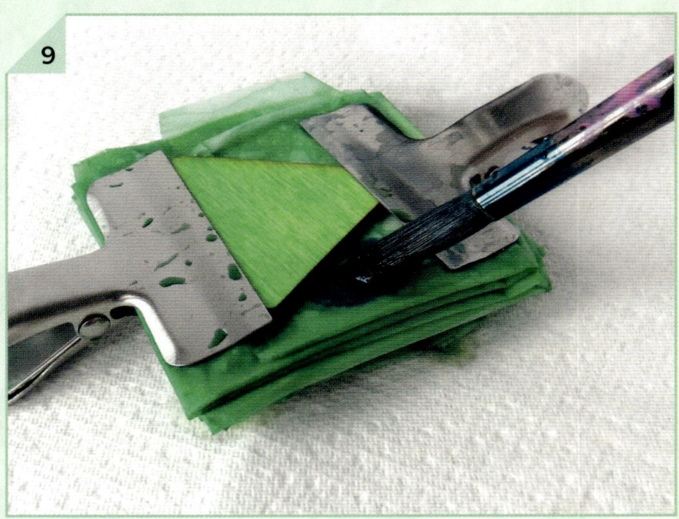

8 Slowly lift the clamped tissue paper up and allow ink to dribble from the end. Lay it on kitchen paper to soak up any excess ink.

9 Add hints of colour using ink on a paintbrush. If the clamped object is too large to dip dye, simply add the paint or dye with a paintbrush or pipette. Spray on extra water if needed to encourage the colours to spread.

10 Leave the clamped tissue paper to dry overnight by laying it on parchment paper until fully dry before unwrapping. Take care not to tear the tissue paper when unwrapping.

11 If you have used only metal clips and not elastics, you can dry the tissue paper at this stage using a heat gun on a low setting. Take care not to burn the tissue paper.

12 Unwrap carefully to see the beautiful, geometrical, inky pattern you have created.

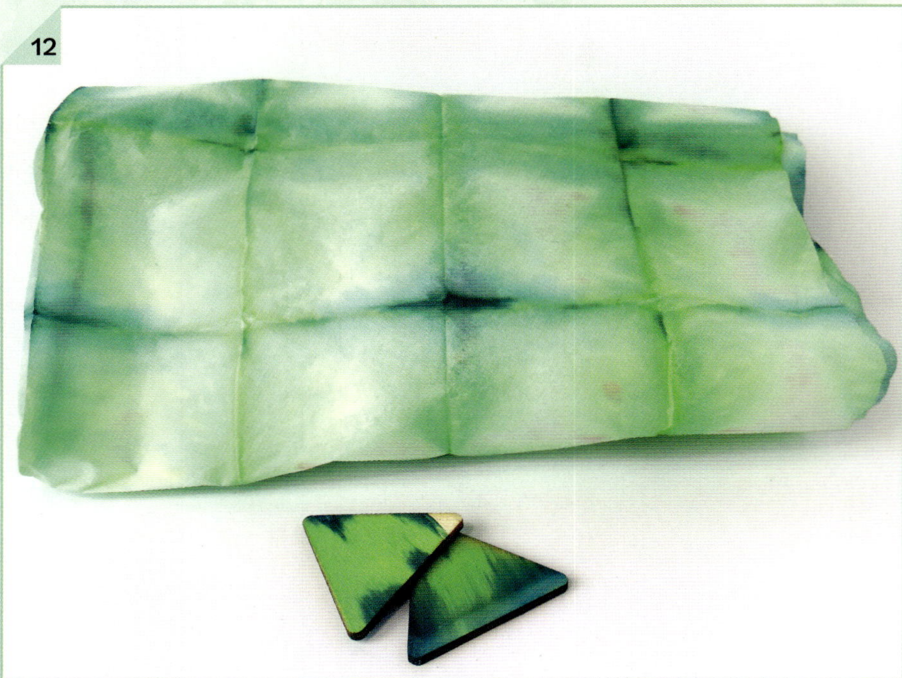

VARIATIONS:

Enjoy creating your own individual geometric designs using the ideas below. These are especially effective when you use dark indigo fabric dye, as the resist patterns stand out strongly against the blue background.

Wooden pegs (a)

Fold the tissue paper into a long rectangle and clip on wooden pegs. To achieve an asymmetrical design, offset the pegs rather than lining them up. Dye, dry and unwrap.

Lollipop sticks (b)

Using lollipop sticks has given tall, trunk-like resists which could be used to represent a forest in the background of a collage.

Clamped skewer (c)

Cut the wide end from chopsticks with sharp scissors and put two over the corner of your folded tissue paper. Secure with a bulldog clip. Fully immerse in the dye bath or dip sections in more than one colour of dye. Leave to dry before removing the clips and wooden pieces.

Clamped coins or curtain weights (d)

Use bulldog clips to secure coins or curtain weights over folded tissue paper and immerse in the dye. Leave to dry before removing the clips. Wipe the coins or weights clean. The result is a repeated circular resist pattern. Depending on the placement of the circular shapes, you can create some lovely flower-like patterns.

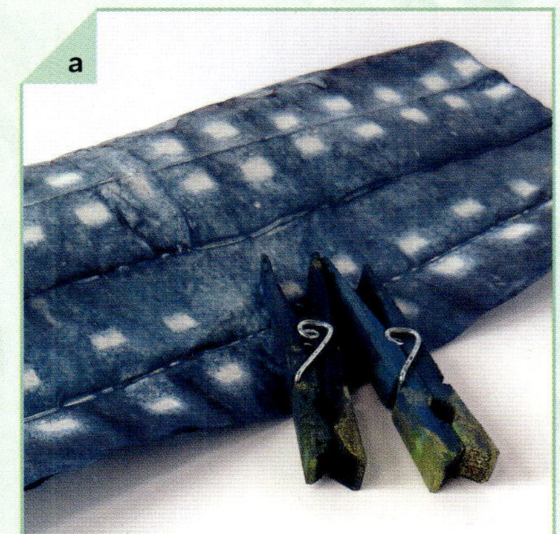

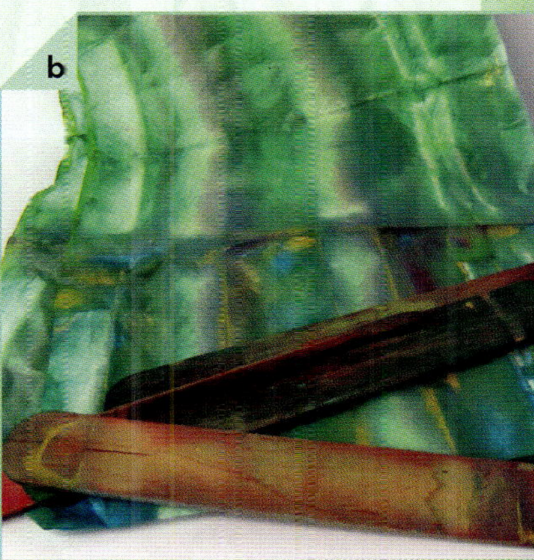

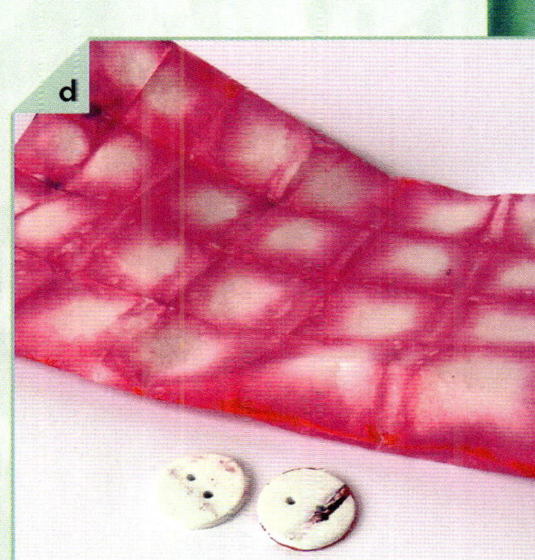

Embrace mistakes

If you have ink leakage from a clamp that was not tight enough, enjoy the unexpected results! This blue sheet was dyed using a small circle, but the results were uneven. However, the patterns look like beautiful moons, so could be used in a collage.

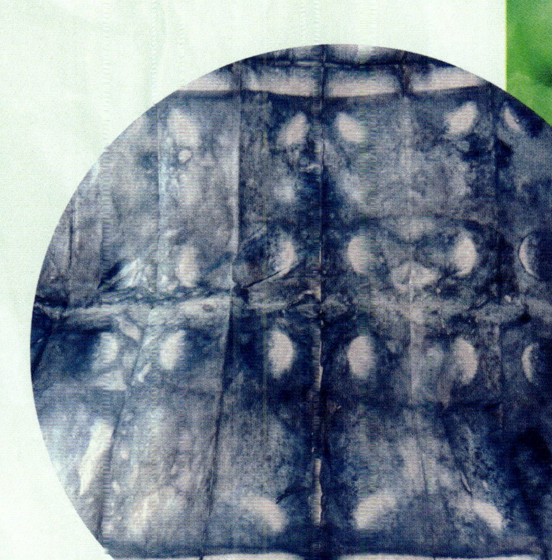

Technique 5:
folding spiderwebs

This is one of my favourite methods of dyeing tissue paper because of the mesmerizing patterns that emerge. This method gives spectacular results and works best on a square piece of tissue paper which is gathered by hand and bound to achieve resist marks.
You can vary the binding type and amount – by doing a simple, single bind to give an individual line, by repeat winding elastic in a straight line to give wider lines or by criss-crossing the elastics to give a more organic result. These designs all burst outwards from the centre of the square of tissue paper.

You will need

Materials

- wet-strength white tissue paper sheets
- fabric dye in a selection of colours
- watercolour inks in a range of colours

Equipment

- spray bottle of water
- disposable plastic gloves
- large silicone mat or plastic tablecloth (to protect your workspace)
- parchment paper
- kitchen paper
- elastic bands or hair ties
- plastic or glass containers for fabric dye
- small and medium paintbrushes
- long-handled paintbrush
- heat gun
- scissors
- apron
- wooden lollipop sticks, small clips and pegs (optional)

METHOD 1: GATHERED

1 Follow the instructions on the dye package to mix the dye solution(s).

2 Spread your tissue paper out on the silicone mat. Fold one edge up to form a square and cut off the excess tissue paper.

3 Pick up the middle point of the tissue paper square with one hand and with the other hand, smooth down the folds. You can put the end of a long-handled round paintbrush in the middle and pull the tissue paper gently down over this. Smooth the sides of the tissue downwards into folds.

4 Working from the centre outwards, add elastic bindings at intervals down the length. Ensure the binding is tight to minimize ink penetration and achieve a clean resist pattern. Remove the paintbrush handle before you add too many elastics!

5 You can vary the type of binding, for example, create single, straight lines or criss-cross. A tight criss-cross binding is very effective at the top of the piece of tissue to create a detailed centre.

6 Spritz the paper all over with water, using the spray bottle.

7 Carefully submerge the whole bound, damp tissue paper in the container of dye, allowing the dye to saturate through the paper.

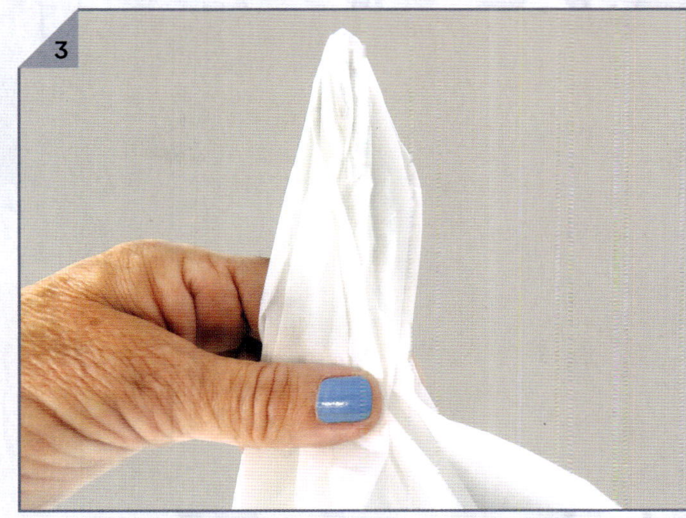

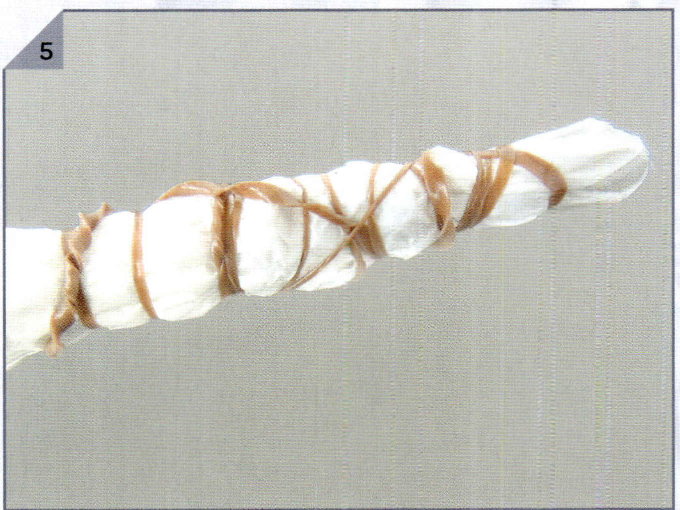

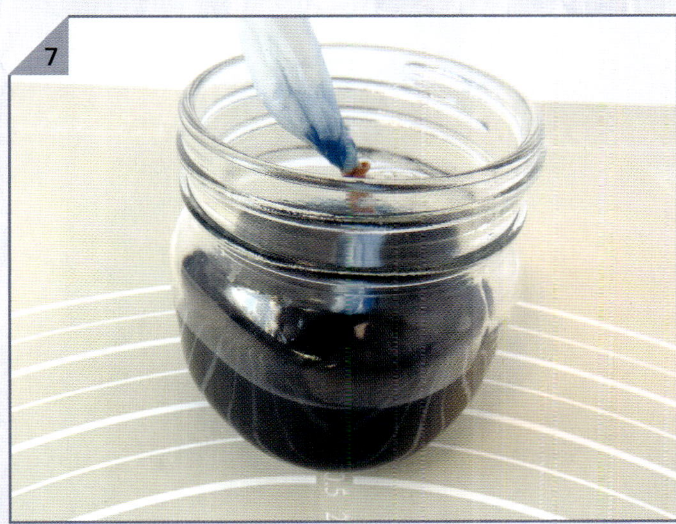

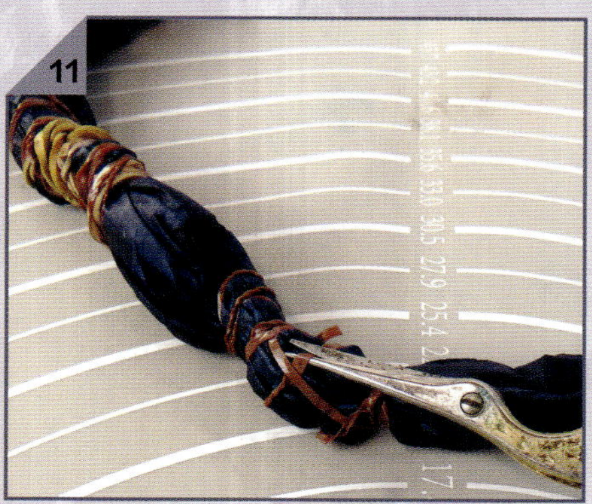

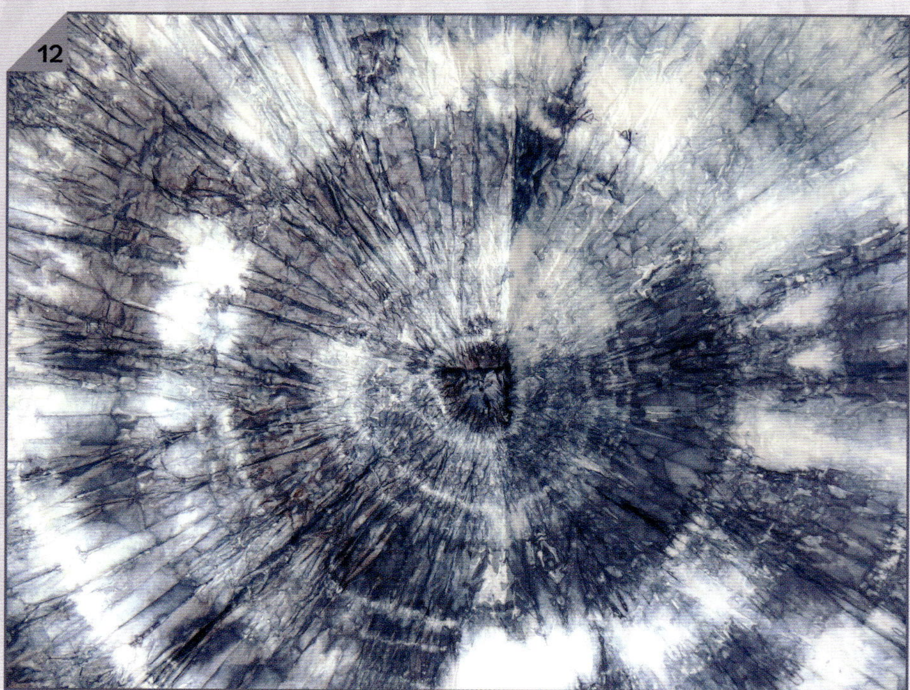

8 Slowly lift the tissue up and allow dye to dribble from the end. Wearing disposable plastic gloves, squeeze gently to remove excess dye. If your tissue is too large to immerse in your dye pot, lay it on a piece of kitchen paper and apply the inks with a paintbrush.

9 You can enhance your design by painting on touches of gold ink as highlights.

10 Lay the tissue paper on parchment and leave it to dry overnight.

11 Unwrap it carefully and cut the elastics.

12 This simple gathered technique achieves some amazing, organic results.

METHOD 2: BUNCHED

Pull the tissue paper over the handle of a long paintbrush, with the middle of the paper at the tip of the handle. Smooth down the tissue and attach elastics so it is bunched. Tie elastic bands tightly at intervals along the length. For neater patterns, be precise with your folds. Roll up and immerse in the dye bath. Remove it and leave it to dry on parchment. This gives a more regular result than the more detailed spiderweb design described in method 1.

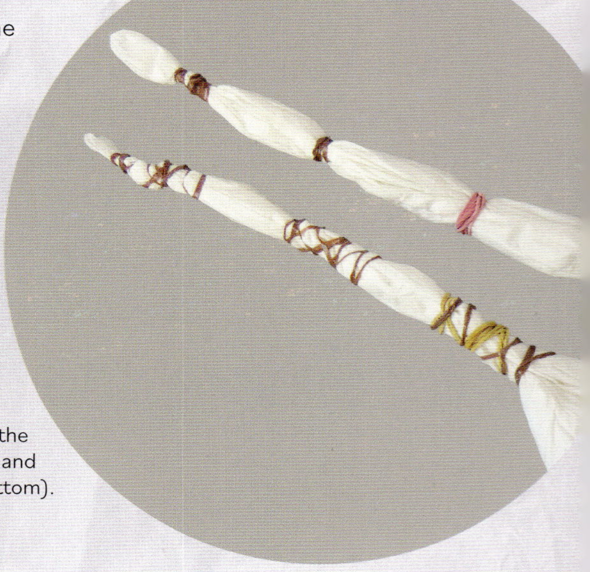

Here you can see the difference in the tying for the bunched method (top) and the gathered method (bottom).

VARIATIONS:

Each of the following designs is created by folding the tissue into an accordion shape for dyeing as follows:

1 Fold the square tissue paper diagonally into a triangle.

2 Fold this triangle in half.

3 Open up the triangle with the right-angled corner at the top.

4 Hold the bottom left corner and fold it up to the middle of the triangle at the top. Press edge.

5 Open up the tissue paper.

6 Fold up bottom left corner to the new crease.

7 Fold this flap backwards on itself.

8 Each time you fold, crease the edges.

9 Keep folding the triangular flap forward and backwards until you meet the middle crease.

10 Repeat the above for the right-hand corner.

11 You should have an accordion-folded long triangle.

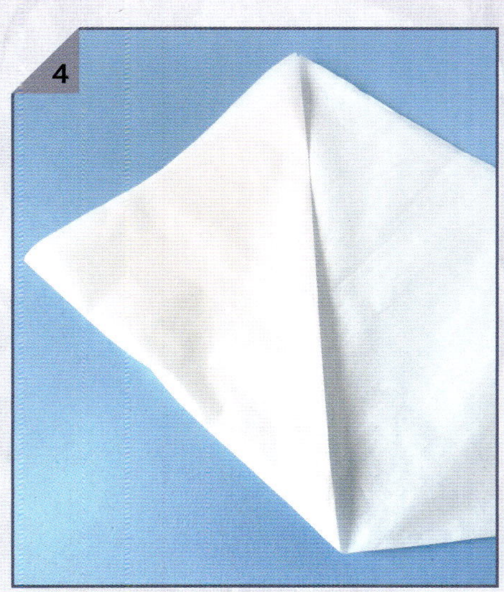

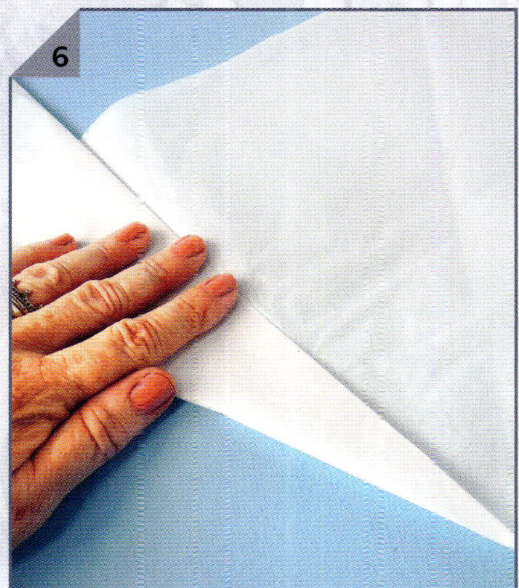

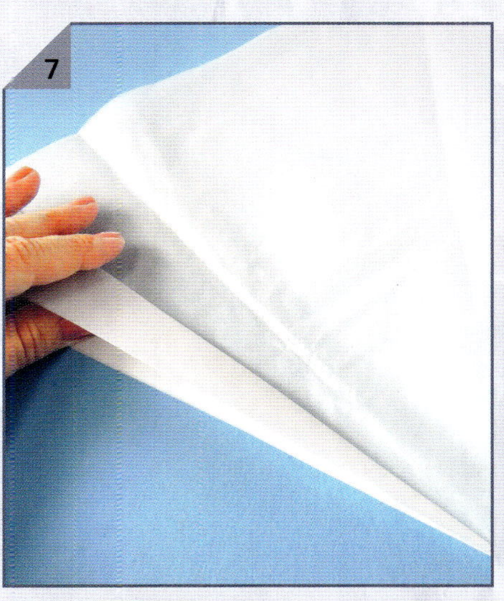

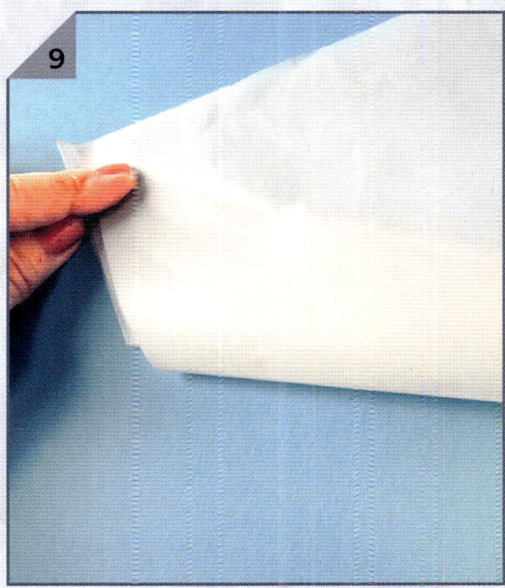

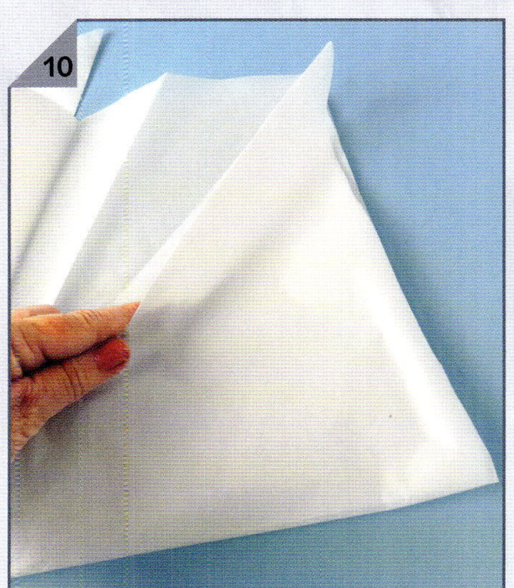

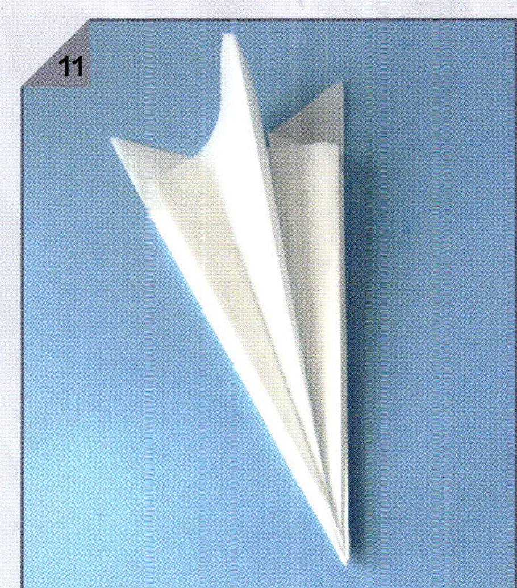

Clip resist

Take the accordion-folded long triangle from the previous page, then add an elastic to the top to secure the tissue paper.

1 Place small clips at intervals along the length of the paper.

2 Roll up the folded, clipped tissue paper and immerse it in a dye bath, or hand paint it.

3 Remove it and leave it to dry on parchment overnight.

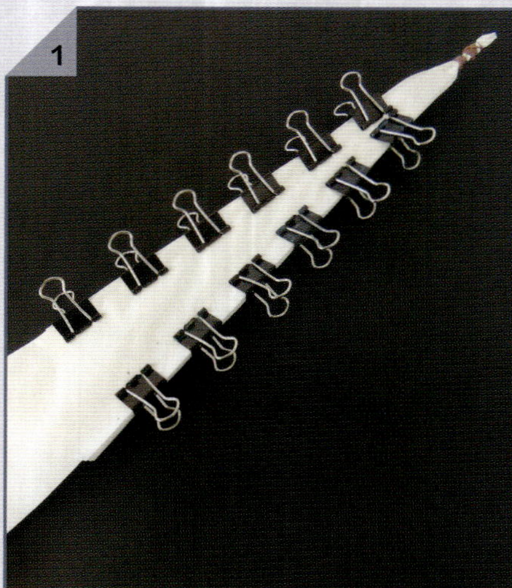
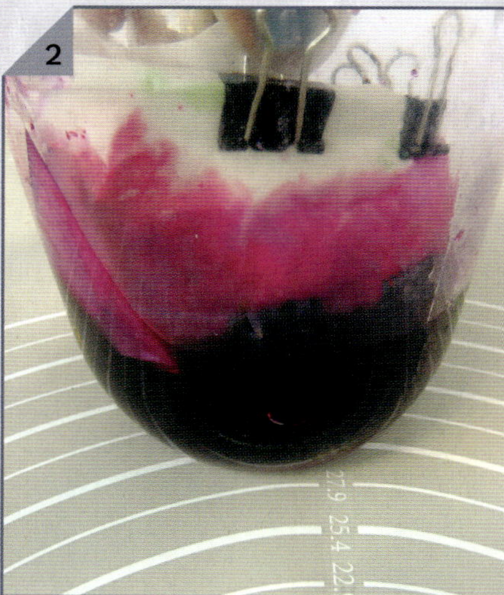
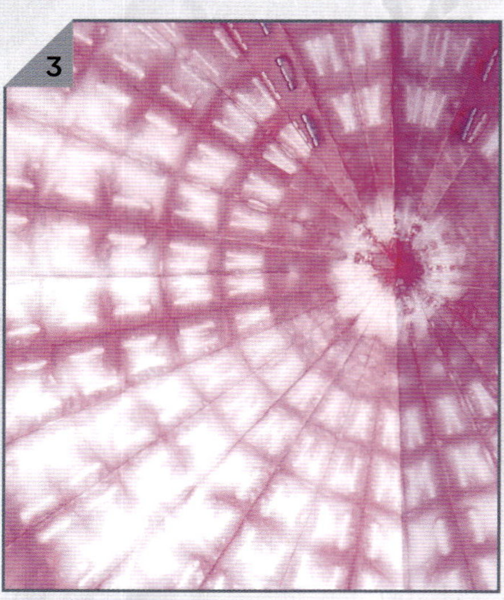

Wooden peg resist

This follows the same method as the clip resist technique above, but with slightly different results.

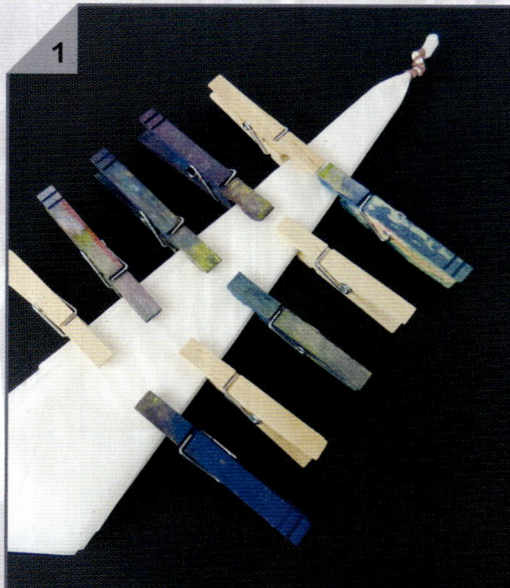
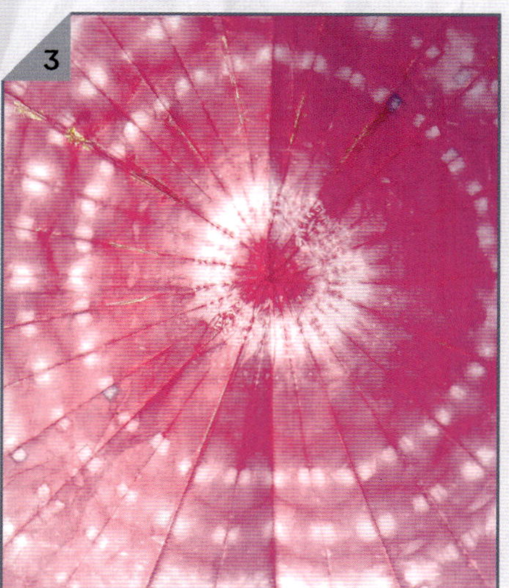

Lollipop stick resist

Prepare an accordion-folded long triangle as above and tie an elastic approximately 3cm (1¼in) from the top (the centre of the paper).

1 Attach lollipop sticks in pairs across the length at intervals. You can vary the lollipop stick size to give wider or thinner resist bands Secure the sticks on both sides with elastic bands.

2 Roll up the piece and immerse it in a dye bath.

3 Remove it and leave it to dry on parchment

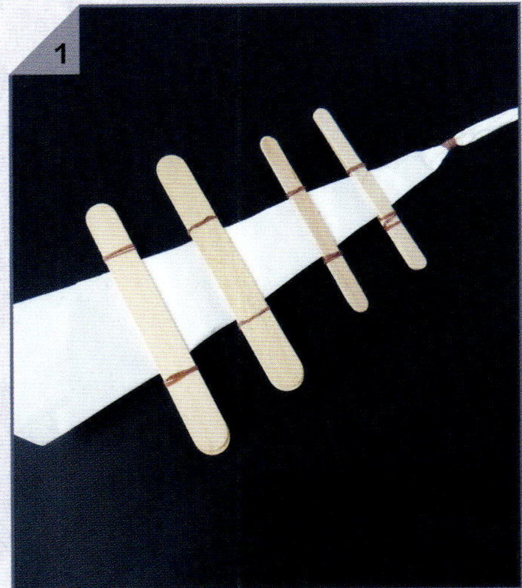

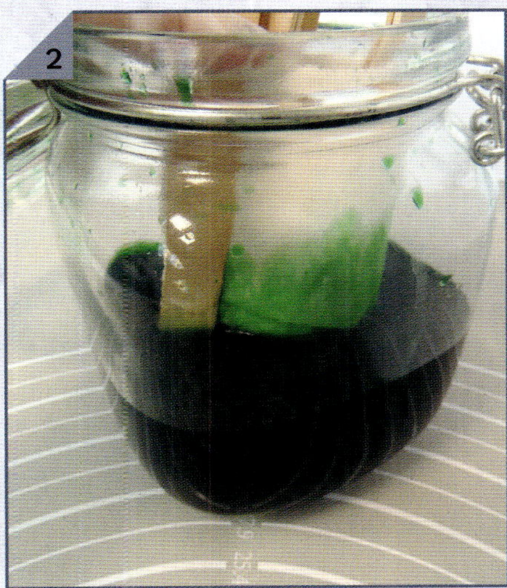

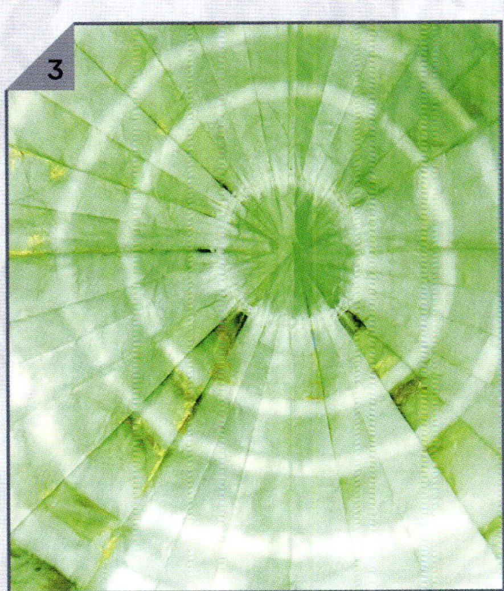

It is effective to dip dye the tail of the long triangle and then hand paint the rest with different colours, for example complementary colours or splashes of gold.

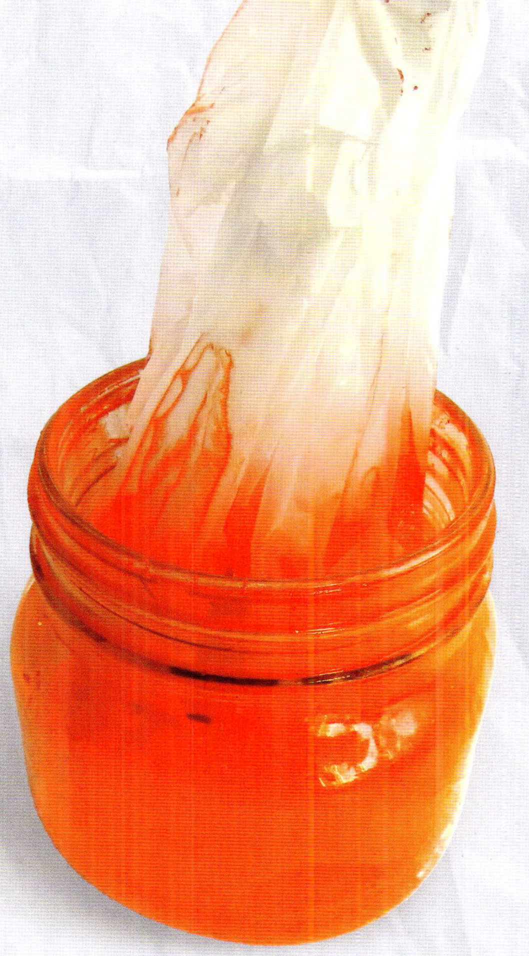

Technique 6:
twisting

Painting flowers is one of my passions and I tend to see flowers in any designs I make. This simple twisting technique gives very organic blossom shapes, and I love to use it as an under-layer for my floral encaustic wax or resin paintings. This technique produces some stunning results, especially if vibrant colours are used. Remember that the inks and dyes will dry a little lighter than they appear when wet.

In project 10 on pages 132–137 you can learn how to create a fantastic floral painting on a wooden board, using your twisted dyed tissue paper as the base. Flower centres can be enhanced, and the painting can be sealed with encaustic wax or resin, both of which will enrich the abstract floral design.

I hope you will enjoy creating this type of design as much as I do. Let's twist!

You will need

Materials

- wet-strength white tissue paper sheets
- fabric dye in a selection of colours
- watercolour inks in a range of colours, including gold for highlights

Equipment

- small to medium-sized empty (recycled) bottles
- spray bottle of water
- disposable plastic gloves
- large silicone mat or plastic tablecloth (to protect your workspace)
- parchment paper
- kitchen paper
- plastic or glass containers for fabric dye
- pot of clean water
- small and medium paintbrushes
- heat gun
- apron

METHOD:

1 Follow the instructions on the dye package to mix the dye solution. If you are using watercolour inks, dilute them with water in cups, according to your desired colour intensity. For stronger hues, use watercolour or acrylic inks straight from the bottle.

2 Place the tissue paper on the protected work surface.

3 Spray the whole sheet with water to dampen – this makes it easier to twist.

4 Select three bottles of different sizes. Take the largest bottle and place it under the tissue paper towards one corner.

5 Place the damp tissue paper over the top of the bottle and pull it slowly down, smoothing the pleats and twisting gently from the top at the same time. Do several twists, tucking the ends around the base of the bottle.

6 Take the next bottle and place it under another free area of the tissue paper. Twist slowly in the same direction as you did with the first bottle. Tuck in the ends.

7 If you have space, you can add a third small bottle with a gentle twist. The centres of the bottles will form the flower centres in your design and the radiating lines around the twist will give the petals.

8 Twist all the bottles in together and tuck all the ends in snugly around the bases.

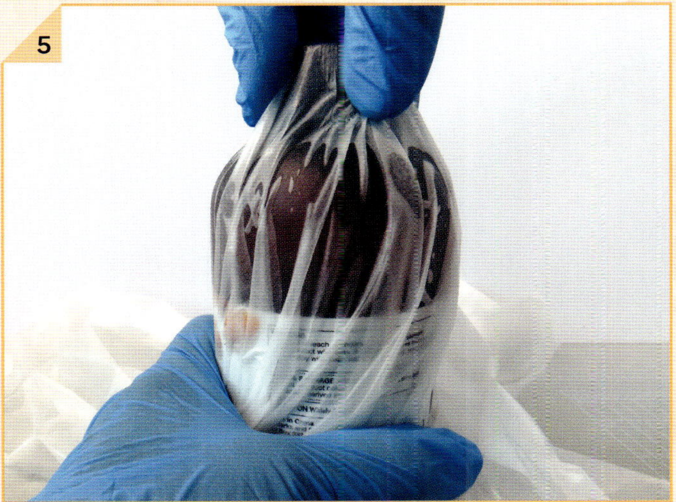

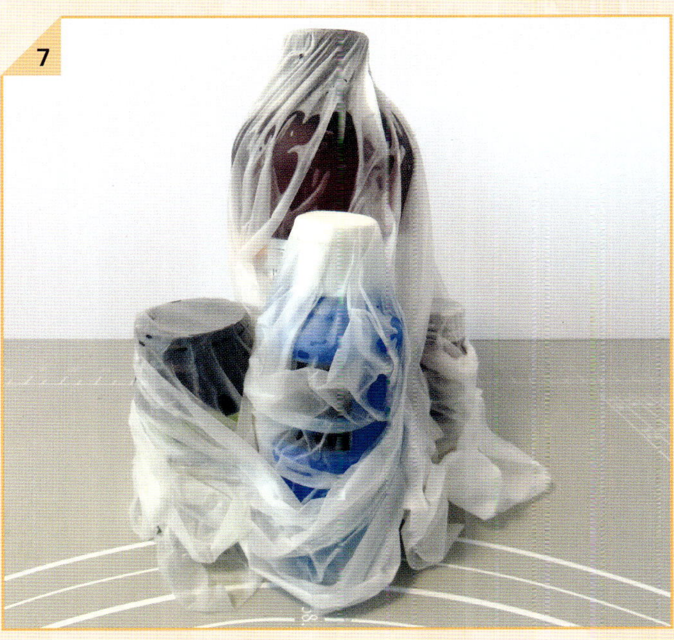

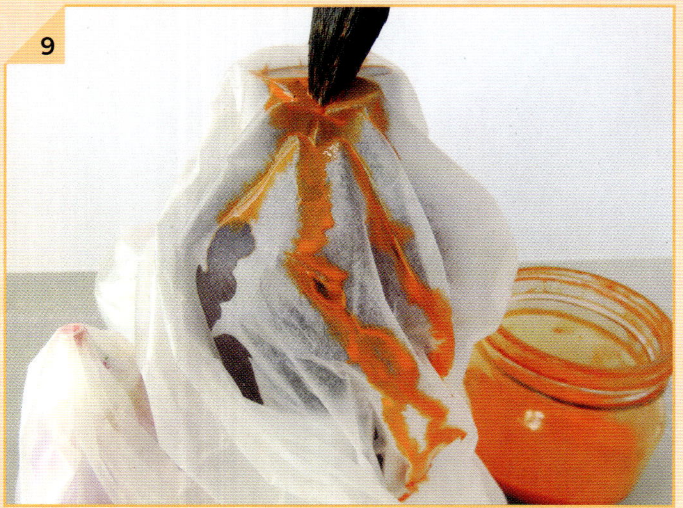

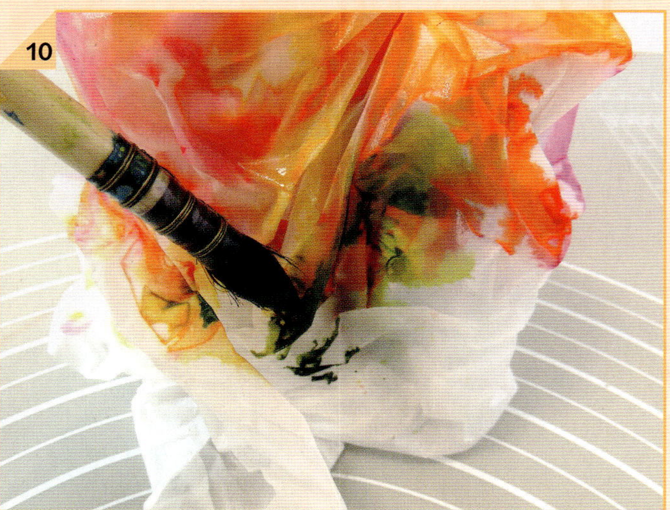

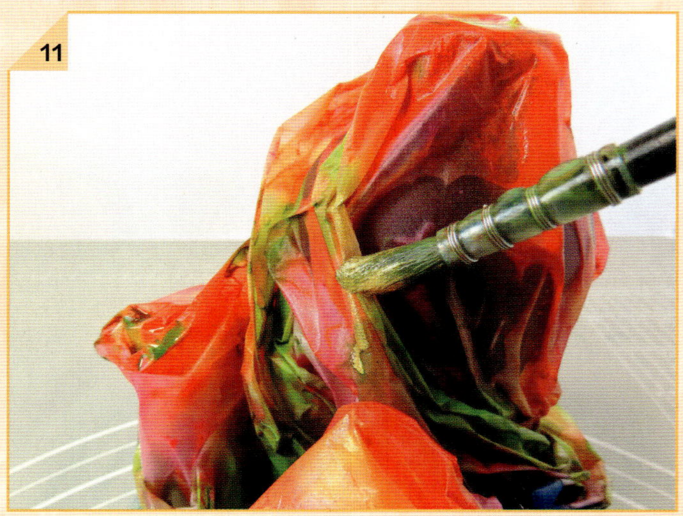

9 Use ink droppers or a paintbrush to apply dye or inks onto the tissue paper. Using a smaller paintbrush, add some ink to the flower centre (the bottle top). Clean your brush in water before adding another colour to minimize contamination. Repeat for the other two bottles.

10 Using the larger paintbrush, swipe on other ink colours around the centres. I use fabric dye to add darker greens and blues to give depth, especially around the edges of the tissue paper.

11 Add further watercolour or acrylic ink, if needed, to the twisted sections, being sure to drop some colour into the folded areas. I love to add gold paint on the creases to give highlights on the radiating petals.

12 Add more water with the spray bottle, if needed, to encourage the colours to mix and be absorbed by the tissue paper. Always keep the paper damp.

13 Gather up the twisted tissue and bottles and set them aside on parchment paper to dry, ideally overnight.

14 Alternatively, if you are impatient to see your design, you can dry the dyed tissue paper with a heat gun on a low setting. Slowly unwrap the paper and dry gently as you go.

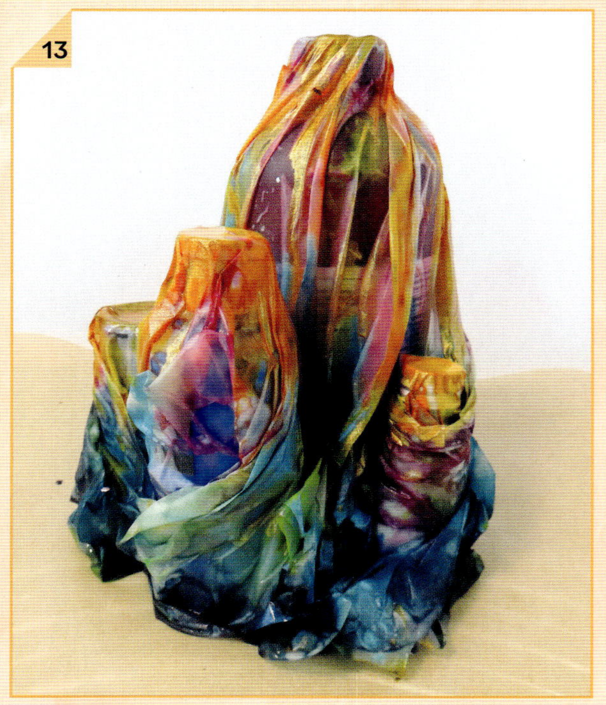

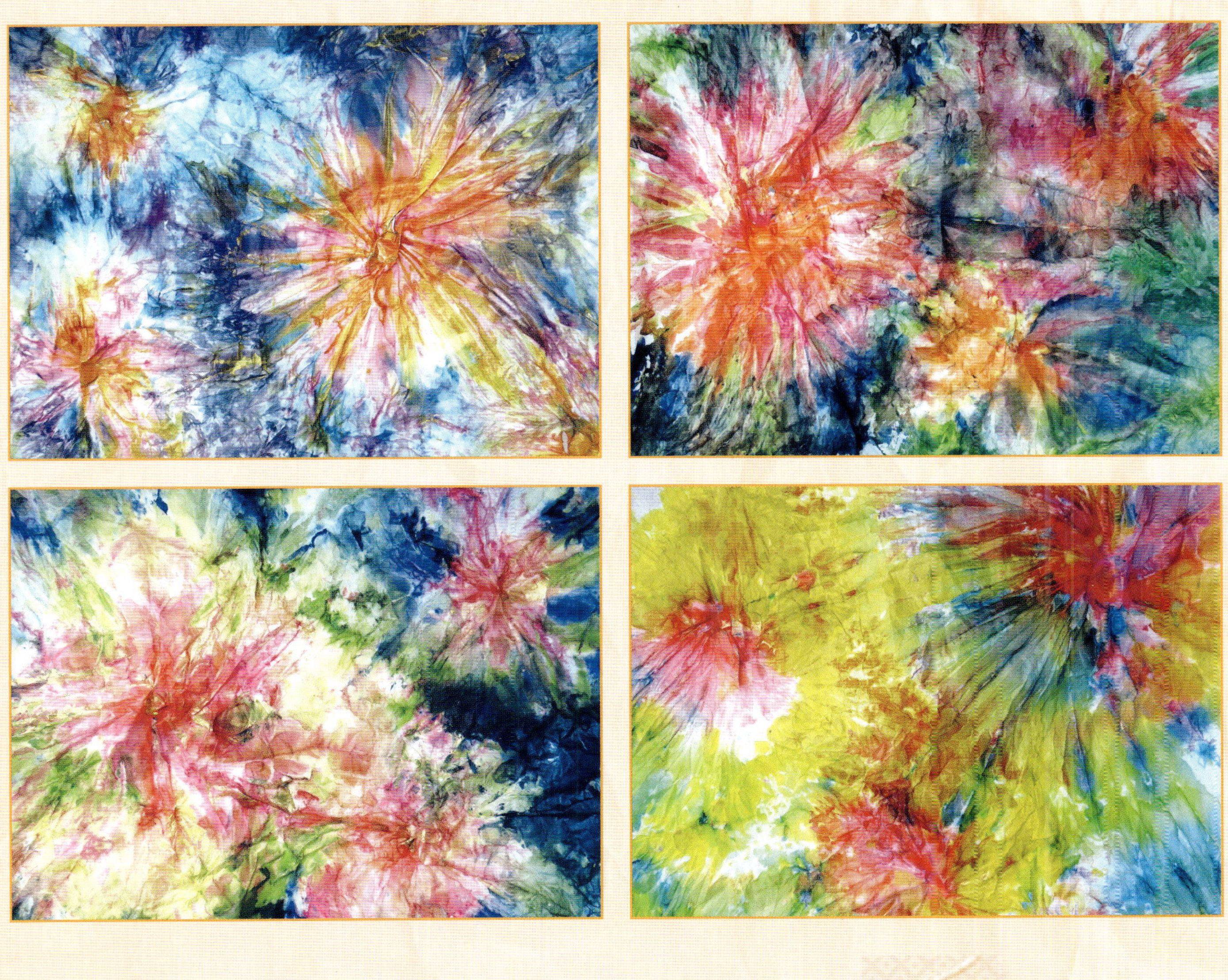

Tip

Open up the sheet when it is partially damp and start to dry
gently with the heat gun. If you leave it too long or over-dry
it with the heat gun, the tissue can stick together and will
need to be gently pulled apart. This comes with a danger of
ripping – if this starts to happen, spray a little water on the
dried section and it should pull apart more easily.

Technique 7:
tie dye

The shibori tie-dye method of tying beans into cloth is called binding.
Small objects like beans are placed on the fabric, then the fabric is folded
and tied tightly around the objects. When the fabric is dyed, the areas covered
by the beans create a resist, resulting in intricate and organic patterns. It is
possible to apply some of this binding technique to wet-strength tissue paper
by tying elastic bands around various objects to achieve stunning dye resist
designs resembling flower centres. These make an excellent starting point for
a painting, since the centres can be further embellished.

You will need

Materials

- wet-strength white tissue
  paper sheets
- fabric dye, watercolour or acrylic
  inks in a selection of colours,
  including gold ink for highlights

Equipment

- a selection of circular objects:
  rubber or polystyrene balls,
  recycled lids and bottle tops,
  marbles, baking beans, glass
  stones and pebbles used to
  fill vases, large beads, buttons
  and circular curtain weights;
  also irregular objects such as
  collected pebbles or stones
- spray bottle of water
- disposable plastic gloves
- large silicone mat or plastic
  tablecloth (to protect
  your workspace)

- parchment paper
- kitchen paper
- plastic or glass containers for
  fabric dye
- paper cups
- pot of clean water
- elastic bands or hair ties
- garden twine or string
- small and medium
  paintbrushes
- small scissors
- heat gun
- apron
- masking fluid (optional)

METHOD:

1 Follow the instructions on the dye package to mix the dye solution. If you are using watercolour inks, dilute them with water in cups, according to your desired colour intensity. For stronger hues, use watercolour or acrylic inks straight from the bottle.

2 Place the dry tissue paper on the protected work surface.

3 Wrap the dry tissue paper carefully over the largest ball and secure it with an elastic band. Take time when tying the objects as the tissue can tear when you wrap an elastic band round it. The tighter you wrap, the greater the dye resist.

4 Spread out any tissue paper folds neatly since this will affect your final design.

5 Take the next ball and place it under another area of the tissue paper. Again, wrap it carefully in the tissue paper and secure it tightly with an elastic band.

6 Continue adding your balls, marbles, lids or other objects across your tissue paper, until you have completed your design. Leave some areas untied, to add depth to your composition.

7 Try adding extra elastics to some tied objects to give a spiderweb effect round them.

8 Now spray the paper and tied objects all over with water, using the spray bottle. This will help the dye to penetrate the tissue paper.

9 Use ink droppers or a paintbrush to apply dye or inks onto the tissue paper. Using a smaller paintbrush, add ink to the flower centres (the circular objects). Clean your brush and add another colour to encourage blending.

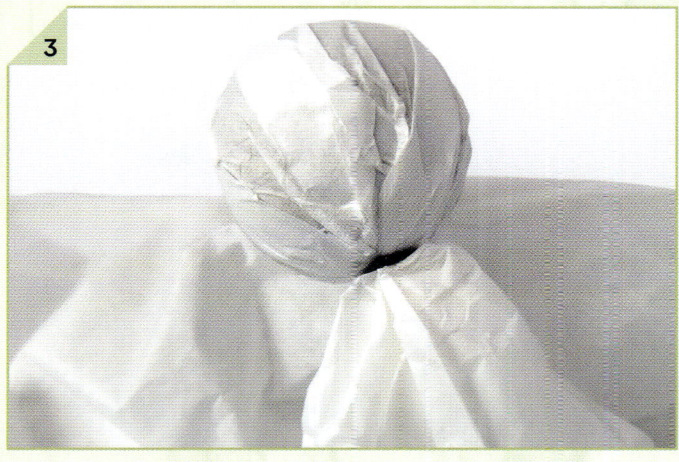

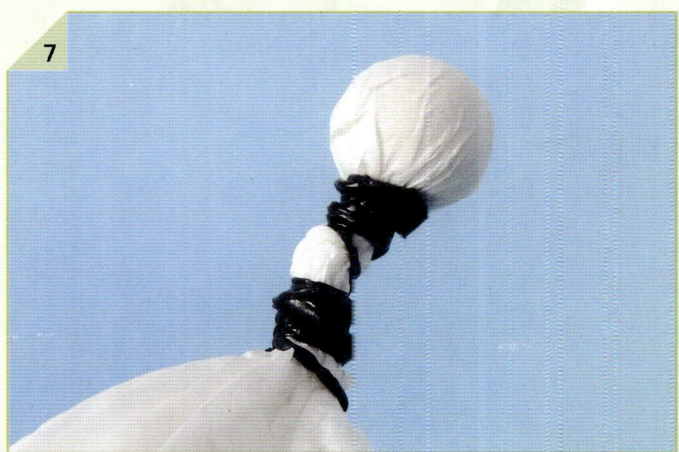

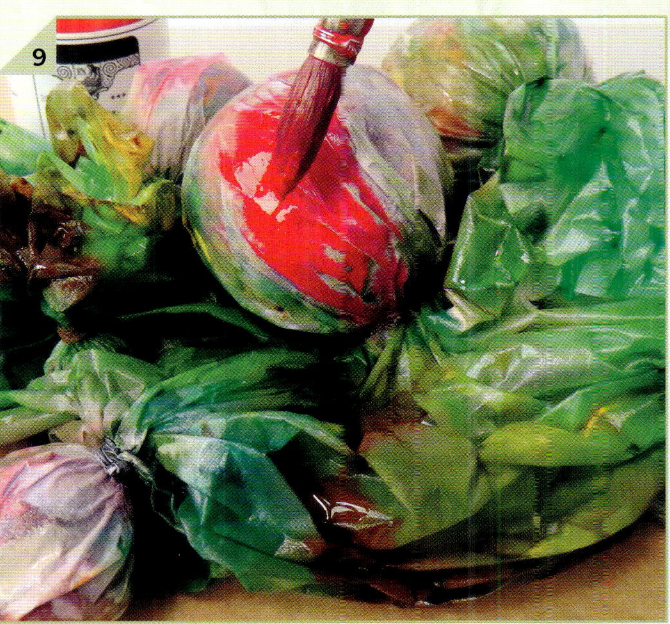

10 Using the larger paintbrush, swipe on other ink colours round the centres. Use fabric dye to add darker greens and blues to give depth, especially round the edges of the tissue paper.

11 Add further watercolour ink or acrylic ink, if needed, to cover the whole sheet of tied paper. Add gold paint on some centres to provide highlights.

12 Add more water with the spray bottle, if needed, to encourage the colours to mix and be absorbed by the tissue paper. Always keep the tissue paper damp.

13 Gather up the tissue paper with the bound objects and and set it aside on parchment paper to dry, ideally overnight. Do not dry it with a heat gun at this stage or the elastic bands will break!

14 Unwrap the tissue paper carefully the next day, using scissors to cut the elastic bands off, and carefully remove the bound objects. The beautiful resist patterns will begin to emerge.

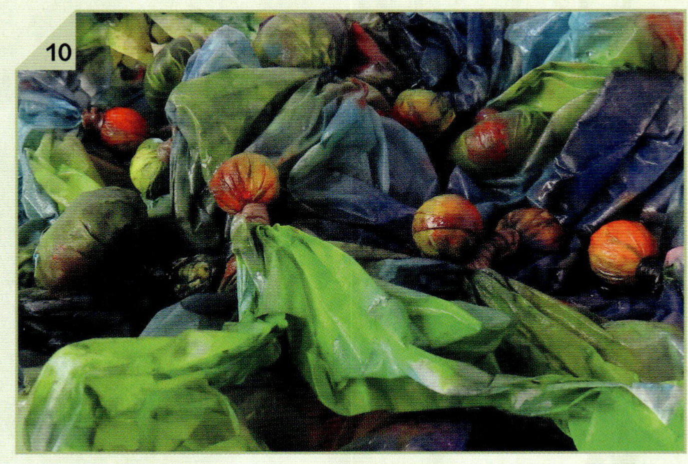

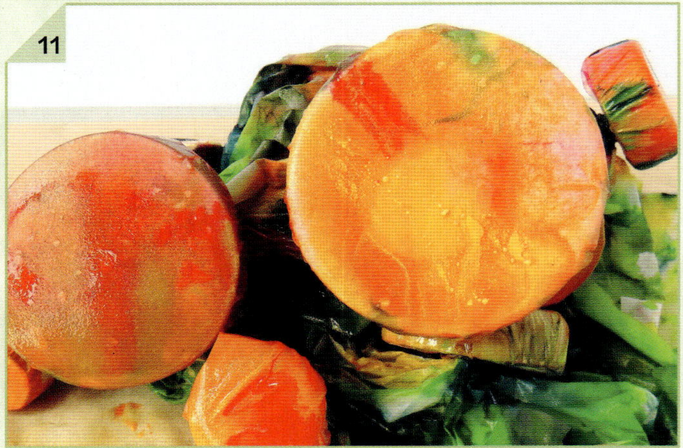

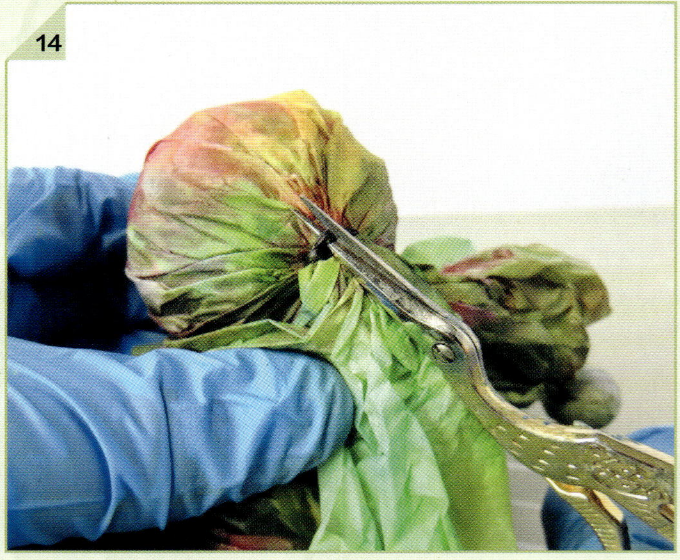

Tip
Used rubber balls, marbles and stones will inevitably have ink on them. Wipe them with wet kitchen paper to minimize contamination in your next project.

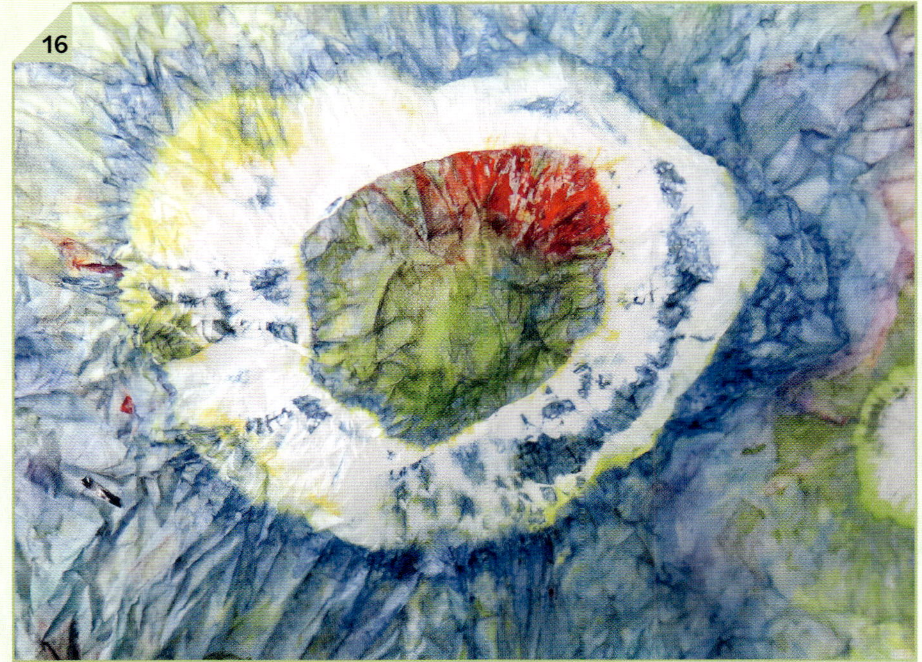

15 You can further dry the unwrapped sheet by hanging it up to dry or by using a heat gun on a low setting.

16 Your results will be an amazing array of tie-dyed floral patterns.

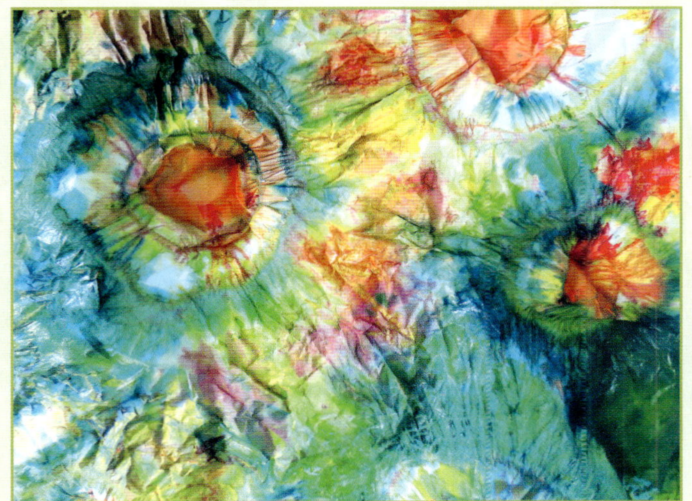

Cluster bottle tops or beans together and vary the size of items used for a more organic design. Try twisting the ball or lid gently before applying the elastic to give more defined lines.
Lids with lined edges can provide beautiful results.

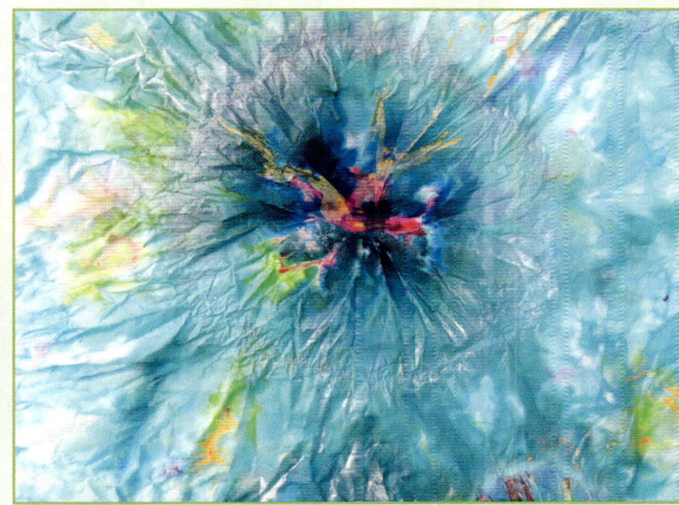

Adding colour to a tissue-covered polystyrene ball gives a lovely organic, veined effect.

EXTRA DESIGN IDEAS:

Unwrapping these tie-dye designs unveils mesmerizing patterns. The intricate folds and shapes transform the tissue paper into a work of art. It never fails to excite me how the colours blend and merge to create a visual feast.

You can use the tissue paper as it is for wrapping paper, but it can also be used to make bookmarks and gift tags or to decorate tealight holders, trays and wooden boxes, as demonstrated in the projects which follow.

In project 10 on pages 132–137 you will learn how to incorporate this type of design into imaginative floral paintings.

Full immersion

If you fully immerse a tied piece of tissue paper in one colour of fabric dye, you can create a stunning, high-contrast design which is more abstract than floral. Use a darker, more intense mix of fabric dye to achieve this. Tie the objects tightly to create bold white resist shapes. This makes an excellent design for wrapping paper.

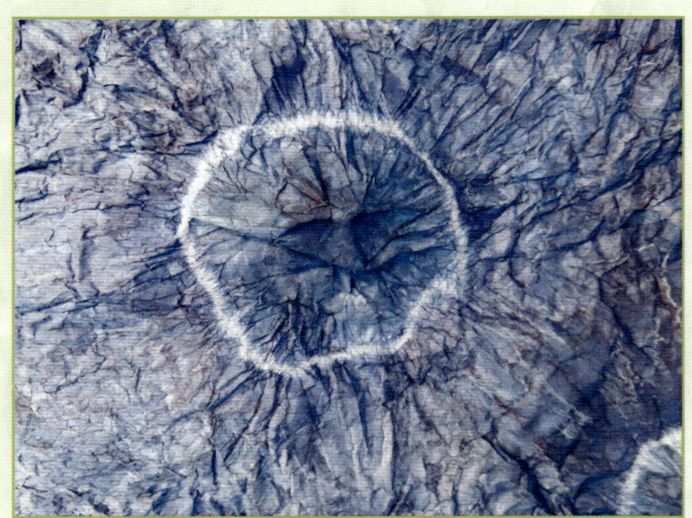

Masking fluid on centres

1 Create a patterned centre to your floral images by adding dots of masking fluid when the tissue paper is wrapped but still dry.

2 Wait until the masking fluid fully dries, then add colour as before by hand painting or dip dyeing to give subtle organic results when the piece is dry.

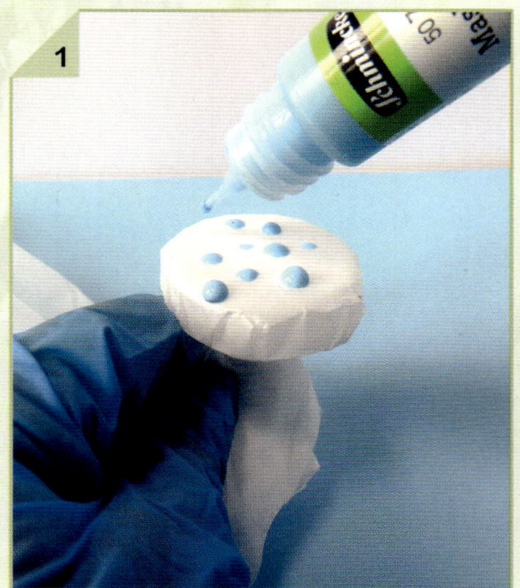

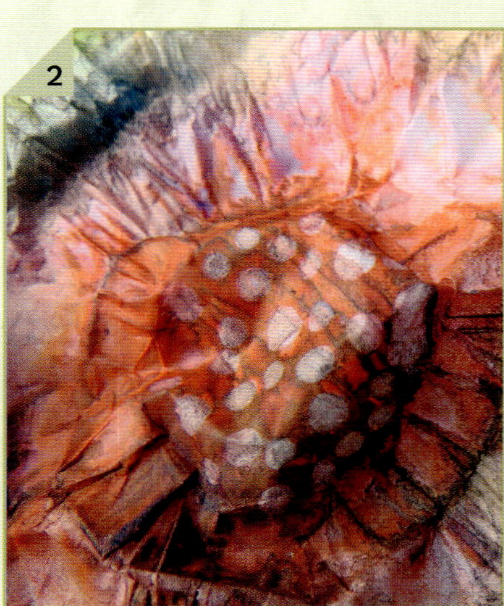

Criss-cross patterns

On larger lids you can criss-cross extra elastic bands over the flower centre to give a different lined effect (right). Also try garden twine or string as a resist (far right). This can give a more subtle resist effect than elastics, due to its greater absorbency.

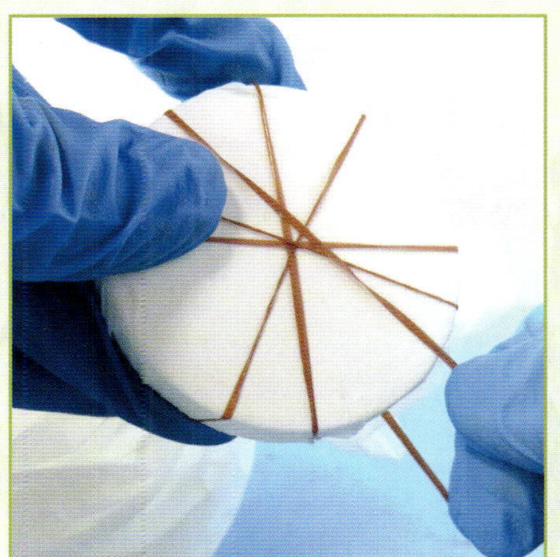

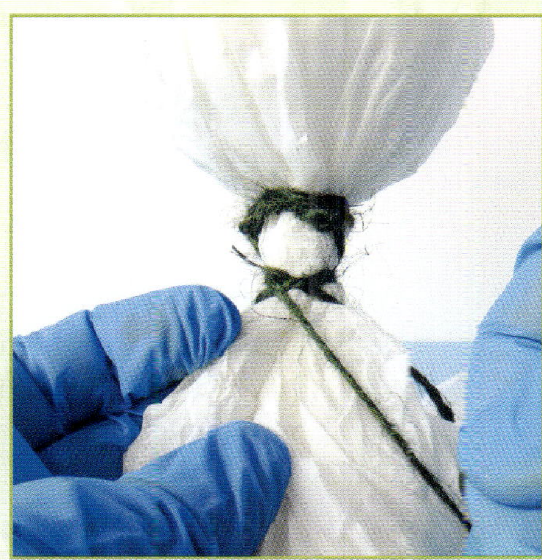

Go large

Use large lids or a child's ball to create dramatic floral centres. Because of their size, it is best to paint these in two stages: first paint the centre and let it dry, then add inks and dyes to the surrounding tissue paper.

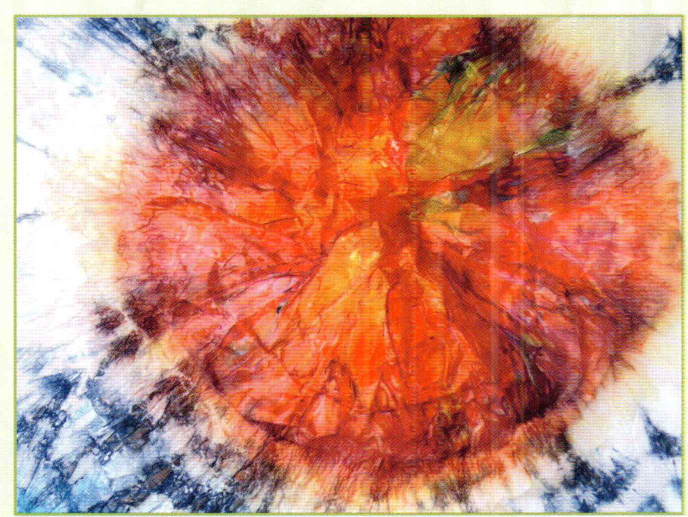

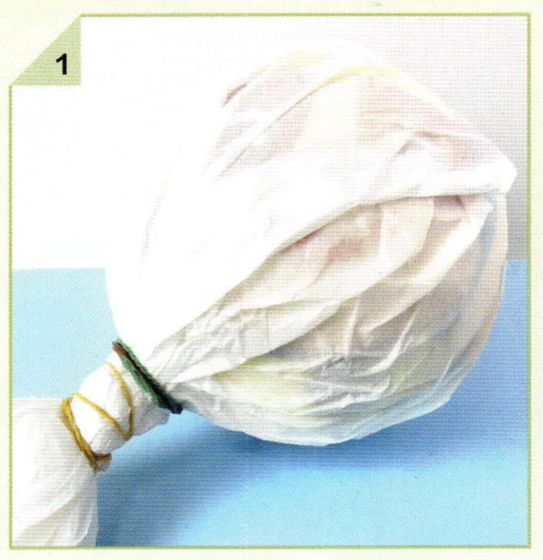

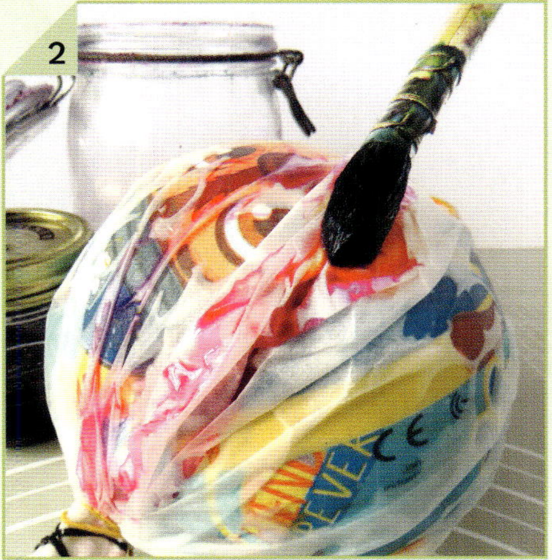

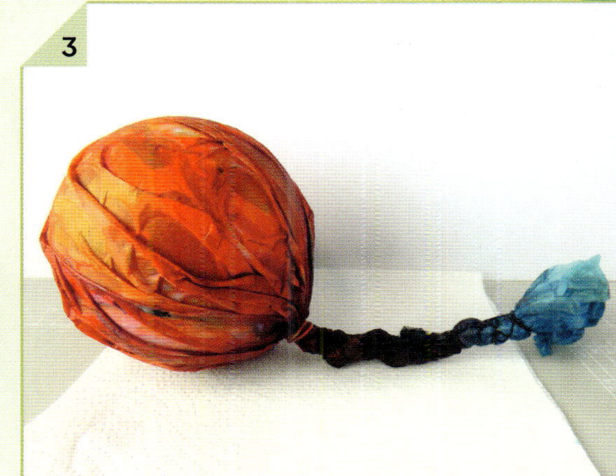

Technique 8:
wax resist paste florals

In this technique I use a wax resist paste and directly paint a design onto the blank white tissue paper. Once this has dried you can combine it with some of the other dyeing techniques, for example crumple or dip dye. The wax resist paste also works well with a wide range of mark-making tools, some examples of which I have included below.
I hope you enjoy the creative process and love your results!

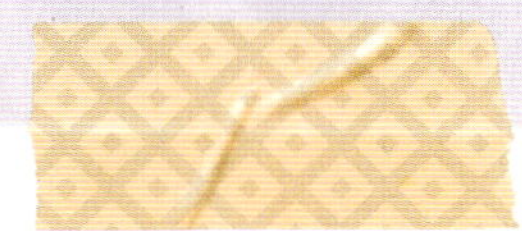

You will need

Materials

- wet-strength white tissue paper sheets
- selection of inks and dyes: watercolour, calligraphy and gold ink and acrylic liquid or fabric dyes
- brushable wax resist paste

Equipment

- spray bottle of water
- disposable plastic gloves
- large silicone mat or plastic tablecloth (to protect your workspace)
- parchment paper
- kitchen paper
- plastic or glass containers for fabric dye
- biodegradable baby wipes
- pot of clean water
- small, medium and large round paintbrushes
- small art sponges
- paper cups for mixing dye
- small wooden spoon or old teaspoon
- small shallow pot for wax resist paste
- apron
- mark-making tools (optional): cotton buds, bubble wrap, round sponge stamps, metal ruler, silicone brush, head massage tool, recycled thin plastic bag, medium ball or balloon, botanical stamp, silicone straw

METHOD:

1 Spoon some wax resist paste into a small mixing pot.

2 On dry white tissue paper, using small and medium paintbrushes, paint on your design. I am painting swirly flowers and leaves, but you can paint any shape you like.

3 Try sponging the wax resist paste or splashing on drops. The paste will create a barrier, preventing the inks or dyes from adhering to the paper in those areas.

4 Leave the paste on the tissue paper to dry overnight. Do not dry it with a heat gun due to the possible emission of fumes.

5 Once dry, if you want to, gently scrunch the tissue paper with the wax paste on it – this gives more wrinkles for the dye and inks to settle into and creates a more organic effect.

6 Follow the instructions on the dye package to mix the dye solution. If you are using watercolour inks, dilute them with water in paper cups, according to your desired colour intensity. For stronger hues, use watercolour or acrylic inks straight from the bottle.

7 You can fully immerse the waxed tissue paper into a dye bath so you have a uniform coloured background with resist flowers.

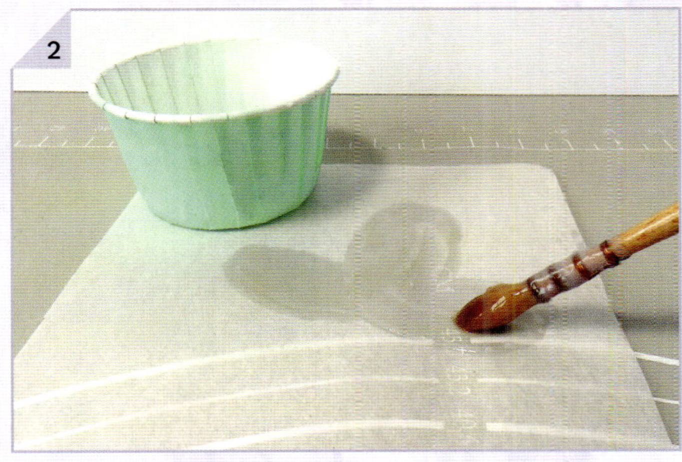

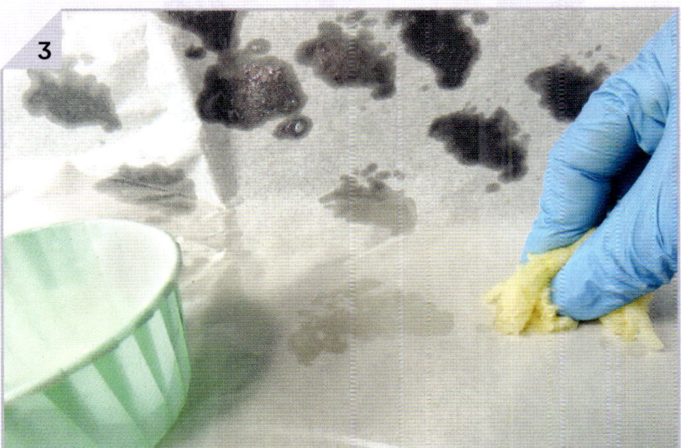

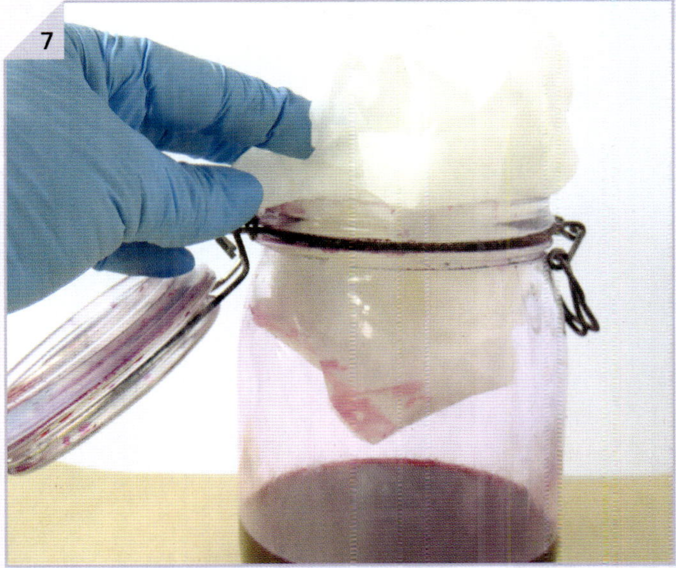

Tip
Use water to rinse the wax resist paste from your brush or sponge.

8 Squeeze out any excess dye then gently roll up the tissue paper and leave it on parchment paper to dry overnight.

9 If you prefer, you can apply the dye or inks to the damp tissue paper using ink droppers, a small paintbrush or a sponge. Place the tissue paper on the protected work surface. Spray the paper all over with water, using the spray bottle. You can create patterns and splatters, or blend colours together. As you paint, keep kitchen paper nearby to blot excess water or adjust the intensity of the colours. This will help you control the flow of the inks or dyes and achieve the desired effects.

10 Add more water with the spray bottle, if needed, to encourage the colours to mix and be absorbed by the tissue paper. Always keep the paper damp.

11 The tissue paper will automatically start to crease and form intricate patterns against the silicone mat, which will add interest and texture.

12 By adding more water to the tissue paper, you can intensify the blending and bleeding effects of the inks.

13 Wash the resist paste off your brushes using clean water.

14 Ideally leave the tissue paper to dry flat overnight or gather it up in a rough ball or gentle twist and transfer it to a parchment sheet. Be patient and avoid touching or disturbing the paper while it is drying.

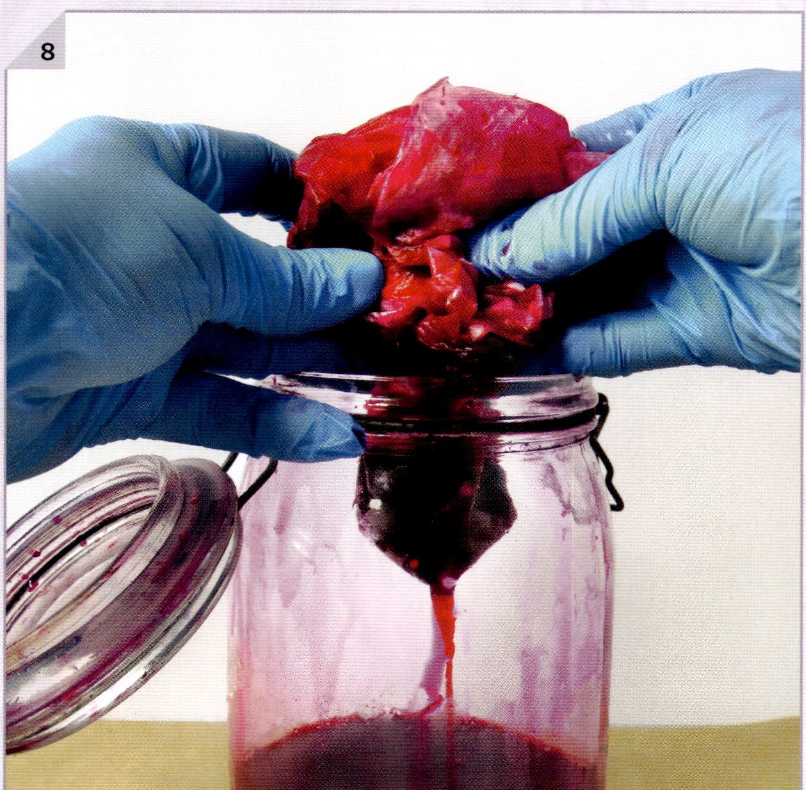

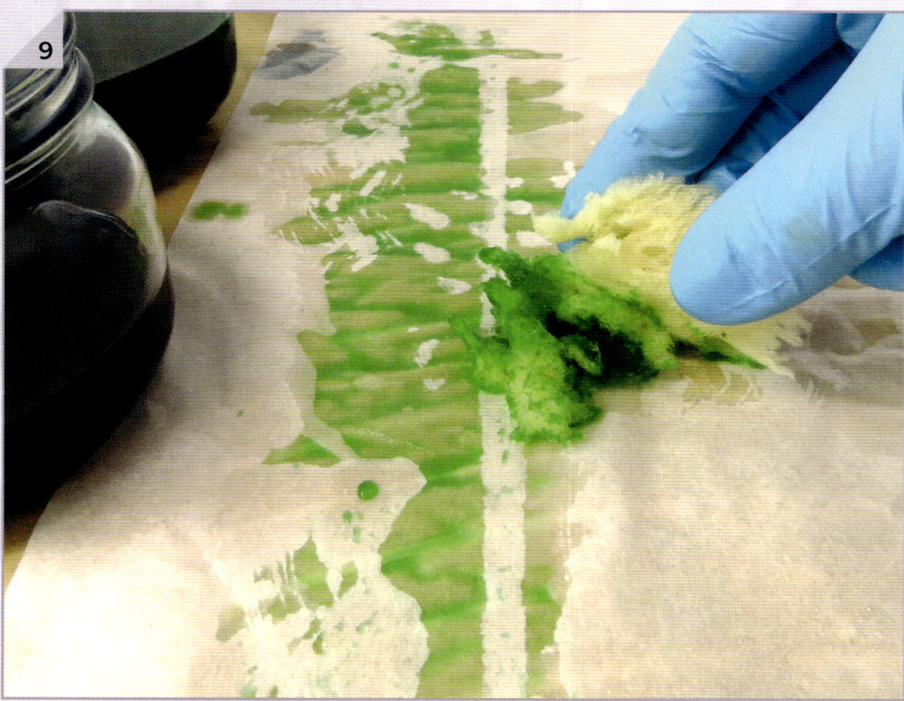

The resist flowers and petals in the
design include mottled parts in the
wax resist areas where, due to the
interaction of the crumpled tissue
paper with the wax paste, some of the
ink has seeped through. This gives a
lovely soft, yet still translucent effect.
These papers can be used straight away
as unique and vibrant wrapping paper
or for other creative projects. You can
also add gold ink embellishments on
the centres of flowers for extra drama.

These wax resist designs work very
well added to glass tealight holders,
glass candle holders or glass bowls
since the resist areas allow the glow of
a light to diffuse through. See project 6
for some examples.

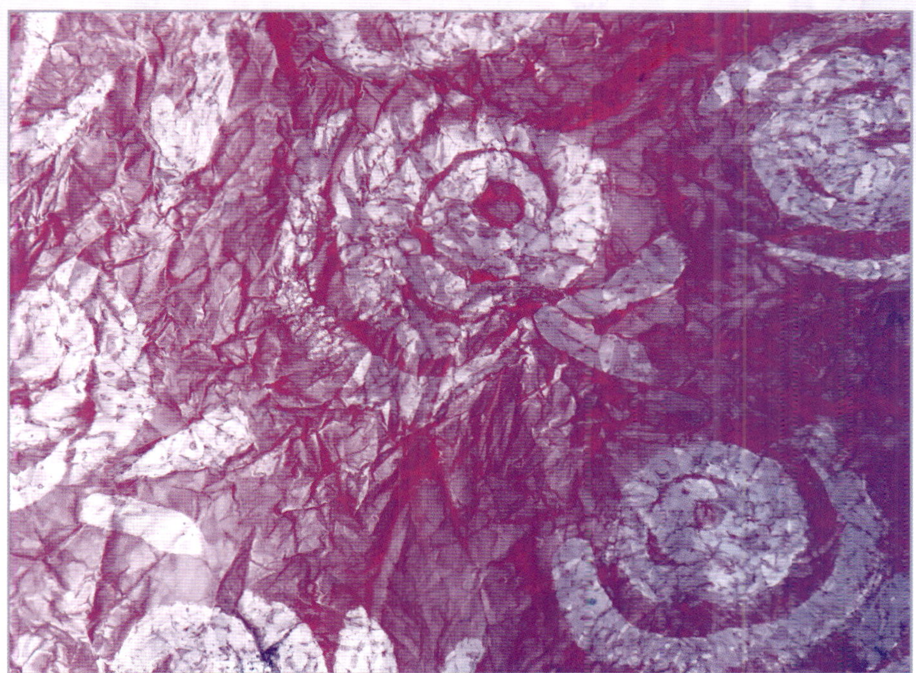

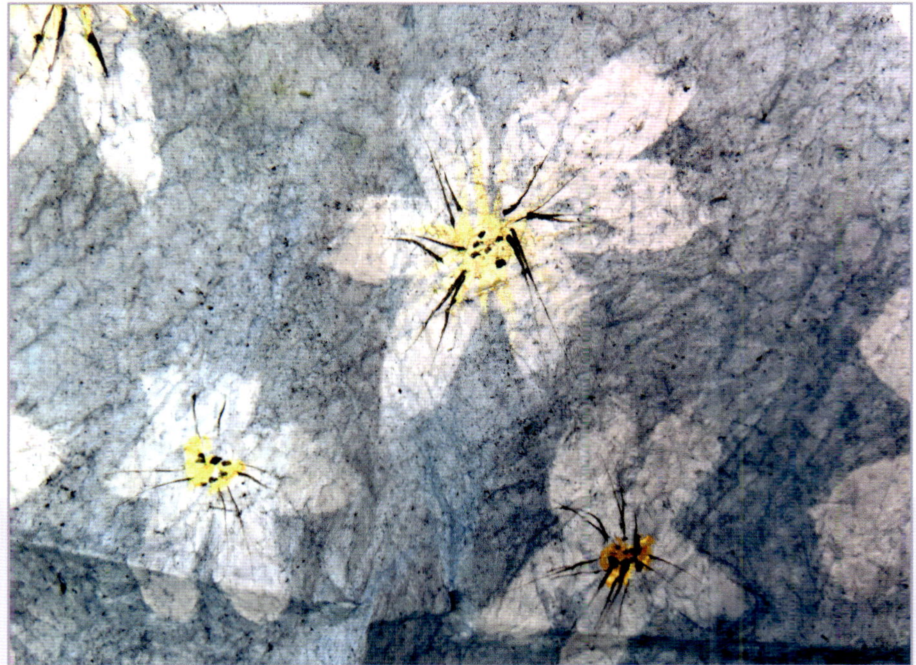

Tip

Experiment with different brush sizes, pressure and patterns
when using the wax resist paste. Keep your paste quite thin for
a better effect.

EXTRA DESIGN IDEAS:

Printing techniques using resist wax paste

1 Turn a small, thin plastic bag inside out and fold it over a child's small ball, retaining folds to act as petals. Secure it with an elastic. Paint on brush strokes of the wax resist paste radiating outwards from the centre of the ball.

2 Press gently and roll the ball a little to make a floral imprint on dry tissue paper.

3 Dye the tissue paper as before and admire the very effective results.

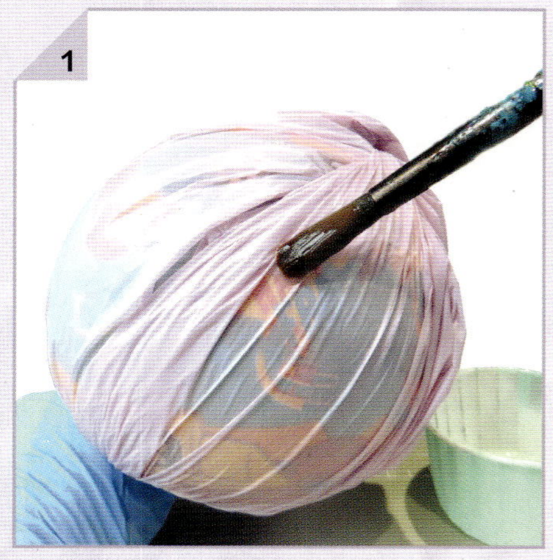

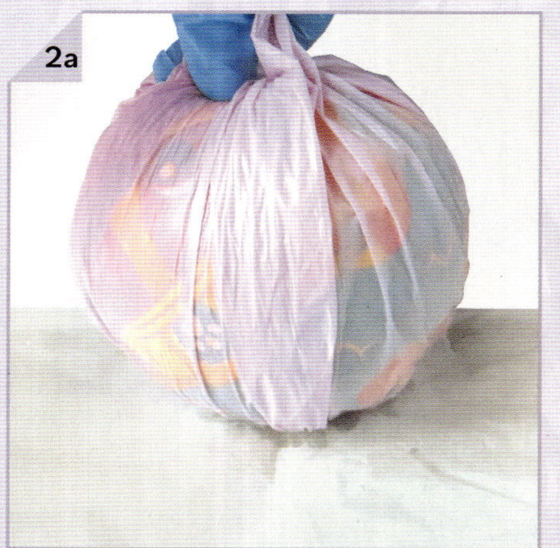

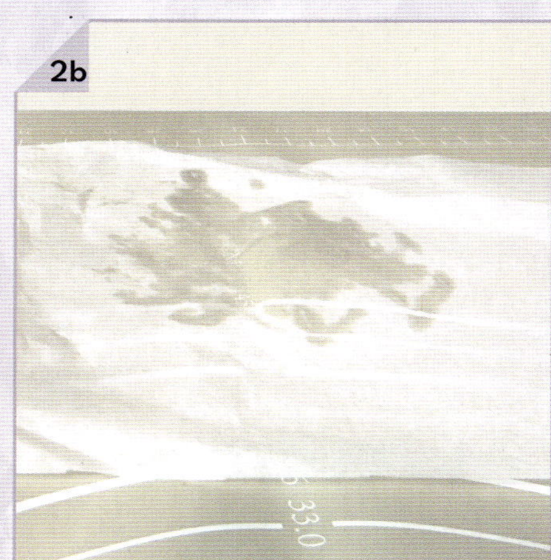

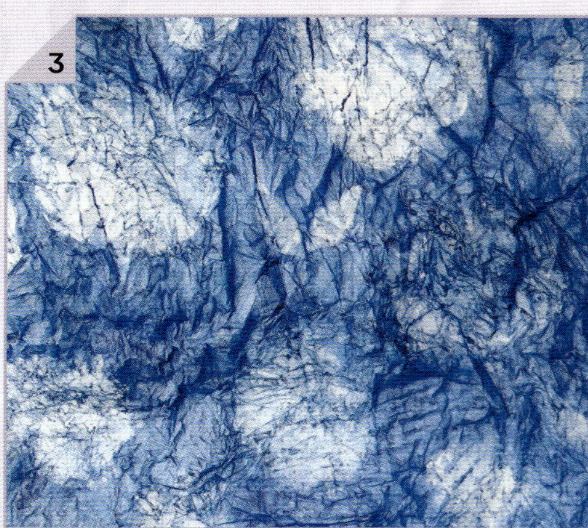

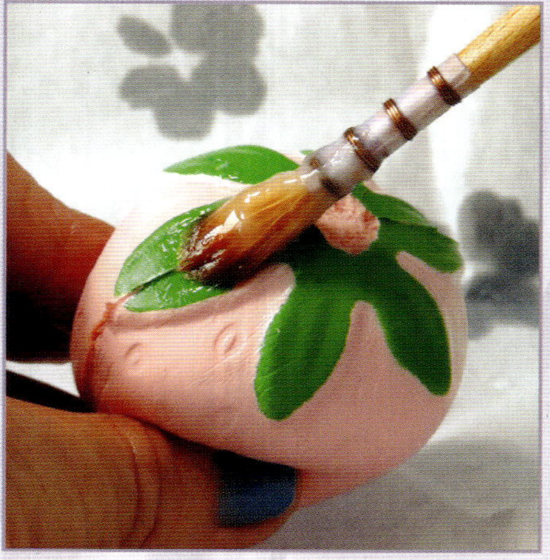

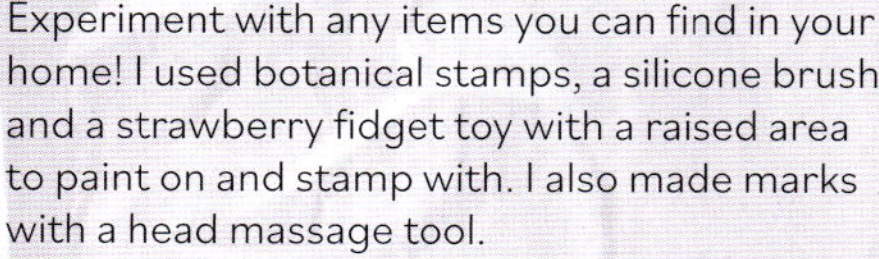

Experiment with any items you can find in your home! I used botanical stamps, a silicone brush and a strawberry fidget toy with a raised area to paint on and stamp with. I also made marks with a head massage tool.

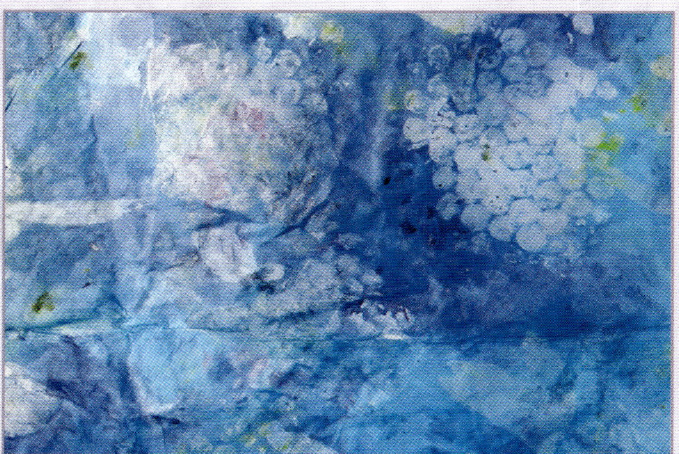

Try wrapping bubble wrap around a ball and printing with it; this gives a lovely soft design.

Abstract designs

Rather than making floral designs,
why not try painting on lines, dots
or other shapes using a paintbrush,
cotton bud or other tools to create
random or repeating patterns. The wax
resist paste is flexible enough to be
used against a metal ruler for straight
lines. I also printed with the end of a
silicone straw to give small hoops of
resist. Use circular sponge stamps for a
spotty pattern.

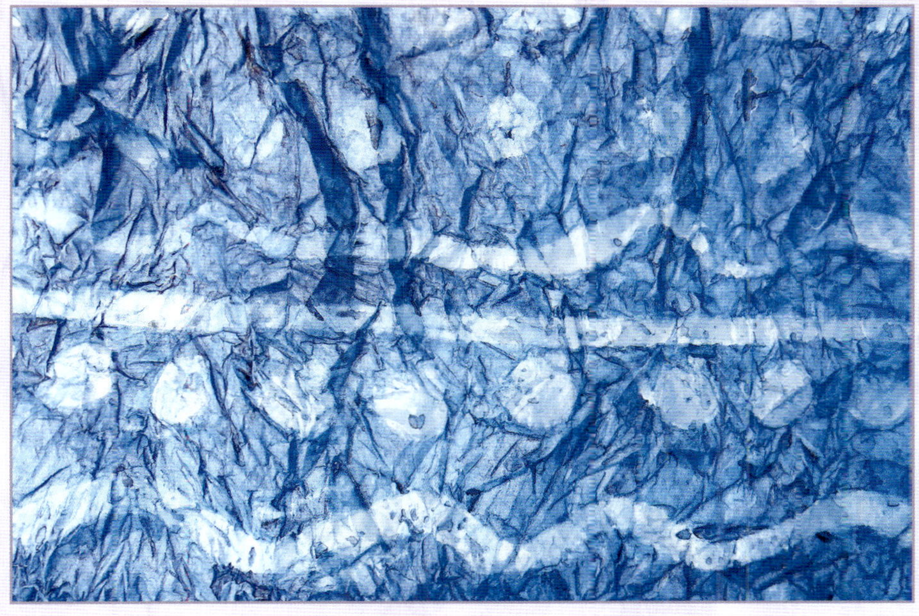

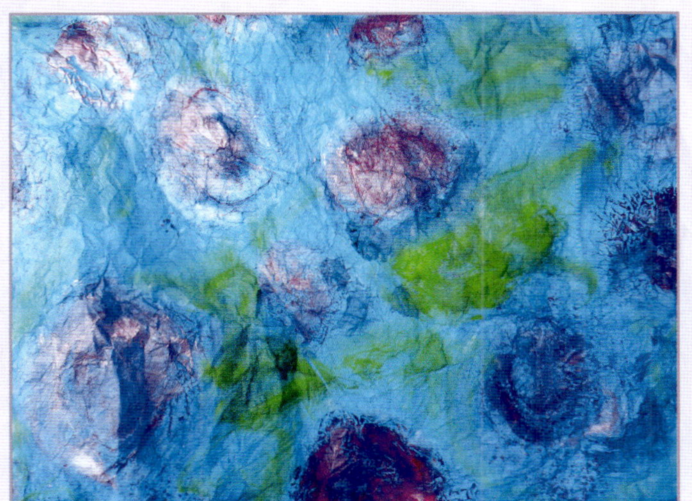

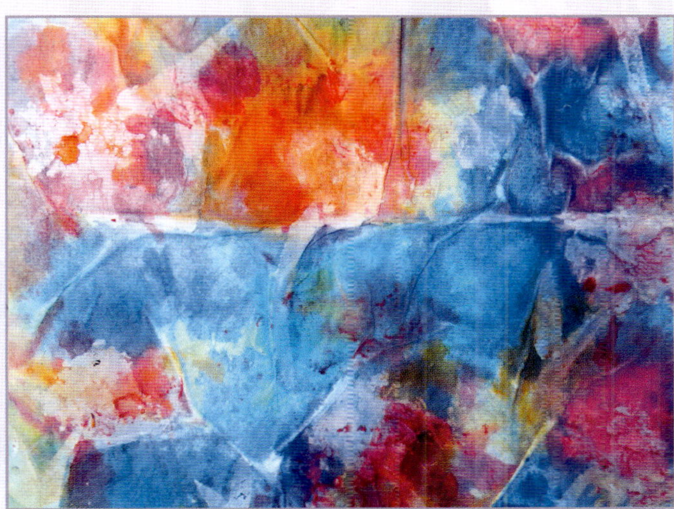

You can also paint additional colour onto dried
wax resist tissue paper.

Technique 9:
hot wax

This technique uses hot melted wax applied directly to dry tissue paper with an encaustic iron tool with interchangeable metal tips. The wax is removed by ironing once the tissue has been dyed and dried. Take advantage of the translucency created by adding your finished tissue paper to glass objects as described in project 6.

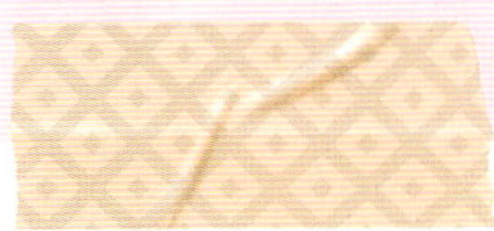

You will need

Materials

- wet-strength white tissue paper sheets
- selection of inks and dyes: watercolour, calligraphy and gold ink and acrylic liquid or fabric dyes
- encaustic medium pellets or clear encaustic wax paint block
- gold paint or gold relief paint

Equipment

- spray bottle of water
- disposable plastic gloves
- large silicone mat or heat resistant mat (to protect your workspace)
- parchment paper
- kitchen paper
- plastic or glass containers for fabric dye
- biodegradable baby wipes
- pot of clean water
- paper cups for mixing ink
- paintbrush or sponge
- newspaper sheets
- dark card or paper
- household iron
- apron
- encaustic hot iron tool: mini-iron with a range of tips

Tip

The encaustic hot iron tool is less flexible than a paintbrush, so experiment on scraps of tissue paper until you're confident using it. It's worth learning this technique as it gives excellent results.

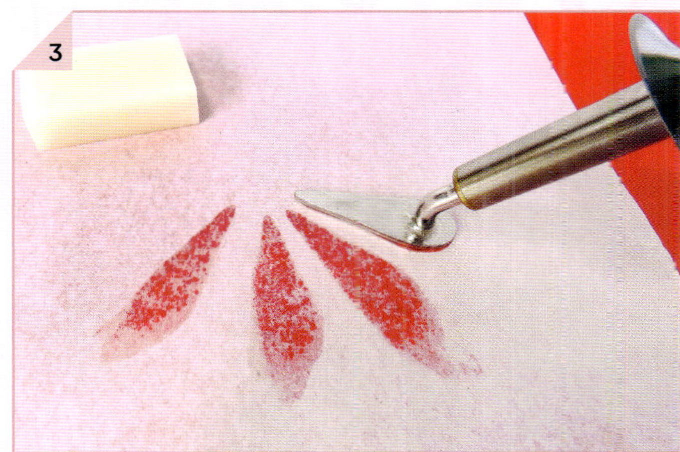

METHOD:

1 Lay down a silicone or heat resistant mat.

2 Plug in your encaustic hot iron tool.

3 Lay the tissue paper over a piece of dark card or paper so that you can see what you are painting. On the dry white tissue paper, using the hot iron tool dipped into a block of clear wax, create some flower or abstract patterns by adding melted encaustic medium to the tissue paper. Repeat patterns work well for this technique. Experiment with different tip sizes and shapes. Use the edge of the tool to create lines and the tip to create dots.

4 The wax will act as a resist, preventing the inks or dyes from penetrating to the paper in these areas. When cooled enough to touch, carefully wipe the tip clean of wax with a piece of kitchen paper.

5 The wax dries immediately so there is no need to wait for your design to dry!

6 Follow the instructions on the dye package to mix the dye solution. If you are using liquid watercolour inks, dilute them with water according to your desired colour intensity. For stronger hues, use watercolour or acrylic inks straight from the bottle.

7 Fully immerse the waxed tissue paper into a dye bath so that you have a fully coloured background.

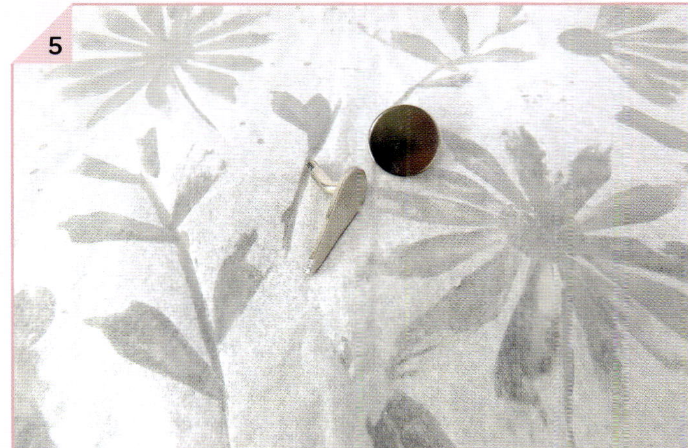

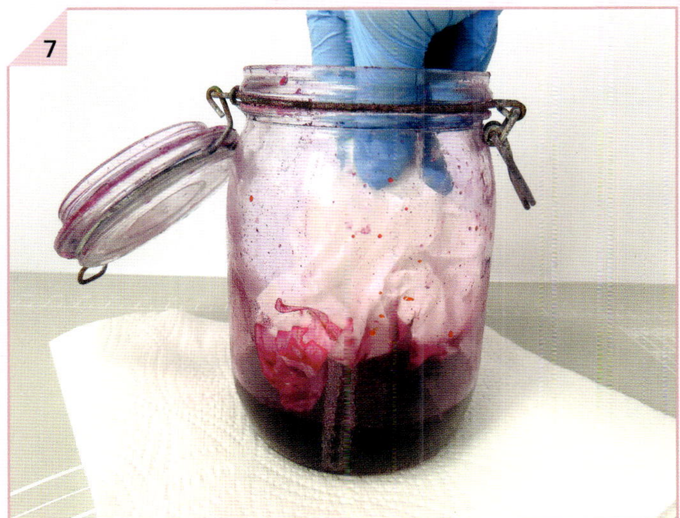

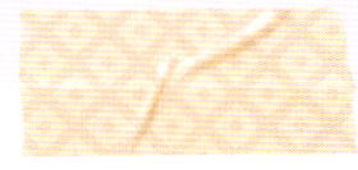

Safety note

The tips on the encaustic hot iron tool get very hot, so take care and do not leave the tool unattended. Do not change the tips or clean them when the iron is still hot!

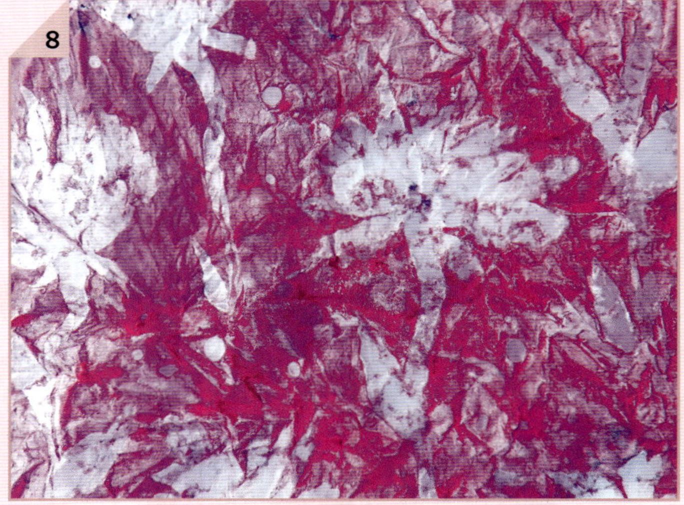

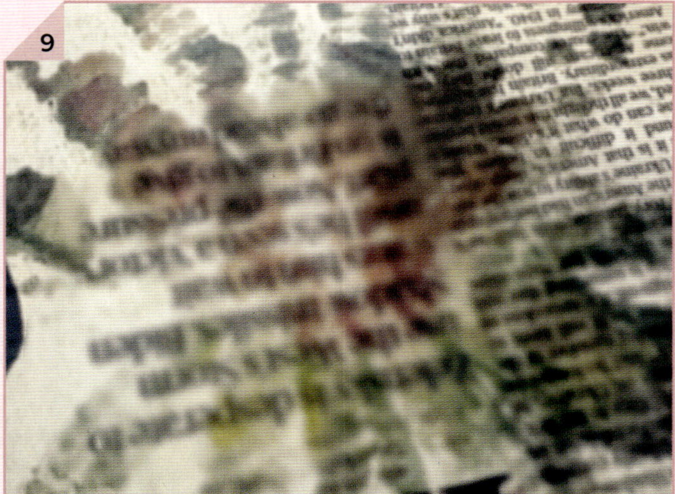

8 Gently wrap the tissue paper into a ball and place it on parchment paper to dry completely overnight. Do not use heat to dry it. Once completely dry, unfold.

9 Place the tissue paper between sheets of parchment paper or newspaper and press it with a household iron on medium heat to melt the wax.

10 Once all the wax has been removed, your design will be revealed. This technique gives a cleaner resist image than the wax resist paste, because the encaustic wax adheres more tightly to the tissue paper before dyeing.

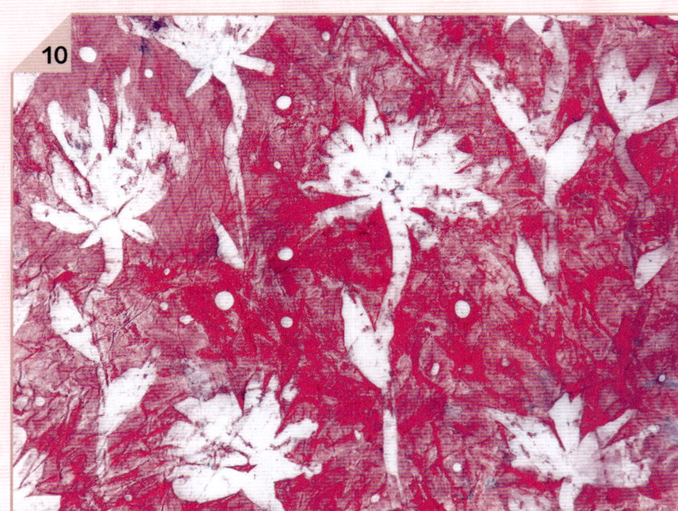

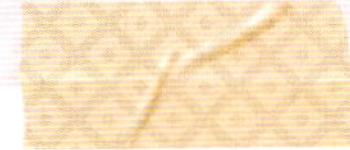

Tip

Experiment with a range of encaustic hot iron tool tips to create different patterns, lines, shapes and dots.

VARIATIONS:

Leaving the wax on can give a lovely organic effect. Gently crumple the tissue to add in small cracks then sponge or directly paint inks over the waxed tissue. This gives a soft, almost marbled, pattern of inks which have dried on the wax. This tissue design will work well with the glass objects in project 6 (see pages 102–111) such as tealight holders, jars, bowls or bottles since the waxy areas will allow soft diffused light to penetrate.

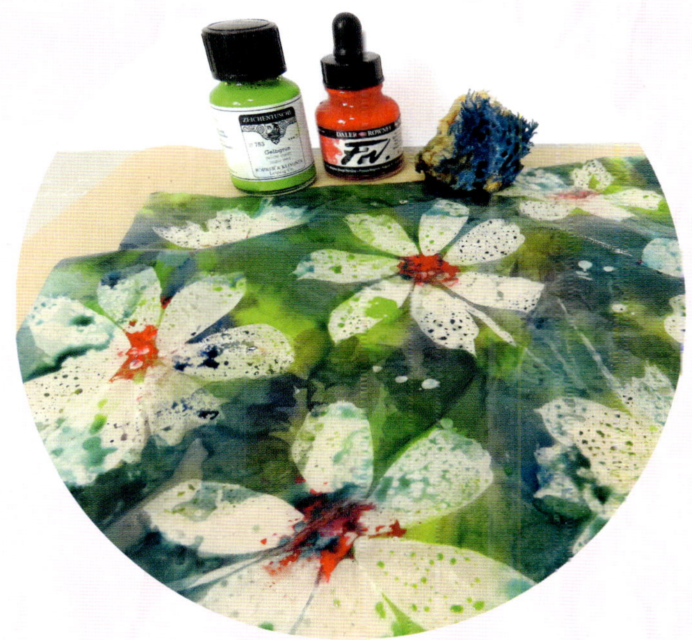

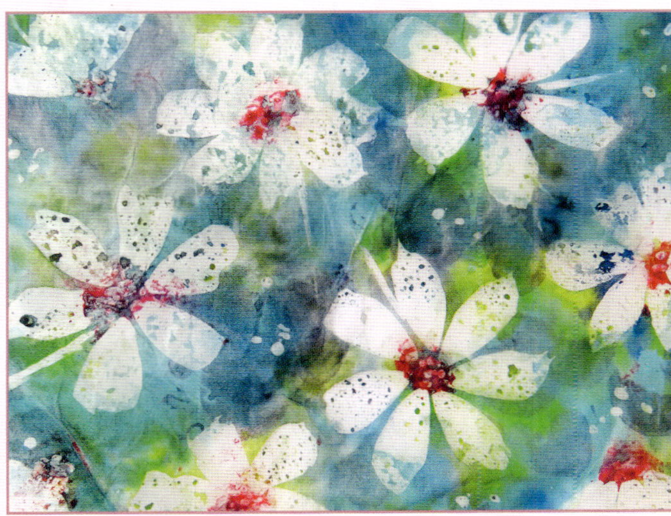

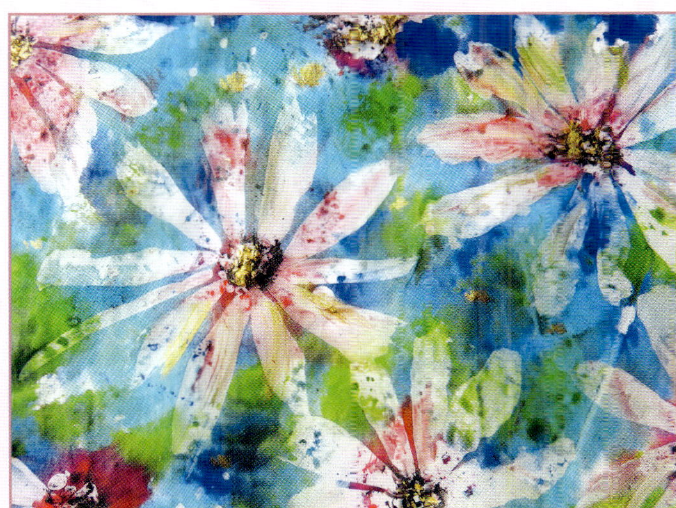

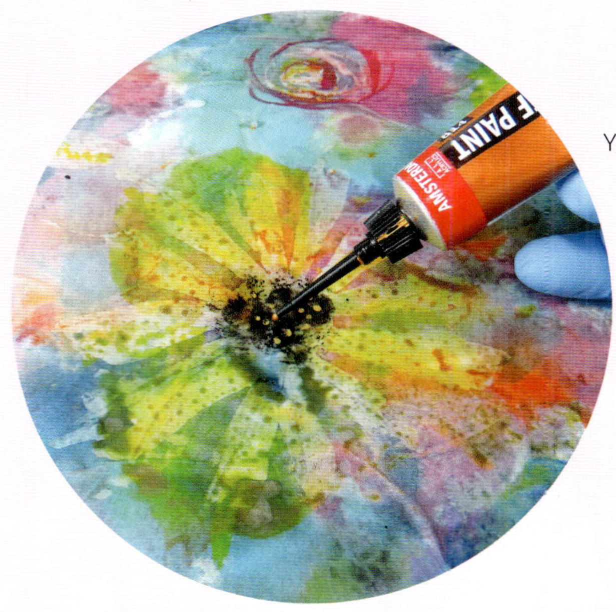

You can embellish these wax resist patterns once dry by painting on gold paint or gold relief paint, if you wish. Some of these wax resist florals were painted on with a natural bristle brush dipped in melted encaustic medium.

Technique 10:
hand-painting flowers

You can create a beautiful image by hand painting a loose landscape on tissue paper to form a meadowscape, using inks and fabric dyes. This style of painted tissue paper acts as a good base for a painting on mountboard, card or a wooden substrate. Details of meadow flowers can then be added by painting on wax or other media once the tissue paper is mounted (see project 9 on pages 126–131).
Here I show you how to create a meadowscape base which incorporates some floral areas.

You will need

Materials

- wet-strength white tissue paper sheets
- fabric dye or watercolour or acrylic ink in a selection of colours
- watercolour fixative spray

Equipment

- spray bottle of water
- disposable plastic gloves
- large silicone mat or plastic tablecloth (to protect your workspace)
- small art sponges or sponge brushes
- plastic dropper
- various sized paintbrushes, including a wider one
- paper cups for mixing inks
- plastic or glass containers for fabric dye
- palette or mixing tray
- kitchen paper
- apron
- biodegradable baby wipes

METHOD: CREATING A MEADOWSCAPE BACKGROUND

1 Follow the instructions on the dye package to mix the dye solution. If you are using watercolour inks, dilute them with water according to your desired colour intensity. For stronger hues, use watercolour or acrylic inks straight from the bottle.

2 Place the tissue paper on the protected work surface. Wet the entire surface of the paper using clean water and a wide brush or the spray bottle. Make sure the paper is evenly damp, but not overly saturated.

3 Using the wide brush or a sponge, sweep shades of green ink in an arc across the lower two thirds of the tissue paper. You can add some splashes of yellow or brown to represent foliage.

4 Sweep on some pale blue across the top section for the sky. You could also add streaks of pink in diagonal lines across the sky. Wash the sponges or brushes in clean water before changing colour.

5 Loosely drop in splashes of vibrant ink to represent scattered flowers, using a plastic dropper or small paintbrush. Work quickly while the tissue paper is still damp. Use a small brush for detailed work on the flowers and a larger brush for broader strokes on the landscape areas. Apply the colours gently and let them blend naturally on the damp surface of the tissue paper.

6 As you work, keep kitchen paper or a cloth nearby to blot excess water or adjust the intensity of the colours. This will help you to control the flow of the inks and achieve the desired effects.

7 Add more water with the spray bottle if needed, to encourage the colours to mix and be absorbed by the tissue paper. Always keep the paper damp.

8 The colours will start to blend and flow. You can use a brush or your fingers to gently manipulate the inks, encouraging the colours to mix and create interesting patterns.

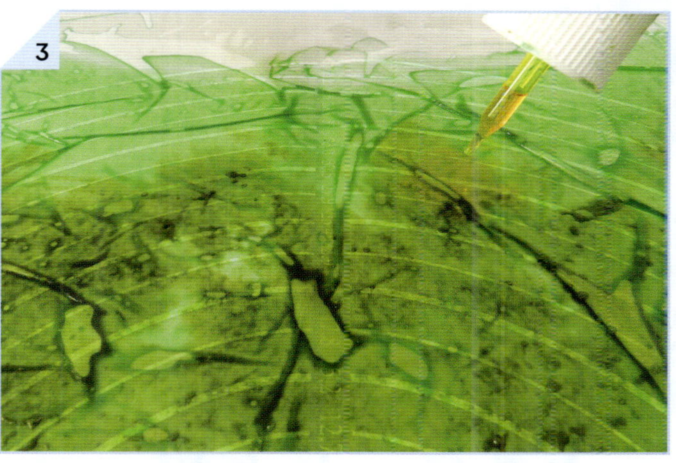

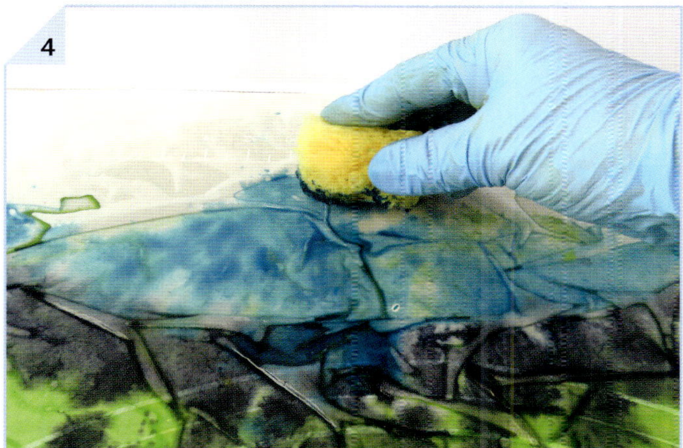

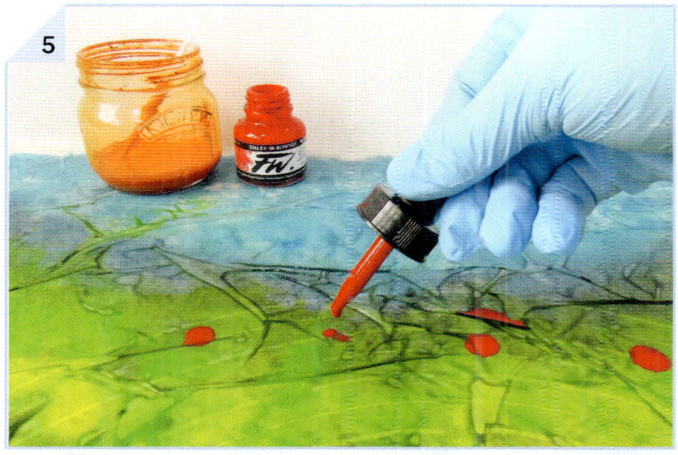

9 The tissue paper will start to crease and form intricate patterns against the silicone mat, which will add interest and texture to your final design.

10 You could add a yellow or gold area in the sky as a suggestion of a sun, but this can be added later, for example by hand painting it as you create a painting on a wooden board using the tissue paper as a base (see project 9).

11 Leave the tissue paper to dry overnight on the silicone sheet. Any wrinkles will be retained, adding interest and texture.

12 If you can't wait to see your design, you can dry the dyed tissue paper with a heat gun on a low setting. Once it is nearly dry, you can hang the sheet up to dry fully.

Now you have the background to a meadow scene. You can adhere this tissue paper to mountboard or a wooden board and paint on detailed flowers, leaves, a sun, trees, birds and clouds to complete your meadowscape. See project 9 on pages 126–131.

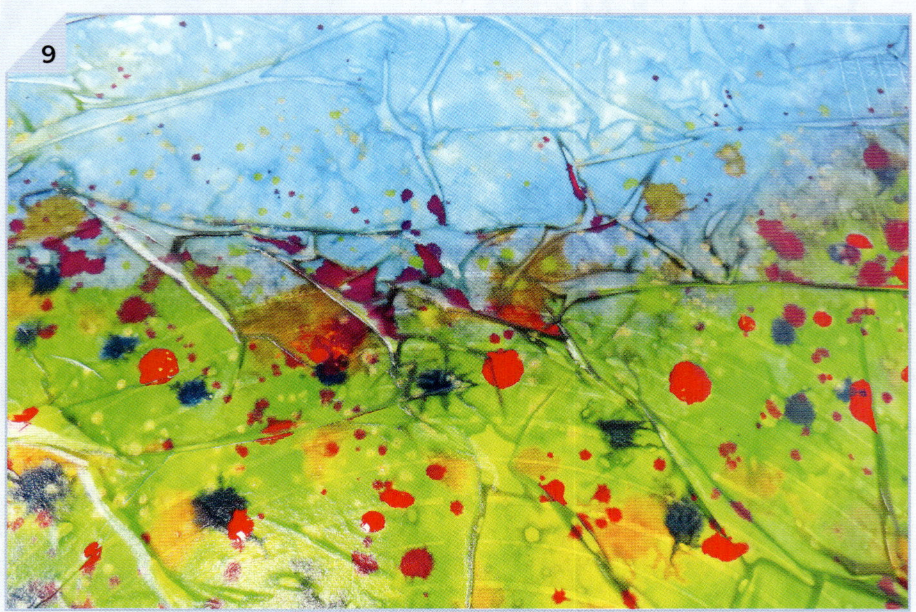

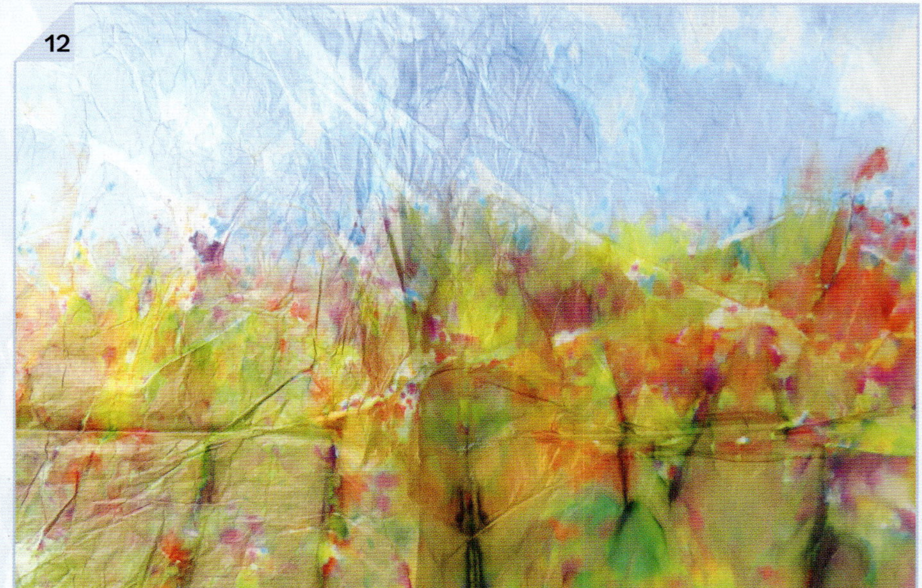

Tips

If you plan to use this dyed tissue paper as a base layer for a piece of art or collage, remember to spray it with a watercolour fixative to minimize the risk of colour fade or bleed.

For even more creases in the tissue paper, put a layer of recycled plastic over the silicone mat before painting the tissue paper.

MARK-MAKING: METHODS WITH DIRECT PRINTING

The way damp wet-strength tissue paper interacts with inks and dyes means that you can paint directly on to it to form general outlines of flowers. Depending on the amount of water added, these may appear very loose and without much detail. You can then cut and mount these on to mountboard, thick card or a wooden canvas and add detail by overpainting with watercolours, acrylic paints or even encaustic wax paints. Or you can print and stencil onto the wet-strength tissue paper – see suggested techniques below.

Mark-making tools

You can use a wide range of tools to make marks on the tissue paper. Enjoy finding mark-making materials from around your home.

- sponge applicators
- circular sponge stamps
- loofahs
- botanical stencils
- bubble wrap
- balloon or ball wrapped in plastic
- silicone tools
- old packaging materials, hessian or other textured material

Tip

Many of the mark-making techniques which follow work best on dry tissue paper, in order to retain the shape of the mark made.

Printing using plastic over a ball

Take a plastic bin liner and wrap it over a small ball or balloon. Now add strokes of ink onto the rounded end and start to print flower shapes directly on to your dry tissue paper. For a more blended look, dampen the tissue paper. To change colour, simply wipe off the excess ink with a baby wipe and add your next colour. To vary the size of flower print, vary the length of ink strokes used. This is a really fun way to create flower images which can then be embellished with centres, leaves and stems.

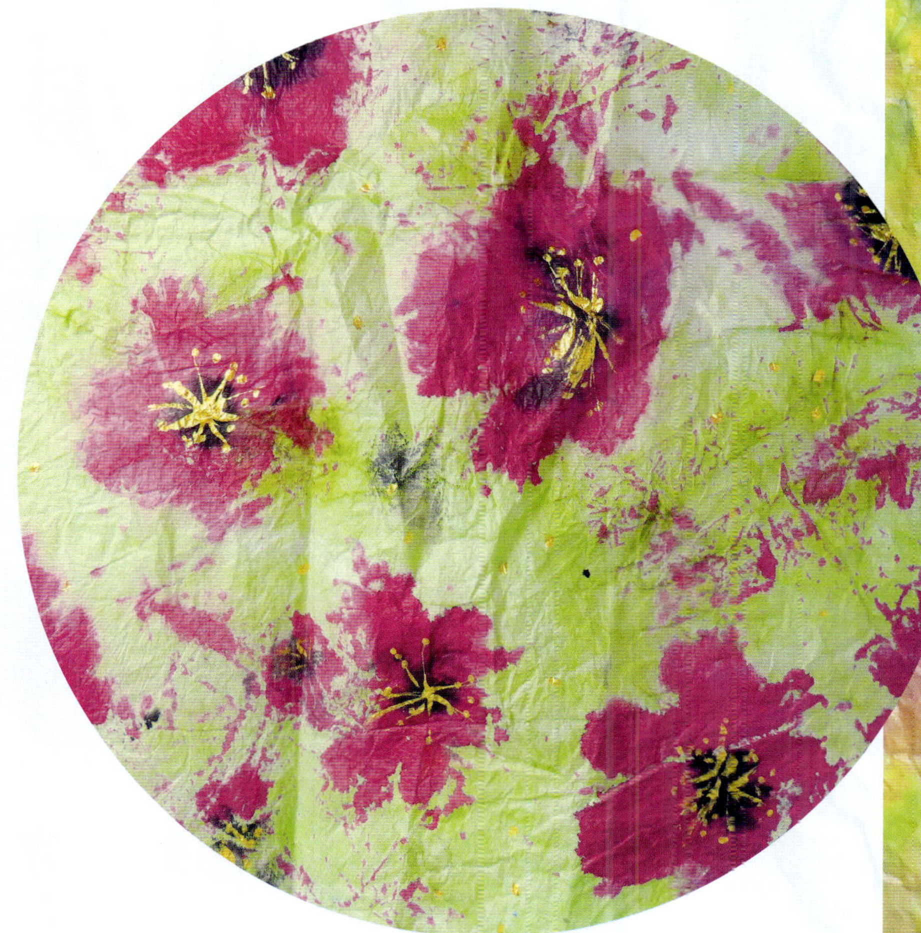

Plastic food wrap or recycled plastic

To achieve organic shapes like branches or grasses, once ink has been added to the wet tissue paper, lay a piece of plastic food wrap over the top and remove it when dry. Try using recycled plastic from bin liners or packaging to create a variety of organic designs.

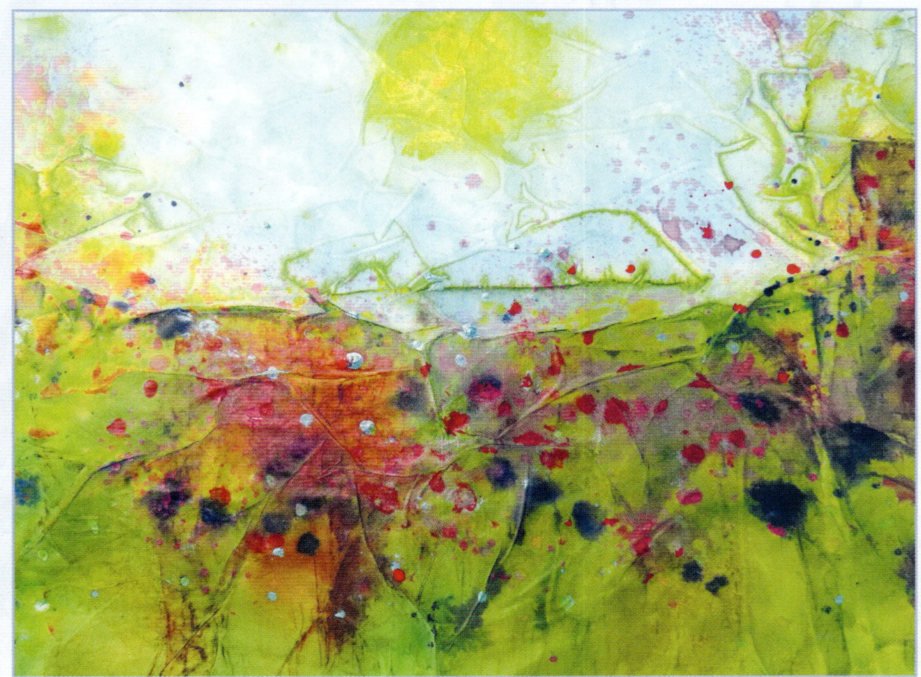

Stencils

Use a plastic stencil with an abstract design on dry tissue paper to give a rock strata formation at the bottom of your design. Dab acrylic or thicker watercolour ink on over the stencil. Remove the stencil and leave to dry.

   I made my own circular stencil out of cardboard. You can also used recycled packaging or print with bubble wrap. Circular foam brushes also print well with the ink.

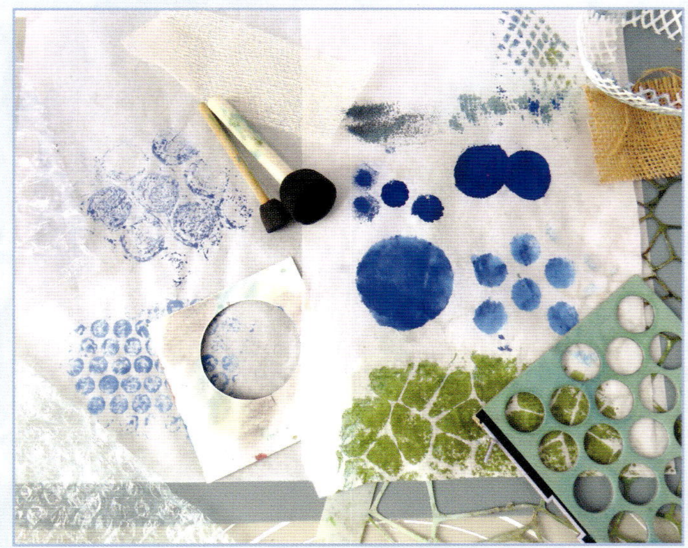

Silicone tools

You can use silicone straws, spatulas, art tools, pot holders and even a head massager to print patterns onto dry tissue paper.

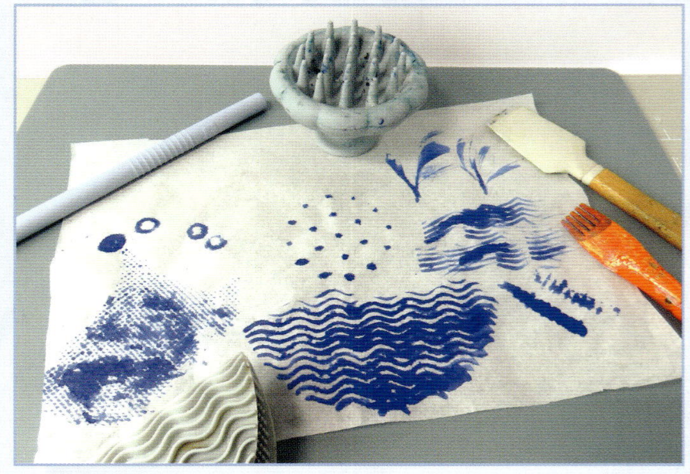

Stamps

I have used shop-bought botanical rubber stamps, alphabet letter stamps, flower shapes for use with icing, a strawberry fidget toy with a flower shape on the end as well as a loofah to print floral images on tissue paper. Twist the loofah to give a swirled shape. These patterns can be repeated. You can print on to white tissue paper, but I find it more effective to dye your tissue paper a background colour, leave it to dry then overprint with a darker colour.

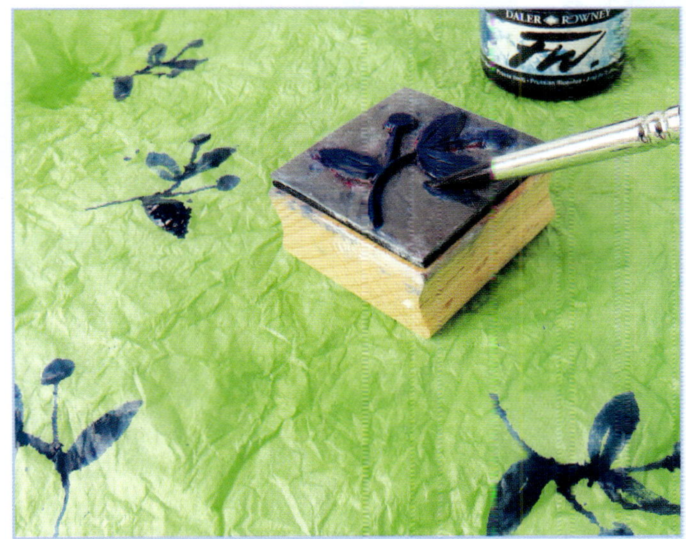

You can also combine the above effects to give patterned papers, or even directly paint on ribbons of colour and gold drops to give an abstract look to your design.

Remember to experiment, enjoy the process, and let your creativity flow. Enjoy the beauty of nature captured in your hand-painted masterpieces!

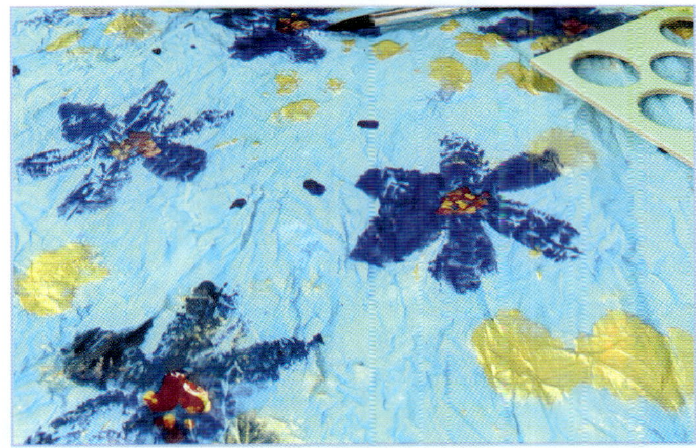

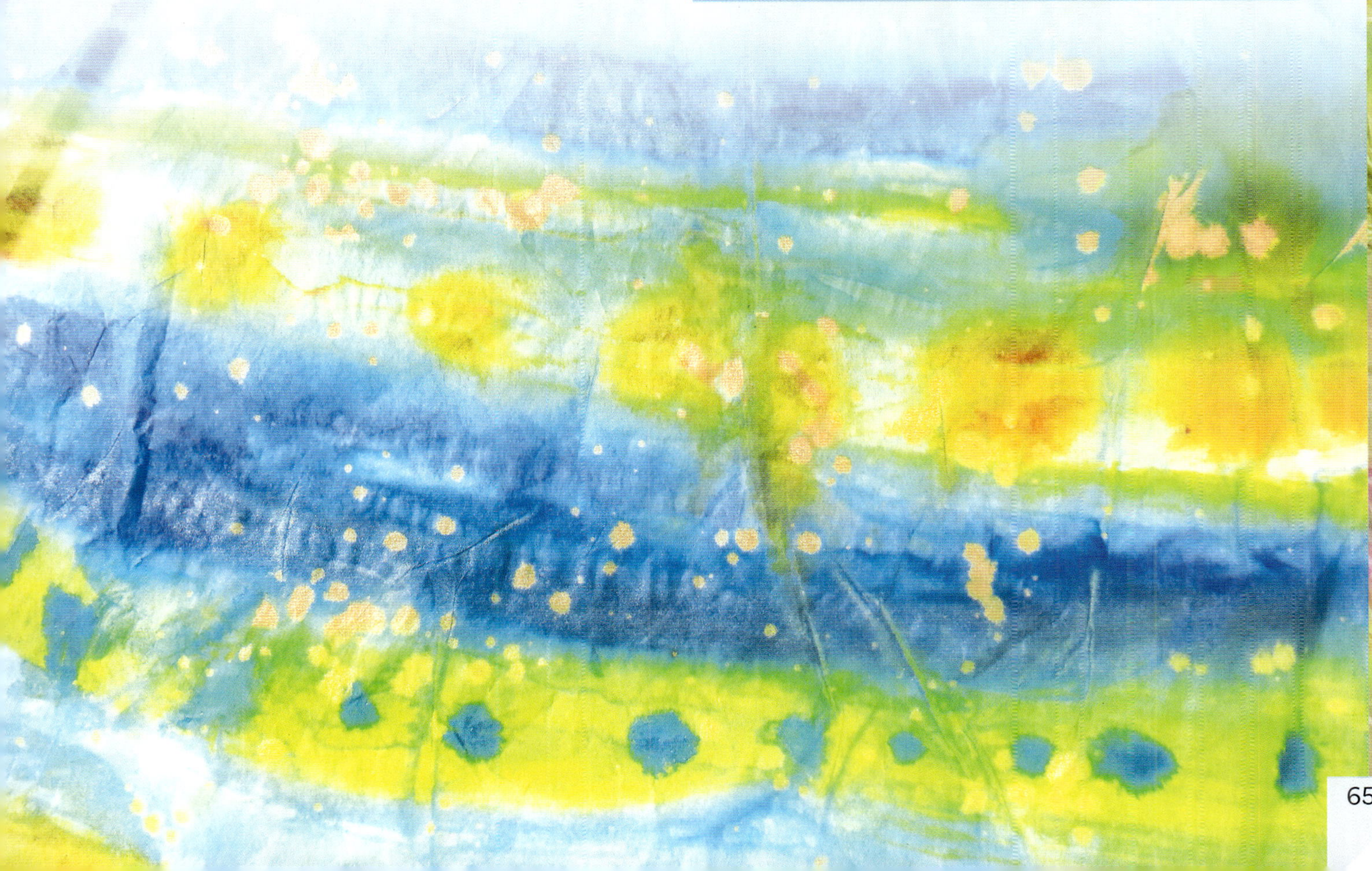

Projects

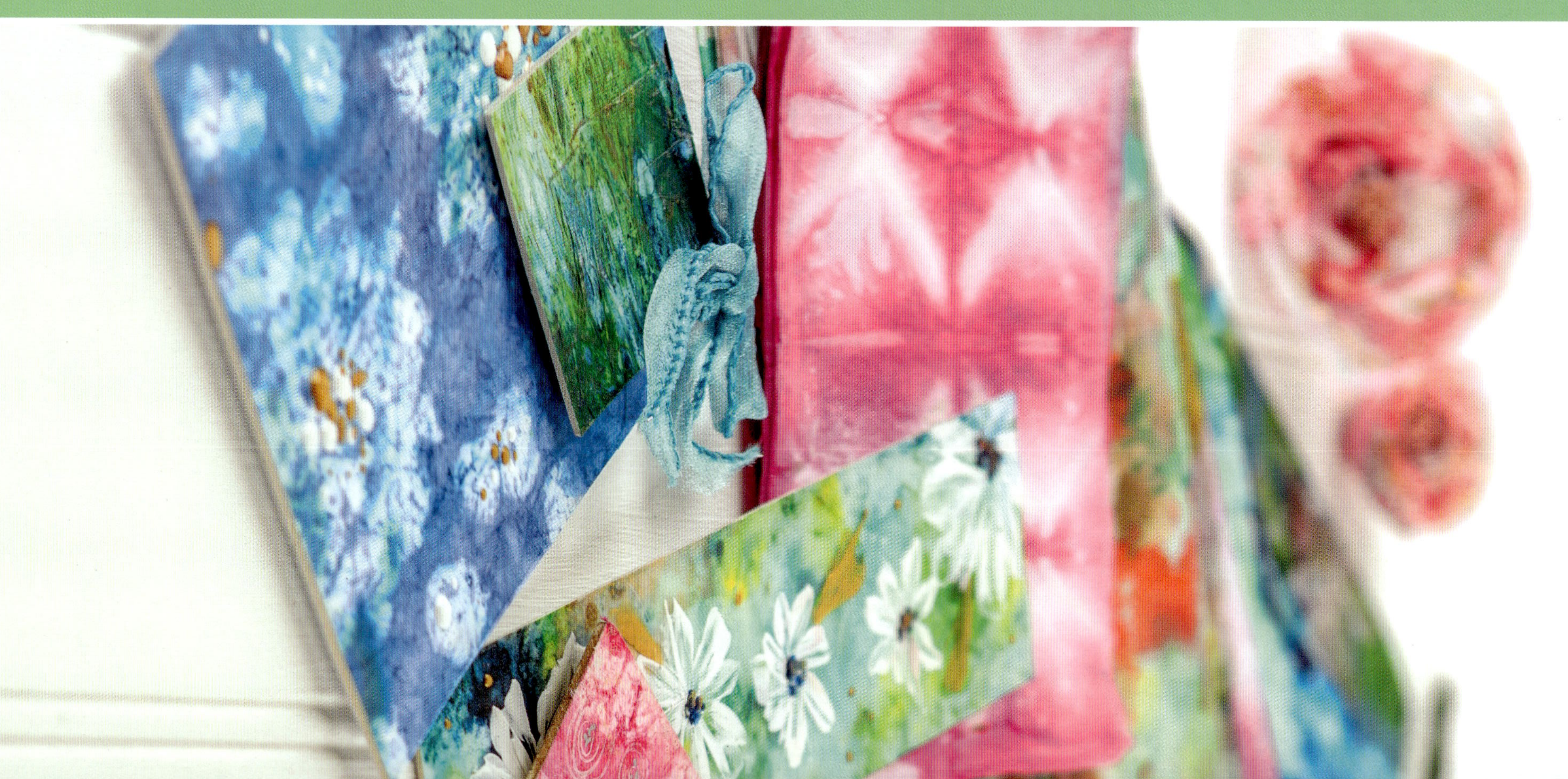

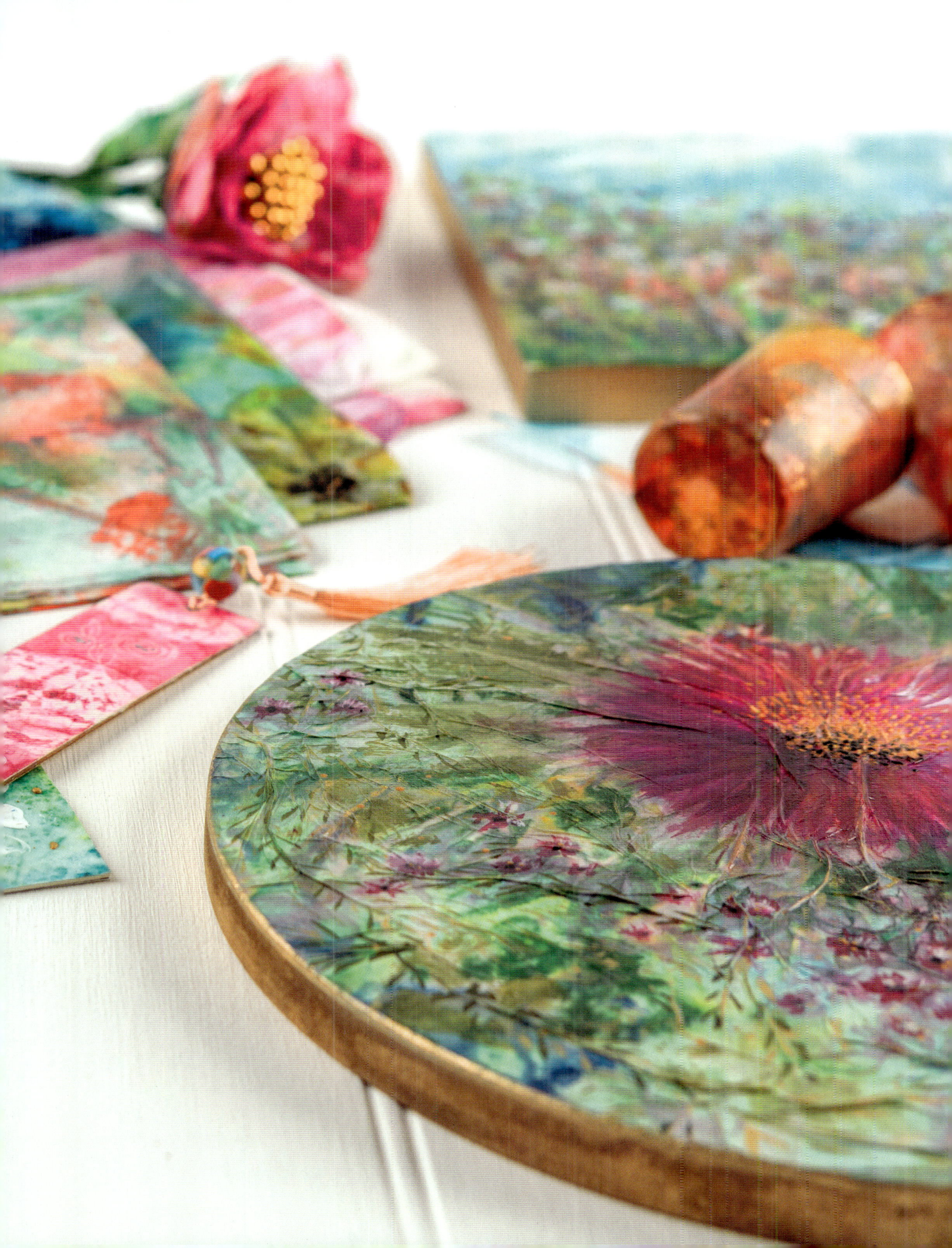

1. Gift tags

Creating hand-dyed tissue paper is a fun and creative way to enhance your gift tags and wrapping paper. The unique colours and patterns of the dyed tissue paper will add a touch of elegance and personalization to your gifts. The recipient will really appreciate the extra thought and effort you have put into the presentation.

These unique and personalized tags will add a special touch of luxury to any gift. The combination of hand-dyed tissue paper and encaustic wax or glossy glue will give them a beautiful, textured finish.

For both the mountboard and the wooden tag, you can further embellish the surface with gold relief paint, as shown. You can also add gold encaustic wax paint to the edges of the tags – refer to project 2: bookmarks on pages 76–83 for step-by-step instructions on how to do this.

Any of the tissue made using methods shown in techniques 1–10 can be used directly to make gift tags or gift wrap.

Tip

Adhere the tissue paper over mountboard or plywood shapes, then trim, seal and add a coordinating ribbon to give a distinctive touch to your gifts.

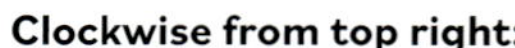

Clockwise from top right:
Precut plywood tag with PanPastel and sparkly Decopatch added; precut plywood tag with gold pen added; large tag cut from mountboard, with grommet and drops of wax; tag cut from mountboard with grommet.

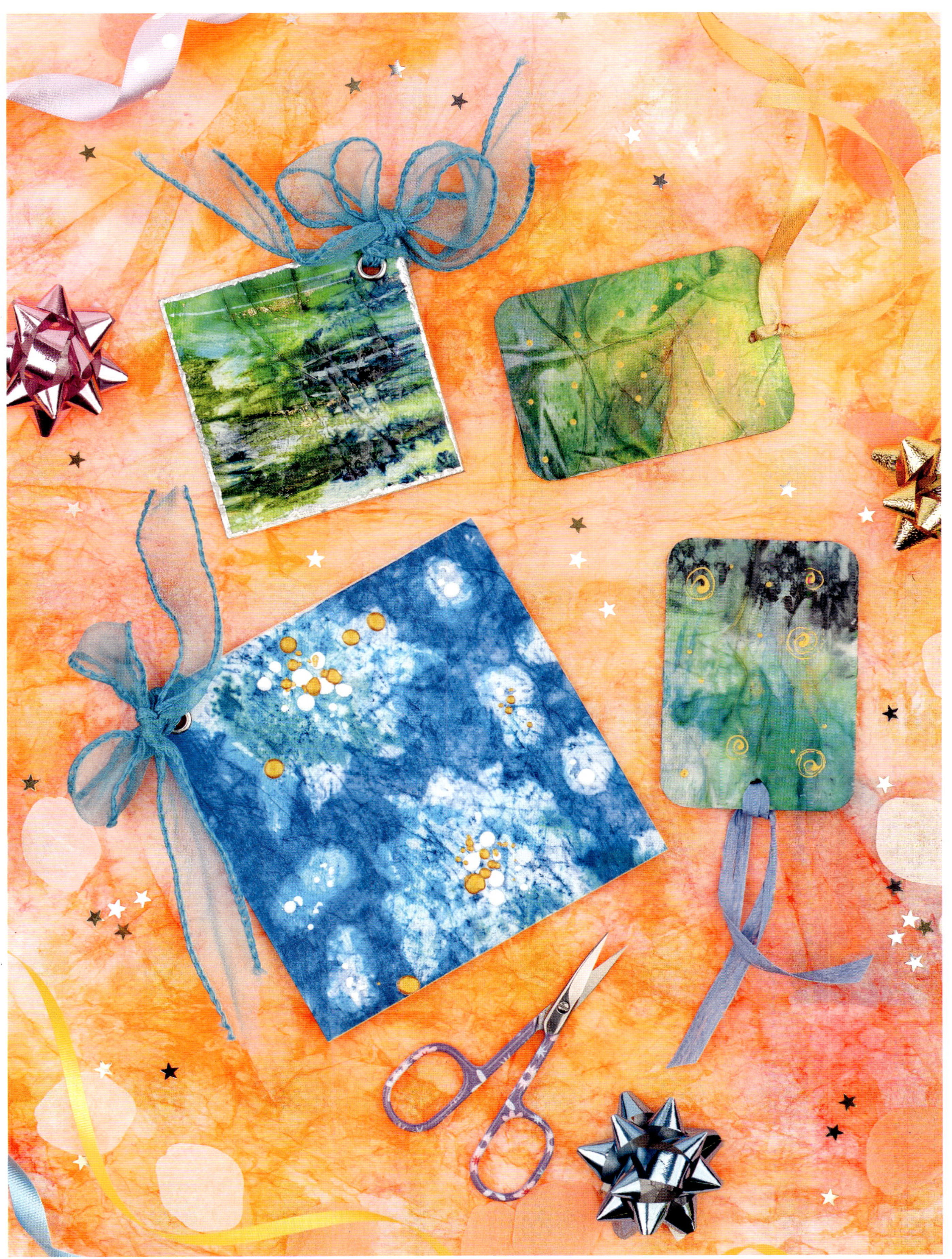

You will need

Materials

- pre-dyed wet-strength white tissue paper
- watercolour fixative spray to seal dyed tissue paper
- mountboard cut to required size
- plywood circles or seasonal shapes
- chalk paint
- wallpaper paste
- parchment paper
- paper
- PVA glue for sealing
- white gel pen, metallic pens or gold relief paint for embellishment
- ribbon or string (for attaching the gift tags)
- solid glue stick
- PanPastels (optional)
- encaustic medium in pellet form (optional)

Equipment

- large silicone mat or plastic tablecloth (to protect your workspace)
- craft knife
- hammer
- sharp pointed metal awl
- sponge or foam brush
- biodegradable baby wipes, for clean up
- cutting mat
- metal ruler
- pencil
- soft lint-free cloth for buffing encaustic tags
- grommet kit with 5mm (¼in) eyelets (optional)

Equipment for sealing with wax (optional)

- metal tin or silicone muffin case
- hot plate
- natural bristle brush for encaustic medium
- heat gun

CREATING GIFT TAGS FROM MOUNTBOARD

1 Prepare your workspace: lay down a silicone mat or plastic tablecloth to protect your work surface from stains.

2 Choose a piece of hand-dyed tissue paper that complements the colours and patterns you would like for your gift tags.

3 Spray the tissue paper with watercolour fixative and give it a few minutes to dry.

4 Lay the tissue paper over the mountboard – it should be larger than the mountboard.

5 Apply wallpaper paste evenly with a sponge or foam brush to the mountboard. Make sure to cover the entire surface evenly.

6 Gently press down to adhere the tissue paper to the surface. Retain the wrinkles for added texture. Pinch the damp tissue paper gently to create more wrinkles.

7 Allow the wallpaper paste to dry completely. This usually takes a few hours, but drying times may vary depending on the brand used.

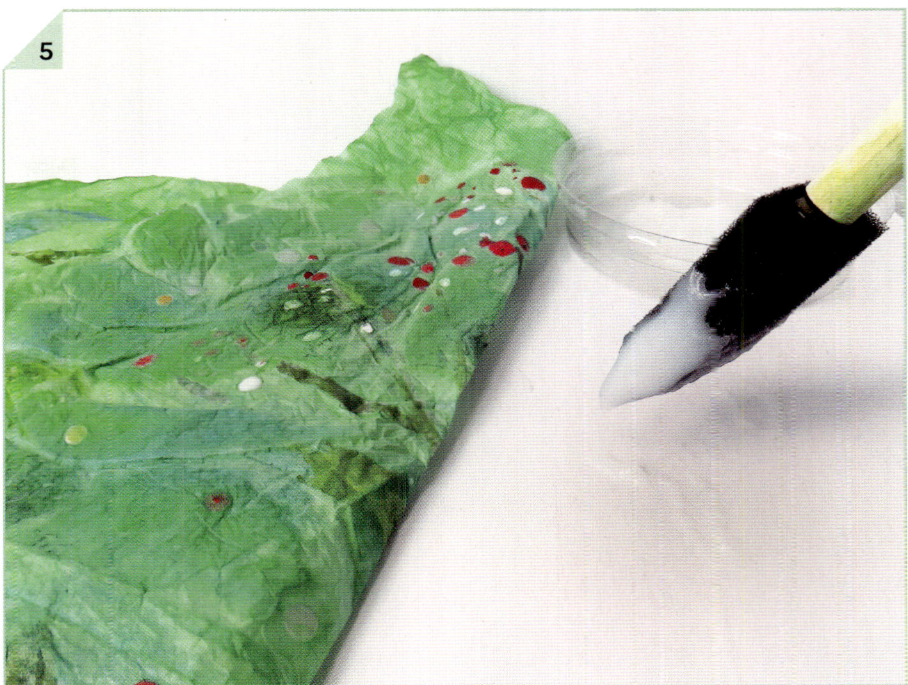

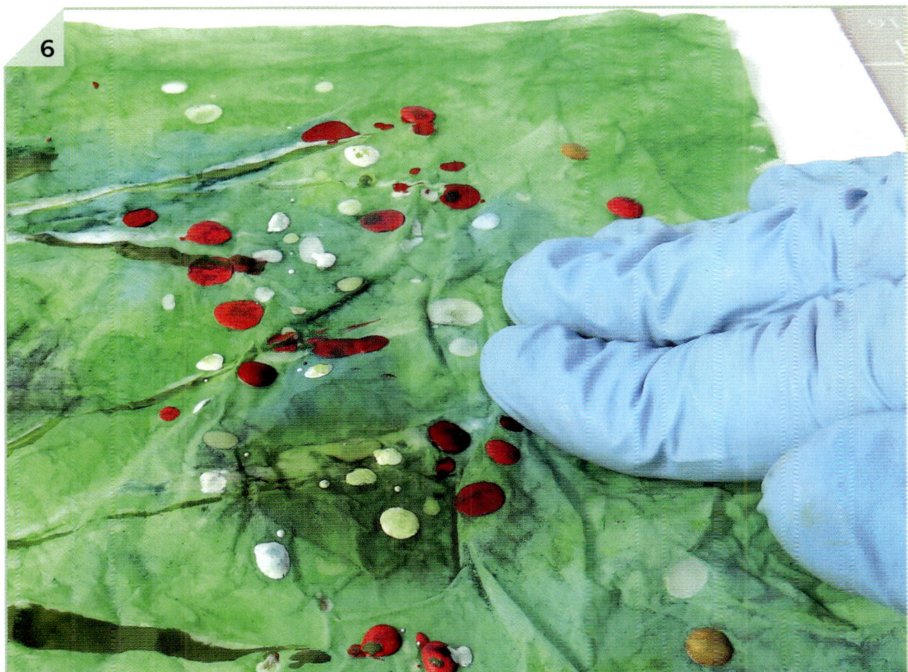

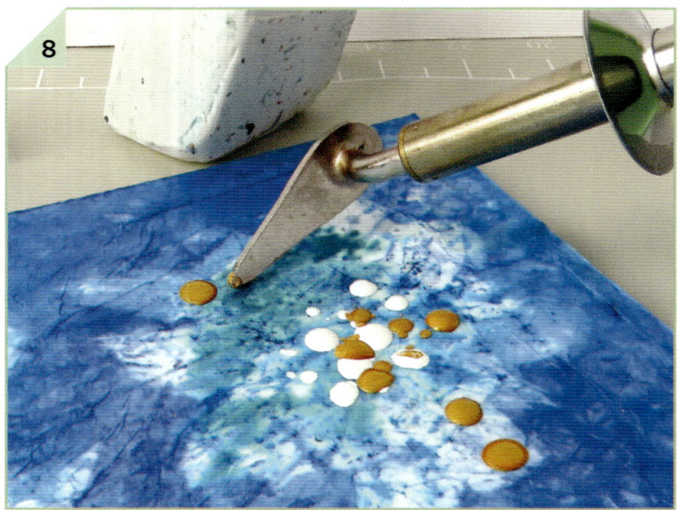

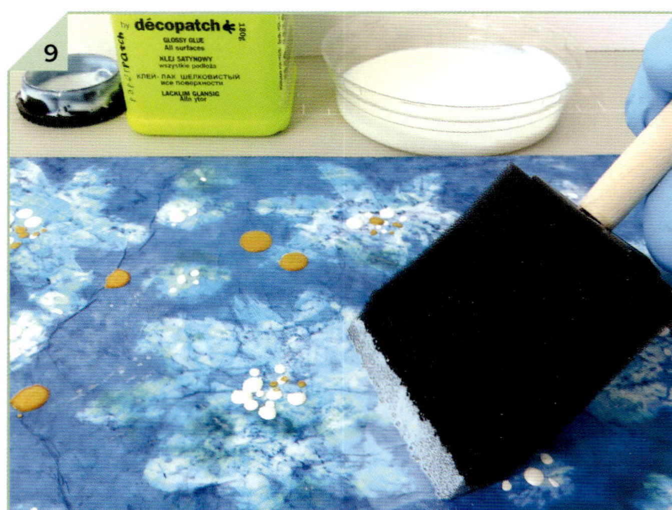

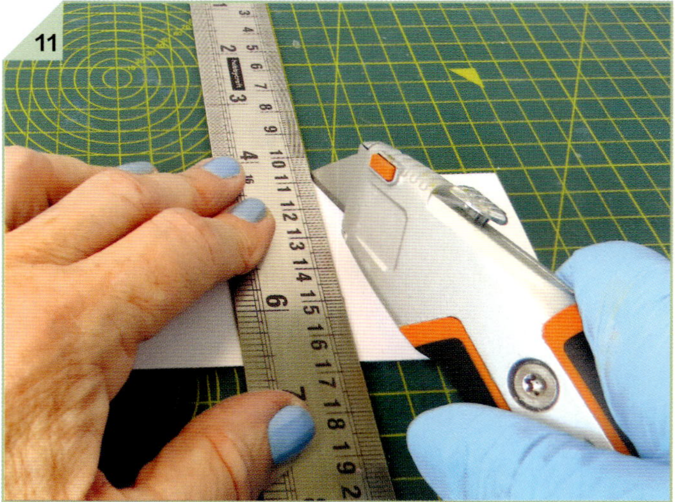

8 Before sealing, you may wish to use a white gel pen, relief paint, PanPastel, drops of wax or metallic pens to add details to your design.

9 Apply a thin layer of PVA glue over the top with a foam brush. This will seal and protect the tissue paper.

10 Cover the entire surface of the tissue paper with the glue, ensuring no edges are left uncovered. Leave to dry fully on parchment paper.

11 Cut the mountboard into tags of the required size and shape, using a craft knife and metal ruler on a cutting mat.

12 For a professional finish, use a grommet kit to punch through hole in the corner of your mountboard tag.

13 Thread a ribbon or a piece of string through the hole to complete the gift tag. Your mountboard gift tags may have paint or ink on the reverse. If so, cut some paper to size and stick it on with a solid glue stick to cover the marks.

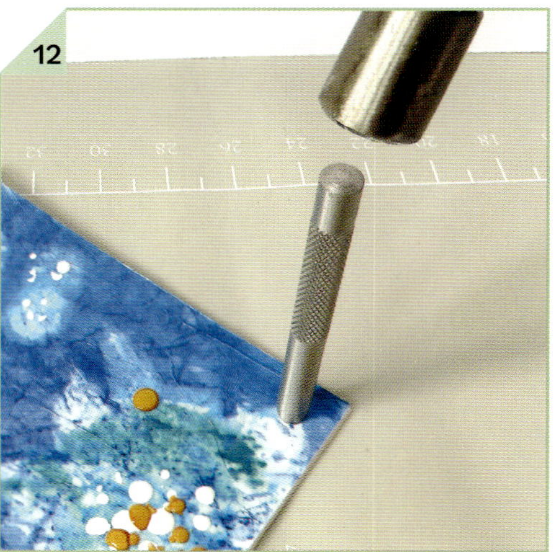

Tip
Once dry, for sealed tissue on mountboard, place on parchment paper and put a heavy book on top; leave overnight to keep flat.

Sealing wooden or mountboard gift tags with encaustic wax (optional)

1 Melt encaustic medium (pellet form) in a metal dish or silicone muffin case on a hot plate or melt the wax in a wax melt pot.

2 Once the tissue paper is in place, apply a thin layer of clear molten encaustic medium over the top of the tissue paper, using a bristle brush. This will seal and protect the paper. Cover the entire surface of the tissue paper with the wax, ensuring no edges are left unsealed.

3 Fuse gently with a heat gun.

4 Once cooled, buff the wax with a soft cloth to give it a shiny finish.

5 Use a grommet kit to punch a hole in the corner of your mountboard gift tag.

6 Thread a ribbon or string through the hole to complete the gift tag.

Tip

Wash wallpaper paste off foam brushes, dry and reuse them.

Safety note

When using encaustic wax, work in a well ventilated area to disperse any fumes. Do not leave the hot plate or heated tool unattended.

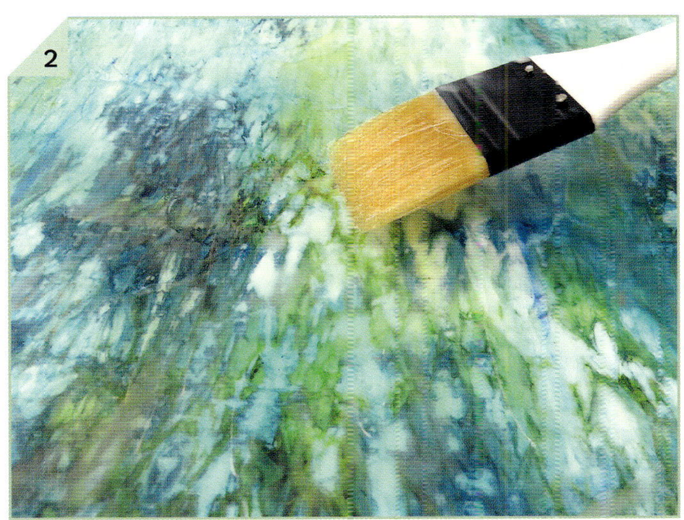

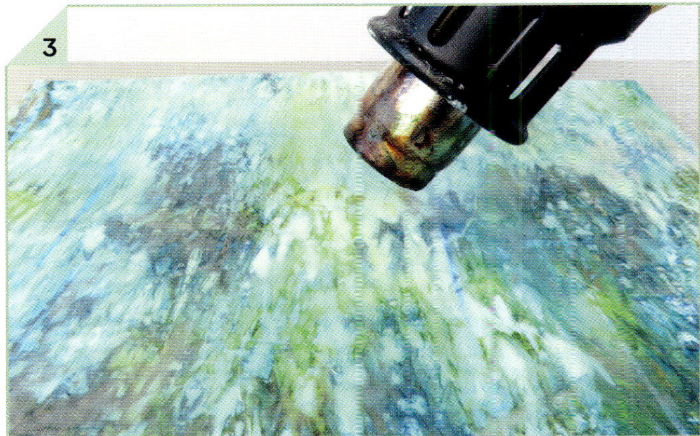

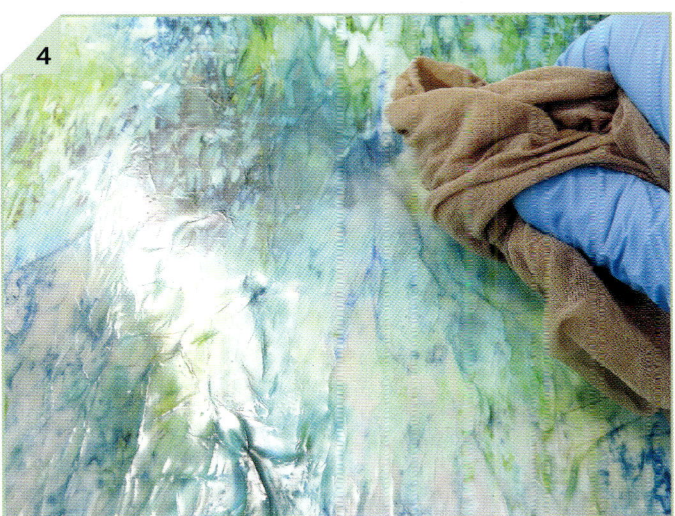

Creating gift tags using plywood shapes with predrilled holes

1 Prepare your workspace: lay down a silicone mat or plastic tablecloth to protect your work surface from stains.

2 Prepare the plywood shapes by painting them with a coat of pale coloured chalk paint, using a sponge brush. Leave to dry.

3 Choose a piece of hand-dyed tissue paper that complements the colours and patterns you would like for your gift tags.

4 Spray the tissue paper with watercolour fixative. Leave to dry for a few minutes.

5 Carefully cut the tissue paper into shapes that will fit over the plywood shapes. Remember to cut the shapes larger than the plywood bases.

6 Apply wallpaper paste evenly to the plywood shapes using a sponge or foam brush. Make sure you cover the entire surface evenly.

7 Place the cut pieces of hand-dyed tissue paper on to the wallpaper paste-coated plywood shapes. Gently press down to adhere them to the surface.

8 Allow the wallpaper paste to dry completely. This usually takes a few hours, but drying times may vary depending on the brand used.

9 Once dry, trim the excess tissue paper from the edges of the plywood shapes using a craft knife to create smooth edges.

10 Before sealing, you may wish to use a white gel pen, drops of wax, PanPastel or metallic pens to add details to your design.

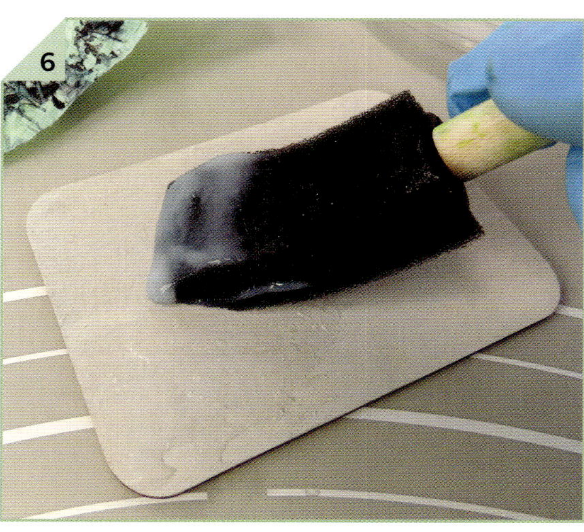

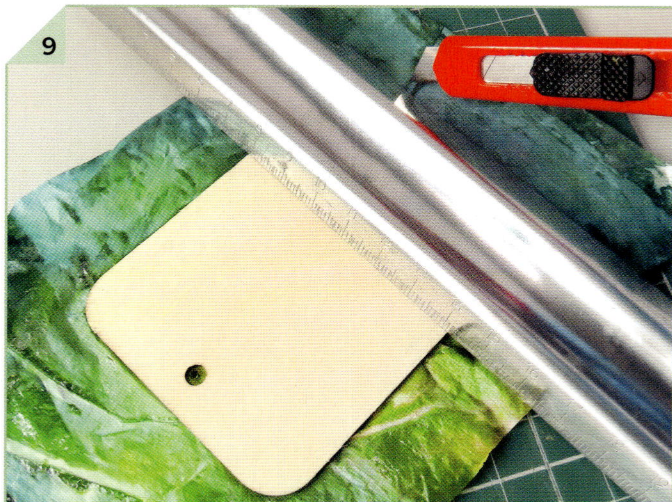

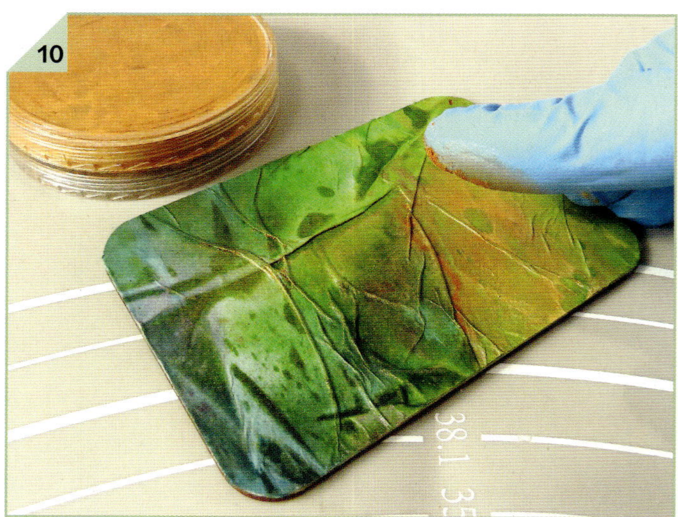

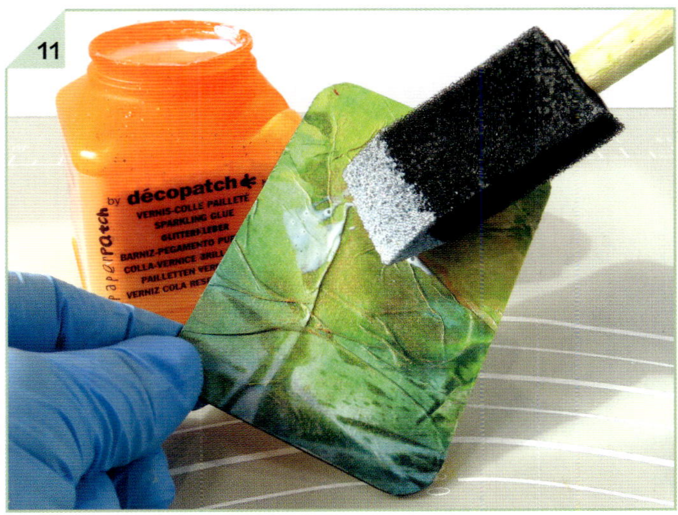

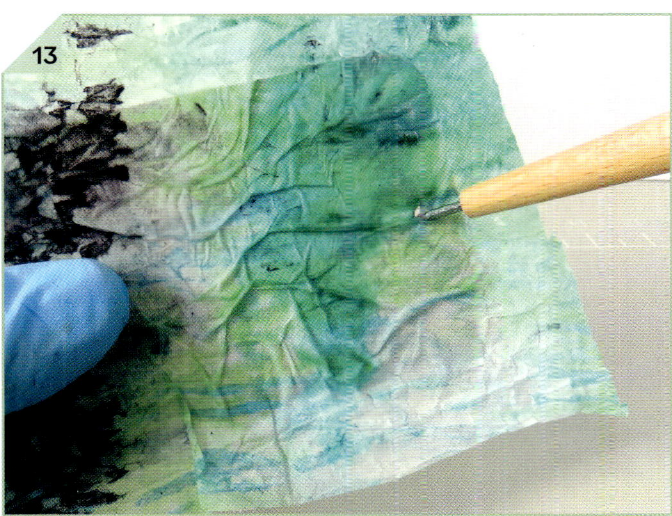

11 Apply a thin layer of PVA glue over the top with a foam brush. This will seal and protect the tissue. Make sure you cover the entire surface of the tissue paper with the sealant, ensuring no edges are left uncovered.

12 Leave to dry fully.

13 Use a sharp metal awl to poke a hole through the dried tissue paper over the precut hole to allow you to thread a ribbon through to complete the tag.

Tip
Normal sticky tape will not stick to wet-strength tissue paper; instead use a solid glue stick when wrapping a gift, or a hair elastic if you are wrapping a bottle, for example.

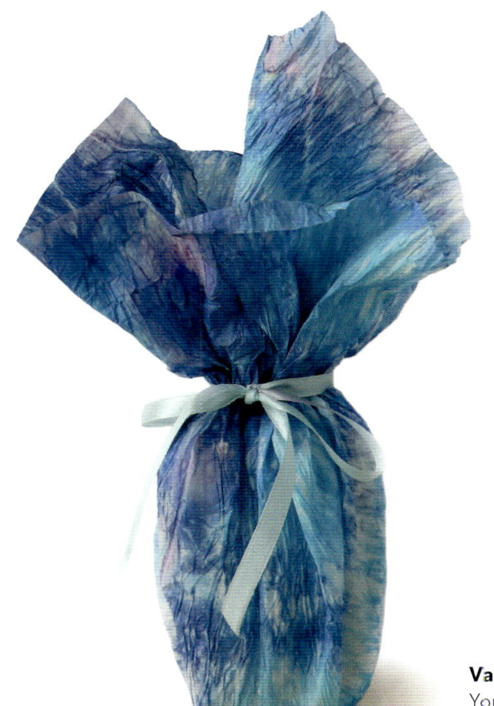

Variation: Wrapping paper
You can use the same techniques to make your own customized gift wrap for all occasions.

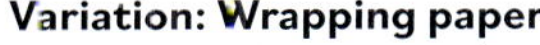

2. Bookmarks

A handmade bookmark combines creativity and functionality. It is a delightful and practical accessory or thoughtful personalized gift for people who love to read. The bookmarks you make are unique pieces of art, which can be admired daily by the recipient.

You will need

Materials

- pre-dyed wet-strength white tissue paper
- watercolour fixative to seal dyed tissue paper
- wooden bookmark with pre-drilled hole
- mountboard
- chalk paint or pale primer/undercoat paint
- wallpaper paste
- parchment paper
- PVA glue for sealing
- white gel pen, metallic paint pens or gold relief paint for embellishment
- ribbon or string and beads
- encaustic medium in pellet form (optional)
- encaustic wax paint blocks (optional)
- PanPastels (optional)
- tassels (optional)

Equipment

- large silicone mat or plastic tablecloth (to protect your workspace)
- craft knife
- hammer
- sharp pointed metal awl
- sponge or foam brush
- biodegradable baby wipes, for clean up
- cutting mat
- metal ruler
- pencil
- masking tape
- scissors
- soft lint-free cloth for buffing encaustic bookmarks
- grommet kit with 5mm (¼in) eyelets (optional)

Equipment for sealing with wax (optional)

- metal tin or silicone muffin case
- hot plate
- natural bristle brush for encaustic medium
- heat gun
- encaustic hot iron tool: mini-iron master with a range of tips

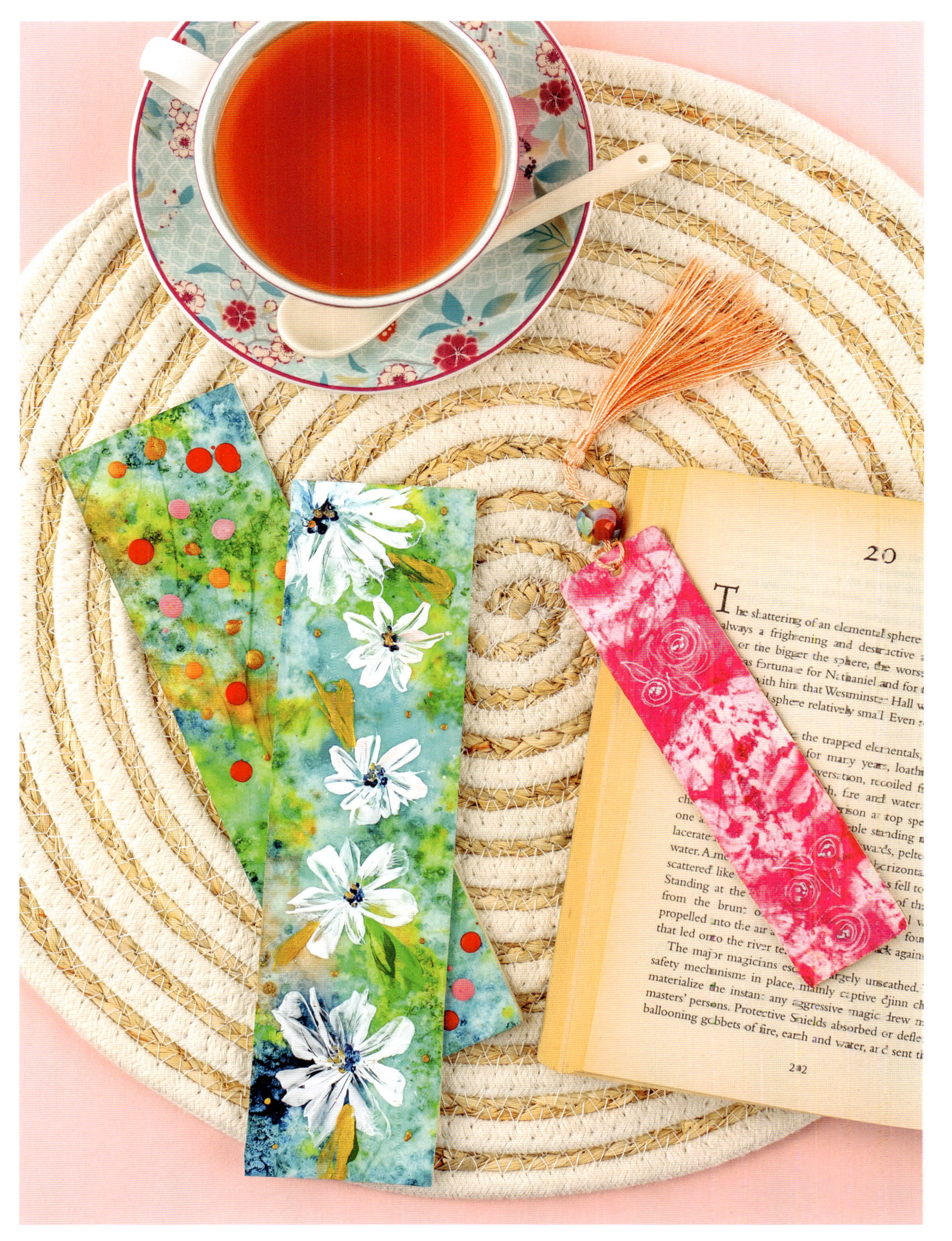

MAKING A BOOKMARK FROM MOUNTBOARD

1 Cut a large piece of mountboard, ideally pale coloured.

2 Cut a large piece of pre-dyed tissue paper to cover your mountboard.

3 Spray the tissue paper with watercolour fixative and give it a few minutes to dry.

4 Apply a thin layer of wallpaper paste to the mountboard using a foam brush.

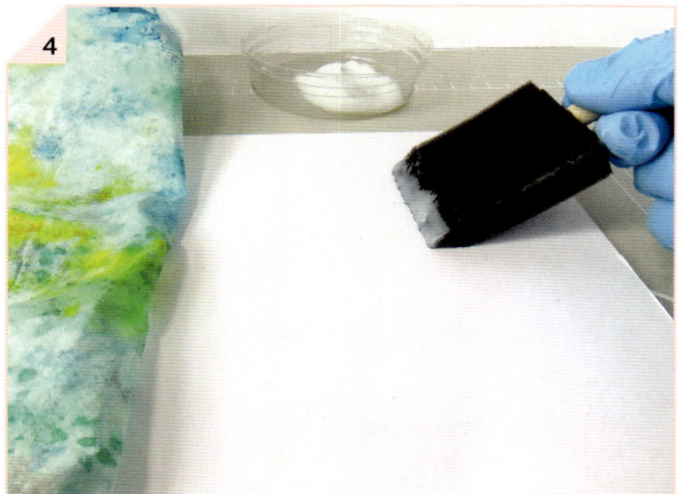

5 Carefully place the tissue paper over the wallpaper paste, smoothing it out to remove any air bubbles.

6 Gently press down to make sure the tissue paper adheres firmly to the mountboard. Retain the wrinkles for added texture. Pinch the damp tissue paper gently to create more wrinkles.

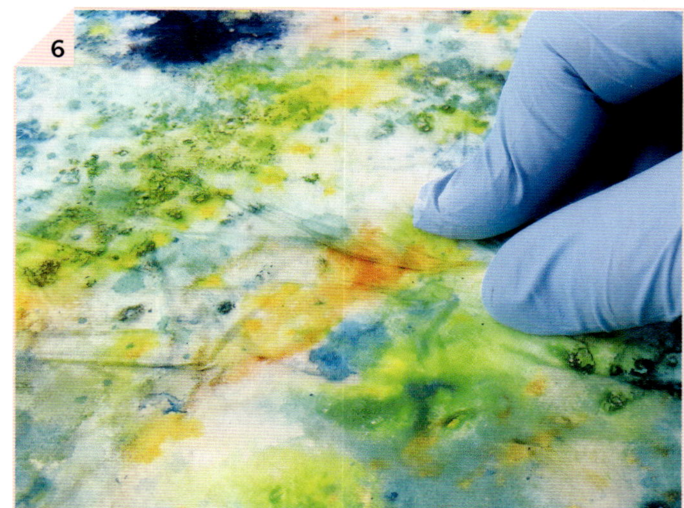

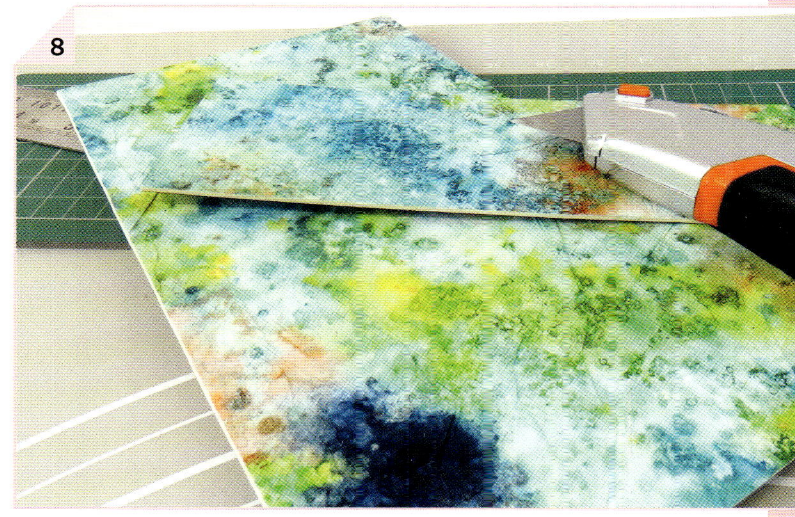

7 Allow the wallpaper paste to dry completely. This usually takes a few hours, but drying times may vary depending on the brand used.

8 Use a pencil to lightly trace the shape of the bookmark onto the reverse side of the mountboard. A typical bookmark size is around 5cm x 15–20cm (1in x 6–8in). Using a craft knife and metal ruler on a cutting mat, cut the bookmark out.

9 Place strips of masking tape on the reverse of the bookmark to keep it clean as you decorate it.

10 You may wish to use a white gel pen, PanPastel, drops of wax or paint pens to add details to your design. Try catching the wrinkles with a touch of PanPastel to highlight them.

11 Apply a thin layer of PVA glue over the top with a foam brush. This will seal and protect the tissue. Cover the entire surface of the tissue paper with the PVA glue sealant, ensuring no edges are left uncovered.

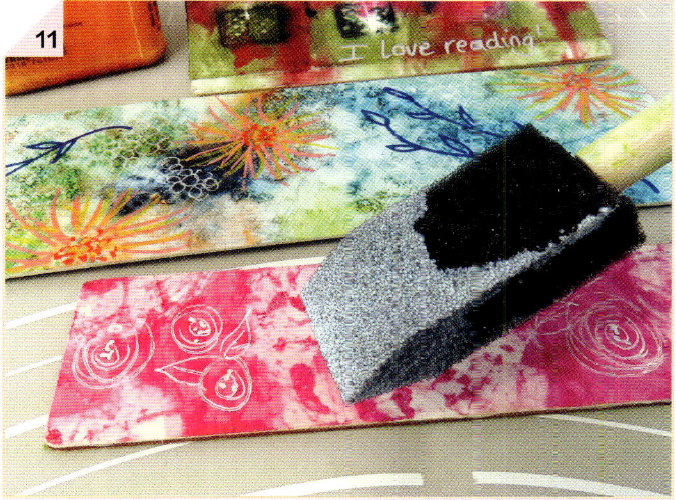

Tip

I tend to cut bookmarks to suit the pattern I like, rather than keep to an exact size.

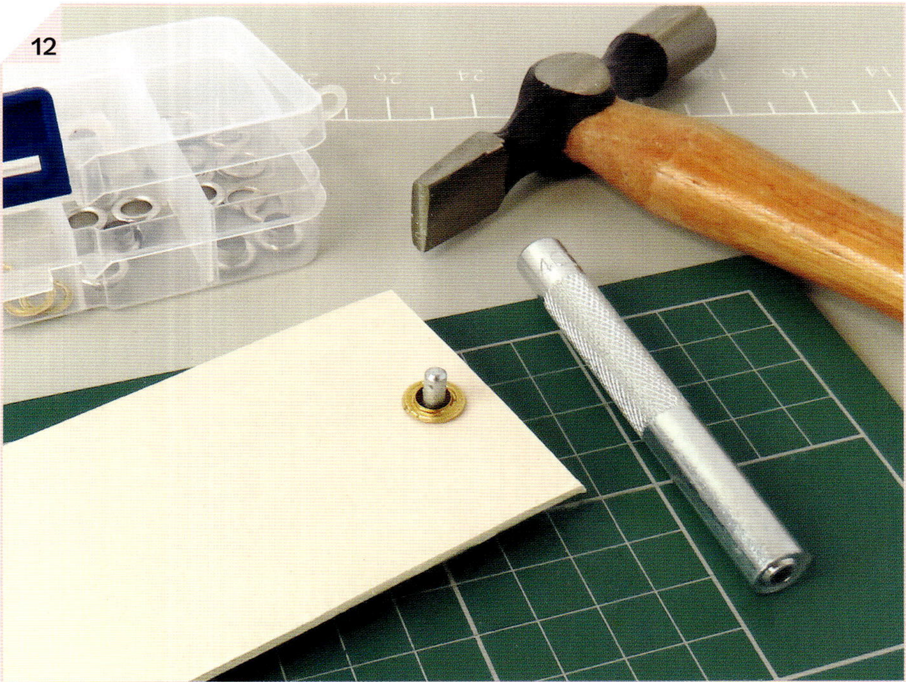

12 For a professional finish, use a grommet kit to punch a hole in your mountboard bookmark. Position the grommet punch in the centre top of the bookmark, hammer to cut the hole and insert the double-sided grommet.

13 Remove the masking tape from the reverse of the bookmark.

14 Thread a ribbon or a tassel through the hole to complete the bookmark.

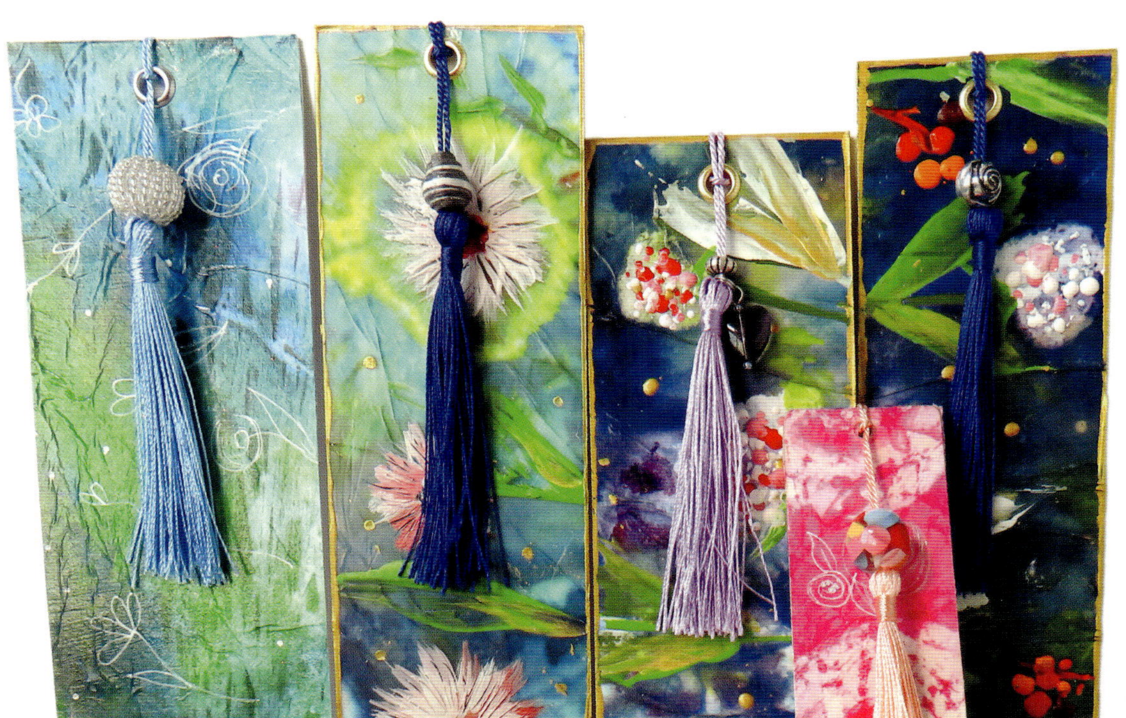

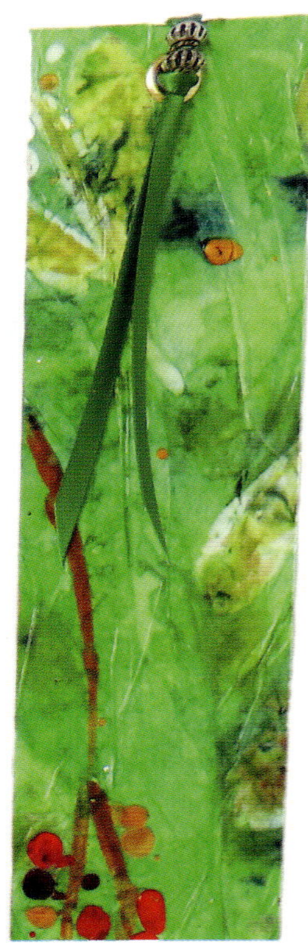

Making a bookmark from precut plywood shapes with predrilled holes

1 Paint the bookmark with a coat of pale-coloured chalk paint or primer paint, using a sponge brush. Leave to dry.

2 Choose a piece of tissue paper that complements the colours and patterns you would like for your bookmark. Spray the paper with watercolour fixative and leave to dry.

3 Cut the paper to a size that fits over the bookmark, remembering to cut larger than you need for the shape

4 Apply wallpaper paste to the bookmark, covering the surface evenly, including the precut hole.

5 Place the cut tissue paper on top, gently pressing down to adhere it to the surface. To create more wrinkles, you can squeeze the paper.

6 Allow the wallpaper paste to dry completely. This may take a few hours.

7 Once dry, trim the excess tissue paper from the edges of the bookmark, using a craft knife.

8 Before sealing, use a white gel pen, drops of wax or paint pens to add details to your design.

9 Apply a thin layer of PVA glue over the top with a foam brush to seal and protect the tissue paper. Cover the entire surface of the tissue paper with the sealant, ensuring no edges are left uncovered. Leave to dry fully.

10 Use a sharp metal awl to poke a hole through the dried tissue paper over the precut hole. Thread a ribbon or tassel through to complete the bookmark.

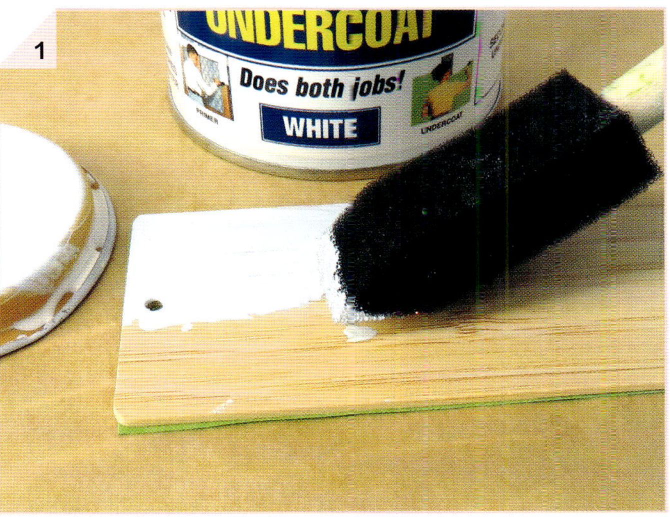

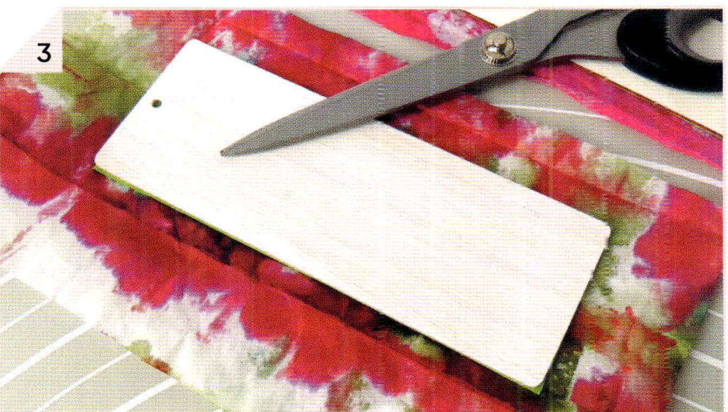

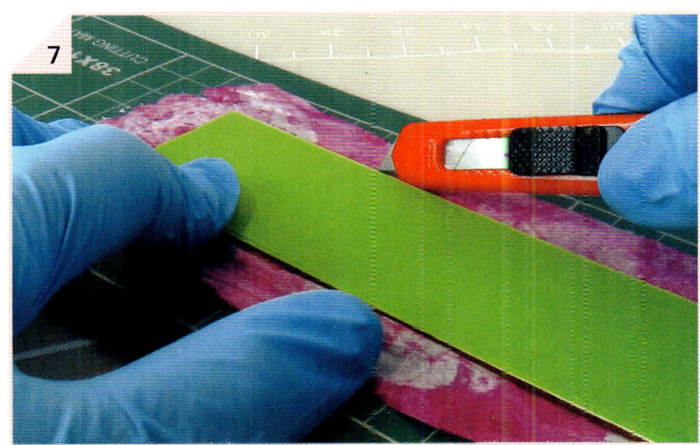

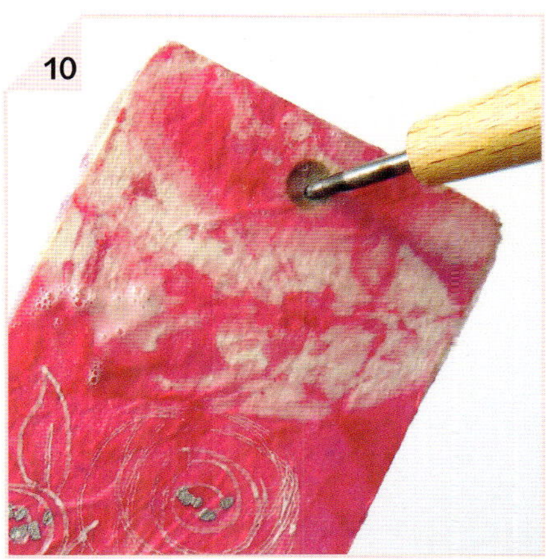

Encaustic wax finish

Seal the tissue paper with clear encaustic medium to add a glossy and protective layer, making your bookmark more durable.

1 Melt encaustic medium (pellet form) in a metal dish or silicone muffin case on a hot plate or in a wax melt pot.

2 Glue the pre-dyed tissue paper onto the bookmark using wallpaper paste. Leave to dry.

3 Trim excess tissue paper as required with a craft knife.

4 Apply a thin layer of clear molten encaustic medium over the top of the tissue paper, using a bristle brush. This will seal and protect the design on the tissue paper.

5 Cover the entire surface of the tissue paper with the wax, ensuring no edges are left unsealed.

6 Fuse gently with a heat gun.

7 If your tissue paper has abstract botanical shapes on it you can paint on flowers with a small petal-shaped tip on an encaustic hot iron tool. This gives a beautiful 3D appearance to the flowers. Add dots for the flower centres. Build up the dots to achieve depth and texture.

8 You can also just drop on dots of wax using the encaustic tool dipped into encaustic wax blocks to create an abstract effect.

Tip

There is no need to fuse wax added directly from an encaustic hot iron tool. See safety note on page 73.

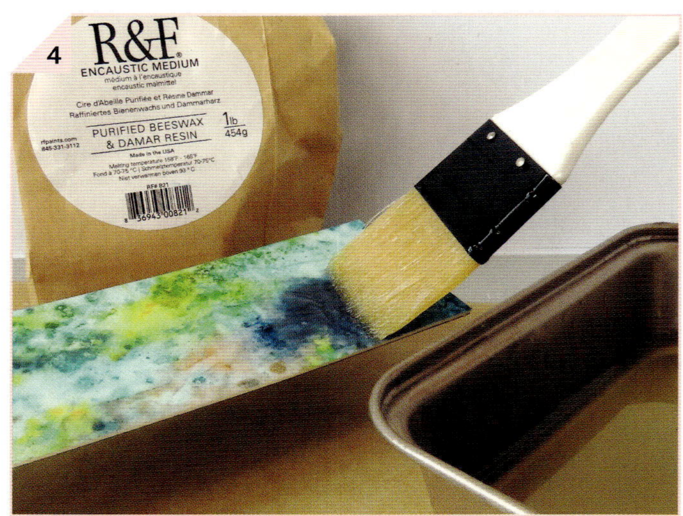

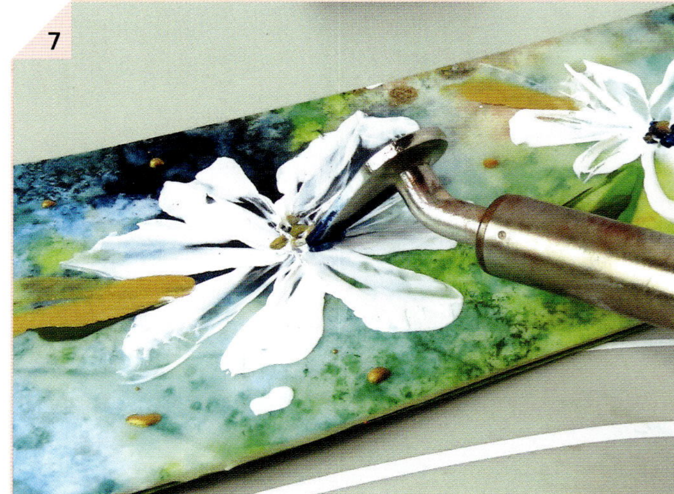

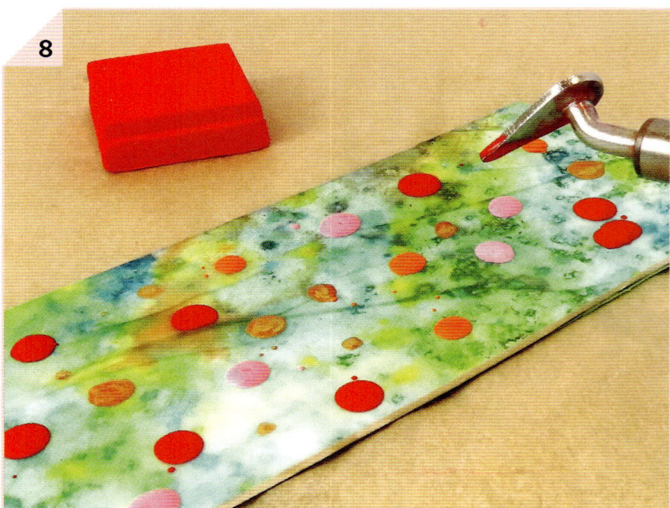

9 Once it has cooled, buff the wax with a soft cloth to give a shiny finish.

10 You can leave the bookmark like this or, for a professional finish, use a grommet kit to punch a hole in the corner of your bookmark. Hammer on a hard surface.

11 (Optional): Choose a co-ordinating coloured tassel and thread it through the hole and loop it over to tie. This gives your bookmark a stylish design.

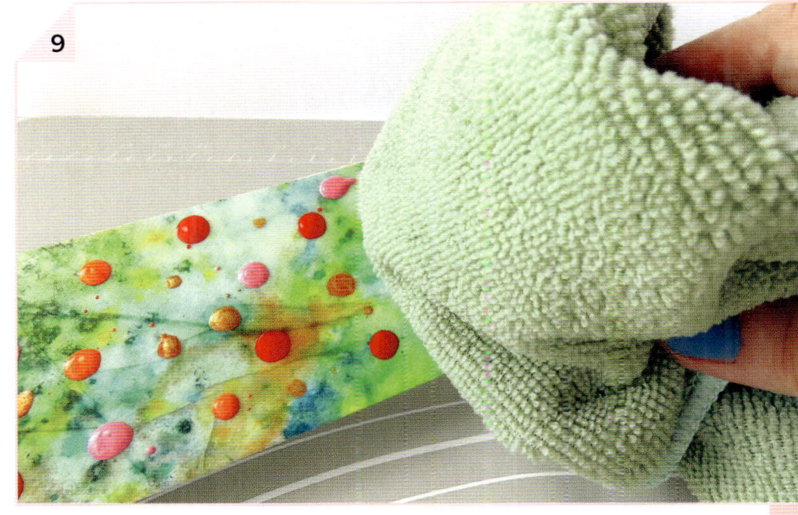

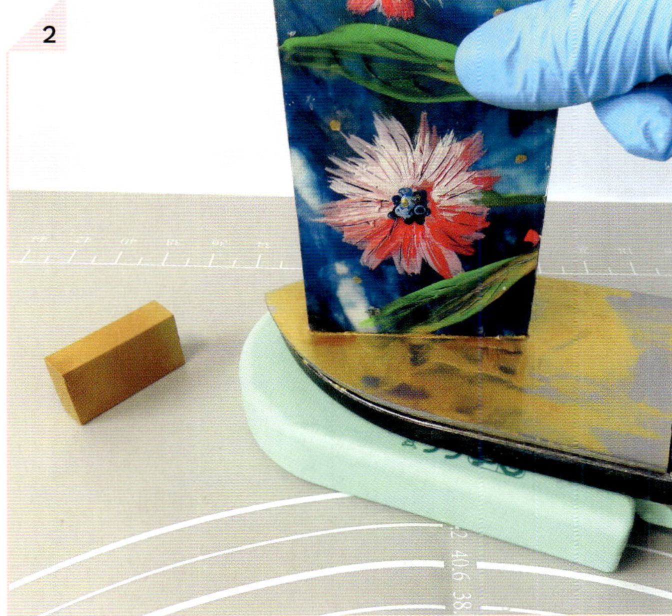

Wax edging

1 Melt gold or silver encaustic wax paint on the heated encaustic iron or on a hot plate.

2 Dip the edges of the bookmark one by one into the puddle of wax. Melt more wax from the block as needed.

3 When all sides are dipped, polish the whole bookmark lightly with a soft cloth to bring out the shine.

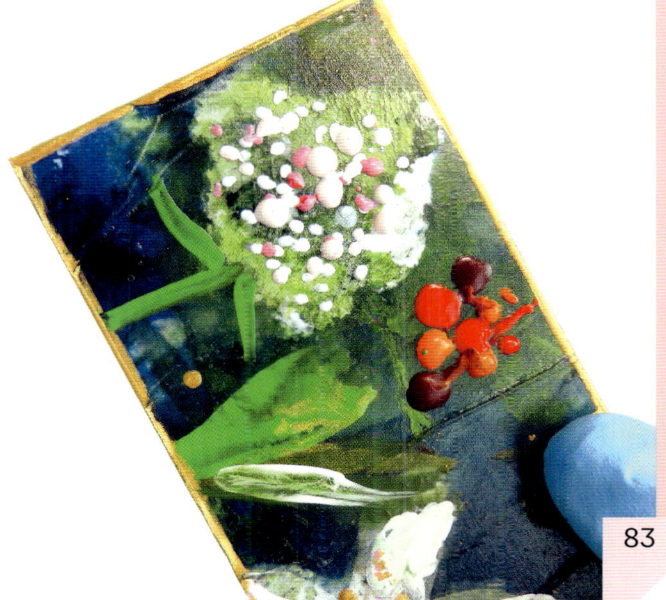

3. Notecards and envelopes

You can easily apply some of the beautiful hand-dyed tissue paper you have created to mountboard to make unique notecards with matching envelopes. These notecards will reflect your personal style and creativity and will be much appreciated by the recipient.

They are perfect for any occasion: thank you notes, invitations or a message to friends and family. Adding matching envelopes elevates these custom cards and will ensure that they become treasured little gifts, long after the occasion is over.

Get ready to unleash your creative side and enjoy the process of making these striking notecards!

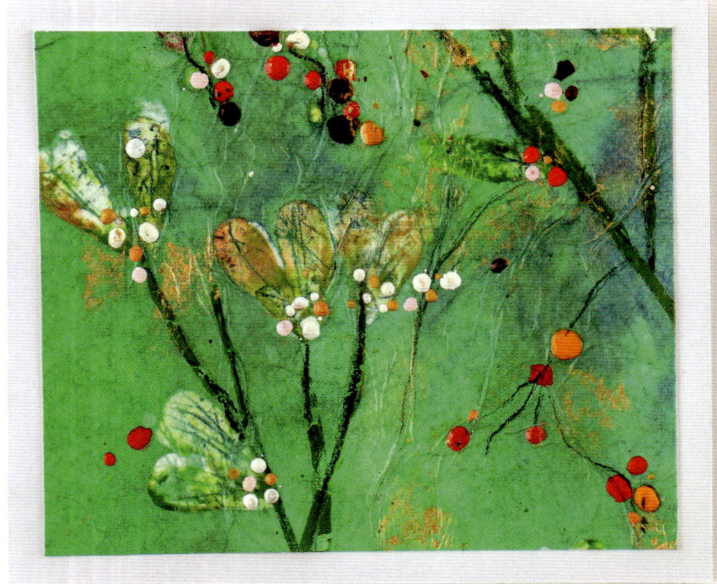

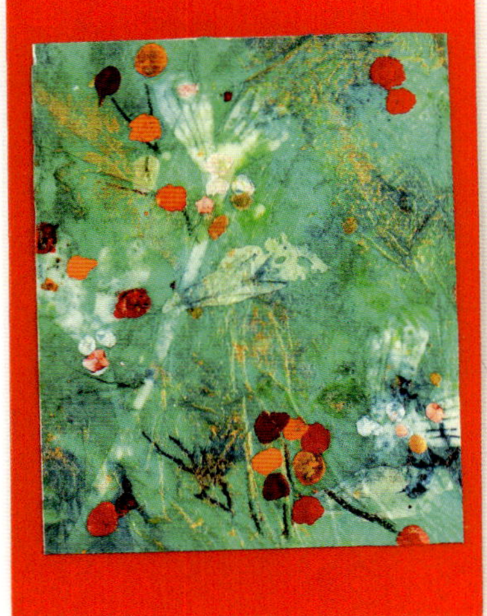

Variation: Christmas cards
You can use the same techniques demonstrated to make your own Christmas cards and matching envelopes.

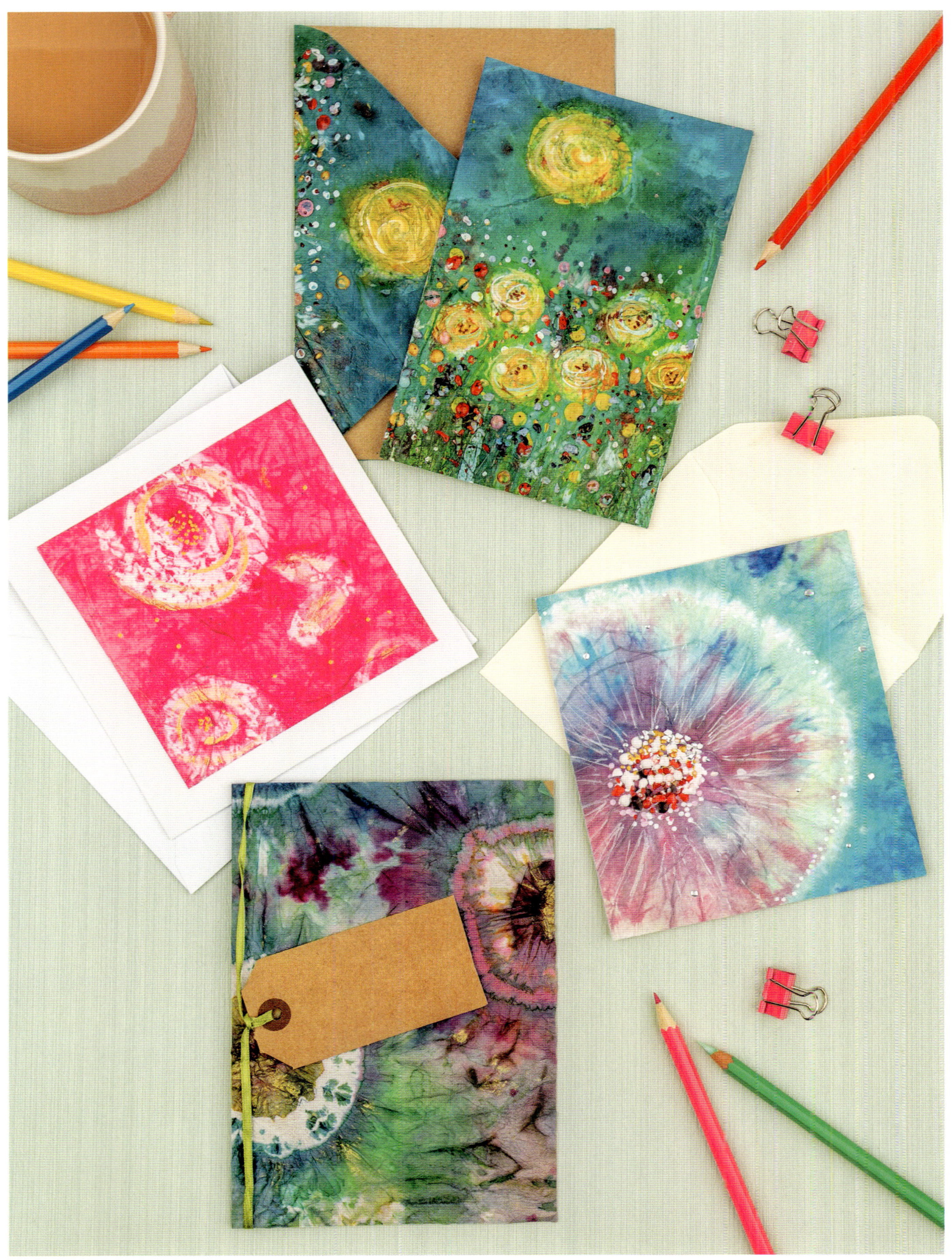

You will need

Materials

- pre-dyed wet-strength white tissue paper
- watercolour fixative to seal dyed tissue paper
- mountboard
- chalk paint or pale primer/undercoat
- kraft or other envelopes for example: 18.5 x 13.5cm (7¼ x 5¼in) on 115gsm kraft paper
- wallpaper paste
- parchment paper
- thin card, A4 – 210 x 297mm (8.3 x 11.7in)
- PVA glue for sealing
- solid glue stick
- encaustic wax paint blocks in a selection of toning colours and gold for highlights
- white gel pen, metallic pens or relief paint for embellishment
- PanPastels (optional)
- encaustic medium in pellet form (optional)
- kraft gift tag and ribbon or string (optional)

Equipment

- large silicone mat or plastic tablecloth (to protect your workspace)
- craft knife
- sponge or foam brush
- disposable plastic gloves
- biodegradable baby wipes, for clean up
- cutting mat
- metal ruler
- pencil
- masking tape
- scissors
- printing roller or brayer
- soft lint-free cloth for buffing encaustic notecards

Equipment for sealing with wax (optional)

- metal tin or silicone muffin case
- hot plate
- natural bristle brush for encaustic medium
- heat gun
- encaustic hot iron tool: mini-iron master with a range of tips

CREATING MULTIPLE NOTECARDS FROM ONE PIECE OF MOUNTBOARD

1 Select the pre-dyed tissue paper you want to use. To minimize colour bleed, spray with watercolour fixative. Leave to dry.

2 Spread wallpaper paste evenly over the mountboard using a foam brush or section of sponge.

3 Lay the dyed tissue paper over the board – smooth it out but retain some wrinkles for added interest. Use a roller or brayer to help it to stick.

4 Leave to dry overnight under a heavy weight.

5 Once dry, trim the mountboard to the desired size using a craft knife.

6 Protect the back of the notecard by using masking tape or cover it with some scrap paper.

7 You may wish to use a white gel pen, gold relief paint, drops of encaustic wax paint or metallic pens to add details to your design.

8 You can also add gold PanPastel to highlight the wrinkles. Apply with a gloved finger.

9 Apply a thin layer of PVA glue over the top with a foam brush. This will seal and protect the tissue paper. Leave to dry thoroughly.

10 Carefully remove the masking tape or protective scrap paper from the back of the notecard.

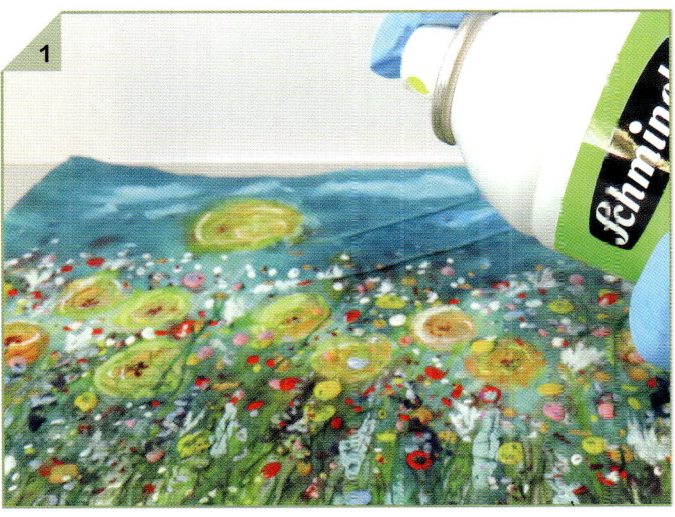

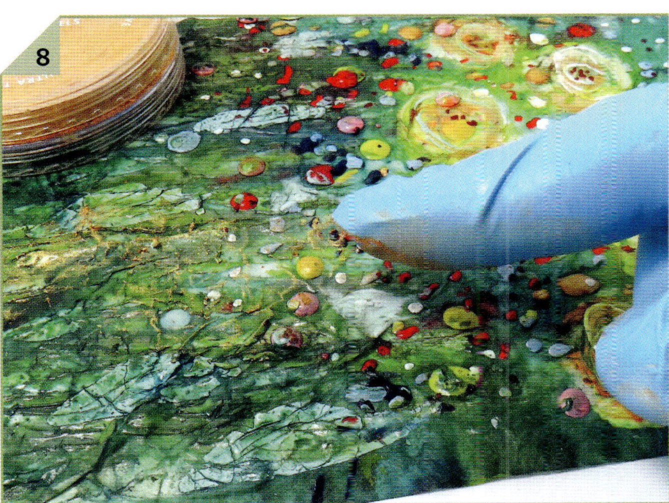

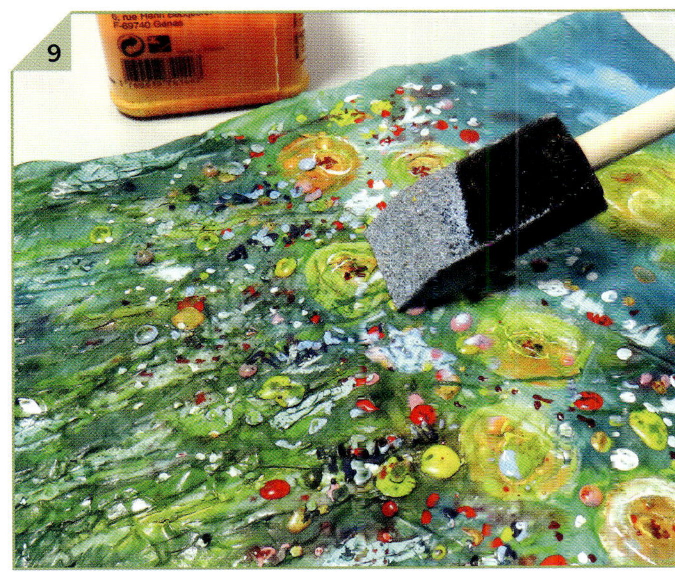

Adding a translucent finish on mountboard

Seal the tissue paper with clear encaustic medium. This translucent finish adds a glossy and protective layer, making your notecard both attractive and durable.

1 Melt encaustic medium (pellet form) in a metal dish or silicone muffin case on a hot plate or in a wax melt pot.

2 Adhere your pre-dyed tissue paper to the card using wallpaper paste. Leave to dry.

3 Apply a thin layer of clear molten encaustic medium over the top of the tissue paper, using a bristle brush. This will seal and protect the paper.

4 Cover the entire surface of the tissue paper with the wax, ensuring no edges are left unsealed.

5 Fuse gently with a heat gun.

6 Add gold PanPastel to highlight the wrinkles and fuse gently.

7 If your tissue paper has abstract botanical shapes on it, you can paint on flowers with a small petal-shaped tip on an encaustic hot iron tool. Applying wax in this way gives a beautiful 3D appearance to the flowers. Add dots for the flower centres. Build up the dots to achieve depth and texture. Gold wax acts as a beautiful highlight.

8 You can also just drop on dots of wax using the encaustic tool dipped into encaustic wax paint blocks to create an abstract effect.

9 Once cooled, buff the wax with a soft cloth to give a shiny finish.

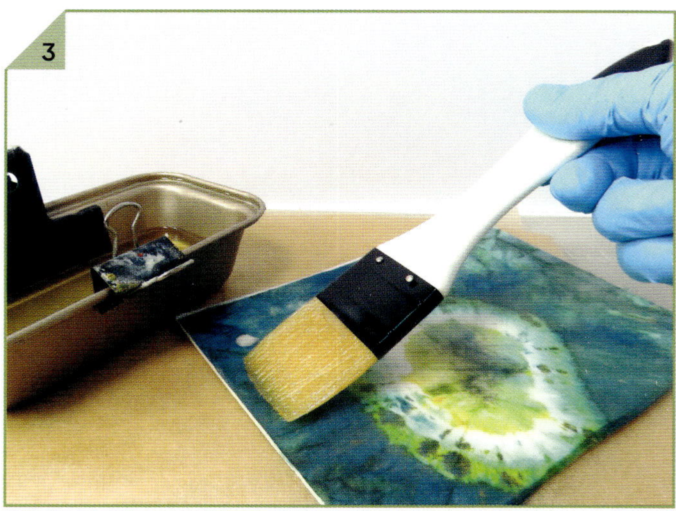

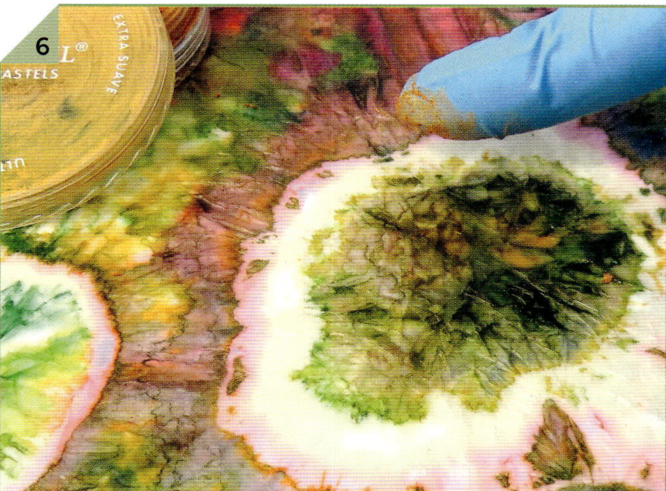

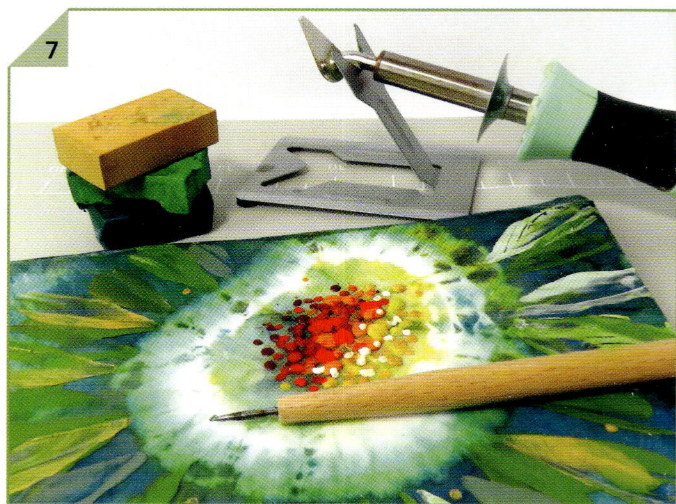

Tip

There is no need to fuse wax added directly from an encaustic hot iron tool. See safety note on page 73.

MAKING MATCHING ENVELOPES

You can also turn your envelopes into works of art!

1 Lay a kraft envelope on a piece of dyed tissue paper. Ensure the tissue paper is large enough so it can be folded over to cover the envelope. My envelopes were 18.5 x 13.5cm (7¼ x 5¼in) on 115gsm kraft paper.

2 Seal the pre-dyed tissue paper to minimize colour bleed, using watercolour fixative. Leave to dry.

3 Use a solid glue stick to adhere the envelope to the tissue paper, ensuring it extends to cover the flap only. Press down firmly to be sure it sticks well.

4 Carefully trim the excess, using scissors.

5 Do not cover the rest of the reverse of the envelope

6 Cut out a piece of mountboard to size to ensure it fits into the envelope. Adhere your dyed tissue paper using a solid glue stick, embellish it and seal it on one side only.

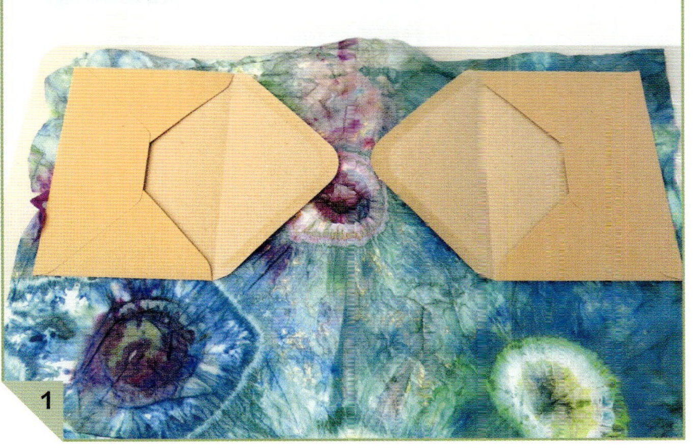

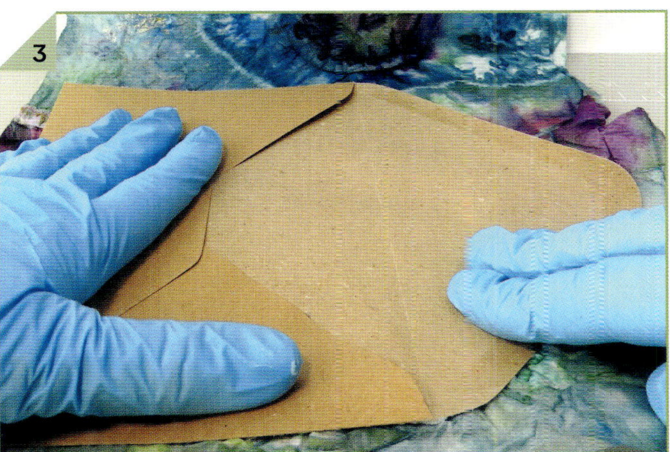

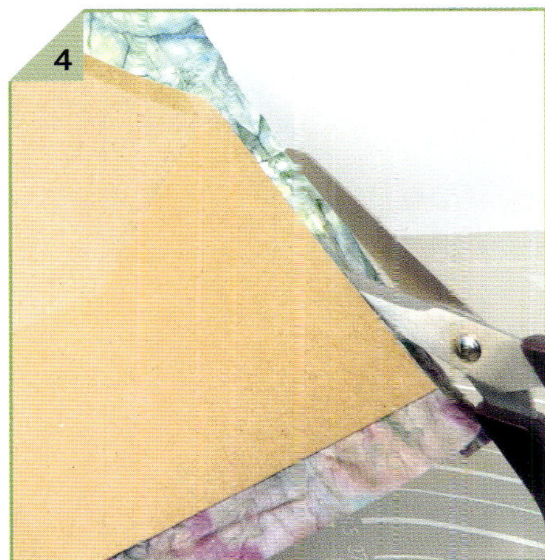

Tip

This process works even with tissue paper on which you have used wax as a resist or embellishment.
You can choose to match or mismatch the envelopes and notecards.

Adding name labels

Since you have covered the front of the envelope with textured, dyed tissue paper, it is unlikely you will be able to write the name of the recipient on it.

One solution is to tie on a kraft or homemade gift tag: either tie it around the sealed envelope or loop the ribbon under the flap before sealing. Then write the recipient's name on the tag. This adds a lovely personal touch.

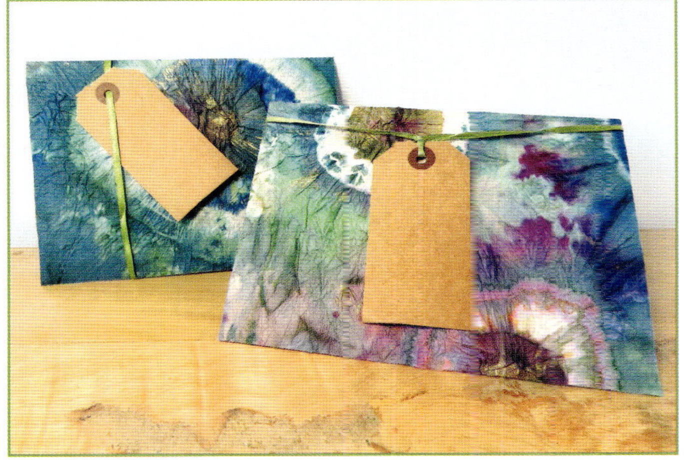

ADDING A TISSUE PAPER DESIGN TO BLANK GREETING CARDS

You can decorate blank, pre-made folded cards using a tissue paper design. These can be used for any occasion for example, birthdays, a thank you note or even Christmas cards.

Additional materials

- blank cards with matching envelopes from a craft store
- encaustic wax paint blocks

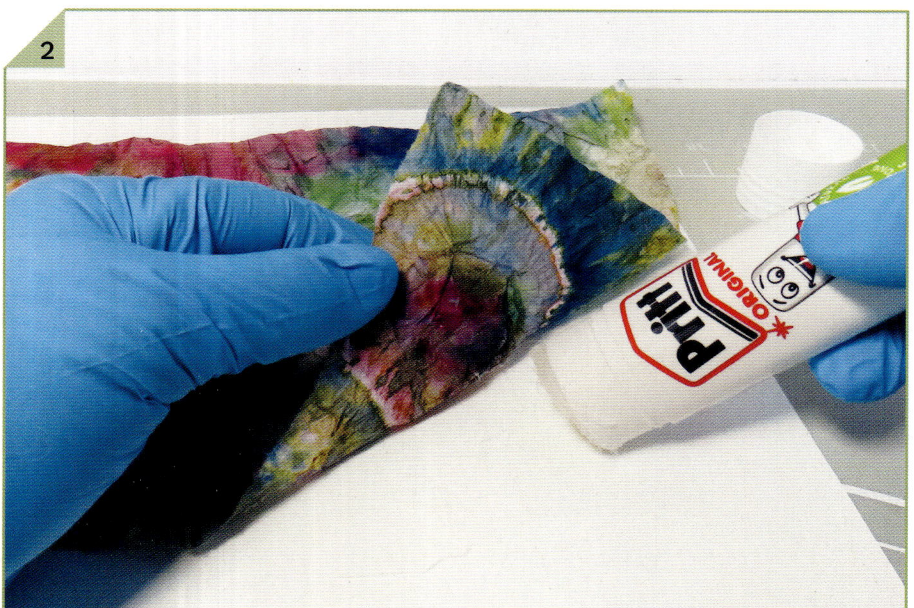

1 Seal the pre-dyed tissue paper to minimize colour bleed, using watercolour fixative. Leave to dry.

2 Instead of glueing the hand-dyed tissue paper to mountboard – stick it onto thin card, using a solid glue stick.

3 Seal it with PVA glue, using a foam brush. Leave it to dry completely.

4 Trim the tissue paper back to the edges of your blank card, using a craft knife and cutting mat.

5 Embellish with paint pens, gel pens or relief paint.

6 Stick to the blank greeting card by using a glue stick and place between parchment paper overnight under a heavy book.

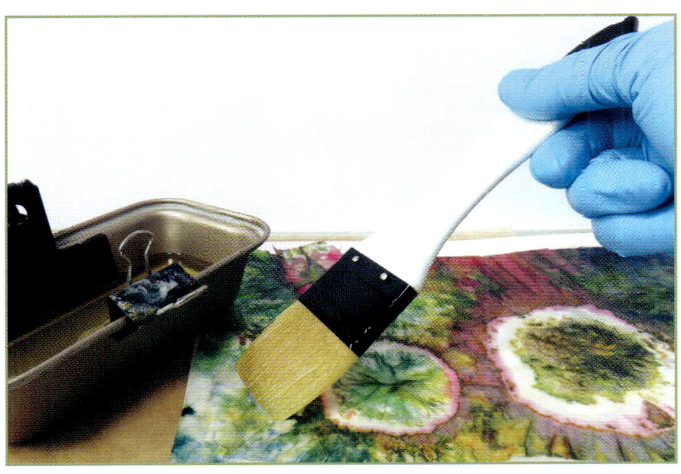

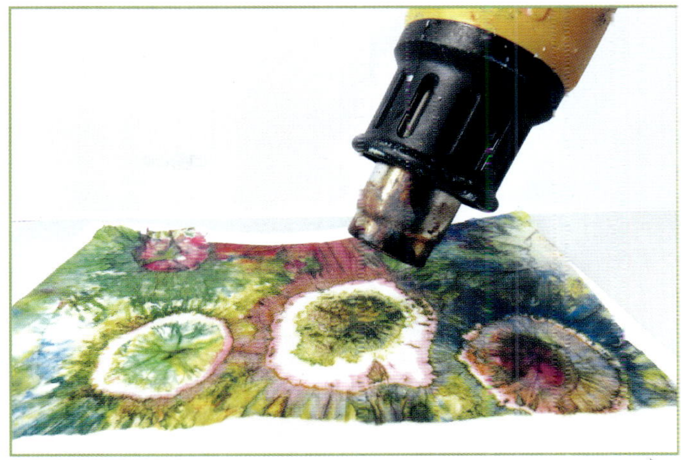

An alternative finish

Instead of using PVA glue to seal (see step 3 opposite), you can seal the tissue paper on card with encaustic medium (above left) and fuse it lightly (above right). Add drops of encaustic wax paint with an encaustic hot tool to create flower centres (right). If you use a graded selection of colour as shown, you can achieve a 3D effect. Trim to size and adhere to the front of your blank greeting card, using a solid glue stick. Buff gently with a soft cloth to make your design shine.

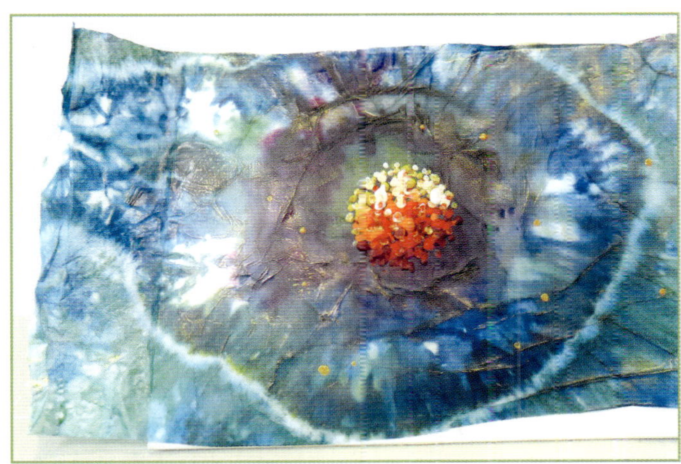

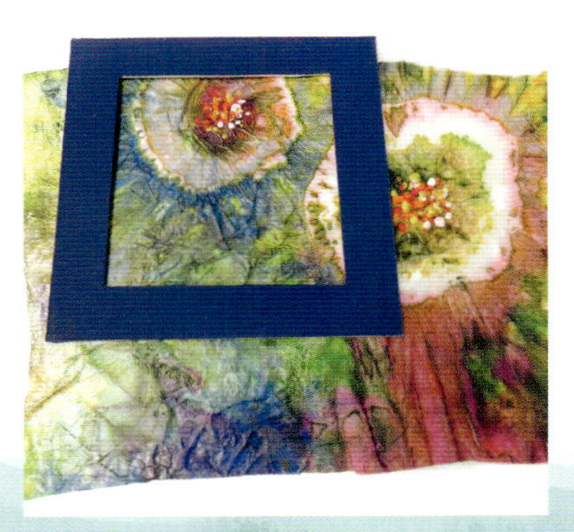

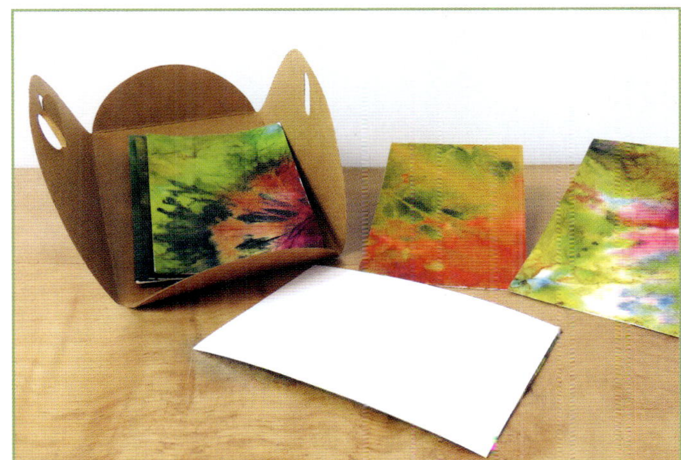

You can also make tiny cards to use for affirmation cards.

4. Serving trays

In this project you will learn step-by-step how to cover a small bamboo or glass tray with hand-dyed wet-strength tissue paper. Once the glue is fully dry, your tray is ready to use as a decorative piece to display ornaments or small plant pots or for practical purposes, such as serving snacks or drinks or practising hobbies on. It would also make a beautiful and unique gift.

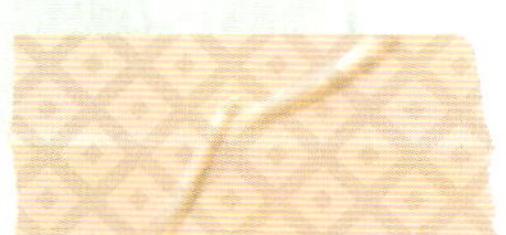

You will need

Materials

- pre-dyed wet-strength white tissue paper, large enough to cover your tray
- watercolour fixative to seal dyed tissue paper
- bamboo, wooden or glass tray
- acrylic medium gloss gel (acts as glue)
- acrylic gloss medium (acts as glossy sealant)
- matt, satin or sparkly PVA glue (optional)
- gold relief paint pen or gold PanPastel (optional)

Equipment

- large silicone mat or plastic tablecloth (to protect your workspace)
- craft knife
- foam brush or sponge
- scissors, large and small
- paintbrush, round ended
- cutting mat
- rubber printing roller (brayer)
- biodegradable baby wipes, for tidy up

Money-saving tip

Use PVA glue as an adhesive and as a top coat!

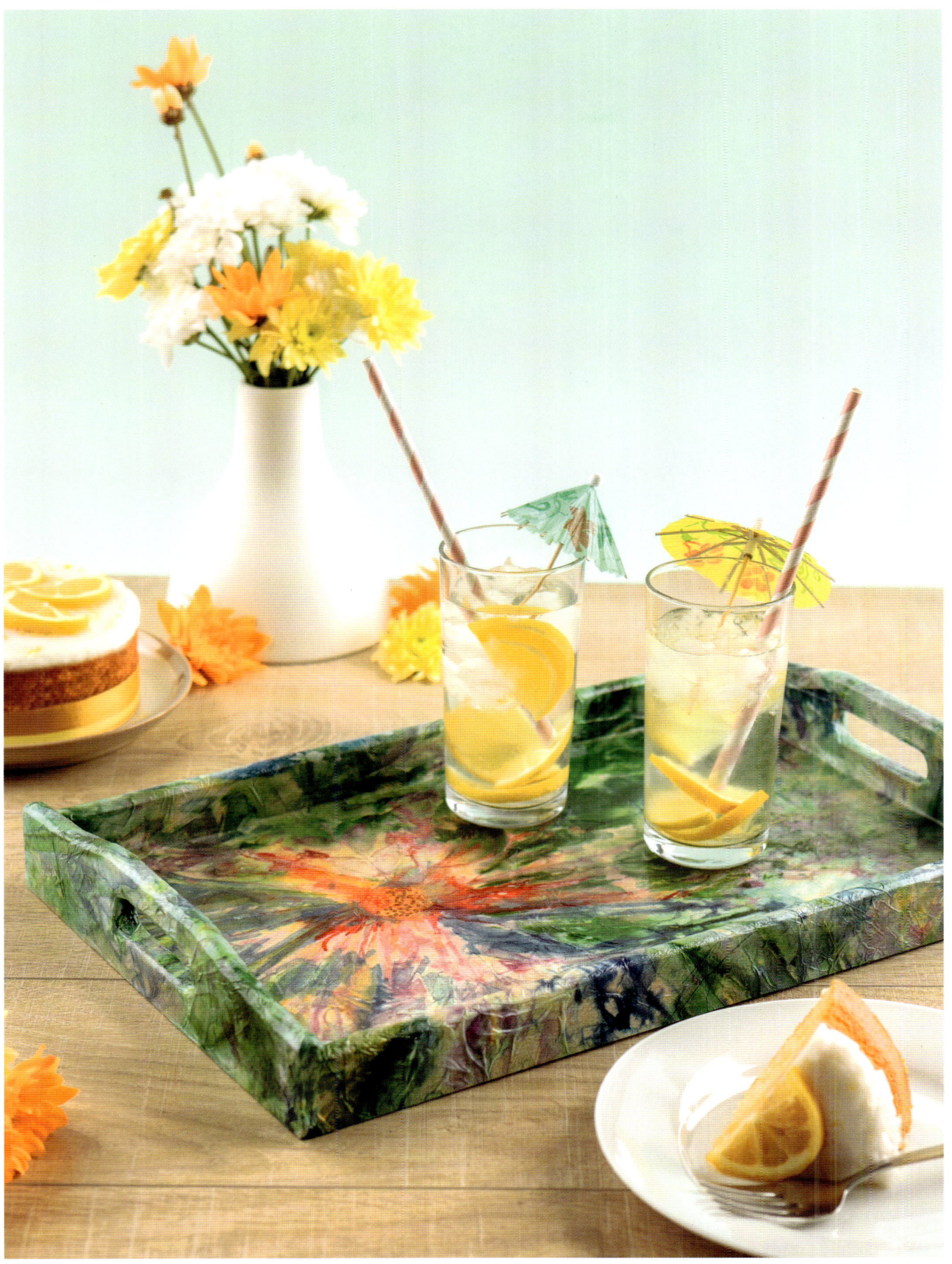

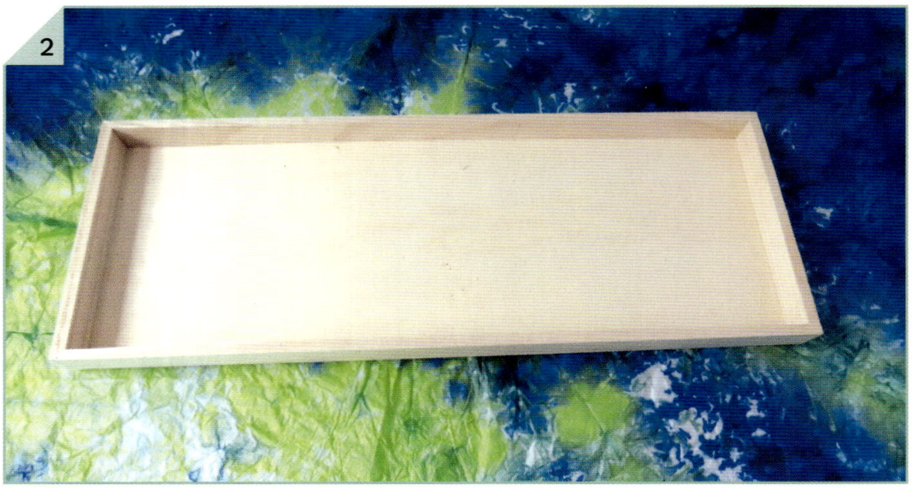

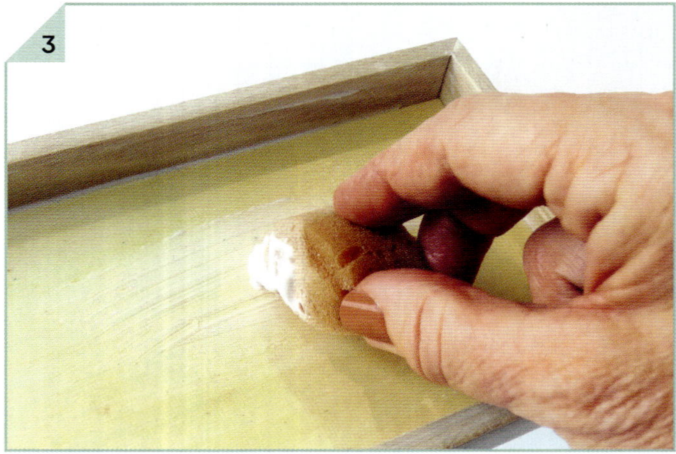

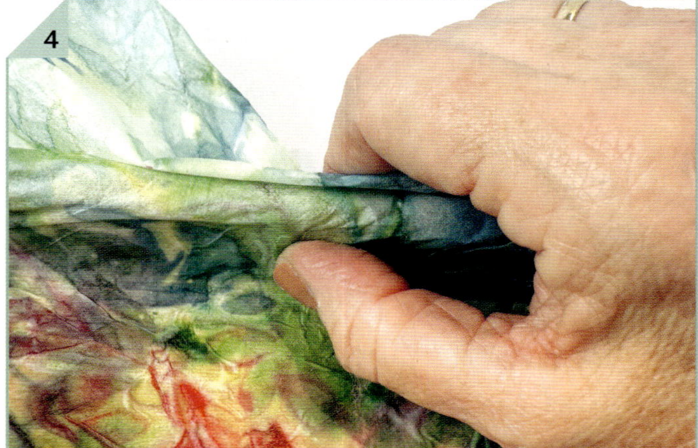

1 Gather your materials and cover your workspace to protect it. Ensure your tray is free from dust or dirt by carefully wiping it with a biodegradable baby wipe.

2 Choose a piece of hand-dyed tissue paper larger than the surface area of the tray (including handles, if present). This allows for easier application and trimming later. Depending on the size of the tray, you can use a coordinating or contrasting piece of tissue paper for the inside base of the tray. You can also decorate larger trays with hand-dyed tissue paper – just ensure you have enough paper of a similar pattern to cover the whole tray. If it is a very large tray, you can dye two pieces of tissue paper with a similar pattern. To minimize colour bleed, spray the tissue paper with a watercolour fixative. Leave to dry.

3 Now apply the adhesive. Use a sponge or foam brush to apply a thin layer of acrylic medium gloss gel onto the inside base surface of the tray. Cover the entire area where you will place the tissue paper.

4 Gently place a piece of tissue paper onto the glued surface. Smooth it out with your fingers or a clean cloth to remove any air bubbles or wrinkles or, if you prefer, retain some wrinkles for added texture and interest. Allow this section to dry. Leave excess paper at the four edges, which can be trimmed later.

Tip

Choose the best piece of the pattern for the inside tray base and apply this first.

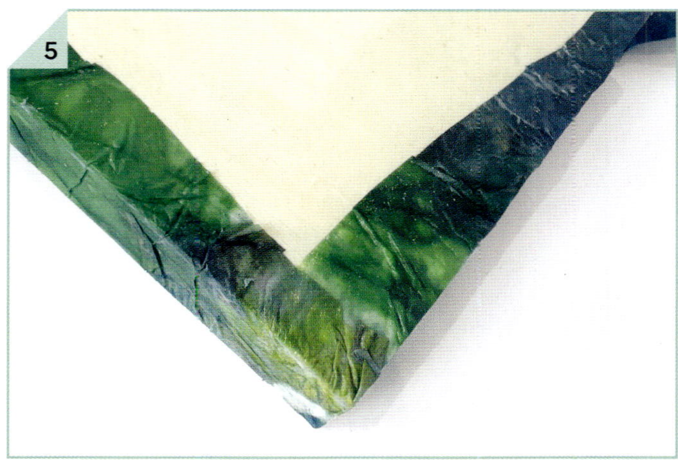

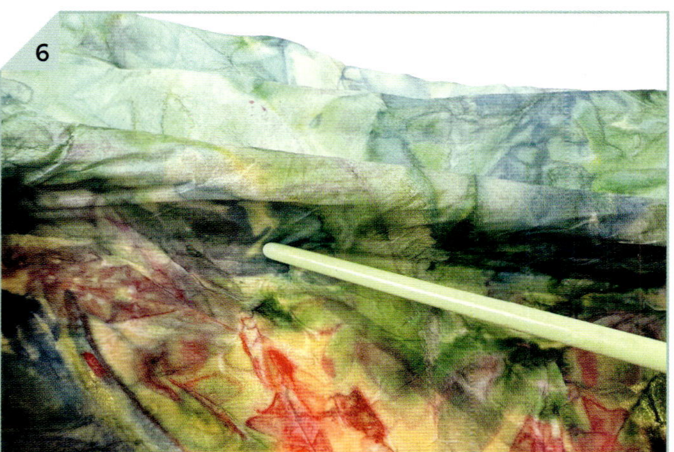

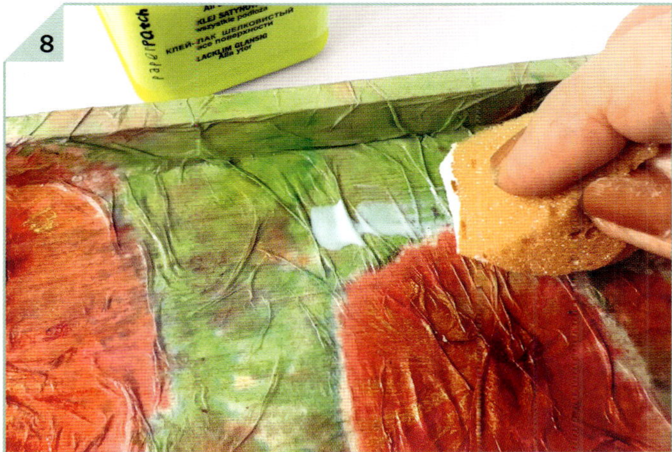

5 Repeat this step for each section of the tray until it is completely covered. You may need to trim excess paper in some sections with a craft knife or scissors, and fold as you go along in others, depending on the shape of the tray – a bit like wrapping a gift. Wipe off any excess acrylic medium gloss gel with a baby wipe.

6 Use a round-ended paintbrush to gently smooth the inside edges and corners of the tray, to ensure the tissue paper fully adheres. You may need to do the gluing in stages, depending on the shape of your tray.

7 Set the tray aside on a silicone mat to prevent sticking, in a well-ventilated area, and allow it to dry completely. This may take several hours or overnight, depending on the type of glue used.

8 Once all the tissue paper is fully dry, apply two thin layers of acrylic gloss medium over the top using a sponge. This will seal it and provide a protective layer. Leave it between coats to dry thoroughly. Make sure you apply the gloss medium evenly and smoothly.

Tip
Save any scraps of hand-dyed tissue paper you cut off in case you need them for repairs later.

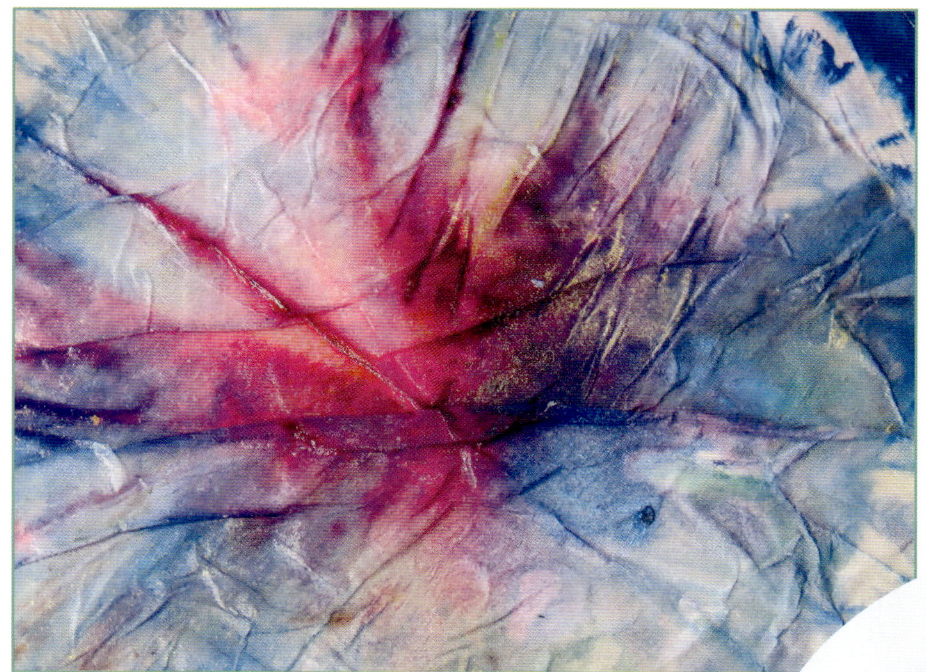

CREATING A GLOSSY FINISH

If desired, you can create a glossy, satin or sparkly finish, by using sparkly PVA glue. You can also add gold PanPastel over the wrinkles to add highlights (above) or use a gold relief paint pen to add dot embellishments to flower centres (right).

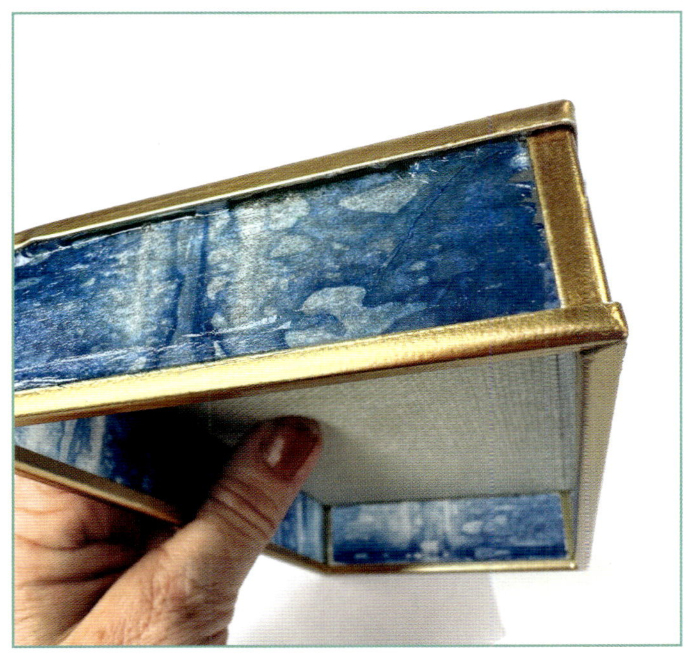

COVERING A GLASS TRAY

The glass trays I have only need their four glass sides covering. Use the same method, as above, to adhere your selected hand-dyed tissue paper. Wipe any excess glue off the glass or other edges, to minimize smears.

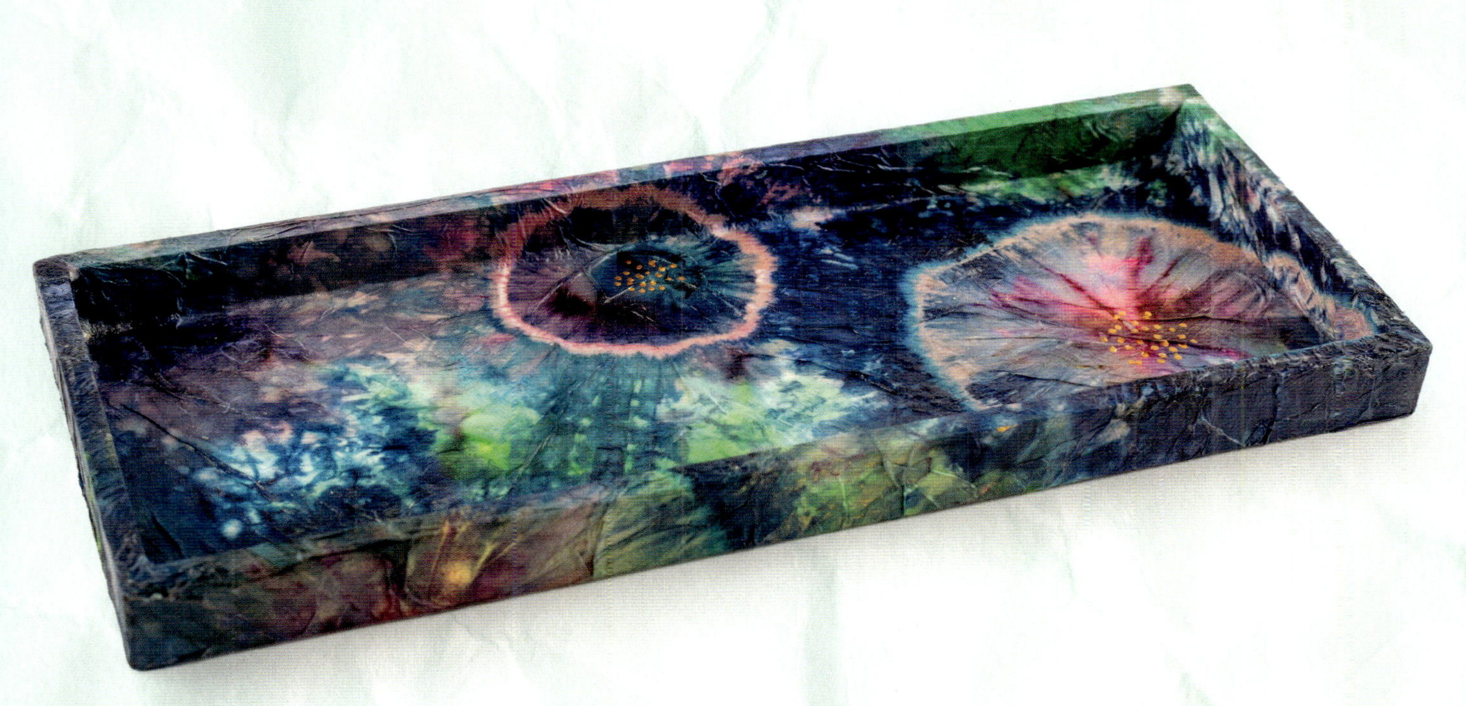

This is a smaller tray than the one demonstrated in the project. It shows abstract floral shapes made using technique 7: tie dye on pages 44–49. A small tray is versatile and can be used for various purposes including serving food and drinks; organizing small items like keys, coins, pens and jewellery; or for showcasing candles or plants.

5. Storage boxes

Gluing hand-dyed tissue paper to a small wooden or thick card box creates a unique jewellery or storage box or a memorable gift.

Experiment with different-shaped wooden boxes or pots, or ones with hinged lids. Larger wooden pots are ideal for plants or stationery. Try upcycling wooden containers from charity shops to give them a new lease of life.

You will need

Materials

- pre-dyed wet-strength white tissue paper
- watercolour fixative to seal dyed tissue paper
- wooden box, open or with a hinged lid
- acrylic medium gloss gel (acts as glue)
- acrylic gloss medium or decopatch glue (as sealant)
- PanPastels (optional)
- gold relief paint pens, beads, sequins or buttons to embellish (optional)

Equipment

- large silicone mat or plastic tablecloth (to protect your workspace)
- biodegradable baby wipes, for clean up
- disposable plastic gloves
- foam brush
- scissors

Money-saving tip
Use PVA glue as an adhesive and as a top coat!

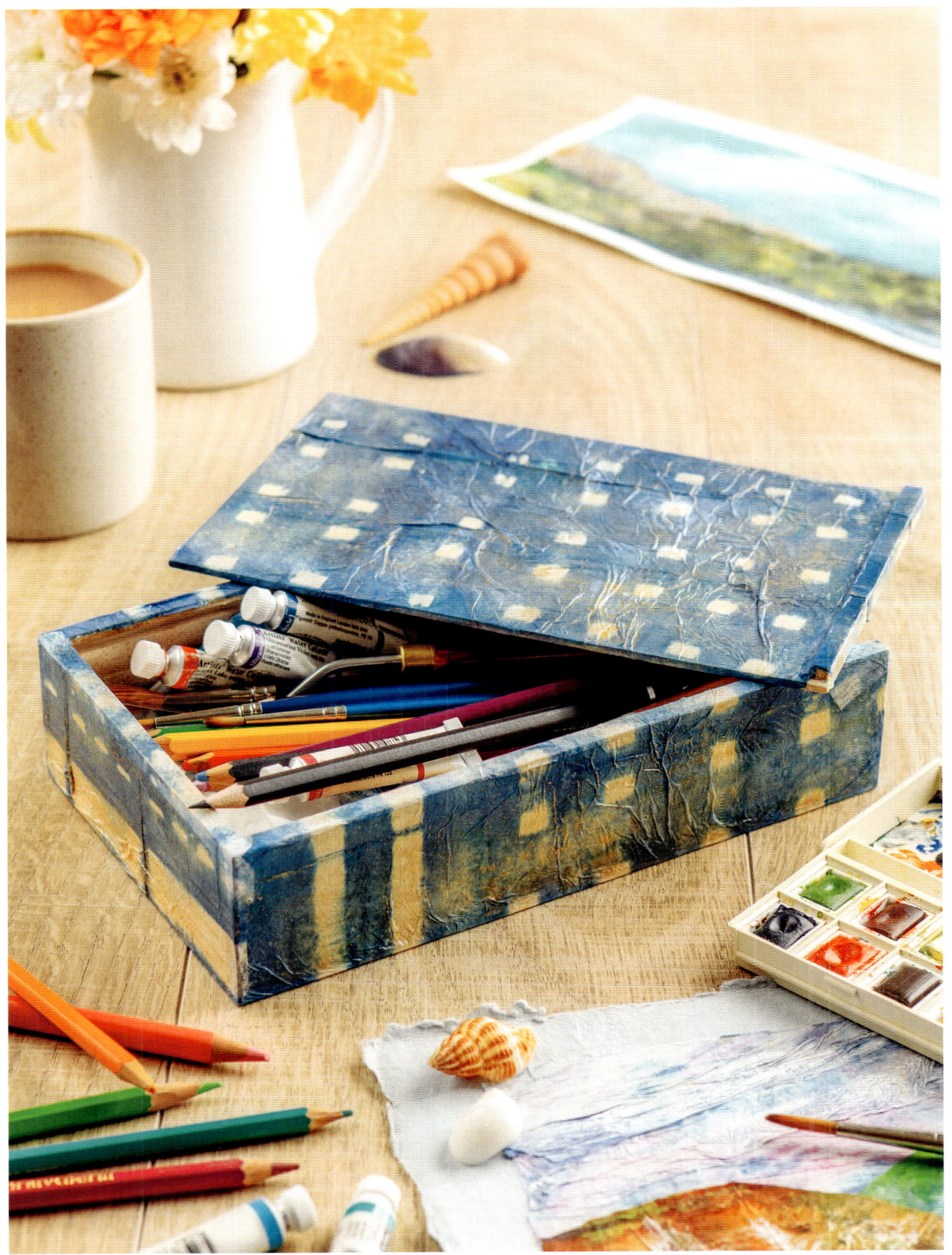

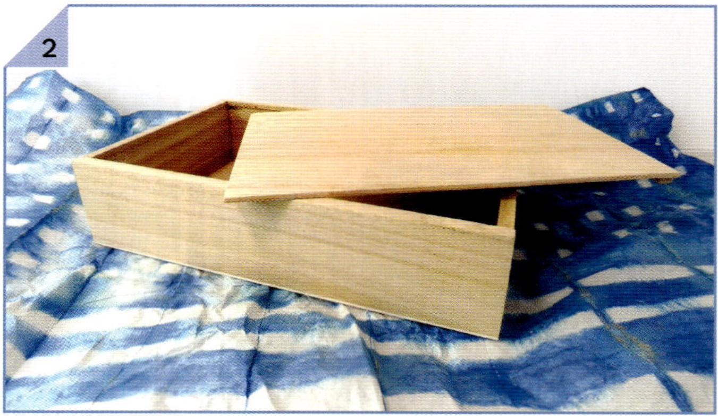

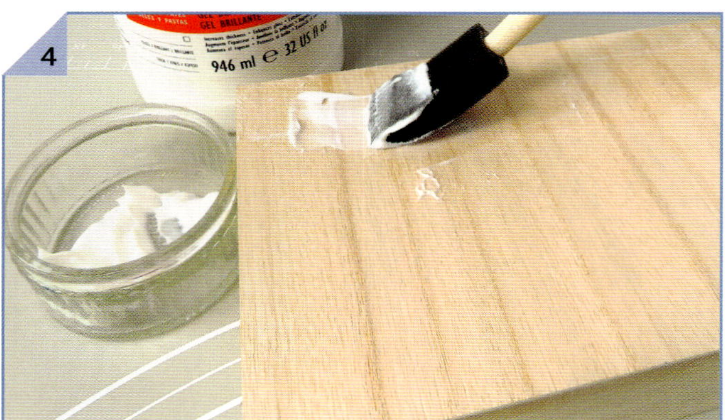

1 Gather your materials and cover your workspace to protect it.

2 Select pre-dyed tissue paper with a suitable pattern to cover the box: a smaller pattern may work better on a smaller box. The tissue must be larger than the box.

3 To minimize colour bleed, spray with watercolour fixative. Leave to dry.

4 Apply a thin, even layer of acrylic medium gloss gel to the base of the wooden box using a foam brush.

5 Carefully place a piece of dyed tissue paper onto the glued section of the box, smoothing it out with your fingers or a clean brush to remove any wrinkles or air bubbles. Retain some wrinkles for character if you prefer.

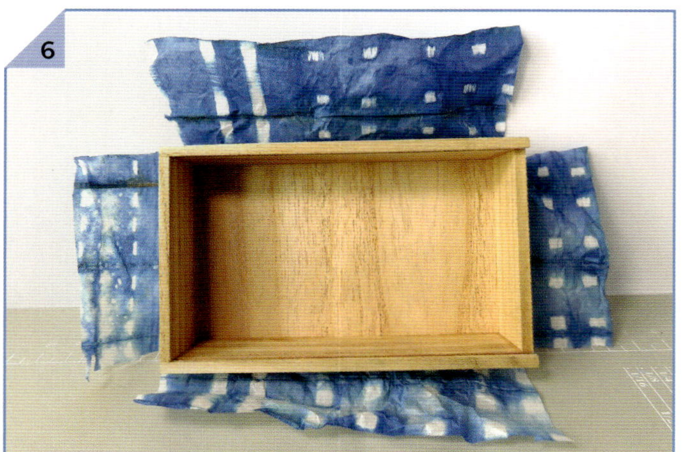

6 Wrap and glue the tissue paper around the box. Wrap it as you would a gift, but you may need to cut into the corners and trim some pieces as shown to achieve neat folds.

7 Add acrylic medium gloss gel to the top edges of the box and press the tissue paper over them. Spread extra gloss gel on the outside of the glued-on tissue paper to help to smooth down the folds. Trim as necessary using scissors.

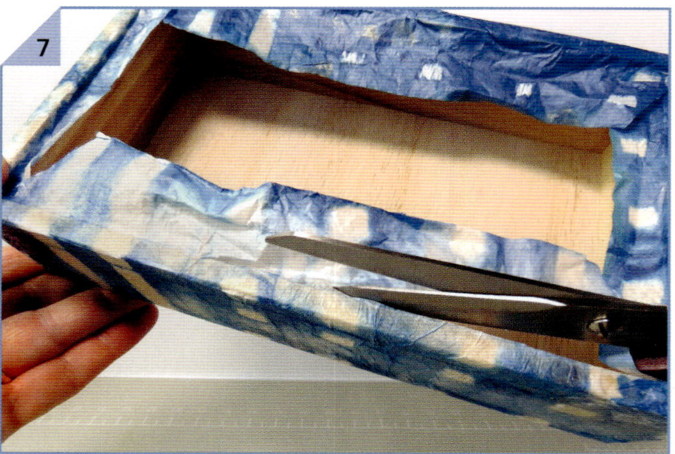

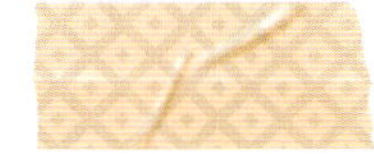

Tip

Cut edges slightly larger than needed and overlayer the folds, to minimize gaps.
Avoid covering hinges with tissue paper.

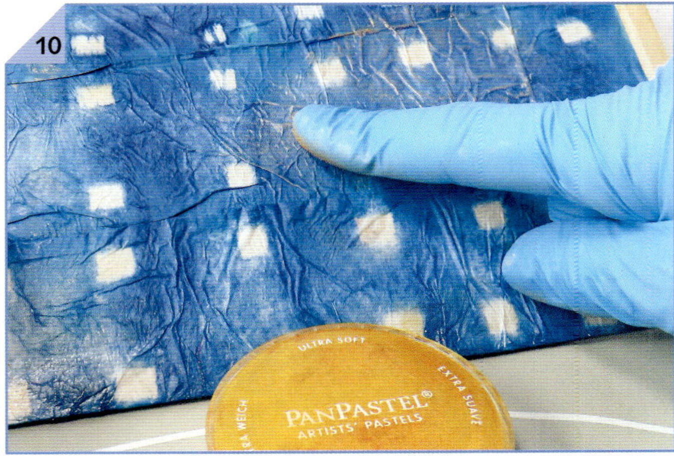

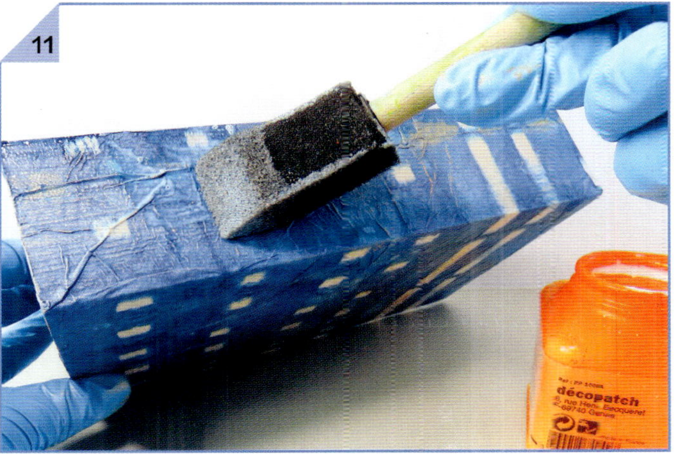

8 This box has a slide-in lid, which is also covered with tissue paper and trimmed.

9 Once the paper is applied to the entire outside surface, let the glue dry completely. This may take a few hours or overnight, depending on the thickness of the gloss gel layer. You may wish to do this wrapping in several sections, for example, the base first, let it dry, then trim any excess using scissors, then complete the sides and top edges. Overlayer any sections which may be too pale.

10 Rub on PanPastel with a gloved finger to highlight the wrinkles and texture.

11 Carefully seal the outside of the container with acrylic gloss medium or sparkly PVA glue for added shine. You may need to paint this topcoat in sections due to the shape of the box. Leave to dry completely.

12 Add any embellishments such as cold relief paint, to further personalize your box. You could glue on small beads, sequins or buttons.

13 Allow any additional sealant or decorations to dry completely.

COVERING CONTAINERS OF OTHER SHAPES

For a cylindrical pot, follow the steps above, taking care to cover curves completely. You can even add dots of encaustic wax to give a 3D effect to floral shapes in the tissue paper.

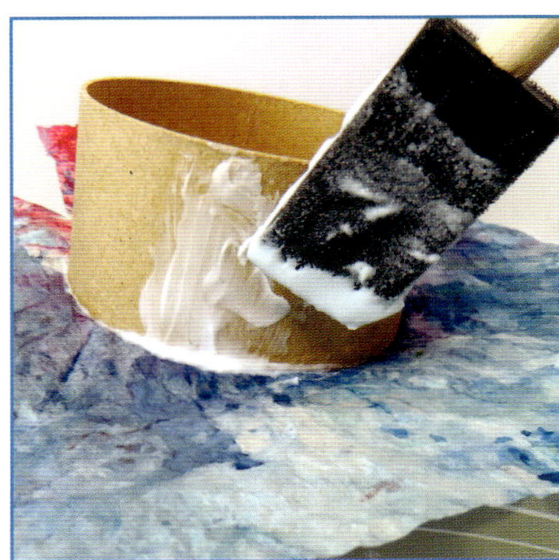

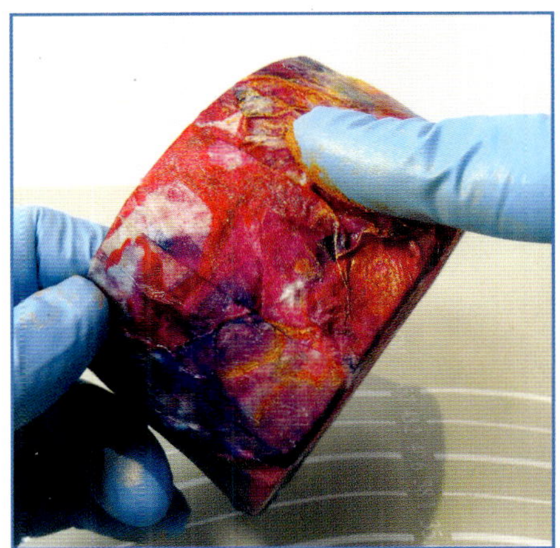

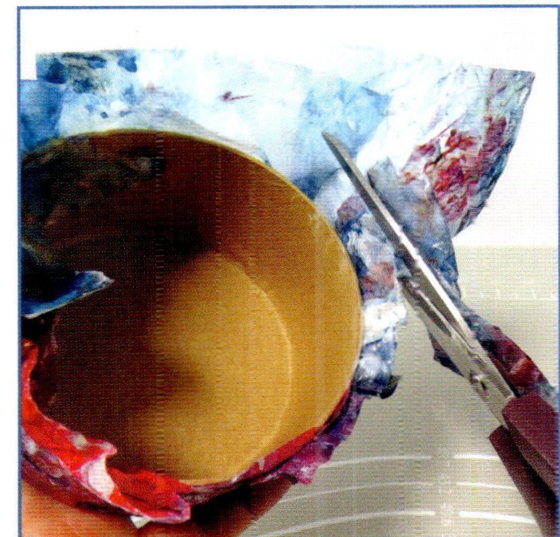

6. Tealight and candle holders

Try creating some beautiful and unique tealight or candle holders using your vibrant hand-dyed tissue paper. This technique involves laying down one single layer of paper to enhance the translucency of the tissue paper (unlike decoupage where multiple pieces of paper are layered).

Try using waxed dyed tissue paper from technique 9 (see pages 56–59) or the hand-painted flowers in technique 10 (see pages 60–65) to give beautiful, soft, translucent results on your chosen glassware.

Experiment and have fun trying this technique on different shaped candle holders. The same principles can be applied to taller jars or pots to hold candles in, for example for use on a wedding table display or for a garden party. Depending on the shape of your tealight holder, you could tie raffia round the top as a decorative bow or to allow it to be hung outside. Enjoy the warm and glowing ambience these little lights create.

Remember the *wabi-sabi* principle: your designs do not need to be perfect. Embrace the golden drips and the unexpected wrinkles!

In this project, the tissue paper is adhered to the outside of the glass holder, so it is safe to use a real flame inside, even if you use wax on the rim or the outside of the object. However, as with all candles, please use with caution and monitor closely.

Once the jars are fully dry, place a tealight inside each jar. Light the candles or switch on the artificial tealight and enjoy the unique and colourful glow created by the tissue paper layers. These make beautiful gifts, especially at Christmas.

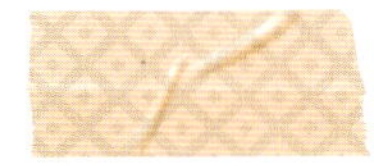

Safety note

Keep tealights away from flammable materials and never leave them unattended.

Caution: make sure there is no overhanging ribbon or tissue inside the jar with a candle flame.

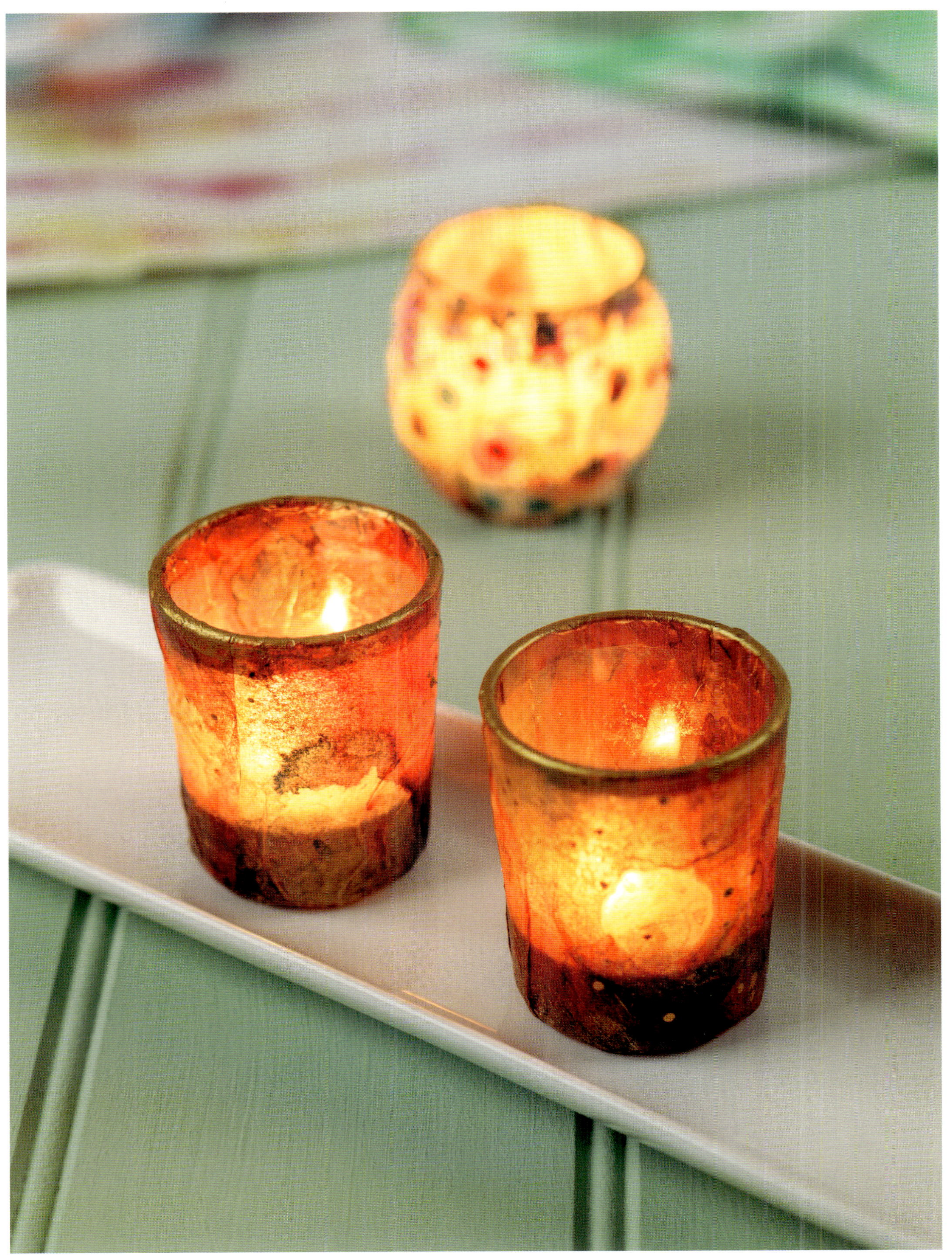

You will need

Materials

- pre-dyed wet-strength white tissue paper
- plain glass tealight holders, candle holders or dishes
- acrylic gloss medium or PVA glue to adhere the tissue paper to the glass
- watercolour fixative to seal dyed tissue paper
- gold relief paint
- gold watercolour ink
- gold PanPastel

Equipment

- large silicone mat or plastic tablecloth (to protect your workspace)
- craft knife
- isopropyl alcohol/alcohol rubbing solution
- foam brush or sponge
- biodegradable baby wipes, for clean up
- paintbrush, medium round and small line
- solid glue stick
- disposable plastic gloves
- jar of clean water
- kitchen paper
- scissors
- cutting mat
- pottery loop tool for removing excess wax

Equipment for sealing with wax (optional)

- glass jar covered with tissue paper layers (see the instructions on the following pages)
- gold, silver or other colours of encaustic wax in block form
- encaustic medium (encaustic medium pellets or block or clear wax paint block, which incorporates dammar resin)
- encaustic hot iron tool: mini-iron master with a range of tips
- heated palette to melt the wax on
- metal tin or silicone muffin case
- small natural bristle brush and fan for painting on wax
- soya wax flakes for cleaning brushes
- heat gun to fuse the wax
- soft lint-free cloth to buff the wax

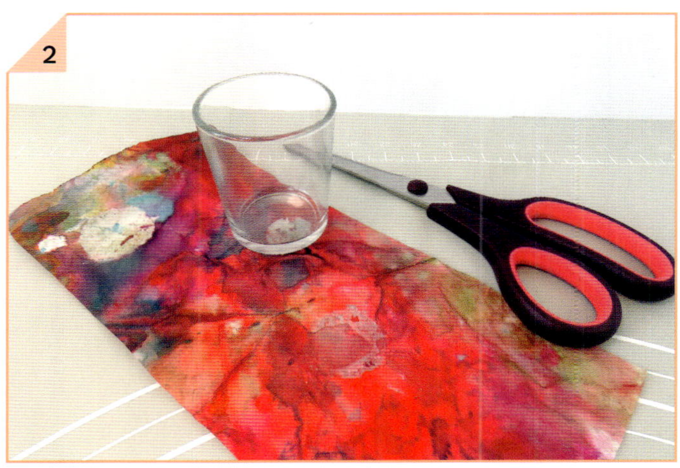

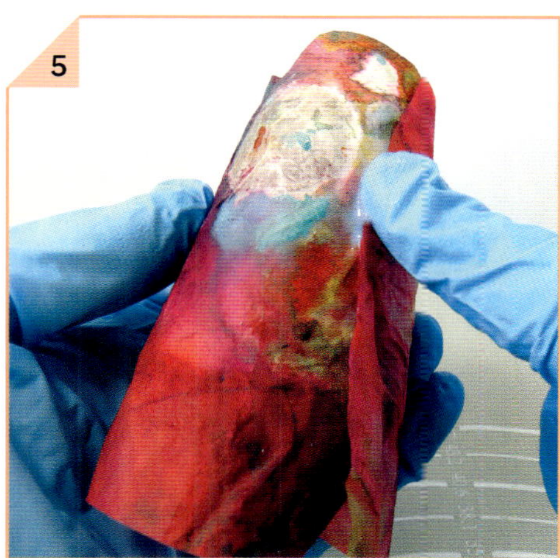

ADDING TISSUE PAPER TO TEALIGHT HOLDERS

1 Remove any labels or residue from the jars. Clean them with isopropyl alcohol on a piece of kitchen paper and make sure they are dry before starting the project.

2 Cut pre-dyed tissue paper larger than the required tealight holder, choosing the part of the design you want to fit well on the shape. Designs with a small pattern will work better on small tealight holders.

3 Spray with watercolour fixative to minimize bleeding and colour fade.

4 Apply acrylic gloss medium as glue: using a small piece of sponge or a foam brush or paintbrush, apply a thin layer on to a small section of the glass jar.

5 Attach tissue paper: lay the straight edge of the paper on the top outside rim of the tealight holder and press it onto the glued section of the jar. Smooth it out gently with your gloved fingers to remove any air bubbles or wrinkles. Some wrinkles can be kept and enhanced later, if you like this effect. Continue until the entire jar is covered in tissue paper.

6 Trim off excess with scissors and wipe away any extra acrylic gloss medium with a baby wipe. If the tealight holder is curved, crease or cut the paper to give a neat finish on the base of the jar.

7 If you have a small gap in the base, cut a circle of tissue paper and add this to cover it.

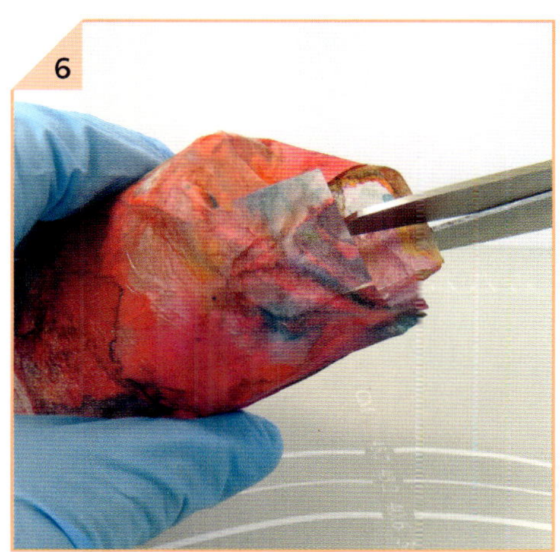

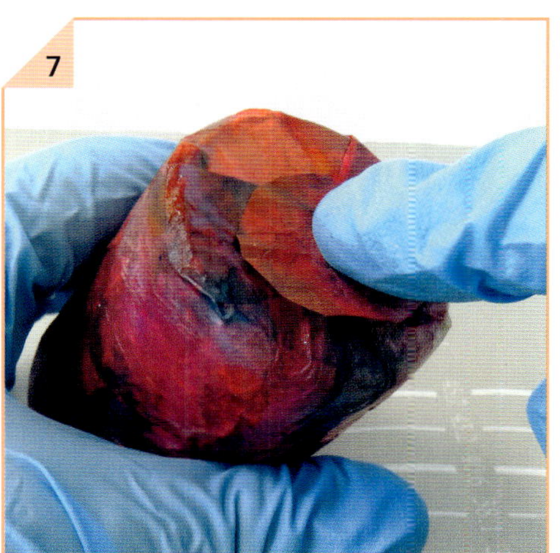

Tip
Save tissue paper offcuts for collages.

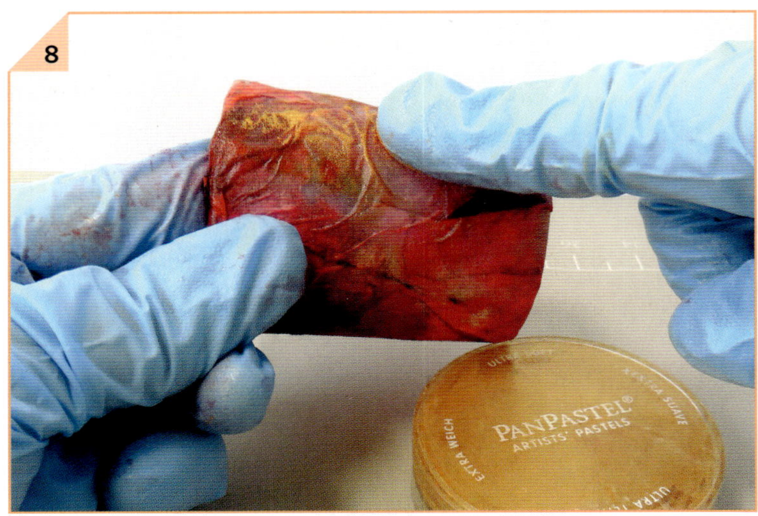

8 Rub on gold PanPastel or paint or gold watercolour ink over the wrinkles to act as highlights. Leave to dry.

9 Seal with acrylic gloss medium: brush another layer over the entire surface of the jar. This will seal the tissue paper and create a glossy finish. Make sure to cover all the edges and corners. You can even use a sparkly PVA glue to add some glamour.

10 Allow the glued tissue paper to dry completely. This usually takes several hours or overnight, depending on the type of glue used. Follow the drying instructions on the acrylic gloss medium jar or glue bottle.

11 Complete your decoration by adding dots or swirls of gold relief paint.

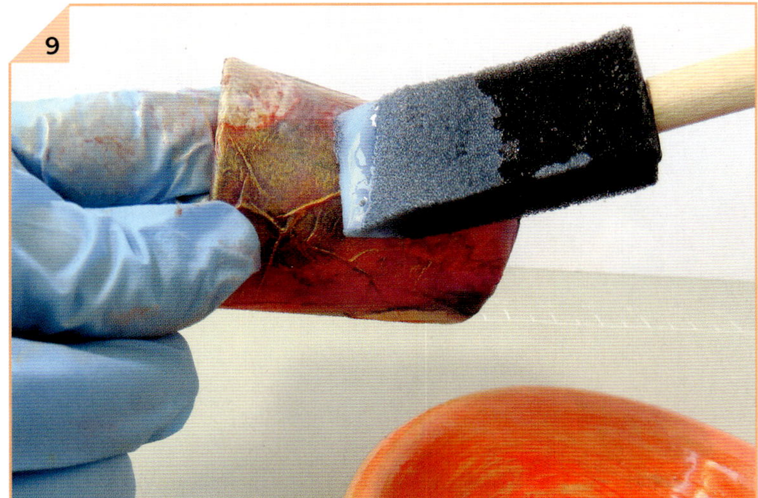

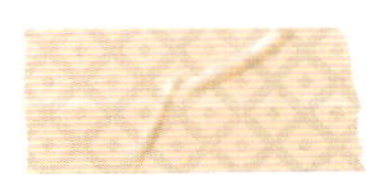

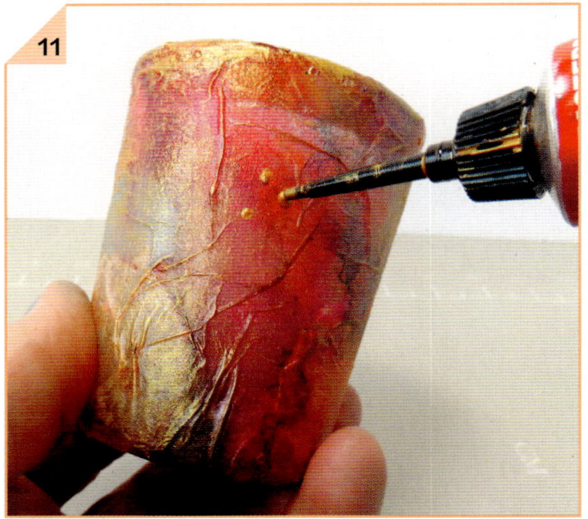

Tip

Add more glow to your tealight holder by using sparkly PVA glue!

Don't worry if there is a small tear in your tissue paper: it is usually possible to carefully slide the open edges together when adhering the tissue paper to the glass surface.

ADDING TISSUE PAPER TO CANDLE JARS

Using waxed tissue paper gives a soft, translucent effect when lit inside, for example with LED string lights.

   Follow steps 1–8 on pages 105–106, cutting a fringe in the top section before folding and glueing it down. Then follow steps 9 and 10 opposite.

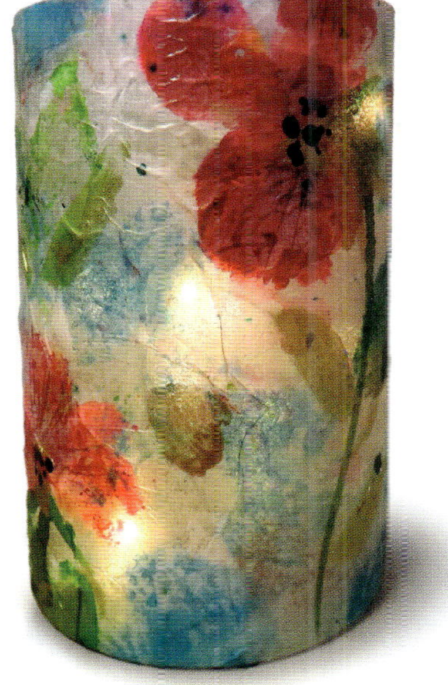

Hand-painted designs look lovely on jars this size. Once the jar is fully dry, place a candle or a string of LED lights inside.

ADDING GLAMOUR TO THE RIM

Add gold or silver around the top rim using wax, gold leaf or metallic ink: ensure that the tissue paper layers on the glass jars are fully dry before proceeding.

Using metallic ink

1 Gently hold the tissue-covered glass jar and carefully paint along the top rim with the metallic ink on a small brush. Apply steady and even pressure to create a consistent line. Drips are fine too for that *wabi-sabi* effect!

2 If needed, you can go over the rim again to make it more opaque and vibrant. Allow the metallic ink to dry completely.

3 Seal with PVA glue, using a foam brush. Leave to dry completely.

4 Use a soft cloth or tissue paper to gently buff the rim of the glass jar. This gives a clean and polished look.

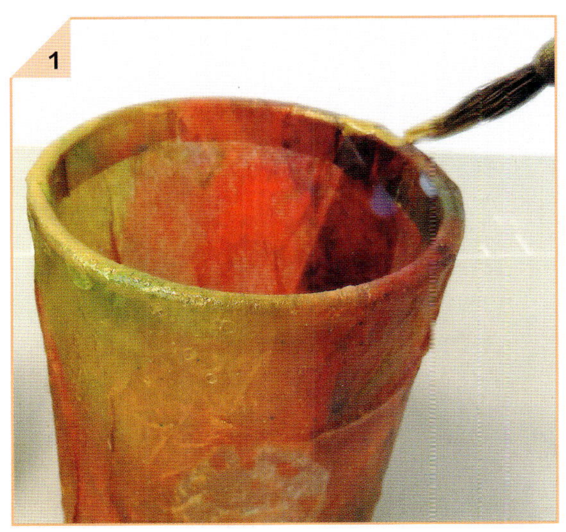

Using metallic encaustic wax

Choose a gold or silver wax that is specifically designed for crafts and can be melted.

1 Melt part of the wax block on a hot palette, add a little clear encaustic medium, and mix.

2 Paint on the molten wax evenly around the rim of the jar, using a small round bristle brush to give a thin layer.

3 Clean the brush with molten soya wax.

4 Fuse the rim of the jar very gently with a heat gun until the wax starts to glisten.

5 Set the jar aside to allow the wax to cool and harden completely.

6 Buff with a lint-free cloth to polish the wax and give a shine.

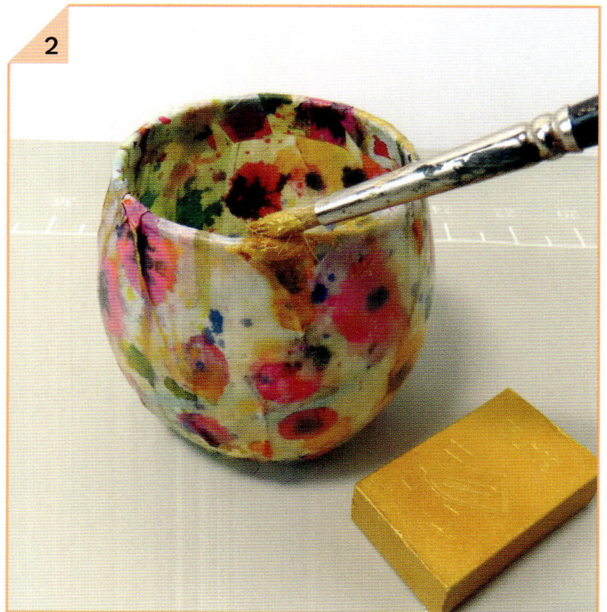

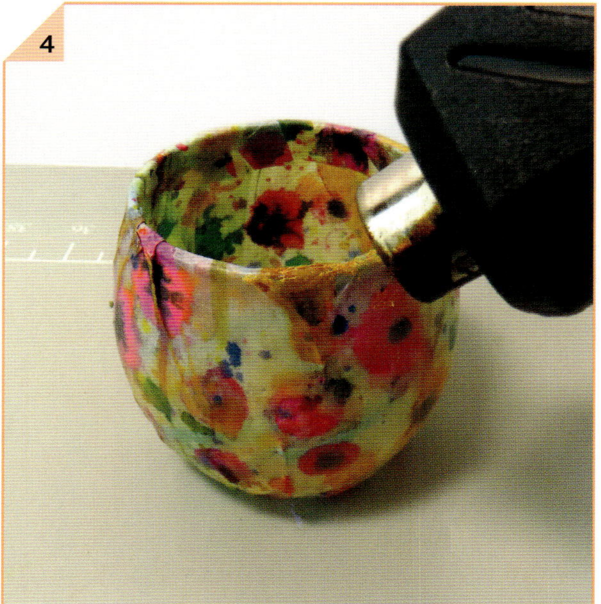

Tip
When the wax glistens, it is fused.

COVERING THE TEALIGHT HOLDER IN ENCAUSTIC MEDIUM

To create a more unusual and tactile finish to your tealight holder, you can add transparent encaustic wax medium to the whole circular surface of the jar or a glass bowl. Encaustic medium, which is beeswax with dammar resin in it, gives enhanced durability and shine.

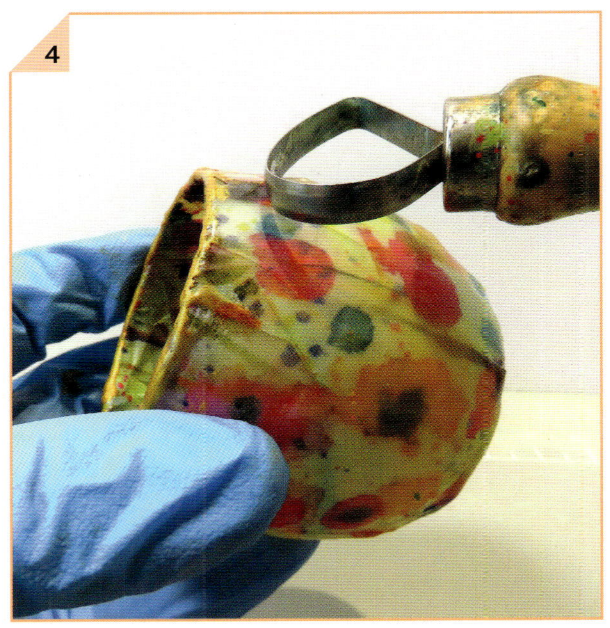

1 Melt the encaustic medium pellets in a metal dish or silicone muffin case on a hot palette (at 93°C/200°F).

2 Paint on the molten wax with a natural bristle fan brush, evenly coating the whole curved side of the tealight holder.

3 Fuse the wax gently with a heat gun until it glistens. Turn the jar around slowly and carefully to achieve this, or stand it upside down.

4 If any extra drips of wax remain, use a loop tool to scrape them off.

5 Set the jar aside to allow the wax to cool and harden completely.

6 Clean the brush with molten soya wax. Buff with a lint-free cloth to polish the wax and give a shine.

Tip

Using a small fan-shaped bristle brush gives a thin covering of wax for added translucency.
The glass jar can get hot when fusing so take care!
See safety note on page 73.

ADDING WAX EMBELLISHMENTS

If your tissue paper has abstract botanical shapes on it, you can paint on flowers using a small petal-shaped tip on an encaustic hot iron tool or using a natural bristle Chinese calligraphy brush, which allows for both fine lines and broader strokes to be created. Applying wax in this way gives a beautiful 3D appearance to the flowers.

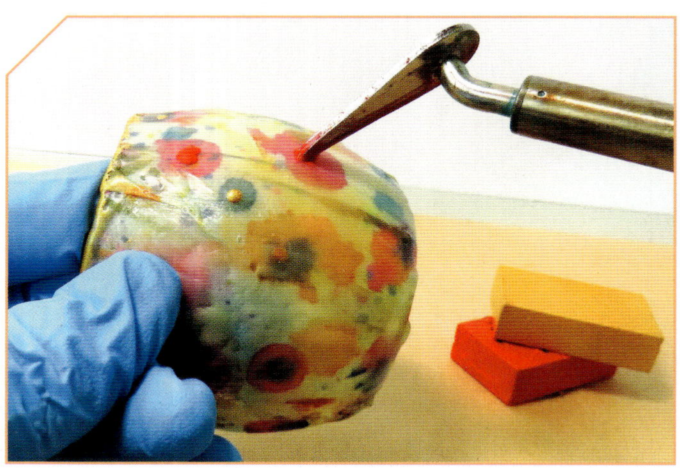

1 Add dots for the flower centres. Build up the dots to achieve depth and texture. You can also simply drop on dots of wax using the encaustic hot iron tool dipped into encaustic paint blocks to create an abstract effect.

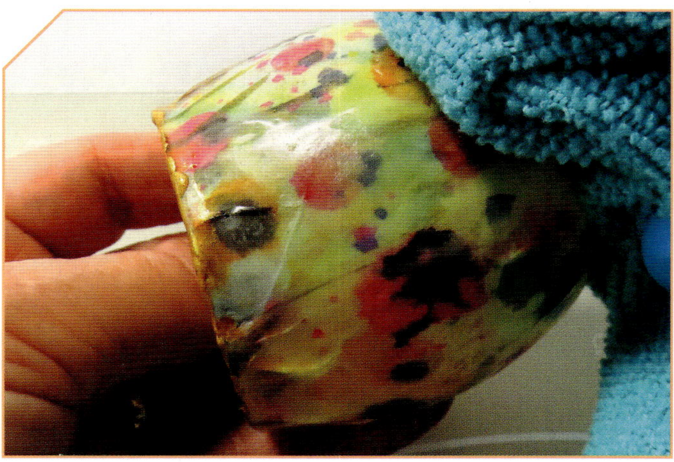

2 Once cooled, buff the wax with a soft cloth to give a shiny finish.

Tip

There is no need to fuse wax which is added directly from an encaustic hot iron tool.

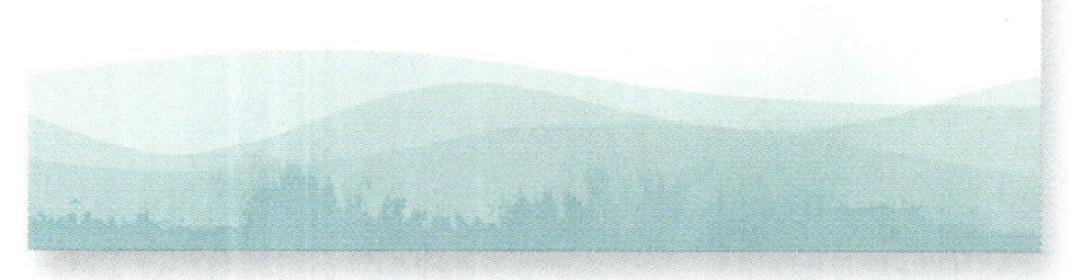

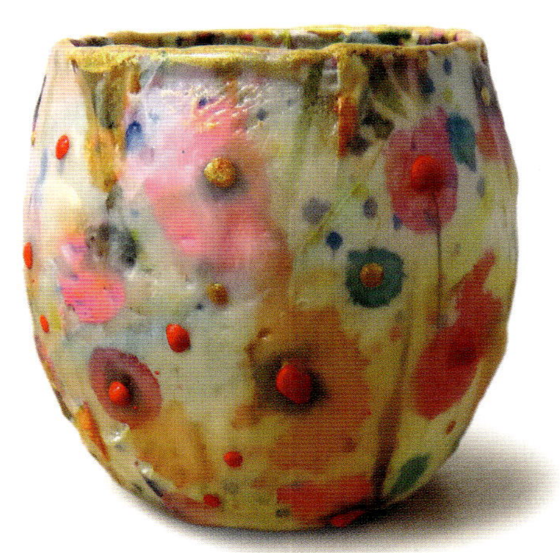

DECORATING A GLASS BOWL

You can follow a similar process to decorate a clear glass bowl with hand-dyed tissue paper and encaustic wax.

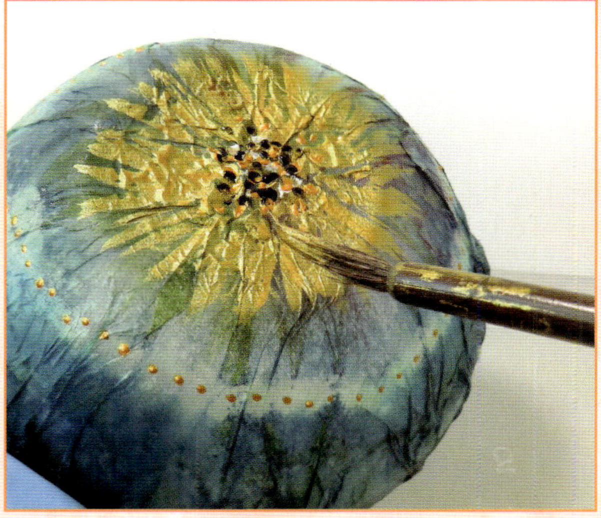

Adding gold ink to the flower on the base.

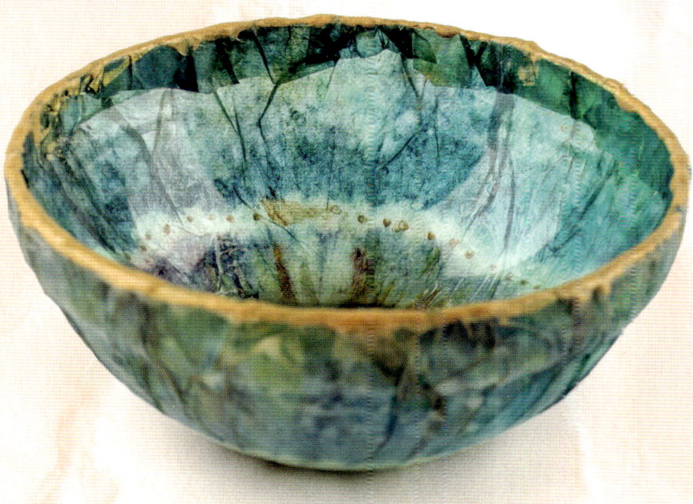

The finished glass bowl.

GOLD LEAF AND EMBOSSING

To create this aged gold effect, once the bowl was covered I added gold leaf. Use 'size' to adhere the thin imitation gold leaf and rub off excess once dry. The edge was further embellished by adding on some gold embossing powder and fusing it with a heat gun to make it sparkle.

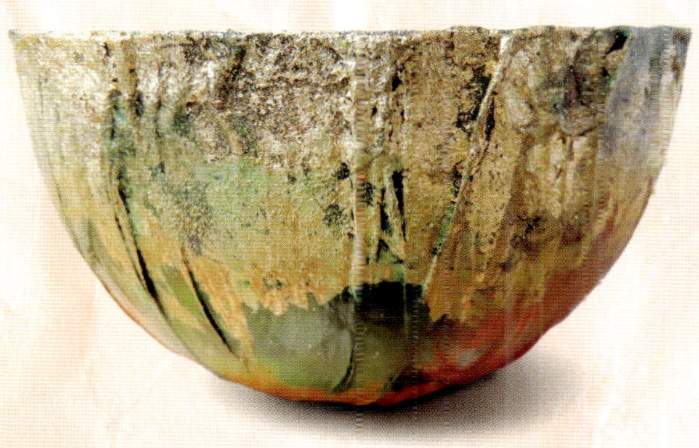

7. Tissue flowers

There are many different methods of creating handmade flowers – some of which are described below. You can create tissue flowers by dyeing petals using plain wet-strength tissue paper (see technique 2: dip dye on pages 20–23), or you can cut multiple petal shapes out of sheets of hand-dyed tissue paper. In this case, I recommend folding the paper to allow you to cut multiple petals at once.

Handmade flowers add charm and ambience to any space when displayed in a vase or a dish. The vibrant paper mimics the beauty of real blooms but, unlike real flowers, tissue flowers are long-lasting and will retain their freshness and shape for many years.

Use them for wedding table décor or buttonholes, or as a creative centrepiece for a special meal. They could also be attached to a gift for a personal touch.

You will need

Materials

- pre-dyed wet-strength tissue paper
- undyed wet-strength white tissue paper
- florist wire for bud, 22 gauge
- fine bullion florist wire, 0.5mm gauge
- wooden skewers
- green oasis florist tape, 1cm (⅜in)
- tin foil
- artificial flower stamens
- gold florist pins
- gold PanPastel
- gold watercolour ink
- selection of watercolour or acrylic inks
- white and green watercolour pencils
- hair elastic or fine florist wire
- iridescent shimmer spray (optional)

Equipment

- small bulldog clips or pegs
- black marker pen
- parchment paper
- large silicone mat or plastic tablecloth (to protect your workspace)
- solid glue stick
- disposable plastic gloves
- pot of clean water
- small spray bottle of water
- small pliers or scissors to cut wire
- scissors
- glue gun and solid glue sticks
- awl or sharp tool
- small paintbrush
- plastic pipette
- paint palette

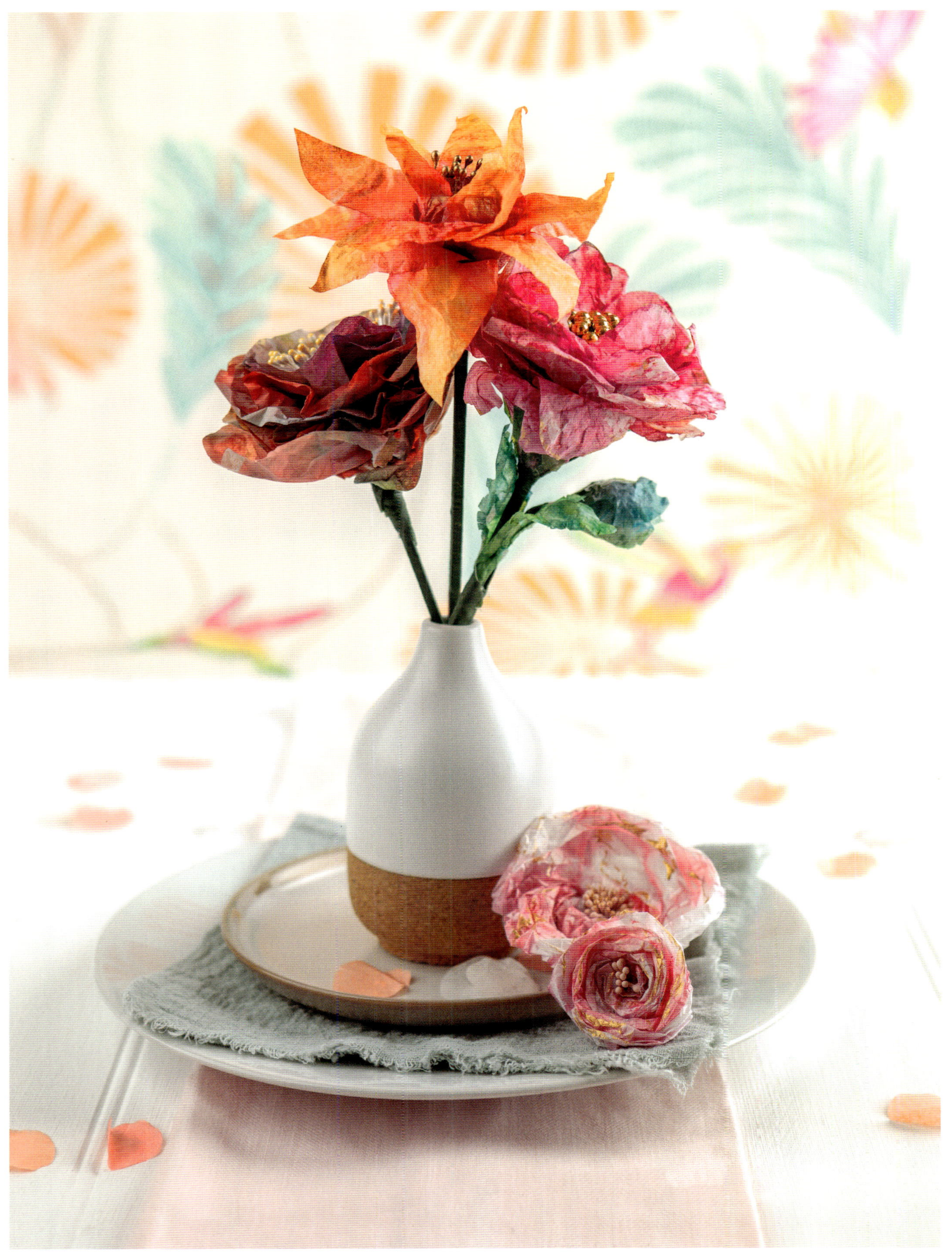

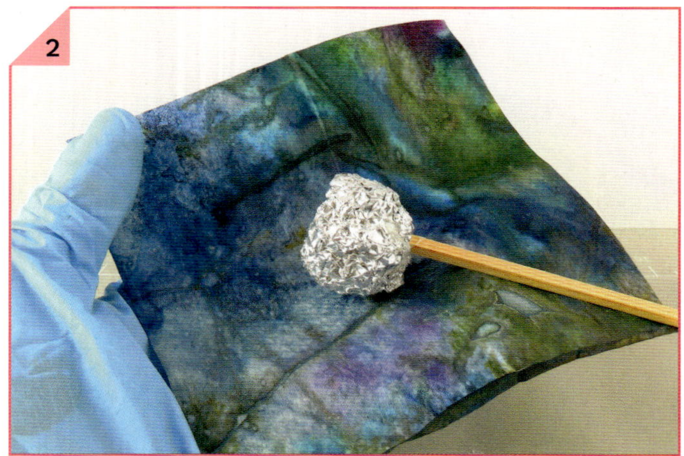 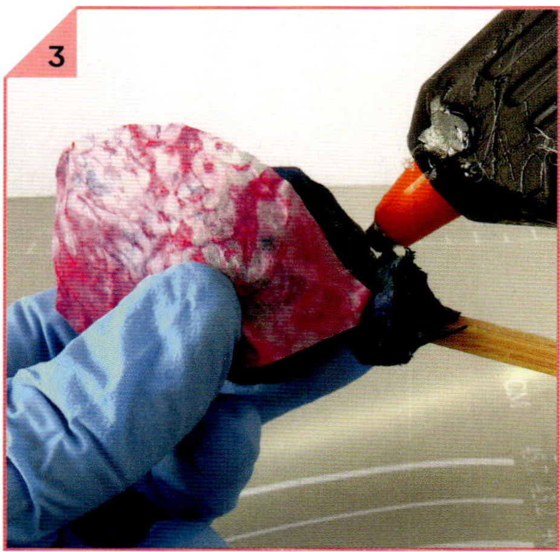

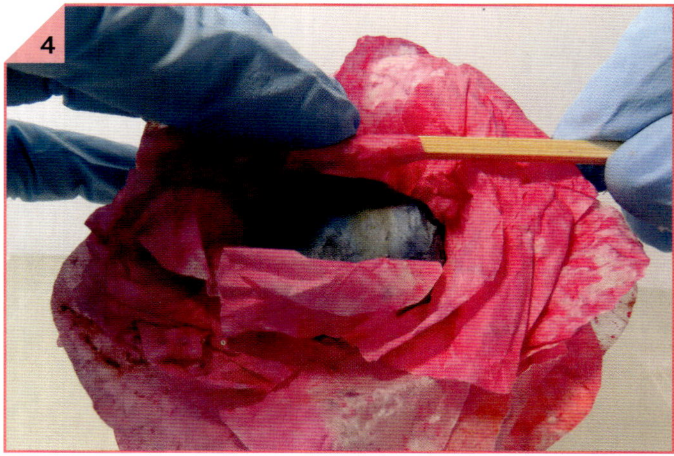 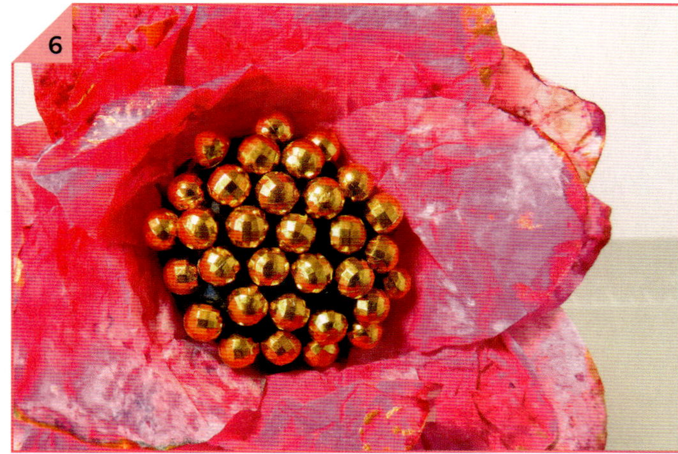

ROSE

Create a beautiful, layered rose with a bud, ready for display.

1 Make a ball of tin foil for your flower centre. Add some glue from a glue gun to the end of a wooden skewer and stick this into the foil ball. Cut out multiple small, medium and large petal shapes.

2 Cover the foil centre with a piece of dyed tissue paper, using a glue gun. Smooth it flat with your gloved finger. Tie an elastic round it to secure it and trim excess tissue.

3 Glue on petals, starting with the smallest petal size, using a glue gun. Add a line of glue to the bottom edge of the petal and add this to the flower centre at the base. You can use the glue gun to add a little glue to the bottom edge of the flower centre if you prefer. Continue to add more to build up the flower, overlapping as you go and moving on to medium then large petals.

4 Keep adding larger petals to create a full flower. Gently shape the petal tips of your flowers by rolling them around a wooden skewer.

5 Paint gold ink with a small brush on the very edges of the petals or add light touches of iridescent shimmer spray.

6 Complete the flower centre by pushing in gold florist pins.

Tip
Take care using a glue gun: the glue gets
very hot!

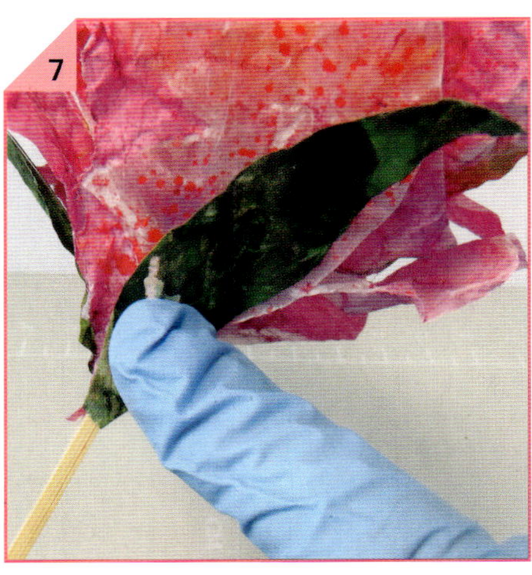
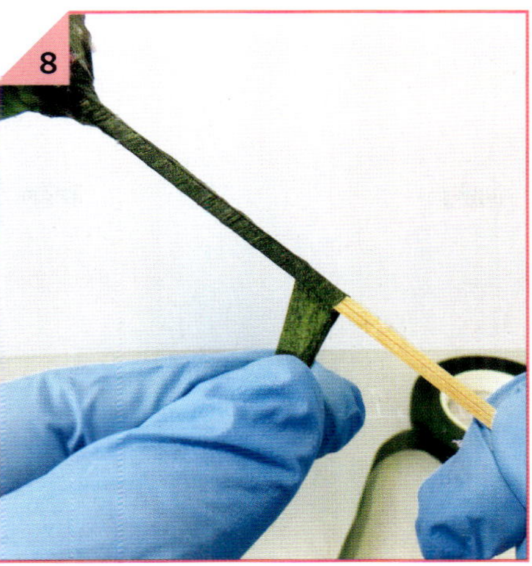
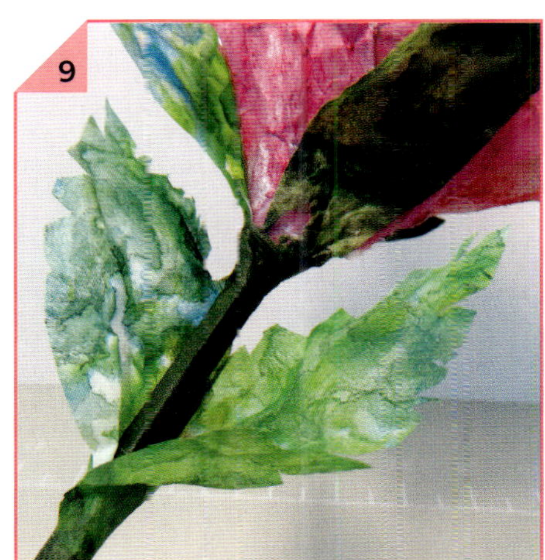

7 Cut out sepal shapes from green-dyed tissue paper and stick the sepals to the base of the rose, using the glue gun.

8 Glue the end of a long strip of green florist tape to the base of the rose and gently twist this round the skewer – continuing to the bottom, stretching it slightly to ensure adhesion. Secure at the bottom with a dot of glue from the glue gun.

9 Cut out leaves from green-dyed tissue paper and stick these on to the stem using the glue gun.

10 Create a small bud by making a smaller ball of tin foil and gluing this onto some 22 gauge florist wire, using the glue gun. Double over the wire to give extra strength.

11 Add the bud's unopened petals and green sepals then wrap the wire with green tape. Attach the bud to the skewer with green tape and glue.

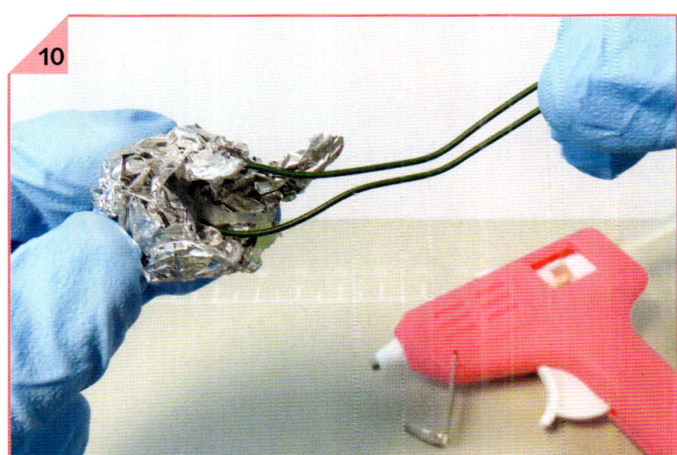

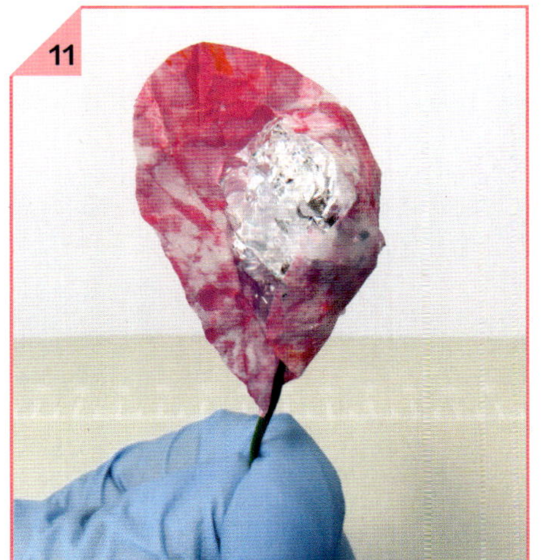

Tip

For petal and leaf templates, see page 144. For extra copies to download, head to the Bookmarked Hub (www.bookmarkedhub.com). Search for this book by title or ISBN: the files can be found under 'Book Extras'. Don't limit yourself to my templates – draw your own petal and leaf shapes.

POPPY

Make a beautiful poppy with a detailed centre and layers of colourful petals.

1 Make a ball of tin foil for your poppy centre. Add some glue from a glue gun to the end of a wooden skewer and stick this into the foil ball. Cover the ball in green pre-dyed tissue paper and secure with an elastic band or wire.

2 Glue artificial stamens around the centre, using a glue gun. Add green and black pen lines in the centre to make it look realistic.

3 For the petals, cut 10 circles of pre-dyed tissue paper, each 11cm (4¼in) diameter. Push them onto the skewer one at a time, gluing each in place with a glue gun. Gently squeeze the petals into shape.

4 Glue the end of a long strip of green florist tape to the base of the poppy and gently twist this onto the skewer – continuing to the bottom, stretching it slightly to ensure adhesion. Secure with a dot of glue from the glue gun.

5 Add touches of glue to the edges of the petals and dust them with gold PanPastel to act as highlights. Dust the centre with PanPastel in the same way.

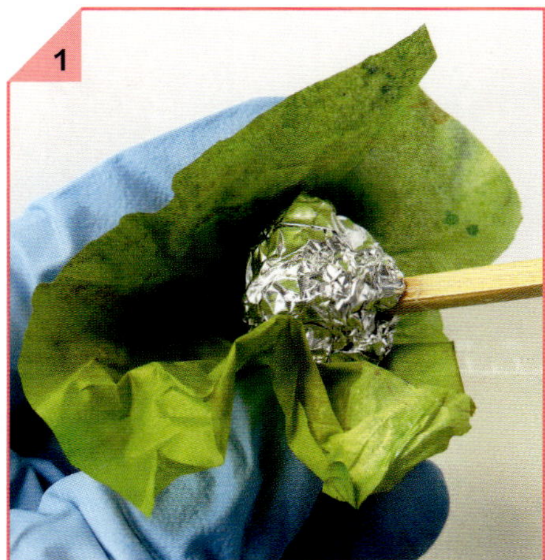

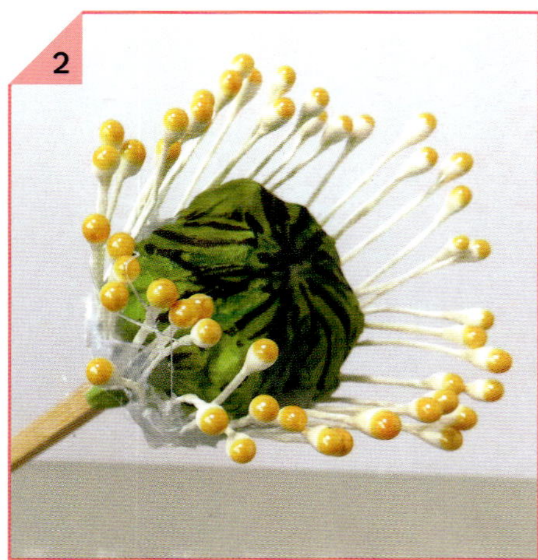

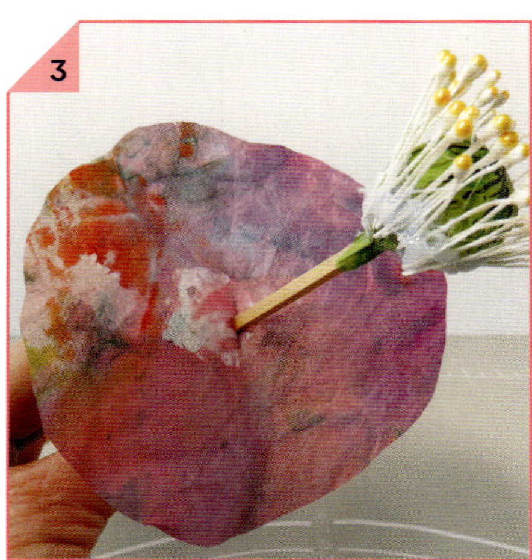

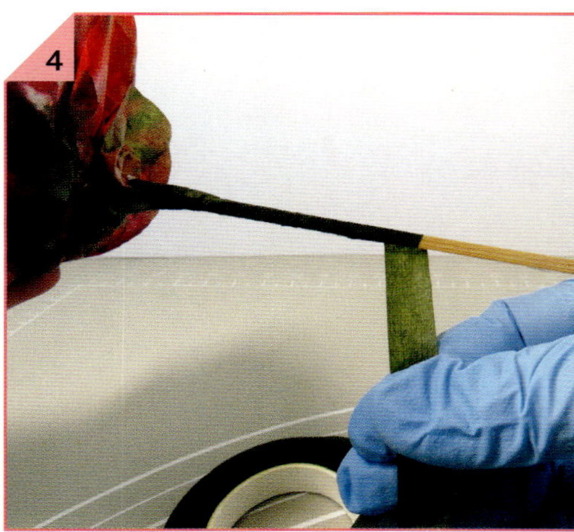

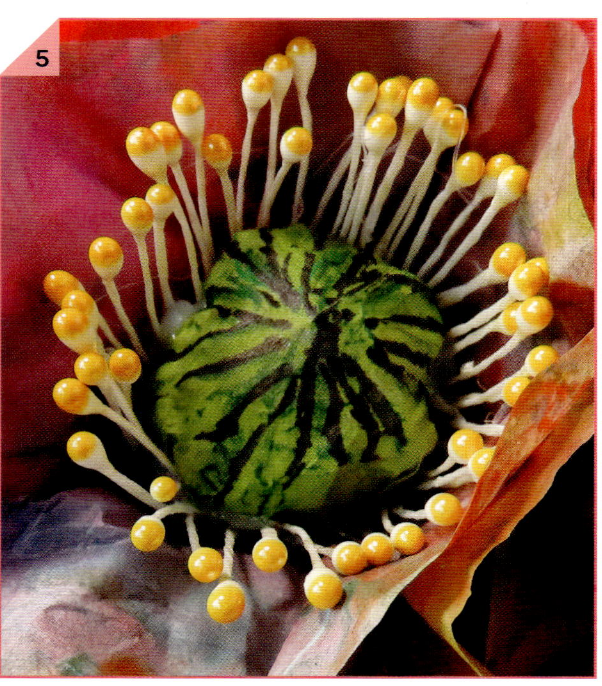

TWISTED FLOWER

Twisted flowers make lovely decorations for wrapped gifts but could also be added to a wooden skewer stem for display in a vase.

1 Create a rectangular bag from dyed tissue paper by cutting a rectangle, for example 18 x 25cm (7 x 10in). Fold it in half widthwise and stick down the sides using a solid glue stick.

2 Carefully turn the bag inside out. Make a small hole in the middle of the bottom of the bag with an awl.

3 Push through some artificial stamens. Glue these in place with the glue gun.

4 Carefully twist the bag round the stamens, folding any edges in and gluing with a glue gun, as needed. Curl a few of the outside petals.

5 Optional: paint highlights of gold watercolour paint on the edges of the petals.

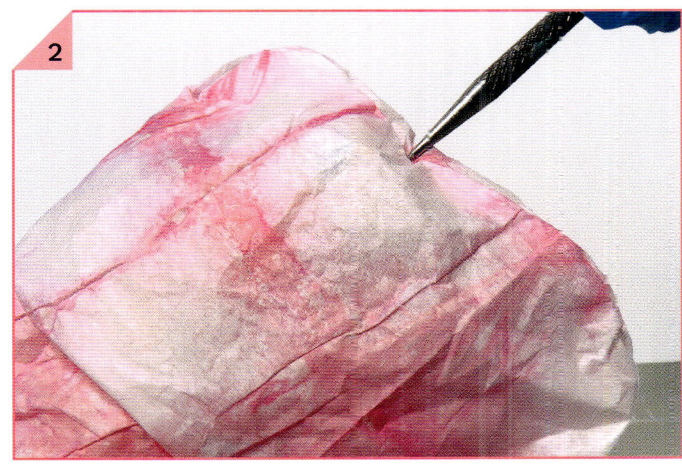

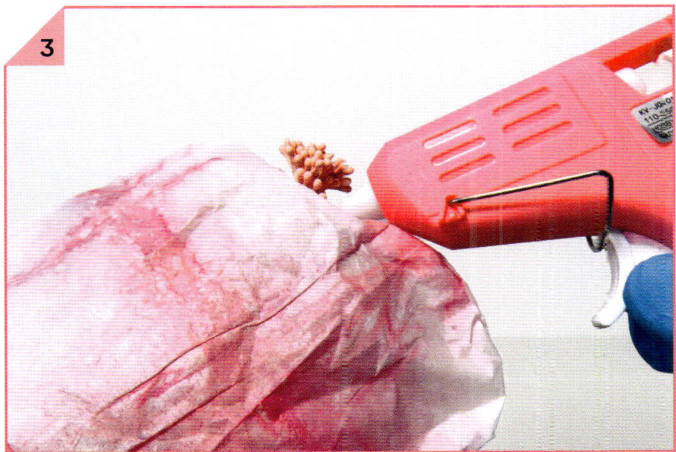

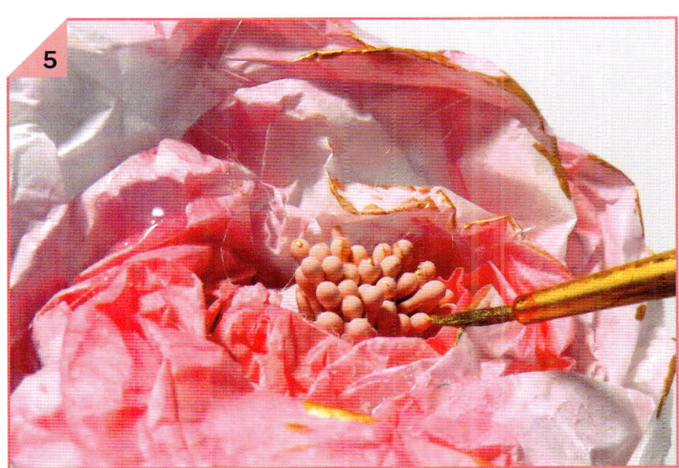

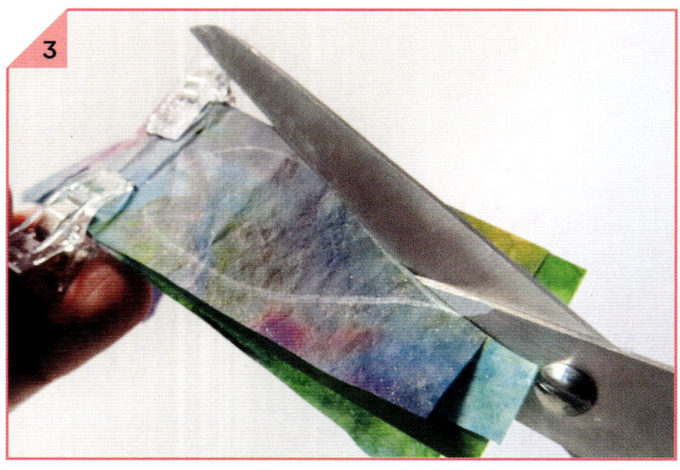

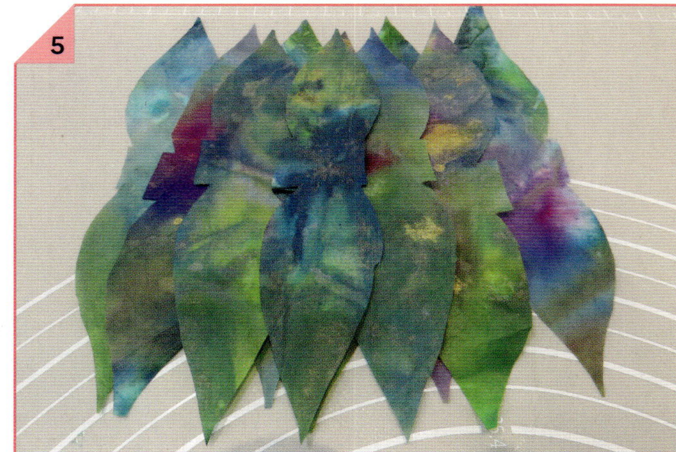

LAYERED FLOWER

1 Cut out three squares of pre-dyed tissue paper 20 x 20cm (8 x 8in) and two squares 15 x 15cm (6 x 6in).

2 Lay the larger squares on top of each other and accordian fold three times. Add a clip or peg in the middle of each side to hold the folds together.

3 Use a white pencil to draw petal shapes with pointed or rounded tips, on both sides of the clips, then cut them out, leaving them joined on to the petal opposite.

4 Remove the clips or pegs and unfold the tissue paper to reveal the joined pairs of petals. Repeat with the smaller squares.

5 Layer the larger petals as shown: place four side by side, then three side by side on top of those, then two, then one in the centre.

6 Add the smaller cut petals on top in the same way. If you want to add stamens, lay them over the middle.

7 Gather the centre of the tissue paper and the stamens together and secure with a thin piece of florist wire. Glue the stamens in place with a glue gun.

8 Fluff out the petals and stamens into a flower shape.

9 Use gold watercolour ink to add subtle highlights to the edges of the petals.

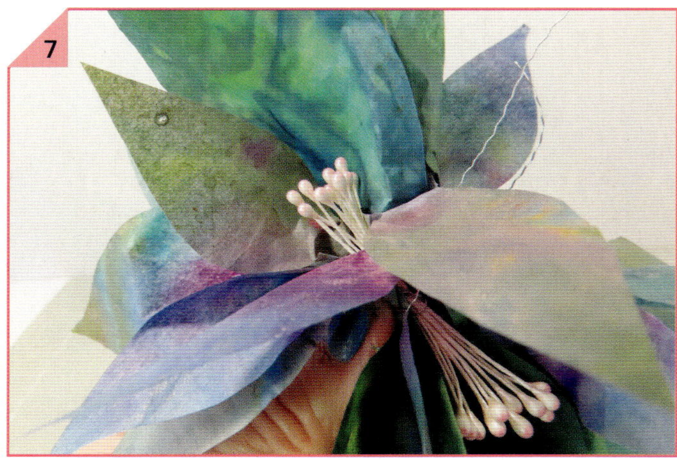

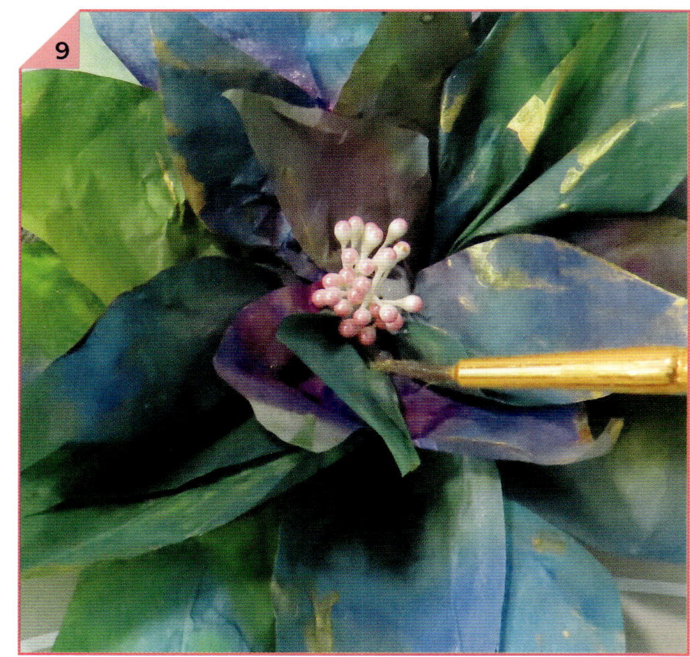

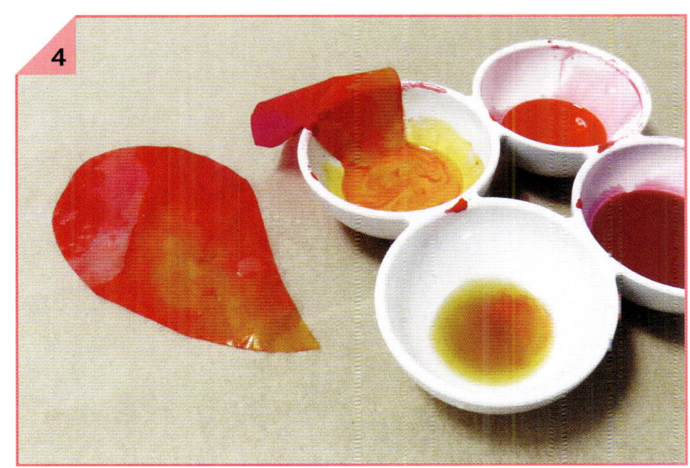

DIP-DYED PETALS

1 Using undyed wet-strength tissue paper, cut out some petal shapes of different sizes.

2 Add a few different colours of watercolour ink or fabric dye to a palette dish and dilute with a little water.

3 Gently dip the ends of the petals into the ink, letting it soak upwards. Spray the petals with water to help the inks spread.

4 Turn the petal around and dip the other end into a different colour, then let them bleed together.

5 Lay the petals out to dry on parchment paper.

6 Attach to a flower centre as in the Poppy example on page 116.

7 Add golden highlights using watercolour ink or PanPastel, if desired.

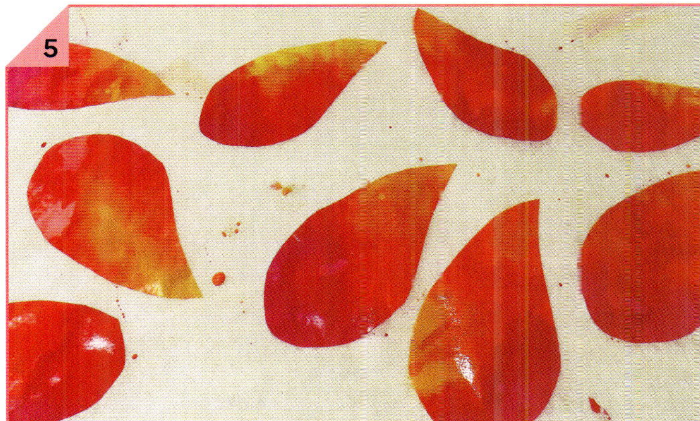

Tip
For curled petal edges, roll an edge round a wooden skewer and press gently. See page 144 for petal and leaf templates.

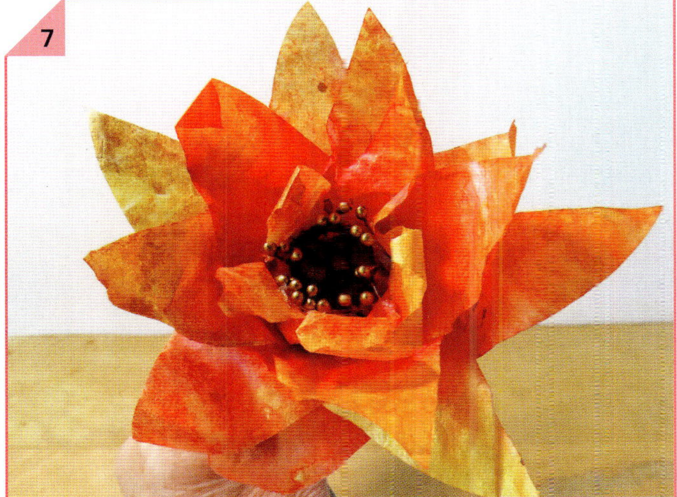

8. Seascape collage

Wet-strength tissue paper is ideal for collage work – enjoy incorporating some of your unique hand-dyed tissue paper into an original abstract seascape, adhered to thick paper. Be bold and imaginative and use unexpected colours, shapes and textures in your design. The finished collage can be displayed as a piece of art, stuck onto mountboard and framed or mounted onto a birthday or other celebratory card.

The pole wrap method used in technique 3 (see pages 24–29) gives inspiring rippled patterns that can be used effectively to represent water.

Top: Chasing Waves.
Bottom: Mountain Echoes.

You will need

Materials

- heavyweight cotton rag watercolour paper or watercolour board
- pre-dyed wet-strength tissue paper
- watercolour fixative to seal dyed tissue paper
- pieces of paper or other materials, e.g. hessian, suitable for collage
- acrylic glazing medium
- bleed-proof white paint or acrylic paint
- pastel crayons, PanPastels and a selection of acrylic paints including gold relief paint

Equipment

- large silicone mat or plastic tablecloth (to protect your workspace)
- foam brush or sponge
- biodegradable baby wipes, for clean up
- metal palette knife
- paintbrush, medium round or oval
- solid glue stick
- disposable plastic gloves
- pot of clean water
- kitchen paper
- scissors
- cutting mat
- sharp craft knife
- masking tape (optional)
- heat gun if required to warm the masking tape (optional)

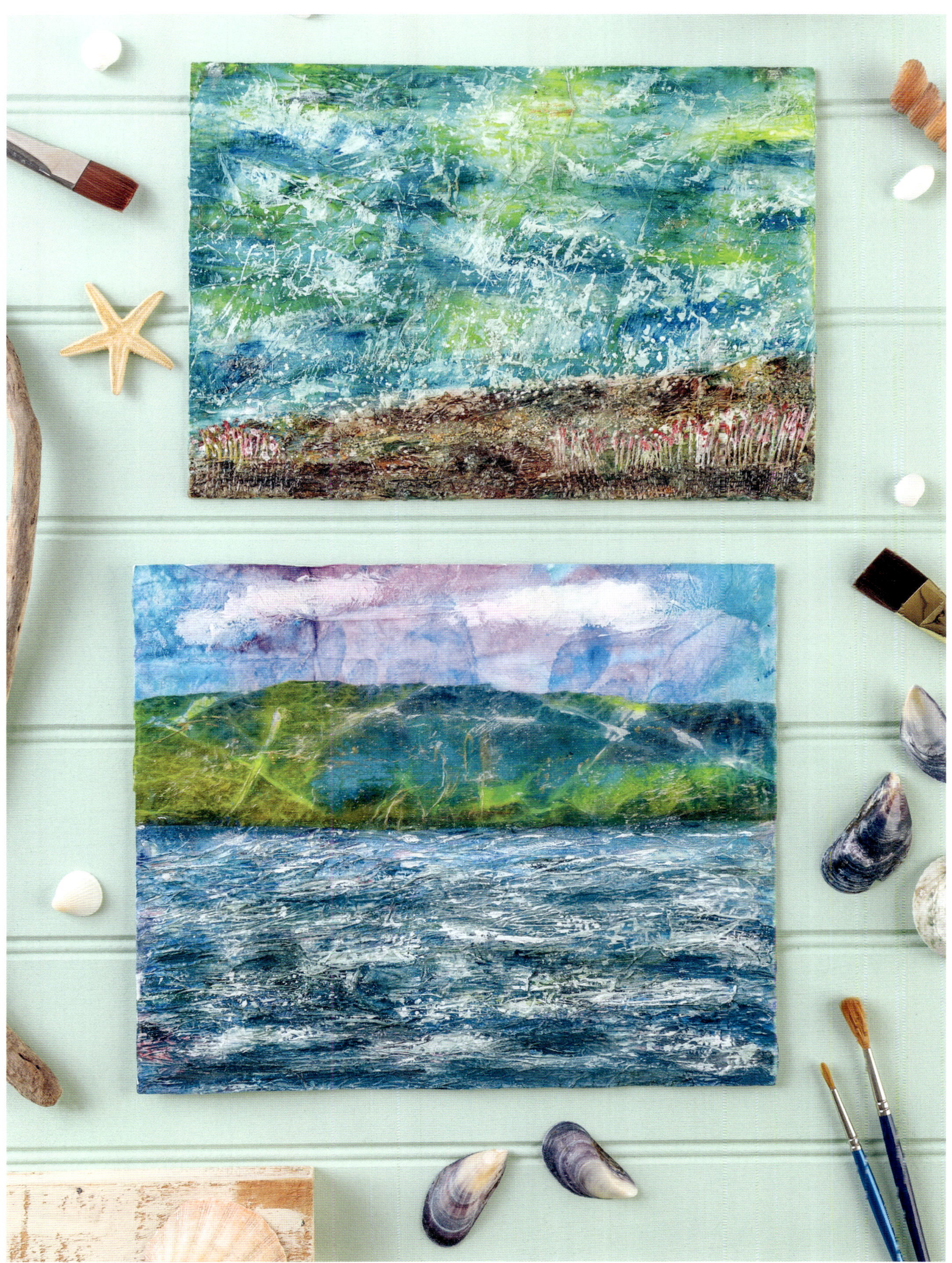

MOUNTAIN ECHOES

In the following steps, I show you how I created my Mountain Echoes collage (bottom image, page 121).

1 Gather your materials and cover your workspace to prevent any glue from damaging the surface.

2 Cut your watercolour paper or board to size and select dyed tissue paper and other collage papers or materials with a suitable pattern to create a landscape. Lay these out roughly over your board. Cut the sections to size with scissors. However, if using wet-strength tissue paper, you can use more easily blendable ragged edges rather than cutting them straight. Tear with the grain or soften the area to be torn with water on a clean paintbrush then carefully separate the section you want.

3 Decide if you want a white border round your painting and, if so, mask off the edges of your watercolour paper or board with masking tape.

4 Spray with watercolour fixative to minimize bleeding and colour fade. Leave to dry.

5 Apply a thick, even layer of solid glue stick to the areas to be covered by the background collage paper. Cover every section fully to minimize unwanted bubbling later. Choose a dyed tissue paper background for each section, e.g. a pale, abstract blue for the sky or pole-wrapped, rippled water for the sea. Try to use the rule of thirds, placing the horizon at either the top or bottom third of the page, depending on whether you would like your focus to be on the sky or the seashore.

6 Carefully place a piece of the dyed tissue paper onto the glued section of the paper, smoothing it out with your fingers to ensure it sticks fully. I prefer to keep as many wrinkles as possible since it adds drama to the sky, sea or land.

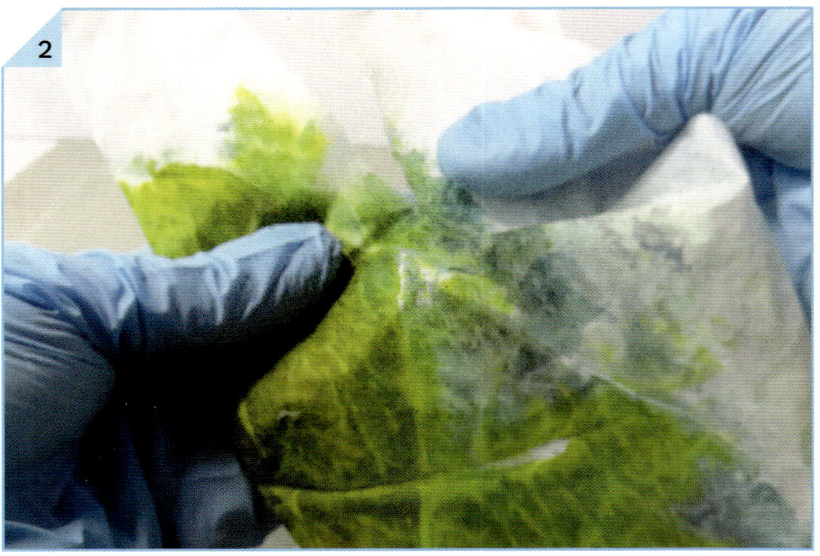

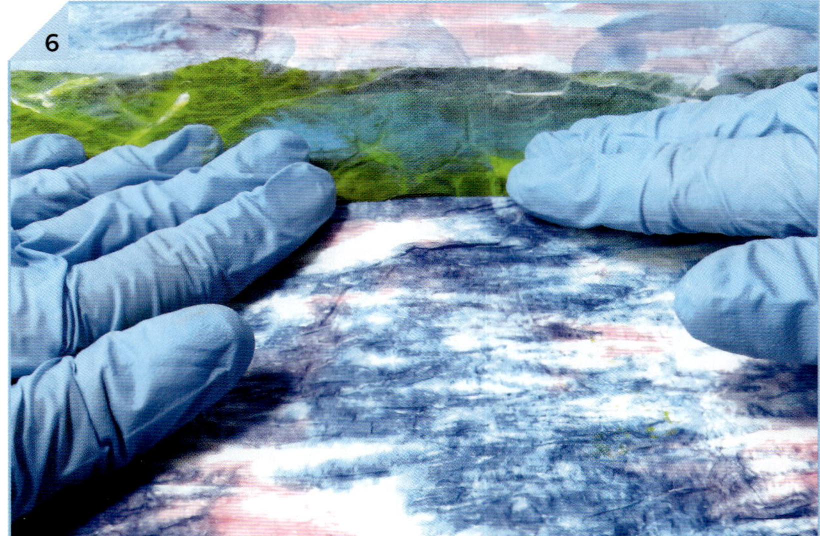

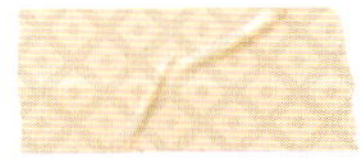

Tip

See the Troubleshooting section for details on how to remove an air bubble (see page 143).
If you are working within a masked border, keep the tissue paper within this boundary.

7 Continue layering the pieces of collage paper using solid glue stick to build up your composition. Look at it from a distance to gain perspective. Try layering thin tissue paper over thicker, patterned papers for diffused translucence.

8 Brush on layers of acrylic paint to enhance the sky, clouds, waves and rocky foreground. You can also use a gloved finger, for example use bleed-proof or acrylic white paint to add in soft clouds.

9 Once the tissue and collage papers have been applied, let the glue dry fully. This may take a few hours or overnight, depending on the thickness of the glue layer.

10 Using a sharp craft knife on a cutting mat, carefully trim any excess tissue paper from the edge, if needed.

11 Add any details to your painting by using pastel crayons, PanPastels, permanent pens or even paints or inks to give depth and contrast, in particular to the rocks in the foreground.

12 A palette knife is very effective for dragging white paint over the wrinkles to give highlights like sea foam on waves.

13 Add further embellishments such as gold relief paint to further personalize your painting. You could add gold leaf on a setting sun, for example. Stencils can also be very valuable in adding detail to collages with acrylic paint. Or you could add splashes of white paint to give a sea spray effect.

14 Carefully and slowly remove the border masking tape if used, warming it slightly with a heat gun, to aid removal.

15 To complete your collage, seal the painting by applying a thin layer of acrylic glazing medium with a foam brush. Leave to dry.

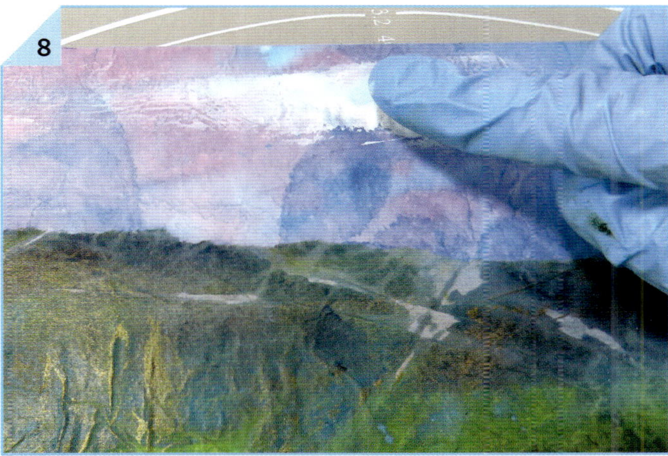

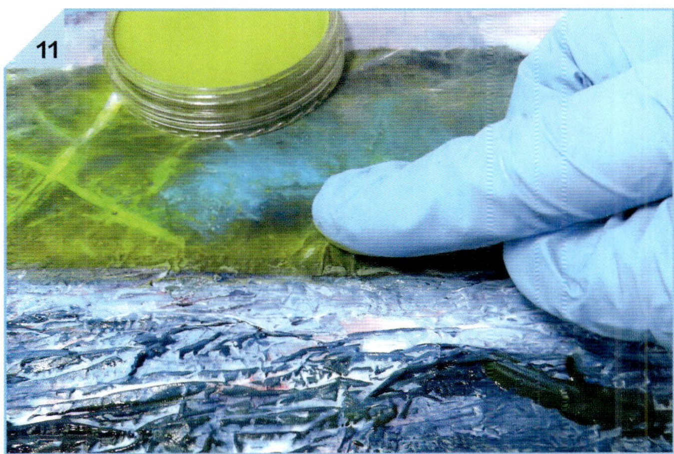

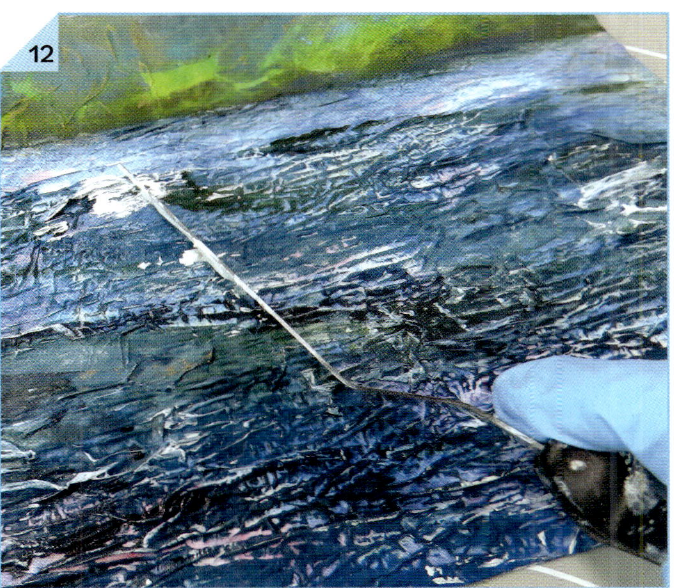

CHASING WAVES
Adding detail in the foreground

These steps are demonstrated on the Chasing Waves collage shown at the top of page 121.

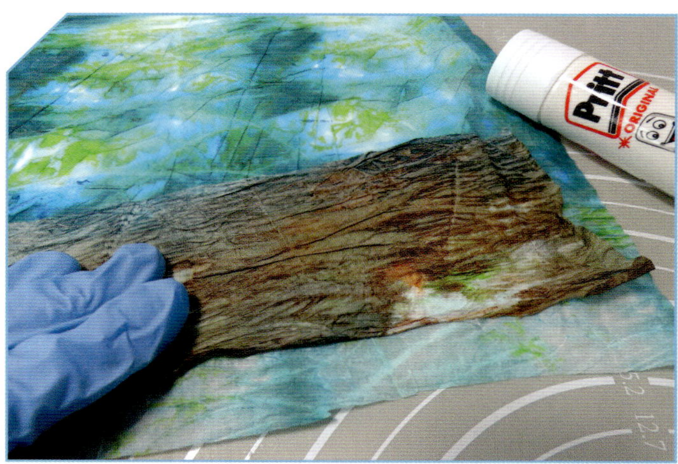

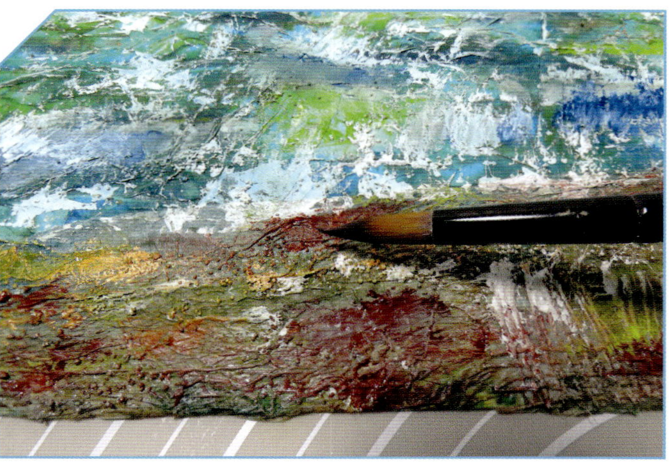

1 Add pieces of frayed hessian or other fabric for texture, perhaps in the foreground to represent rock strata or plants. Layer the different materials to create a visually dynamic collage. For a seascape it is effective to have darker colours in the foreground and lighter colours towards the horizon.

2 Paint layers of acrylic paint to enhance the sky, clouds, waves and rocky foreground.

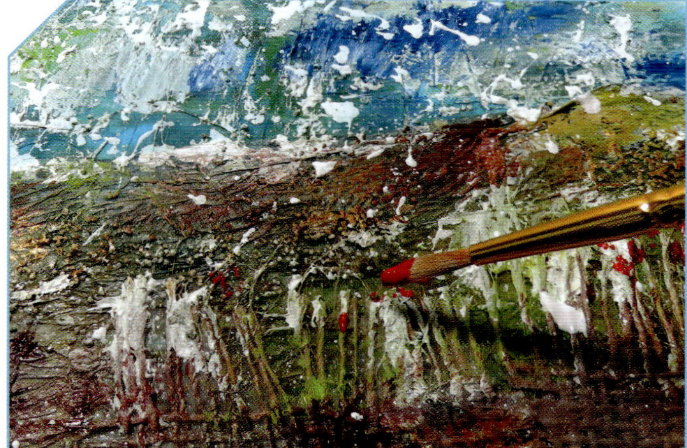

3 Once dry, embellish the foliage with red and pink acrylic paint to give a loose floral effect.

Tip
Start sticking as soon as you have inspiration, rather than worrying about it being exact. Remember you can always cover up a section.

CREATING TEXTURE USING ADVANCED TECHNIQUES

ADDITIONAL MATERIALS AND EQUIPMENT

- birch cradle board
- gilding wax or chalk paint for the edges of your board
- a similar collage could be created using a long, narrow, wooden cradle board panel, ideally sealed with a stain block primer then painted with chalk paint
- PVA glue
- silicone sand

- sandpaper 150 grit
- wooden spoon
- tar gel
- acrylic glazing medium
- wooden skewer
- masking tape
- palette knife

1 Adhere the tissue paper to the wooden board using wallpaper paste and a foam brush.

2 Spray with watercolour fixative to minimize colour bleed. You can also use acrylic paint to enhance your design. Select green and blues to add depth to your sea and mountains.

3 Once dry, trim any excess tissue paper with a craft knife.

4 Tape the edges of the board with masking tape to protect them.

5 Use bleed-proof white paint or gesso by dragging it over the wrinkles with a palette knife to create highlights. Also rub in dark PanPastels to add depth, or gold PanPastels for highlights. Splash on white paint to add sprays of sea foam.

6 Mix a teaspoon of dry silicone sand into half a teaspoon of PVA glue. Scrape this over the surface of the painting with a palette knife. Leave to dry. This adds excellent texture to the rocks and waves, especially when highlighted with white paint.

7 Drizzle trails of clear tar gel across the waves with a wooden skewer, to give thick reflective ripples on the water.

8 Seal the painting with acrylic glazing medium using a foam brush and leave to dry.

9 Remove the tape from the board and gently rub the edges with sandpaper to remove any small extra pieces of tissue paper. I seal the edges of my wooden panels with gold gilding wax, rubbing this on with a finger and leaving it to dry.

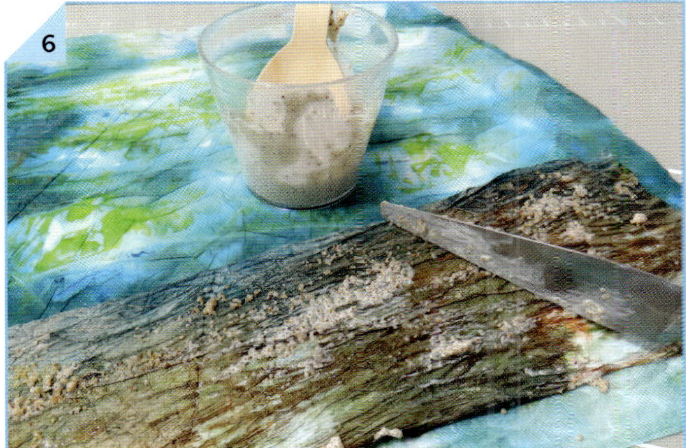

Tip

On a wooden panel, use tissue collage as the underlayer, then add encaustic wax and paint. Effective texture can be developed. Minimize use of acrylic paint, gel or glues when using encaustic, due to incompatibility.

9. Meadowscape on board

In technique 10, we learnt how to paint a loose impression of a meadow scene on a large sheet of wet-strength tissue paper. Here we use this technique to create a stunning, waxy meadowscape on wooden substrate, using encaustic wax.

Choose a rectangular wooden panel which suits the size of your tissue paper and create a meadow scene to fit. The method below shows how to create your floral scene by embellishing the tissue paper with encaustic wax flowers. However, you can paint flowers, trees and leaves with acrylic or watercolour paints, then seal it with acrylic gloss medium.

Since we are using encaustic wax, you must use a solid wooden substrate, not canvas. You also need natural bristle brushes when working with hot wax; synthetic brushes will melt.

You will need

Materials

- birch cradle board 25 x 51cm (10 x 20in) and 19mm (¾in) deep
- pre-dyed hand-painted meadowscape on wet-strength tissue paper (see technique 10 on pages 132–137)
- watercolour fixative to seal dyed tissue paper
- pale chalk paint or primer/undercoat
- wallpaper paste
- recycled round lid
- encaustic medium in pellets
- encaustic wax paint blocks in floral and foliage colours, gold and white
- gold gilding wax or chalk paint for the edges of your board
- brown or other recycled paper
- watercolour pencil, black or green (optional)
- PanPastel in gold for highlights (optional)

Equipment

- large silicone mat or plastic tablecloth (to protect your workspace)
- foam brush or sponge
- biodegradable baby wipes, for clean up
- disposable plastic gloves
- scissors
- cutting mat
- sharp craft knife
- heat gun
- masking tape for the edges of the board
- encaustic hot iron tool: mini-iron master with a range of tips
- hog bristle round brushes, small and medium, Chinese natural bristle brush and a 3cm (1¼in) wide flat brush
- heated electric palette with metal tins, silicone muffin cases or a wax melt pot
- pottery loop tool
- metal awl or other sharp tool
- soft lint-free cloth for buffing

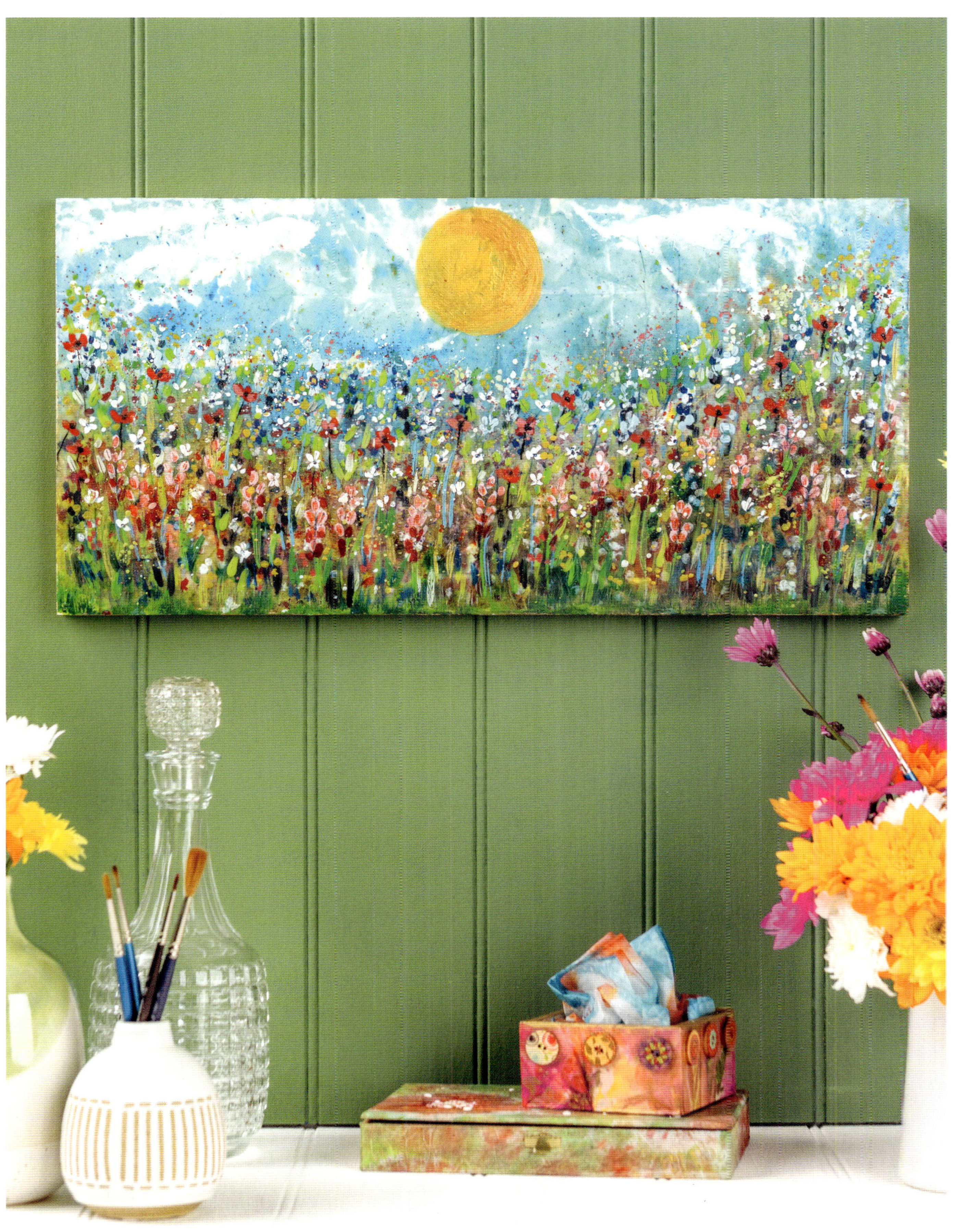

1 Tape the edges of your board with masking tape. On the reverse, use more masking tape to secure a piece of brown or recycled paper to minimize marks and to protect it during the painting process.

2 My board was painted with gesso when purchased, however, you can prepare your surface by painting it with a coat of pale chalk paint or white primer/undercoat. This will give a more even finish to your work and protect the wood. Leave to dry. Repeat with a second coat and leave to dry completely.

3 Select your meadow tissue paper. If you feel you want to add more areas of colour to it, then just drop or sponge on more watercolour inks. Leave to dry.

4 To minimize colour bleed, spray with watercolour fixative. Leave to dry.

5 Use a foam brush to spread wallpaper paste over the top third of the board. Carefully lay your dyed meadow tissue paper over the wooden board, leaving some overhanging at the edges. Smooth the tissue down as you go, checking it adheres. As always, keep some wrinkles for added texture and interest in your painting.

6 Continue sticking down the rest of the meadow background to the board. Leave to dry overnight.

7 Check the tissue paper is stuck down well – add wallpaper paste to any corners or edges which have not fully adhered. Leave to dry completely.

8 Lay your board on a cutting mat and using a sharp craft knife, trim the excess tissue paper from around the four edges.

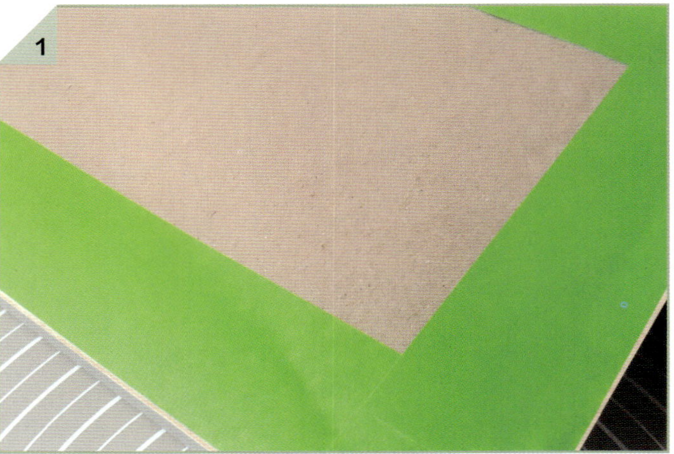

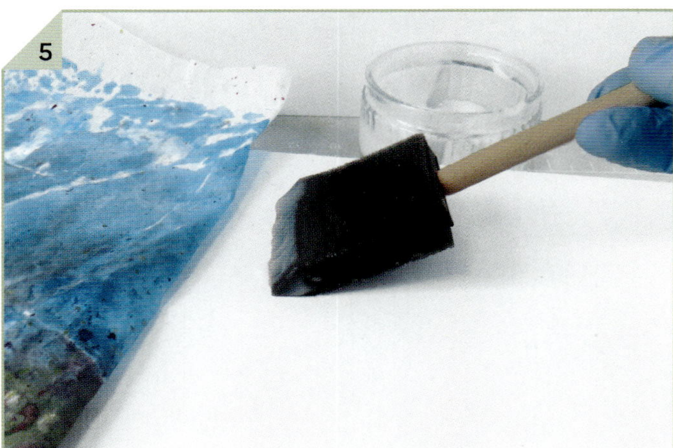

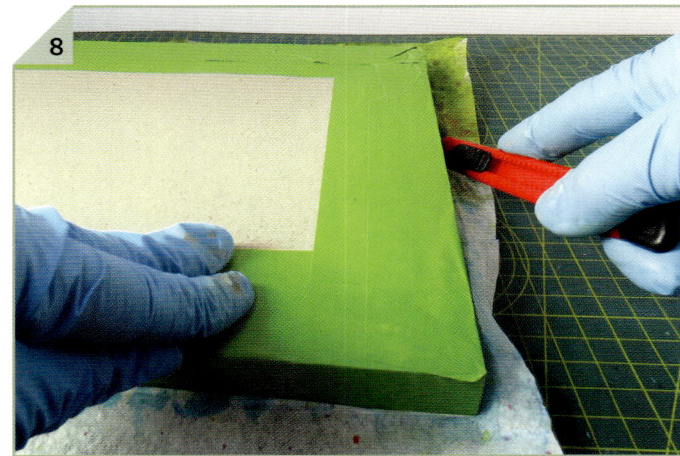

9 Melt your encaustic medium pellets in a metal tin on a hot palette or in a wax melt pot.

10 Using a flat natural bristle brush, paint a thin layer of clear melted encaustic medium over the whole board. Paint right past the edge of the board – we will clean any edge drips later. Hold your heat gun 2–3cm (¾–1¼in) away from the surface. Fuse gently until the wax glistens and any tiny bubbles and brushmarks melt away.

11 Repeat with a second layer of encaustic medium. Fuse gently again. Your wax may appear cloudy after fusing, but it will become clear when cool.

12 Use a watercolour pencil to draw some suggestions of branches and stalks.

13 Melt some of the encaustic wax paint blocks on your heated electric palette and using a medium round hog bristle brush, start painting on petal shapes and flowers. You can mix the wax colours on the hot palette. Add flowers to where you made the pencil stalk marks.

14 Use a smaller bristle brush to add smaller flowers. You could add a scattering of red poppies using a brush or encaustic hot iron tool.

Tip

Avoid using any acrylic products with encaustic wax, as they are incompatible. See safety note on page 73.

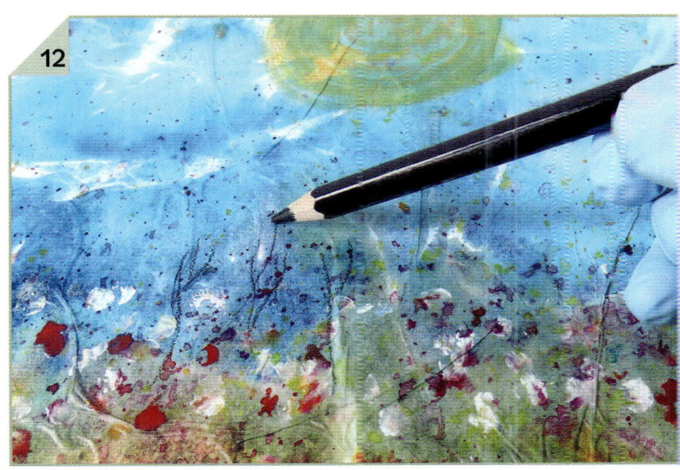

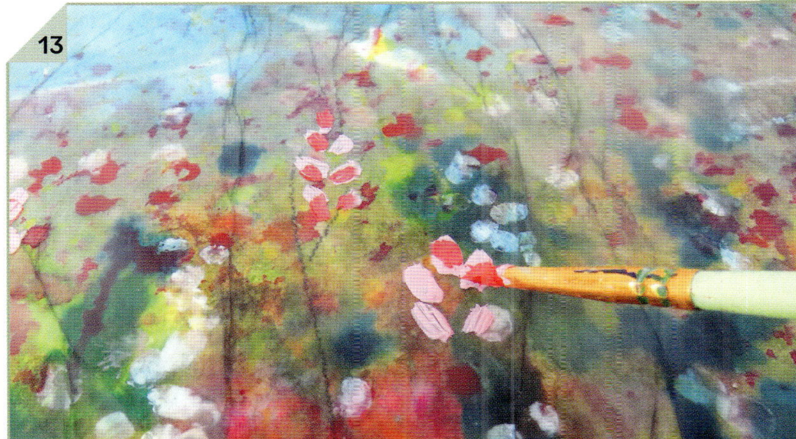

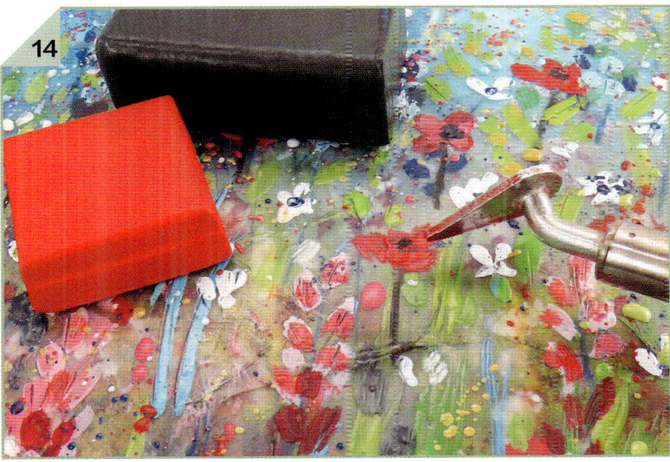

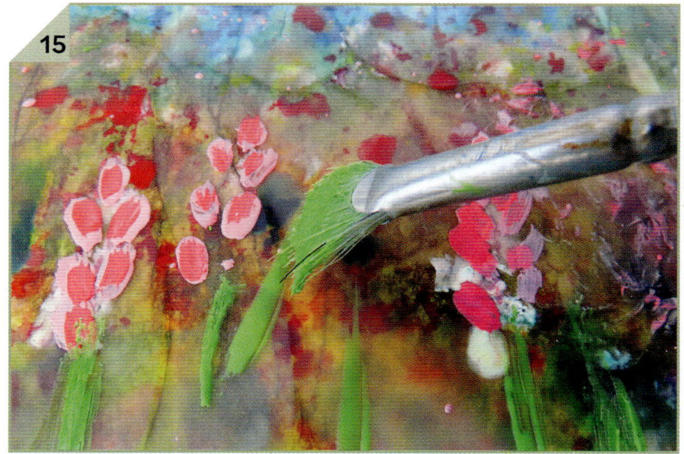

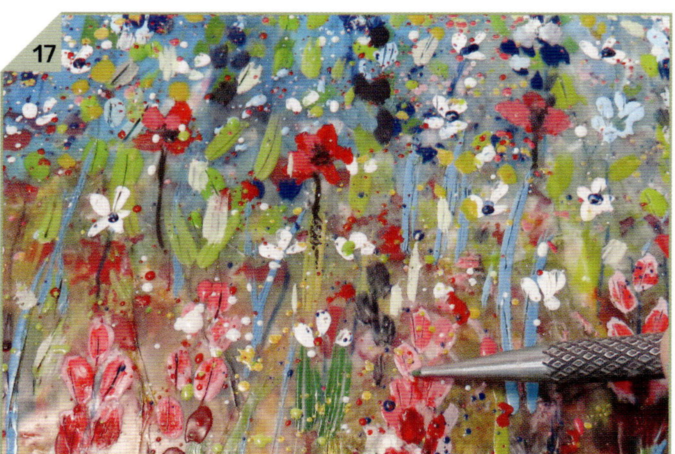

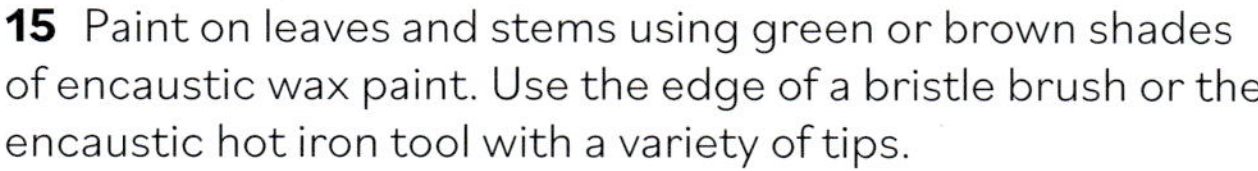

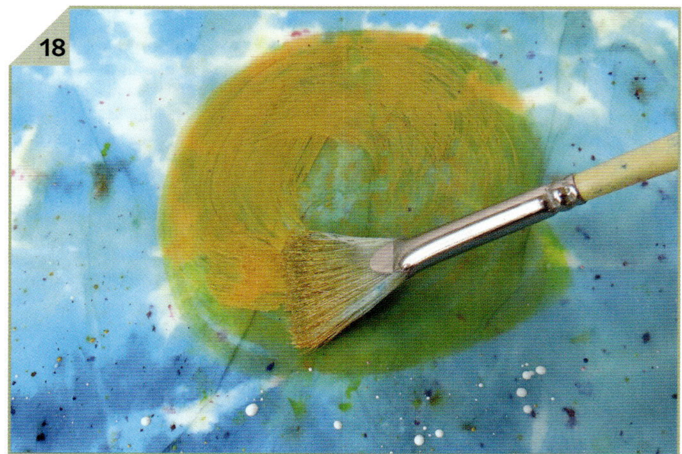

15 Paint on leaves and stems using green or brown shades of encaustic wax paint. Use the edge of a bristle brush or the encaustic hot iron tool with a variety of tips.

16 Fill your board with a variety of flowers and foliage. Experiment with different colours to create a vibrant and lively meadowscape.

17 Use an awl or other sharp tool to scrape some veins into the petals and leaves. This adds to the realism and texture of your painting.

18 You can add a large circular golden or yellow sun into the background. Draw round a large lid with an awl or other sharp tool as a guide. Using a medium round natural bristle brush, apply melted golden wax and fuse it gently with a heat gun to retain some texture.

Tip

Remember the *wabi-sabi* principle when creating your meadow: the flowers and leaves do not have to be perfect. Suggest a flower-filled field by building up layers of texture and colour. Knowing when to stop is the challenge with this type of painting!

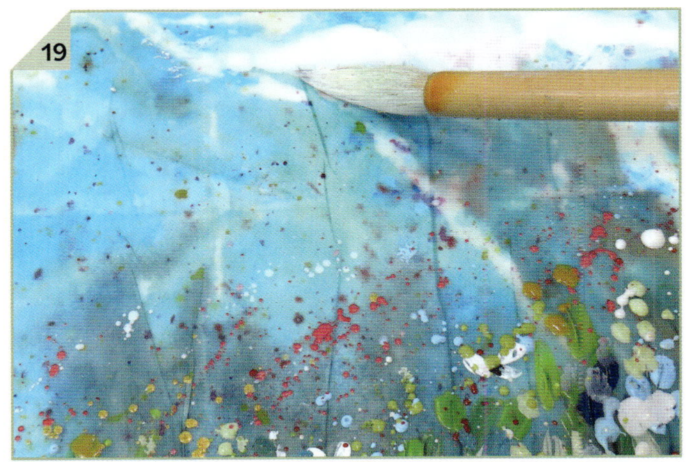

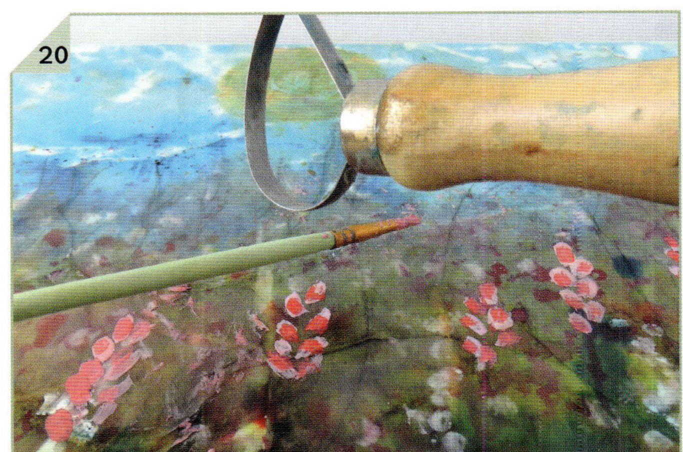

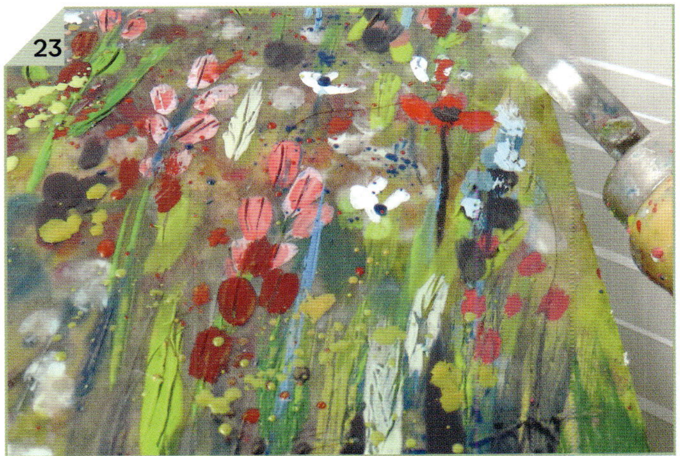

19 Using white encaustic wax paint on a Chinese natural bristle brush, paint on suggestions of clouds. Use a heat gun on a low setting to gently fuse and soften the cloud edges.

20 Splash melted wax drops across the painting by loading a small round brush with some coloured wax mixed with some clear encaustic medium. Hold the brush over your painting and tap the handle with the pottery loop tool so droplets fall onto the painting. This gives the meadow a hazy, ethereal feel.

21 Add golden highlights to the sun and some leaves by rubbing on gold PanPastel with a gloved finger and gently fusing.

22 Complete the painting by gently fusing with your heat gun on a low setting. You do not want to melt the flowers and texture that you have created. If there are any areas you are unhappy with, you can gently scrape off the wax with the pottery loop tool.

23 Gently heat one edge of the board at a time, with a heat gun set to a low heat, then drag a pottery loop tool down the side to remove and discard any excess wax.

24 Once cooled, remove the masking tape and backing paper from your board.

25 Finish the edges of your painting by adding gold gilding wax with a cloth or your finger. Rub this on right up to the edge of the painting. Alternatively, you can paint on chalk paint in a colour of your choice.

26 Let the painting cool and cure for 24 hours. This allows the wax layers to fully harden and adhere properly. Then polish the surface of the painting with a soft, lint-free cloth to give a gentle sheen.

Enjoy the creative process and the beauty of nature that you have captured in your hand-painted masterpiece! To maintain the painting's luminosity, buff it occasionally with a soft lint-free cloth.

10. Abstract flowers on board

Using the abstract designs created by twisting (technique 6 on pages 40–43) and tie dye (technique 7 on pages 44–49), you can create your own floral painting. Having pre-dyed tissue paper ready for the background means you are not starting with a blank canvas – there is already colour and pattern, which is an excellent starting point for your floral art. Look at your tissue paper designs and visualize flowers blooming from them. Where can you see a flower centre? Where can you see petals or leaves? These are the areas you will embellish.

This type of design works well on any size and shape of wooden board. Circular boards are especially effective. Just choose a piece of tie-dyed tissue paper to suit the size and shape of your board.

If you do not want to use encaustic wax, see the alternative methods below.

You will need

Materials

- birch cradle board just smaller than your pre-dyed tissue paper
- abstract tie-dyed wet-strength tissue paper (see technique 7)
- wallpaper paste
- encaustic medium in pellets
- encaustic wax paint blocks in floral and foliage colours, gold and white
- gold and black relief paint to add stamens to flower centres
- gold gilding wax or chalk paint for board edges
- watercolour fixative
- primer or pale chalk paint
- PVA glue
- bleed-proof or acrylic white paint for highlight on flowers
- watercolour inks for highlights, petals and leaves e.g. pinks, gold and green
- brown or other recycled paper

Equipment

- large silicone mat or plastic tablecloth (to protect your workspace)
- foam brush or sponge
- biodegradable baby wipes, for clean up
- disposable plastic gloves
- masking tape
- 150 grit sandpaper
- pot of clean water
- scissors
- cutting mat
- sharp craft knife
- heat gun
- encaustic hot iron tool: mini-iron master with a range of tips
- natural bristle 3cm (1¼in) flat brush, round brushes, small and medium, Chinese calligraphy brush (all natural bristle)
- heated electric palette with metal tins, silicone muffin cases or a wax melt pot
- pottery loop tool
- soft lint-free cloth for buffing

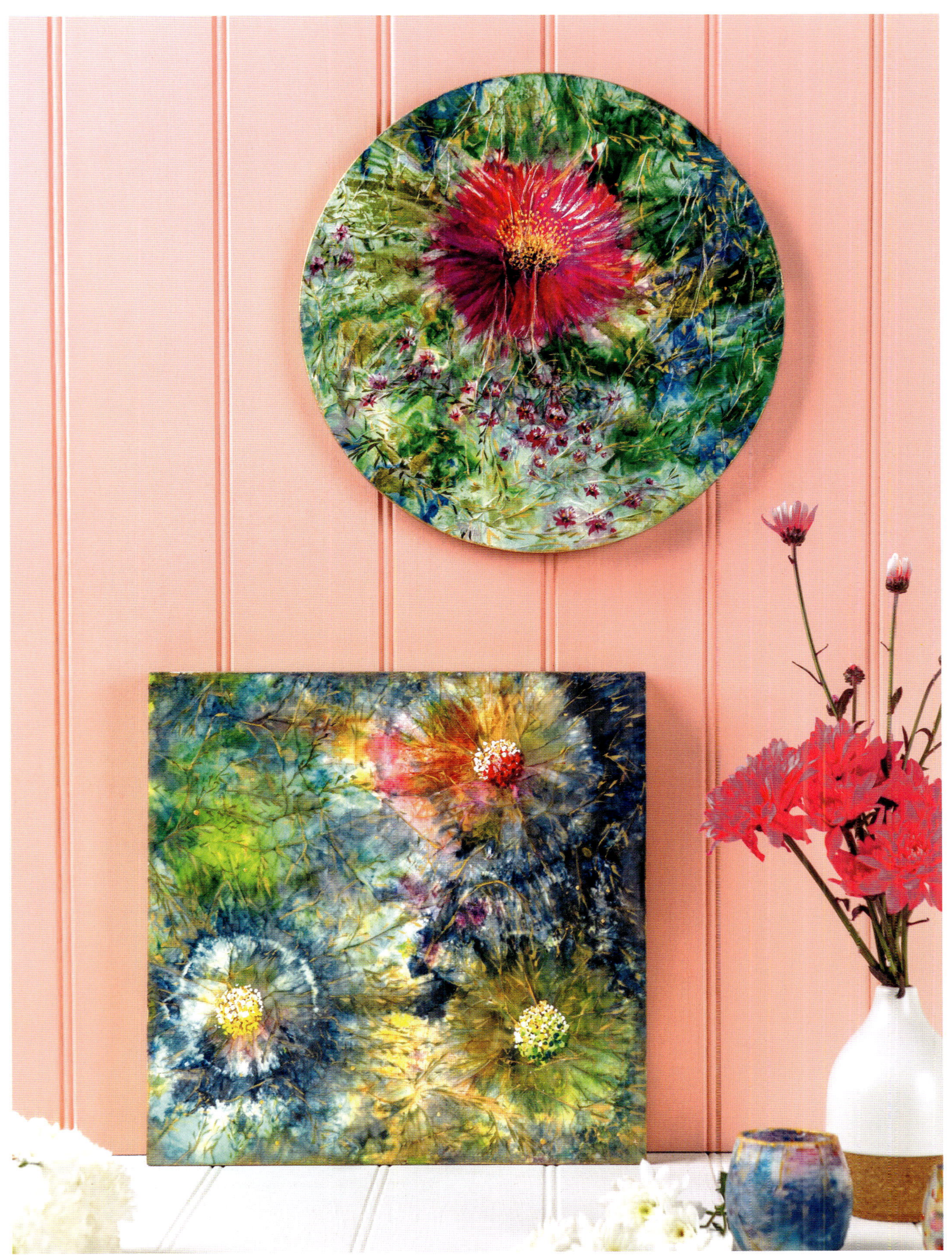

FLORAL DESIGN ON SQUARE BOARD, SEALED WITH ENCAUSTIC WAX

1 Tape the edges of your board with masking tape. I used a birch cradle board measuring 30.5 x 30.5cm (12 x 12in), 4cm (1½in) deep. Secure a piece of brown or recycled paper to the reverse of the board with masking tape, to minimize marks and to protect it.

2 My board was ready-primed with gesso, but you can prepare your surface by painting on a coat of pale chalk paint or white primer. This gives an even finish to your work and protects the wood. Leave to dry. Repeat with a second coat or and leave to fully dry.

3 Spray pre-dyed tissue paper with watercolour fixative to minimize fading and bleeding of the colour. Leave to dry.

4 Your tissue paper should be larger than your board. Use a foam brush to spread wallpaper paste over the top third of the board. Carefully take your dyed tissue paper and lay it over the board, leaving some overhang at each edge. Smooth the tissue paper down as you go, ensuring it adheres to the surface. Aim to retain some wrinkles for texture – this works well for a floral painting.

5 Continue this process, sticking down the rest of the tissue paper. Leave to dry overnight with a heavy object on top to ensure strong adhesion. Use parchment paper between the tissue paper and the heavy object, to protect your design.

6 Check the tissue paper is well adhered – add wallpaper paste to any corners or edges which have not fully stuck.

7 Once fully dry, lay your board on a cutting mat and carefully trim the excess tissue paper from round the four edges with a sharp craft knife. Gently rub away any small bits of tissue paper on the edges using 150 grit sandpaper.

8 Embellish the raised veins by painting on gold watercolour ink. Keep your Chinese brush flat and drag it over the veins to catch the wrinkles. Then use a smaller brush to paint in small gold or green leaves attached to these veins.

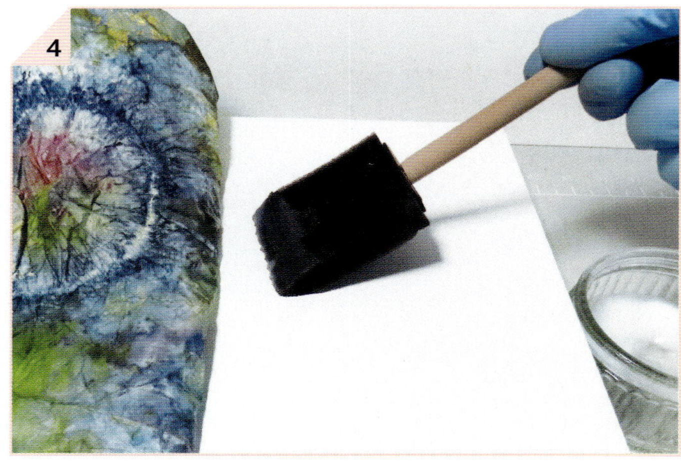

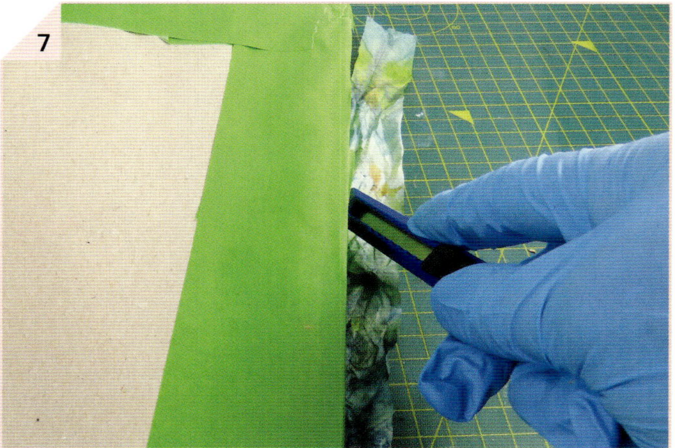

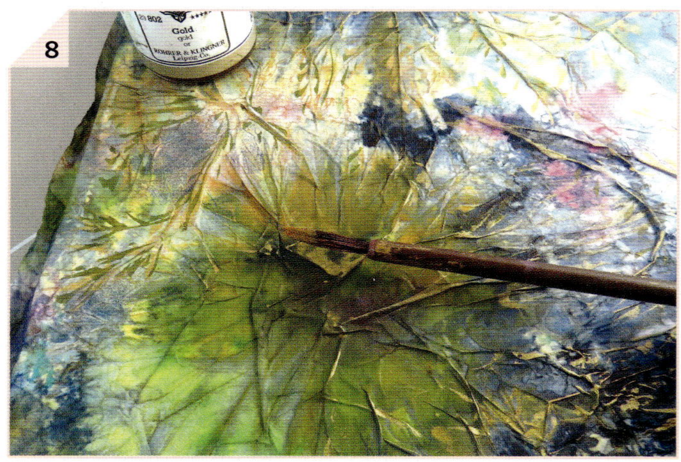

9 Using a wide, flat natural bristle brush, paint a thin layer of clear encaustic medium over the whole board and fuse gently with a heat gun. Fuse only until the wax glistens. Check for any gaps and repeat with a second light layer of encaustic medium. Fuse again lightly. Be sure to paint on the wax past the edges of the board – any drips will be removed later.

10 Embellish the parts of the design which suggest flower centres by melting wax on the encaustic hot iron tool and adding drops of coloured wax to form a round shape. Imagine where the light is coming from and, for example, put darker tones on the left, merging to medium in the middle with lighter drops of colour on the right. Add some drops of gold wax to the top right for highlight. You can scrape off any extra wax you don't like by using the pottery loop tool. There is no need to fuse drops added with an encaustic hot iron tool.

11 For additional texture, drip on melted wax drops across the painting. Dip your brush in the melted coloured wax, then use another brush to tap the paintbrush so that drops fall.

12 Complete the painting by gently fusing with your heat gun on a low setting. You do not want to melt the flowers you have created.

13 Finish the edges by gently heating one section with the heat gun on a low heat, and dragging a pottery loop tool down the side to remove any excess wax.

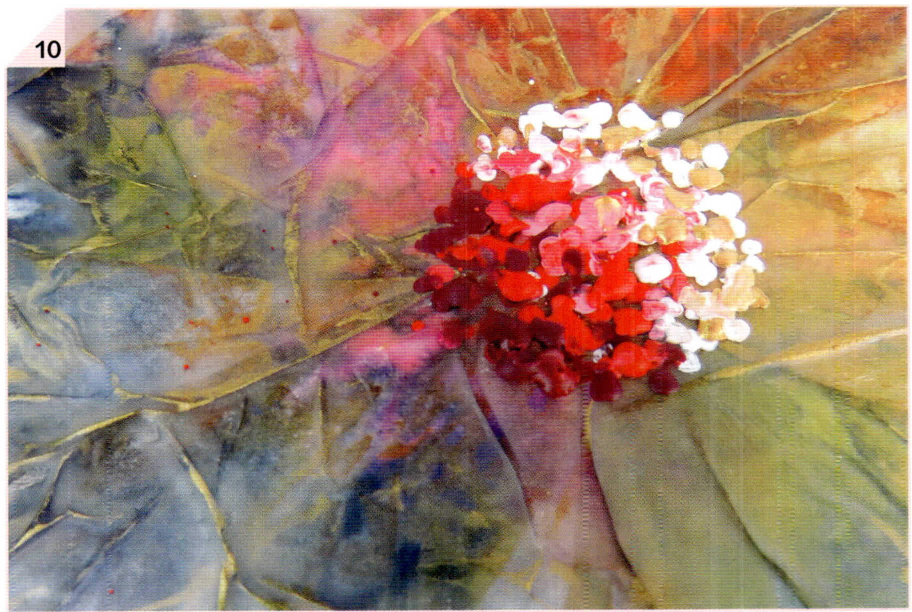

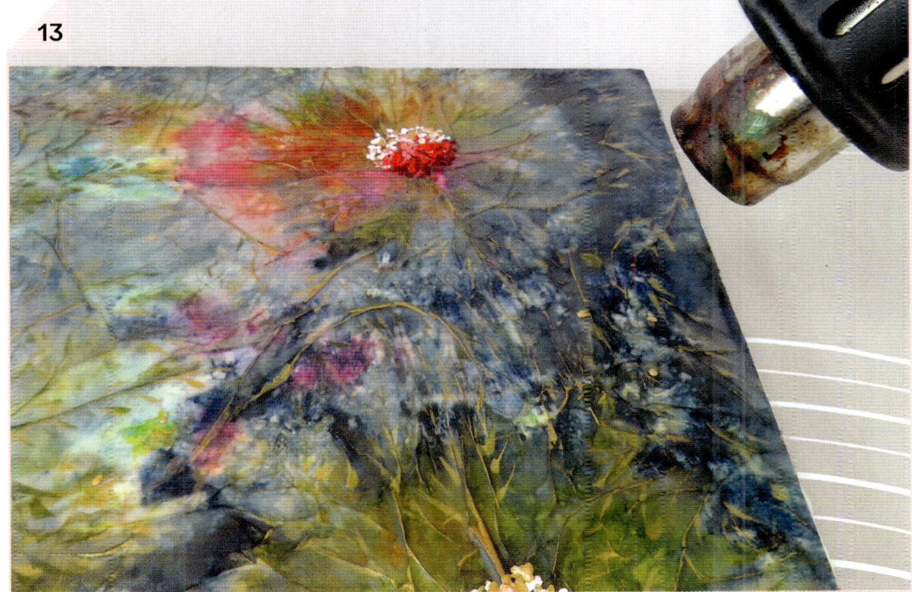

Tip

Remember to spray the dyed tissue paper with a watercolour fixative to minimize the risk of colour fade or bleed.
Melted wax is very hot so splashing it could be dangerous. See safety note on page 73.

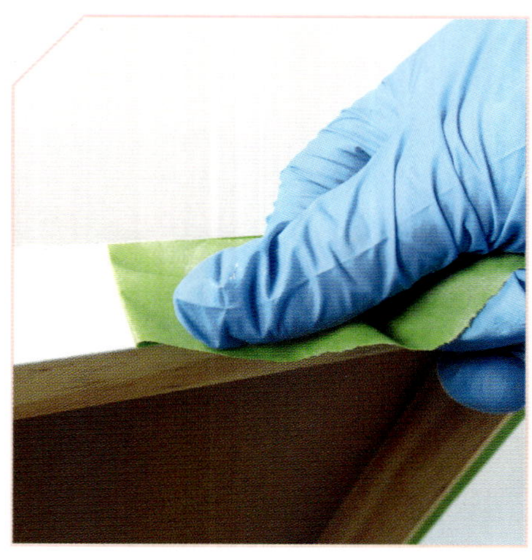

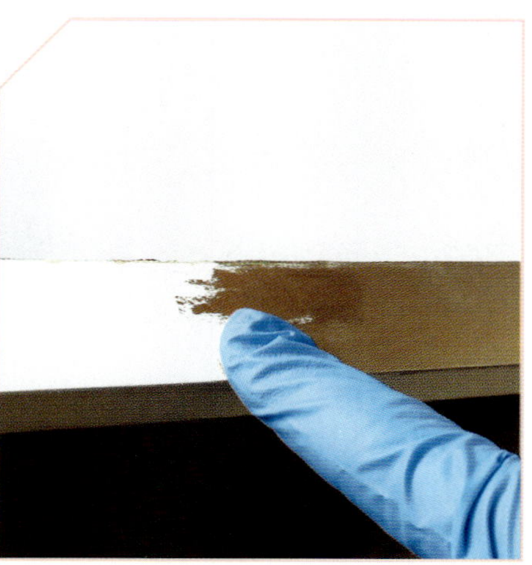

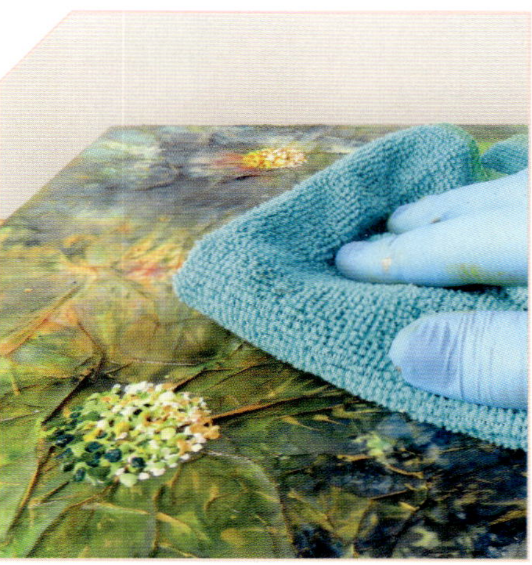

14 Once cooled, remove the masking tape and backing paper from your board.

15 Finish the edges of your board by adding gilding wax with a gloved finger or by applying chalk paint with a brush.

16 Let the painting cool for 24 hours then polish the surface of the painting with a soft lint-free cloth to give a gentle sheen. To maintain the painting's luminosity, buff it occasionally.

FLORAL DESIGN ON ROUND BOARD, SEALED WITH PVA GLUE

If you prefer to create your flower painting without encaustic wax, you can adhere the tissue paper to your wooden substrate as above, then embellish the flower centres with acrylic paint or ink and seal with PVA glue.

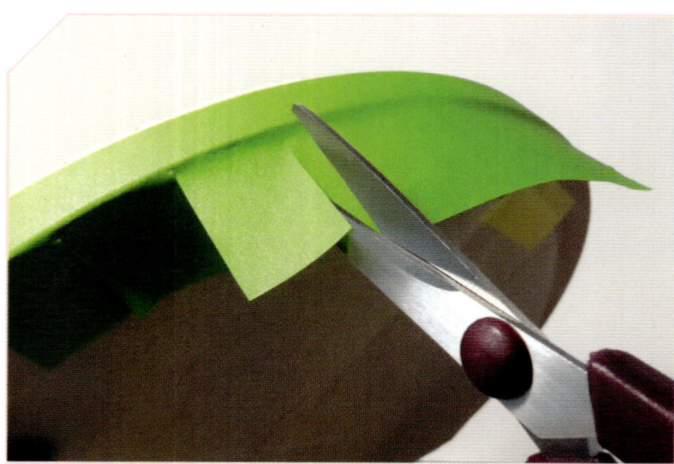

1 Tape the edges of your board with masking tape. I used a circular birch cradle board, 30cm (11¾in) in diameter and 2cm (¾in) deep. Secure a piece of brown or recycled paper on the reverse of your board with masking tape to minimize marks and to protect it.

2 Prepare your surface by painting a coat of pale chalk paint or white primer using a foam brush. This gives an even finish to your work and protects the wood. Wipe any drips from the edges with a baby wipe. Leave to dry. Repeat with a second coat and leave to dry. Rinse your foam brush under water immediately to allow for reuse once dry.

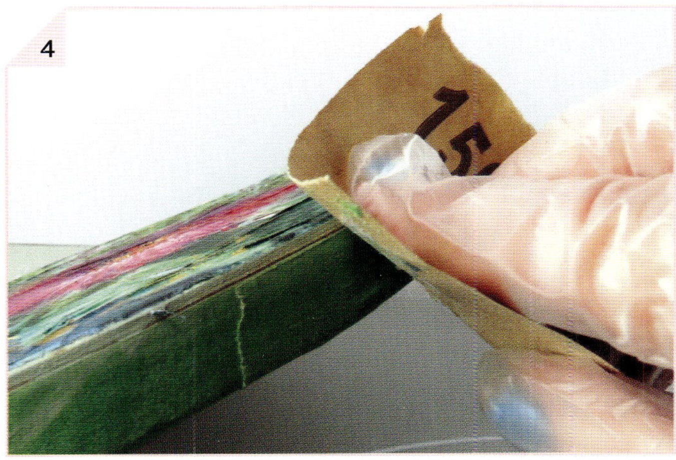

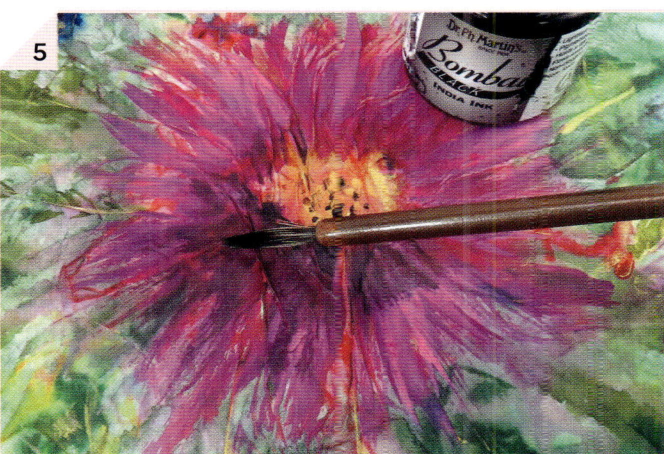

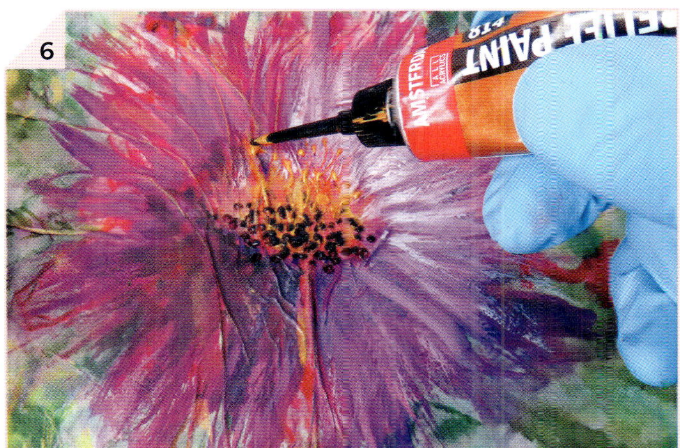

3 Follow steps 3–7 on page 134.

4 Gently rub away any small bits of tissue paper on the edges with 150 grit sandpaper.

5 Embellish the parts of the design which suggest flower centres, painting on petal details with watercolour inks in shades of pink. Use some white paint for highlights. Add smaller pink flowers.

6 Add stamens with gold relief paint to the large flower centre. Add black dots of relief paint in the centre to add depth.

7 Hold your Chinese brush flat and drag gold ink over the raised wrinkles to highlight them.

8 Paint in small leaves along these lines using green and gold ink. Leave to dry.

9 Using a foam brush, paint on two thin coats of PVA glue to seal the painting.

10 Once dry, remove the masking tape and backing paper from your board.

11 Finally, complete the edge of your board by rubbing on gilding wax with your gloved finger. Remove any excess gilding wax with a baby wipe.

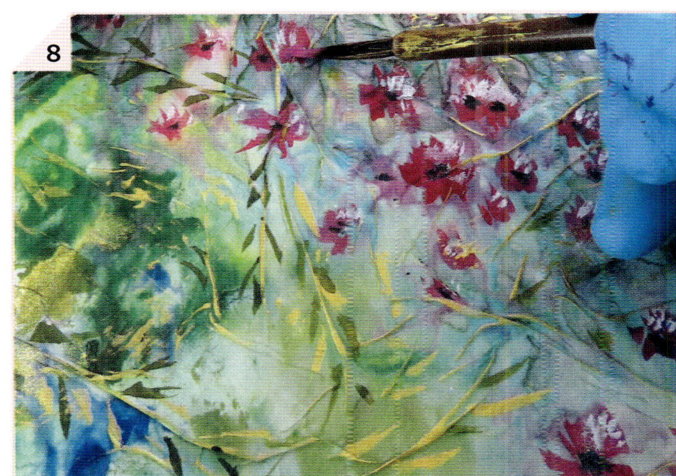

Inspiration

Here are some ideas to show you the range of vibrant art, cards, tealight holders and trays you can make, using hand-dyed tissue paper as your starting point.

Be bold and creative!

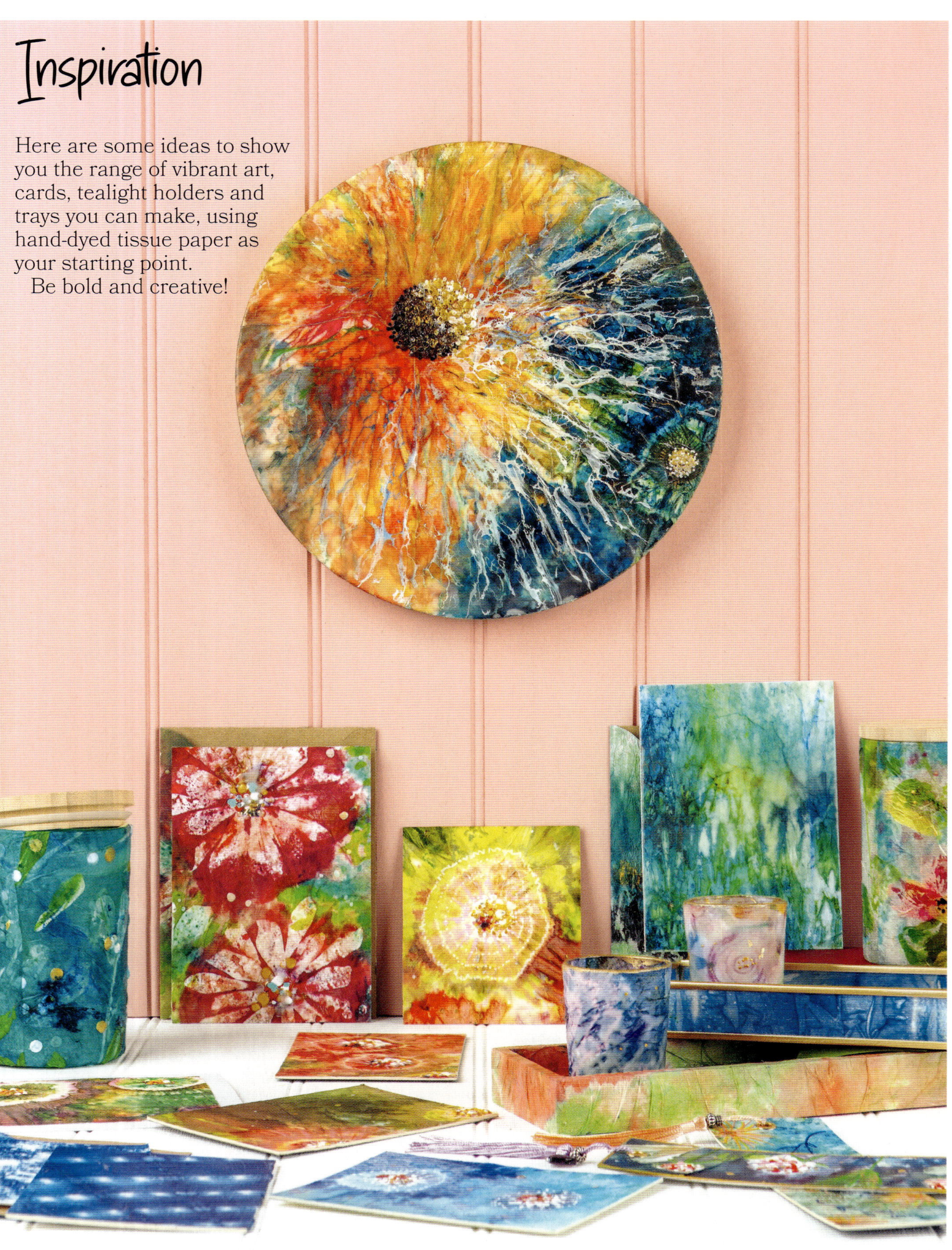

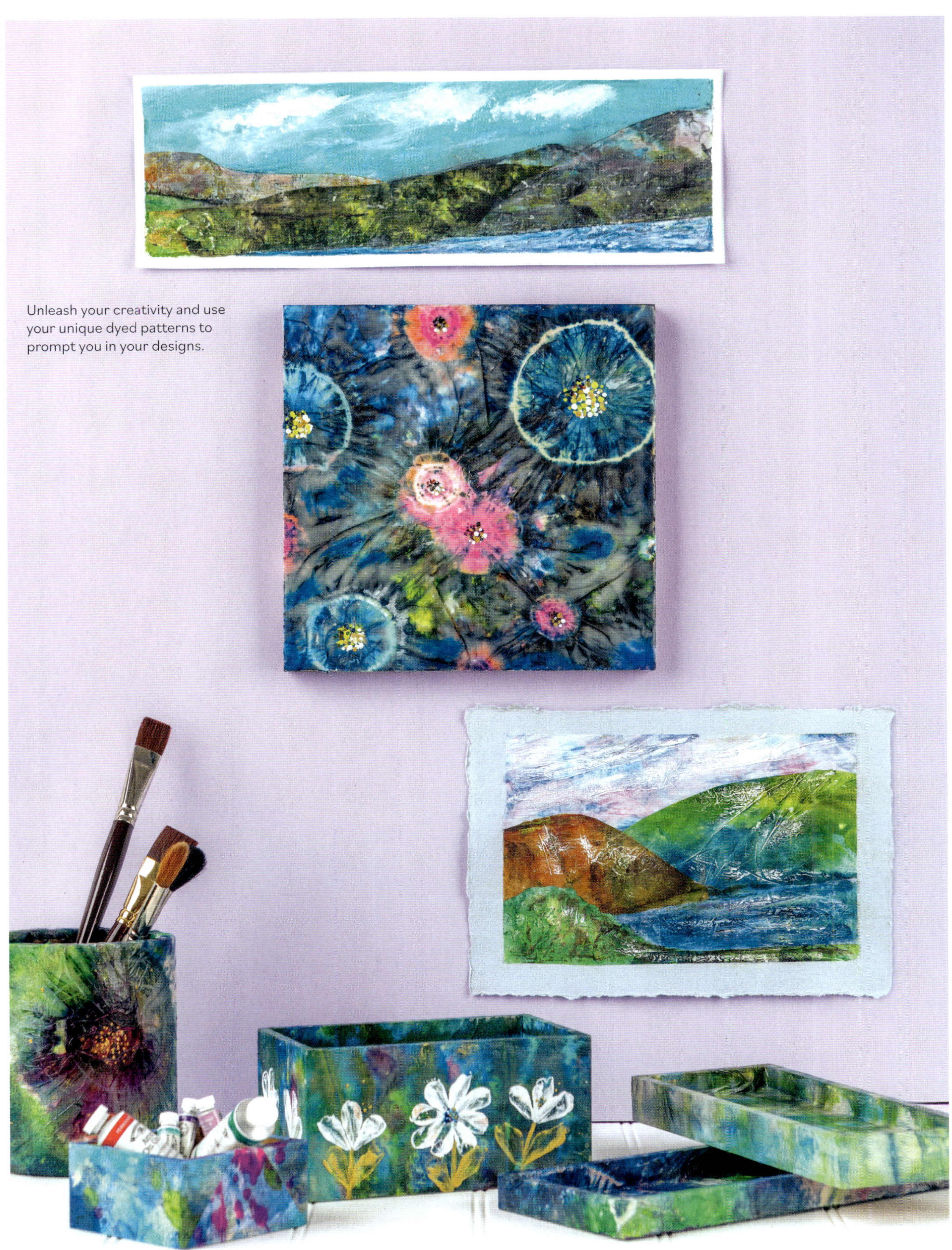

Unleash your creativity and use
your unique dyed patterns to
prompt you in your designs.

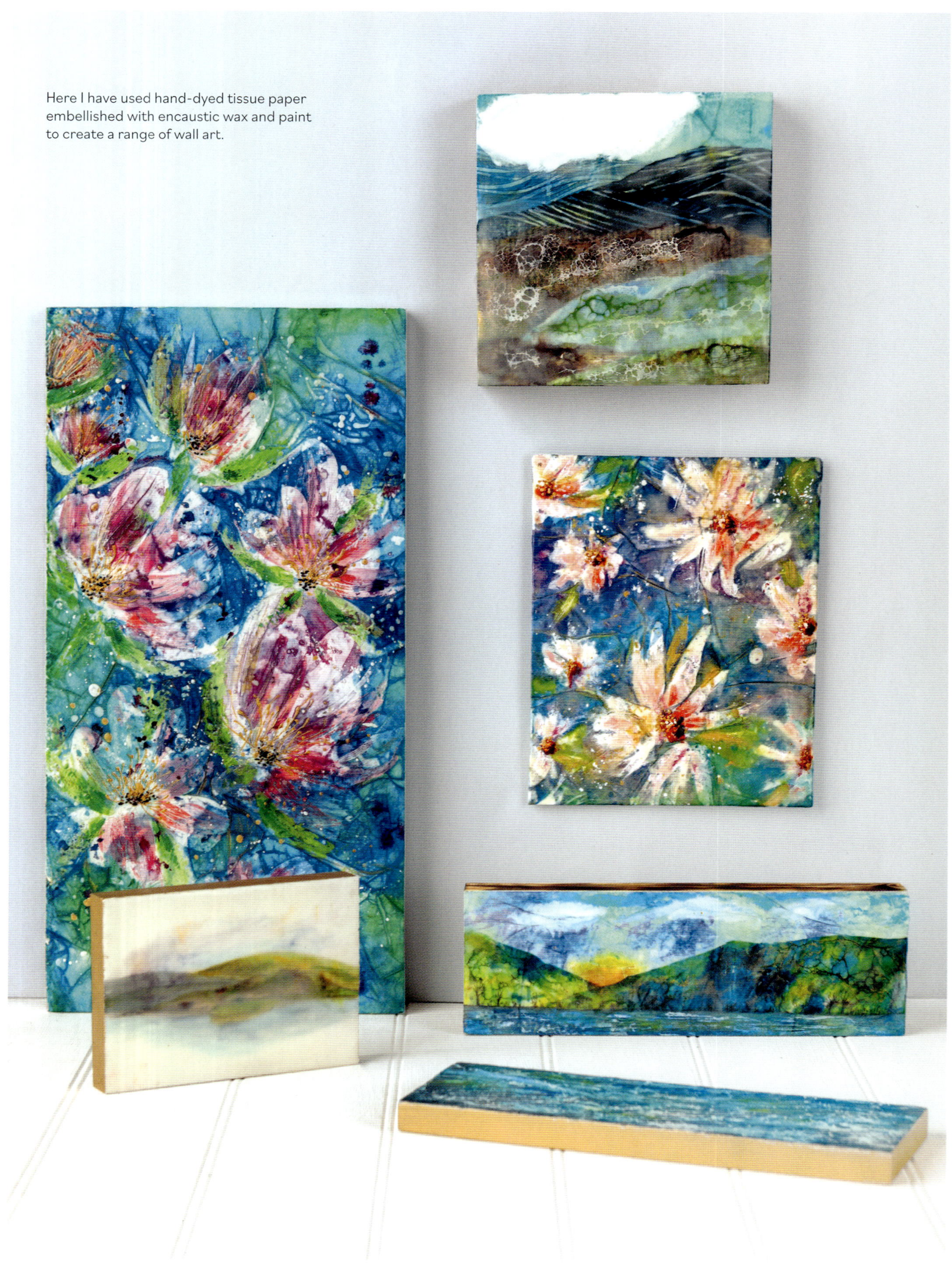

Here I have used hand-dyed tissue paper embellished with encaustic wax and paint to create a range of wall art.

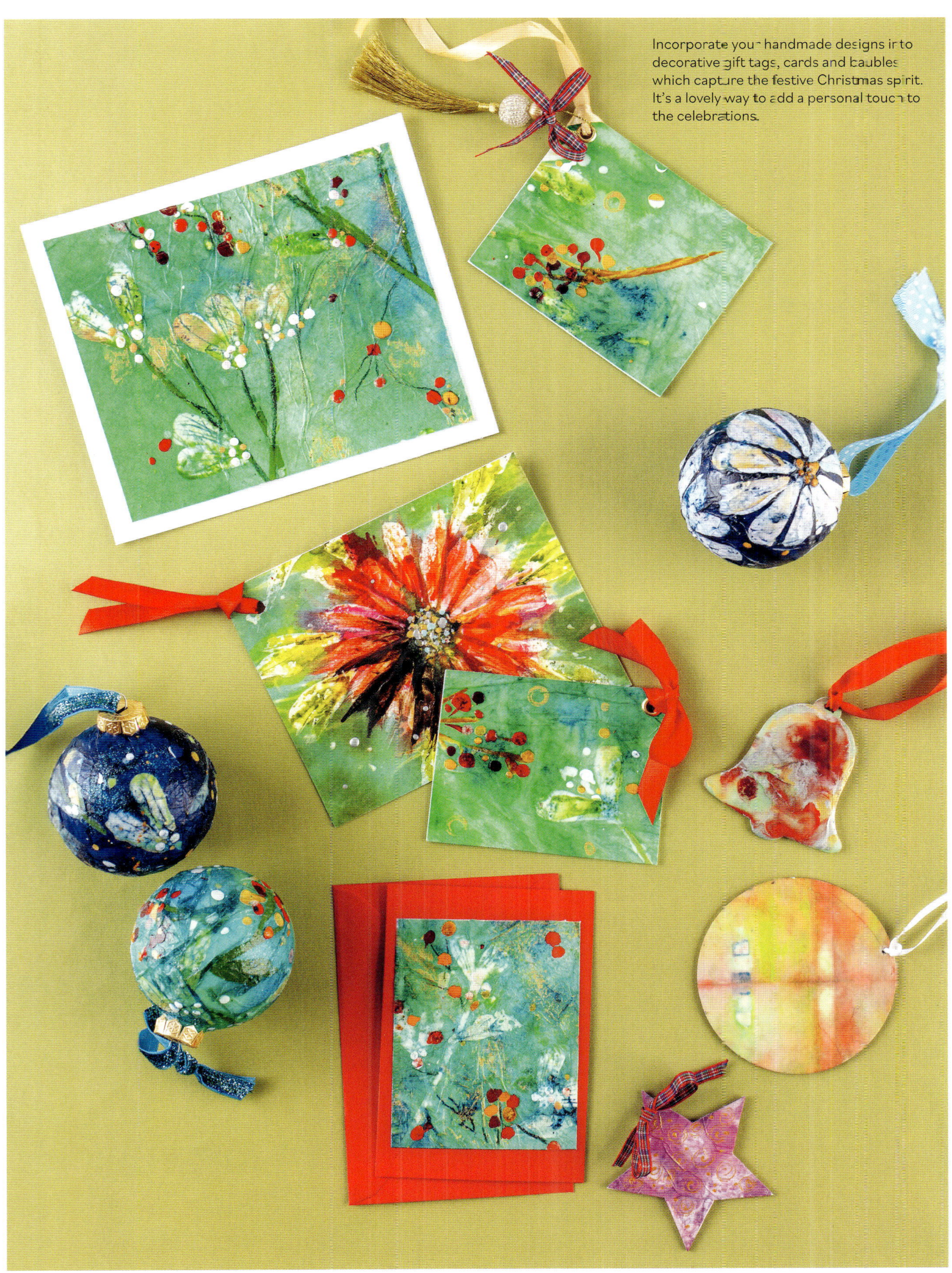

Incorporate your handmade designs into decorative gift tags, cards and baubles which capture the festive Christmas spirit. It's a lovely way to add a personal touch to the celebrations.

Troubleshooting

Here are a few common problems you might encounter. Don't worry – there are solutions. Wet-strength tissue paper is very forgiving, and any small repairs can be done easily and will never be noticed. Make sure you have the following to hand:

- pot of clean water
- wallpaper paste or acrylic gloss medium as glue
- metal pottery awl or pointed wooden skewer
- small rounded paintbrush
- small sponge
- small scissors
- offcuts of matching dyed tissue paper for repairs

FILLING GAPS

If you have a small gap in your tissue paper or a section that is too pale, for example, you can patch it with another piece of tissue paper. Dampen the patch you need to add and soften the area to be torn with water on a clean paintbrush, then carefully, using the brush, tear a small section of tissue paper large enough to cover the gap. Try to colour match as much as you can, but you can always add further colour if needed to hide any areas, so do not worry too much. Place some wallpaper paste over the gap and lay the patch over it, smoothing it down with your finger or a small piece of sponge.

FIXING TEARS

Dampen the tissue paper edges very slightly and push them together over the tear, then seal them with wallpaper paste. If you must make a join, try to join with a ragged edge rather than a straight one, since it will be less noticeable.

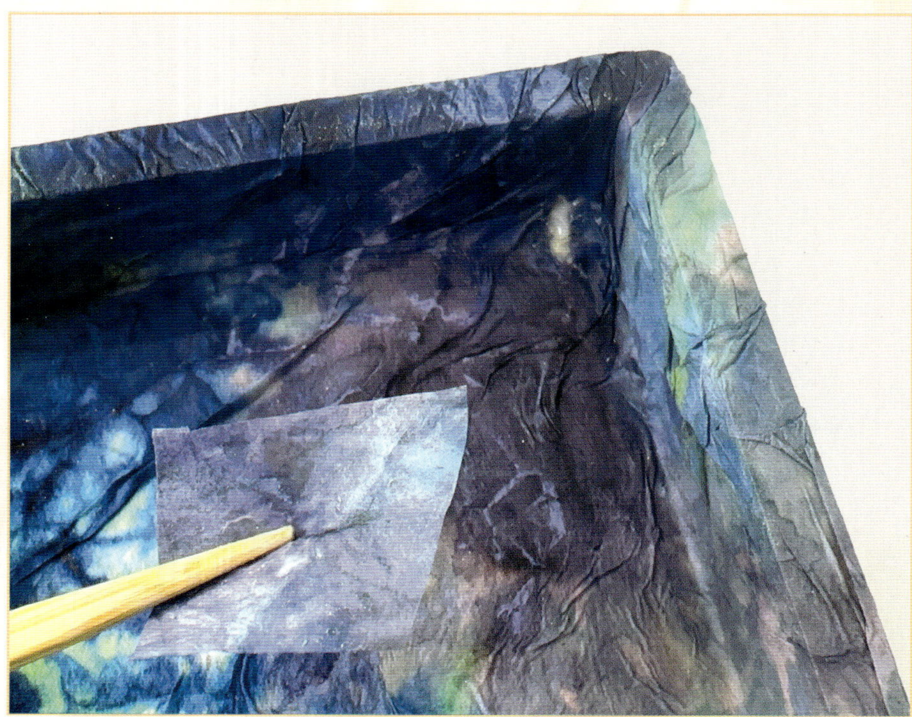

Adding tissue paper for repair.

REMOVING BUBBLES

When you have a bubble on, for example, a tray where the tissue paper has not stuck down fully, you can fix this by piercing the bubble with a sharp pointed metal awl or the sharp end of a wooden skewer. Apply some wallpaper paste and massage it in so that some goes under the bubble. Press down firmly to get the bubble to stick down. Finish the repair by smearing more wallpaper paste over the bubble. Press down to flatten it.

You can also use this method to remove bubbles when you are adhering tissue paper with PVA glue in a collage.

OFF-CENTRE GROMMET HOLE

If you find that the grommet hole you have punched is not perfectly central on a bookmark, trim the edge of the bookmark to make it narrower but with the grommet hole central.

COVERING HANDLES ON A TRAY

Handles can be tricky to cover; it's best to cover the handle gap completely with the tissue paper then, once this is dry, cut through the tissue paper and fold the edges in, sticking as you go. Use a wet paintbrush to soften the tissue paper as you cut through the gap. Stick down the cut tissue paper around the insides of the handles, using wallpaper paste. Cut off any excess with small scissors. The joins will not be seen once the tray is complete.

Using a sharp tool to pierce a bubble.

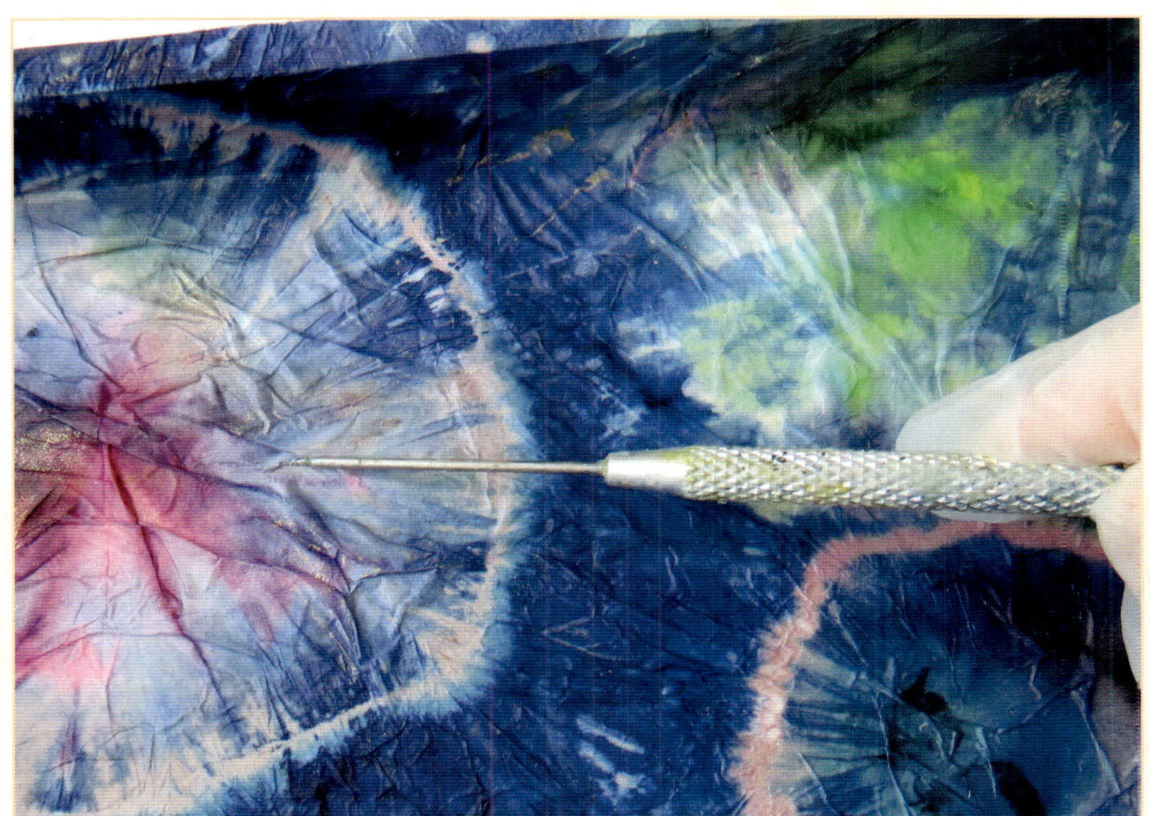

Templates

Here are some petal and leaf templates for project 7: tissue flowers. They are reproduced at actual size. For extra copies to download, head to the Bookmarked Hub (www.bookmarkedhub.com). Search for this book by title or ISBN: the files can be found under 'Book Extras'. Don't limit yourself to my templates – draw your own petal and leaf shapes.

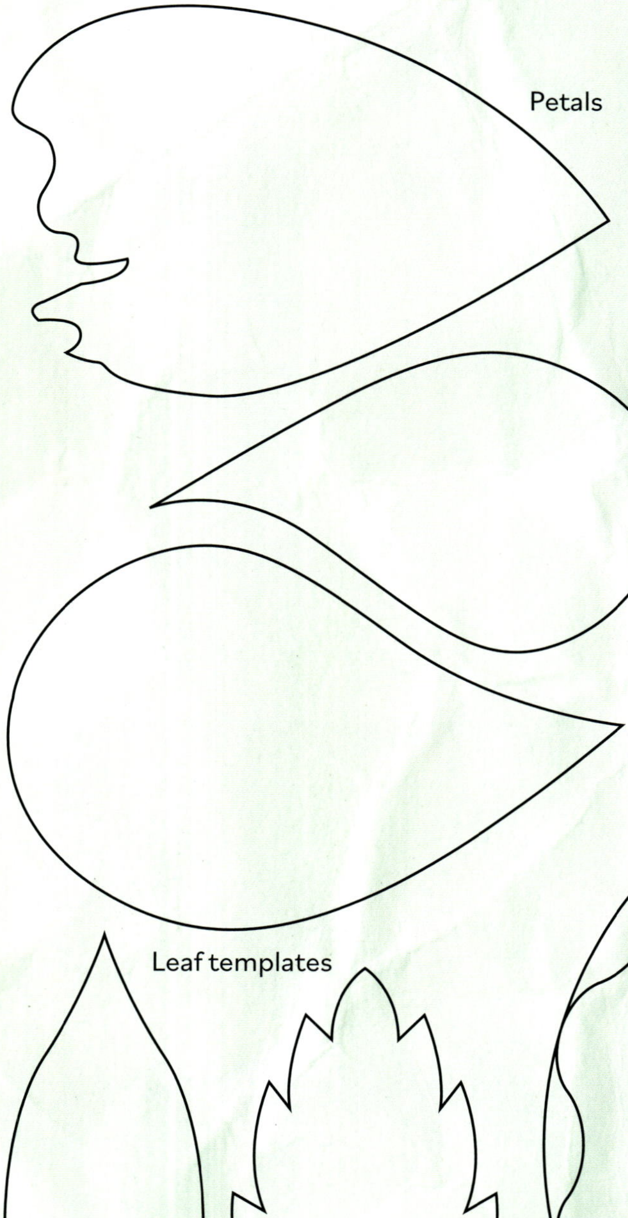

Petals

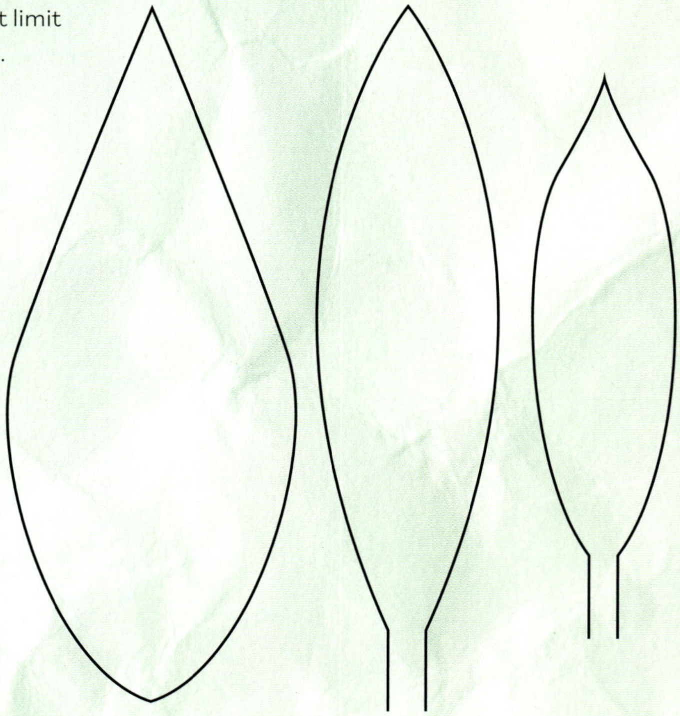

Pointed petal/dip dye

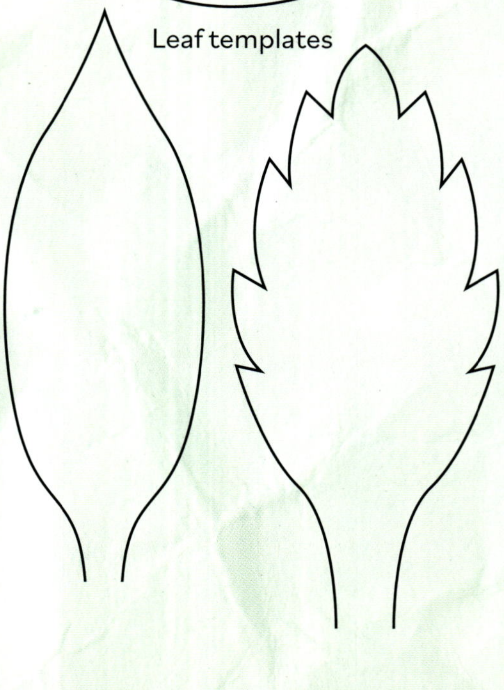

Leaf templates

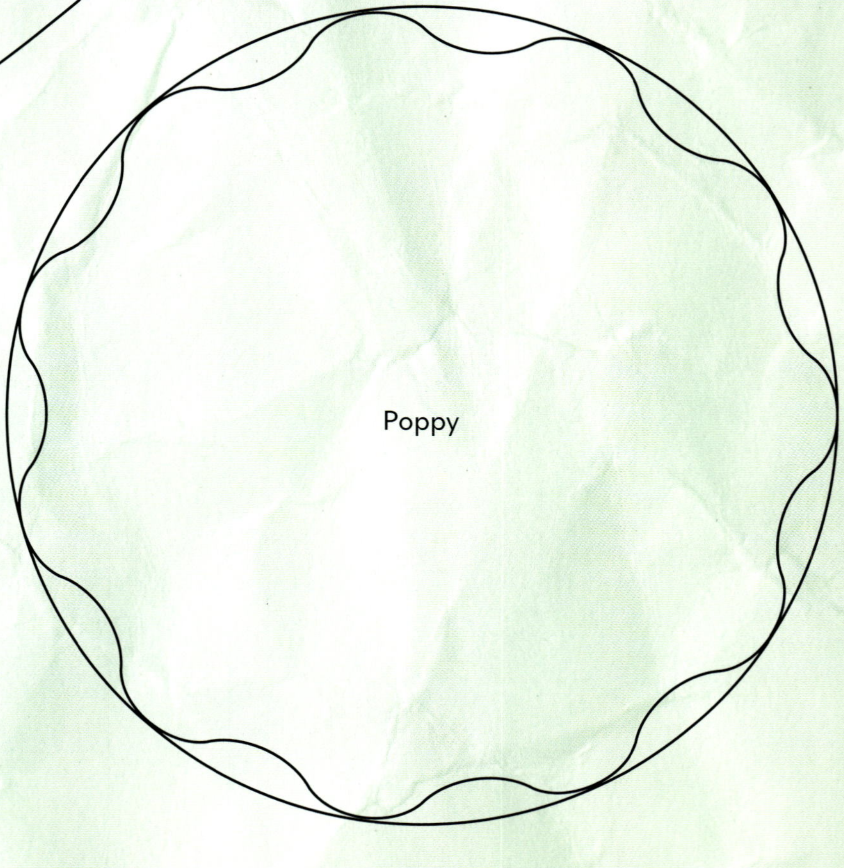

Poppy

Life According to the Soul

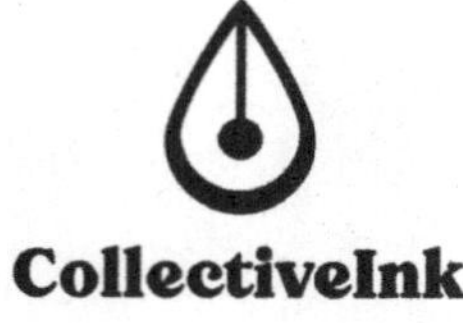

CollectiveInk

First published by Sixth Books, 2026
Sixth Books is an imprint of Collective Ink Ltd.,
Unit 11, Shepperton House, 89 Shepperton Road, London, N1 3DF
office@collectiveinkbooks.com
www.collectiveinkbooks.com
www.6th-books.com

For distributor details and how to order please visit the 'Ordering' section on our website.

Text copyright: David Allen 2025

ISBN: 978 1 917704 87 8
978 1 917704 90 8 (ebook)
Library of Congress Control Number: 2025939445

A CIP catalogue record for this book is available from the British Library.

Design: Lapiz Digital Services

UK: Printed and bound by CPI Group (UK) Ltd, Croydon, CR0 4YY
Printed in North America by CPI GPS partners

The manufacturer's authorised representative in the EU for product safety
is: eucomply OÜ – Pärnu mnt 139b-14, 11317 Tallinn, Estonia,
hello@ eucompliancepartner.com, www.eucompliancepartner.com

We operate a distinctive and ethical publishing philosophy in all areas of our business, from our global network of authors to production and worldwide distribution.

Life According to the Soul

Awakening the Hidden Connections
Between Your Life and Your
Soul's Eternal Truth

David Allen

6TH
BOOKS

London, UK
Washington, DC, USA

Table of Contents

Table of Contents

Section 8 From Beginning to End

Dedicated to my beloved Sandra
who went home on 26 March 2016.
I know where you are.

Introduction

Imagine a single breath – yours, mine, or that of a stranger born centuries ago. It begins, it ends, and the cycle repeats across billions of lives. What does it mean to exist in this fleeting moment between birth and death?

What does it mean for us, navigating a physical existence filled with joy and heartbreak? We are enveloped in an amnesic state, focusing our attention on the present and shielding us from dwelling on who we were before, or the inevitability of death. This is a remarkable feat.

Who were you before birth? Who will you be after death? The expanse of time surrounding a life dwarfs its brief duration. Will the vast stretch of time after death mirror the eternity before we were born?

There are approximately eight billion people alive today, and in just 120 years, every one of them will have been replaced. Every one of them will be gone. The planet will be filled with entirely new people, and I find that thought profoundly striking.

Where does our sentience originate? We know we live briefly, but why? Is God the answer? Perhaps, but humanity has worshipped many gods. Major religions honour distinct deities, each prescribing unique social and political structures and commandments. They cannot all be identical, yet they may not be truly different either. Is the assumption that only one belief is correct a product of our limited understanding?

We are born into a body that perceives itself as separate. Connecting with others is a skill we must learn, relying on senses beyond the obvious to communicate. Yet, to all intents and purposes, we feel alone – trapped within our minds, which absorb ideas about the world and ourselves that shape our emotions, comfort, and happiness. For some, this solitary existence and the challenge of forming meaningful connections is a profound struggle.

This book is not merely an academic exercise. It builds on existing knowledge to show that we are not alone – that our sentience is the soul's, inherently connected to others. This understanding makes life's traumas more comprehensible. The mind's isolation and persistent loneliness can merge with the soul's connectivity, offering perspective. These questions have driven my work for decades, culminating in a realisation that compels me to share my findings.

That's why I wrote this book now, twenty years after beginning this work and twelve years after its conclusion. The time feels right. I strive to listen, embrace guidance, and heed the inner voice that one morning urged, "Do this." The mind's loneliness can be eased by the soul's connectedness, and we can receive guidance once we learn to listen.

These insights stem from thousands of hours of testimony – stories of past-life memories, spiritual awakenings, and profound connections shared by ordinary people like us. The amnesic state we are born into is superficial, but memory is eternal, woven into the fabric of existence. By revisiting these memories, we can reset our perspective, gain understanding, and reconcile the flaws of human biology with the enduring peace of the soul.

These revelations reveal that we are two melded into one: a physical body fused with an immortal soul. The body delivers pleasure, pain, and senses – touch, taste, sight, and hearing – along with emotions that powerfully shape our behaviour. The soul provides higher sentience: self-awareness, compassion, and the capacity to love.

One part of us dies: the complex biological body returns to dust, mingling with the earth's ancient remnants. Yet the sense of "I am" – our core essence – endures in a different form, realm, and perspective. When you gaze at a cloudless sky, marvelling at the universe's countless stars, the understanding of "I am" sharpens, if only briefly, before physical reality reclaims your focus.

Text cannot fully capture the emotions or vivid "being there" sense that clients describe. In past-life sessions, they may observe events like an immersive film or relive them, feeling the physical sensations anew. Chapter 4 vividly illustrates this: a woman under hypnosis, recalling a life as a man, expresses profound feelings of sexuality and sensuality. Such genuine, emotional experiences underscore the reality of these memories.

The transcripts offer a fresh perspective on modern life and its beliefs, particularly around gender. Gender confusion is a significant issue today, with much uncertainty about why some feel misaligned with their bodies or behave differently. These revelations provide a new dimension to this personal and social topic. Clients consistently describe a gender preference during incarnation (here, I use "gender" interchangeably with "sex", as they do). Incarnations clearly involve experiences as both sexes, a diversity essential to soul growth.

Often, the gender for the next incarnation isn't an issue, quite often people do express a preference, but it's no big deal, but some have a firm preference and don't like the idea of incarnating as the "other one", though they know they need to embody those experiences eventually into their overall growth.

Section 1 is where we discuss your immortal soul joining with the foetus. Elsewhere in the transcripts you'll read about the work of souls who fix problems with the joining or prepare souls to be able to do this better. However, the principle take from Section 1 is that there are two component parts, the human brain, and your immortal soul. For older souls, maintaining a healthy life balance is much easier but for younger, less experienced souls, difficulties arise when the human side overpowers the nature of the soul. Such loss of control can also happen when souls take too little energy with them in a life, and you'll see references to this in the transcripts. The combination of an inexperienced soul and low energy use makes this outcome much more likely. In essence there are no evil souls but there are evil humans, driven to that by a corrupt belief system or mental illness.

What happens when the human side dominates, and the soul's influence wanes? This often damages soul energy, requiring repair upon returning to the spiritual realm – hence the Healing Shower: a process of renewal described in Chapter 4; human behaviour hinges on our beliefs.

The life may fail, in the sense of soul advancement, and one reason why some have so many more incarnations than others. We see, from the difficulties expressed in Chapter 5, that repeats can be common and extensive. Rather like being held back in school for another year again and again until you pass.

From the human perspective our behaviour is dependent upon what we believe. In my book *The Sophisticated Alcoholic*, O-Books 2011, I explain in detail how our belief set creates unwanted and damaging behaviour. It's not just behaviour with alcohol that is affected, but all our behaviour. Belief is all important, it engenders emotion which in turn develops and then drives a behaviour deigned to satisfy those emotions, almost regardless of how damaging or evil it might be.

We are, as humans, incredibly easy to manipulate through our belief system. We can be convinced to believe anything because of the capacity of the human mind to adopt and act upon external stimulus. It's no surprise when you understand the discomfort some souls have towards their future physical gender. Combined with a narrative that encourages the belief that one can change it, some will take the opportunity given by a narrative, that is supportive, to modify their entire behaviour and sometimes their physical person.

Given a situation where our soul has lost the ability to moderate the human need to satisfy emotions, themselves driven by belief, people can engage in such damaging or unconventional behaviour. When this happens, our immortal side suffers in its attempts to regain some influence.

Within these transcripts is one explanation as to why some people have this inner sense of being in the wrong body and if that is understood then it becomes much easier to deal with. That won't be the case for all those who profess that state because the attention and extensive support for changing yourself, in some cases, irreversibly, will encourage the same behaviour by others for quite different reasons. Also, it's important to understand that if the formerly agreed lessons aren't learnt, the same or similar challenges will be repeated in future incarnations.

I also want to address privilege. In today's world privilege is often associated with monetary wealth or influence. It is often alleged that we are all born equal, which is quite obviously untrue. If you consider that privilege really ought to be all encompassing and connect that to the many examples in the testimonies in this book, it opens a perspective on it which is helpful to you in this life by aiding your understanding that adversity, where that exists, is necessary for your spiritual growth and personal development.

If you then consider the scope of privilege, you may see that where you might be less privileged in one area, you might also have a degree of privilege in another.

For example, I might have dreamed of opening the bowling for England (apologies for the cricket analogy), but at under 1.98 metres (6'6"), that was never an option. On the contrary, I was born with an active and able mind which has contributed to my life being on relatively smooth ground. That is certainly another form of privilege.

The clear message from these testimonials is that many lives offer many experiences of privilege in its broadest sense. Some lives with adverse conditions such as low economic freedom, or poor health, may be balanced by comradeship and the love of those around you, your equals.

One of the most common questions people ask prior to their sessions is, "Why am I like this?" They are usually referring to an aspect of their lives they are unhappy with, but the realisation that it was a choice, sometimes a recommendation, and that it has a greater purpose is a reassuring understanding.

To have a life could be seen as the greatest privilege of all and an acknowledgement of that is spiritually and psychologically soothing.

How to Read This Book

This book weaves together lifetimes of exploration through the awe-inspiring memories of clients I've guided across past lives and spiritual realms, revealing a hidden dimension of existence that fills a void in our understanding.

The revelations of people come in different forms. Sometimes, in this process, I'm very clear about where they are and what they're doing, and the questions and answers you see will largely reflect that. At other times, people go their own way, and it can be a little confusing as to what's really happening, so I will interject and clarify the scenes to help you more easily see where these experiences fit into the overall scheme of things.

Prior to these sessions I gather some information from the client which includes a list of those people closest to them or important in their lives. This is to help with the identification of souls they will encounter along the way. Also, I ask them to list the questions about their life that they want answering and at the end of each session, not included in the transcripts, I always check with them to see if any of the questions remain unanswered or not completely answered. On occasion, I'll use this information in the sessions to clarify identity or direct towards an answer they seek or pursue a conclusion to an event which is of extraordinary interest. Overwhelmingly though, I allow people to find their own way.

Where you see **Narration**, an explanation or clarification follows. Sometimes for broader understanding I may refer to the works of Dr Michael Newton to fill in gaps. I'll be specific when and where this happens. Explanations are concluded with **End of Narration.**

Narration

Dr Michael Newton (1931–2016) was a pioneering hypnotherapist and author whose groundbreaking work in Life Between

Lives (LBL) hypnotherapy profoundly shaped the field of spiritual regression. His books, *Journey of Souls* (1994) and *Destiny of Souls* (2000), present detailed case studies from clients who, under deep hypnosis, recalled memories of the afterlife, soul existence, and spiritual realms between incarnations. Newton's meticulous documentation of these sessions revealed consistent patterns – such as soul groups, councils of elders, and the soul's journey of learning through reincarnation – offering a structured framework for understanding human existence beyond the physical. His founding of The Newton Institute for Life Between Lives Hypnotherapy formalised training for practitioners, spreading his methods worldwide. Newton's work has influenced countless spiritual seekers, therapists, and researchers, providing a foundation for exploring the soul's purpose and fostering a deeper appreciation for the interconnectedness of all life.

People describe evaluations, research options and places and things they do when in their spiritual home. Throughout the text, I've used the descriptions applied by Michael Newton, such as the Council, the Library and Life Selection for consistency of terminology and clarity. Although people will give slightly different descriptions of these activities, a common naming convention will be helpful to the reader to know what's going on. They are specific names pertinent to these explorations and as such are capitalised in all the text.

End of Narration

Occasionally, I will allow an entire conversation to run freely. Some people are deeply connected with their past lives, and the continuity of these discussions can be very helpful. Often, I ask similar questions, but responses vary, so I've retained all the questions. Sometimes, to maintain continuity with a particularly interesting account, I'll present the entire conversation as it happened.

Names used are not people's real names, nor are the initials. Where names are mentioned within the testimony, I have altered them to protect the anonymity of the individual, as explained, but everything else is directly from the recorded testimony. Clients share their experiences under their anonymised names, but spiritual or past-life names may emerge during sessions. I use "people" to describe both their human and soul identities, such as when souls meet their Council.

Names and place details are often a close approximation, sometimes misinterpreted between the information source and the client. Sometimes, the investigative mind can find a person's name or a place name from the past and sometimes not. Either way, it doesn't help much. If the name exists, then we know of it and so might the client, if it doesn't it may be a misinterpretation or not yet known. Most importantly, it's the benefit the client gets from a better understanding of their existence that counts.

The testimony that appears in the text comes from directly transcribed audio files recorded at the time of the client's LBL (Life Between Lives) or PLR (Past Life Regression) session. Every client has formally agreed to their testimony being used in helping others understand the nature of their spirituality. The testimony comes from people who are deeply relaxed and experiencing something quite new.

Text cannot fully capture the emotion or hesitancy in clients' voices. To enhance readability, I've removed repetitive stutters (e.g., "um, um") while preserving the testimony's meaning. Nothing material is removed, and nothing is added.

The intention of this book is to show you a broader aspect of your existence so that you might more easily come to terms with your own life and your inner beliefs. We begin by revealing part of the journey back in time in the womb. It is the first question I ask that has no direct connection to the person they are today or their current life experiences. One question seeks that connection from before conception, from before any current existence became a reality. I ask at what month of the pregnancy did the soul join with the foetus.

The answer to that cannot come from even the earliest memories of the current existence, yet people do answer, often without hesitation, as if it is a known fact residing in a different set of memories – those we are normally unaware of.

The first part of the book will focus on the past to engender a sense of awe and wonder that people can be so clear and descriptive about a past life. A part of discovering our spiritual home lies in the lives we have lived, though in isolation they do not connect with the "everything" in the same way as with complete spiritual understanding. The past lives people have experienced provide the detail and clarity that confirm the broader reality of our spiritual existence.

This part is important. As a practising hypnotherapist, I had been largely dealing with the more practical issues people faced, helping them use their own ability to relax and reorganise some subconscious priorities and beliefs – such as stopping smoking more easily. The second speciality of my practice was finding and adjusting the behavioural drivers of those who use alcohol excessively and can't stop, even though they know it is damaging to them.

My book *The Sophisticated Alcoholic* (O-Books, 2011), edited by eminent Consultant Psychiatrist Dr James Kustow, explains this process in detail.

At some point, I chose to enter the field of Spiritual Regression. I can't easily explain why I felt the need to do that, but there is an inner voice – inner guidance – that we can easily mistake for random thought. As you read this book, you'll realise that help is always there if you listen to it, and it will help you recognise that not all your brilliant ideas are necessarily your own.

My first Past Lives session was a revelation. As the client described a past life in vivid detail, my heart raced, and I realised this was as real as the sunrise that morning – a glimpse into a truth beyond our everyday reality. Everyone must do something for the first time, and this was mine. Since then, of course, I've conducted hundreds of them – thousands of hours in helpful interrogation – but that wasn't the case then. Inducing trance is a learnt technique that most people could master, but in this process, we were stepping away from known reality. The first time I asked a client to describe a past life, it was a pivotal moment for both of us. The description of a former life – a seemingly impossible series of events recounted in detail in response to my questions – was transformative. It was only then that I realised this was real in every sense.

This is why an understanding of how and what people can recall will also be helpful – to allay concerns, to prove the process, and to stimulate your desire to know more.

The book is divided into sections and chapters. The sections cover major parts of the exploratory process, and the chapters present the evidence from people upon which our understandings are based. Different individual transcripts add a little more to the understanding of each section, aiming for as much completeness as possible.

Each section will raise issues. They do this by exploring the transcripts of my conversations with clients – my questions and their answers. Each set of experiences will be prefaced by an explanation of what is to come, followed by the verbatim conversation. Where it is necessary to provide additional explanation within the conversation, I'll do so, ensuring you know it is my interpretation of what is being said and not part of the verbatim transcript.

One of the principal objectives of the book is to help you make sense of your broader existence and apply this knowledge to your own life. Issues raised will be discussed at the end of each chapter, and the entire section will then be summarised to encapsulate the salient points simply.

Join me on this journey to uncover the eternal truths of your soul.

Section 1

First Connections: Introduction

The hypnotic induction is a process that helps clients to achieve the necessary level of relaxation and detachment from their conscious mind. It's akin to those fleeting moments just before you fall asleep or the seconds after waking, just before a vivid dream fades completely. It's when brilliant ideas emerge or solutions to long-standing problems suddenly appear. However, just achieving this state isn't enough. Dr Michael Newton's years of work showed that practising memory recovery improves recollection of the spiritual realm or past lives.

During the process, we explore real childhood memories in depth, such as asking what's in someone's pocket or telling them to look inside a school desk when in a memory of being in a classroom. The development of such techniques dramatically improves recollection and recovery of long-lost memories.

We'll typically regress to 12 years, 7 years and then to the youngest memory they have before seeking memories of the client's period in the womb.

All these memories are real, in the sense that they happened in the client's current life. Even the womb experiences are unarguably part of this life. Scepticism, hesitancy, or concern about the session fades when recovering "real" life memories, making the process doubly effective.

The womb period, however, offers the first glimpse of a connection we're normally unaware of. Our soul existence is revealed when the first non-worldly question is asked.

Our immortal spirit connects with the physical human foetus sometime after conception. From the great deal of work already completed in this area, we know that older, more experienced souls tend to join the foetus a little later than younger souls.

Critically, this question is the first one that is not about "real" world things. It's not something from the current life which, hitherto all previous questions had been. It is the first one that requires soul memory to answer – the very first bridge between this life and the immortal soul's existence.

Most people answer promptly and instinctively.

This section, consisting of five short chapters, delves into the profound and often mysterious connection between the soul and its physical host during the prenatal phase, as revealed through hypnotic regression sessions. Each chapter presents a unique perspective from individuals – Rosemary, Alice, Oakley, Urban, and Wendy –guided by the facilitator, DA, to recall their experiences in the womb. These accounts illuminate the soul's varying degrees of comfort, awareness, and intention as it integrates with the developing foetus. Drawing on themes from Dr Michael Newton's research, the narratives explore the timing of soul-body connection, the soul's freedom to depart, and its subtle interactions with the mother's emotions and physical state. Together, these chapters offer a rich tapestry of insights into the spiritual dynamics of incarnation, setting the stage for deeper explorations in later sessions.

Section 1

Chapter 1a: Rosemary Aldridge

DA: Moving back now, it's a time just before you were born. Feel this dark, warm, moist environment. I'll ask you a couple of simple questions. First, can you tell me if your arms and legs are reasonably comfortable?

RA: They're not particularly comfortable, but I consider it better than being out. I'm a bit tall in there.

DA: Is it better in there or out here?

RA: I'm very uncomfortable, really.

DA: Can you hear or feel your mother's heartbeat?

RA: I can hear it.

DA: Can you sense your mother's emotions from time to time?

RA: All the time.

DA: Are you able to influence her emotions occasionally? For example, to calm her when she's stressed?

RA: It's as if whatever I do, she doesn't notice. It's like being on a rough sea.

DA: I'll ask a few questions about your joining with this body. Now that you've spent a few months inside it, do you have any feelings about this body that you'd like to share?

Narration

This marks the first recognition of two entities: the soul and the foetus's physical body.

End of Narration

RA: I don't like it at all. It's very uncomfortable. It's toxic. She's not at home in her body, so she doesn't really want to be there herself anyway.

3

DA: I'm asking about your body – the question is about how you feel in your body.

RA: Oh, okay. How do I feel in my body? I don't like it. It's an increasing sense of being imprisoned. I'm going to have as little contact with it as possible until I have to be in it fully.

DA: Do you spend much time away from it?

RA: Almost all the time. But I'm battling because the ones teaching me want me to stay. My whole world revolves around this process – going through it and understanding it from every angle.

DA: At what point in the gestation period did you first join with this foetus?

RA: I was connected from the moment of conception, but I can increase or decrease that connection. I nearly left it altogether at two months.

DA: Why was that?

RA: I didn't want to face it. I wanted to run away. I don't like the earth very much.

Narration

After the initial connection, souls may leave their human hosts during early gestation when their presence is less needed. Once connected, the soul and body are linked, but the soul retains freedom to depart. Not all soul energy is used in an incarnation – the amount varies with the soul's advancement, with experienced souls leaving part of their essence in the spiritual realm, a timeless home we never fully leave.

End of Narration

RA: It was impulsive. It felt like I did something and then regretted it. I tried to stick it out, but all the time, I just wanted to leave.

DA: But in making that initial connection and joining with the human brain, was that easier or more difficult than usual?

RA: I'm just listening… It was easy because I've done it so many times. But there's a kind of desperation too – like, "Here we go again." I put shutters down in my mind. My challenge is to hold the full awareness I have when I'm not in a body, but I skip it when I'm in one. I've been training to do that.

DA: Why did you choose this body?

RA: I'm not sure I did.

DA: That's okay. We can come back to that later. Can you—

RA: I chose to be a woman.

DA: Would you say you normally choose female incarnations over male ones?

RA: No, I feel better in men's bodies. It's safer.

DA: Can you discern any difference in character between your soul and this body?

RA: I'm not quite understanding you.

DA: It doesn't matter. If there's no answer, it's fine to say "I don't know" because your memories will become clearer as we progress. That's good.

RA: There's someone else there – a twin. I can see that. I feel guilty about taking this body because someone else had an option on it too. I can feel that envy strongly. I feel grief around it. That makes sense in many areas of my life. I feel I took this position, so now I must give a lot away because of what I took…

DA: Okay. I want to return to this later from a clearer perspective – not while you're in the womb. We'll revisit this issue when you have a clearer view.

Chapter 1b: Alice Archer

DA: Moving back, it's a time just before you were born. Feel this dark, warm, moist environment. I'm going to ask a couple of easy questions. First, Alice, can you tell me if your arms and legs are reasonably comfortable?

AA: Yes.

DA: It's nearly time for you to be born. Can you hear or feel your mother's heartbeat?

AA: No.

DA: Can you sense your mother's emotions from time to time?

AA: Yes, I think she's happy.

DA: Are you able to influence her emotions, for example, if she were under stress?

AA: No.

DA: Now that you've spent a few months inside this new body, do you have any feelings about it that you'd like to share? For example, will you find it interesting to work in this body?

AA: I don't really have any feelings or thoughts.

DA: That's okay. It's fine to say so. If I ask a question and you don't know, just say you don't know. When did your soul's consciousness join with this foetus? At what point in its growth?

AA: I think it was late – maybe just before birth.

DA: Which month?

AA: Eighth or ninth.

DA: Is it usual for you to join late or was this a special case?

AA: Just the way things worked out.

DA: Do you think this body is a good match for your soul's consciousness?

AA: It's okay. It's a little confused and nervous.

DA: Can you discern any character differences between your soul and this body?

AA: It has potential.

DA: Do you know why you chose this body?

AA: It likes to help others.

Chapter 1c: Oakley Howell

DA: Now, we'll move to a time just before you were born. As you feel my hand gently touching your forehead, you'll be in your mother's womb, just before your birth. Tell me, Oakley, are you comfortable? Are your arms and legs reasonably comfortable? I know it can be cramped in there.

OH: No, it actually feels like there's quite a lot of space.

DA: Okay, that's good. I'd like to ask a few questions about this time. Can you hear or feel your mother's heartbeat?

OH: Yes.

DA: Can you feel your mother's emotions from time to time?

OH: Sometimes, not very often.

DA: If you sense she might be stressed, are you able to influence her emotional state at all or is it just something you're aware of?

OH: No, I can't influence her.

DA: Now that you've spent a few months inside this body, do you have any feelings about the new foetus that you'd like to share? For example, do you think you'll find it interesting to work with this body?

OH: I will find it interesting, but... I feel a sense of... not being entirely happy about leaving my home.

DA: What was the choice of this incarnation – why did you choose to do it at this time? Why this particular body? It doesn't matter if—

OH: It seems to be about... the emotion... What I'm feeling is that I'm going to Earth to help, to make a difference in other people's lives. But at the same time, I feel trepidation that I won't be strong enough to help them directly – maybe only indirectly.

DA: Let me ask about the joining. Was integrating with this body easy or difficult this time?

OH: I found it easy.

DA: Do you think this body is a good match for your soul's consciousness?

OH: I think so.

DA: What month did you first join this foetus?

OH: About April, I think. So, which month of the pregnancy would that be? Maybe the third – about a month or two.

DA: Was this particularly early for you? Do you normally join at one or two months?

OH: No, it's about normal for me.

DA: Can you tell me why you chose this body? Is that clear to you now?

OH: Not quite clear, no.

DA: That's okay. While we're here, is there anything else about the joining or working with the body that you'd like to share? Anything that comes to mind?

OH: I'm starting to feel my mother's emotions now. She has mixed feelings about carrying me because she's quite old. But I know she'll be a perfect mother. She'll nurture me to the point where I can be of value down here.

Section 1

Chapter 1d: Urban Ogden

DA: And it's the time just before you're about to be born – not a minute before, but a day before. I want to ask you a few questions about this experience. Can you tell me, are you comfortable? Though it's rather cramped inside the womb, are your arms and legs in a reasonably comfortable position now?

UO: [No response recorded.]

DA: Some interesting questions: can you feel, hear, or detect your mother's heartbeat in any way? If she's under stress or happy, can you sense that? Does it come through to you? For example, if she's very happy, what sensations do you get? And if she's upset, can you detect that? Is there anything you can do to influence it – make her feel more peaceful – or is it something you have no control over?

UO: It feels like I don't have control.

DA: You don't have control?

UO: It feels that way. It's like I'm trying, but no one's listening, so that's why it feels like that.

DA: Urban, tell me, at what month in the pregnancy did your spiritual soul join this foetus?

UO: First, second, maybe third – around there.

DA: Do you always remain with the foetus?

UO: No.

Narration

Urban's ability to leave the foetus confirms Dr Michael Newton's findings that the soul's energy retains freedom to depart after the initial connection, with part of the soul remaining in the spiritual realm.
End of Narration

10

DA: So, where do you go when you're taking a break, as it were?

UO: Back to the others. We're making sure the time is right for each of us to go to our place.

DA: Was this particular joining with this foetus an easy transition for you?

UO: Yeah, of course.

DA: Is it always that easy?

UO: Yeah, always. I was just about to say that.

DA: Do you feel that the body your soul will work with in this lifetime is a good match for your soul's consciousness and personality?

UO: Yeah.

DA: Is there anything else about this time in your mother's womb that you think might be important to this process today that you'd like to share?

UO: I can't think of anything. I just let her know from time to time that she should have a different type of nutrition because it would be good for the baby. It's like a signal I'm sending out to her, and she responds.

DA: Is it mental or physical?

UO: No, it's mental – but not mental as we understand it. It's like a signal from my heart to her heart.

Chapter 1e: Wendy King

DA: And it's now the time just before you were born. I'm going to ask you some really easy questions. First, Wendy, can you tell me if your arms and legs are reasonably comfortable?

WK: Yes, I think so. I know it's probably a little cramped in there because it's nearly time to be born.

DA: Can you hear or feel your mother's heartbeat?

WK: Yes, I can feel it's time to go. One wonderful thing about being in this memory is that we can hold time for a while. So, even though birth is probably imminent, time at this moment is standing still.

DA: I'd like to ask you some questions about your time in the womb. Can you feel your mother's emotions from time to time?

WK: Yes, I can.

DA: Do you sense when she's stressed or happy?

WK: Yes, I think she wanted a baby.

DA: Is there anything you can do to calm her emotional state if she's upset?

WK: I can't think of anything.

DA: That's okay. Now, Wendy, you've had a chance to spend several months inside this foetus. Do you have any feelings about the body you're in now that you'd like to share? For example, do you think you'll find it interesting to work with this body?

WK: I think I will.

DA: Is the body a good match for your soul's consciousness?

WK: Yes, I think so. I sometimes wonder why I chose it, though.

DA: Was the integration process easy or difficult?

WK: I think it was easy. Having made up my mind to go with it, I found it easy.

DA: What are your impressions over the last few months with the brain you've been working with?

WK: I think this brain is quite good, but not really very original.

DA: That's good. What month did you join the foetus?

WK: June.

DA: And how old was the foetus at that time?

WK: It was born in December.

DA: Three months in?

WK: Yeah, three to four.

DA: Can you discern any character differences between your soul and this body?

WK: I think this body's a bit weak-willed.

DA: How does it compare with other bodies you've had in other lives? For instance, it's female – is that different for you?

WK: I think so. There've been various... sometimes men, sometimes women.

DA: As I ask these questions, you'll notice an impression will occur to you as the answer. It might be crystal clear – an image, a sound, something you know to be true. Sometimes you'll be uncertain, and it's okay to say "I don't know". What's revealed will be pertinent and relevant to you. Why did you choose this body?

WK: I'm not sure. I see a life that's fortunate in many ways – easy in some ways, incredibly difficult in others. It's sort of divided in two, if you know what I mean.

DA: That's good.

First Connections: Summary

The chapters in this section reveal the complex and individualised nature of the soul's prenatal experience, highlighting both common themes and striking contrasts. Rosemary's intense discomfort and resistance to her body contrast with Alice's detached neutrality, suggesting differences in soul experience or energetic commitment. Oakley's sense of mission and early joining reflect a purposeful incarnation, while Urban's casual confidence and subtle influence on his mother's nutrition point to a seasoned soul's ease with the process. Wendy's acceptance of her body, tempered by awareness of its limitations, underscores a balanced perspective.

Collectively, these accounts align with Dr Michael Newton's findings on the soul's variable timing and freedom during gestation, illustrating how souls navigate the transition from the spiritual realm to physical embodiment with unique motivations, challenges, and connections to their human hosts. These foundational insights pave the way for further exploration of the soul's journey in subsequent sessions.

The Past: Introduction

Prepare to embark on an extraordinary journey through the annals of the soul, where the veil of time is lifted to reveal the awe-inspiring tapestry of human existence across centuries. The past-life experiences of Nora, Elias, Rachel, and Theodore offer a breathtaking glimpse into the eternal voyage of the soul, each narrative pulsating with vivid sensory details, emotional depth. and spiritual revelations that will captivate and inspire.

These four distinct experiences – spanning the gritty streets of seventeenth-century London, the golden fields of a nineteenth-century farm, the enigmatic tropes of an otherworldly encounter, and the poignant struggles of early twentieth-century America – unfold like chapters in a cosmic saga, inviting readers to bear witness to the soul's resilience. complexity, and interconnectedness. As you delve into these accounts, anticipate profound lessons on love, loss, gender. sexual cognisance in the opposite gender, and the futility of self-destruction, each session illuminating the soul's purpose and the transformative power of understanding one's eternal nature.

Prepare to be moved by the raw humanity and spiritual grandeur of these revelations, which promise to ignite a sense of wonder and curiosity about the timeless journey we all share.

Chapter 2: Nora Thornton

This chapter presents a vivid exploration of Nora Thornton's past-life regression, guided by the facilitator, DA, through a hypnotic trance that unveils two distinct lifetimes. The session begins in a bustling seventeenth-century London street, where Nora recalls her life as Nell, a woman immersed in a vibrant yet impoverished community.

The narrative then shifts to a contrasting twentieth-century experience as Katrina, a young woman on holiday in an African country, grappling with feelings of disorientation and unease. The seamless transitions between these lives, and the return to Nell's story, highlight the soul's ability to navigate multiple incarnations, each marked by unique emotional and sensory details.

This transcript illustrates the profound connection between Nora's current self and her past lives, offering insights into the soul's continuity and the lessons carried across time. The session culminates in Nell's poignant transition from a life of hardship to the serene embrace of the spiritual realm, underscoring the transformative power of past-life recall.

> **DA:** Nora, is it day or night?
>
> **NT:** Day.
>
> **DA:** Hot or cold?
>
> **NT:** Lovely and warm.
>
> **DA:** Are you outside or inside?
>
> **NT:** Outside.
>
> **DA:** Do you know if you're in a city or town?
>
> **NT:** I think it's a city.
>
> **DA:** Are you alone?

NT: No, there are people all around. It's busy.

DA: How are you dressed?

NT: Long skirt. Sort of quite scruffy.

DA: Small or large?

NT: Quite small. It's like an old-fashioned street. People are calling; it's all quite raucous, quite friendly, but sort of shouting. It's like I would imagine an old-fashioned London street.

DA: What's your name?

NT: I don't know.

DA: What year is it?

NT: Oh, a long time ago. People around? Mm.

DA: Do you know what they're saying?

NT: London. It's London. London accents, rough London accents. Old-fashioned clothes.

DA: Is anybody near you?

NT: Yeah, people bustling around, carrying things.

DA: Are there shops?

NT: No, there are barrows with fruit and vegetables in them. But no, I don't think they're shops. They're houses.

DA: Are you standing near a house?

NT: I'm in the middle of the street, and they're very close on the other side.

DA: What are the houses like?

NT: Little, or wooden.

DA: Who's the nearest person to you?

NT: There's someone in a window upstairs. They're leaning out of the window.

DA: Can they see you?

NT: The window, the top window, is overhanging. I think I might have to move back a bit. Yeah, they can see me now.

DA: How old are you?

NT: I think I'm – I don't know – I'm not young. Forty, maybe, but yeah, I think I'm forty.

DA: What are you wearing on your feet?

NT: Some funny sort of scruffy shoes. They're almost like little boots.

DA: Are you wearing a hat?

NT: Yeah, it's white. It's more like a sort of cotton bonnet thing. Worn out, filthy, grubby. My arms are covered; teeth are bad. Missing teeth. A lot of them are missing. I think I've got six on the top and about four on the bottom, and they're dirty-looking teeth. I don't ever clean them.

DA: Are you hungry?

NT: No. Not hungry.

DA: Do you live nearby?

NT: Mm, I live in the street. I know all the people around me.

DA: What's on your mind?

NT: Mary in the upstairs window. I don't know.

DA: Just look around. See the people. If you see someone you know, just look at them until they become a little clearer. And then they may… Whilst you're doing that, I'll just have to turn the microphone up a little bit.

NT: I'll just keep looking around.

NT: There are dogs there too. Stray sort of dogs.

DA: As soon as you remember your name, just tell me what it is. Is there anybody here close enough to talk to?

NT: Mm.

DA: Walk over to them and talk to them. Say something.

NT: His name's Jack.

DA: What have you said to him?

NT: Just said, "Hello, Jack."

DA: What was he saying?

NT: He's teasing me. Like flirting teasing, but we know it's just… jokey. You know, it's not serious. It's just jokey.

DA: What does he say?

NT: He tells me I look lovely as ever and he's called me Nell. He's got fruit and vegetables.

Narration

You'll recall that Nell didn't know her name initially, but it was revealed to her by Jack. This is a useful way of obtaining such information.

End of Narration

DA: Ask him what year it is.

NT: 1610.

DA: Nell, how do you feel?

NT: I feel safe. I'm where I belong. It's home, and I like all the hustle and bustle around me. There are children. Lots of them.

DA: Are any of them nearby?

NT: Yeah, there are children playing in the street as well. And mine are playing with… Some of them are playing with other children. There's lots of laughter and… It's a happy place. We're all very poor, but it's happy. It smells.

DA: What does it smell of?

NT: Rotten, nasty. But we don't really notice it because it's always there. There's water in the streets. It's not raining. Dogs are scavenging. I think they're stray dogs. I don't know. We don't have baths. We all look really scruffy and shabby, run-down.

DA: Now, all I want you to do is, you're looking around in the street. Close your eyes, as now. And we're going to move again. I don't know whether it'll be backwards or forwards. We'll be in another place in a moment. As you move through the tunnel of time, your eyes close. Be in the sense of drifting, moving through time. And you open your eyes again. We'll be in another place. Open your eyes and look around. And tell me, is it daytime or nighttime?

NT: It's night. Clouds, clouds in the sky there. Full moon. Hot, balmy.

DA: Are you outside or inside?

NT: Outside.

DA: Are you alone?

NT: No. I don't know who it is.

DA: Are you male or female?

NT: Female.

DA: How are you dressed?

NT: Got a skirt on. It's like tropical weather.

DA: What kind of skirt is it?

NT: Short. And I've got a sleeveless top on.

DA: What's it made from?

NT: Just like a fine sort of cotton material.

DA: Look at your arm. What colour is your skin?

NT: Really brown, lovely suntan.

DA: How old are you?

NT: Quite young. Thirties, maybe twenties.

DA: What's your name?

NT: Karina, Katrina. I think it's Katrina.

DA: How many people are here?

NT: One. One Black man.

DA: What's his name?

NT: It begins with M.

DA: What's he wearing?

NT: Trousers and a short-sleeve shirt. Light-coloured trousers and a patterned short-sleeve shirt. We've been out. He's, my partner.

DA: Are you married?

NT: No. I'm single.

DA: Have you known him long?

NT: No. Not long.

DA: What do you feel about the situation?

NT: Lost. That's all it is. But I know I shouldn't be there. I don't care.

DA: Why are you there?

NT: Because I want to be. We're just… we're not standing that close. And we're talking, not about him and me, but just things in general. I'm on holiday. I live in England.

DA: Where are you on holiday? What's the name of this place?

NT: I'm in an African country, but I don't know where. There's lots of nighttime noises around. Not scary, but like insect noises. And things screeching, you know, not frightening though.

DA: What are you talking about now?

NT: We've been out for a meal. We're talking about the meal. And I know I should go. I'm trying to get away. But I don't know where we are, and I don't know how to go home.

DA: How did you get there?

NT: Taxi.

DA: What's happening now, Katrina?

NT: He's trying to persuade me to stay with him. I'm starting to get a bit frightened because I don't know how I'll get from there. I should have stayed with my friends. I'm not frightened of him. I think it's best if I stay. Get a taxi home in the morning.

DA: Where would you stay? Is there a house there?

NT: Yes.

DA: It's his house, is it?

NT: Yes.

DA: Are you inside the house?

NT: No, still outside. I'm staying. I've decided I've got to until I find out where I am. Then to stay.

DA: What are you both actually doing?

NT: Walking to the house.

DA: Are you talking?

NT: Mm. He says there's wine in the house.

DA: Just relate to me the conversation as it occurs.

NT: He doesn't normally have wine in the house, he's saying, but he has got some. And I'm thinking that's all right. The house looks quite nice.

DA: What year is it?

NT: Don't know. It's 1990. No, no, no. Don't know.

DA: Tell me what's happening.

NT: I'm going in the house. And it's chaos in there.

DA: In what way?

NT: It's just a shambles and untidy. Quite scruffy. The man who lives on his own and doesn't... just doesn't get round to doing anything. Lots of washing up, piled up, and clothes everywhere. Not nasty, just a shambles.

DA: Just keep describing what's happening as it occurs.

NT: I'm sitting down.

DA: Just keep talking about things.

NT: I'm sitting down. He's opening a wine bottle. He's got two glasses. He's poured the wine. I'm feeling uncomfortable though. I don't really want to be here. There's no phone. There's no phone in the house, because I've asked. I've changed my mind, and I think it's best if I go home. But there's no telephone in there to call a taxi. I'm feeling quite uncomfortable, really. No, I shouldn't be here. No, he's been okay about it. Been a gentleman.

DA: What's happening now?

NT: I'm feeling very uncomfortable about staying. But he's been a real gentleman. I say I'll sleep on the sofa. And he says, no, it's all right. He will. I'm feeling safer. I shouldn't be here. It's okay. It's okay. He's saying he wants to show me around tomorrow. But there's no car. I don't understand.

He says he can borrow one. He wants to show me around. I'm with friends, and I say I can't. He says they can come, too. But there's too many of us. There's four of us.

DA: What are your friends' names?

NT: Catherine. Melanie. Elizabeth.

DA: And where are you now?

NT: Sitting down.

DA: Just close your eyes. And we will move again. Tell me, is it daytime or nighttime?

NT: I'm back in the same street.

DA: Are you new?

NT: Yes.

DA: How old are you now?

NT: Forty. I'm not really sure, but I don't know how old I am. I'm about that, though. I don't know when I was born. I don't keep records, really.

DA: What's happening around you?

NT: The street's quieter now. People are going home. There's little dogs scavenging.

DA: Are there any children near you?

NT: No, not really. Children, they sort of do what they want, really. It's difficult to feed them, though. No, no money. We have bread. With fruit and vegetables. Don't really have meat. Children are sick a lot. I'd like to do more for them, but I can't. I haven't really got anyone to ask to help. Just struggle on.

DA: We need to move forward. To the most recent place. To an appropriate point in your life.

NT: No, I can't leave. This is where I belong. I should stay here. I have children to look after. I worry about my daughter. She's very weak and pale.

DA: What's your daughter's name?

NT: Mim. She's nine.

DA: Is she near to you?

NT: I'm in the house now. She's sitting down. She's very pale and quiet. I'm smiling at her. She's trying to smile back, but her heart's not in it. She looks so sad. She's got long brown hair. I'd like to be able to do something nice for her, but I can't. Because there isn't the money.

DA: Look very closely at her. Look very closely. Look closely into her eyes. Look deep into her eyes.

NT: We both know she's not going to live. She's got something bad. Chest problems, coughing. I can't afford medicine. And I'm just thinking, well, when it happens, it'll be one less mouth to feed.

DA: How do you feel about that?

NT: Well, I know it's going to happen. And I think I've accepted it. She's eating bread, just dry bread. Some broth. And I keep thinking of her having something warm inside. That would be good.

DA: And now, I want you to close your eyes at that point. I don't want you to stay as now. But I want you to move forward. Move forward to an appropriate other time in your life. A time of significance. When you are there, open your eyes and tell me what you see.

NT: I'm not well.

DA: How old are you?

NT: I'm old, but… I'm forty-something, but I'm old. Been a hard life.

DA: Where's Mim?

NT: Mim's died. Mim's gone. But that's okay. I knew it would happen. It was the coughing. The chest. It's what did it. Still in the same house. There's more space in the beds now. One person less. Try to wash clothes. If I hang them out, they're just as dirty. I do my best. I've lost a lot of weight.

DA: Now, I want you to move forward. I want you to move forward to your bed.

NT: I've got a deep pain in my chest. Hurts. I've been in bed quite a long time. Neighbours are coming in to see me. Very kind. I'm ready to go. It's hot and I'm sweating. Bright light. Peaceful. I can hear birds. There's grass. I've never ever seen grass before. I feel all light. I'm me, but I'm different. I'm clean. There's lots of people. I don't know any of them, though, but they know me. It's like I'm being welcomed. They're all really pleased to see me. It's all very happy. Everyone looks well, and they're smiling and laughing. It's all green and sunny and beautiful trees. And it's just so new to me. I've never seen anything like this. I only know towns. I only know my street.

Chapter Summary

Nora Thornton's regression session is a striking testament to the soul's multifaceted journey through time, uniquely capturing the emotional depth and sensory richness of two distinct past lives. The vivid portrayal of Nell's life in 1610 London – a world of raucous camaraderie, poverty, and familial devotion – contrasts sharply with Katrina's fleeting, disoriented experience in a 1990s African setting, marked by uncertainty and a yearning for safety.

The fluid movement between these lives, reveals the soul's ability to retain and recall intricate details across centuries, from the smell of rotting streets to the chaos of an untidy house. Nell's story stands out for its emotional weight, as Nora grapples with the loss of her daughter, Mim, and the harsh realities of survival, only to find profound peace in her spiritual transition. This session's uniqueness lies in its blend of gritty historical immersion and modern introspection, offering Nora a deeper understanding of her soul's resilience and the enduring human spirit amidst adversity.

Chapter 3: Elias Young

This chapter delves into a concise yet evocative past-life regression session with Elias Young. Unlike extended past-life narratives, this session offers a brief glimpse into Elias's life as Geoffrey Sinclair, a nineteenth-century farmer overseeing a harvest in a rural setting. The vivid sensory details – fields under a late afternoon sun, workers in white coats, and the distant farmhouse – emerge with remarkable clarity, showcasing the soul's ability to recall fleeting moments from a distant incarnation.

The session's brevity, a hallmark of LBL's focus on broader spiritual insights, underscores its unique purpose: to touch upon a single life's essence before moving toward a deeper understanding of the soul's eternal journey. Elias's reflections on his contentment and familial ties provide a poignant snapshot of a life grounded in simplicity and duty.

Once again, the clarity and detail of the recollections is amazing.

DA: Now, firstly, tell me, is it daytime or nighttime?

EY: Daytime.

DA: Are you alone or with others?

EY: With others around.

DA: But not actually with you, no? Is it cold?

EY: Warm. We are outside, and we are in fields. It's a farm, I think. Men have got white shirts and white coats.

DA: Like they used to look? How old are you? Don't know? Trying to focus – are you working there with them?

EY: No, I think I'm in charge of them. I'm not one of them – on a paddock set.

DA: Are you male?

EY: I think I'm a farmer.

DA: What's your name?

EY: Geoffrey or Jess.

DA: What year is it? I don't know – that's okay. Sometimes when I ask you a question...

EY: 1897.

DA: Thirteen?

Narration

I didn't hear clearly so am checking if it's eighteen or thirteen

End of Narration

EY: I'm not sure about that. It just seems not coming to me.

DA: Yeah, sometimes when I ask you a question, the answer might not immediately be there, and it's okay to say "I don't know", but of course, it will come to you at some point, as will your age.

EY: There are no tractors – it's horses. That must be old.

DA: Is the farmhouse nearby?

EY: No, it's in the distance.

DA: But is the land you're on – is it all part of your farm?

EY: No.

DA: So, what's happening at the moment? I mean, men are working – what are they actually doing?

EY: I think we've just got the harvest in. We've been getting it in.

DA: So, this is something – having a break, standing around? This is something which is quite usual for you? This is, in effect, your life. What time of day is it?

EY: Late afternoon. The blokes are happy – they've had a good day's work.

DA: And, presumably, it's nearly over as well for them, is it?

EY: They like working for me.

DA: Are you happy?

EY: Yep, I'm happy, they're happy.

DA: Okay, are you married?

EY: I don't know. Can't move away from the scene with the blokes, the farmhouse.

DA: That's okay because it's late afternoon – it's nearly time to end the work for the day. So, it'll be quite quick and easy for you, as you stand there, to move to the point where you go back to the farmhouse, go back home, go back to have tea. Let's just move quickly back up to the house.

EY: There's a wife and two children.

DA: What's your wife's name?

EY: Mary.

DA: What's your surname?

EY: Sinclair?

DA: And the children – what are the children's names?

EY: The girl's called Rose, and the boy's called Martin.

DA: How old are they?

EY: The boy's six, the girl four.

DA: How old are you?

EY: Thirty-seven?

DA: Just tell me a little bit about how you feel about your life.

EY: It's fine. My wife's a good wife, but she's not my soulmate.

DA: Do you have a good living?

EY: Reasonable. I'm not rich – it's comfortable.

DA: Would you say that you were content with your contribution in your life – that you were doing?

EY: I like the land. I like what I'm doing.

DA: How do you prefer to be called? Is it Jess or Geoffrey?

EY: Geoffrey.

DA: Geoffrey, we're now going to move to the last day of your life. In a moment, I'm going to count to three, and when I reach the number three, you will be in the last day of your life, and I'm going to ask you some questions about that as I begin to count now.

Chapter Summary

Elias Young's regression session stands out for its succinct yet richly detailed portrayal of a single past life as Geoffrey Sinclair, a 37-year-old farmer in 1897. The session's unique brevity, characteristic of Life Between Lives explorations, captures the essence of Geoffrey's existence – marked by the satisfaction of a good harvest, the camaraderie of his workers, and a comfortable, if unremarkable, family life – without delving into extended narratives.

The clarity of Elias's recollections, from the warmth of the fields to the names of his children, Rose and Martin, highlights the soul's remarkable capacity to access precise memories from a distant era. Unlike deeper past-life explorations, this session's fleeting focus on a single moment underscores its role as a stepping stone to broader spiritual insights, offering Elias a glimpse of his soul's grounded resilience and the quiet fulfilment found in a life of honest labour.

Chapter 4: Rachel Carter

The exploration of gender and sexuality is a cornerstone of human experience, deeply intertwined with questions of identity, embodiment, and personal growth. In modern society, discussions about gender fluidity, identity, and the spectrum of sexual expression dominate cultural and philosophical discourse, reflecting a growing recognition of the complexity of these concepts.

Within the framework of reincarnation and soul development, as presented in Rachel's past-life regression, gender preferences take on a profound spiritual dimension. Souls, as amorphous beings of pure energy, are not bound by physical forms but choose to incarnate as male or female to experience the unique pleasures, challenges, and perspectives each offers. This choice is not arbitrary but essential, serving as a mechanism for karmic balance and spiritual evolution. Experiencing both male and female incarnations allows souls to cultivate empathy, understand power dynamics, and integrate diverse aspects of existence, in an era where gender norms are increasingly questioned.

Rachel's description of sexual arousal, copulation and orgasm as a man comes from a perspective that can only be experienced through living that life again, with the ability that only deep and immersive memories can facilitate.

This perspective underscores the undeniable necessity of embodying both forms to achieve a holistic understanding of life, offering insights that resonate with contemporary debates on identity and equality.

DA: Are you on a street or a road somewhere, in a city or a town?

RC: No. It's kind of stuck in time. I don't see buildings or trees. It's alone and nothing.

DA: Is it hot or cold?

RC: It's neutral.

DA: Let me ask you a few questions about yourself as you are there. Do you know if you're male or female?

RC: No, I don't know. I feel neutral.

DA: Look at your left arm and hand in this memory. You can just lift the hand up in the memory and look at it. Tell me, what colour is the skin?

RC: Reddish.

DA: Do you have any clothing on the arm?

RC: No.

DA: Do you have any clothing on the top part of your body?

RC: Can't see, no.

DA: Is your hair long or short?

RC: Short.

DA: Are you wearing any clothing on the bottom half of your body?

RC: No. No clothes.

DA: So, if you look down at your body, you can tell me if you're male or female.

Narration

There was a snort and a bit of a giggle from the client.

End of Narration

DA: Okay, so what happened there?

RC: It's not female.

DA: Male?

RC: Yes.

DA: Okay, you can tell that. Why?

RC: I can see dark hair.

Narration
This was obviously a surprise to her, and the giggling contin-
ued for a bit.
End of Narration

DA: And? Yes. That's okay, you're doing very well. Are you
a big man or a small man, in height and size?

RC: It's not big. It's average.

DA: Are you young?

RC: Yes, it's athletic.

DA: How old are you?

RC: Thirty... thirty-nine, thirty-seven.

DA: So, you're an adult male?

RC: Yes.

DA: Is there a reason why you aren't wearing any clothes? Is
that normal dress for you?

RC: I'm in a sort of laboratory. It's just white.

DA: White floor and white walls?

RC: Yes, nothing. It's like empty space. There are no trees,
nothing. It's just confined.

DA: Are the walls there?

RC: Yes.

DA: Is there a door in the room that you're in?

RC: Yes, I see a door.

DA: Why are you in a room without any clothes on?

RC: I don't know.

DA: Is it an experiment?

RC: No, no. It's kind of an experiment or something.

DA: Do you feel that you spend quite a lot of time without
clothes?

RC: I'm not cold, so no, not a lot of time.

DA: What's your name? It doesn't matter. If it's not clear
at this moment, it will become clearer in a little while.

How do you feel? Are you anxious or are you very comfortable and happy where you are?

RC: It feels like I'm okay with that.

DA: Do you know why you are there?

RC: It's kind of – yes, it's volunteering. I wasn't pushed there.

DA: Do you know what you're volunteering for?

RC: No, no.

DA: Okay, that's fine. Information will come to you. Look at your fingernails and toenails. Are they short?

RC: Yes.

DA: Are they well kept?

RC: Yes.

DA: Is your skin in good condition?

RC: Yes.

DA: Are you muscular?

RC: It's not that hairy, or the body is quite bald. I wouldn't say it's muscular. It's slender and nice-looking. Nice.

DA: What year is it? It's okay, it's okay. When it comes to you, if that appears to you, you can just tell me as and when it occurs. The same as your name – as soon as you know your name, then you can tell me. How long do you expect to remain in this room? For example, are you waiting for something to happen?

RC: I've been caught there by surprise. There is so much in the open now.

DA: There's so much what?

RC: There's something. There's a purpose.

DA: Okay, let's focus a little bit more on the body. Do you have any facial hair?

RC: No.

DA: If at any time you're unsure about the answers, you can always either look, or you can use your hands to touch your body to sense and feel.

RC: When I touch my face, it's like a little bit of feeling. It's shaved, short hair.

DA: Shaved, but it's not shaved today?

RC: No, it's kind of a little bit of hair.

DA: How many days would you say?

RC: Just one.

DA: Just one day?

RC: One or two. I mean, it's just, like, very, very short.

DA: Okay, look at your arms now and tell me the colour of the skin. Are you dark-skinned or light-skinned?

RC: No, it's light. It's light skinned.

DA: Light-skinned. Okay. Look at your abdomen, your tummy, and tell me – is it, what you would call athletic? No hair?

RC: No hair.

DA: But is it plump?

RC: No, it's quite athletic. It's well-built. It's not skinny. I feel it's a good, muscly body.

DA: Is it a strong body?

RC: Yes.

DA: Okay, look at the penis again. Is it circumcised?

RC: No, it's not. No. Okay. It's not. No. It's normal.

DA: Are there any hairs on the legs?

RC: Yes. Yeah. Yeah, there are.

DA: Okay.

RC: It's darkish hair.

DA: What is it that creates a reaction from you when you either talk about or look at the penis on this body?

RC: I want to laugh.

DA: Eh?

RC: I want to laugh.

DA: You want to laugh? Why is that?

RC: I don't know. It's strange to me.

DA: What did it do for you? Yes. Of course. What did it feel like?

RC: When I touch my head, my tummy, I feel very nice and strong. It's strong. It's a good body. I like it. And generally strong.

DA: Okay. What do you feel when you touch your penis? Well, it's yours – you can do what you like.

RC: I feel like… I feel testicles in my hand. Yeah? Yeah.

DA: What does it feel like when you do that?

RC: It's a nice feeling. Okay. It's not a bad feeling, but it's kind of pleasurable.

DA: If you continue to do that, can you feel a sense of excitement?

RC: If I continue, I think I will.

DA: Well, continue, because how many opportunities do you have to do this? So, continue. Tell me what's happening.

RC: Well, my penis is aroused. I don't know. I'm supposed to move. Yeah.

DA: It's what?

RC: It's aroused.

DA: It's hard. How does that make you feel?

RC: Kind of whole. Myself.

DA: Is it a satisfying feeling?

RC: Yes. Myself.

DA: Are you still caressing?

RC: No. I'm just enjoying being there and feeling myself in that body.

DA: If you continue to caress it, what do you think will happen?

RC: I don't want to continue.

DA: Okay. Why is that?

RC: I think it's not that – I'm not there for that.

DA: Okay. But this is quite a unique experience for your physical self in this current life. So, you have the opportunity to explore it as far as it can go. What is most important is what you learn from what you feel.

RC: I like my hair.

DA: You like your hair. This room that you're in – how big is it?

RC: It's round.

DA: Are there tables and chairs in it?

RC: No.

DA: So, you have nowhere to sit?

RC: No.

DA: Is there a toilet?

RC: No.

DA: Is there a door?

RC: A grey door. Yes.

DA: Is it a door that you can go out of if you want to?

RC: I can try that door. I can try it.

DA: Okay. Go and see if the door will open.

RC: Yes. It opened.

DA: What's outside the door?

RC: Light.

DA: Is it a door to another corridor or a door to outside the building?

RC: It's not outside. It's somewhere inside.

DA: Is it another room or a corridor?

RC: It's another room, corridor – something, again, around.

DA: Can you walk down it?

RC: No.

DA: Is it the kind of place where it's okay or expected or alright to walk around naked?

RC: Yes.

DA: Do you still have an erection?

RC: No.

DA: Okay. So, let's go explore. Just walk around, tell me what you find.

RC: No humans.

DA: There's nobody at all in the building?

RC: I see strange – not people. There are different creatures.

DA: What kind of creatures?

RC: Silver suits, like black eyes, big heads.

DA: Are they aware that you're there?

RC: Yes.

DA: Can you communicate with them?

RC: Kind of, yes. I can.

DA: So, can you ask them what you're doing there?

RC: I can ask. They won't tell me, for some reason.

DA: See if you can find a way out of the building.

RC: Okay. There's a corridor. I see, under the corridor, some greenery.

DA: Okay, so walk out of the building and into the open.

RC: Okay.

DA: Is it still a neutral temperature? Is it warm still?

RC: Yes, like tropics.

DA: Okay. So, leave the building. Is anybody trying to stop you?

RC: No.

DA: Okay, just leave the building. Have you come out into woodland or jungle or an open area?

RC: Yeah. Lots of trees, greenery.

DA: Okay, so just go wherever you sense is the right way to go.

RC: Now I see where it was. It was like something metal – like, yeah, in the tropics. Where I came from, like a base or something. Strange. Which is unusual, just to have in the forest or tropics.

DA: Okay, we can keep moving away.

RC: Okay.

DA: Are you still quite comfortable with the fact that you're naked?

RC: I'm fine, yeah.

DA: Yeah, okay.

RC: No problem.

DA: Keep going until you find something of interest. Maybe it's a village or a town or another person or perhaps a river.

RC: Yeah. Bridge.

DA: You come to a bridge. Is it a bridge over a river?

RC: Yeah, quite high. So, I can see down – it's quite high, a bridge.

DA: Is there anybody around?

RC: No, no one.

DA: If you cross the bridge, can you get down to the riverside, by the side of the river?

RC: No, I just crossed, and there's – it's still a cliff. I'm crossing the bridge.

DA: Can you tell me your name yet?

RC: I don't know why I have this name. I had Nathan. I don't know why.

DA: Nathan? Yes. Well, I'll call you Nathan until something better comes up – if anything better does turn up – but this is often the way that it happens. Tell me, Nathan, what year is it?

RC: Nineteen… nineteen-third, something nineteenth century.

DA: What country are you in?

RC: It's tropics somewhere. Could be Africa? No, not Africa.

DA: How do you feel in yourself? Are you scared?

RC: No. Comfortable, yes. Okay, just – okay, yes. Strange no one there, and I just want to run.

DA: So, keep walking, or if you want, you might even want to run. Can you run?

RC: Yes.

DA: Then run and tell me how strong the body feels.

RC: Very strong, I can run, I can jump and feel air in my lungs. Very nice, very nice feeling.

DA: How does the body – compare the feeling of the body of Nathan with the body of RC?

RC: It's wider and breathing more – more air into lungs.

DA: Tell me more about the differences in how you feel.

RC: It's – feeling is very, very strong and almost like... like... almost like a – yes, like, very confident, strong body and not scared at all of anyone. Skin is very thin.

DA: Sorry, can you say that again?

RC: It's the skin – sort of, I feel like there's not much fat on the skin. It's sort of like...

DA: Very light and muscular?

RC: Yeah, yeah, very – yeah, and muscular. And, yeah, quite – I see more muscular myself, like jaws, most muscular – you can see.

DA: Do you feel that having a penis feels better?

RC: Feels nicer. Feels like it's – when I draw my attention to it, it feels like it's normal, nice. But it's not about the penis – it's about this, the whole body, the strength of it and sort of abilities of that body.

DA: Now, Nathan, I'm going to count from one to three, and when I get to the number three, in this life, you're going to move forward – move forward to a point in time when you encounter other people, perhaps a normal time. So, as you are, if you're still running, you can stop running, and in this memory, you can just close your eyes. I will count to three; when you open them, you will move forward to the point where you are in contact with some people, preferably including females as well. And that could be – it might be in ten minutes' time, or it might be fifteen minutes' time, or it might be years, I don't know. You just move forward to the appropriate point as you close your eyes in that memory now, and

I count one, two, three, and open them again, and there
are some other people there. Nathan, tell me where you
are and what's happening.

RC: Yes, I see – red-haired woman.

DA: Are you still naked?

RC: No, something is on me.

DA: What are you wearing now?

RC: Just simple something – cotton clothes.

DA: Describe – is it a cotton shirt, trousers, or just a loincloth?

RC: Yes, it's just – it's just a grey colour. Yes, I have very
grey trousers.

DA: Do you have underwear on under the trousers?

RC: No, just – just – just these clothes, very light.

DA: Do you have anything on your feet?

RC: No, no, no – nothing.

DA: Anything on the top half of your body?

RC: Yes, I have top – yes, like shirt, very loose.

DA: Are you wearing a hat?

RC: No.

DA: Okay, where's the woman?

RC: In front of me.

DA: Okay, are you speaking to her?

RC: No, not this moment, no.

DA: Okay, go to her and speak to her. How old is she?

RC: She is – is in her thirties.

DA: How old are you now?

RC: Thirty-six.

DA: Do you know what year is it yet? You said nineteen-
something. Is that any clearer now?

RC: Nineteen eighteen.

DA: Nineteen eighteen. Is the woman a woman you know?

RC: I have close feelings to her.

DA: Oh, so she's – she's somebody you're close to. Is she
close in the sense of a lover or a sister?

RC: I love her.

DA: So, she's – okay, your partner, in effect.

RC: Yeah.

DA: How long ago was it that you were in this – this place naked? I mean, how much time has passed?

RC: Five minutes.

DA: Oh, so it's very shortly after. Where did you get the clothes from?

RC: I've – it's sort of in the place where people have to have clothes. I found her. She's also in cotton – long dress.

DA: Are you close to her?

RC: Yes.

DA: I mean, physically – have you, as you've moved towards her, have you become very close?

RC: Yes, I – I can feel her, like, very, very close.

DA: Do you want to kiss her?

RC: I can kiss her. Yes.

DA: Does she respond?

RC: Yeah. Yes.

DA: What's her name?

RC: Irene. Irene something.

DA: Irene.

RC: Yes, Irene.

DA: Where are you going to go with Irene?

RC: Just talking and walking. We are in the forest now.

DA: When was the last time you had sexual intercourse with Irene?

RC: I can't remember that.

DA: Is it something you want to do now?

RC: No. Not now. I feel warm, but I want to talk.

DA: Okay. What do you want to talk to her about?

RC: Be close to her and ask her where she was. Yes. Yes. Yes. Just enjoy being next to her for some time.

DA: Do you want to, as you're in the body of Nathan at the moment, do you want to explore the sexuality of manhood with Irene?

RC: Yes.

DA: Yes. In which case, we can move forward in time. Again, I count to three. And when I get to three, you will both be in a place where you will be able to enjoy a sexual relationship. As I count to three now: One, two, three. Where are you both?

RC: On the grass.

DA: On the grass, and presumably there's nobody else around?

RC: No.

DA: How do you feel, Nathan?

RC: Warm. Nice.

DA: How do you feel toward Irene?

RC: Very close.

DA: Are you aroused?

RC: Yes.

DA: Does she know that?

RC: Yes.

DA: Are you both fully clothed?

RC: No. No, I'm… I'm trying to… not the bottoms.

DA: I just – I want you to now just put time on – actually, hold for a minute. Everything can stop in time. And I want to allow you the opportunity to empty your mind of preconceived morality, preconceived notions – notions that you have in your adult physical life as RC that are necessary to survive in a social environment. But in this environment, in this memory, they're interfering because they, in relation to things that are very unusual, are causing you to make judgements at each stage. So, at this moment, you can let all of those go completely – no preconceived notions. So, nothing you say about this encounter will seem the slightest bit odd or unusual. What is most important is that you have a sense of what it feels like. Okay, so we can take time off hold now and continue where we left off. So, explain to me exactly what's happening now.

RC: Kissing. We're kissing. Feel her hair – very long and red colour, and curly. Freckles – she's got freckles. I like touching her.

DA: Okay, where are you touching her now?

RC: Breast. Breast.

DA: What are you touching with hands now?

RC: My hands and nipples. Feel her nipples.

DA: Where are her hands?

RC: She's touching my back and then my bottom.

DA: Are your trousers off?

RC: Yes.

DA: And you are erect? Try and leave the judgements behind.

RC: Yes. We're out. Yes.

DA: Okay, carry on.

RC: It's a nice feeling.

DA: Is it – for you, tell me, is the intensity of the feeling important?

RC: It's amazing. It's amazing. It feels very intense.

DA: Is it different to the feeling you would have as Rachel, as a woman?

RC: Very different.

DA: Can you explain the difference?

RC: I kind of give – I'm giving my warmth and my strength, my body, to her. And I feel her very – I feel strong. Her body is – I can feel the strength of my body that I hug her and that she's a woman.

DA: Okay, so how far have you got? Have you penetrated yet?

RC: Yes.

DA: I want you to continue now until ejaculation. And I want you to tell me what that feels like. It's okay – if you feel it intensely in your body, you can still let that show. That's fine. Just go as you would do until ejaculation. Has it happened?

RC: Yes.

DA: Tell me what it felt like.

RC: Very relieving and sharper – sharper than a woman.

DA: Yes, that's okay. Is it a unique experience to be able to compare the differences? In what way sharper?

RC: Stronger, sort of elaborating – sort of feeling, also, that I am dominating her. Important, I think.

DA: What does that feel like?

RC: Just when I care for her, and this is the most important dominating. I take care because she's weaker, and I'm stronger. Protect... a protecting feeling.

DA: In that memory, Nathan, you can just close your eyes. I'm going to count to three. And when I reach the number three, you will move instantly to a completely different life. Now, this life can be as a man again or as a woman.

Chapter Summary

Rachel's past-life regression as Nathan illuminates the profound spiritual significance of gender preferences in the journey of the soul. By incarnating as both male and female, souls gain access to a spectrum of physical, emotional, and social experiences that foster growth and karmic balance.

RC's experience highlights the visceral differences between male and female embodiment, particularly in terms of strength, arousal, and relational dynamics, such as the interplay of dominance and protection. This narrative resonates with modern discussions on gender, where the fluidity and diversity of identity challenge norms, yet it also underscores an essential truth: the necessity of experiencing both male and female forms to fully comprehend the human condition.

In a world grappling with issues of equality and identity, this perspective offers a timeless reminder of the value of empathy and the interconnectedness of all experiences, urging us to honour the essential roles that both genders play in shaping a complete and balanced existence.

Chapter 5: Theodore Lang

The cycle of life, death, and rebirth carries profound implications for the soul's journey, particularly when patterns of failure, such as repeated suicides, dominate an individual's incarnations.

Theodore's story reveals the futility of such self-destructive behaviours, which, far from offering escape, merely postpone the inevitable confrontation with unresolved lessons. In the spiritual framework of reincarnation, suicide does not end suffering but ensures that the soul must return to face the same challenges again, repeating the cycle until mastery is achieved. This perspective is especially relevant in modern times, where mental health struggles and feelings of isolation fuel rising rates of despair.

TL's experience underscores the interconnectedness of all beings, a truth obscured by the illusion of separateness in physical life. By recognising that failure through suicide only perpetuates the need to relive these lessons, we are reminded of the importance of perseverance, empathy, and connection in breaking free from cycles of self-sabotage, offering hope and purpose in addressing contemporary issues of loneliness and mental health.

DA: Firstly, tell me, is it daytime or nighttime?

TL: It's daytime.

DA: Are you inside or outside?

TL: Outside.

DA: Are you alone or with others?

TL: I'm with my family.

DA: So, who's actually there?

TL: My son, my wife, and, um, my daughter.

DA: How old are you?

TL: I think I'm 35.

DA: What's your name?

TL: Um, Jack.

DA: What's your wife's name?

TL: Um, Melissa.

DA: And what's your daughter's name?

TL: Henrietta.

DA: How old is she?

TL: I think she's six.

DA: This outside, you're with the family, is it a holiday?

TL: No, we're just walking along the street.

DA: So, are you outside in a town? Or was it a residential street?

TL: No, it's a town. It's like a high street.

DA: Is it, are you walking down there for a purpose? Is it for shopping or are you going to see somebody?

TL: It seems like a sort of Sunday walk, I think. There's a lot of people around. A lot of traffic, but it's like, you know, horse and cart vehicles.

DA: What year is it?

TL: I want to say 1902, something like that.

DA: And what country are you in?

TL: I think it might be America.

DA: Jack, what do you do for a living?

TL: I think, I think I might be a lawyer.

DA: Well, you could probably see your dress. As you're walking down the street with your family, is it a very wide street or a narrow street?

TL: It's quite wide.

DA: How are you dressed? Would you say you were smart, well-dressed?

TL: Yeah, I'm wearing, like, a stovepipe hat, I think. I've got a moustache, black.

DA: Can people acknowledge you as a person? Do you know people, many people there?

TL: I feel like we haven't lived here very long, in this town.

DA: What's the name of the town?

TL: I'm not sure. I mean, I think if…

DA: It will just come to you in time, and if we're still at this stop, if it just occurs to you, then you can just tell me. What will happen is as you become more and more immersed in this memory, the reality of being there will become stronger and stronger, so that you will feel your weight as you step forward, as you walk. You will feel the physicality of being, and these things will come to you, but they're not enormously important at this moment. So just have a look around and tell me what kind of shops you see.

TL: I see a butcher, and a store that sells goods, like leather goods, I think.

DA: Is Melissa very close to you at the time, physically? I mean, is she next to you?

TL: Yeah.

DA: Is she saying anything to you?

TL: No, I can feel a certain tension between us.

DA: Do you know why that is?

TL: I think I'm often in a bad mood. I'm very cold. I have trouble expressing my emotions.

DA: How about today? Are you in a good mood?

TL: Not really. I feel proud of my family, but I don't feel like I want to be nice to them. I don't want them to know that I'm proud.

DA: Okay, Jack, we don't need to stay here too much longer because we are going to move in this life, and we are going to move to the very last day.

TL: To the town. The name that comes to me is Heightsville. Like H-E-I-G-H-T-S-ville.

DA: In a moment, I'm going to count to three. When I reach the number three, you will be in the very last day of this life as Jack. As I begin to count. One. Two. Three. Now, Jack, tell me, is there anything going on around you that might suggest your physical death will come this day?

TL: There's water nearby, and I'm drunk. I'm near the sea, I think. Like the town near the water, near the sea.

DA: How old are you on this last day of your life?

TL: I'm not that old. Fifty-something. Fifty-three, something like that. But I'm alone. I mean, I don't think I even have a wife anymore.

DA: What about your daughter?

TL: I don't know where she is.

DA: Tell me what's happening at this moment.

TL: I just feel really unhappy. I don't want to live anymore. I think I've lost everything.

DA: Just move very quickly now to the point of death. And right through that to the other side. Jack, you've just died. Where are you? What can you see?

TL: I... I'm just... I died in the water. I drowned. I can't...

DA: Where are you looking at the scene from? Are you above it?

TL: I think I'm just watching my body fall to the bottom of the water.

DA: Was that a deliberate act?

TL: Yeah, I just kind of gave up. I think I was hoping to fall in, and I kind of did, but yeah, I did it. It was deliberate, really, yeah. I simply care.

Narration

As we will see later, suicide is a repeating pattern in the lives of TL. He'll realise later that these acts of self-sabotage serve no purpose as he'll just have to repeat the lesson in another life.

End of Narration

DA: What do you think about the life that you've just lived?

TL: It wasn't that good. I mean, I just didn't really share my family, but I love them. And I don't know what happened, but they ended up leaving me. I don't think… I think maybe they died. I think my wife died. I'm not sure about my daughter. She just went off and had her own life.

DA: As you look upon this scene after death, how do you feel now?

TL: I'm just happy to be free again.

DA: You're pleased it's over?

TL: Yeah.

DA: Your spirit has been through this many, many times before. And soon you will begin to return home. Now this is a… or was a lonely death. Something that you were content to happen. An incarnation that you couldn't complete for whatever reason. But now, you are fully connected to your soul state. Directly connected, in fact, to the highest consciousness of your mind. As an eternal, timeless being, you will remember incredible details about your immortal life between lives. And thus, you will be able to respond to my questions about your soul existence quite easily. Now, tell me what is happening now.

TL: I'm just seeing a lot of lives I've had, all happening at the same time.

DA: Do you still have a visual connection with the death, this last death?

TL: Sorry?

DA: Do you still have a visual connection with the last death? Are you still looking down on the sea?

TL: Well, I can still see that life, yeah.

DA: Are you moving?

TL: I'm floating. I'm, yeah, I'm floating.

DA: We are now going to a place of expanded awareness as you move upward into the loving realm of an all-knowing spiritual power. Even though you are only at the gateway of this beautiful realm, your soul will feel the joy of being released. Everything will become very familiar to you as we progress further because this peaceful realm embodies an all-knowing acceptance. You are now beginning to move away from the earth's plane in perfect comfort. So, tell me, are you, how far away from your body are you now?

TL: I can see the earth and, you know, I'm way above the earth.

DA: In which direction are you moving? Are you moving backwards looking back from where you've come from? Are you moving forwards?

TL: Yeah, I'm going backwards.

DA: What kind of sensation is it? Are you being pushed, pulled, just floating?

TL: I feel like I'm being pulled.

DA: Soon you will receive divine help in releasing all remaining residual negative energy from your physical life. You will be entering your eternal home where we can talk about your immortal life between lives and all the lives you have lived before with objectivity and understanding because this is a spiritual realm of planning and harmony. What I want you to do now is to continue to offer a commentary on what's going on so that I know exactly where you are at all stages.

TL: Well, I've... I just feel these presences behind me, a presence of people, some beings behind me. But I'm still looking back at where I've come from.

DA: Is the earth plane, the Astral Plane still visible, have you moved beyond it?

TL: It's fading, I mean it's... I'm now just surrounded in this light.

DA: What kind of light?

TL: It's just really, it's really white.

DA: Are you still moving?

TL: No, no, I'm not now. I'm just interacting with these, you know, these people. I'm kind of now... I'm seeing where I am, it's taking on a more definite form, I can see mountains, and we seem to be gathering on a hill. Okay, I can now see that one of these people is my dad in this life now. You know, he's dead.

DA: Is he communicating anything to you?

TL: Well, I feel like he's very pleased to see me. But I feel like we can't really be together. It's like, he's just there, but he's not going to really stay.

DA: That's okay. How many other people are there?

TL: About ten.

DA: Are they in front of you or to the side of you? Where are they in relation to you? Are you looking at them directly?

TL: Yeah, but there's like a separation between me and them. I just feel now that I didn't really do what I was supposed to do in the life I've just had. So, I feel that I mean, these people, they're like my family, but they're disappointed. But they love me, nonetheless.

DA: Did any one of them seem to be more important than any of the others?

TL: Well, I can see somebody I know in this life, Erica.

DA: How does she present to you? Obviously, she presents as female, but does she present the same way as she looked in a kind of human physical form or is it something you just know from the soul energy who it is?

TL: Well, it's to do with her hair, I think. The length of her hair.

DA: Describe how she manifests to you, for example.

TL: Well, she's just dressed in white, like a one-piece robe, and she's just looking at me.

DA: Is she bathed in light?

TL: Well, I wouldn't say bathed in light, no, just… it's like on, like, a hill, but there's a light source behind her coming from the sky, I suppose.

DA: Is she communicating anything to you?

TL: Well, I feel that… that we… that we have a lot to do. I mean, in other lives, there's a lot that we still have to do together. Maybe she was my wife in the life I just came from.

DA: Does she seem to be more important than any of the other people there?

TL: Yeah.

DA: What's happening to you at this moment? I mean, this light that was around you, is that still there?

TL: Well, no, it's more just like a sort of an earthly environment, as I said, with mountains and a hill, but it's not Earth, it's just like a setting that we've created just to have this meeting. We could have been at anything; it's just a peaceful setting.

DA: Is anybody else communicating anything to you?

TL: Well, there's like a sort of a more of an authority-type figure, like a male energy, who's explaining that I need to go back, and, you know, try again. This wasn't what I was, you know. I wasn't supposed to kill my son, but it's about learning to love.

Narration

Here, TL has his first realisation that he'll need to experience all these difficulties again in a new life. This is the first time he mentions killing his son, and we don't know how or why. There are likely many acts undertaken in this life that he shouldn't have done, so this is just one of them. We need to pursue what's best for him now, so that event is no longer important.

End of Narration

DA: Is this person your guide?

TL: Yeah, I think so, yeah.

DA: What's his name? You can ask him if you're not sure.

TL: Well, the name that comes to me, it doesn't seem right somehow, it's Dysmarn, I don't know, it's something like that, but I can't really pronounce it, you know.

DA: What's your spiritual name?

TL: What comes to me when I think of that is the name Aletha.

DA: You can always check this with Dysmarn, if that's the nearest we're going to get to a name that we can pronounce, that will do. You can ask him and check that. You can check that with the entity who played Erica in this current life.

TL: I think this is something I keep doing. I mean, I keep losing people who are close to me, and then I just end up on my own and start killing myself.

DA: Has this happened before? In other lives?

TL: Yeah, I think so, yeah.

Narration

Here we have confirmation that suicide has been a recurring thread and is preventing his soul existence from advancing. Ironically, it's a lot like school or college when one must repeat a year. In this context, the repeats will continue until he successfully navigates a life and can move forward. In his groundbreaking work in *Journey of Souls*, Dr Michael Newton explores the advancement of souls in detail, and it is a very useful reference.

End of Narration

DA: What's happening now with the people that were near or around you?

TL: Well, I'm among them now, it's like I've been welcomed back, but I think my daughter is there, but I can't really communicate with her.

DA: Is Dysmarn saying anything to you?

TL: Well, he's just reinforcing the idea that the lesson that I need to… that I need to be able to express love to the people in my life, which I don't do.

DA: Is there anything you need to do now? Do you need to go, for example, do you undergo any kind of review?

TL: Well, I think I am reviewing it now. I mean, you know, I think that's what we're doing, we are reviewing the life together, and I can just see all the moments where I chose to be cold.

DA: Is this just in the most recent life or are you looking at moments from other lives as well?

TL: Well, I can see, like, a whole… it's almost like a sort of a fountain, like this enormous fountain in the sky. In each kind of trail of water from the fountain is like a life, so I can see all these lives, but the one that I'm really focusing on right now is one I just came from.

DA: Okay, so tell me, what are the important sections of that life that are being shown to you now?

TL: Well, like when I'm being touched by my wife, I mean, just like on the face, and I just pull away, or even as a child, I would keep my distance from my own family, my family of origin.

DA: Are these just instances or memories of that life that you, that just appear to you, do you review them just kind of in isolation, or is anybody else commenting as these appear? For example, does Dysmarn, does your guide see these as well? Is he making observations, is anybody else making observations when they come up?

TL: Well, right now, I just seem to be experiencing it with my guide, but he's not really making any comments, no, he's just there with me. It's like what he said about the need to express love, I'm now seeing the moments when I didn't, when I could have done.

DA: Can you also look at moments from this current life that has passed with him? Are there any similarities?

TL: With which life?

DA: The current life you're in as TL.

TL: Yeah, I mean, this sense of not being able to connect to my family, not really loving Erica the way she deserved.

DA: Rather than tell me that, are you... are you seeing instances as you did with the life when you were Jack, are you seeing instances just coming up impromptu, as it were, of where these things have occurred?

TL: Well, I can kind of home in on this life. I mean, the branch or the fountain, I can home in on this life.

DA: He's not making any observations. I mean, you could, of course, ask him, am I doing it all over again?

TL: I do think that a lot of the lives I'm seeing did have a lot of similarities. It's like something which I'm not really getting about what I should be doing.

DA: How many times have you committed suicide in life, in your lives?

TL: Well, I mean, I see quite a lot of recent lives, or just, like, not even suicide but just giving up and becoming drunk and not looking after my health, that's a kind of suicide. But it's always because I seem to end up on my own. I lose the people who are close to me.

DA: Are any of them there? That are playing a part in this current life? Are any of the people that are around you now, have they played a part in this current life?

TL: Well, this... I want to say, this energy, I can't really connect with it, it's... I feel like she has been in this current life.

DA: What, as Erica?

TL: No, this is the one who was my daughter.

DA: Henrietta in the last life, is she in this current life as well?

TL: Yeah, I mean, I think... I feel that it's somebody I knew a few years ago, but she's not in my life now.

DA: Was she important to you at the time when you knew her in the physical life?

TL: Yeah, yeah, very important.

DA: Who was it?

TL: I think it was Rachel.

DA: She's a friend?

TL: She was somebody I liked, but she didn't feel the same way about me.

DA: Okay. But she was a friend?

TL: Yeah, for a while, yeah.

DA: Aletha, how many lives have you had?

TL: Ah, I mean, hundreds, a lot. Yeah, I mean, thousands maybe.

DA: Is this issue of sharing a love, is that something you've been working on for a long time?

TL: Yeah, it seems like it's almost like the last great lesson that I need to learn.

DA: Is it proving troublesome?

TL: Yeah. Yeah.

DA: What's happening now?

TL: Um, it's like some kind of structure is forming that's helping me to understand what it's all about. What it's... why I need to keep coming back. I said structure, I mean, like... Yeah.

DA: Describe the structure to me as it forms.

TL: Well, it's like… I guess it's forming a sort of a sphere, but it's made up of… I mean, it's transparent, and I can see all these, like, connections. And I think each… it's almost like the structure of a brain, like with all these neurons. But it's not a biological thing. It's just like a pattern of energy, if you like. But it's this idea that we're all connected. All these neurons inside the sphere are people, are souls.

Narration

TL is now beginning to understand the connectivity that exists between all of us, that in our isolated lives we do not recognise. For him, this is an important understanding.

End of Narration

DA: Can you see the connections? Do you look closer as it becomes more visible, easier to see?

TL: Yeah. But it's… there's so much, it's like we all, not all of us, but so many of us fail to realise these connections, that it's like our brain creates this illusion that we're just totally separate from everybody else, everything else. And then we just do what we want to do, and other people and other things are just antagonistic forces that are stopping us from doing what we want to do.

DA: How does it make you feel to see this representation of the interconnectivity between all things?

TL: Well, it just seems so obvious now. But it's the way that we become trapped inside these physical bodies, and it completely prevents us from feeling these connections. Well, it makes it very difficult. But that's, like, the whole point is to connect even though we feel separate. But it's like, from this perspective I have now, it seems so obvious that we're connected. But the thing is to know other people's pain is so clear now. But when I'm in my own, when I'm embodied, all I can experience is my own pain. But the thing is to... is to try, almost trying to feel other people's pain and to heal their pain.

DA: Is a part of what you feel the last remaining big lesson? Is the part that you have great difficulty with, in physical incarnations, that of experiencing and creating empathy?

TL: It's being able to stop focusing on myself and my own pain. But it's really difficult. But I feel that in this life, I mean, the one I'm having now, that I really have an opportunity to really... to really make progress. That I don't have to... I'm getting closer. But it's still very difficult.

DA: Okay, that's fine. Is Dysmarn actually saying anything else to you at the moment? Is he still talking to you?

TL: Well, I'm just observing because he's not really making any comments, no. I'm just, you know, looking at this myself. I'm not really hearing anybody else making any comments or anything.

DA: Is everybody else still there?

TL: Well, yes, I'm aware of them on the periphery.

DA: They've kind of stood back to allow this process to unfold.

TL: Yeah. Yeah.

DA: Keep commenting to me on what you're seeing within this sphere of connectivity and what you feel from it. Whether there's any change in the way that your energy feels, whether it's getting stronger, changing any form as a result of being aware of this sphere. Whether there are any parts of it that you look at more closely. If you can try and keep me up to date with what's going on and, of course, for you, for the recording later as well.

TL: Okay. Well, I'm just getting the sense that I'm thinking of certain people, I mean, like religious figures, can see the importance of this… of this overcoming the separation. I'm thinking of Jesus and Buddha, who recognise the other people's suffering. So, this… in this sphere, and it's like, I mean, it's not even a sphere, it's just this vast web that each of these points is like a point of light. But there's, like, spaces of… it's not a space, like a connection, it's like these threads that connect each of these points of light are dark. And what we need to do is to sort of illuminate that… that connection between each of us.

DA: Are there some areas of this huge web where there is some illumination?

TL: Yeah. So, there are some. There are lots of places where the darkness is much less intense. And some… so I was seeing, like, you know, like one of these nodes, I mean, it seems like it could be Jesus, and the connections between this node, this light, and all the others around it is completely, I mean, there's no darkness, it's just these huge waves of light connecting everything, every other light around it.

DA: Is this web real-time? I mean, are there things, are there awarenesses being created as you see it? Is it?

TL: Well, I just think these are, like, these are not beings being created, they are beings that exist.

DA: But the awareness between individuals of the belonging to the whole, is what you're looking at, is it kind of like a map which is something that was drawn, a snapshot in time, or is it real-time where, as people become aware of their connectedness, a new light, the dark thread becomes a light thread, that sort of thing? I'm just wondering if it's real-time you're observing it, if you like, the awareness of humanity as it evolves, as it changes.

TL: It is changing. It seems to be a representation that has… it seems to have taken this form so that I can understand it, but at the same time, it's also connected to… it's also representing in real-time what is actually... but I mean, it's not like there's any sense of time, like, you know, some of these lights lived thousands of years ago, somewhere, somewhere in the future, but it seems like the whole purpose is to just create nothing but light in this sphere.

DA: Is your current incarnation, your current life a part of that web? Can you see you, in effect?

TL: Well, yeah, I can see... I think a representation of me, but what I see is this representation of my life now within this vast sphere, it's not even the right word, it's like infinite, but it's as if all these connections.

DA: Are your past existences, your past lives there as well?

TL: Yeah, I mean, everything's there, every soul, every being, but there's so much darkness, so there's so many of these points of light that are just isolated, they're surrounded by darkness.

DA: Do you have a role to play? Is that part of your physical learning in this incarnation to improve that situation?

TL: Yeah.

DA: Is that something that you feel that you may be able to do now that you're aware that it exists?

TL: Yeah, it's just, it's something about understanding that... that I am, that we're all really the same, we're all equal, we're all part of the same thing, the same web, and it's like we need to shed light on others, so it's getting over this illusion that all there is, is just ourselves, which so many people believe that really all there is, is just them, everything else is like alien and threatening and, you know, needs to be conquered, beaten, but we have, at the same time, there is a tremendous amount of love that happens between people, but I'm really having trouble in this life feeling that or experiencing that or expressing that.

DA: Can you ask if this current life is kind of going to plan, or are there difficulties, or would they have stood a possibility of derailing it yet again? Is it supposed to be difficult up to there and something, that is, that you need to resolve? Essentially, I want you to ask if your life is going according to how it ought to run, according to the general template of what was expected?

TL: Yes, it is. It's going… it's unfolding as it should, as I was going to say, as we planned it. I'm not sure who we are, as I guess, as Dysmarn, well, I mean, it's fine, the plan.

DA: So, the plan would have included difficulties again with relationships?

TL: Yeah.

DA: The plan may well have included a point in your life where you were going to be become more aware, perhaps even in the process today?

TL: Yeah, this was something which, this was something which had been planned to happen around this stage in my life.

DA: Who was involved in the planning?

TL: Well, it's the two who I saw recently, Erica and Rachel.

DA: Did Dysmarn take any part in this plan?

TL: Well, in the planning process, but not in the actual unfolding of the plan.

DA: I mean in the actual planning process, not when you joined with the foetus, when you began this incarnation, but prior to that, because it was a fairly short time, in wherever time might be a relevant concept, from your life as Jack, which ended probably somewhere around 1922, 1923, to your existence now, which was only a few years before reincarnating again in such a short period of time. Were you a part of the plan to put you back into a life with the same difficulties to give you another opportunity to complete properly as opposed to giving up. For example, were you consulted with the plan?

TL: Oh, yeah, I mean, it was… this was mainly my plan, I think, so it's like understanding… it's from this perspective, when I'm able to see the lives I've had, and I'm aware of the same problems I experience and the same inability to really overcome these problems, so now it becomes that, you know, that I need… so I try again.

DA: So, what did you put in this life, what did you incorporate in the plan of this particular life, this particular body that you chose? What did you put in that to make it different this time round? I mean, the difficulties were still there because you still have to overcome those, and you've experienced some of those relationships already in your life, so what was going to be different in this life to help you overcome?

TL: Well, it was going to be harder to really find that family unit, which in previous lives I found quite easy, and then it would have been, like, a question of expressing love to my family, which I wasn't able to do, but in this life, I haven't had a family, so in a way, it becomes easier to; it becomes easier to identify the problem because I find myself alone, I don't have a family that I can take for granted and ignore, so what I've experienced, what I wanted to experience in this life, was having these, these people, but then I lose them very quickly.

DA: Were they in on the plan?

TL: Yeah, I mean, it was all… it was all kind of agreed upon, even with… even when I was a child, with when I was… when my parents divorced, for example, but it's been harder in this life to find that kind of… that… but it's like, it's been harder to find a stability in terms of relationships.

DA: Because it was supposed to be?

TL: Well, yeah, so I would end up being alone a lot because my relationships would not last, and so then I would have more time to realise what I was doing wrong, whereas in previous lives, I was in these relationships for a long time, so…

DA: Without having to bother to cultivate them, as it were?

TL: Yeah, just taking them for granted, and, but so I can think of one life where… it's a different life where my wife died, but my daughter was still there, but I just completely shut down. She would come back home every day from school, and this was, like, I don't know, like nineteenth century, and I would just ignore her. It was almost like I was so angry with my wife dying, I took it out on my daughter, and I would hear her cry at nighttime, but I wouldn't go to her.

DA: Because in this particular life, you have a huge amount of time left, you've only had it for 41 years.

TL: Well, yeah, and this is, like, a… this is very much a transitional stage I'm going through now in my life. It's all about coming to realise these things that I'm… I've been talking about today.

DA: What's happening now?

TL: Well, I'm just… I'm just trying to understand the life I'm living now, so I'm, I'm not currently really thinking about focusing on the space between lives.

DA: Is Dysmarn still there?

TL: Yeah, he is now.

DA: What about everybody else? Are they still in the background or are any of them coming forward to you?

TL: Um, well, yeah, now I'm focusing on them now, so now I'm among them.

DA: What's being communicated to you?

TL: I'm not really understanding why… I don't really understand why I need to go back. I mean, it seems… it seems somewhat pointless.

DA: When you say go back, what do you mean?

TL: I mean, go back and have another life on Earth.

DA: After this particular one? Or after the last one?

TL: The one where I drowned, it's like, I feel that I'm being encouraged to go back, but it seems like, what's the point?

DA: Well, you were obviously persuaded because you're back in another incarnation now.

TL: But there's a real resistance to the whole process.

DA: I want to create the opportunity for your friends and the group of people around to come in and just communicate whatever they want to you now, so that you can just let them in and just let them speak to you, communicate whatever they want in terms of emotions or concepts, so can you let them in now and just listen and tell me what's being communicated to you?

TL: Well, they're saying that… they're asking me to let them in, that, I'm so afraid of, I'm so afraid of being disliked, being judged, but they're saying that there is… that what matters is just that connection, that it's… that all the judgement is all something in my mind, that it's like a chimera, it doesn't really exist, so it's… so they are explaining that it's kind of easy when we're in this… in this realm, it's easy to express that love for each other, but it's much more difficult on Earth, but that's really the whole point, it's that… I just get that sense of because it's so difficult to overcome our own mind, our ego, if you like, when we're inside a body, it takes a tremendous amount of power sand effort, a tremendous amount to show love for others, you know, it's easier to show love for one person, but then it's like, try showing it to ten people or a hundred or a thousand or everybody, the whole world, that becomes so insanely difficult, but that's just it, it's because it's so difficult, but by doing it, that's how we really become... that s how we get back to God, but it's like, the process of going through it is what makes us evolve, I mean, as souls rather than as people, yes, but we can't do it in the spirit realm because it's just too easy, it's all so... in a sense, we don't really evolve there.

DA: It's self-evident there.

TL: So, we kind of, it's almost like we stagnate, you know, everything's so easy, but then we come here, and it's like completely different, it's just really hostile, but it's trying to remember that what is self-evident in the spirit realm, it's remembering it when we're down here.

DA: Well, you won't have to remember because you've had the experience, so you will feel it much more easily than before, and you will retain the ability to directly connect with Dysmarn, particularly with him, maybe with others as well, so the part of the links, part of the connectivity has been established.

TL: Yeah, but I'm also weighed down by this animal body, and even the brain, you know, we think we are our brain, but we're not, the brain is this kind of weight that we carry around that can just act like a barrier to what we really want to do.

DA: Are there any good things about having a physical body?

TL: Well, yeah, it's those kinds of things, like feeling warmth on the face or the pleasure of eating, but it's so easy to get kind of lost in those sensations and then we come to the point where all we want to experience are these pleasant bodily sensations, but that's not the point, that's not really what we are supposed to be doing down here.

DA: Well, aren't you all... do you still have this high-level connection, is there anything else that you need to explore there at this moment, or do you think that perhaps for now we've... we're drawing to a natural conclusion?

TL: I'm not sure, I mean, I don't know, I don't feel like necessarily that anything's being concluded, but...

DA: Is there anything else that you might feel that you need to know, that you want to ask, or you want to explore while you're there? Remember, this is not a one-time thing because you've opened a connection, it will remain with you always, but having experienced the enlightenment and understanding of what the reality of your immortal existence is will have a dramatic effect on the way you feel about your physical life as well.

TL: I'm asking... I'm asking Dysmarn how, when I'm down here, how I deal with... how I'm supposed to deal with the pain that I feel, and he's saying, like, that... that pain is just part of the experience, it's not even something that you can necessarily get rid of, well, I guess it's like... it's acting in spite of... in spite of the pain.

DA: Is that helpful?

TL: Yeah, it's just very difficult because I see two... it's almost like two different expressions of my... of who I am in this life, and there's the way that... the way that I have been and the way that I want to be, but it's very difficult letting go of all this... all this crap I carry round with me from the past.

DA: You may well find that it will become easier to do because only you carry it with you and only because you want it, and this change of perspective that's happened today will alter that.

TL: Yeah.

DA: Is there anything else that you specifically need to ask? I know often people will say because it's such... it is such a lighter experience in being back home that it's quite nice to have to stay there, but you still have a life to live, are you ready to return?

TL: I think so, I just keep focusing on this issue of pain, you're living with carrying pain around with you with me, but I'm not really getting... I'm not really getting a clear sense of how to... how to let it go.

DA: Maybe that's the point, let it be something for you to discover.

TL: Yeah.

Chapter Summary

Theodore's past-life regression reveals the profound futility of failure through repeated suicides, a pattern that has trapped his soul in a cycle of unlearnt lessons across numerous incarnations. Each act of self-destruction, whether deliberate drowning or neglectful self-harm, proves futile, as it merely resets the stage for the same challenges to be faced again in a new life. TL's journey underscores the spiritual truth that lessons, particularly those involving love, empathy, and connection, must be completed for the soul to advance. His vision of a vast web of interconnected souls highlights the illusion of isolation that fuels his despair, offering a stark contrast to the reality of universal connectivity. In a modern context, where suicide rates reflect deep societal struggles with loneliness and mental health, TL's experience serves as a poignant reminder that giving up only prolongs the journey.

By embracing the interconnectedness of all beings and persevering through pain, individuals can break free from cycles of failure, finding purpose in the pursuit of love and understanding that transcends lifetimes.

The Past: Summary

The past-life regression sessions of Nora, Elias, Rachel, and Theodore weave a rich mosaic of the soul's past incarnations. Despite being largely limited to just former lives, themselves discrete and separate from the whole, except for Theodore, each narrative illuminates unique facets of human experience while converging on universal themes of growth, connection, and resilience.

Nora's vivid recollections of life as Nell in 1610 London and Katrina in a 1990s African setting reveal the soul's capacity to navigate starkly different eras, grappling with poverty, loss, and disorientation, yet finding solace in the serene embrace of the spiritual realm. Her journey underscores the continuity of the soul across time, where hardships forge resilience, and love endures despite adversity.

Elias Young's brief yet evocative glimpse as Geoffrey Sinclair, a nineteenth-century farmer, captures the quiet contentment of a life rooted in simplicity and duty, highlighting the soul's ability to find fulfilment in modest moments of honest labour.

Rachel Carter's exploration as Nathan, a man in a mysterious tropical setting, delves into the profound spiritual significance of gender embodiment, revealing how incarnations as both male and female foster empathy and balance, offering insights that resonate with contemporary questions of identity.

The following heart-wrenching account of Theodore Lang's repeated suicides as Jack in early twentieth-century America exposes the futility of escaping life's lessons, emphasising the interconnectedness of all beings and the necessity of perseverance to break cycles of despair.

Together, these experiences illuminate the soul's purposeful navigation through diverse lives, each marked by unique challenges yet united by the pursuit of love, empathy, and understanding. In a modern world wrestling with isolation, identity, and mental health, these stories offer a timeless reminder of our shared humanity and the eternal quest for connection, urging us to embrace the lessons of our past to shape a more compassionate future.

Section 3

Death: Introduction

The following five short chapters focus on the point of death, that time when the physical life has passed, and the soul existence is realised.

This section is important because there are many questions about it, particularly concerning the connection, if any, that one's spiritual self retains the life that's just ended.

What is surprising, well at least for me, was the complete detachment from the confines of a physical existence. Most people simply want to get on with it and go home, a term used to describe the passage from physical reality to the spiritual realm. When asked about comforting those remaining, or dwelling for any time the usual response, paraphrased, is "no, I'm done here, let's go".

The process doesn't dwell on death, because the experience can be real enough to cause symptoms, such as pain, or coughing, to be felt when no such physical threat exists. It lends credence to understandings that the brain controls everything and can both create pain and conceal it, if only we knew how to properly control that.

The section is for you to understand that death is but a gateway and although many may hold that concept as a belief, to listen to people actually experiencing it is revelatory.

Chapter 6: Lois Pennington

Lois Pennington (LP) revisits the final day of a life as Fred, swiftly shedding all connection to his earthly existence with jubilant detachment.

DA: Fred, while watching the cottage, close your eyes. We'll move to the last day of your life. When you're there, open your eyes and tell me what you see.

LP: I'm lying in bed, wearing striped pyjamas. The mahogany bed has a high end with scroll ends – resembling a sleigh bed but not quite. A chest of drawers holds framed pictures. A tall window has net voile curtains and heavier curtains on a brass rod, pulled back with tassels. It's a grand room, surprising after my wellingtons. The yellowish wallpaper looks aged. I'm wondering where my bird is.

DA: Is anyone else in the room?

LP: A woman stands by the door to my left, with a round brass knob. She wears a black dress, white apron, and a bonnet with a frill.

DA: How old are you on this last day?

LP: Eighty-two.

DA: Is anything happening that suggests your death will come today?

LP: I can't get out of bed, and this woman, attending me, looks worried. There's a dismal expectancy, but I feel all right. I'm really worried about my bird. By the window, there's a polished stand, about four feet tall, with a horizontal bar – a coat hanger for jackets, not for the bird. She's by the door, holding a bowl with a sponge or cloth.

DA: We'll move to the point of death soon, but first, I'll ask your unconscious mind to block all external noises except my voice. Now, Fred, move to the point of death. What's happening?

LP: I'm going backwards, falling. The room grows paler – dimmer yet brighter. I'm falling into a shaft of light, not a tunnel.

DA: Do you feel pain?

LP: No. I'm ready. I don't want to be there anymore.

DA: Move through the process of death, past it, to the other side. Tell me when that's happened.

LP: It has. Everything's bright – very white light with amorphous shapes, perhaps people, at the edge.

DA: Are you still in the room?

LP: No, I didn't think of it until you mentioned it.

DA: Are you stationary or moving?

LP: I feel stationary.

DA: Do you sense being up or down? What do you see around you?

LP: I'm hovering.

DA: What's below you?

LP: It seems odd, but I'm on a cloud, with green fields below. I feel in the sky. It's strange.

DA: You've died, rising from your physical body, as your soul has done many times. How do you feel? Any sadness or happiness?

LP: No sadness. I'm delirious, amongst friends, being guided.

Chapter Summary

Lois, as Fred, swiftly began the journey home, too eager to linger for further questions. From the last day of Fred's life to his death and beyond, her jubilation at shedding physical limitations reflects a common elation in this process.

Chapter 7: Ulysses Archer

Ulysses Archer (UA) explores the final day of a life as James, accompanied by Peter, a local vicar, and an old woman, revealing a peaceful departure with minimal attachment.

DA: James, sitting in your chair, close your eyes. Move to the last day of your life as James. When you're there, open your eyes and tell me what you see.

UA: I see an old woman and Peter. I'm lying in my bed in the cottage.

DA: How old are you?

UA: Sixty-nine.

DA: Is anything happening that suggests this is your last day?

UA: Peter's holding my hand, crouched down, with a woman standing behind him.

DA: Do you have an illness?

UA: Just age. Just life.

DA: How do you feel?

UA: Sad for these people.

DA: And for yourself?

UA: I have no feeling.

DA: Any pain?

UA: Just tiredness. Weakness. I can't breathe properly. I can't speak – I can just think.

DA: James, move quickly to the point of death and pass through it. Tell me when that's happened.

UA: It's happened.

DA: Where are you now?

UA: I'm standing up.

DA: Can you see yourself lying on the bed?

UA: Yes, but I'm thin, and I'm standing, in my twenties.

DA: Are you standing or floating above your body?

UA: I'm upright, floating quite high.

DA: Can you still see Peter and the woman?

UA: The woman left as I passed. Peter's still there.

DA: What do you think of this life?

UA: Proud. Happy. Could have been happier, but I dealt with what was. I'm floating high, seeing the cottage with smoke from the chimney.

DA: Have you decided to move?

UA: I don't know. The cottage is getting smaller. I'm dressed smartly now, as a younger person.

DA: What's below you now?

UA: The church.

DA: Are you still moving?

UA: Yes, slowly, perhaps a bit fast.

DA: Are you facing the direction you're moving?

UA: No, I'm looking down, moving upwards, still above my cottage, seeing the whole village. It's quite nice.

Chapter Summary

James's rapid departure from physical existence shows no lingering attachment, his spirit swiftly ascending with a sense of pride and acceptance.

Section 3

Chapter 8: Alastair Nunn

Alastair Nunn explores the violent death of Jez, highlighting a brief attachment to unfinished tasks before embracing spiritual release.

DA: Jez, we don't need to stay here long. Move to the last day of your life. On the count of three, you'll be there. One, two, three. How old are you on this last day?

AN: Thirty-three.

DA: Is anything happening that suggests your death will come today?

AN: No. There are people, marauders, violence.

DA: What was that?

AN: My body's tingling. Pain in my right collarbone – not severe – and my left ear. I think I've been hit with something blunt – a staff, club, or cudgel, perhaps.

DA: How do you feel now?

AN: Drifting off. Achy. Limbs tingling.

DA: If this is painful, we can move quickly. Go to the point just after you've died and tell me when that's passed.

AN: Yes.

DA: You've passed, rising from your body, as your soul has done many times.

AN: I haven't finished what I was supposed to do.

DA: You may feel brief sadness, but you'll soon return home. Where are you in relation to your body?

AN: Floating above.

DA: Is anyone near your body?

AN: No.

DA: What do you see around you?

AN: Something temple-like. Torches. Commotion outside. Big stone, crystalline things – obelisks. I see what hit me – a mace with a smooth end, smooth stone.

DA: Can you still see your body?

AN: Yes.

DA: How far above it?

AN: Twelve, fifteen feet.

DA: How do you feel about that death?

AN: Bad. I didn't do what I was supposed to. More to be done.

DA: You're in your soul state, connected to your eternal consciousness, ready to recall life between lives. Before moving further, do you want to stay – to say goodbye or address unfinished business – or go now?

AN: I'd like to stay.

DA: What do you want to do?

AN: Soak up the atmosphere.

DA: Anyone you want to communicate with?

AN: Others are here, but they're not talking. They look old.

DA: Anyone you want to comfort?

AN: No.

DA: Take a moment to view this scene. Any disorientation will pass. As you breathe, you'll sink deeper into the trance. Are you still looking at your body?

AN: No.

DA: What's happening now?

AN: I've drifted away.

Chapter Summary

Jez lingered briefly, not to comfort anyone but to absorb the scene, perhaps seeking understanding. Isolated in a violent conflict, he had no close ties. Souls typically feel no lasting connection to a life now irrelevant, a pattern seen in other cases.

Chapter 9: April Oakes

April Oakes revisits the grim final day of a life as Harry, revealing fleeting compassion before his soul's eager transition.

DA: Move to the last day of this life as Harry. On the count of three, you'll be there. One, two, three. How old are you on this last day?

AO: Thirty.

DA: Is anything happening that suggests your death will occur today?

AO: Yes, I've got chains around my ankles, and I'm… I think I'm ill.

DA: Where are you? Is the setting familiar?

AO: I'm sitting in what feels like a cell.

DA: Are you alone, or are there others?

AO: No, there are others, in a mess with buckets of water.

DA: What year is it?

AO: 1923 comes to mind, but I'm unsure if it's right. I feel I've lost a child.

DA: What do you think of this life?

AO: It's been awful. Treated terribly throughout. Agony in my bones, not allowed to…

DA: We needn't dwell here long. Move quickly to the point of death, through it, and tell me when it's passed.

AO: I'm lying down.

DA: Have you died?

AO: Yes.

DA: You've passed, rising from your body, as your soul has done many times. You may feel brief sadness, but you'll soon return home. Where are you in relation to your body?

AO: Just above it, I think.

DA: Is anyone around who cares for you? How do you feel about this life?

AO: No one notices anyone dying because everyone's dying.

DA: Harry, what are you feeling?

AO: I'm at peace to die. Glad to die.

DA: You're in your soul state, connected to your eternal consciousness, ready to recall life between lives. Before moving further, is there anything you need to do here? It seems not. Are you ready to move on?

AO: Yes, I wanted to help the others, but…

DA: Can you do that?

AO: No.

Chapter Summary

Harry's life as a prisoner in squalid conditions was marked by suffering, yet a fleeting desire to help others lingered. Attachment to this painful life faded quickly, with his soul ready to move on.

Chapter 10: Kylie Vernon

Kylie Vernon explores the final day of a life as Beth, defined by loneliness and frailty, finding profound peace in her soul's release.

DA: Close your eyes. Move to the last day of your life. On the count of three, open your eyes, and you'll be there. One, two, three. How old are you on this last day?

KV: Seventy.

DA: What's your name?

KV: Beth.

DA: Is anything happening that suggests your death will come today?

KV: It's all dark. The curtains are drawn. I want the sunlight in.

DA: Where are you?

KV: In bed.

DA: Is it your own bed?

KV: Yes.

DA: Describe what's happening and how you feel.

KV: I'm very weak. No energy at all. I don't feel ill, just weak.

DA: What do you think of this life?

KV: Awful. Full of loneliness. I feel I've been in penance.

DA: Were you well yesterday?

KV: No.

DA: Do you have an illness?

KV: I don't think so. I don't feel ill, just weak.

DA: What time of day is it?

KV: Midday.

DA: Is it unusual to be in bed at midday?

KV: Until the last two weeks, yes.

DA: Has this weakness grown over the last two weeks?

KV: Mm-hmm.

DA: Is Stan still alive?

KV: No. He died years ago at 40.

DA: Have you lived alone since?

KV: Yes.

DA: Did you still run the shop?

KV: For a while, yes.

DA: Do you have friends?

KV: I've got friends now.

DA: Is anyone else in the house?

KV: Yes.

DA: Who's that?

KV: A lady brings my lunch. I don't want it.

DA: Does she always bring your lunch?

KV: Yes. I think she's my neighbour.

DA: Have you been frail for a while?

KV: Mm-hmm. For a long time. I've just had enough. I've given up.

DA: Do you feel pain?

KV: No. Just exhausted and tired.

DA: Beth, move quickly through your death and tell me when it's passed.

KV: Oh, yes.

DA: You've died, rising from your body, as your soul has done many times. You may feel sadness, but your spirit is experienced.

KV: No, I don't feel that.

DA: Because it was such a bad life?

KV: Mm-hmm. I don't feel it.

DA: Do you want to go home quickly?

KV: Mm-hmm.

DA: Where are you in relation to your body?

KV: I can't see anything.

DA: Are you moving?

KV: No, I can't see anything. Oh, hold on. There's grey light. It's better. Oh, yes, light. I feel different. I feel young again. Oh, my, I feel young again. Fresh air. Flowers I can't recall the last time I smelt flowers. I'm at peace.

Chapter Summary

Beth felt no remorse for her lonely life. Her experience reflects a common pattern: profound elation and peace upon leaving hardship, as the soul embraces vitality and freedom.

Chapter 11 Myrtle Lambert

Myrtle Lambert revisits the sudden death of Neville, revealing brief frustration before his soul's eager return to spiritual freedom.

DA: Neville, we don't need to stay here long. Move to the last day of your life.

ML: This is the last day of my life.

DA: Is anything happening that suggests your death will come today?

ML: No. I'm sent alone to look for something, but I can't recall what.

DA: Continue your task, searching or doing what you were doing.

ML: I'm trying to determine if there are hostiles around. I'm on the edge of a village, I think.

DA: What should you do next?

ML: I'll move slowly to the edge of the orchard.

DA: Have you reached it?

ML: Yes.

DA: Hold your position, Neville. At the orchard's edge, what do you see?

ML: A garden and a house the orchard belongs to.

DA: Will you move into the open to see who's in the house?

ML: I'll go into the garden to pass through and beyond the house. I believe the occupants are friendly.

DA: What are you doing now?

ML: Walking up the path to the door.

DA: Continue, providing a commentary so I know where you are and what's happening.

ML: There's a porch over the back door. I've changed my mind and decided to knock to see if the woman of the house is home.

DA: Any reply?

ML: No one comes, so I open the door, and that's as far as I get.

DA: What happens?

ML: I sense someone was on the other side with a gun.

DA: Move quickly through the death to the other side and tell me when it's passed.

ML: Yes, it's passed.

DA: You've died, rising from your body, as your soul has done many times. You may feel sadness, but your spirit is experienced. Where are you in relation to your body?

ML: Quite a distance from it. I've left it behind, briefly continuing to go through or around the house to discover what lay beyond.

DA: Can you see your body?

ML: Yes, if I turn and look.

DA: Can you see who shot you?

ML: Yes, the woman of the house.

DA: Is anyone else in the house?

ML: No.

DA: How do you feel?

ML: Annoyed.

DA: Why?

ML: It was my ineptitude, and I had to leave so suddenly.

DA: You're in your soul state, connected to your eternal consciousness, like a vast repository of your existence's knowledge. Before moving further, is there a reason to stay, or are you ready to leave?

ML: I'm ready to leave.

Chapter Summary

Neville's sudden death brought fleeting annoyance, but, as with other souls, once freed from the physical body's constraints, he was eager to return home.

Section 3

Death: Summary

Death captures the soul's liberation from physical existence through varied past-life regressions. Fred (Chapter 6) departs a frail but comfortable life with delirious joy, unconcerned for earthly ties. James (Chapter 7) leaves a peaceful village life with pride and minimal attachment, ascending swiftly. Jez (Chapter 8), despite a violent end and unfinished tasks, lingers briefly before drifting away. Harry (Chapter 9) escapes a grim prison, his fleeting compassion giving way to peace. Beth (Chapter 10) sheds a lonely existence, embracing vitality. Neville (Chapter 11) moves past a sudden death with momentary frustration, eager for home.

These accounts reveal a universal pattern: whether emerging from suffering or serenity, souls feel unshackled from the physical realm. They show little desire to remain, instead experiencing profound freedom and an eager pull to their spiritual home, affirming the soul's eternal essence.

Section 4

The Journey Home: Introduction

Section 4, The Journey Home, presents four compelling accounts of souls transitioning from physical existence to the spiritual realm, each guided by David through the intricate process of leaving earthly ties behind and reconnecting with their eternal essence.

These chapters – following Douglas, Isadora, Wanda, and Antonia – illuminate the diverse pathways souls take as they navigate the liminal space between lives. From the immediate release of physical burdens to the restorative processes like healing showers and the heartfelt reunions with Primary Soul Groups, this section captures the universal yet deeply personal nature of returning to the spiritual home.

Each session reveals the soul's resilience, the guidance of spiritual entities, and the profound sense of belonging that awaits, offering a rich tapestry of experiences that underscore the continuity of consciousness beyond the physical plane.

Chapter 12: Douglas Heath

The Journey Home follows Douglas Heath's transition from a traumatic death in a past life to the spiritual realm.

Continuing from his abrupt end, Douglas undergoes a cleansing "healing shower", a process some souls experience to repair energy damaged during incarnation, as described by Dr Michael Newton in *Journey of Souls* and *Destiny of Souls*. The session culminates in his first meeting with his Primary Soul Group, a close-knit cluster of souls with whom he shares a profound connection.

This chapter explores the movement away from earthly ties, the restorative power of the healing shower, and the joy of reuniting with familiar spiritual companions.

DA: Is it hot or cold?

DH: Hot.

DA: Are you inside or outside?

DH: Inside.

DA: Are you alone?

DH: I'm dead. A bomb just went off – possibly Second World War. I'm not feeling the pain in my head. The top right side feels missing.

DA: That's fine. Hold time still for a moment – nothing moves, no pain, just memories. Where were you during this event?

DH: I think it's London.

DA: What were you doing?

DH: I was just a normal man.

DA: Civilian?

DH: Yes.

DA: What's your name?

DH: I don't know.

DA: With time on hold, there's no pain. It's just memory. How old are you?

DH: About 40.

DA: What were you doing before the explosion?

DH: I was in my house, I think. I don't recall.

DA: If any information, like your name, comes to you, tell me. Your name is especially important.

DH: My surname is John.

DA: John. And what year is it?

DH: 1943 or 1944.

DA: Be more specific when you can.

DH: I'm thinking 1944, but the war ended in '45.

DA: Resume time now. Return to the situation. If there's pain, we'll move beyond the point of death quickly.

DH: I'm already there.

DA: Where are you in relation to your body?

DH: Above.

DA: What can you see?

DH: Rubble.

DA: Can you see your body?

DH: Yes.

DA: Is the injury as you described – a head injury?

DH: Yes, but it's on my left side.

DA: Was anyone else in the house?

DH: No.

DA: How do you feel about having just died?

DH: Nothing really. Not sad or happy, just observing.

DA: Some feel brief sadness, but your soul has done this many times, and you'll soon return home. Anything else about your death or feelings?

DH: Maybe I didn't fulfil my life, possibly because I died young.

DA: Are you moving, Douglas?

DH: I think so.

Narration

Sometimes, the past life's name remains unknown, so I use the client's given name (changed for anonymity). The current conscious mind enables seeing through both memory and current identity, with no cognitive dissonance regarding names.

End of Narration

DA: Can you still see the destruction?

DH: No, it's gone.

DA: Are you moving in the direction you're facing or backwards?

DH: In the direction I'm facing.

DA: Does it feel like floating or a pulling sensation?

DH: Both.

DA: What can you see when you look back?

DH: The distant scene. I'm not bothered about it.

DA: How far from the scene are you?

DH: Thirty feet, maybe more.

DA: Is your movement steady or accelerating?

DH: It's gentle.

DA: Have you moved further?

DH: No, I've left.

DA: What's happening?

DH: It's like a shower, but not water – golden light.

DA: Where's it coming from – above, beside you or behind?

DH: It's like a wall I'm passing through.

DA: What do you feel?

DH: Warmth. It's cleansing, making me lighter.

DA: Are you alone? Do you sense anyone else?

DH: No.

DA: Describe the feeling of this shower. What's changing?

DH: It's warm, tingly, energising.

DA: Does it start at your head or feet?

DH: It's all over.

DA: Coming from the outside in?

DH: Like I'm passing through a wall of it, everywhere.

DA: How strong and energetic do you feel, percentagewise?

DH: Very strong.

DA: What do you think of the life you've left?

DH: A bit of a waste of time.

DA: Allow this process to complete.

DH: Okay.

DA: What's happening now? What's ahead?

DH: Blackness, intermingled with golden hues.

Narration

Souls use part of their energy in incarnations – less for advanced souls, more for newer ones. Younger souls' energy may be damaged, requiring a "Healing Shower" to repair it. As we're exploring memories, I often suggest moving through this quickly, though some, like Douglas, progress rapidly on their own.

End of Narration

DA: Are you moving?

DH: Maybe.

DA: Do you feel you've been here before?

DH: It doesn't feel like home. I'm not aware of familiarity.

DA: Scan ahead for anything beyond blackness. Can you see beyond your surroundings?

DH: I think I can see into the distance.

DA: What's behind you?

DH: The barrier wall.

DA: To your left?

DH: The wall's length.

DA: To your right?

DH: The same.

DA: Any point of light in the distance?

DH: Not yet, but my hands feel very energised.

DA: One hand or both?

DH: Both.

DA: Are you moving or stationary?

DH: My hands are very hot, almost lifting themselves, full of energy.

DA: Let that energy spread through your aura, so it's not uncomfortable. Do you sense another spirit?

DH: Not yet.

DA: How do your hands feel now?

DH: Same but not aching.

DA: Are they radiating a colour?

DH: Gold.

DA: Golden light?

DH: Yes. I'm not sure I've got fingers anymore.

DA: We're continuing the re-energising process. Let it complete. What's happening?

DH: It's like shedding a skin, leaving the 3D behind.

DA: Is your light still golden?

DH: Yes, entirely.

DA: Are you ready to go home?

DH: Yes, but I don't know where to go.

DA: Do you see any points of light or a large area of light?

DH: I'm trying too hard.

DA: Let it happen naturally. Look at your horizon and tell me when you see light. Begin moving forward if you can. What's happening?

DH: I'm free, like swimming in the blackness, doing acrobatics.

DA: I'll ask your guide to assist. Your guide, always with you, offers spiritual comfort. On the count of three, your vibrational awareness will rise, and your guide will appear. One, two, three. What's happening?

DH: I'm not sure if it's my imagination. He looks Chinese, perhaps with a beard, a big round face, maybe a warrior.

DA: Is your guide male?

DH: Yes.

DA: Is he communicating anything?

DH: Strength.

DA: Ask what you need to do to get home.

DH: Think of myself flying like a dart.

DA: What's your guide's name?

DH: Perhaps Shukoshi, S-H-U-K-O-S-H-I.

DA: Ask him to help you get there.

DH: I feel dart-shaped, flying at great speed.

DA: Is Shukoshi with you?

DH: I'm not sure. I don't think so.

DA: What's ahead?

DH: Something large and orange, like a sun, not too bright to look at.

DA: Is it directly in front?

DH: Yes, huge.

DA: Are you moving toward it?

DH: Yes, very quickly.

DA: Do you sense Shukoshi?

DH: No, he just helped me start, gave me strength. I need to merge into that ball.

DA: Have you reached it?

DH: Yes. It feels like all beings are here.

DA: What can you see around you?

DH: Orange.

DA: Just orange?

DH: Yes.

DA: Any different shades?

DH: No.

DA: Do you still sense other beings?

DH: Yes.

DA: Are any close to you?

DH: I think so.

DA: Can you touch anyone?

DH: No, you feel them, like flame-shaped forms.

DA: Are the shapes distinct? Can you separate one from another?

DH: The heads are distinct, but the rest merges.

DA: How many are there?

DH: It feels like a lot.

DA: Is any one more significant?

DH: Yes, one in front.

DA: Describe this being.

DH: It resembles the mask from *Scream*, but not frightening, with a bushy white beard, like a wizard.

DA: Is there an entity within?

DH: This is the entity, showing a face for my benefit.

DA: Do you recognise the energy?

DH: Perhaps an old teacher.

DA: Are the shapes becoming clearer?

DH: Slowly.

DA: Is Shukoshi there?

DH: No.

DA: Call for him in your mind, and he'll come.

DH: I only see faces now, no bodies.

DA: How many are significant?

DH: About a dozen.

DA: Are they in a line, semi-circle, or bunched together?

DH: A sea of thousands, but my particular ones are a group of about 12.

Narration

This group of 12, a typical size, is his Primary Soul Group. Douglas's reference to "my particular ones" shows early recognition of their close connection.

End of Narration

DA: How far are you from them?

DH: Close, almost touching distance.

DA: Start with the face furthest left. What colour do they present?

DH: Originally orange, now emerald green.

DA: Male or female?

DH: Male, I think.

DA: Who is this, based on their energy?

DH: Maybe my friend, Barley.

DA: What do you sense from him?

DH: Friendship.

DA: Can you feel that being so close?

DH: Yes.

DA: Move to the next. What colour?

DH: Pink.

DA: Gender?

DH: Female.

DA: Identity?

DH: Possibly my mother.

DA: Ask her for confirmation. What response?

DH: I don't know.

DA: Did she respond?

DH: No.

DA: What do you feel from this energy?

DH: Not my mother, perhaps a past girlfriend or helper.

DA: Look closely at this being. Now, pick the most important one – by colour or emotion.

DH: Middle, slightly right, with white energy.

DA: Gender?

DH: Male.

DA: Identity?

DH: Fatherly energy, likely my father.

DA: Is he communicating?

DH: Just confirming it's him.

DA: What emotion?

DH: A tower of strength.

DA: Is Shukoshi near?

DH: If I want him. He's not in this group, just a guide.

DA: Where is he?

DH: Back towards the wall.

DA: Look at the other beings. What's most prominent?

DH: Middle to the left, second row back – my mother's face.

DA: What do you sense?

DH: Mischief and fond warmth.

DA: Is she communicating?

DH: Just those feelings.

DA: Continue identifying them.

DH: Next to her, changing from brown to purple, is my wife, young and happy.

DA: What's she communicating?

DH: Love, understanding. She knows me.

DA: Ask why this process feels slow.

DH: Maybe I'm not relaxed enough.

DA: Hold time briefly. Focus on your breathing. Deep breath in, out slowly, longer than the in-breath. Again. Deep breath in, out slowly. Once more, fully and quickly in, out slowly. I'll touch your forearm. Drift deeper, letting apprehension go. Resume time. Look at the beings. What do you sense?

DH: Next to her, left, is smaller but powerful – my friend Paul, a rock for me.

Narration

Maintaining a deep trance for hours is challenging. When trance lightens, indicated by struggles with detail, I use techniques like breathing exercises to deepen relaxation, ensuring clear memory recall.

End of Narration

DA: Do you feel familiarity with this process?

DH: No.

DA: Continue describing people.

DH: I don't know the white-bearded one, like Gandalf from *Lord of the Rings*. He's significant.

DA: Does he say anything?

DH: He emanates authority but is kind.

DA: How do you know? Can he answer questions? Ask about the significance of your foot loss and back pain in your current life.

DH: He laughs at "Gandalf". His name's Rosen or similar. He's an overseer.

DA: Ask about those issues.

DH: I chose them, possibly due to prejudice against disabled people.

DA: An ongoing theme in past lives?

DH: More like trying it out, to see what it's like.

DA: Ask how many lives you've had.

DH: Three I might learn about, but more overall.

DA: Total lives?

DH: More than three, but I'm given three.

DA: Has the scene changed?

DH: No.

DA: What's Rosen saying?

DH: Our group are playful children, mischievous, fun.

DA: Is that your nature?

DH: Yes.

DA: Ask to assess the life just ended – did you achieve what you should have?

DH: That life with the head injury wasn't fun, mundane, not going anywhere.

DA: Why choose that life?

DH: For more opportunities to express myself. It was a time of conformity.

DA: How to channel your playful energy now?

DH: By leading by example, not being told.

DA: Were you getting an answer?

DH: I'm seeking my life's purpose, but I must find it myself.

DA: Is the environment the same?

DH: It's dark, not clear.

DA: I expected it brighter. Is everyone still there?

DH: Yes.

DA: Shukoshi?

DH: No, he's not in my soul group. Rosen is the chief guide.

DA: Is Sarah there?

DH: Yes, but I haven't seen her.

DA: Can you identify others?

DH: Fletcher's at the front, right, with my brother Andrew behind him.

DA: What's happening?

DH: I'm laughing – it's like nothing's happening, as expected.

DA: Maybe that's fine. Ask Rosen about the fear causing self-deprecation and lack of fulfilment. Why experience these?

DH: To overcome them. I'm unsure of their origin.

Narration

Sessions prioritise client benefit. Clients submit questions post-booking, and I ask them when opportunities arise, as now. We may end intriguing threads due to time limits and client focus, not research.

End of Narration

DA: Ask Sarah about lessons from your relationship.

DH: We help each other grow.

DA: Has she appeared in other lives?

DH: Likely all have, but I don't know how.

DA: Ask Sarah.

DH: She has long, dark hair, possibly into occult or sorcery.
We may have been burnt for it in medieval times.

DA: Is she your soulmate?

DH: One of them. All these people are, but she's a favourite.

Chapter Summary

Douglas's journey home encapsulates the spiritual transition, beginning with his departure from a violent death in 1944 London, marked by indifference to his unfulfilled life.

The healing shower, a wall of golden light, cleanses and energises his soul, repairing damage from incarnation and restoring vitality, a process vital for newer souls as noted by Dr Newton. His meeting with his Primary Soul Group, a cluster of about 12 souls including familiar figures like his father, mother, and friend Barley, brings a sense of connection and playfulness, guided by figures like Shukoshi and Rosen.

This journey – from movement away from Earth, through the restorative shower, to the joyful reunion – underscores the soul's eagerness to shed physical constraints and embrace its eternal home, a pattern central to the spiritual realm's welcoming embrace.

Rosen, and his soul group – including familiar figures like his father and mother – reaffirm his spiritual connections, guiding him toward home with joy and familiarity.

Section 4

Chapter 13: Isadora Glenn

This exploration delves into the moment of passing for Isadora, the release from earthly burdens, and the reunion with her Primary Soul Group in a realm of light and harmony. Through their dialogue, we witness Isadora's emotional and spiritual evolution as she navigates this familiar yet awe-inspiring return home, offering readers a glimpse into the eternal connections that shape her soul's journey.

DA: You've just died and moved away from your physical body. Now, you've been through this experience many times before. As you progress, your memory will improve. You may sense some brief sadness or remorse at this moment, but from what you've just said, I suspect that you are now happy.

IG: Yes.

DA: All the pain has gone?

IG: Yes.

DA: Tell me where you are in relation to your body. Are you still in the same room?

IG: I'm hovering over, looking down.

DA: How is your son taking it?

IG: He's actually quite relieved.

DA: This must be a great relief.

IG: That's what I've been waiting for. That's why I'm hovering, because I want to see their faces.

DA: Is there anybody that you would like to try and touch or contact, just to say that everything's okay?

IG: No.

DA: You're just happy to leave them, and that life's done and dusted, as it were – finished, time to move on?

IG: I can see they're okay.

DA: I'll just ask you one more time: is there anything that you feel you need to do here or is it just time to go?

IG: Just time to go.

DA: Have you started to move away from the earth yet?

IG: Yeah, it's a cloudy thing.

DA: As you leave, do you feel – is it like you are being pulled, or is it just kind of floating?

IG: It's like being sucked into a tube.

DA: In what direction are you moving? Are you moving in the direction you are facing, or are you moving backwards? Which way are you facing – are you facing behind you, where you have come from or are you facing in front of you where you are going?

IG: In front of me.

DA: If you look back, can you see anything of the earth?

IG: Nothing.

DA: Now, you have been this way before. Just keep moving and know that you are going home. Are you moving quickly or slowly?

IG: Quick.

DA: Is that changing? Is it speeding up or is it the same speed?

IG: I think it's speeding up.

DA: As you find yourself moving higher and further away, is the space around you getting lighter or darker?

IG: It's getting lighter.

DA: Okay, tell me when you can see far into the distance beyond your immediate surroundings.

IG: It's like moving towards the sun.

DA: Is it just a large globe of light you can see?

IG: No, it's not. It's just light.

DA: Just light. As you continue to move towards it, you may be able to differentiate – there may be lots of points of light or one large light.

IG: I can't see anything.

DA: Is it just bright light?

IG: Yeah, that's okay.

DA: Are you still moving?

IG: No, it's slowed down.

DA: Tell me what the light feels like. Is it around you?

IG: No, not yet. I think I'm standing in some kind of gate of some sort.

DA: Is there anybody else there?

IG: Yeah, it's a cloud man. It's just a fog.

DA: Do you sense any other beings present?

IG: Yeah, it's lots of them, but I can't see them.

DA: Do you have to go through the gate?

IG: Yeah, but I think the fog man is trying to stop me. I'm going too fast, I think.

DA: Okay, you can just take your time. You don't need to hurry.

IG: But I want to hurry.

DA: The cloud man, the fog man – is he communicating with you?

IG: Yeah.

DA: So, what is he saying to you, or what is he communicating to you?

IG: He wants me to slow down.

DA: Okay, well, just do that for a while. You have plenty of time. You might ask him why he wants you to slow down.

IG: Because I'm always hastening everywhere. I can't learn anything if I'm running.

DA: Is he your guide?

IG: I think so.

DA: What's his name?

IG: He's laughing at me. I don't know. You can ask him. Yeah, but I can't – I don't understand what he's saying.

DA: Try and repeat the sound that he's making for his name to me if you can, and I'll try and write something down.

IG: It's a feeling. It's a sound of some kind. I think he said "Joy".

DA: You think it's—

IG: Joy. It's a feeling. His name is a feeling, but it says "ComeJoy".

DA: What is your spiritual name?

IG: Estrella.

DA: Can you spell it?

IG: E-S-T-R-E-L-L-A.

DA: Estrella, have you gone through the gate yet?

IG: Yeah.

DA: Who else is there?

IG: Many.

DA: How many?

IG: Oh, I can't count, the people are everywhere.

DA: Are they all expecting you?

IG: No, it's like just passing through. It's like a big train station.

DA: Is ComeJoy still with you?

IG: Yeah.

DA: Continue your journey with him until you get to where you need to be. Tell me about ComeJoy. He is obviously represented to you – you said "he". Is he represented as male?

IG: Yeah, mostly.

DA: If you look at him closely, is he showing any features, or does he remain amorphous?

IG: He's got a golden cape. He's white – white and golden. It's like the cape that the Pope uses, a robe, some kind of robe.

DA: Has he got any facial features?

IG: No, not yet.
DA: Is he holding your hand?
IG: No.
DA: How far away from you is he?
IG: Pretty close. I can almost touch – he's touching my shoulder.
DA: Ask him where you're going.
IG: To my group. They're waiting for me.
DA: Can you see them yet?
IG: Yeah.
DA: How many of them are there?
IG: It's one to my right and three in front, and just behind them, there's one or two – two, I think.
DA: Does one of these seem more important than any of the others?
IG: Yeah, one in front.
DA: The one in the centre of the three in front of you – let me ask you a few questions. How does this entity present itself to you – as male or female or amorphous?
IG: Male.
DA: What colour is it? What are the colours associated with this entity?
IG: Yellow.
DA: Is he communicating anything to you?
IG: He's so bright, I can't look at him.
DA: Can you sense any communication from him?
IG: Yeah, he's happy to see me.
DA: How does that make you feel?
IG: I don't know who he is. I can't recall who he is.
DA: That information will come to you shortly. We need to allow some time for this to happen, but what I want to know is if you're getting any sense of communication from him. What do you sense from him other than he's happy to see you?

IG: He's some kind of partner or brother. He has some kind
     of moral brother, I think.
DA: Okay, let's look at the others and then we can come
     back to him. The entity to his right – let's say to your
     left, you're looking at them on the left side of him –
     tell me firstly whether the entity represents as male or
     female.
IG: It's a female.
DA: What colour is she?
IG: Yellow.
DA: Is she also quite bright?
IG: No, not so bright.
DA: Is she communicating anything to you?
IG: Yeah, but not – she's just happy to see me, but not so
     intensely.
DA: What's her name?
IG: Olga.
DA: Olga.
IG: O-L-G-A, I think. That's all – it keeps repeating.
DA: Is she playing a part in your current life, the current
     physical life?
IG: I think she's my mum.
DA: Okay, all of this will become very much clearer as we
     spend time here. But now let's go to the entity that is to
     your right-hand side from the way that you're looking.
     These are the three that are in front – we have the very
     strong yellow light of the male in the centre and the one
     to the right of that. Firstly, let me ask you if that entity
     is presenting as male or female.
IG: Male.
DA: And what colour again?
IG: More green – greenish-yellow-green.
DA: Is he communicating anything to you?
IG: Yeah, he says that it's nice to see me and he's here.

DA: He's here in this life as well?

IG: He says that he's supporting me.

DA: What's his name?

IG: I-I can't, I don't know.

DA: Okay, we can come back to that. Is he playing a part in your current life?

IG: Yes.

DA: Who is he in this life?

IG: He's my partner.

DA: Ah, which is – how do you say that – Alan? And moving round now, you said there was an entity also to the right, on your right-hand side. Is that entity still there?

IG: Yeah.

DA: Does the entity present to you as male or female?

IG: It's a small female.

DA: What colour?

IG: Pink, really, like almost white.

DA: What's her name?

IG: Rosa.

DA: Rosa. Is she communicating anything to you?

IG: She says hello.

DA: Is she playing a part in this current life?

IG: Yeah, I think so.

DA: Who is she in this life?

IG: Janet.

DA: She's Janet. Now, you said there were a couple standing behind?

IG: Yeah.

DA: Tell me a little bit about them and who they are.

IG: It's almost – the ones in the front are blocking my view.

DA: Okay, let's come back to the male entity – the very bright yellow entity in the centre – and tell me what his name is now.

IG: I can't tell, I don't know.

DA: That's okay.

IG: He's saying something.

DA: Just allow the communication to come into you, and then you will understand.

IG: It's got something to do with plants.

DA: Is he playing a part in this current life for you?

IG: No, I don't know – no, he's not.

DA: Does he play a part in some of your lives?

IG: He's not there, and he's not – oh, it seems like he's in the distance, in the background.

DA: Is ComeJoy still with you, your guide?

IG: Yeah.

DA: Where's he?

IG: To my left.

DA: Ask any of these – your friends, your group, any of these entities – anything that you want to. You can meet them, greet them, hug them, whatever you want to do. Just follow your feelings and your sense and what they want to do. So, you can ask questions – just tell me what's happening, what's going on, so that I know, so that it's on the recording.

IG: Everyone wants to talk at the same time. They're just like me – they want everything really fast. It's just blah, blah, blah – I can't figure out what – I can't – the words are just coming.

DA: Well, you can tell them to hang on – one at a time. You can exercise some control over what's happening.

IG: The one in the front, the strong light—

DA: Yes.

IG: His name is Timian.

DA: And how is Timian important to you?

IG: He is my son.

DA: Ah, he's the son you're going to have. How does that make you feel?

IG: Weird, because we've never had a laugh together before.

DA: Okay, he's obviously very strong, very close. Is he your soulmate?

IG: Yes.

DA: Is there anything that you'd like to ask? Is there anything that you'd like to ask anyone else?

IG: Not at this moment. I want to know who the two in the back are.

DA: Okay, ask – you can ask Timian to move aside a little bit, or you can move forward through them and tell me who the two in the back are.

IG: They're quite small, like child-sized, but they seem so skittish, like they're kind of scared. Are they new in the group? Maybe – I think they're new in the group.

DA: What colour are they?

IG: The one that I can hardly see has got some darker blue, I think, and the one in the front, he's got a somewhat greyish—

DA: Which is the blue one – the one on the left or right?

IG: The blue one is on the left. I think.

DA: I heard you were telling me about the two entities at the back – are they still there?

IG: Yeah.

DA: Have you got any more information about them?

IG: No, they seem very shy.

DA: Is there anything else that you want to talk to your friends about at this time?

IG: No, no, no other than I'm happy to see them.

DA: Is ComeJoy still there?

IG: Yep.

Chapter Summary

Isadora's journey reflects a universal experience of transitioning from the physical to the spiritual realm, marked by a sense of release and joy.

Guided by her spiritual guide, ComeJoy, Isadora moves swiftly through a tunnel of light, encountering her Primary Soul Group in a vibrant, harmonious space. The reunion with familiar souls, including her son Timian, her mother Olga, her partner Alan, and others, brings a mix of excitement and curiosity, tempered by the calming presence of her guide.

This chapter illustrates the profound comfort and connection found in the soul's return home, offering a serene yet dynamic glimpse into the eternal bonds that define Isadora's spiritual existence.

Chapter 14: Wanda Kirby

Wanda's session offers a vivid exploration of the soul's transition from physical life to the spiritual realm. Unlike typical journeys, this experience stands out for its poignant reflection on solitude as a purposeful lesson, as revealed by Wanda's guide, Finn. The familiar yet mystical landscape resembling Stonehenge and the enveloping mist create a unique backdrop for Wanda's reconnection with her soul group, highlighting the interplay between past lives and present challenges in her spiritual evolution.

DA: You can move quickly past the point of death in this memory. You have just died. And tell me, can you see your body? How far away from the body are you?

WK: Quite near. But separate.

DA: Is anyone else near your body now? Are there other people there?

WK: Yes.

DA: Tell me what's going on.

WK: I think some people laid me onto a gate or something to carry me back.

DA: What do you feel about this at this moment?

WK: Sorry that it was rather soon.

DA: How do you feel about your death?

WK: I don't mind too much now.

DA: Do you wish to remain a while longer to perhaps say goodbye to somebody? Or to attend to any unfinished business on Earth? Or would you prefer to leave right now?

WK: I'd like to go now.

DA: Now as you move away from your body, please describe everything that happens so that I can stay with you. Have you started to move away yet?

WK: Yes.

DA: As you leave, do you feel a pulling sensation or just a floating?

WK: Mainly floating.

DA: Are you facing the direction in which you are moving or are you moving backwards?

WK: Facing.

DA: As you turn back, what can you see below as you move away from the earth's plane?

WK: The earth.

DA: Literally. Is that a surprise to you?

WK: Yes, because I've obviously moved quite quickly.

DA: Tell me when you can see far into the distance, beyond your immediate surroundings. And tell me if you can see anything.

WK: It's almost like I'm back on that hill again. Grass.

DA: Is anybody approaching you?

WK: I'm kind of anticipating it. I feel rather excited.

DA: Tell me what you can see as you look around you.

WK: Looks a bit like Stonehenge. Grass with stones. But it's the atmosphere. It's the feeling of the familiar.

DA: What do you sense? What does your own energy sense from this place?

WK: That I know it very well and I love it. I'm just waiting for the others.

DA: Do you feel a sense of growing stronger as you stay in this place?

WK: Yes, I think I need a bit of rest. R&R.

DA: Rest and recuperation. This is quite a normal process of replenishment of energy. And we can just allow that to take its course. Because you can already sense that there are those waiting for you to become ready.

WK: I just wonder why anybody's ever afraid of dying.

DA: Tell me what is happening and what you can see and feel.

WK: Familiar people.

DA: Are they there?

WK: Yes.

DA: Are they in front of you or to the side?

WK: They're kind of round. Front, side, and back.

DA: How far away from you are they?

WK: They're very near now. It's lovely to see them.

DA: Does anybody come forward first? Are any of these sensed or felt to be more important than the others? Or more significant to you?

WK: Yes.

DA: Look at that spirit and describe what you see.

WK: I can't really see. I feel. I know the essence of that person.

DA: Who is it?

WK: I think it's kind of my other half.

DA: What's happening now?

WK: We're all talking about what had happened.

DA: Tell me what's being said.

WK: It's not really like language. It's kind of... We're just all of us so happy to be together.

DA: What do you feel at the moment?

WK: Rather envious of myself, if you see what I mean.

DA: Is your guide present?

WK: I think at the edge.

DA: Look toward the spiritual entity that you think is your guide. And tell me a little bit about this spirit. Your sense or feeling of this spirit.

WK: Kind but a bit stern. I'm not sure if I did very well.

DA: Do the spirits around you give you a sense of gender? Does your guide give you a sense of gender?

WK: A man.

DA: What's his name?

WK: I don't know.

DA: You can ask him.

WK: I think it's Finn.

DA: What's your spiritual name?

WK: Alestra.

DA: Alestra, what's happening now?

WK: It's quite difficult to see. There's a mist.

DA: Are your friends still near you?

WK: Yes.

DA: Can you touch them?

WK: Yes. They help me.

DA: Are they still around you in a complete circle?

WK: Yes.

DA: How many of them are there?

WK: Sort of quite a crowd, really. About eight people, I think.

DA: About eight? Choose the one you sense is most important to you. Go and touch them.

WK: Yes.

DA: And when you touch them, tell me what you sense. Who they are. Whether you recognise them.

WK: He's got what sounds like a German name. Ernhard.

DA: Did this spirit play a part in your current life?

WK: I'm not sure. I don't know.

DA: What do you feel about Ernhard?

WK: I feel he's a man. And I'm a female.

DA: Is he communicating anything to you?

WK: Not in words. No.

DA: In communicating concepts or ideas, what do you sense is coming from him? You may be receiving information in a sense which is not words. I understand that. But to make sense for us and for the recording, you need to translate into words what the communication is.

WK: Yeah. I think… I think I have known him now. I think he was Bill. Bill was him. I'm sorry, I'm not very good at talking about it. It seems to me that I have to be alone so much.

DA: Where does that sense come from? Who's telling you that?

WK: I think Finn is telling me.

DA: Can you ask him why?

WK: He says I've… I've had to learn how to be cut off from things, from people, and manage by myself. So, people go… I don't think it's always been like that.

DA: Move around the other souls that are with you at this time, and you may find that if you go up to touch them, to touch energies, and what I'd like you to do is to just tell me what you can about each of them as you go around. So just pick perhaps the next one that appears to be most important to you other than Ernhard, touch them, and tell me what you sense about them and what they may communicate to you.

WK: I think Michael, my son.

DA: What's his spiritual name?

WK: I think it's Michael.

DA: What's he communicating to you?

WK: That we have done a lot of things together in the past.

DA: Does he mean over many, many lives?

WK: Yes. Yes, he does. I think the four of us in this life now were close to start with, as it were, and now we have to separate up a bit.

DA: Move from Michael to the next spirit and touch them and tell me about them and what they may be communicating to you.

WK: Louis. I've known Louis all his life, and he's a very close friend, I think.

DA: Is he communicating anything to you? If he isn't, it doesn't matter – we can just move on.

WK: Matt, his father. He's a very gentle soul.

DA: Is he communicating anything to you?

WK: He's a comforter.

DA: What's Matthew's spiritual name?

WK: Hal.

DA: Move to the next person.

WK: That's Ernie.

DA: Ernie, did you say?

WK: Yeah.

DA: Is he communicating anything to you?

WK: She's a she.

DA: She. And she is a she too. And she's representing herself as female in a spiritual sense as well?

WK: Yes.

DA: Is she representing anything, saying anything to you?

WK: I think she's saying we should have done this earlier.

DA: What's her spiritual name?

WK: Judith.

DA: Now I know that there is often a huge amount that you're experiencing and that is going on, and it's really – I know it's very comfortable for you just to be involved in that – but you really have to tell me something, otherwise there's nothing on the recording.

WK: No. I don't – I don't know. I don't think there is very much going on, actually. That's the odd thing. It's just a sort of atmosphere.

DA: How would you describe the atmosphere?

WK: Like a sort of mist, you can lean on.

DA: Okay. Let's move round to the other spirits because I want to know who these eight people are. Let's move to the next one.

WK: Diana. Diana was her name. We were young, and the wood that we started off in was our particular wood

DA: What's Diana's spiritual name?

WK:I just know her as Diana. She died, I found out, quite a long time ago. Young – well, fairly young. She had – I met her when I was 12. She had a lot of influence.

DA: How long were you friends?

WK: Well, she was three years older, and I was evacuated another time in the war. She was going to be an actress. So, I did that too when I grew up.

DA: Is she communicating anything to you in particular now?

WK: No, not – just glad to see each other. I didn't know she was dead, but I looked her up online.

DA: Move to the next person and tell me who they are.

WK: Barney.

DA: What's Barney's spiritual name?

WK: William, I think.

DA: Is he communicating anything to you?

WK: He's saying he's alright because he's one I worry about, but he seems to be okay.

DA: Okay, let's move on to the next one.

WK: Carla.

DA: Who's Carla?

WK: She lived now. That's the lady I met when I was 17, 18 – that age. She was a refugee.

DA: What's her spiritual name?

WK: Laura.

DA: And is she communicating anything to you?

WK: She's saying that we've met again.

DA: Ask her what she means by that.

WK: I think she's been born again in this present life. I met her in 1948, so I suppose she could be.

DA: Is she currently incarnating now?

WK: Yes, I think so, but I don't know who she is.

DA: Ask her.

WK: She could be Anne. I'm not sure. I don't find this easy at all.

DA: Just let it happen. Just let it happen. Have we any spirits left that we haven't interrogated, as such?

WK: I'm not sure.

DA: We'll move to the next one, and if it's somebody new, that's fine, and if it's somebody we've already been to, that's also fine because we'll know.

WK: I think it's one of my friends. I have two friends called Audrey. Now I think it's – I think I know which one it is, but I'm not sure.

DA: Is she talking to you? Does she communicate anything to you?

WK: Her name's Mary, and she's having a difficult time now in this life. I don't think I'm helping her enough.

DA: Is Finn still there?

WK: Yes, on the edge.

DA: I think he's a bit of a sink-or-swim merchant. Tell him that you have a number of questions, a number of things you'd like to find out, and ask him whether there's anything that you can now do to help that.

WK: Yes. I want to ask him if I'm on the right path.

DA: What is he saying to you?

WK: He says it's the right path for me, and part of it is this feeling of becoming more alone.

DA: Are you comfortable?

WK: Not really, no.

DA: You can adjust and move. Are you physically comfortable?

WK: I'm getting cold, actually.

DA: Right. Let me get you a blanket. Would you like a comfort break or —

WK: Yes.

DA: Okay, just sit there for a bit. I'll get the blanket then. What we'll do is just rest your head back for a minute. Okay. And just close your eyes. This will be quite easy for you to do because as soon as you open your eyes again, you'll be able to go and use the loo, come back, we'll cover you with a blanket, and we will be able to return to exactly the same place that we left quite easily. Okay, open your eyes, and I'll show you where the loo is. Just sit there – first door on the right.

WK: Okay. I suddenly felt terribly cold. It sometimes does happen, right?

DA: This should sort you out.

WK: Thank you.

DA: It's okay. That's good. Okay. Just rest back.

WK: I'm not sure that I'm getting very far.

DA: And close your eyes. Right, now you don't have to think of anything. Let me move that up a little further. Right, so what we're going to do – just close your eyes and we can retrace and quickly move back to where you were before. Now you will remember a little while ago how your body relaxed quite easily when your eyes felt quite tired, and you remember how you drifted down into a nice relaxed state, and you will also remember how you checked all around your body and let all the tension go from all the muscles, and we went quickly back into this wooded, beautiful woodland area where you sat and you left your body, and you recounted and relived some memories, and we went back and back again down through your childhood where we stopped at a couple of points, and then spent a little bit of time in the womb, and we came from there and moved back to a life as James as a 20-year-old standing in the room, and then we moved through to that accident which ended James's life, and from there you moved away, and you could see the earth as you moved away, and you moved to a place of recuperation so your energy could be replenished and repaired, and then your friends came to see you, and that is where you are now. Is Finn still there?

WK: Yes.

DA: Is he communicating anything to you?

WK: Not a lot, really.

DA: Still drifting down deeper and deeper with each breath you take, it will become even more relaxed, more comfortable, and the more that happens, the clearer will be the messages. I want you to ask Finn to take you to a place of review where, as the spiritual entity Alestra, you can review your progress and actions of the past and actions of the present and ask him if you are able to do that.

WK: Yes.

DA: And if he will take you there now?

WK: Yeah, okay, he says.

DA: Then go with him and tell me what is happening.

WK: I was standing looking at – like a television screen. It seems a little incongruous, and he seems to be saying that I've got a way to go yet. It seems to have been such a long time since Bill died.

Chapter Summary

Wanda's journey unfolds in a distinctive setting that evokes both familiarity and introspection, with the Stonehenge-like landscape and a tangible mist shaping her experience. The encounter with her soul group, including figures like Ernhard and Michael, is marked by a profound sense of reunion, yet it is Finn's guidance on embracing solitude that sets this session apart.

This chapter captures Wanda's struggle to articulate non-verbal spiritual communications and her gradual acceptance of her path, offering a nuanced perspective on the soul's need for both connection and independence in its eternal journey.

Chapter 15: Antonia Zest

Antonia's session unfolds with a distinctive emphasis on the restorative process following a challenging life. The immediate engagement with a healing shower and the tender intervention of a female healer highlights the session's focus on energy repair, setting it apart from typical soul group reunions. The playful interaction with mischievous spirits adds a layer of levity, revealing Antonia's need to reconnect with her lighter, less serious side as she navigates her spiritual homecoming.

DA: Now, before we prepare to move further away from your body and begin the journey back, can you just describe to me exactly where you are now in relation to your body?

AZ: Okay. I'm still sort of hovering under the ceiling of the hut. I see her lying there. But I also want to move forward now. She's fine.

DA: That will just begin to happen as I talk to you. Now, if you started to move, are you ... What is the sensation? Describe the sensation of movement. Is it ... Is it as though you're being...

AZ: I'm floating slowly, gently, in a meandering way. I follow a direction, but it's not straight. It's as if I'm enjoying it.

DA: As you look back from where you've come from, what do you see?

AZ: I see the hut and the forest around. There's lots of forest there.

DA: Are you moving faster?

AZ: It's as if I'm up to the last clock.

DA: Well, that's okay. You can do that if you want to.

AZ: I'm rising. I'm rising. I see the sea.

DA: Continue to describe to me everything that is happening on this journey, so that I know where you are, and I can stay with you.

AZ: I'm in a space that is … It's like a shadow, but I can feel, I can sense the light. I feel slightly pulled to the right.

DA: Is your speed constant or is it still accelerating?

AZ: It's hesitant. It's … I don't know why. I want to, but it's as if I have to be slow.

DA: Okay.

AZ: But it's as if something's nudging me to … Yes, it goes faster now. It goes faster. And straight. There is something greyish, lighter. It's like a wall that is not a wall. Anyway, we'll pass just through it. And that's light. It's beautiful. I'm slowing down again. There's a place I need to go to. It seems as if it's quite close. And it's an entrance to a house or space. And I'm getting a shower.

DA: Where is it coming from?

AZ: Oh, is this … It comes from above me and around me

DA: What do you sense and feel as it touches you?

AZ: It's warming me and it's as if it's taking away those dark … It's to, in a way, get rid of the debris of my last life.

DA: What colour is the shower?

AZ: It's white.

DA: Completely white?

AZ: It's flickering like bluish silver.

DA: Is it touching you all over or just from the top or the sides?

AZ: No, it washes all through me. It's as if I feel my skin but also there is none. I feel that I want … It's not light. It's something else. It's not light. And yet it goes through me and relieves me. But it's enough shower now. I feel tired.

Narration

Once again, we have a very good description of a healing shower, though it can appear as different things to different people. The consistent factor is that it repairs the energy damaged in the life just lived.

End of Narration

DA: Are you moving again?

AZ: At the moment just sitting there and there is somebody there who just puts a hand on my head.

DA: What do you sense from this person when they touch you?

AZ: Kindness and gentleness. As if she's feeding me with something. As if the kindness is feeding me.

DA: Does this entity appear to you as a male or female? Do you sense it?

AZ: It's female. It's female.

DA: If you look closely, can you define a shape? Can you describe her?

AZ: Yes, she's wearing … Well, she appears to be wearing some dark red … She's one of the healers who looks after souls who have just come in.

Narration

Souls have specific roles, which we'll discover more about later. In this case the energy damage had been noticed and quite unusually some additional attention seems to be necessary.

End of Narration

DA: Is she communicating anything to you?

AZ: Only that everything's fine now and that I will move on in a minute. Yes, it feels good. I'm ready to go further now. So, I'm standing at the … I feel … I know where I'm pulled. But again, it's slow. It feels as if I used to move much faster. But I'm on my way again. I need some sort of greyish, whitish field. There were other shapes moving. And I follow the stream first, but I'm faster now. And I know that that's where I have to go. I have to take that stream but follow fast. And it's like I need to veer off to the left now.

DA: Okay.

AZ: There's some place there. It's weird. It looks as if there is a wall and then a roof. Like an overhang, flat. But when one enters, there's only that one wall. And one just goes behind it and then there is a large space. Just white, greyish white, light. And there are shapes there.

DA: How many shapes are there?

AZ: They're clumped. I can't…

DA: You can move closer. They may become more defined.

AZ: I can't quite see anybody. They all seem to hide.

DA: Do you sense anything from them? Mischief?

AZ: I do. But I'm aware that behind me, to my left, there's my guide. I haven't seen him yet, but I sense his presence. But they are hiding from me.

DA: Are they playful spirits? Playful entities?

AZ: They are. They are playful. It's as if now they're all surrounding me. I can't discern anybody but they're surrounding me and…

DA: What do you sense from them?

AZ: They're fond of me. And they like making a bit of fun of me because I'm so serious. It's as if they're whirling around me and I'm … And I stop. I'm not supposed to stay. It's okay to be with them, just to touch base with them. To feel that mischievous spirit. Remind myself that I have that as well. But I'm not supposed to stay at all.

DA: You can stay for a bit. See, try and look at the entities. They're closer to me. They're playful. Tell me what you can detect. The good way to do this is to ... You may well notice that one of them might seem to be more important than the others. It might be slightly brighter, or it might be slightly bigger. Or it might just seem to you that it's a little more important than the others.

AZ: One of them was this close. And she's a little female.

DA: What's her name?

AZ: Isima.

DA: Is she playing a part in your current life?

AZ: No, she isn't. She was my sister in the previous one, but she's not in my current life. None of them is in my current life.

DA: What's your spiritual name?

AZ: Suva.

DA: Is your guide still nearby?

AZ: He's somewhere around. He's somewhere behind me still, but he doesn't want me to ... No, I need to...

DA: Just call him to you. Just ask him to come to you. I'm calling him. Yes. What's his name?

AZ: Randell. R-A-N-D-E-L-L.

DA: Now, Suva, you indicated that you weren't needed to stay here for too much longer.

AZ: Mm-hmm.

DA: But I'd just like to ask you ... of the independent entities that are around you that clearly know you, do you know how many of them there are? Can you count them for me?

AZ: They're about seven, eight ... Hang on. Eight.

DA: And as you are now becoming more familiar with their presence, can you tell me what colours they show to you? Are they all white or are they different colours?

AZ: No. Two are green. There's a yellowish-green one. And there's pinkish and there is a blue one there.

DA: Which colour is Isima?

AZ: Isima is the light blue. She's the one with light blue with a white radiance.

DA: And what colours does Randell emit?

AZ: He's dark green. Very dark, bluish green.

DA: Do you sense that when you've been elsewhere and done the other things that you need to do, you'll then be able to come back and join them and spend a bit more time with them?

AZ: I think so, yes.

Chapter Summary

Antonia's journey stands out for its vivid depiction of energy restoration, marked by a cleansing shower and the gentle touch of a healer. The encounter with a playful soul group, led by the light blue Isima, introduces a unique dynamic, encouraging Antonia to embrace her mischievous spirit. This chapter underscores the importance of healing and balance, offering a compelling insight into the soul's capacity to recover and rediscover joy amidst the complexities of its eternal path.

Section 4

The Journey Home: Summary

The journeys chronicled in Section 4 weave a narrative of spiritual homecoming, marked by the soul's liberation from earthly constraints and its reintegration into the harmonious realm of eternal consciousness. Douglas's rapid transition through a golden healing shower, Isadora's swift passage through a tunnel of light, Wanda's introspective pause in a Stonehenge-like landscape, and Antonia's restorative encounter with a healer and playful spirits collectively highlight the multifaceted nature of the soul's return.

The recurring presence of guides – Shukoshi, ComeJoy, Finn, and Randell – underscores the tailored support each soul receives, while the reunions with Primary Soul Groups emphasise the enduring bonds that anchor these spiritual voyages. This section reveals the dynamic interplay of healing, guidance, and connection, illustrating how souls, regardless of their earthly experiences, find solace and purpose in the embrace of their spiritual home.

Reviews: Introduction

The soul's journey unfolds through reflection and the mapping of lessons across countless lives. Section 5: Reviews, invites readers into the sacred process where souls assess their earthly paths, guided by the Council or archival exploration. These sessions – spanning Esther's orb preference, Hope's fear of past lives, Rebecca's karmic loops, Abigail's Hybrid Soul insights, and Isabelle's symbolic visions – reveal spiritual evaluation's depth. In the modern day, amid algorithm-driven distraction and post-pandemic isolation, such reviews resonate. They mirror our need to pause, find clarity, and navigate loneliness, identity, and purpose. While tailored to clients' needs, not research, these transcripts show how introspection anchors us, offering wisdom for today's complex world.

The Library

The Library, sometimes called the knowledge store, is where clients review former lives from their soul's perspective. Imagine working in a small branch of a global company, then moving to head office to see the whole operation. Some souls need this perspective; others do not. Unlike the immersive experience of reliving past lives, the Library offers detachment, like describing a play rather than acting in it. Clients perceive records differently – screens, immersion, or telepathic insight – based on their expectations. The focus is understanding, not the mechanism.

The Council

The Council is a formal evaluation, overwhelmingly positive, where souls are guided, not judged. Typically involving five members led by a senior figure, its setting varies, but encouragement dominates, as seen in Isabelle's jewelled elders. Dr Michael Newton's *Journey of Souls* and *Destiny of Souls* (Llewellyn Press) detail soul progression, colours, and seniority. Guides remain silent, offering support, while detailed descriptions of the Council members validate clients' experiences, grounding spiritual memories in earthly reality.

After a life, some souls require reflection, though not all. These sessions prioritise clients' needs over research, so explorations may shift to follow their benefit, not curiosity. This section illuminates how Esther, Hope, Rebecca, Abigail, and Isabelle navigate their soul's growth, offering universal lessons for connection and purpose.

Chapter 16: Esther Newton

As her spiritual self, Maya, Esther navigates the spirit world with her guide, Blackhawk. Her journey begins with a reunion with her Soul Group, including her sister-in-law Dinah and friend Inara, before transitioning to a significant meeting with the Council. The session culminates in the knowledge store, which Esther refers to as the Library, where she reviews past lives to uncover lessons for her spiritual growth. The knowledge store emerges as a critical space for Esther, reflecting her resistance to modern methods and preference for traditional orbs, offering a unique perspective on her soul's development.

DA: Is there any particular place in the spirit world that you would like to go to first? Or would you like to rejoin your friends right away? Okay, as you've said that you would like to move on, and with the help of your guide, let's go and join your friends, your Primary Soul Group. And tell me when you see them, Maya. Now I know that this is a fantastic experience for you, but you will want to know about this in detail later. And if you tell me, it will be recorded.

And although you will remember well, the recording doesn't miss anything. So, tell me what's happening at the moment.

EN: My sister-in-law is there. She's in a dark suit and she's very cross.

DA: Who is this?

EN: This is my sister-in-law, Dinah, on the earth plane in this life. And she's cross because she's been waiting a long time for me.

DA: What does she say to you?

EN: Oh, thank God we've been waiting for you. We thought we were going to miss you again. She's not, she's not on my path. She's not a body person. She doesn't take such difficult assignments.

DA: Has she ever helped you in your assignments?

EN: Yes.

DA: Did she help you in this last life?

EN: I don't know. I think she wasn't there because she's been waiting.

DA: What colours do you sense from her?

EN: She's yellowish green.

DA: Now you've got that initial introduction over with, are there others that you wish to see?

EN: Her sister is there.

DA: Dinah's sister?

EN: Yeah.

DA: What's her name?

EN: In this life, it's Inara, but she's dead in this life.

DA: What was Inara to you in your last life?

EN: We were at university together, in this life.

DA: This life?

EN: Yeah.

DA: What is she saying to you?

EN: We thought we were going to miss you again, and there's so much to catch up on.

DA: Are these the only two souls that are there?

EN: Yeah.

DA: Is your guide still there?

EN: Yes, but he's off, just waiting.

DA: Is he off to one side or the other?

EN: To my right.

DA: Do you see any other light?

EN: Oh, lots, but they're away.

DA: Are there any others that are coming to you?

EN: No, just these two.

DA: Is this what normally happens?

EN: Yes, the more times you come, the less you see people that you know when you get back, because we're all doing different things.

DA: Dinah, is that Dinah's spirit name or earthly name?

EN: No, that's this life's name.

DA: What's her spirit name?

EN: I don't know.

DA: Do you know Inara's spirit name?

EN: It's the same, Inky, yes.

DA: You call her Inky?

EN: Yes.

DA: Oh, right. Well, do they tell you that there's anything you need to do now?

EN: Oh, they just want me to go with them and have some fun, because they know it's not been fun this time around again.

DA: And what kind of things would they call fun? What kind of things would you do?

EN: Playing, just playing, but I can't go with them. I've got reporting to do. I've got to go and report. They're so naughty.

DA: So, what do you tell them?

EN: That they'll have to wait.

DA: And what do they say?

EN: They're fed up because they've been waiting, but they know because the guide is coming near now.

DA: What does he say?

EN: Nothing, but they're backing off, and they hope we'll see each other again, but they don't know. They're waiting for their assignment, but they don't know if I'll be near them.

DA: Well, it seems as though it is time now for you to move
   to another place in the spirit world. Is that the case?

EN: Yes.

DA: Do you know where you're going?

EN: I'm going to report.

DA: To the Council?

EN: Yes.

DA: Okay. Have you started going to the Council?

EN: We're there.

DA: Now tell me where you are.

EN: It's like a cathedral. It's like it's hewn out of this white
   marble rock, and it's uneven, but it's like a cave, yet it's
   light.

DA: Are you inside?

EN: Yes.

DA: Where is your guide in relation to you?

EN: He's standing next to me on my right.

DA: Are the Council members there?

EN: Yes.

DA: How many of them are there?

EN: Five.

DA: Does one of them appear to be a spokesperson?

EN: Yes, the blue one.

DA: How are they arranged?

EN: It's like a horseshoe.

DA: Are they in front of you?

EN: Yes.

DA: How far away are they?

EN: About 6 metres.

DA: Can you see each Council member quite clearly?

EN: No, they're just lights.

DA: Starting from the left-hand side, as you face them, with
   these five Council members, what is the predominant
   light of the one furthest on the left?

EN: It's green.

DA: And the one next to him on the right?

EN: It's white.

DA: And the next person would be the one in the middle. Is that the spokesperson?

EN: Yes, it's the blue, that sort of violet blue. He's the lightest. The brightest as well.

DA: And the person on the right-hand side of him, as you look?

EN: He's white.

DA: And the person on the farthest right?

EN: He's small and white.

DA: What is the first thing you hear in your mind, and who addresses you first?

EN: It's the blue one. He's not talking to me; he's talking to Blackhawk.

Narration

Blackhawk is her guide, introduced earlier in the overall session.

End of Narration

DA: And you understand what he is saying?

EN: It seems to have been something about them waiting for me.

DA: What does Blackhawk reply?

EN: That my spirit sisters had interrupted, and they always do, and he's irritated with them. But you mustn't be angry with them, because they're young, and they're excited, and they've been waiting for me.

DA: Is the session about to get underway?

EN: Yes.

DA: So, once they've found out why you were a bit late, and about your spirit sisters, what's being asked now? What's being discussed?

EN: They're talking about my achievement.

DA: And what are they saying about it?

EN: That they think I've done a fair job, but if I'm serious about this, I really need to think about my next incarnation and increase the complexity. Because although I was frightened at the end, I had a very privileged life in China.

DA: Is this something that you feel you want to do?

EN: Yes.

DA: Do they talk about the fact that you did decide on a relatively privileged life in China?

EN: No, I went to be with Ho Fun, but I never found him.

Narration

This is the first mention of Ho Fun, but as we were busy on more important Council matters, I didn't follow up as it was just an aside.

End of Narration

DA: Does your guide have any input?

EN: No, he's gone.

DA: Is it still the main Council member who's addressing her?

EN: Yes.

DA: Just before we move on, the one on the right at the very end, the small white one.

EN: He's getting quite excited about something and being told not to interfere. He's trying to lessen the impact of what the blue one is telling me.

DA: If you look at the blue guide, do you see anything about or on the light, the objects, or for that matter on any of the Council members?

EN: They're all wearing a kind of box.

DA: When you say box, what do you mean?

EN: It's like, it might be a thin cigarette case from the 1920s. It's sort of boxy.

DA: You say they're wearing them. How are they wearing them?

EN: They're just in front of them.

DA: On a table?

EN: No, on their shape.

DA: Is it possible for you to just walk a little closer? We've taken time out now, so there are no questions. Just to take time out.

Walk a little closer and see if you can see these boxes more clearly.

EN: Yes, they're thin, like a cigarette case would have been.

DA: Is there anything on the boxes?

EN: No, they're just plain.

DA: You can return to your position where you were before, and we can continue the Council meeting. And tell me what else you're being asked or told.

EN: I'm told I need a new assignment. I need to go and think about where the gaps are.

DA: What gaps are they talking about?

EN: The gaps in my development.

DA: Okay, can you be a bit more specific as to what they are?

EN: I've been too passive. I need to be more adversarial. And I need to advocate for others, because I didn't do that. I didn't do that when Mao came. I was silent. I just didn't try to resist that ridiculous person. I just hid by my husband. And my musical talents were smashed. And my hands, my hands were all knotted by my back.

DA: Do you feel that your Council members are justifying what they're saying?

EN: Yes, but they know I need a rest. I need to recharge. I need to think about that life.

DA: Do the Council members make any comments about your current state of advancement compared to all your former lives?

EN: Just that I need to ratchet it up a bit, take on something more, and speak, and change things.

DA: Look carefully at your Council right now, Maya, and tell me how they feel you are doing in your current life.

EN: They're pleased. It's gone from one extreme to the other. I've made a lot of people think. I've made a lot of people uncomfortable.

DA: Do they tell you, or do you sense that they feel you addressed all the issues or are there some issues that are still not quite properly addressed?

EN: Oh no, there's work to do.

DA: And what do they say that work is on?

EN: Myself.

DA: In what respect?

EN: That I have to learn to love myself, and to be still, and to give respect to myself.

DA: How do you feel knowing that?

EN: The question isn't relevant.

DA: Is there anything more to the Council?

EN: To keep on with this work and not underestimate its value on the earth plane. More and more people will come.

DA: Do you sense at all that there is a higher being in this room with you and the Council members?

EN: Yes.

DA: Do you have any sense of who that might be?

EN: [No response provided.]

DA: Do you think that that message that they've given you is going to be useful in your current life?

EN: I don't know.

DA: What are your overall feelings about yourself as the Council meeting draws to a close?

EN: [No response provided.]

DA: Is there anything else you wish to say to the chairperson before we leave the Council?

EN: I got the message.

DA: Good. Is it time to go, or do they want to talk about past life incarnations, even previous ones?

EN: I don't know what to say about … The life in Rome was very hard, and the life … I don't know the name they call it, but it's Jerusalem now.

DA: That was softer. Do you choose to be one gender more than another in your lives?

EN: Yes.

DA: Which one is that?

EN: Male.

DA: Why do you think that is?

EN: The bodies are better. Women's bodies are rubbish. They're too short. They have too much pain. I'd like to be a man.

DA: How do you feel you met your objectives when you were in lives as a man?

EN: The respect was better.

DA: Your soul objective, I mean.

EN: It was easier, because you weren't fighting the body, and people listened more, because you had the power.

DA: Did the power feel good?

EN: No. I didn't know the power until I didn't have it. It's difficult to gain power in the other body.

DA: Where were you during your first life?

EN: In a cave.

DA: Were you male or female?

EN: Female.

DA: Was that a long life?

EN: No, short. I was burnt.

DA: Your Council said that you were doing a fair job in this life.

EN: Yes.

DA: Does that make you feel that you're accomplishing something?

EN: Must be. It's difficult to reconcile it with the brain in this life. The brain is limited.

DA: One of the things that you will be able to do, Maya, in particular, is remember this in great detail in due course when you return. And you will remember that things needed to be a little more difficult. And you will remember that you need to love yourself a little more. But for now, what I'd like to know is, is there anything else that you can recall or that you were being told from your past lives that will help you to achieve what you need to achieve in this life?

EN: No.

DA: Is your Council meeting over?

EN: Yes.

DA: Is it time to move to another place? And if so, where would you like to go?

EN: I've got to go to the knowledge store.

DA: When you go there, do you go alone, or are you conducted by your guide?

EN: No, my guide goes with me, but he knows I know how to get there, so it's kind of perfunctory.

DA: How does this area of study appear to you as you approach it?

EN: Drawers and filing cabinets and screens. And they know that I hate it. I hate all this stuff. Why can't they just go back to the old ways?

DA: What were the old ways?

EN: With orbs. I think it's funny. It's preparing you for the next time. And the earth thinks it's so clever with all its gadgets. And they've lost the art of communication by telepathy. And all those silly things they have to communicate with, and they still miss it. If only they'd tune in and use their minds.

DA: You said they thought it was funny. Who's they?

EN: The people that run the knowledge store.

DA: Are there any other souls near you?

EN: Many, buzzing about.

DA: Tell me what you see around you at this moment, other than the filing cabinets and screens you've already mentioned.

EN: Small toys and things that shouldn't be here. They're not supposed to be in the store. It's supposed to be clean and focused. But these young souls, they just push it all the time. And they bring their toys. And now they're being scooted along.

DA: What mechanism are you going to use to review your lives? Will you be reading or viewing?

EN: Viewing.

DA: Now you're clearly here to do some work. What life are you going to review first? Let me just put time on hold for a moment or two, so you can think about what you're going to do. I want to ask your body that is here in this room. It is comfortable. Think about what you're going to do. And I will be back in a moment.

DA: Can you tell me, Maya, what work it is that you're about to do, what you're going to review?

EN: I'm going to review several lives and find the thread to make the other life clearer.

DA: How do you go about doing that?

EN: I want to go and find the orb.

DA: Are orbs still there?

EN: Yes, but they're dusty at the back. All this technology nonsense. I don't want a screen. I want my orb to look into. To work with my orb.

DA: Do you sense that you will be able to do that?

EN: Yes, if I persist.

DA: I'm just going to put time on hold for a moment. And I'll ask if you'd like me to put the chair back a little further.

EN: No.

DA: Okay. Thank you. I'm comfortable now. What lives are you reviewing?

EN: My life in China.

DA: And just tell me the salient points of what you need to find out about that life.

EN: The unanswered question is why I didn't stand up, why I didn't resist. The answer is fear. It's an earthly problem. It's not one we have other than on the earth plane.

DA: What other lives do you need to look at?

EN: My life in Rome as a slave.

DA: Male or female?

EN: Male.

DA: And how was your beauty a problem?

EN: As a beautiful man? That men and women wanted to possess me as a slave. And they were cruel.

DA: Possess you sexually?

EN: Yes.

DA: What lesson comes from that life?

EN: That it's about my body lesson. That I've had the fabulous body, and it got me into loads of trouble. And while I complain about the bodies, I know why I continue to choose them.

DA: What choice did you have in Rome?

EN: Um, just two.

DA: And when you were in Rome in that life and you were a slave, how could you change what you were?

EN: I couldn't.

DA: How could you reject advances?

EN: I couldn't.

DA: Did your body enjoy the advances?

EN: No.

DA: None of them?

EN: No. Not the ones from ... They weren't from love. They were from greed and possession. There was no kindness.

DA: But as a man, have you had a time in your incarnations where you've experienced physical pleasure alone?

EN: I don't know.

DA: What other lives do you need to look at?

EN: None. I need to move forward.

DA: Did you manage to do this using the orb?

EN: No. Just through talking to you.

DA: Where are you now?

EN: Still there.

DA: Have you viewed any of these past lives?

EN: Yes, as we're talking.

DA: How do you see them? Do you re-experience them?

EN: It's like our television.

DA: Would you, if you wanted to re-experience it?

EN: No. It's all in shorthand now, at the time as part.

DA: Are they archived in some way?

EN: Yeah. And the people who want them in the orb are getting fewer. And they're laughing at me. Yeah.

DA: If you wanted to expand the archive to a real life, could you rejoin that life temporarily and feel what you felt then?

EN: No.

DA: Other than this life with you, are there any other themes or areas of study or anything that's of particular interest to you that you'd like to do now?

EN: No.

Chapter Summary

Esther's session, under her spiritual name, Maya, provides a rich exploration of her soul's journey through the Council and the knowledge store, or Library. Her initial reunion with Dinah and Inara highlights the dynamics of her Soul Group, while the Council meeting reveals her progress and challenges, particularly her passivity in a past life in China and the need to advocate more assertively. In the Library, Esther's preference for orbs over modern screens underscores her struggle with earthly limitations and her desire to reconnect with deeper, telepathic communication. The session concludes with insights into her lives in China and Rome, pointing to unresolved lessons about fear, power, and self-love that Esther must address to advance her spiritual path.

Chapter 17: Hope Yeoman

Hope explores her wide spiritual landscape, beginning with a heartfelt connection to her guide, Orrgon, and progressing to the ancient Library where she encounters a significant book. Her journey continues to the Council, a place of higher guidance, where she confronts deep-seated fears and dichotomies in her life. The Library proves to be a pivotal space for Hope, revealing past lives and insights that challenge her to face her struggles with isolation, control, and the desire for freedom. This transcript captures the raw, unfiltered nature of her testimony, reflecting both the emotional intensity and the spiritual depth of her experience.

DA: It's fine. You can do anything here. Just feel everything.

HY: I feel like...

DA: What's he saying to you?

HY: He's just ... He's smiling. He's knowledgeable and ... quiet. Intelligent smile. Calm. Deep. Calm. His beautiful brown eyes. We're just communing. It's such ... an ache in here. He's standing outside my garden. It's like there's a ... It's as if he's on the other side of a dry-stone wall. It's my garden. My space. He's just outside it. He can choose to paint my garden... or he can choose to paint what I think is his space. Which is open ... It's like I imagine somewhere like, say, Cornwall ... with dry stone walls and open fields and pasture. Very, very green. But ... not far. A very short distance and then it's just open sea. Cliffs and open sea. And that's what he ... He can choose to paint those ... or that scene, or my garden, or ... just the green and the pastures ... and the walls. There's a house. He's got a house over there. Built of the same rocks. Stone. It's like a … It's like I imagine, like you see, a croft. It's low and close to the ground but very homely looking. And that's his house. That is his garden.

DA: You can … You can ask him into your garden if you wish.

HY: He's saying, no, that's your garden. That's your space. I'm happy to look at it, that's yours.

DA: That can remain yours. But if you wish…

HY: He says you can come into mine. You can come and see the paintings.

DA: What's his spiritual name? You can always ask him.

HY: It's Orrgon. Orrgon. Orrgon. I thought he said Argon.

DA: Ask him to spell it.

HY: O-R-G-O-N. Orrgon. O-R-R. Two Rs. O-R-R-G-O-N. Orrgon. He … He can take me … He can take me to the Library. He says he can take me. I feel … If I want, he'll take me to the Library. He was a bookworm. I learnt to be a bookworm with him. He's offering to take me to the Library.

DA: Then go.

HY: He used to take me to the Library when I moved. We used to go Saturday mornings together. But this is … this is a bigger Library. This is a more ancient Library. This is … volumes and volumes. He's climbing some wooden steps. Like … like you see … It's almost like pulpit steps. But it leads into this … or through and around this vast … vast … wonderful … collection of … books and maps. And … It feels very, very old. I can feel him walking ahead of me up these steps. I'm not sure if I'm walking up them yet. With him. I must be. Because I'm now on a level … I didn't feel myself walk up. But I'm now on a level with him. Where he is … doubting again.

DA: Just focus on what's happening.

HY: He's put a … There's a big … What do you call it? Like a lectern. But crossed between a lectern and a table. Yes, the book is slightly tilted. But it's too heavy to be on something less solid than it is, and it's … huge. Oh. I don't know. It's about a metre tall; it looks like … It's got clasps and … gems on it. And … it's … heavily … very heavily bound. It's not frightening. It's not daunting looking at it. But I feel it's very significant. Okay.

DA: Does he want you to go and look in it?

HY: He's inviting me to. Just … with his hands. Just … indicating the book. He's standing to the side. As I'm standing … I have to move in that direction to open it. Am I ready to open it? He's indicating … He's not saying anything. He's not giving me anything more than just … calm assurance and … telling me it's in my own time. At the same time now looking back … for … Is it Lois or my mother or someone else? To also reassure me.

DA: Then begin to open the book.

HY: I've moved him in front of it. I'm feeling … all the cover. It's … it's so … There are so many … It's metal … and jewels … and … material and … I can't make the colours out there. But I don't think that's necessarily important. I can just feel the things. I can … maybe I have to feel my way into the book. There's a single clasp in the middle. The clasp feels very heavy all of a sudden. When I made the decision to open it … it was as if a sudden weight settled down, and … It's holding my arms down on the book. And not allowing me … No, not allowing me. I'm not being prevented. I'm preventing myself. Gosh. It feels so heavy.

DA: Hold the book again ready to open it.

HY I can't lift my arms to it.

DA: Now you can open the book. And tell me what's inside.

HY: I've still not got past that clasp. My mother gave me permission to open it. She told me I could give myself permission to open it. It's so big. And you can do that. It's so easy because it will just open when you want it to open. I feel pretty spacey at the moment. I can't find what will give me permission to pull that cover back.

DA: Oh, that's easy. You can.

HY: What stops me? Pig-headedness. Stubbornness.

DA: Remember, Rihanna, you are completely safe. Enveloped in this golden shield of light. It will keep you protected from all things. And just as soon as you decide to give yourself permission … The book cover will just open.

Narration

Rihanna is her spiritual name. Also, you'll notice me interject with a safety protocol which was introduced during the hypnotic induction, so she knows what it means and how it can protect her. I felt it was necessary to get past this obstacle. You'll see other interventions later in the process.

End of Narration

HY: I can't myself. I've reasoned that. I've remembered that there is nothing to fear. Only fear itself. I've set up the fear. And I can walk through it at any time I want to. And find that it was … an illusion. If I understand, then it can't hurt me. Nothing will hurt me. There is nothing to fear. Only the fear that I set up and I know I can go … I know I can create. I know I can create. I've created my garden. I've created my space. I've created something really beautiful. I have it in me to … create the illusion of fear. And I have the ability … to remove that creation if it doesn't suit me. If it doesn't suit my purpose. I can remove that fear. And open to all that I need to open to.

To learn. To move on. To grow. To progress. To move towards that light, I'm still trying to get to.

DA: Let's come back to the book. The book's still here. Let's open it. And just open it.

HY: I've opened the cover but I'm not looking at what's there at the moment. I need time ... to get past that. But it will be exciting. And stimulating. And enlightening. Gosh, I want that so much. My mind has taken up that position again. And moving me towards, gently towards ... that book.

DA: Take that strength from Lois and use that to help you to look.

HY: I'm looking ... I'm at the book. I'm looking into it. But it's not a page. It's like a ... It's like a ... a sort of well. But it could be a well or a screen. If it's a well, it's not dark. It's got life and colour there. Maybe it's a ... a sort of screen.

DA: Well, we can call it a screen.

HY: Yeah. I'll call it a screen. Um ... But it's something I can enter. Yeah. To enter into it. To move ... I'm moving into it. I don't know how I'm doing that, but I'm moving into it. And it's ... It's a ... it's a ... just a ... comfortable ... country ... gentle rolling hills. It's just something to give me some comfort. A breathing space for the moment. Ah, I see. I'm not actually in it. It's... The book is still here. It's a page, but it's like a live page, and it draws me in, and then I feel part of that page, and then I can turn it. I can turn that page now. To the next one. That was just to gentle me in. There are people in this one.

DA: Do you recognise them?

HY: They're coming out of the page. They're coming ... They're part of a scene now. They're ... Ah ... excited. But I can't make out individuals.

DA: What's their dress like?

HY: It's more like I'm seeing them as ... colour. Light colour rather than ... I can't see their sort of recognisable forms.

DA: I understand. Do you sense anything about the period in which these people lived?

HY: Greek Roman time maybe? It's warm.

DA: Is one of these people you?

HY: Yes, I think so. There's a very beautiful, tall, olive-skinned, black-haired woman. Probably ... I don't know. In her twenties. In her prime. Very, very beautiful. Very ... graceful. I can't ... I feel she's me. I don't feel part of her, but I feel she's me.

DA: As you focus on this scene and as this scene unfolds ... the essence of it will become clearer and clearer. Almost as if you were watching a television programme. Or a live play on stage. And as the scene unfolds, I want you to tell me what is happening between these people.

HY: She's quiet. Where she is, is a quiet place, but she's ... The surroundings are busy. It's a busy place. But where she is, she's calm and quiet. I feel she's holding something here. A basket or a container of some sort. No, not a basket. They used to call them amphoras or something. Held oils. That sort of thing. Yes. Something like that. That's what it feels like. And it's a busy, busy, busy place. People, it's like a market. I have a feeling it's beside a temple or something of that nature. A holy place or something. There's activity all around. But not with her. She's calm. She's graceful. She's just in the scene, but not in it. It's as if she's separated herself in some way. Or she has the ability to separate herself from the busyness of life. The wheeling and dealing that's going on in this marketplace. Perhaps the cruelties that are going on there.

DA: One of the interesting things about this entire process is that at any time you might want to, you can actually be her again in this scene. Instead of looking upon the scene from a distance, you can see it through her eyes. And you can feel what she feels.

HY: I'm doing that now.

DA: And you can tell me a little bit about her. For example, what's her name?

HY: Juliana.

DA: And as Juliana now, tell me, why is it that you feel so separate from what's going on?

HY: I'm simply but quite richly clothed. I have a feeling that I'm slightly superior to these people. I'm separating myself, but I'm naturally separated from them because I have a different world, but I actually like to watch what they are doing. It's interesting. They seem to be alive. They live. I feel, for all that I am, beautiful. People tell me I am beautiful. I know I am beautiful. I am graceful. I am rich. I am comfortable. I have a secure life. Yet I spend time standing here. I pause in my activity to watch what goes on out there. People milling. People touching. People reacting. People laughing. People being ... I feel very ... I am fortunate that I'm sad that I'm so separated.

DA: As Rihanna now, Rihanna, do you see any similarities between your life as Juliana and your life as Hope?

HY: I do. I feel totally separate. As Hope, I'm separating myself more and more. But I don't like it. I want to be part of ... I want to feel as other people feel. I want to ... I want to be part of life and not standing to one side like Juliana's doing. I feel alone. Alone as Hope.

DA: Rihanna, turn the page.

HY: Coming back to being Rihanna. I'm turning the page again. Oh, this is strong. I'm straight into being a man.

I've been a very strong … fearless … warrior type. A disciplined soldier. Ancient … I thought at first Roman, but I think it's … some other period. Before Rome? I'm not clear, yeah. Possibly. Let me feel it more. Middle Asia. Middle East, Middle Asia, Middle … Persia. Somewhere there. Somewhere in that realm.

DA: What's the name of the soldier?

HY: Baranda. Gosh. I'm so big and powerful.

DA: Are you Baranda now?

HY: I'm Baranda.

DA: What does it feel like?

HY: I can do anything. Question nothing. I … What's there not to do? I do as I wish.

DA: Baranda, tell me a little bit about yourself.

HY: I am close to … a local warlord who rules this region. We've known each other since we were boys. And … I can do no wrong. I am his right-hand man. We do as we wish. We are both very strong. He came to power quite at a young age. My power … comes along with his.

DA: What is his name?

HY: Akron.

DA: What are you doing now, Baranda?

HY: I'm looking out with Akron. From his castle. We're looking into a valley. It's a rich, green valley with a river … flowing into it from the mountains, which are … in the distance, but not more than a day's ride. They're close. They mark one extreme of Akron's land. We are considering what's beyond that. We finished … we finished reinforcing his lowland areas. We know and have fixed the boundaries there. But we're wondering if we can extend them … over this mountainous route.

DA: Do you have a strong army?

HY: We have a very strong and loyal army. It's not large, but it's made up of … men who are loyal to Akron … and this land … and their families.

DA: What is the name of this land?

HY: I don't get the name.

DA: Baranda, tell me what you do for your recreational pastimes.

HY: We ride, we hawk, we hunt. We lie with women. I have a beautiful wife, but she understands. I look after her. She is comfortable. We love each other, but … but I'm a man. She's happy, I'm happy. We have a child on the way. Which makes me very happy. She has servants to care for her. She should be well. She should be safe.

DA: When you lie with women, how does this happen?

HY: Because they like me. I'm charming, I'm strong, I'm large, I'm … powerful. Women like power. They fall for it. They want to give themselves to me. I've never taken a woman against her will. Even in battle, following battle. She must want … she must want me, but they always do. Hey. Who wouldn't?

DA: As Rihanna, do you see any similarities between Baranda and Hope? Or are they quite opposite?

HY: They are opposite.

DA: Is there more to do here or is it time to turn the page? We can turn the page. Okay, don't do it for just a moment and you can use the time… to breathe slowly … and deeply … and drift deeper … and deeper … and deeper … into the trance. That's right. Down … and down. And as you do that … you will actually feel more and more comfortable … and more and more at ease. You can now turn the page.

Narration

These sessions are long, and people tire. When that happens, their trance begins to lighten and the memories fade. I have just paused the process for a moment to deepen the relaxation a bit, you'll see other examples of this as we progress.

End of Narration

HY: I've turned the page, but I'm not seeing anything yet. It's misty and gloomy. It's cold. There's a child … in ragged clothes. Victorian sort of style, but ragged. Crouching next to some baskets against cold bricks. She's cold. But she's waiting there.

DA: What's she waiting for?

HY: She's … she's waiting for someone to find her. She's … she's lost her people.

DA: What's her name?

HY: Sarah.

DA: Sarah?

HY: Sarah. She's so frightened. She's got to wait. She knows she's got to wait.

DA: How old is she?

HY: Nine.

DA: And what date is it?

HY: 1837. I'm waiting. Where is he?

DA: Have you joined? You are now Sarah.

HY: Yes, I'm Sarah. I'm looking. There's plenty of people rushing around. They're cold. They're running to do what they have to do and get home more. To do their job. It's only me here, still … next to this basket. I'm so cold. I'm so cold. I'm so cold. I'm waiting.

DA: What's in the basket?

HY: I don't know. It's not mine. It's rags. I don't know. It's not mine. I'm just here next to it. I can hide almost. People won't see me. But I can wait. But I don't know what I'm waiting for. I'm waiting for someone. I don't know where my family is. I've lost them. But I've got to wait here. If I wait here, I'll be safe. If I wait here, someone will find me. If I wait here, I'll be safe. Someone will find me. It's dark. Who's going to find me? I don't know how long I've been here. I don't know where I am. It's busy. It's … there's water. In here. It's like a … It could be a dockside or something. I don't know I know it's cold.

DA: What time of year is it?

HY: Winter. I have no shoes. No warm clothes. But I seem used to being cold. I'm used to being hungry. I don't know. It doesn't matter. I have no food. I'm always hungry. Who will find me?

DA: Sarah, just move forward in this existence to a significant point. Just move forward in time. What's happening now?

HY: No one found me. I'm still here on the rags. I'm too tired. I'm too cold. I'm too tired. No one found me. No one found me.

DA: There's Rihanna. Rihanna. Come back out, Sarah. And just look again at the scene; separate. That poor child. Are there any similarities between Sarah and Hope?

HY: It's being alone, never connecting. I'm so tired. Being a child, never going beyond a child. Never fulfilling the promise. The promise that was in that young life. It could have been so much more than it was. Yet lay there, died alone. Cold, tired of life at such a young age. And no one finding her. Until it was too late.

DA: Let's turn the page one more time.

HY: I'm going to need a break.

DA: That's okay. Right, so what we'll do … Do you want to turn the page one more time? No, we'll do the break first. Just put time on hold. It's really easy to do. I'm going to count to five. When I count to five, your eyes will open. And you'll be able to get up. Go to the loo, have a drink, whatever you want to do. But you will still be in this deeply relaxed state. Although you will have complete control over all of your faculties. When you return and sit in the chair, I will count from five back to one. And as soon as I reach the count of one, you'll be back again standing in front of this book, waiting to turn the page. But for now, one, two, three, four, five. Slightly spaced. It's okay.

Narration

One of the necessities of long sessions is the occasional need to use the toilet. We know this, so the ability to break for a few minutes and resume the deep relaxation needed has been rooted in her subconscious as a part of the hypnotic induction process. If this isn't done beforehand, such breaks could cause long delays.

End of Narration

HY: Thank you.

DA: I'll pour you some water while you're out there.

HY: Yes, please.

DA: Are you warm enough?

HY: Uh-huh. Clinging to my tissue.

DA: There are plenty more.

HY: That's better.

DA: Place your arms on the side of the chair.

HY: Yes.

DA: Place your arms on the side of the chair. Five, four, three, two, one. Turn the page.

HY: Oh, it's a bright scene. It's like the prairies. I think it is the prairies. I almost don't believe this, but I'm galloping bareback on this beautiful horse. I am an Indian. I'm a boy, young man.

DA: How old are you?

HY: Eighteen.

DA: What's your name?

HY: Redfeather. This is my favourite, my fastest, my beautiful pony. Freedom. I can gallop for hours. My horse and I. Oh, such freedom. It's so beautiful. The country, the space is the same as in this, and here, it's just wide open and free. At one with everything. It's just wild. I'm so happy when I'm doing this.

DA: How do you feel about your body?

HY: Well, I'm fit, strong, young, lithe. I can jump on my pony without thinking. Just, I'm there. I think it and I'm there.

DA: What are you wearing?

HY: Just, just something to cover this up.

DA: What is it exactly? Can you describe it to me? How does it fasten?

HY: It's, it's, it's soft leather. Soft, it's like, it's from deer, deer. Yeah, and it just ties, they tie at each side. Tie it strong.

DA: What's used to tie it with, is it...?

HY: It's just the same, it's the leather, in like a, it's a thong.

DA: And how long is it?

HY: Oh, my legs are free. To feel the wind, the sun. It's hot, it's beautiful. I'm returning to my family now. By the river. There are children playing. There are my friends. It's so peaceful, so loving, so at one. We're at one with everything, our surroundings, our animals, our people. We have no fears. We just are. We are part of the land we are in. We're not separate. But I have fun all the same

DA: As Redfeather, are there many other young men your age?

HY: Yes. Oh, yes. Sometimes I ride with them, sometimes I ride alone. Sometimes we have fun, sometimes we go hunting. Sometimes we watch the girls. But mostly we like to go riding. To ride like the wind.

DA: Are you officially a man?

HY: No, that's coming soon. I'm preparing.

DA: What happens when that, when that, what, tell me how that happens.

HY: I'm taken to the forest, to the wilderness. I have to set up my own shelter. I spend several moons there. I learn about myself, my spirits, my guides. I come close to my animals. I can return a man. I prove myself. I can be strong on my own, so I can be strong enough to support others, take away my children. And be strong for the tribe. It's very important. If I failed, if I ran away, if I ran home, I would have failed. I'll be as the women; I will have failed. But I'm strong, I know I can do it, I will do it. I'll have my horse, my beloved pony, and my knife. I shan't be afraid.

DA: Are you looking forward to it?

HY: I am, I am.

DA: When you, when this is completed and you take a wife, how does that happen?

HY: She and I must choose each other, and then approach our chief, our leader, our chief, for permission. He consults with the elders. If they all agree, we may marry. To marry, there is a ceremony. During which we enter the water, and we pour water ceremoniously, each over the other, to wash away our former lives, and to become one.

DA: What is the name of your tribe?

HY: The Tambetans.

DA: When you succeed through this ceremony, you take a wife, is there a home provided for you, or is it...?

HY: I provide the home.

DA: You provide the home?

HY: I will have hunted and got the skins for myself. I will have carved, cut and carved the wood. I will have built the fire, stones. I will have bought, found or made the items we need. I have to have a place ready for a wife.

If I cannot do that, I cannot take a wife. I cannot do that unless I have spent my time out in the wilderness and proved that I can do it.

DA: Now, as Rihanna, what similarities do you see between Redfeather and Hope?

HY: The wish for freedom. The wish to be independent. To be creative. To be able to care for myself. To be at one. With all there is.

DA: Is there a difference in how this is achieved? Because it seems for Redfeather, this is already organised. If you do this, then you get this. Are there similarities with Hope or is that quite different?

HY: Hope cannot see the way to do it. There is no structure to do that. She is lost, trying to find the structure, the key, something that will allow her those freedoms. A sense of freedom.

DA: What is it that she needs to do?

HY: To have spent time in the wilderness, but she feels that she's done that.

DA: As you stand looking at the book, do you feel now that there is a need to look any further at this moment in time? Or do you want to turn another page?

HY: No, I'm done now.

DA: Who is near you?

HY: My father and my mother.

DA: I'm going to ask that your most senior guides make themselves known to you. Whether that be Lois, or Orrgon, or somebody else. I'm going to count to three. And when I count to three, your most senior guide will appear to you. As I begin the count. Now. One. Two. Three. And tell me, who is it that's there?

HY: Forming only slowly. I need more help.

DA: What's happening at the moment? Is Lois still there? Is Orrgon still there? Is the book still there?

HY: I feel like I'm that child again, waiting for someone. It's just misty. I feel lost and afraid. I want someone to find me.

DA: Is it possible that you could find somebody else? That you could look for them? If you leave your hiding place.

HY: I'm afraid. If I don't stay here, they won't find me.

DA: But you could leave a marker there, couldn't you? Of something. Something that's yours, or … and come back. You could always return at intervals. To check. Leave some sign that you were there. But maybe … if you could go out, then perhaps you will find them.

HY: I want to, but I'm so afraid.

DA: What would have to happen for you to be able to do this?

HY: To leave my place?

DA: Yes, what would have to happen?

HY: I need someone to get me. I have to get over the fear of leaving that place. I have to go and reach out. I know I want to. But why can't I? What stops me from reaching out?

DA: Take my hand and go with me. What's happening, Sarah?

HY: It's good to have someone to hold their hand now. Someone wants to help. Yeah, I'm just a bundle of rags. Somebody wants to help, and I want them to.

DA: Well, just let that happen.

HY: I've never allowed myself to let go. I couldn't before.

DA: But you're completely safe here. You are protected. Fully protected.

HY: If I let go, everything else crashes. I'm holding everything up.

DA: Are you sure that's true?

HY: I feel like it is. I don't want to do it anymore. I want to nurture me now. I need to nurture me to move on. I think. But I don't know.

DA: Where are you now?

HY: I've left the little girl behind.

DA: Okay.

HY: I'm still here. I'm just going to sit back in the chair. Thank you. I'm still here. I don't know if I'm Hope or Rihanna.

DA: Okay, let's come back to Rihanna.

HY: I'm afraid there's no one there for me. I know there must be, but I'm afraid there isn't. I've been ... alone ... so long and so often and ... I can't believe that there is somebody there. But I've lost the ability to ... reach out and invite them in. That's how it feels.

DA: Right, just for this moment now ... we're going to put time on hold. And I want you to go even deeper into the trance. I'm going to count down from ten to one. And as I count down ... you will feel yourself ... drifting way, way down. Even deeper than before. Ten. Nine. Eight. Seven. Six. Five. Four. Three. Two. One. Deeper and deeper. Deeper and deeper. Still drifting down. Deeply, deeply relaxed. And protected and safe. So deep. That's right. Even deeper. Down you go. Down, down, down. Really, really deep. All you can hear is the sound of my voice. All you can respond to is the sound of my voice. It is the only thing ... at the moment which is filling your world. Just my voice. As you drift deeper ... and deeper. Your body is relaxed. Every muscle is completely relaxed. You have no ability at all ... to create any tension in any muscle. You just cannot do it. Almost as if the ... messaging connections between your muscles and your brain ... have been temporarily switched off. You are completely relaxed. If the tissue weren't on the side of the chair ... it would fall from your hand. If I lift a hand... you cannot do anything. You're just completely relaxed. You cannot move any muscle. You're completely relaxed. Deeper and deeper. Now, in a moment ... I'm going to tell you something very, very important. But it's something that you will not remember. The only thing. As Rihanna... Rihanna, I'm talking to Rihanna. Would you like to go somewhere ... where you may be able to ask questions ... or receive some kind of evaluation?

Narration
Another pause to deepen the relaxation.
End of Narration

HY: Yes.
DA: Do you know where to go for this? Or is there somebody close to you that can take you there?
HY: I don't sense anyone around me.
DA: Tell me what you can see. Is your surrounding light or dark?
HY: It's not dark.
DA: Tell me what colours you see around you. Is there a different shade of lightness around you?
HY: A lavender purple light has opened up to me.
DA: Is it communicating anything to you?
HY: I'm feeling waves of the light. Washing it towards me. And over me. I'm drawn to it. I've come out of the dark. I'm into a... sort of an ethereal realm. It's like marble, but not marble. White. It's... reaching up into the heavens and away into the distance... but close too at the same time. I have someone to my left. I don't know who. I sense others in the room.

Narration
We've arrived at the Council.
End of Narration

DA: Are these others in front of you or behind you?

HY: They're in front of me. And... I feel I know them, but I... I don't see them, but I sense them. I don't... I feel I know them.

DA: The spirit that is behind you and to your left... is this your guide?

HY: I feel that to be so.

DA: Can you... can you look and see if there's any... presentation of form to you?

HY: I can feel him.

DA: It's a him?

HY: I feel it very strongly.

DA: What's his name? What's happening with these... entities in front of you?

HY: They're waiting for me to be more conscious of... them. To be more within the room.

DA: That will happen in a very few moments. As you become more and more acclimatised to this place... it will become very familiar to you.

HY: I have seen it before. I have seen it before. There's... They're up higher. I thought they were lower at first, but they're not. They're up higher. And there's a... The marble below them is... It can show me scenes. It's not... it's not at the moment, but it can show me scenes. But I can see these... five... beings.

DA: Are they becoming clearer to you?

HY: Slowly.

DA: Does any one of them seem to be more important than the rest?

HY: I feel I should say the centre one, but there's a woman to the left and there, that seems to be the first that's come into focus.

DA: What colour is she?

HY: She's green... and lavender.

DA: Is she communicating anything to you?

HY: She seems to be saying, don't worry, don't worry. You're fine, you're safe. Be with us, that sort of thing. I think the others are all men. Male.

DA: What colours are they?

HY: I seem to see white at first, but then if I wait... and concentrate... I start to pick up other colours within the white. And... now the one to the right... is... more pale blue, grey, pale blue, silver. The one in the centre is becoming more golden than white. Gosh, there's a red to his right. Between the centre one and the woman. Very... red. And there's a deep resonance coming from it too, a deep... sound. It doesn't interfere, it's not interfering, it's just a deep resonance. The one in the middle between the outer right.

DA: It doesn't matter for the moment. Has any communication begun yet?

HY: Only with this woman. But no, no. Peter is telling me to go forward. I step in an area... which is... I can only describe it as a light bath, or a light shower. Which raises my vibration. I keep tracking myself down as well. Let yourself expand and receive. I can't believe these people are here for me. The one with the golden light is saying that they are here for me. They are here to help and to guide me. Not to be afraid. But I'm not afraid of them. I must be afraid of what they can give me. Is that it? I seem to be stuck.

Narration

Peter is a member of her Primary Soul Group.

End of Narration

DA: Ask them what it is that you need to learn here in this existence.

HY: I'm putting up barriers to hearing. I am doing that, but I don't want to.

DA: That's okay, we'll just let them subside. Where do you feel the barriers? Do you feel them in your body?

HY: It's like a resistance. Oh, yeah. Yeah. It's like a wave of something comes over me. It takes me down a peg again. I have to build back up to where I'm able to.

DA: We can help. Take my hand. Hold the wrist. Do you sense?

HY: I sense.

DA: Where it's holding you in your body.

HY: Where it's holding me in my body.

DA: Just place my hand there and I will take it away. You're going to leave. Now ask that question again and listen to the answer and tell me what's happening.

HY: I'm here to learn to be strong. To overcome weakness. My sense is too soft, too hurt. So, I have to learn strength. I'm asking how I can do that. The red one. Yes. The red appears to be there to give me the strength to bind me to the earth. To the lower emotions. But I feel they're too strong. And it's that. It's a sense of that that stops me. Getting through these barriers. Getting past these things. Being manacled to the lower emotions. And not connecting more with myself. And rejuvenating. Revitalising. Connecting with my guides. Connecting with Council. Because I am so caught up in the details of life that I can't or won't. It takes so much effort to get to those places where I can revitalise. He feels too strong for me, but this Council must be the Council that is giving me the best. So why don't I understand that?

DA: Were the lives that you explored earlier in the Library, Juliana and Sarah, were these lives to learn the same lesson? And were they not successful? Is it a lesson you're finding difficult to master?

HY: Yes.

DA: What about the lives of Baranda and Redfeather who were quite the opposite? Where it was ordered, they knew exactly their place, they had power and control.

HY: They feel wonderful. They feel free. They feel strong. Juliana was separate. Sarah never had the chance to go beyond needing.

HY: Maybe the lives, the strong lives have given me too ... No, I don't understand. What did they say? No, I can't get past this. It's like an anachronism; it's like mutual exclusion. I need to find strength, so I need to be bound to more, or do I? To more earthly things. But the fact that I am prevents me from connecting to the help and guidance, the reality in themself, that is the holder that I need to tap into, I need to get to.

DA: This is Hope talking, isn't it? This is not Rihanna. Okay, just listen to what the Council is saying and just tell me what they're saying. You can always evaluate it afterwards when you listen to the recording. It's important you relate what is being said to you.

HY: I am trying to clear the fog from my mind to understand what they're saying, what they're doing, what they're telling me.

DA: Well, just tell me what they're telling you and clear the fog later.

HY: But I can't hear it, I can't feel it.

DA: Ask if there's anything you can do to help this.

HY: He's saying you have an expectation of failure, which is preventing me from understanding or hearing what I'm being offered from the Council. He's telling me to park my scepticism, to put it somewhere else and then listen.

DA: Shall we do that then? Okay. Just put time on pause. And drift deeper and deeper into the trance. Down, down and down. And as you drift down and just enjoy this really comfortable relaxation, I want you to imagine that you have a white, soft, fluffy cloud hovering above your head. It's white and soft and fluffy. And tell me when it's there.

HY: It's there.

DA: Right, now this is fascinating and really interesting. Because what I want you to do, Hope, is to think of all the things that could be preventing you from hearing the Council's words as Rihanna. All the things that might be getting in the way. All the negative feelings, negative emotions. Scepticism. I want you to round all those things up and put them into the cloud. Now what's really interesting about this is it doesn't really matter if you run out of things, or you can't find any more. Because your unconscious mind will be finding these negative elements and putting them in the cloud as well. So even though you may not be able to discover any, your unconscious mind will be clearing the negativity and putting it all into the cloud. And you can tell that's the case because if you look at the cloud now, you'll see that it's starting to darken. And the cloud will darken with the negativity from you And it's coming from you and going into the cloud, so scepticism into the cloud. You might be able to find a bit in you, but your unconscious will find a lot more. And this happens really quite quickly because if you look at the cloud, you'll see it's going darker and darker and darker. And very soon it's going to be black. It's full of all the negativity and scepticism, self-doubt, low self-esteem, all. And you can feel it leaving your body and going into the cloud and the cloud will now be inky black. Really, really black. And if you look right at the centre of the cloud, you'll see a pinpoint of white. Can you see that? As you focus on that pinpoint of white.

it will get bigger and bigger. Until you see that it's not actually a pinpoint of white, it's actually the sun. This time a helpful, caring sun burning away the cloud from the centre, burning away the negativity. And it's getting bigger and bigger and brighter and brighter. And you can feel a safe warmth of it, but it's not damaging to you. And as it glows brighter and burns away this blackness of your negativity, the cloud will have completely disappeared. Just tell me when it's finally gone and you're looking at a brilliant clear sky. Right, I'm going to talk to you again now as Rihanna. And you're in the Council chamber. And you'll be able to hear everything clearly. And tell me what's being said.

Narration

I'm using a block clearing technique here to help Hope get out of her own way. As you can see this works well and usually does. It's a standard hypnosis technique.

End of Narration

HY: The golden one says, well done, young lady. You've cleared that at last. Welcome. They're going to play something for me on this screen. Okay. In front of them. Beneath them. It's looking at my life. It's… it's showing… it's showing me when I was small as a child. I'm playing in our back garden. Where we used to live then. I'm happy, actually. I'm… I'm always happy outside. I'm happy with the trees. I'm happy… I'm playing with the pond. I'm with the water. I'm with the fish. I'm with the cat. Dog. Grass. I seem to have trouble moving beyond that. It's… it's such a lovely place to be. But I am moving on. I'm moving into… I'm getting older. I'm seeing the real world, but I want to keep going back. It was… it was… it was safe. It was a familiar place. I was close to... what I understood. I don't understand people very well. I... limit myself in my... schooling. I have more intelligence than I used. I was too lazy, too soulful. But I also had no thoughts, no vision for... no vision of what I might do. It's as if I constantly hark back. The future has to happen, but I don't want it to change from being... safe and comfortable and what I know. So... I was kick-started into it... when I fell pregnant with my son, so I had to become an adult. I had to be... live in the real world and take responsibility. And I did. And I have done, and I took responsibility for my husband, I took responsibility for my mother. I took responsibility for the finances, I took responsibility for my job, I take responsibility for my... pension, I don't... And yet I don't want to take responsibility. I want to go back where it was easy.

DA: Are they showing this to tell you that it's... time to let go?

HY: I think they're telling me it's easy to let go. Because I pull the responsibility towards me. I keep taking it from others. I want to take the responsibility for them, which is strange because I had a... this hankering back to being a child. And yet I pull... I want to control things, perhaps. And yet I don't like controlling things because then I'm exposed, because if I control things... You can create the illusion of not being exposed. Yes.

DA: What are they saying to you now?

HY: They're saying take comfort. You're ready to release these now. And to allow... to be secure that you can just allow... and be happy still. No, I need more than that. Why do I... I seem to be... They're showing things that are... contradictions that I feel. On one hand, I don't want to control. On the other hand, I do control. I take control. On one hand, I want to be open and to be... open and loving and… free in myself. On the other hand… I'm inhibiting myself. I'm the one who… Everything is dichotomy. Everything has its opposite, so I'm pulled this way, and I'm pulled that way. But they've said it's time for you to let go. Now time to let go. But which do I let go of? I let go of it all.

DA: Well, you let go of what you don't want. And embrace what you do. Ask them what Alan is doing in your life. What his role is as you haven't met him yet. In this spiritual journey.

Narration
Alan is a friend who appeared earlier in the session.
End of Narration

HY: I'm asking the question, but I'm needing to wait for the answer. I'm getting a great… sense of…weight… here. I'm asking them to show me on the screen what this means. I'm hoping to clear the emotion before I can see anything.

DA: That's okay. I can help you clear that quite quickly. We've done this before, haven't we? How does it feel now?

HY: What they showed me… was that the relationship mirrors… those dichotomies. The extremes. Sometimes good. Sometimes bad. Very little in the middle. We never seem to pull in the same direction at the same time, or really so it ends up as a confusion. The same as my life has been confusing for me.

DA: What's his role in your life? Dichotomies?

HY: No. He is a strong character. He appears to be a strong character. But I know he has weaknesses.

DA: What's happened?

HY: Back to getting nothing. Back to being alone. I've shut them off again.

DA: It's okay.

HY: Why do I do it?

DA: It's okay. It's okay.

HY: It's like there's a complete brick wall that I can't get past. I just can't get past. It's setting up my expectations.

DA: You've been past it several times.

HY: I keep leaping back this side of it. Is it because I'm meant to be this side of it? Am I meant to struggle with this? Am I meant to not see that side? Because that's how it feels... at times. Is this what I'm meant to be? Is that the purpose?

DA: Not according to what you've been told so far.

HY: I'm afraid that might be the case.

DA: Let's deal with it. Let's deal with the emotion that's going on. Let's deal with the sadness that's going on.

HY: The sadness. That's it.

DA: Just feel it subside.

HY: I've put up so many masks. So many layers.

DA: Just feel the sadness drain away. Just put your hands on the side. Now just... allow yourself to relax again. I'm going to count down from five to one. You just allow yourself to relax. Even more. Five, four, three, two, one. Just allow everything, every thought to leave your mind. To drift out of your mind completely. That's right. That's good. Just relaxing, going deeper and deeper and deeper. Now, Hope... as you're now resuming this relaxation... and sensing the peace and comfort that comes with it... just relaxing. No need to think about anything else at all. No need to think or worry or anything like that. Do you feel at this moment... that we've done as much as we can today? Okay, still deeply relaxed. Still deeply relaxed. Now in a few moments I'm going to count from one to five. And when I do that... as I begin the count... your whole being... will begin the journey up to... fully conscious wakeful awareness.

Chapter Summary

Hope's session is a testament to the complexity of her spiritual and emotional journey. Through her interactions with her guide, Orrgon, and her exploration of the Library, Hope uncovers past lives – Juliana, Baranda, Sarah, and Redfeather – that mirror her current struggles with separation, strength, and unfulfilled potential. Her time with the Council reveals a persistent battle with fear, scepticism, and the dichotomy between control and freedom. Despite moments of clarity, Hope's session concludes with unresolved tensions, as tiredness prevents a full resolution. The Library stands out as a crucial space for her self-discovery, offering glimpses of the lessons she must integrate to move forward. This chapter leaves Hope at a crossroads, poised for further growth in her spiritual journey.

Chapter 18: Rebecca Andrews

Rebecca offers a profound glimpse into the workings of an advanced soul navigating the spiritual realm. Rebecca visits the Library to review records of her past life as Hilda, then engages with the Council to evaluate her soul's progress. The session also explores her spiritual role as a healer of damaged souls, revealing her expertise in energy work and incarnation preparation. The Library stands out as a pivotal space for Rebecca, where she seeks to understand and break free from recurring life patterns, illuminating her journey towards wholeness and conscious remembrance.

RA: I've chosen to return to a temple where I spend much time. It's a very circular building. If it were placed on Earth, it would resemble a circular structure with steps leading up to it. It's a place where records are kept. I'm back looking at my records, searching. I don't want to waste time. I just want to find this thing related to Hilda. I want to ensure, in some pattern, that it's completed now and removed from the records. It's about some sort of glitch or something that happened.

Narration
Hilda is a past life name.
End of narration

DA: If you're looking at the records, can you tell me how they are presented to you?
RA: They're like choir stalls in a church, arranged in levels. There are beings who look after them. You can access

them purely with your mind, setting an intention and seeing it. Or, if I see it in a language, I could walk up and look, like in a Library with books indexed by symbols. You can feel a frequency for your own identity. I can sense it, then travel to the information I need. The records aren't really written. When you touch them, they draw in the energy you want to focus on.

DA: The other beings there, can you describe them to me?

RA: The beings who manage the place are very wise. They've seen much life on many planets but specialise in this recording or energetic management. You can contact them using a vibrational key or a symbol, and it's like getting online with them.

DA: So, the record of your life as Hilda will be there now? Is that the one you're looking for?

RA: Yes, I'm going to imagine, because it's easy for me having just come from Earth, a television set in my mind, and I'll intend to see that record.

DA: What do you want to find out about the record? You've just lived the life.

RA: I want to see what's actually being recorded. I want to understand how this recording process works. Having just come through that journey, I want to see how it's being documented.

DA: And how is it recording? Is it as you expected?

RA: I see many symbols, like hieroglyphs, and I'm wondering, what is this for? Why are we recording everything? There's confusion about the purpose of these records – not here with the archivists, but on Earth, where their purpose isn't understood. They're really the basis for research. I can see what I wanted to research as Hilda, and I can view it like a map to see what's evolved, what's grown, and how that information could influence how children choose to incarnate. Many death patterns are stuck in bodies, and people carry them back. There are many loops happening on Earth, tied to how bodies are imprinted.

DA: Does the recording of Hilda's life give you the information you seek?

RA: Well, I've just taken myself through one of those traps. I've fulfilled my own prophecy, gone around one of the loops, and I'm checking now to see if I've done it again. I've done this so many times; I must be able to find the way out. It's like breaking the mould.

DA: If this loop is continuing, has it been going on for some time?

RA: I've been doing it for a long time. Many souls have, but I've certainly done it a lot. I've done it from this level to try to move something forward. It's almost like something in the DNA, imprinted into people's body patterns. It's about when I wondered if I was the German man or the woman. The DNA could possibly be adjusted so the memory of wholeness, connectedness, and source doesn't leave us when we incarnate. We wouldn't get lost in matter. When Hilda looked at the German man, I was trying to remember we're all one at a certain level. If we had remembered that it would have changed everything – the soldier would have realised he was killing himself. I would have connected more deeply with our oneness. It could have broken the spell of separation, healing it, I suppose.

DA: Do you spend much time looking at archives between lives or is this important because you've just returned?

RA: No, I'm very interested in archive work generally, particularly regarding how the body is programmed for the next life in its cellular memory and genetics – what's included.

DA: Are you saying there's a choice to leave some memory there, or should it start completely fresh?

RA: That possibility is coming to Earth to make all things new.

DA: What happens when stuff is carried over into a new body that should be left behind? Is that an error?

RA: No, it's not an error. It just is, if you remove judgement. It's been that way for a long time, but it's also possible to change. New streams of consciousness are giving souls the chance to incarnate without history, without preconception. You don't need to learn the old ways – it's no longer necessary to separate spirit and matter. It's about coming fully as souls into body, remembering consciously. We'll have a history but know it, say goodbye, and choose a new path with fuller knowledge of the bigger self.

DA: How many lives have you had?

RA: Thousands?

DA: Do you know exactly?

RA: I'm getting a figure in the five digits, starting with a three – 34,981, that's what comes to mind.

Narration

Most souls have had thousands of lives, and this number isn't a surprise though it is on the high side. The fluency of the descriptions and the awareness and the numbers of incarnations would suggest that she is an older and quite advanced soul.

End of Narration

DA: Okay.

RA: If we hadn't gone through the fall of man, I wouldn't have needed all those lives, not necessarily.

Narration

Sometimes we get obtuse references that are off the current subject and as such aren't followed up.

End of Narration

DA: It's all a story. What was your first incarnation?

RA: Being a star.

DA: On a star?

RA: No, being the consciousness of a star, a point of light.

DA: Have all your incarnations been on this planet or have some been elsewhere?

RA: Some have been elsewhere. I'm living others simultaneously now as well.

Narration

We haven't had much information on Hybrid Souls yet and this is the first mention of them. Essentially, some souls incarnate on different planets, different dimensions and in areas where we don't have the concepts to be able to understand them. The earth is popular because it is so physical, violent and at the same time compassionate. Learning is quicker here because of the intensity of the existence, but there are much easier places to live a life, even if it is one, we cannot properly understand.

End of Narration

DA: At the same time, you're here? How much energy have you brought into this body?

RA: Rebecca knows how to top it up, but I didn't bring enough.

DA: As a percentage?

RA: Maybe 20%. Mostly, I'm studying.

Narration

This has been mentioned earlier but it's the first time it has been explicitly referred to. Bringing only 20% of one's energy into a life is another big clue that the soul is quite advanced, but as she says, it seems not to be enough. So mistakes can still be made.

For the more advanced souls, incarnating in more than one place at a time comes up occasionally.

End of Narration

DA: Some of your energy is back in the spirit world, and you're using some elsewhere. Where else are you using it at this moment?

RA: I can't get a name. It's far out in space.

DA: Not on Earth?

RA: No, it's like these libraries, perhaps with the records. I'm in a university doing research, like science.

DA: Returning to Hilda's life, are you satisfied that the recording properly represents what occurred? Is it a verbatim, minute-by-minute record?

RA: No, people think it is, but it isn't exactly. It's like music with lots of sound – you take the main melody. It's what's relevant to the soul, what enhances evolution.

DA: Does this knowledge help when choosing a new life?

RA: In the past, it's been a reference. But I'm experimenting with not using it – screening out pre-existent awareness to see what I could tap into, like a deeper version of what's happened on Earth with veils down. It's about evolving a life with an area screened off.

DA: Is your guide with you? How do they present themselves – male, female, or amorphous?

RA: They can be anything. Right now, they look male.

DA: Because it's easier to refer to. What's his name?

RA: He says, just say P; the rest is unimportant. An initial of sorts.

DA: Is he communicating anything else?

RA: He's responsible for much scientific development and research brought to the planet. He's a teacher, really.

Narration

We divert here because it just seems appropriate. As she explains, she helps souls whose energy has been severely damaged by their earthly incarnation.

End of Narration

DA: What role do you usually take in the spirit world when not incarnated?

RA: Preparing young souls for incarnation and dealing with casualties from Earth, like running a casualty department, rehabilitating souls. I do much transition work between dimensions and lives.

DA: Tell me more about preparing souls for incarnation. What does it involve?

RA: If it's for Earth, it involves reviewing records with the soul. But with some I'm working with now, I'm doing the opposite – helping them move into pure consciousness, using colour temples to remember themselves as points of light. It's like planting a new seed of consciousness, as Christ said, to make all things new.

DA: Is this before or after an incarnation?

RA: When they return, I meet them as needed, resting and healing their energy field, gradually helping them remember who they've been. Then we discuss what gives them space to play and create. Play is a great healer – souls can explore fantasies in the spheres without huge consequences, like children in a playgroup. I help them freshen up, especially those with trauma, like from wars, to rest and play.

DA: Let's talk about replenishing soul energy. How does that happen when souls return damaged from life experiences?

RA: For a soul returning exhausted, it's like they're on a hospital trolley. The body and energy field are built on divine geometry, light, colour, and sound. A prism-like ball above directs light frequencies to realign the energy field by resonance. For specific damage, like to kidneys, I direct a point of the prism to shift colour frequencies and restore balance. That's a main technique.

DA: How do you know when it's completed?

RA: I read the frequencies. The person's energy field returns to pure white light.

DA: Are there times when energy is so damaged you can't fully repair it?

RA: I might not be able to, but in the universe, everything is repairable.

DA: So, if you couldn't do it, you'd get help?

RA: Specialist workers would step in. Sometimes the soul needs to work through some of it. Spiritual law guides how much light and what frequencies are used, directed by masters. I follow that guidance.

DA: With preparing souls for reincarnation, what's your role?

RA: Much of it is checking the energy field is prepared, similar work.

DA: So, your work focuses heavily on energy, ensuring it's right?

RA: Yes, it's about working with the light to reinstate it, not letting beliefs or thoughts obscure it. Illumination can happen instantly if the mind allows, tied to remembering our core identity.

DA: Let's return to the looping question later. For now, when you return from incarnations, do you ever attend an evaluation process?

RA: Yes, I always do, even in my sleep state on Earth. It's not a big deal for me; I do it anywhere. I've done it in the last six months.

DA: Take me through the last time this happened after your last incarnation – how it occurred, who's there, and what you discuss.

RA: My teacher, P, is there.

DA: Okay.

RA: There's a Council, like 12 elders. I don't go until I've rested, meeting friends informally.

DA: Then it's about focusing – what's been happening, Rebecca? Tell me what they said. Is it a specific place you go to?

RA: It's a place created in the mind, like big columns of light representing rainbow colours. I know it well.

DA: In your last evaluation in spirit form, how many elders were there?

RA: The same 12.

DA: Were any of the 12 more prominent? How are they represented to you?

RA: Sometimes they're discrete, barely visible, always fully present but not always the ones I communicate with most. That's left to the team member advancing my work.

DA: What are they saying about this last life?

RA: They're asking, have you done it enough times? Can you allow yourself to move on? Do you believe you've earned the right?

DA: When they say, have you done it enough times, what are they referring to?

RA: Going into a body, experiencing separation to remember wholeness.

DA: Explain that more, as I'm not quite clear.

RA: It means incarnating physically, having a veil over my consciousness, then spending a life trying to remember my origins and connectedness with all life. It's experiencing that we're one, despite physical boundaries.

DA: Is this learning still ongoing in your current life?

RA: Yes, until today. When they asked at the end of my last life if I'd done it enough, I felt I hadn't got it right, so I needed to do it again.

DA: How do they feel you're doing? Do they think you should have resolved this earlier?

RA: They smile, saying it takes as long as it takes – up to me. They note I give this freedom to others but not myself, asking when I'll allow it. They mention I felt guilt for taking a body, thinking someone else missed out, so I keep giving away my turn.

DA: Ask them how they feel you're doing in this current life.

RA: They say I'm free, but I need to catch up consciously in the human mind, bridging it.

DA: This has been a long-term attempt.

RA: All my life, I've been healing separate parts, trying to fit them together.

DA: It seems many lives have had the same objective.

RA: Yes, like a big explosion long ago where I lost awareness, took on guilt, and have been piecing things together since. In a body, I lose insight, but now I'm back enough to bridge and integrate it, over thousands of years.

DA: In this existence, aside from the repeating lesson, this body has had issues with addictive eating and weight problems. How much is from this life versus your soul's journey?

RA: About 80% is tied to this journey about memory.

DA: So, 80% is part of the soul task?

RA: Yes, 80% is carry-over from history.

DA: From previous existences?

RA: And my unwillingness to allow myself the memory of wholeness, the love of connectedness.

DA: When you chose this existence, how much of these issues – addictive eating, weight problems, compulsive behaviour – were you aware of before taking the body?

RA: There's confusion here. I need help. Something's blanked out, like missing information, so I can't answer yet.

DA: The question is, were the compulsive behaviours you struggled with part of your lesson, known beforehand, or just from this life?

RA: It's not just this life. It was alcohol in another life – an energy translated as eating here.

DA: What's the purpose of taking bodies with compulsive behaviours?

RA: It strengthens the will, setting boundaries on who I am, mastering elemental energies of the physical body tied to Earth. If the ego pulls stronger than my soul because I haven't bridged it, it draws me into habits. It's about holding soul frequency in matter, retrieving myself from getting lost in it since the fall of man.

DA: Will this life end the looping?

RA: Yes, it can, if I decide. It's very close.

DA: If the looping ends, will the compulsive traits also end?

RA: Yes, if I decide it's over, the rest will follow. Last year, I lost a stone, hit a plateau, but couldn't hold it – wanted to eat normally, not excessively, but found it too hard without simple pleasures like cappuccino. I wasn't strong enough to go further.

DA: Is it possible to eat normally and lose weight?

RA: That sounds good, but I wonder if I'm allowed to overdo it – am I allowed?

DA: Is it possible?

RA: I'm hearing yes, it is possible, like a counsellor confirming it.

DA: Is this the counsellor in violet?

RA: The whole group says yes.

Narration

Violet is the colour of highly advanced souls, those that have no need to incarnate further so they provide guidance and help for others.

End of Narration

DA: They're emphatic then.

RA: Yes, a resounding yes, then quiet – they say, over to you.

DA: Is that for me to ask another question?

RA: To me – they're saying, "Over to you, Rebecca."

DA: Have compulsions been a feature of many recent existences?

RA: Extremes have – having much or nothing, wealth or poverty. Impulsiveness has caused me the most trouble, not considering enough before acting.

DA: I'm still exploring the link between your impulsive traits in this existence and other lessons. You can be whoever you want – eat and behave normally. Is this struggle essential to your learning, and did you know it beforehand?

RA: At the level of intention, yes, I can. But no, I didn't know it would be this intense.

DA: So, it's been exacerbated by this life?

RA: It was a latency but didn't have to manifest.

DA: The potential for damaging traits was there, depending on what happened?

RA: Yes, and in the future, it's about not having those latent traits – a clean slate. But I looped with them still in.

DA: How many times have you done that?

RA: Well, there seems to be Nine very significant times, it's like leaving a deep track in.

DA: How close are you to resolving this now?

RA: I think as we're doing it, we are resolving it.

DA: What are the Council doing now? They've shut up for a while.

RA: You know what they say, Rebecca, the further you go, the more you work out yourself, so…

DA: What about P, What's P's role in this?

RA: He's saying to look at the body scanning department, like an x-ray or ultrasound. Scan it with light from my third eye, like a camera over my body print.

DA: What's it revealing?

RA: In my pituitary glands behind the eyes, there's not enough light, giving me a prejudiced view of life. I can feel it.

DA: Why not change it to receive enough light?

RA: Yes, I'll ask for a laser of light to bring the missing frequency, like surgery on the pituitary. That's P's gift – helping me pinpoint what changes the frequency. It affects my thyroid, which I'm on thyroxine for, balancing metabolism and other glands.

DA: Is that corrected now?

RA: Yes, I get a yes.

DA: What else does the scan show?

RA: Something in my throat – trauma from births and deaths, holding me back from speaking out or using my voice fully.

DA: Ask for an energy repair to that too?

RA: Yes, I will. P's saying to look at a past life in Vienna, the opera singer, for insight about giving myself permission to have my voice back, connected to the throat.

DA: Should we look at that life now?

RA: I know I was a man, an opera singer, well-known but not from the heart, out of touch with my soul.

DA: We can review it in the Library or revisit the life. Which is quickest?

RA: I'll imagine it like a play and speak to myself as that singer.

Narration

We return to the Library or at least her impression of it.

End of Narration

DA: Let's go to the archive for the opera singer section. You're male – what's your name? What was the opera?

RA: It's like "Lieb", L-I-E-B, fairly clear.

DA: When did this life take place?

RA: I see 1860-something, 1870. I see a grand piano I loved, hearing Bach's music, preparing for a performance with acclaim. But my emotional life was a mess. My teacher was jealous, and we had a strange, possibly gay relationship.

DA: With your teacher?

RA: Yes, some depraved sexuality, not pleasant, but I think it was a gay relationship.

DA: Is that relationship significant for what's carried over in your throat?

RA: Yes, because it was dangerous to use my voice. Someone, maybe him, messed up a performance with lighting when I was expressing fully. I couldn't remember the words, was drinking, fell down steps, possibly broke my neck, and ended up in a wheelchair. After that, no one cared about me – just my voice. I was disgruntled, mean, living through my ego's gift.

DA: How old were you when this accident happened?

RA: Towards 40, very insecure.

DA: What do you need to understand from that existence to repair the throat energy?

RA: That when you come from the heart or spiritual connection, you're safe. The gift flows through you, but it's not who you are – it's not status.

DA: Do you need to revisit this life in more detail?

RA: I need to revisit a decision I made.

DA: What was the decision?

RA: That it's dangerous to fully express myself or my voice – it can kill you.

DA: When was that decision made?

RA: As I fell down those steps, drunk, ending the enjoyment of my life, like dying.

DA: Was that true? Does it need to be true?

RA: No, it doesn't, because here I am. I could delete this record, as I suggest for others, and reinvent a new scenario.

DA: Check your throat again, ask for the energy to be repaired, and see if it's possible now.

RA: I see a band of gold around the throat, like a connection – the bridge. The voice is the bridge, representing my soul. It's being mended, with a gold band around it.

DA: Allow that healing to complete and tell me when it's done.

Chapter Summary

Rebecca's session traces her exploration of the Library and Council, shedding light on her identity as a Hybrid Soul with thousands of incarnations. Her focus on the records of her life as Hilda reveals a persistent loop of separation and guilt, which she seeks to resolve through understanding DNA imprints and cellular memory. The Council's evaluation encourages Rebecca to move beyond these patterns, while her role in the spirit world – preparing and healing souls – underscores her advanced spiritual capabilities.

The session's return to the Library to review a past life as an opera singer in Vienna highlights the healing of her throat energy, symbolising her reclaimed voice and soul expression. Rebecca emerges close to breaking her cycle, poised to integrate her lessons with newfound clarity.

Section 5

Chapter 19: Abigail Zale

Abigail's session centres exclusively on her interaction with the Council, a pivotal encounter that addresses her soul's progress and challenges. Accompanied by her guide, Rendon, Abigail engages with the elders to reflect on her lessons of loneliness and independence. The session also touches on her identity as a Hybrid Soul, with incarnations split between Earth and other non-physical realms of tones and light. The Council serves as the focal point for Abigail's exploration, offering insights into her current life's heaviness and her struggle to connect with humanity, illuminating her spiritual journey towards balance and acceptance.

> **DA:** So, where is it important for you to go now?
> **AZ:** I need to meet the elders first. I need to meet the Council first.
> **DA:** Okay. Does … does Rendon support that?
> **AZ:** He's … he's … yeah, he's … he's coming with me.

Narration
Rendon is her guide.
End of Narration

> **DA:** Okay. Well, let's go then. When you get there, describe the surroundings to me.
> **AZ:** It's like … there are columns. Columns, yeah? Columns there, sort of slightly raised like a step. And there they are. One, two, three, four, five. One is in the corner.
> **DA:** Are they facing you in a line?
> **AZ:** Well, it's a bit of a semi-circle.

DA: A bit of a semi-circle?

AZ: Yeah.

DA: How far away from you are they?

AZ: Well, two or three metres. I'm fairly close. I can still see all of them.

DA: Who is the most important?

AZ: Ah, it's the one in the middle. It's big. It's bigger than the others. And he grins.

DA: Does he present as male or female?

AZ: He's a male.

DA: Describe him.

AZ: He's … it's … he is … he is not tall in measurement, but he has a presence that makes him feel very tall. And he's got a radiant yellow gown, if you like … of course, he doesn't wear a gown, it's just … he likes that. He likes that yellow and all that. I like him very much.

DA: Is he wearing anything else?

AZ: Oh, he's wearing this big black wig, which makes his hair stand out … it looks as if he has hair like a huge afro. He's having fun with me. He's very friendly, he smiles. And he has something around his neck.

DA: Move closer and have a look. Have a closer look and describe to me what it is.

AZ: It's a bird. It's a bird, like … rising. A bird just taking off. And then some dahlias, which reminds me of the phoenix.

DA: What is he communicating to you?

AZ: He's sort of telling me that it's good to have me back. He knows it was tough last time. He's sort of patting me on the back a bit, welcoming me. And it was as if in the last life I had to learn to be on my own. And I certainly did.

DA: Was it a successful lesson?

AZ: Yes. Yes, it was successful.

DA: What else do they have to say to you?

AZ: That I should go and plan my next life. That I've been doing okay in the last one. It was about being independent, learning how to cope with loneliness.

DA: What about this one?

AZ: Oh, in a way, I think that was a preparation for this one. Because in this one, I will be lonely.

DA: Do they have any observations to make about how you are progressing in this life?

AZ: They say I'm doing all right. I shouldn't worry too much. But there are things I don't understand in this life.

DA: You can ask them.

AZ: And I want to know why I've never been able to think something through. I can't plan ahead properly. I can only think so far, and then it's all gone. And then I follow my impulse. And it's gone okay. But it's as if I'm not using my mind properly.

DA: What do they have to say about that?

AZ: I could do it if I wanted to, but I don't want to. I don't understand why I don't want to. It's as if I was given this mind to explore things but not to go too deep. There's so much to explore that I can't take the time to … I don't know.

DA: And what's the primary lesson for this life?

AZ: To take things as they come. Learning to accept things as they come. But I don't know. I think I'm getting too high and coming into my head too much.

DA: Just stay with the imagery of the Council and remember to allow your breathing to help you relax even further. That's right. Still going down. You can put time on hold in the Council whilst you allow yourself to drift further and further down. As I place my hand on your arm, you will find that very helpful in just drifting down and down and down. That's right. Deeper and deeper.

AZ: Now it's something about learning that I don't need to be in cells all the time. I like being nowhere. I don't need to … I can be with people and just be among them without leaving. I can play second fiddle. That's part of my learning in this life. But it's not about being on my own or being a leader. I can just be … I don't have to distinguish myself in any particular way. But I say I don't need to be so serious all the time.

DA: Is that how you see yourself in your physical life, as a serious person?

AZ: It's as if I was almost born serious. I can make fun, but rarely. I'm very serious. I feel in this life everything's very heavy.

DA: Are they suggestive?

AZ: It feels as if … maybe I've taken on a bit too much.

DA: Was this life designed to be easier than the last one?

AZ: No. It was a different aspect that I wanted to explore. It was, in a way, loneliness amongst people. But it's a lot heavier than I thought it would be.

DA: Are they saying to you it doesn't necessarily have to be that way?

AZ: They remind me that I didn't take that much energy.

DA: How much energy did you take?

AZ: About forty … Forty per cent. That's why it's heavier than … You see, the body is strong. The body could probably have taken more energy. I think I was a bit rash. I tend to do that. I tend to be a bit reckless sometimes. Spontaneous? Spontaneous is a nice word for it, yes. So sometimes I just jump and think it will be fine.

DA: Whilst you're with the Council, let's explore this sense of feeling that you had of not belonging on Earth. Does that have a substantive basis in that you haven't incarnated on Earth very often? Or is it something else?

I suppose the question is, are most of your incarnations on Earth?

AZ: Yes, most are on Earth. But I have also incarnated in other places.

DA: But they are the exception rather than the rule?

AZ: No, it's about half and half. It's as if everything else is easier than Earth. Yes, I didn't take quite enough with me.

DA: Okay, let me ask you some questions about your incarnations in general. How many times have you incarnated on Earth?

AZ: Actually, not that many times, I realise. Maybe a few hundred.

DA: How many times elsewhere? It would be similar if it's about half and half. There'd be a few hundred times in other places.

AZ: No, no, no, it isn't. It's where I go for an easier ride. That is about the same number of times, but maybe not so much. But there are other places I go. Other places.

DA: What's the name of the place you go to more often if it's not Earth?

AZ: It's not Earth. It doesn't have a name. It's a space with tones where ... it's not music, but it's where one works with tones. Like every colour has a tone, every soul has a tone. And so, I realise this is more recreational. This is not incarnation. I don't incarnate anywhere else. There is no body anywhere else. So, if incarnation means becoming flesh...

DA: Or, well, not necessarily. It could be becoming energy, but in a different place.

AZ: I'm getting around quite a bit. I like being in this place with tones and ... There's another place. It's about creating with light, creating with the awareness that is there. Making structures of buildings.

DA: So, what prompted you to take on another very heavy physical incarnation on Earth?

AZ: I need to learn to connect to human beings better. I find that difficult. And there is something that is ... I can't help it. This feels strange. Human beings ... even though I've been there quite a few times, it's not ... I can't really connect with them. It's as if there's always something I don't get about them.

DA: But you connect with Peter?

AZ: We have ways of connecting with each other, but we are not connected all the time. Not at all. At other times, we are very much like strangers. We know each other, but we are different. Different from each other. But also different from the people around us, which is strange.

Narration

Peter is a helpful soul from an adjacent Soul Group.

End of Narration

DA: Of your earthly incarnations, how many would you say were male and how many female?

AZ: I've been more male. But usually when I was a man .. No, also when I was a woman ... No, I think it's about half and half. But my preferred mode is definitely male.

DA: Why do you prefer it?

AZ: Simpler. Men are so much simpler in their understanding. So much clearer. As a woman, things always seem incredibly complex. And it's very difficult to find a place where you can be free as a woman. It's much easier to be free as a man.

DA: So, what made you choose a woman's body this time round?

AZ: It's been too long in a man's body. It was time again to explore. Sort of the time when women were struggling for freedom. That was really important in this life. The feminist movement. To participate in that and to see that there are things that can be achieved.

DA: Which gender do you prefer physically? The woman's body?

AZ: I like the woman's body. Somehow, I myself am ... I feel myself as more male. Of course, I know I'm not. I'm both. But male is my preferred guise.

DA: Have the Council anything more to tell you?

AZ: They tell me I don't have enough energy to see it through, but I do not need to worry about that. Which is a great relief.

DA: Do they have any suggestions as to why you feel that you don't have any motivation for things in this life? It's difficult to get going.

AZ: No, I didn't want to become anything in particular. I know that what I'm doing is okay for me. And that I have the motivation when I need it for my own goals in life. And everything else is like a distraction from ... It's not quite clear, but it's as if it's about knowing as much as possible, rather than getting bogged down in one thing in particular.

Chapter Summary

The thread of choice about being male or female seems to demand a balance over time, perhaps a sort of Karma. It may be why some people feel uneasy about their gender in the current life, yet it must be completed as originally planned. The soul state, of course, is pure energy, though when we see soul mates or Council members, or guides, their representation as male or female is helpful as it connects to a degree of familiarity.

Isolation and the sense of being alone is something we all have to contend with.

Chapter 20: Anna Yarrow

In the journey of the soul, few moments are as profound as the first encounter with a guide who ushers us into the spiritual realm. This chapter, nestled within the section "The Journey Home", presents a vivid transcript of a client's experience meeting their guide and a council of elders. Through Isabelle's session, we explore the transition from earthly uncertainty to spiritual connection, a process that resonates deeply with modern feelings of isolation and the search for purpose. Her encounter with a radiant figure named Ishmail and a diverse council offers insights into guidance, destiny, and the soul's role in today's world.

As a jeweller, Isabelle's keen eye for detail enriches the imagery, reflecting how our unique perspectives shape spiritual experiences. This transcript invites readers to consider how spiritual connections can anchor us amidst life's transitions, offering clarity and courage for the path ahead.

DA: Is anything happening?

AY: There's a man there. Tall. Intense blue eyes. Long white beard. Long white tunic. He's wearing a long white tunic.

DA: How far away are you from him?

AY: Erm … a few yards. But he's welcoming. He's got his arm out to welcome me. Now it's as if he's got his arm around me.

DA: How do you feel at this moment?

AY: Uncertain. Like, where am I?

DA: I'm sensing your uncertainty. Can you see anything past him?

AY: Erm … yes, it's a lot of light. I'm seeing what look like light versions of poplar trees. Like an avenue. I'm walking down an avenue of light.

DA: Are you still with this person? Are you walking with him? Is he on your right-hand side or your left-hand side?

AY: He's on my right. He's talking to me.

DA: He's talking to you?

AY: Yes.

DA: Is he holding you?

AY: Yes, he's got his left arm lightly over my shoulder. He's just guiding me and talking.

DA: Can you understand him now?

AY: No. I seem to be talking back, but I can't hear. He's laughing.

DA: Are you still walking down the avenue?

AY: Yes.

DA: What's happening now?

AY: Oh, we've come to a door. It's a very old door, but it's not. It's a door of light. He's opening it, and we're going through it, and we're in a big room. It's like a church of light.

DA: Tell me a little more about this person. Look at him. From the top down, describe the details that are presented to you.

AY: Yes. He's like a wizard; what I'd call a cosmic wizard. He's very tall, above human height – six foot seven, something like that. Very long hair. He's absolutely covered in glaring white. Very large eyes. An old face, but it's beautiful – a beautiful face. High cheekbones. Slim nose. Chiselled chin. I can vaguely see ears; they're a bit pointed. Slim neck. I can't really see the body that well. He's covered in a white tunic, like a white cloak and long dress in a way. He has a belt around it, which is again white, like rope. Shoes which are pointy

– very pointy shoes. Again, they're all white light. He shimmers with stars in it. Stars seem to shimmer around him. He's very friendly. He feels like someone I've known forever.

DA: What's his name?

AY: I've got two names. The first one that comes is Ishmail. Behind it, there's a name, Merlin. But the main name is Ishmail. I begin to hear his voice – a very deep voice. It's suddenly come in, very reassuring. He's pleased I can hear him now.

Narration

The name Merlin and the wizard-like appearance may be caused by conscious interference, but there is a better name in Ishmail, so we'll go with that.

End of Narration

DA: What's he saying?

AY: "You're okay now. You're safe. You're in the right place. It's okay." That's it.

DA: Is he your guide?

AY: Yes.

DA: Is he your most senior guide?

AY: Yes. I'm checking. Yes. Confirming. Yes.

DA: What is your name?

AY: Yes. Isabelle. I'm being called Belle. Isabelle.

DA: What else is going on around you, Belle?

AY: I see people busy. I'm seeing people in a kitchen – a kitchen of light, making food. It's like a monastery, actually – a monastery of light. There's a church area, an area where people are sleeping, a garden, an office. It's like a monastery of light.

DA: Can you ask him what it is that you should be doing now?

AY: Okay. He's saying very clearly, "We're going to see the council." He's taking me down a passage. I know I'm sitting with him opposite a group of what looks like wise elders. And they do look very strange. They don't look human at all.

DA: Are they in front of you?

AY: Yes.

DA: Are they seated? Are you seated or standing?

AY: I am seated, as is my guide. He's seated next to me.

DA: Is he to your left?

AY: He's on my right.

DA: And how far away are the elders?

AY: They're quite close. It's like a trestle table. They're in chairs which are very high-backed. There seem to be about five or six. They have very pointed faces, like the face of a hound, which is strange to me. Piercing eyes. They have hoods. They're very dark blue.

DA: Are they all the same colour?

AY: No. The two in the centre are midnight blue. The ones outside them are wearing dark green. And the two at the outer ends are wearing a deep, deep pinky-red – cloaks with hoods.

DA: Are they wearing hats?

AY: Yes. Tall, pointy, quite Egyptian-looking, actually. And they have a point that comes down the brow. Their brow is very high. They're very old – exceedingly old, billions of years. I can't describe how old they are.

DA: Are they wearing any adornments?

AY: Yes. They seem to be wearing ... There's a pendant, which is like a star. It has a garnet in the centre. This is one of them.

DA: Which one?

AY: This is to the right side of my body – in front of me, but to the right side of my body.

DA: Is he one of the two centre ones, one of the two blue ones?

AY: He's the right-hand one. He wears a star, which has a cabochon-cut garnet in it, with diamonds around. I'm a jeweller, David. That's probably why I'm seeing this On a long chain, this pendant is very powerful.

DA: You're going to remember, in every detail, this pendant and the details of other pendants. And at a later time you'll be able to draw them. What is the other blue council member wearing? Does he have a pendant as well?

AY: Yes, but it's not a pendant. He's got a brooch around the neck – totally different. It's like a lily; with such detail I could hardly describe it. It's stunning. The petals are like pink and gold enamel, like shot silk, colours reflecting into each other. Then there are diamonds, with an orange-pink centre stone. It's actually a sapphire. I can describe it to you afterwards, but it's a sapphire. It's a very beautiful lily, like a water lily.

DA: What about the other members?

AY: If I go to the ones in green – no, he's different, completely different. He's wearing a necklace, like an Egyptian one, all turquoise cloisonné set beads, like cells – a chest necklace covering the whole chest area, thickly interwoven with turquoise and carnelian beads. Now I'm looking at the man on the right, the guide in green on the right. He's got a staff, and the staff has a black tourmaline at the top – very powerful, with energy glowing off it. He's got no jewels on, very plainly dressed but in this deep green. There's a ferrule to the staff where the black tourmaline is set, covered in garnets – just covered in garnets – and then it's a long oak wood staff. When I look at the ones at the very outer edge, they're completely plainly dressed. The one on the right does have a brooch, like a Celtic brooch, all silver, very intricate.

DA: Whereabouts is the brooch on his body?

AY: It's on his left breast, on the left lapel, as I saw it.

DA: And the other person on the far outside?

AY: It's very different. The outfit's changed – it's turned silver, glowing silver, like a space suit. They're very beautiful, stunning beyond human beauty. It could be male or female – very androgynous. They're wearing this long gown with a very tall hat, but they're completely different, like someone from another dimension. They say they're from Sirius, the star system, and they tell me I'm doing a great job on Earth. "You're doing fine."

DA: Which one are you speaking to?

AY: This is the one on the far left, the person who's from Sirius, a star person, as I'd say. I've been given a name – Andorus. This is the Sirian person, the star person. They say they're a guide and they're here for me now, at this time. I'm coming back to the centre. I seem to have walked along this row of people and studied them. I'm now sitting back down next to Ishmail, next to my main guide. I have to say, Ishmail is my Earth guide. He's confirming to me, "I am your guide at this time on Earth. I've always been your guide while you've been on Earth." I've gone quiet.

DA: Let's just allow the meeting to progress. You've obviously gone to the council for a purpose. Let's see what they want to say to you.

AY: The one to my right, in the centre, in the dark blue cloak, is speaking. He's saying, "You've got a job to do, and you've got to do it. Don't be afraid. Let go of your fears. It's going to be a whole lot better than you could possibly imagine." He's speaking of my time on Earth now and from here on. He's saying, "You feel very alone at the moment, which is why you've come to do this work." He's saying I've come to a junction in my life, and the first half of my life is complete – I'm making a full stop. He's saying, "The new has now begun. Your new life is now happening." And now he's saying again, "You've got nothing to fear. Let go of all that fear. Stop worrying." He's handing me a glass orb. It's gone into my body, just below my navel, into my sacral chakra. It feels like a record of what's going to happen from here on. Oh, he's sitting down again. It's gone quiet. I'm sitting down again. It's quiet.

DA: Is there more to come?

AY: I was wondering. Someone's trying to stand up – they're sort of wavering. It's the councillor to my far right in the pinky-gold cloak.

DA: Do you know his name?

AY: He's Ishmael. That's the one that's Ishmael.

DA: What's he saying?

AY: He's saying he called me to come and that, David, you're my vehicle to talk to them. He's saying, "We welcome you." He's smiling. He's got teeth – they're all sort of silver and golden, very weird to me. He's smiling. His eyes are like white silver, like silver lights. He's got a very straight nose, pointy ears again, high cheekbones, chiselled chin, big, slitty eyes, but they're quite big. He's saying, "Peace be with you." He keeps saying, "Peace be with you. We're glad to see you. We're welcoming you." Now he's sitting down. It's gone quiet again. Every time they speak, I go to the table and really listen to them, and then I go back to my seat. It's all quiet again. To my left, the elder in green to my left is standing. I'm standing up again. I'm walking to the table.

DA: His name?

AY: Carlo. He's saying some history. He's saying, "You are thousands of years old. You come from far out in space, the essence of you." He says I'm an intermediate soul. He keeps saying, "You've had to spend quite a bit of this life so far feeling alone, and you have been a very independent soul. At times, you've found this really tough because your human side wanted to be a social connected being, but you are a very independent soul, and you've done well. You've survived being alone from the human element." He says my aura colour is mostly very dark blue – midnight blue – with some electric blue. There's some turquoise there. My main aura colour is deep midnight blue, then electric blue, and at the very outer edge, it's pale blue, then white. That is my actual true aura. He says I'm a counsellor for souls individually who choose to come to me. People come to me by invitation – I have to wait for them to come to me, not introduce myself.

DA: Is that in your spiritual existence, your role as a spirit, or the role that you have in this life?

AY: It's human. It's my role in this life. Yes. He says I'm doing well, quite advanced. I'm pausing because he's fading – he's stepping back and coming forward again. This is because of my energy; I got a bit tired for a moment. He's saying, "You're doing a good job." Oh, he's coming out with something about soulmates. He's saying, "Yes, yes, yes," and he keeps trying to get it straight to my heart because right now my heart energy is glowing very pink. He's pointing his finger at my heart energy and saying, "William Street is your soulmate. Believe it. William Street is your soulmate. Do not doubt this."

Chapter Summary

Isabelle's session unveils a transformative journey from uncertainty to affirmation, guided by Ishmail, a towering figure shimmering with star-like light. As they traverse an avenue of light into a monastery-like realm, Isabelle meets a council of ancient elders, each adorned with symbolic jewels reflecting her jeweller's perspective. The council's messages – releasing fear, embracing a new life phase, and affirming her soulmate connection with William Street (a romantic interest) – address her loneliness, a sentiment shared in today's disconnected world. Her role as a counsellor, waiting for souls to seek her, mirrors modern challenges of patience and purpose. This transcript is rich with vivid descriptions and emotional depth.

Section 5

Reviews: Summary

Esther, Hope, Rebecca, Abigail, and Isabelle each traverse unique spiritual landscapes, revealing the multifaceted nature of soul development. Esther reconnects with her Soul Group and reviews past lives in the Library, grappling with passivity and self-love.

Hope's emotional journey through the Library and the Council uncovers past lives that mirror her struggles with isolation and control, leaving her at a crossroads. Rebecca, an advanced Hybrid Soul, heals soul energies and seeks to break cycles of separation in the Library and the Council, nearing resolution. Abigail's singular focus on the Council addresses her loneliness and Hybrid Soul experiences, guiding her toward acceptance. Isabelle's radiant encounter with her guide and the Council, enriched by her jeweller's imagery, affirms her new life phase and soulmate connection.

Collectively, their experiences weave a tapestry of lessons on fear, connection, and the soul's relentless pursuit of wholeness in an often-disconnected world.

Section 6

Life Selection: Introduction

Section 6: Life Selection explores the intricate process of choosing a new incarnation, distinguishing itself from Section 5's retrospective soul reviews by focusing on the proactive orchestration of lives. Across four journeys – April's sensory-driven choices, Oliver's nurturing support, Edmund's soulmate reunion, and Ivy's reluctant growth – clients reveal diverse motivations, from love and duty to discipline and purpose. We'll discover, through the memories of these four people how this happens, what prompts it, who decides what, and other aspects of this impending renewal.

The stories illuminate the soul's agency, encouraging readers to embrace intentional living and spiritual evolution.

Few aspects of this special journey inspire more questions than this one. How did I get here? Why am I who I am? Why is life so difficult? If one incarnates again and again, how is the next life decided? It's an area of great interest.

Chapter 21: April Allen

Introduction

April's journey as Naya distinguishes itself through its immersive pre-life planning, unlike the retrospective soul reviews of others in Section 5. Guided by the subtle Gag, she explores three potential lives via sensory experiences, prioritising familial bonds and a soulmate over dependency or medical paths. In today's uncertain world, April's deliberate choices inspire reflection on the soul's agency in shaping life's purpose.

DA: When you decided to take this life, we know it's several hundred years since your last one. In earthly terms, that's a long time, but it matters less in the spiritual world. What prompted you? How did you know it was time?

AA: My guide or soul group members informed me it was time to consider it.

DA: That it was time to take another life?

AA: Yes, you're gently told to think about it.

DA: When a new incarnation is planned, does it just happen, or is there significant organisation involved?

AA: There's a lot of organisation going on, but it happens behind the scenes.

DA: Can you share what you know about it?

AA: It's like a vast operations room where everything must align. Time masters – highly evolved souls – manage it quietly, like Gag, who stays unobtrusive.

Narration

Gag is her guide.

End of Narration

DA: Laid back?

AA: Yes, though dour rather than severe. As a child, I saw him as a dapper 1920s gentleman with spats, a cane, and a tasselled scarf – clearly, he enjoyed life once.

DA: Let's return to the organisation of the new life. How far do these background souls coordinate, especially with those intertwined in your life?

AA: They're usually from the same soul group or cluster, not a distant place of learning – I hesitate to call them schools, as that feels too earthly.

DA: When does this process start?

AA: After you're told it is time.

DA: Or have you ever initiated it yourself, saying you're ready?

AA: No, I've never initiated it. You're prompted because leaving is for evolution, not choice.

DA: So, it's a coaxing process?

AA: Yes, subtle encouragement to evolve.

DA: You know it's necessary, but do you ever try to avoid it?

AA: Yes, I've said I'm not ready.

DA: What's the response?

AA: They give you time, never pushing. Eventually, you realise it's needed – a form of self-discipline.

DA: When you agreed last time, walk me through the process.

AA: You're taken to a circular space outside your usual sphere, where you're shown potential bodies and lives.

DA: When you chose this life, how many options were there?

AA: Three.

DA: Is this place like a building?

AA: No, a sphere in space.

DA: Are others present?

AA: Just the controller, operator, and my guide.

DA: How are these lives presented?

AA: Like a 360-degree cinema screen. You can step in, feel sensations – smell, taste, touch.

DA: You step into the person, not just watch?

AA: Yes, if you choose, to experience the five senses.

DA: Did you do that with all three?

AA: Yes, I always do.

DA: With this life, did you experience any painful moments?

AA: Some, but not the worst – they protect you from that.

DA: To keep you committed?

AA: Yes, it's gentle persuasion, subtle control.

DA: What about the two lives you didn't choose?

AA: They were both females. One was an invalid in a wheelchair in America – that was too dependent. The other was like this life, a potential doctor, but I rejected it, questioning Western medicine's drugs and side effects.

DA: Why avoid the invalid's life?

AA: I needed physical freedom, not reliance on others.

DA: Did you sense this life was their preferred choice?

AA: No, any of the three was fine – it was my decision.

DA: What did you experience about this life's outline?

AA: Walking with my father by the Thames in 1950s London, seeing bomb sites. My loving grandfather, cousin Terry, like a brother, and my evolved mother who wears bright blue but belongs to another cluster.

DA: Does your mother appear often?

AA: Yes, in about half my lives.

DA: Are organisers scouting for roles, like "Who'll be April's mum?"

AA: Sometimes. I was lucky – my childhood was happy, with a loving family and joyful Christmases.

DA: How far into this life did you see?

AA: Into my 80s, so I'll live long.

DA: Did you carry pre-life knowledge, like your depression as a teen?

AA: Yes, I knew I'd meet Martin at 50, and waiting caused depression starting at puberty.

DA: When did you meet Chris, your first husband?

AA: Around 22 – he was a doctor.

DA: Was that a learning experience?

AA: Yes, relationships are my lessons. Chris exposed me to Western medicine's pressures, which I questioned.

DA: What ended your relationship with Chris?

AA: His strict, religious upbringing led to issues after marriage. His mother, born illegitimately, never received love, so couldn't give it, affecting him, as a psychiatrist explained.

DA: That was a clear reason to end it – a significant challenge.

AA: Yes, a lot of pressure as a young woman.

DA: Were you sexually naive before Chris?

AA: Yes, my generation feared unwanted pregnancy. Naivety lasted until my late teens or early twenties.

DA: Did you know Chris's issues would arise?

AA: Yes, I was aware before choosing this life.

DA: Were major life points, like relationships, preset?

AA: Yes, including three key relationships, with Martin as my soulmate at the end.

DA: But you don't fully recall that in life?

AA: No, though I checked it beforehand.

DA: How did you choose this life?

AA: I said, "I'll take it," then discussed roles with my soul group, deciding who'd support me and how.

DA: Is the foetus already chosen, or do you wait?

AA: It's prepared, but I'm not told how. You're informed when it's time.

DA: Hence the complex organisation?

AA: Yes, especially with souls born before you, leaving partial energy behind.

DA: What happens when it's time to go?

AA: You're taken to a restful place, then sent through a reverse tunnel to integrate with the foetus.

DA: Describe the place of rest.

AA: Dark, quiet, peaceful, warm, reassuring.

DA: How do you rest?

AA: Through a meditative state.

DA: Are others there?

AA: Yes, but you're in an isolated cell, like a beehive.

DA: How are you called to join?

AA: It happens subtly – you're suddenly with the foetus.

DA: Are you aware of travelling?

AA: Yes, a sense of movement.

DA: What part of the foetus do you connect with first?

AA: The brain, near the pituitary gland, where lobes meet.

DA: Was this joining easy?

AA: Yes, smoother than some, where you feel less welcomed.

DA: Have you had difficult joinings?

AA: Some require more soothing and reassurance.

DA: Can joinings fail?

AA: Only in cases like miscarriage or stillbirth, not from a healthy foetus rejecting a soul.

DA: How long does joining take?

AA: It's gradual, requiring continual reassurance and gentleness.

DA: Can you join partially, rest, and continue?

AA: Yes, you can join anytime, even late, and pause as needed.

DA: Was your joining late?

AA: Yes, around eight or nine months, but easy.

DA: Could you leave and return after joining?

AA: Yes, even after birth, especially when the baby's young.

DA: Do you visit Earth as a spirit between lives?

AA: No, I prefer the spirit world and have no desire to return, even for beauty, as I can experience it there.

DA: Do others visit Earth?

AA: Yes, some choose to.

Chapter Summary

April, as Naya, navigates a meticulous incarnation process, selecting her life from three sensory-immersive options with Gag's guidance. Rejecting dependency and medical careers, she embraces a life of familial love, her soulmate Martin, and relationship lessons despite foreseen challenges like teenage depression and a strained marriage. Her late foetal integration reflects a balance of choice and spiritual structure, urging readers to find resilience in purposeful living.

Chapter 22: Oliver Hart

Introduction

Oliver's journey, as Hannah, centres on the pull of her spiritual home, a stark contrast to the life selection deliberations of April or the introspective reviews of Section 5's clients. While others weighed life options or past lessons, Hannah's reluctance to leave her nurturing haven stems from love for soulmate Christine, whom she supports as a mother in this life. Her focus on spiritual rest and reciprocal bonds sets her apart, resonating with modernity's quest for authentic connection amid digital overload, inviting readers to reflect on the soul's balance between duty and serenity. We know of the complex organisation needed in order to support a life in a way that not only aids the principal soul but also meets the objectives, as much as possible, for the supporting roles in the new incarnation.

DA: What else is important for you to do now?

OH: I must use my talents in every way possible to nurture others – that's what matters most.

DA: I meant in your spiritual home, with this expanded awareness. What might you do? Spend time with friends, explore, or review your life?

OH: I don't like leaving this place anymore. I've no urge to push beyond it.

DA: Do you feel this is your last incarnation or is it uncertain?

OH: It's uncertain, but it could be my last, or nearly so. I prefer being home – this planet's exhausting.

DA: When you chose this incarnation, what prompted it? You're busy, teaching, loving your spiritual home – then something sparks another life. Was it your decision, a suggestion, or collective?

OH: I returned not for myself but for others, volunteering to support a soul group member, Christine, my mother in this life.

Narration

Most recollections, particularly around choosing the next incarnation are seen from the perspective of the client directly. In this case, however, we see an example of an associated incarnation whose primary purpose was as a "supporting role" in someone else's necessary new life. The important souls in one's life are roles agreed to by others, whether that be a parent, child, lover or other.

End of Narration

DA: So, this incarnation was driven by your role in Christine's life?

OH: Yes, absolutely.

DA: How was it organised?

OH: Christine craves intense emotions, reincarnating in tough lives to grow quickly. She's strong-willed, and I love her, so I support her when I can.

DA: Did Christine request your help, saying she needed support for this incarnation?

OH: We met as a group – guides and souls – in a round room, relaxed, planning together. Some volunteered, but it's a complex matrix of life paths enhancing each other, not just hers.

DA: Is there a specialist group handling the intricate details?

OH: Yes, stronger souls oversee it, ensuring everything fits.

DA: If Christine or another asked for help again, might you incarnate to assist, balancing your desire to stay home?

OH: Yes, we reciprocate, helping loved ones grow.

DA: So, love outweighs your wish to stay, prompting incarnations?

OH: Yes, we're love, eager to uplift those we cherish.

DA: When you agreed to help Christine, was the human body unknown since the embryo wasn't yet formed? Is that common, unlike choosing a specific body or gender?

OH: I needed to join at a specific point as a male to support her.

DA: If the pregnancy had been female, would another soul have joined?

OH: Yes, a female might have overwhelmed Christine.

DA: Was that why she had you later in life?

OH: No, it was about timing, not age – I gave her strength to endure Earth's miseries, preventing despair or madness.

DA: How's the celebration with friends progressing?

OH: Time isn't linear here. I'll join them, and it'll last as we wish – I can access it anytime.

DA: With your strengthened connection to Tamsin, what else do you want to explore in this higher consciousness?

OH: I have questions, but I'll resolve them intuitively now.

Narration:

Tamsin is his guide.

End of Narration:

DA: Anything else to share?

OH: I'm here to help another soul group member, but this human's path is unexpected. He lacks the urge to parent, having nurtured in spirit yet I'm unclear if a child's soul would connect.

DA: You can ask Tamsin.

OH: I'm trying, but there's no answer yet.

DA: You can persist with guides – don't always accept their silence.

OH: She says another group member might incarnate through me, but it's not essential. It's clearer now – I'm here to help, so I might assist twice.

DA: What's happening now?

OH: I'm facing questions I haven't answered. They'll come clearer here, but I must boost my energy and reform spiritual relationships, adjusting to my state.

DA: Have we reached a natural conclusion for now?

OH: I'd like to contemplate this world a bit longer.

DA: I meant for this session – have we explored enough for now?

OH: Yes, nurturing defines me – partners, children, parents. My adopted son, Sam, from a related soul group, chose me. He's advanced, with big tasks ahead, and I'll support him.

DA: You can return here anytime now.

OH: I know, and I'll need time for all this to unfold.

Chapter Summary

Oliver, as Hannah, reveals a nurturing soul driven by love to incarnate for soulmate Christine, her mother in this life, despite yearning to remain in her spiritual home. Volunteering in a collaborative soul group meeting, she chose a male body to provide strength for Christine's intense emotional journey. Her role extends to supporting adopted son, Sam, an advanced soul, while grappling with unresolved questions about further nurturing. Oliver's journey underscores the power of reciprocal love and intuition, offering a beacon for finding purpose and connection in a fragmented world.

Chapter 23: Edmund York

Introduction

Edmund's session, as Edward, illuminates the orchestration of his incarnation to reunite with soulmate Pauline, a vital thread in Section 5's exploration of soul reviews. His emphasis on cosmic timing over bodily choice, driven by a longing to protect her, distinguishes this chapter. Reflecting the need to search for a meaningful connection amid digital transience, Edward's journey invites readers to consider the soul's enduring commitments and the call to share spiritual truths.

DA: You're comparing notes with others. Has Diana incarnated this time?

EY: No, not this time.

DA: How did your current incarnation, as Edmund, manifest? How did you know it was time to reincarnate and choose it?

EY: Timelines converged between me and Pauline.

DA: So, it was organised to meet her needs?

EY: We had to unite to protect her.

DA: Why this body? Was the choice significant?

EY: Just a body in her environment. She's older, so it was easy to select – I knew my destination.

DA: Was this incarnation about getting the timing right for Pauline?

EY: Yes, that's what it was.

DA: To meet your soulmate?

EY: I missed her before, long ago. It's been a long wait.

DA: Can't you meet her in your spiritual home?

EY: No, she wasn't there. We kept missing, like planets out of orbit – no clue as to why.

DA: Were most incarnations without her?

EY: Yes, making this time crucial.

DA: She's in the spirit world now – what part of her is there?

EY: She's still on Earth, in another incarnation.

DA: Another life?

EY: I'll wait until she's done, then we'll return together.

DA: Will future incarnations unite you?

EY: No more incarnations. We'll stay in spirit.

DA: Is that fixed, or could it change?

EY: It's fluid, not stone, but feels set for now.

DA: Have you met spirits who no longer incarnate?

EY: Many – lots don't return.

DA: What determines ceasing incarnation?

EY: Being more useful there than here – it's that simple.

Narration

He means more useful in the spiritual realm than on Earth, but it's also to do with attainment and seniority. Once souls have advanced to a particular level, they have no need to incarnate again and can spend eternity in the spiritual realm.

End of Narration

DA: You've had countless incarnations. Can you estimate a number?

EY: Numbers don't matter. I've been a sailor, many roles – details aren't key.

DA: Do past incarnations hold value, shaping you?

EY: They're jigsaw pieces, forming me. Pauline was the missing piece – now the puzzle is complete.

DA: You asked about your purpose as Edmund. It seems it was organised to share a life with Pauline.

EY: Yes, but now I must tell others about this world. With my time left, I have to explain there's another realm.

Chapter Summary

Edmund's incarnation was orchestrated to reunite with Pauline, aligning timelines to safeguard her after countless lives apart. His choice of body was secondary to this cosmic rendezvous, and with their reunion achieved, he now feels complete. Resolved to forgo future incarnations and remain in spirit, Edmund dedicates his remaining time to revealing the existence of another realm. Echoing the current yearning for authenticity, his journey inspires readers to pursue profound connections and embrace their role in unveiling life's deeper truths.

Chapter 24: Ivy Graham

Introduction

We see a playful soul's nudge toward maturity. Guided by Joy, her prankster ways meet a council's stern push to incarnate, shaping her as a healer. This chapter's focus on reluctant growth mirrors the modern day's struggle with distraction and avoidance, urging readers to embrace responsibility and purpose, finding balance between freedom and the soul's deeper call to evolve.

DA: Let's discuss how you chose this life as Ivy. How did you know it was time to reincarnate?

IG: I was told to do it.

DA: Who told you?

IG: Joy, my guide, though higher entities decide.

DA: Higher than Joy?

IG: Yes, entities far above me.

DA: Did you meet them?

IG: Yes.

DA: What happened? You were in your spiritual role, then summoned. Did Joy tell you to go?

IG: He fetched me. I was pranking, doing nothing, and they tired of it, saying I needed this life to grow.

DA: Were you irresponsible, like your fun-loving group?

IG: Yes, we're all a bit like that.

DA: Did you have roles, or could you just play?

IG: Our group learns fast, meant to teach, maybe guide, but we're too young, too reckless.

DA: When Joy found you idling, what happened next?

IG: I dodged him, tricking my way out, but got bored. When I stopped, he was annoyed, shaking his head – I knew why he came.

DA: Did you go with him right away? Where to?

IG: To a church-like place, serious and daunting.

DA: Describe it.

IG: It's a place of judgement, like a doom-laden court, scary and solemn.

DA: How many were there?

IG: Three – one high up front, one left, one right.

DA: Are you in a structure? Sitting? Are they?

IG: It's like a court, floating yet structured, not quite a place.

DA: Were the three waiting when you entered?

IG: Yes, ready for me.

DA: How far away were they?

IG: About ten metres.

DA: Did Joy stay?

IG: Yes, watching from behind, to my left.

DA: Describe the main judge – male or female?

IG: Male, big, dark, scary, like he's angry.

DA: What colour is he?

IG: Blackish, with golden-brown around – meant to be happy, but they're cross.

DA: Do they have faces or features?

IG: Vague, similar shapes.

DA: What colours are the other two?

IG: Dark grey, less intense, but still upset with me.

DA: Who speaks?

IG: The one in front.

DA: What does he say?

IG: Not much, just that my antics must stop, and I know he's right.

DA: Word for word, what does he say?

IG: "You can't keep doing this. Go to the world and learn."
He calms, turning green.

DA: Is he less scary now?

IG: Yes, I'm happier.

DA: What else does he say?

IG: They've chosen a body, urging me to take it. They say
I'll learn heaps and make them glad.

DA: Your response?

IG: I feel cornered but say yes – I'm up for adventure.

DA: Does that lift your mood? Their colours now?

IG: They're blue, calmer, and I'm content.

DA: Do they have your best interests at heart, like parents?

IG: Yes, I've pranked too much. They know I learn fast and
waste that gift.

DA: You agree to the life – what's next? One body chosen?

IG: Yes, no choice given.

DA: Did you see what the life held?

IG: They promised nature, greens, space – room to grow,
perfect for me.

DA: How do you prepare?

IG: Joy takes me to a library to study.

DA: Describe it.

IG: Like a vast library, full of books.

DA: Are they books, screens?

IG: Books. Joy picks nature ones to keep me engaged – I
love them.

DA: Are they like earthly books?

IG: Full of pictures – flowers, plants, things I adore.

DA: Did Joy reveal the life's details?

IG: No, they're just keeping me curious.

DA: How long did you study?

IG: A while, no rush.

DA: Did you have to read everything?

IG: Joy said browse, no pressure – wise, as I'd bolt otherwise.
I read about horses, new to me.

DA: From past lives?

IG: Yes, they're thrilled now.

DA: Did you know it was a female life?

IG: Joy hinted, not in words – through feelings.

DA: Could you preview the life's path?

IG: If I did, it's hidden now, like a secret.

DA: Was there a place to review past lives?

IG: Yes, but I skip it – boring.

DA: You never review?

IG: No, once done, I'm out.

DA: After studying, what's next?

IG: They say it's new, something I'll figure out alone, not
told upfront.

DA: How do you do that?

IG: I must slow down, notice small things, embrace a gentle
pace.

DA: Were you excited?

IG: Yes, horses and nature sounded like a holiday. They
laughed, knowing better, but we're all happy.

DA: Then what?

IG: I return to my group, say goodbye, see you soon.

DA: When were roles, like Atemia as your son, decided?

IG: They knew, but I didn't – they tricked me.

DA: Were you uninterested?

IG: Yes, too busy pranking, ignoring details.

DA: Might knowing more have helped?

IG: Probably.

DA: A lesson there?

IG: Absolutely.

DA: How was the goodbye?

IG: I detached, kept it simple – see you, gone – to avoid
pain.

DA: Did you know who'd join your life?

IG: No, I didn't care enough.

DA: After goodbye, what happened?

IG: Joy took me from there to a transition place, like a train's sleeping berth. I lay down, drifting into life.

DA: When did you join the foetus?

IG: I saw the tiny body, didn't like it, and drifted off.

DA: Where to?

IG: A waiting room, just Joy and me. He's firm, tired of my antics, urging calm.

DA: Was this life long after your last, maybe thirteenth-century Endar?

IG: I think so, but I'm vague.

Narration

Ivy incarnated as Endar in a former life.

End of Narration

DA: Avoided lives between?

IG: Maybe one was offered, not sure.

DA: You could check in the library – part of being responsible?

IG: Maybe.

DA: Let's talk to Atemia. He's your son-to-be. Ask his role.

IG: He'll test me, learning what I know. It's my task to teach, proving I've paid attention.

DA: Was he in your Endar life?

IG: Yes, a doctor, present but distant.

DA: Why did you expect a daughter, not a son?

IG: Joy's fed up with my pranks, maybe tweaking me.

DA: What challenges await in this life?

IG: Focus and learning – that's it.

DA: Your illness and fatigue – was that expected?

IG: Joy knew, I didn't.

DA: Why was it vital to face this?

IG: To learn healing's slow pace, not flighty, as I'm training to heal and teach.

DA: Like Endar's long illness, unresolved?

IG: Different – Endar was stubborn, ignored nature.

DA: Is this a repeat lesson?

IG: No, it's richer, filled with what I love, building on Endar.

DA: They threatened you to listen – real or a nudge?

IG: I don't know, don't want to.

DA: What does Atemia say?

IG: He laughs, pats my hair, calls himself the true healer, saying it's fine.

DA: Will he be your son to guide you?

IG: No, I'll guide him, teaching to show I'm listening – everyone's pleased.

DA: How many lives have you had?

IG: Around 200, I see.

DA: Is taking new lives always a struggle for you and your group?

IG: Yes, I dodge them.

DA: You prefer your spiritual home?

IG: Yes, physical lives are tougher.

DA: Where the learning lies?

IG: Probably.

DA: Is there a future role, like healing or teaching?

IG: Likely both – teaching and healing.

DA: Is your maturing, long overdue, happening now?

IG: Yes.

DA: Good thing?

IG: Must be – I dislike dodging tasks.

DA: Will Atemia and friends be proud if you mature? Have they outgrown you?

IG: Yes, I've held the group back.

DA: Want to change that?

IG: Yes.

Chapter Summary

Ingrid's reluctant shift from prankster to healer, nudged by Joy and a stern council, defines her incarnation as Ivy. Chosen for nature and growth, she learns focus amid illness, guiding son, Atemia. Echoing today's battle with distraction, her journey – from dodging to embracing duty – urges readers to slow down, heed life's lessons, and nurture soulful purpose in a frenetic world.

The choice to take a new life is always with the person themselves, and often they have a choice, however, in this case a little pressure was brought to bear in the manner of ''you will volunteer, won't you?''

Life Selection: Summary

Section 6 traces the pre-incarnation journeys of four souls, each navigating life selection with unique intent. April, guided by Gag, chooses a life of familial bonds over dependency, foreseeing challenges like depression. Oliver, as Hannah, incarnates to support soulmate Christine, nurturing others while yearning for her spiritual home. Edmund aligns timelines to reunite with Pauline, dedicating his life to sharing spiritual truths. Ivy, nudged by Joy, matures from prankster to healer, guiding Atemia through illness. Reflecting the modern day's quest for authenticity, these narratives highlight the soul's deliberate design, urging readers to find purpose amid life's complexities.

Section 7

The Spiritual Realm: Introduction

Section 7, The Spiritual Realm, offers a profound exploration of the soul's activities between incarnations, presenting four distinct yet interconnected journeys through the spiritual realm. Each chapter – focusing on Alastair Nunn, Katherine Vale, Oscar Hammond, and Annie Zeigler – reveals unique roles and lessons, from guiding energy to healing souls, teaching spirit-human synergy, and researching incarnation processes.

Together, these narratives illuminate the intricate tapestry of soul development, showcasing how individuals navigate their spiritual responsibilities and prepare for earthly lives. Key moments, such as Alastair's philosophical training, Katherine's soul-healing revelations, Oscar's teachings on human-spirit integration, and Annie's collaborative research, underscore the diversity of spiritual purposes and the shared quest for growth. This section inspires readers to reflect on their own spiritual paths, embracing the balance of duty, learning, and connection in the eternal journey of the soul.

Chapter 25: Alastair Nunn

The following conversation explores, a little more fluidly, the experiences of Alastair as Jez. Alastair delves into guiding energy, mentoring young souls, and wandering worlds like Lim-mo.

DA: Are there any places that you can go to or things that you can do that might help in investigating your past lives? Other than these meetings, can you tell me if there are other activities that you would normally engage in in the spirit world, such as training or evaluation?

AN: Yes.

DA: Can you tell me what they are?

AN: Training, but it's not skills. It's tools. It's ways of doing things. It's attitudes. Beliefs. There's no evaluation.

DA: Do you work with tools or energy?

AN: Energy.

DA: What do you create with this energy?

AN: I can't say. It's a feeling.

DA: Do you work on creative ways of using energy?

AN: Yes, but what the energy does, it inspires or guides it, coaxes or coaches it. It's not easy. It's not corporeal. It's like a, what guides the mob, but positively?

DA: Yes, I understand. Are you familiar with other souls perhaps, or even outside the spirit world, where souls practise their skills in manipulating energy to practise creating both animate and inanimate objects?

AN: No, the energy we use is for guiding the animate objects, shaping their progress.

DA: Tell me, Jez, other than your guide, do you have any other teachers in the spirit world, other than Marcus or Paul?

AN: Yes.

DA: Who are they?

AN: Ce. (Pronounced see)

DA: Can you spell that?

AN: C-E.

DA: Is this a male or a female?

AN: Male.

DA: And what kind of teaching do you get from Ce?

AN: Philosophy. How to know which is right.

DA: Are these teachings done with you alone or in a group?

AN: Group.

DA: Does the group usually consist of just your own soul group or other souls?

AN: No, many.

DA: So, it's like a large open lecture forum?

AN: Yes.

DA: What would be the flow of a typical class session?

AN: He teaches by questions. There are no right or wrong answers, just outcomes. He teaches debate, ethics.

DA: One of the things that we need to do to help you with the questions you want answered is to get some advice and assistance from either Paul or Marcus about the karmic flows in your existences. Is there a place where you can find that out?

AN: Yes.

DA: What kind of place would this be?

AN: Mountain.

DA: Would your guide and protector be with you?

AN: Yes.

DA: Is it possible for us to go there now?

AN: Yes.

DA: Can you describe where you are?

AN: Shrine on a mountaintop.

DA: And who else is there?

AN: Ce, Marcus.

DA: And no Paul?

AN: No.

DA: And are you facing them?

AN: Facing Ce.

DA: And Marcus is where?

AN: Eight o'clock.

DA: Is anything being communicated to you now?

AN: I've got to make my own mind up. I'm not getting any advice.

DA: Can you ask questions?

AN: Yes.

DA: Can you ask them to show you any karmic influences in this life as a result of your past lives?

AN: I'm being shown the sea. Every question gets a question back.

DA: Can you ask them if there is a place you can go to where you can review the activities of your past lives in private?

AN: No, not yet.

DA: Is there something else you have to do first?

AN: It's getting stormy. My hands are getting hot.

DA: Is there somewhere else you need to go to?

AN: No.

DA: Is there something else that you would like to do now? Are Ce and Marcus still there?

AN: Marcus is.

DA: Is he communicating anything to you?

AN: No, just a vague sense of disapproval.

DA: Can you ask him what it is that you need to do?

AN: Get on with it. He won't say what.

DA: Let me ask you, Jez, what forms of recreation do you prefer when you're not being evaluated by counsellors or undergoing specific training?

AN: No, nothing.

DA: Is it just training or evaluation?

AN: Yes.

DA: Do you play with your soulmates? Do you have the discussions that we've already spoken about?

AN: Yes, that's the nearest it gets. There is camaraderie, there is teasing.

DA: Do you play some games?

AN: No time.

DA: Do you ever visit other dimensions outside your home area for the purposes of recreation or study and reflection?

AN: Yes.

DA: What places are these? Different space, different worlds, different places. What do you do there?

AN: Relax, wander. But it's all part of the training, I think.

DA: Can you tell me any of the names of these other worlds?

AN: Two worlds close together. One has rings. Lim-mo.

DA: As a spirit, do you ever visit places you have lived on Earth in physical incarnation?

AN: Yes.

DA: How do you do that?

AN: You just think and you're there.

DA: Can you tell me, Jez, what would be your description of the comparison between Earth and one of the other worlds that you regularly go to?

AN: No people, barren, but beautiful.

DA: Have you ever incarnated on another place other than Earth?

AN: Yes.

DA: What was the name of the place?

AN: Lim-mo.

DA: And what was your incarnation as? Can you describe to me what your incarnation was as on the world of Lim-mo?

AN: No body.

DA: Another body?

AN: No, no body.

DA: No body?

AN: No flesh, no…

DA: It's just energy?

AN: Yes.

DA: This is actually an incarnation, do you feel, or is it as a spirit?

AN: I don't know.

DA: Are there other beings on this planet that are just energy?

AN: Yes.

DA: How many of them are there?

AN: Lots.

DA: Have you incarnated there many times?

AN: Don't know.

DA: Would you say it was easier or more difficult than Earth?

AN: Easier.

DA: What makes Earth so difficult?

AN: The variety of souls, the good and the bad and the worse.

DA: Would you say that on balance you incarnate more on Earth than the other places or the other way around?

AN: Earth.

DA: What makes you decide to incarnate on Earth other than Lim-mo which is an easier place?

AN: Earth is a battlefield.

DA: Is there any difference in physical technology between Earth and Lim-mo?

AN: No physical in Lim-mo.

DA: Is there anyone in your life today on Earth that has incarnated with you on Lim-mo or another world?

AN: No.

DA: As you continue to breathe deeply and relax, you drift even deeper into the trance, I'm going to give you a few moments now and what I want you to think about is how you made the decision to incarnate in the body that you have now. I will then just ask you some simple questions about that. So, I'm going to give you a few moments just to think and consider that. Now I'm going to ask you a few simple questions about the choices for reincarnation. Can you tell me, Jez, how are you notified it's time to reincarnate and who tells you that?

AN: A guide tells you.

DA: Is that Marcus or Paul?

AN: Marcus.

DA: Would you describe your desire to reincarnate again as being strong, moderate, slight or a bit resistant to it?

AN: Resistant.

DA: A bit resistant?

AN: Yes.

DA: Sometimes you have to. You lose touch.

DA: Have you ever said you were not ready for a new life?

AN: Yes.

DA: What were the circumstances when that happened and what were the results?

AN: An easier path chosen.

DA: Do you go to the place of life selection alone or with your guide?

AN: With the guide.

DA: Are you aware of any other higher beings working in the life selection place?

AN: They're there, they're not known though.

DA: Describe the surroundings of this place and tell me what you see and do.

AN: Colonnades, like a big Roman temple. Oracles, all to help in the choosing. Advisers if you need them. Doors, thousands of doors.

DA: How many body choices are available to you?

AN: I don't know.

DA: Do you have a choice?

AN: Sometimes. If the path is difficult then you have more choice.

DA: Well, how about the last time you did this? How many choices did you have?

AN: Two.

DA: Could you describe both of those choices starting with the one that you didn't choose?

AN: Female. Not good-looking. Intelligent. Able.

DA: How much of the planned existence of this life do you get to see?

AN: Two or three key events.

DA: What were the key events in the life of this body, the female body?

AN: Political. Something political.

DA: When you say you get to see two or three key events, is that shown to you as if it's on a TV screen or a screen of some sort or are you able to enter the body and experience them?

AN: Neither. Like a memory, as if it happened.

DA: Where do you have to be for these memories to be made available to you?

AN: The selection place.

DA: Can you describe to me the immediate surroundings? Is it, do you sit down somewhere or—

AN: You lie down and sleep.

DA: And is it during the sleep where these choices are presented to you?

AN: Yes.

DA: Do you have an opportunity to get advice about which choice might be better for you?

AN: Yes.

DA: Who do you talk to about that?

AN: A guide, but there are specialists.

DA: Do you usually use a specialist?

AN: Only if the way is difficult.

DA: Do you sense at any time that it's felt by others that one particular choice is the one you should take?

AN: They are presented differently. Normally there is no strong preference.

DA: Is the choice left entirely up to you?

AN: Yes. Though sometimes there is some coercion.

DA: On the times when there may have been some coercion, have you ever gone against that and actually chosen an alternative?

AN: No.

DA: What is your sense, your feeling when you make the choice?

AN: Trepidation. Nothing ever goes to plan.

DA: Do these three, the key events that you see in the life, and you would have seen two or three key events in your current life, do they always happen, sometimes happen or does it always get mixed up somewhere?

AN: Mixed up.

DA: What were the key reasons you chose this body?

AN: It was the best that could be got, but not the best within parameters allowed.

DA: What was the fundamental point? What is the learning that you need to achieve in order to advance?

AN: To be able to do the best without frustration, with limitations, and to be happy about it.

DA: And how do you think you are doing so far with those objectives?

AN: Okay.

DA: What did you learn before you came to the place of life selection that helped you make the decision for a certain body?

AN: Depends on the course and the requirements of the soul.

DA: In some of your training or your class work, do you get an opportunity to review past lives and how well you did?

AN: I don't remember.

DA: Speaking about this body, Jez, what percentage of your total energy did you bring with you into this current body?

AN: Sixty.

DA: Do you think you brought enough to complete the goals you established for your body?

AN: No.

DA: If that was perhaps a mistake, how much more energy do you think you would have needed?

AN: Twenty.

DA: Another twenty?

AN: Yes.

DA: Is there any way that you can increase the amount of energy?

AN: Yes.

DA: How do you do that?

AN: Chi.

DA: Chi?

AN: Yes.

DA: Can you actually change the proportion of energy that comes from your spirit or is it a question of making the best use of the energy you've got?

AN: Maybe five, ten per cent more than you need to manage.

DA: So, are you saying it's possible to get a little bit more energy but there is a limit on how much more you can take?

AN: Yes.

DA: What is your primary mission in this life and has it changed from what you saw in the life selection room?

AN: Changed.

DA: Can you tell me what it's changed to?

AN: More helping and guiding, less doing and achieving, frustration.

DA: Can you pinpoint anything particularly different between your initial exposure to what this life might do and what has actually happened? I'm talking about the key areas. Have any of these key areas changed dramatically and could you tell me how that happened and what they were?

AN: I was supposed to be in the military.

DA: When was that supposed to happen in this life?

AN: Twenties.

DA: What do you think happened to change that?

AN: My body got selected wrong.

DA: What do you mean by that?

AN: The world changed.

DA: Of all the bodies that you've incarnated in in the past years, which one was your favourite, and can you tell me why that was?

AN: My favourite just fits the job.

DA: Which life was that? Which body was that?

AN: Chinese.

DA: Were you male or female?

AN: Female.

DA: And what was particularly enjoyable about that life?

AN: Clarity. Everything was simple.

DA: What was your name in that life?

AN: Ling.

DA: Ling. Was it a long life? Yes. And when did it take place? What period?

AN: Sixteen hundreds.

DA: Would you describe that as a fairly easy choice life?

AN: Yes.

DA: How would you describe your current choice as being easy, medium, difficult or hard?

AN: Hard.

DA: What makes this choice hard?

AN: The goals exceed the abilities.

DA: Your goals you said, let me just tell you what I have written down because we need to make sure that we've got this right. But your goal in your life is really to be for helping and guiding for others, but initially when you selected the body you thought that it would be more individual achievement. In terms of what you need to do in order to advance, which of those two things is the most important?

AN: Helping and guiding.

DA: And are you saying that to really achieve what you need to is beyond you? Or do you think you're achieving it reasonably well?

AN: No, it's beyond me.

DA: Why do you think that is?

AN: Personality.

DA: Do you think that knowing this, and this you will remember at the end of this session, do you think that knowing this will help you to achieve these goals better?

AN: Maybe.

DA: I'm still very keen to find out what you learn and how you learn things about your previous lives and whether or not there's anything from your past lives affecting you. So, you've told me about a couple of past lives, so clearly you have the memory of them. Can you just go somewhere to sit down and think about them, or do you talk about them with your soul group, or do you speak to guides or other people about your past lives and when do you do this?

AN: All of those. And when you feel the need.

DA: Can we go to a time when you did that so I can find out more about what happens?

AN: Yes.

DA: Let's go to a time when you were last in the spirit world, when you were looking at this aspect of your spirituality and your previous existences and tell me on this occasion, how is it being conducted? Who else is there other than you?

AN: Marcus.

DA: Is it just you and Marcus?

AN: Paul.

DA: Marcus and Paul.

AN: There's a pool, water, memories get played back.

DA: How is this actually done?

AN: I don't know.

DA: Are they played back in your mind?

AN: No, on the pool.

DA: On the pool?

AN: Yes.

DA: What is that?

AN: Like a video, but it has your intentions and thoughts.

DA: Now on this last time when you did that, what past lives did you feel you needed to review, the whole group of you feel that you needed to review?

AN: Not so much life by life, but by sets of intentions. Good intention, bad intention and outcome.

DA: So have there been many lives where you failed in your objective completely?

AN: Never completely.

DA: Have there been any where you've actually succeeded extremely well?

AN: Well, yes. Nothing complete though. Never complete.

DA: Is your progress, your advancement progress, slowish, medium or are you advancing fairly quickly?

AN: Okay. I've only been here three times recently.

DA: What do your helpers say to you if you were to ask them that question? How well am I progressing? Would they say you're doing okay or you're a bit slower?

AN: They'd avoid the question.

DA: Oh, right.

AN: I don't believe the rate of progress matters, just that it happens.

DA: Tell me a little bit more about this last session, this last review. Do you sort of put a number of past lives collectively together and draw something from that?

AN: Yes.

DA: And what was drawn from it on this occasion?

AN: Sometimes the expectation and intent doesn't get a desired result, but it's the expectation and the intent that makes the difference and the passion with which you follow them. Intention is everything.

DA: Do the outcomes and effects of your past lives affect this current life?

AN: To a lesser extent.

DA: Have you identified any major karmic influences that need to be addressed?

AN: No.

DA: Does this process of review help you towards your reincarnation selection when the time comes for that to be made?

AN: Sometimes. It depends on the purpose of the incarnation.

DA: Do you fully understand the purpose before you go to the selection?

AN: Not always.

DA: If you don't, you've already said there are people that you can ask.

AN: Yes.

DA: Do you think it would be more helpful if you had a fuller understanding?

AN: Yes and no. Some things just need experience.

DA: Of all your activities in the spirit world, with your soul group members, perhaps other groups, the large training classrooms, all of these things, are there any areas in that that you usually feel that you should do but you tend to avoid?

AN: Yes.

DA: Which bits do you avoid?

AN: I don't like the straight up argumentative stuff. I'm adept at battle, but I don't like the precursor, the sabre-rattling, the politics. I avoid that.

DA: While we're here in this very special place, Jez, is there anything else, anything at all, that you would either like to do, any place you would like to visit, or anything else you would like to tell me?

AN: Your questions, they assume a structure that there isn't. Classrooms, forums, it's not that structured.

DA: Try and explain to me how it is so that I understand better.

AN: There is a path that has to be walked, and it's not a straightforward path. Sometimes a step may be to do with passion with which you do something. Sometimes a step may be your ability to just let things go by, and not so much structure. Speed or progress is not as relevant. Only few get to the destination, so there's no point in rushing.

DA: What's a destination?

AN: I don't know, just that there is one. There are more advanced souls than I, who can tell?

DA: Have you ever felt able to ask one of them?

AN: You never get an answer.

DA: Are there any other things that you do, however structured or unstructured, that we haven't spoken about?

AN: Yes.

DA: Would you like to tell me about them?

AN: Feelings are more important. In some ways, we're being tempered to react in the right way, through experiences, lifetimes, so that the right thing will happen at the end.

DA: Do you have a role as such in the spirit world? Perhaps a specialism or anything of that nature?

AN: Coach and guide and helper.

DA: Who do you coach and guide?

AN: Those I find on the way.

DA: Can you tell me a little bit more about that? There is a higher purpose, and it needs to be actively pursued, otherwise you get lost on the way. Do you ever help or guide very young souls?

AN: Yes.

DA: How young would they normally be?

AN: Two or three incarnations.

DA: Do you ever get to work with brand-new souls?

AN: No.

DA: Do you know any souls that do?

AN: No.

DA: So how would you typically help a young soul?

AN: As you might train a puppy. Try to keep their nose on the path. Avoid the obvious pitfalls.

DA: Do you ever adopt the role of guide to another very young soul?

AN: No. Two or three incarnations usually. I tend to specialise there.

DA: Does this work take up a lot of your time in the spirit world, as far as time has any meaning, that is?

AN: No. Just occasionally. It's not the amount of effort. Just the correct placing of that effort.

DA: Would you say that you personally incarnated frequently, or infrequently, or somewhere in the middle?

AN: Infrequently.

DA: Is there anything else that you feel we should talk about, or anything that I've missed?

AN: No.

DA: Would you like to return?

AN: Yes.

DA: I just want to ask you a couple of questions now, prior to this incarnation, and will return. I'd like you to explain what you were doing just before you left the spirit world to incarnate into this current life.

AN: Teaching.

DA: Were you given any triggers, or red flags, or anything like that to help you remember the importance of certain events?

AN: No.

DA: Can you tell me how you were supposed to recognise and remember significant people in your life?

AN: No. Intuition. It gets easier with more incarnations.

DA: What was the most meaningful aspect of your last prep class before you incarnated?

AN: It was all to do with the change that's happening, how to keep up. What's different.

DA: In this particular incarnation, Jez, would you characterise your attitude towards your rebirth again as being joyful and full of anticipation, general indifference, or cautious or reluctant?

AN: I suppose I'll have to do it if I have to.

DA: How do you feel about all that you have learnt?

AN: It's coming on.

DA: Now before we close and leave the spirit world, I want you to take a last look around, and just one more time tell me if there is anything of significance that we may have missed that you would still like to discuss.

AN: The place looks older than it used to.

DA: Which place is that?

AN: The meeting places.

DA: The meeting places where you meet? Who?

AN: The soul group, lectures. It's more run-down than it used to be.

DA: Are you ready to return?

AN: Yes.

Chapter Summary

The chapter begins by gently asking Jez about ways to explore past lives and what they get up to in the spirit world. Jez shares that they dive into training – not about skills, but about tools, attitudes, and beliefs, with no tests to worry about. Instead of tools, it's all about energy, which Jez uses to nudge and inspire living beings – a tricky but rewarding task they describe as a positive guiding force. A wise teacher named Ce leads group discussions on philosophy, sparking debates with questions that are designed to elicit outcomes as opposed to answers.

Hoping to understand his karma, Jez visits a serene mountaintop shrine with Ce and Marcus, where answers come as riddles. Fun isn't a big focus, apart from some light-hearted teasing with soulmates but he has little time for games.

He loves wandering other worlds like Lim-mo, a stark yet stunning place where he once lived as pure energy. A place where life was simpler than Earth's mix of souls. Earth feels like a tough battleground, yet it's where Jez often returns.

In a grand temple-like space, guided by Marcus, Jez picked his current incarnation from two paths, aiming to help others despite expecting personal triumphs. Recalling a clear, simple life as Ling in 1600s China, Jez contrasts it with today's challenges, where goals feel out of reach. By the use of a memory pool, a way to experience former lives rather like the earlier descriptions of the Library, they review intentions with guides Marcus and Paul, learning that passion matters most.

With his specialist role as a helper to newer souls, Jez sidesteps arguments, embracing a winding, unstructured path toward a mysterious goal.

Chapter 26: Katherine Vale

Katherine's journey stands out for its focus on healing damaged souls, a specialised role distinct from the energy guidance of Alastair in Chapter 27 or the life selection of Section 6. Her work with foetal soul connections and reflections on love and responsibility reveal a deep yearning for spiritual home. Katherine's story inspires readers to find purpose through nurturing and resilience.

DA: Okay. Where would be an appropriate next place to visit?

KV: You know, I think you're going to have to push me on this, because I'm quite happy just to stay here. So, I think just prompt me a bit. I'm sorry. I feel like I've been gone so long. Yes, I know things that I have to do. And do you know, I'm actually a soul healer over there. All right, I never knew that. You know, souls, physically damaged souls that go over, I actually help heal them.

DA: Tell me about that. Tell me how you do that.

KV: It's your energy vibrations. As you see me, as you see my soul, you know, I've described it. Let's say, let's take a foetus. All right. Now, this foetus has come into life and it's damaged. Its soul is damaged before. I'm talking about a little foetus.

DA: How would that happen? What kind of things would cause that to a brand-new foetus, a brand-new soul that's joined with the foetus?

KV: The connection, right? It's the connection didn't happen. Right.

You know, like in genealogy, you will get like a chromosome, a missing chromosome that will create Down's syndrome or other physical abnormalities in babies because it starts off very young with the spirit. Right. When it enters, if it doesn't enter it properly, right, the connection isn't there. So therefore, the soul is damaged before it's even ... I'm not talking about stillborn. I'm not talking about babies that live for an hour or so.

I'm talking about a couple of weeks, just very, very young souls. We're not young souls. The foetus is young. The spirit has not connected properly, and it damages it.

DA: What's the result when that happens? What happens to the life, the physical life?

KV: The physical life. Right. Because the foetus is still young and not really conscious.

Do you understand that? Yeah then a new spirit has time to come in and take over. But before the new spirit can go in and take over, we have to get the old one out. Because you cannot, in a new baby, you cannot cross spirits over. Right? You have to get an old damaged one out before you get a new one in.

DA: And is that what you do?

KV: Yes. Not so ... I don't arrange for the new spirits to go into the foetus, but I take the old ones out and we help heal the spirit.

DA: How do you do that?

KV: With light vibrations.

DA: Is the other part of the spirit, the damaged part, is the other part, the part that's in the spirit world, is that there with you?

KV: No, that's in another place. That doesn't know because the soul is damaged. It's not like me describing you about John. If his soul, this part of his soul in the spirit world come down into the … Oh, jeez, I'm not making sense. This is really difficult.

I described to you, I told you about John's energy, didn't I?

Narration

John is her soulmate, discovered earlier in the session.

End of Narration

DA: Yeah.

KV: He couldn't connect because it was damaged. When we take the soul energy of the foetus over the damage, the soul cannot connect with it because it's damaged. It has to be healed. Yes, it is aware, right, but it cannot come close to it. No, we have to repair it first before we get them together.

DA: Are there any times when you can't get the damaged energy out?

KV: No.

DA: You always manage to do that?

KV: Yeah, it's really successful. There might be that, once we've got the soul out, that because the soul surprisingly can be so badly damaged from it, that we might not be able to repair it completely. So, there might be a fraction of a minute, not even a … You wouldn't even notice it, but it's still good. And once it's joined with the healthy, once we've repaired it, once it's all as one, the soul, then it's diminished. It doesn't affect the soul at all.

DA: So, the last little bit over a period of time when it's joined actually becomes okay or is corrected over time?

KV: Yeah.

DA: Is that how it happens?

KV: Yeah, straight away. Because, as I say, it's very, very rare that happens. What? Do you know, I've just forgotten what I was saying. Yeah, because the job of repairing the damaged soul is so important that there's only a few … No, there's only … with any kind of healing from any part of the soul, there's specialist soul spirits that do it.

DA: Okay?

KV: Now, you also cannot do it if I've only got part of my soul there and there. I can't do it. I have to be a whole soul.

So, you do it between lives. Right, okay. So, therefore, there are people that we train so that when I'm not around or any of us aren't around because we can't do it, then these other souls in between their lives do it, their lifetimes do it.

Narration

As we've discovered, in any incarnation only a part of the soul's energy is used whilst the remainder remains in the spiritual realm. Katherine explains that the task of removing damaged soul energy, caused by a failure to connect with the human foetus requires 100% of soul energy and can, therefore, only be carried out by souls who are entirely between lives and not those incarnating. Katherine also trains and prepares newer souls to take on this work, so there is always a resource available.

End of Narration

DA: What name would you give that work? What name is given to it? Does it have a description?

KV: It doesn't have a name. It's … no, it doesn't have a name.

DA: That's okay. You don't have to fight anything.

KV: No, I was just looking. No, it doesn't have a name.

DA: How late, how old can a baby be before it's not possible to get the damaged energy out?

KV: Three weeks is absolute maximum and even then, it can be dodgy. But three weeks, two weeks is all right when it should. But three weeks is absolute maximum. Anything over the three-week mark we don't touch.

DA: So, what happens then?

KV: You've got a damaged soul into a baby. All right.

DA: And what's the consequence of that?

KV: Depression. Maybe a child that has depression. A lot of negativity and dysfunction in life and that.

DA: Can you recognise, does it happen sometimes when the physical foetus is still in the womb or does it always have to be in those couple of weeks after birth?

KV: No, never in the womb, always after birth.

DA: So, even though the connection has been damaged when the soul first joined the foetus, it remains that way until birth and then you get the damaged energy out and it's replaced with a new soul.

KV: Yeah. There's a reason for a baby being delivered on term or over. Everything has a reason, everything. God, it's to do with the development of the foetus and the awareness of the soul in the foetus. Because you're taking over the host body, even though it's in the womb, it's not developed, its brain is not developed. This is why I said to you about the brain not... did I say about the brain not functioning? Not having, yeah it's mine, but the foetus isn't aware of things and it's not, it's not, it doesn't do that, it hasn't got that in the womb so therefore it has no awareness. After birth, and this is why the cut-off time is three weeks because this is when a baby's brain starts ticking and it doesn't become, you know like when you feed a baby, it's... suction is, what do you call it, it's automatic.

Narration

KV is attempting to explain a very complex process which embodies concepts we don't have, so she is really struggling to make sense of it to me. Because I have discussed this with her after the session, I can add some explanation. The process she is describing is the joining of the soul with the human foetus, which we know from multiple testimonies can occur anytime from the development of the human brain to just before birth. The time she is referring to is the three weeks after birth which is the deadline for soul energy to be removed when it has been damaged in some way by the joining process. She says the process used is very successful and doesn't know of any failures. It's a very specialist role and the only one I've encountered who does this.

End of Narration

DA: Yes, yeah, it's an automatic response.

KV: That's it, well that goes after two, three weeks, right, and this is why, and then it affects the soul.

DA: So, in the, I mean is that, has that happened to John's incarnation in this life?

KV: No, John chose his incarnation.

DA: Okay, so the joining was okay and it's the negativity that's occurred since then that's been a problem?

KV: Yeah, yeah.

DA: So, what, I mean could you...?

KV: He actually said to me physically, he cannot believe that anyone would choose this life, and I said, but you must have done, right, because you are here, that's what he said to me physically, spiritually, right. He tells me something different, because he wants to progress.

DA: If, is there any way that you could, I mean in your physical incarnation with the knowledge that you've got now, do you, are there any signs that you can tell from people that they, they in fact were the result of going over time with the damaged connection that couldn't be fixed?

KV: No, I don't see any. Not until adulthood.

DA: Would you, would you know people that were adults that, where this was a problem?

KV: What, in my physical life?

DA: Yeah.

KV: Yeah, my daughter Mary, she's had a friend called Michael. He suffers with ADHD. Yeah, him, very good example.

Although he suffers with that and he's on medication, he, what he does is that he does things, he knows that they're wrong, but he cannot stop himself doing them, right. He's in prison at the moment, I mean they're no longer friends, haven't been, and he's, they've been friends ever since they were little, and yet, he came to live with us for a while last year or the year before because he was homeless, and he was, I couldn't fault him, he was a good scout, he's a lovely lad anyway, but when he split up, he sent a text to Mary's boyfriend saying that he was having a relationship with Mary while he was living with me, and that was utter crap, but, and I thought, why did he do that? Why does he, he, I don't know how to say it, because inside I instinctively knew he was a good person, inside his soul was good, and yet he was doing all this stuff that he could not help himself doing, right, that was all bad negative stuff. So yeah, he's a prime example.

DA: What are souls, the other part of the energy, that's still in the spirit world, where, well, because Treymar knows this with John, that he knows that the energy's damaged and he can't do anything about it, and the connection's gone, where this occurs, this is quite normal for the healthy energy that's still in the spirit world to be aware that something has gone wrong in the incarnation. Is there anything at all that they can do about it?

KV: No, not once they've got past three weeks, nothing, no, or not to my knowledge, because then, because my job is dealing with changing, taking out the bad spirit from the body, and we have to do it before the foetus's three weeks old, anything after that, it belongs to somewhere else, and I suppose, I've never thought about it, I suppose I could go and find out about that, but I've, I deal with babies, I don't deal with young children and adults, that belongs to someone else.

Narration

Katherine explains that her role is very specific and limited as in, that's my job and anything else will be someone else's job. Because of this rigid demarcation of duty, it's not so easy to explore vertically. She has no knowledge about work done outside the parameters of her specific job.

End of Narration

DA: It is something that you might want to find out about. You've had 5,000 lives, where are you on the advancement scale of souls, have you moved quite a bit, are you around the middle somewhere?

KV: I don't know.

DA: That's okay, it's okay not to know.

KV: I hope I'm near the end.

DA: Why's that?

KV: I've had enough.

DA: What have you had enough of?

KV: This lifetime. If I compare my life to other people's I haven't had a hard time, but to me, I have had a horrible time, and I just don't want to be here anymore, I don't want to come back anymore, I've had enough, and I've spent an awful lot of years just wanting to go back home, right, so no, I don't want to come down here,

I don't like it down here, and I know that I've got to, and I just hope I'm near the end. John is, John's only got a few more lifetimes.

DA: What happened when you chose this life?

KV: What do you mean what happened?

DA: How did that occur?

KV: Oh, I had, do you know, I had a choice of three lifetimes of what I could choose.

DA: What were they? Where did it happen? Can you describe it, just go, take me, walk me through, if you like, step by step of how, firstly, how you knew that it was time to go and make a choice?

KV: I was getting restless.

DA: In yourself?

KV: Yeah, within myself, and I felt I wanted, I didn't want to stay where I was, I was getting bored. And not so much bored, no, because you're never bored, there's always something to do. But it was like, not a restlessness like in the physical world, it's a different kind of restlessness. It's almost like knowing that it's your time. Do you understand that?

DA: Yeah.

KV: And I don't know if I projected a thought or somebody must have been picking up, but I had a visit and was asked if I wanted to go back, and I said yes.

DA: Who visited you?

KV: The person that, there's people that take us and show us, you know, life, you know, lifetimes. Right, I don't know, hold on. I call them the arrangers, because they're the ones that arrange it.

Narration

The organisation required to get lives to fit in with other lives in any incarnation is a complicated exercise undertaken by spe-

cialist senior souls. Sanu (her spiritual name, revealed earlier in her session) calls them the arrangers, for the reason she states.
End of Narration

DA: Okay.
KV: All right.
DA: Was Treymar involved?
KV: Your whole group is involved.

Narration
Treymar is a senior guide, discovered earlier in the session.
End of Narration

DA: Was it really?
KV: Hold on a minute. No. It depends on what lifetime you have and who you want to come back and what their lessons are. In this lifetime, I would say I've had half of my group come back. And what is done is we all look at lessons. First of all, I'm taken off individually. All right, me and John, because he's my guide, and also my soulmate, we're taken off first. And talked about what lessons needed, need to be learnt, and all the rest, like that kind of thing. And then interviews are held with other soul group members as to what it is they need to learn, and whether they want to incarnate with me, and that, and what place they will have, and in my life. I am actually not so much aware.

I wasn't, I don't think the person whose life is incarnating for the experience, if you like, isn't told about who's coming down and who's who. It's your soul group members, they know.

Narration
We've seen elsewhere that this is a complicated business and no one soul, at the levels of soul we are talking to, knows the

whole process. We know that many other souls are involved, and their learning needs should be met as well as Katherine's learning needs.

End of Narration

DA: So, are you saying that this incarnation is essentially for you, and your soul group members are there to take part to help you go on?

KV: Yeah, yeah, even though they've got lessons to learn. This is why I say they're interviewed individually as to what they want their lives, what they need to learn. So, so even though they choose their lifetimes, it's arranged so that they come within my, my friendship group, or my relationship group, or whatever people you come in contact in your life that have an impact on it.

DA: Has it happened to you whereby somebody else has got the main lesson, and then you get interviewed to see what part you want to play in that?

KV: Oh yeah, we all go through it. We all go through it, yeah. Because I could come down, right, there might be another soul group member who the lesson is for them. It's their time to incarnate again, and the lesson is for them. But also, I might want to come down because it's something that I need to learn. So therefore, the arrangers have to arrange. If you want 10 members of your soul group to come down, they have to arrange all these lifetimes for all 10 of us. And that's a really complicated thing to do because they all have to, there's so much organisation about it, because they have to find a lifetime that will suit the soul. Do you understand that?

DA: Oh yeah, very much, yeah.

KV: Yeah, and find them within the vicinity, you know, the appropriate lessons to be learnt, and all that. Oh, I wouldn't want to be an arranger, it's too much like hard work.

DA: So, when it came time for you to make a choice, did you go somewhere to do this?

KV: Oh yeah, yeah. They can either come to you, or it's like a building with a desk, and a bit like an office, it can be. The setting depends on you, if you want them to come to your house or your garden.

DA: What actually happened the last time when you chose this life?

KV: Oh, I went to them. Although he initially came to me and said, like, you're getting restless, like, do you want to incarnate again? I went to them, I made, I don't know if you would call it an appointment, but you go, went to them. There's a desk with a book in it, so the book must mean something.

DA: You said you had the choice of three lives?

KV: This time I did, yeah.

DA: This time how was that choice presented to you?

KV: On a wall, in pictures.

DA: What, still pictures or movie pictures?

KV: Still pictures, but you knew what it was. Instinctively, you knew what it was. Don't ask me where, I don't know.

DA: Tell me what the other choices were.

KV: I chose the middle choice, because I thought I've had enough. Right, I had a choice of an easier life. Right, where?

DA: What was that, was that male or female?

KV: Oh, right, female. The other, it was, there's three pictures, I chose the middle. The one on that life was the male life, all right. This one, the first life was the female life, this one's the female life. The hard one was the male life.

DA: Okay, so what was it about the male life you didn't like?

KV: Too hard, I didn't want a hard time again. I just wanted, I didn't want an easy time, because I thought you don't, you don't learn anything if you have an easy time. But I couldn't, after the last time, I just couldn't cope with another lonely life.

Unless you've been there, it's so awful.

Narration

People often wonder why their lives might be hard or short, where they are treated unfairly and violently, for example, children killed in wars, or severe deprivation. A part of that answer lies here. To know compassion, you must also know hardship and this choice of difficulty is the real meaning or karma. It isn't something done to you by a vengeful God, but something you choose for yourself.

End of Narration

DA: Did you get, do you get an idea, some knowledge about what the life was going to be like?

KV: Yeah.

DA: And what was it about the male life that was, that was difficult for you, that you didn't want?

KV: I won't say it's on par with John, but it's very, very difficult.

DA: Sorry, do you prefer incarnating as male or female?

KV: Female.

DA: And you say most of your incarnation has been female?

KV: Yes.

DA: You will have incarnated as male at some point?

KV: Yes, we all do. Yeah. All of us do.

DA: But you prefer the female?

KV: Yeah.

DA: Okay. With the first female life, the left-hand picture that you didn't take either, what was it about that life that decided you against it?

KV: Too easy.

DA: All right. Okay, so give me a projection from your memory of what the life was like.

KV: Oh, you had everything you could possibly want. No money worries, beautiful home, easy life, 2.4 children, car in the driveway, husband coming home every night. It was too easy, there were no lessons to be learnt.

DA: Have you ever opted for the easy one? Because you didn't want another messed up life.

KV: Yes, I do that after I've had a particularly hard life, yes. I'll do it that way. Yeah, I do that after I've had a hard life.

DA: Okay, and what was it about this life? What was the lesson? What are the lessons that are so important about this particular existence and that will be learnt as a result of the difficulties that you face in this life? What was important about choosing this life? Why did you feel you needed to do it? What was it you had to learn?

KV: Responsibility. Oh, I never knew that. Responsibility.

Narration

This is the second time in this session where Katherine was surprised by her own revelation. I can't replicate the emotion, or the audible aspect of surprise expressed when information is given to her which she didn't expect. It happens quite a bit in these sessions.

End of Narration

KV: Oh dear, oh. It's funny because I was knowing and thinking about this like before I came here, and the answer is nothing like I expected what I thought I'd come here to learn. It's responsibility for the life of a soul, which are my two children, my two daughters, all right, it's about nurturing their souls and giving them the love and security, Jesus, I'll be coming back, that they needed for their lesson to come down here.

No, it isn't me that's, anyway. That's one, this life was chosen because it wasn't just one lesson. All right.

It's about surviving, even though you think there's other people that have got it worse than you, it's about surviving within your capabilities. I've never had anything in this lifetime. I've never had anything. I've had no love, no money. I've struggled, lost friends that fought my friends. So, you know, it's like you've lost your whole supportive, your support group who keep you going. You've lost nearly all of them.

And that quiet, I think this has been quite harsh lessons. Again, it's no different to the last life, it's very lonely. All right, but this time I've been given responsibility.

DA: How do you think you're doing?

KV: I'm still here. I'm still here.

DA: Is there any way you can get a review, get another second opinion of how you're doing, as it were? Would you like to do that?

KV: Yes, I would actually.

DA: Well.

KV: What, do I ask or do you ask?

DA: Well, just ask Treymar to arrange it for you. He's always there.

KV: He will, but he's not happy about showing me. Because there's still lessons for me to learn, he's worried that if he shows me how I'm doing, that I might relax and think, oh well, done it, you know, all's going well. And take it a bit for granted.

DA: Okay, well he's, he's going to this time, this has nothing to do with me, it's over to you and Treymar to decide what you want to do.

KV: Yeah, he's going to show me a little bit.

DA: Okay. How is that done?

KV: It's like a movie screen. I'm not seeing anything at the moment. He's not happy about doing this, but he's doing it because I've asked. And he sees, he's...

DA: Well, just make it clear to him that you...

KV: It's important for me to know.

DA: Yeah, only what's important for you to know, yeah.

KV: He says, he says I'm doing really well. Well, he says, it's funny, you always see the negative, you don't see the positive, but it isn't so much as what's being shown as the feelings, what's coming at you from what you're being shown. And what I'm being shown is the main two of my daughters and the job that I've done with them, I've done well.

Alice came back, she had her own lessons to learn, but she had the security of me. Yes, I know I've made mistakes, but really, basically, I've done well. But it's not over yet.

He says all of it, I know anyway. Up to now, it's okay. It's not about surviving.

It's about learning from the experiences you've had. And he said these experiences weren't bad enough. Anyway, not for me to say that I'm here.

DA: Okay, you know, one of the things that you'll be able to do quite easily after today is to open a channel with Treymar, his spiritual self, anytime you want to.

KV: Really? So, can I shut down the physical self? If I shut down the physical self, his physical connection with me, can I still have the spiritual connection separate? Absolutely. Right. That's what I wanted to know, because I don't want the physical connection anymore.

DA: You can do that.

KV: Right.

DA: You need to be firm with the physical connection. And it may be, you can check because I say he's there anyway, that it may be that that's part of your learning and it needs to be there as well. But that's something. Right. What you certainly can do now is to open this channel with John.

KV: How do I do that?

DA: All you do is just empty your mind, raise your energy vibrations, and he'll be there.

KV: Right.

DA: And you can do it instantly. You don't have to meditate. You can do it on the bus, probably best not to do it driving a car in case you get distracted. But it's something that you'll be able to do.

KV: Do you know, this has been him being here has been a learning curve for me on things from relationships, things that you put up with, because you're craving to be loved. And you put up with the most awful stuff, which now I'm so humiliated about with him. I will not put up with it, it is unacceptable to me.

Now as to the reason is why I want the physical to stop, because it's unacceptable to me now. And if it wasn't because of who he is, and I didn't know any different, that this would have stopped a long time ago, the physical self. So, it has been a really important learning this.

DA: You've got complete control over it.

KV: I never knew that though. I kept asking him, I kept saying to him, go away, just go leave me alone. Don't want you here. And it just wouldn't happen, because I didn't know how to switch it off. But I did after I spoke to you, I switched it off, because something happened. And I was told off.

And then I said, well, I only want it switched off for one day just to frighten him a bit. And then they brought him back, like dropped the barrier. And then he did something else.

And I said, that's it, I've had enough now. It ends, all of it ends. And I got told off, you cannot use it like this.
You cannot decide, you know, switch it on, switch it off. It stays on or it stays off no more. So, I know that when I cut the physical connection, it's got to stay off. I've got to be sure that's what I want.

DA: Yeah, yeah. But the reality is you can allow in or stop what you want. You can switch it on or off if you want to. May not be the best thing to do. I mean, I don't know the answer to that, but all I know is you can do that. But you can also, what's more important is that you can open the channel to Treymar in spirit form. You can ask your guide, because he's always there. What's happening now?

KV: No, I'm listening to you. All right. I was just thinking it's lovely to have someone so special don't you think?

DA: Yes.

KV: I've never had that on Earth.

DA: But we've all got that.

KV: Yeah, but I've got it over there, not here. All right, and you crave for it when you've got a horrible life. All right; you crave it down here too. All right.

DA: Maybe horrible is just a question of how you perceive it.

KV: Yeah, it's horrible. No, not compared to other people's, no.

DA: So, you have a physical relationship on the horizon?

KV: Apparently so, yeah.

DA: When is that going to happen?

KV: I don't know. I haven't got a clue.

DA: You can ask.

KV: It wasn't him that told me; it was a friend. Because you know, I've got psychic friends and that. And my friend said, I've been feeling for a while now you're going to have a relationship and it's going to be well worth waiting for it.

DA: Check it out on the call.

KV: He knows.

DA: All right, he knows. We'll ask him when.

KV: Within four weeks.

DA: There you go.

KV: All right, where am I going? I didn't even know I was going out.

DA: Well, ask what you like about it.

KV: What I like about it?

DA: Yeah, ask the kinds of questions. Do you have any other questions about this impending relationship?

KV: Is he going to be faithful? Oh, no question, no doubt. Yeah.

He's not going to be like any relationship I've had before. He's going to be genuinely gentle. And a quiet person. But strong. Stubborn. Very proud. He sounds a bit like John actually. Very proud. Very loving. When he loves somebody, this person, when he loves somebody, gives his all. All right, so yeah. I'm going to be loved. Oh, maybe I won't need to go home then or want to go home then for a while.

DA: But your daughters love you.

KV: Oh, yeah, you know what I mean. That's different, isn't it? That's different.

I know they love me, but it's like a relationship love you need, isn't it?

DA: And a physical love.

KV: Yeah, physical love, yeah.

DA: Because that's how we're built. That's how the physical side is wired up. It works that way.

KV: We don't need that when we get over there, do we? Oh, wow.

DA: Well, it's a good question.

KV: No, the physical love is different to the soul love.

DA: Yes.

KV: It's completely different. There's no comparison because it is stronger, it is powerful. And unless you've experienced it, you can't even describe it.

Because with the soul love, you feel that all the time. It's there all the time. No matter where you go, no matter what you're doing, you feel it all the time.

On the physical love, you don't feel that all the time. You know you're loved, but you don't feel it all the time, do you?

DA: No.

KV: Yeah, but you do.

DA: It's a good way of explaining it.

KV: All right. Yeah, you do over there.

DA: When in between incarnations, do you ever pop down to look at the planet again? A holiday? Take a visit?

KV: No. No, I don't like it here.

DA: Do you sometimes incarnate purely because of the physical pleasures that can be gained here?

KV: Yes, I have done. When I wanted the easier life between hard lives, yes, I have.

DA: When you did that, did you prefer to be male or female?

KV: Male, because I didn't have to work hard. That's it.

DA: What other reasons were there?

KV: I like the physical sex. Oh, my God.

DA: Is that more intense as a male than a female?

KV: Oh, what, from a man's point of view? I just enjoy it more as a male, right in between lives, yeah.

DA: When was the last time you incarnated for that purpose?

KV: Oh, gosh, I can't remember. Long, long time. It's been many lifetimes.

I don't do it often because you have one that if we all have to incarnate as one or the other, because we have to experience both sexes, right? So, my chosen sex is as a female. It is nice to come back as a male for a difference, but isn't my chosen sex, mine is as a female.

And it's nice to have a change every now and then. So, I choose the easier lives as a male because I haven't got to work hard and, you know, it's just nicer.

DA: Lots of shagging.

KV: Yes. Depends what lifetime.

DA: Well, you can go visit, I mean, because you can go and pop in on any lifetime you ever had and actually be there, if you wanted to.

KV: I've been to six, right? But how do I go? How do I, well, even when I'm not under hypnosis, I can do that.

DA: I think there isn't really any reason why you shouldn't be able to do that, because hypnosis is self-hypnosis anyway. This is a condition that you have achieved yourself. I've just facilitated the processes and the techniques just help you to get there, but you can certainly get there by yourself. The questioning helps as well because you have so many memories. But your mind sometimes doesn't know which ones to throw at you. So, it does so in answer to my questions. And your guide, Treymar, is listening to my questions and is aware of my presence and what we're doing and why we're doing it. So, you can visit another life. It's when already deeply relaxed and when already in the trance, it's easy to do it because all you would have to do is just close your eyes and on the count of three, one, two, three, you can go back to another life.

DA: Male or female?

KV: Female. Riding a horse, you know, a bit of fox hunting. Gosh, I don't like this life, it's not me. I'm used to being poor.

DA: What's your name?

KV: Sharon.

DA: What year is it? I'm not sure. Okay, it's there, it's there. It will come; it's just a memory that's taking the time.

Okay, well, as you're riding the horse, Sharon, just close your eyes. And this time I'll direct you. Now, I want you to go back to the last easy life you had as a man. One, two, three, open your eyes and you're there. Don't keep it to yourself.

It's the life before Beth, is it?

KV: Yeah, I was a man then. Okay. So, it's still the early 18... it's before, it's late 1700s.

Narration

Beth was a former life.

End of Narration

DA: What are you doing at this moment?

KV: Not a lot, I'm a landlord, I own my own land, inherited property, shall we say. I've got servants, wife, children. I can come and go as I please. I have a string of women.

DA: What's your name?

KV: Stanmore. Stanmore.

DA: What's your, is that first name or second name?

KV: Surname, my name's Burt. Burt Stanmore.

DA: Okay, how old are you, Burt?

KV: At present, I'm a very overweight 30-year-old. But that doesn't stop the women.

DA: Why do they keep doing?

KV: Oh, well, you treat them well, they treat you well.

DA: Is this a good life?

KV: I would say so, yes. Wouldn't you? It's a bit arrogant, isn't he?

DA: Well, you can be him and get into that skin and feel the sensations that he feels while you're there, because this was you.

KV: I'm not sure I want to, I actually don't like him, I think he's a bit arrogant.

DA: What was the lesson of that life? Or was it an easy break? Was it one of your intermissions?

KV: Yeah, it was an intermission. This is why I chose somebody, a lifetime that you didn't want for anything, because money makes life easy. Emotionally, I had a wife who adored me. And she did, she, or I thought she did absolutely adore me. She never showed any difference. My children, my daughters, very, very proud of them. Very proud. Just so beautiful, intelligent, and just really lovely girls. And I didn't have to work hard.

Well, I didn't work at all. I had people doing it for me, and I was very wise with business. I wasn't stupid. I was hard with business, could be hard with my wife. But I had to be. Otherwise, you know, I think she would have had me spend the lot. No.

DA: So not a bad man?

KV: No, no, no, just a bit too confident. No, not a bad man at all, no. Wouldn't hurt anyone, no. I think I was proud of what I had. And the arrogance came out of me being proud of what I had. Of the standing that I had in the community.

I wasn't mean, I was a fair person. And people respected me for that. And that was important to me. So no, this, I definitely chose this for an easy life. Because there were no lessons to be learnt in this life. If they did, I don't remember them. So long ago, very long ago.

DA: So what year is it again?

KV: Late 1700s, early 1800s, if that.

DA: Have you got a year?

KV: I would say 1770.

DA: And whereabouts do you live?

KV: Oh, we're in England.

DA: England, what county?

KV: Durham, definitely Durham, got an accent.

DA: Okay, so your string of women, everybody in the house knows about it?

KV: Oh goodness, no, no. And it's not a string of women, there's two other than my wife at the moment. There's been others along the way, but only one at a time. I can't deal with all that.

DA: And it's absolutely secret?

KV: Totally, but none of them know about each other.

DA: All right, I mean, what about your wife, does she know?

KV: No, oh no, no. It hurt her too much, I wouldn't want her to know. But she doesn't like sex.

DA: Sometimes that happens.

KV: Yes, it does. Yes, it does. So, I'd, I'd keep, if I didn't care about her and didn't love her, I wouldn't care whether she'd know or not. But I do care about her, and I do love her, and I don't want to hurt her. But I have needs, and I'm not going to force her to do anything she doesn't want to do.

DA: That's a principled standpoint, is it?

KV: Yes.

DA: Looking on that life as you are now, could, can you see that as a principled position, as a valid position?

KV: There's no other option.

DA: Okay. When you've spent enough time as Burt, you can go anywhere you want to go. Where do you want to go now?

KV: I want to be with John.

DA: Okay, go there then. Is he there?

KV: He's taken me to the crystal cave again, but I don't understand why.

DA: Well, give it a few moments and maybe you will. Keep telling me what's happening.

KV: When he took me to the crystal cave before, it was just the crystals, right, around the walls. And yeah, you saw them, and there was water like a little lake in the middle. And you know, Enya, her voice was resonating around the things, and we just sat in the boat in the middle of the lake for a while. But he's just taken me in again, and all the crystals have just lit up. Oh my god, I didn't expect that. Oh. Oh, there's energy. He's standing back. He's standing back against the wall, and I'm in the middle of the cave, and all this energy. Oh my god. Oh my god. Did you know that crystals, I never knew this, that every crystal, as much as you've got reflexology, massage, acupuncture, all the alternative therapies, do you know how important crystals are? I didn't believe in them. But each of them is on a different point, because for healing, for giving me energy throughout my body. Oh my god, I never knew that. Never knew it. I'm just going to stand here for a moment. It's a different type of energy. It's like, it's not like the energy of your soul, or anything like that. It's like, it's a very hard, intense energy. Oh, you can't take too much of it for too long. Okay, we're coming back out. Oh, I feel different. I feel like I'm glowing. My soul is absolutely glowing. It's just weird. It's just, I feel a bit tired, actually, I feel exhausted.

DA: Yeah, that's normal.

KV: I'm just going to sit on the grass, I feel actually drained and exhausted. Oh, he's picking me up and carrying me. So, we're not finished yet. Oh, he's made a bed of leaves and put a blanket over them and put me under a tree. Oh, he's just laid me on the blanket and just sitting by me while I'm just resting. Oh my god, my soul is absorbing the energy. It's just happening very gradually and very slowly. Oh, I've got a headache now.

I'll sit out, I'll give him a cuddle. He's lovely.

DA: Is it time for you to return?

KV: He's lovely.

DA: Do you want one last cuddle? He knows it's time for you to come back as well.

KV: Yeah, he knows.

DA: Okay, when you're ready to come back, just say, I want to come back.

KV: I want to come back.

DA: Okay, Katherine, I'm just going to count to five. As I count from one to five, you'll move closer and closer to the water surface in a fully conscious way full of awareness, really quite quickly.

Chapter Summary

Katherine, (spiritual name Sanu) a soul healer, removes damaged soul energy from foetuses using light vibrations when a joining goes wrong and trains others for this critical task. She chose her current life for responsibility and nurtures her daughters despite feelings of personal loneliness rejecting an easy life this time round. She took some time to revisit past lives, including an indulgent male incarnation. She also learns from John in a crystal cave about energy healing. In her current life she finds herself eagerly facing a new relationship. Katherine's journey reflects a common quest for authentic connection and duty.

Chapter 27: Oscar Hammond

Oscar's journey centres on teaching spirits to navigate human minds, a role distinct from Katherine's soul healing or Alastair's energy guidance in Section 7. While others focused on personal lessons or healing, Oscar's expertise in spirit-human synergy highlights the challenges of incarnation. In today's complex world, his insights inspire readers to seek harmony between spirit and body.

DA: What is your usual role when you're wholly in spirit, in between incarnations, when you are not on a planet? What is it that you do in your spiritual home? What role do you adopt?

OH: I teach.

DA: What do you teach?

OH: I teach … people … spirits … and people. They're so … they're so strongly linked … that it's… I teach… the spirits to understand … how to work with the human mind … the brain … and the emotions. There are many that need to understand this.

DA: Is this one of the reasons why … when I asked you earlier about … your joining with this particular physical foetus … you said it was very easy. Because it's something that you teach … and that you're very familiar with.

OH: Yes. Yes, that's right.

DA: What kind of difficulties do spirits have … in joining?

OH: The younger spirits have many problems … with .. coordinating with the chemistry … of the humans. They need to understand what to expect. They also need to understand … that the sensory … powers of the humans

... are a huge diversion ... and can ... can mess things up a lot. They need to know that.

DA: Is it just joining ... or is it also ... about the ongoing ... management of this connection?

OH: Yes, it's about the ongoing management ... of the connection. Yes. Absolutely.

DA: So ... where ... are there instances, for example ... where ... souls ... can't control the human? Or they have great difficulty doing that? Or some of them lose their grip?

OH: Yes, they can definitely lose their grip. Especially with ... so many poisons that they have on the earth. As well, it's ... they have the drugs ... chemicals. All of these things can ... do great harm ... to the synergy that's needed ... between the spirit ... energy ... and the brain.

DA: Is this ... for more advanced souls ... is this ... easier? Are they more successful in managing it ... because they have the experience and the understanding?

OH: Yes. Very much.

DA: What happens when a joining goes wrong? Or if it doesn't work? Just the initial joining with the foetus ... where somebody has such huge problems ... that they aren't actually able to complete?

OH: There's different levels. There's people ... that simply say that they feel detached from ... their body and start hating their body. People that feel detached from other people ... detached from the human race. It can have many manifestations. And sometimes ... can definitely result in what the humans call madness.

DA: Is there any time ... early in the process ... where it can be reversed? Where you can kind of undo it... when the initial joining starts with the foetus... and there's so many problems ... that it's ... the soul comes back out again ... or it has to change or something? Does that happen?

OH: The spirit can be healed ... but ... there is ... a problem with ... with this happening a lot. Dysfunction between the human ... and the spirit. This is happening ... a lot. It can be redressed ... personally ... with the help of the guides ... and the spirit in the human. But it's also very important ... to do this on a mass... level through ... consciousness changes.

DA: Are all young souls ... do they all get the opportunity to ... to go through your... the classes ... before making their ... for example, their very first joining?

OH: Oh yes, they must do this. And their understanding is then ... evaluated ... to see their suitability. But they can never be fully prepared ... for what they will experience. We just try as ... as best we can.

DA: I suppose a part of ... not being fully prepared ... would kind of defeat the ... purpose of it because ... part of it is for ... them to learn ... themselves ... from the experience. The whole point of the incarnation is to ... gain experience. So perhaps I could never be ... you can never be fully prepared ... because there wouldn't be any point. I'm just ... kind of thinking ahead really. It wasn't a question.

OH: That's correct. Prepared is ... prepared is a loose word in this context. It's an understanding ... that they must be taught ... on how to work ... with the body of a human. It comes with practice. And that's one of the reasons why we do it.

Chapter Summary

Oscar, a spiritual teacher, instructs young souls on joining and managing human bodies, addressing challenges like sensory distractions and chemical interference. He explains how a failed joining can cause detachment or madness, reversible through healing or collective consciousness shifts. Despite preparation, experience is key, reflecting the need for balance and understanding in navigating life's complexities.

Chapter 28: Annie Zeigler

Annie's exploration of soul incarnation research sets her apart from Oscar's teaching or Katherine's healing in Section 7. Her collaborative study with a small group delves into refining human body integration, contrasting with others' broader roles. In the need for greater understanding, Annie's work inspires readers to embrace purposeful learning and spiritual collaboration.

DA: When you're back home, in your spiritual home, what kind of things do you do there? What role do you have?

AZ: I'm learning ... I'm learning about human beings. About how human souls adapt, or how souls adapt to the human body, and how to refine access to the human body and become more skilful in entering and sharing that with the others.

DA: Is it kind of a course, so that you can...

AZ: You could ... you could say that, yes. It's ... it's about teaching ... finding out and sharing it with others. But it won't be the last. It's just one part.

DA: Are there other souls doing this as well? Do you...

AZ: Oh, yes. Yeah.

DA: Do you share things as a team, as it were? Or do you work very much individually?

AZ: We are a small group. We are three who do this kind of research. And I know now that two of the initial group are the two ones in green.

DA: In your initial cell group?

AZ: In my initial group, when I arrived, there were the three ... there were the two in green and we three are doing that kind of research. But there is somebody else who … it's the … it's only the first step of incarnating. Because once you are incarnated as a soul, there are still things you need to monitor. And I still have difficulties with some of those. It's not … of course I know how to incarnate, and I know how to do that, but it's somehow making the whole thing into some sort of easily understandable concept. But the other courses I do, the tones are one thing, sort of. There is always some, some little project going, which is fun. I'm aware that my mind has all sorts of ideas, and I know that is not the right place for them.

DA: What are their names, the names of the other two people that you work with, the other two souls?

AZ: One is Erwin, the other is Neruda.

DA: Do you ever incarnate in the same life or do you kind of take it in turns?

AZ: No, we are not together in our lives. We meet up again after we've done our tour.

DA: Okay, so kind of one of you would incarnate and come back and then somebody else would … after a period?

AZ: The others might be incarnated at the same time, but we don't meet up in this life.

DA: I'm really keen to find out how the current life was put together.

AZ: How that…

DA: How that happened. Where the volunteers came from to interact with you in this life. And just to generally to explore that. But before that happens, what I want you to do is to just put time on hold and just focus on your breathing and relax deeper.

AZ: I think before that I need to go to the toilet.

DA: Okay, that's exactly why I was going to help you on hold. If you give it just a moment, I'm going to count to five.

When I reach the number five you will be able to get up, open your eyes, go down, use the loo, come back to the chair. When you rest back in the chair again, I would just place my hand on your forehead and say, go back and you will immediately return to the spirit world where you are now. So, if you can, take the break…

One, two, three, four, five. Just drifting down deeper and deeper. And go way down. So, I'd like to explore with you how you chose this life. Why you chose this life. What did you know about what organisation had to happen to get everybody in place? Suva, tell me initially, when did it become apparent that it was time to incarnate again?

AZ: That was fairly soon after Mina died.

Narration

Suva is Annie's spiritual name.

End of Narration

DA: It didn't take long. What prompted it? Was it you or did Rendon come to say to you, it's time to go again?

AZ: No, we both agreed. Because this life is in a way a continuation. I don't know what kind, it's a preparation for something else.

DA: Who was involved in it? Did it involve Erwin and Neruda as well? The other souls that you work with on the research or was it just something between you and Rendon?

AZ: It was, it was more something between, it has nothing to do with them. It's, it's as if that is, as if this is part of the, the research project as well.

Chapter Summary

Annie describes her primary role in the spiritual realm as a learner and teacher focused on understanding how souls adapt to and incarnate into human bodies. She works as part of a small group of three souls, including herself, Erwin, and Neruda, who conduct research on the initial stages of incarnation. Annie explains that this research involves refining the process of entering a human body and sharing these insights with others, though she acknowledges the difficulty of simplifying such complex spiritual processes into clear concepts. The group does not incarnate together in the same lives but reunites after their respective "tours" to share findings. Annie also mentions other ongoing spiritual projects, such as exploring "tones", which she finds engaging and fun, though she struggles with managing the influx of ideas that arise.

The chapter transitions to Annie's current incarnation, which she reveals was planned soon after the death of a figure named Mina. This new life, decided upon in collaboration with a soul named Rendon, is described as a continuation and preparation for a larger purpose, potentially tied to their ongoing research. Unlike her research group, this incarnation primarily involves Annie and Rendon, with no direct involvement from Erwin or Neruda. The chapter concludes with Annie's reflection on the purposeful nature of her incarnation, underscoring its role as part of a broader spiritual project. This exploration provides a detailed look at the soul's activities in the spiritual realm and the deliberate planning behind incarnations, setting the stage for further inquiry into the organisation of her current life.

Section 7

The Spiritual Realm: Summary

Section 7 weaves a rich narrative of spiritual roles and incarnational planning, with each chapter offering a unique perspective on the soul's eternal journey. Alastair's energy guidance and philosophical training reveal the importance of intent and mentoring, while Katherine's soul-healing work and personal sacrifices emphasise responsibility and resilience. Oscar's teachings on spirit-human synergy address the challenges of incarnation, advocating for balance, and Annie's research into soul adaptation highlights collaborative learning for spiritual progress. Key moments – Alastair's shift to guiding, Katherine's crystal cave healing, Oscar's insights on failed joinings, and Annie's purposeful incarnation – illustrate the diversity of spiritual tasks and the shared pursuit of growth. This section encourages readers to find purpose in their challenges, embrace spiritual connections, and trust in the soul's timeless quest for harmony and understanding.

Continuity, Chapter 29: Edward Lawson

The descriptions below present a remarkably complete and unbroken tapestry of a spiritual regression session, offering a depth and coherence that sets it apart from the more fragmented excerpts of earlier chapters.

Edward embarks on a trance-state odyssey that unveils the intricate contours of his soul's eternal journey. Unlike partial glimpses provided elsewhere, this chapter captures the full arc of a single session, where past lives, spiritual reviews, interactions with review council, and profound exchanges with guides emerge organically, weaving seamlessly into a naturally developing landscape.

Edward's memories surface vividly – from a Second World War airfield to a medieval Cathar existence and a prehistoric fireside – each arising unprompted, as if drawn by an unseen current. His encounters with Athelia, his soul companion, and a council of authoritative guides unfold spontaneously, their comings and goings painting a dynamic spiritual realm that only a cohesive, uninterrupted narrative can reveal. This chapter's wholeness allows readers to witness the fluid interplay of memory, emotion, and insight, illuminating the timeless continuity of a soul's quest for meaning and connection.

DA: That's fine. We will continue to move back to a still younger time. Moving back and back. We're going to move right back to the time just before your birth, when you were in your mother's womb. You will find this a very easy transition to make because you are already so young. We will just spend a few minutes there before we move onto our next stop. So, continue this step down, all the way back, right back into your mother's womb. This is the time just before your birth. Feel this dark, warm, moist environment. Let me ask you just a couple of questions about it. Firstly, can you tell me if your arms and legs are reasonably comfortable?

EL: Yes, I'm a bit crouched up. I'm fidgeting.

DA: Can you hear or feel your mother's heartbeat?

EL: Mmm, Just there.

DA: Can you feel your mother's emotions from time to time? Now you've had a chance to spend a few months inside this body, which is you. Do you have any feelings about the body that you would like to tell me about? For example, do you think you will find it interesting to work in this body?

EL: I think you need to ask me that again.

DA: Do you have any feelings about the body that you're in?

EL: It's protective, but I'm waiting to get out.

DA: We don't need to stay here for very long, but I'd like to ask you, at what point did you join this foetus? How far into the pregnancy was it before you joined?

EL: I'm getting three months. Three to four months.

Narration

Once again, these questions about joining with a foetus mark the very first connection between the physical body and current life memories.

End of Narration

DA: Is this body a good match for your soul's consciousness?

EL: Yeah, we're happy together.

DA: What kind of reception did you get when you joined? Can you explain what the feeling was when you first joined this foetus?

EL: It feels like I just entered, maybe through the shoulder blades in that area, and just spread out like a web. Or, if you want, perhaps like a mould or something, just growing and intermingling, dry rot, just starting from a core and expanding.

DA: What were your feelings about your reception? Was it something that was welcomed, or was it difficult? What was the sensation there?

EL: No, it was fine. It was a good combination from the start.

DA: Was the integration quite easy to do?

EL: Yes, it was almost as if it was waiting for me to arrive.

DA: Did you sense any particular sensation from the body, from the foetus, when you actually joined it? Did it change in any way?

EL: Not that I recall. No, I can't say that it did.

DA: Can you discern any character differences between you and this body that you've joined? No. How does this foetus, this body, compare with other bodies that you've had in the past?

EL: I'm not even sure that I've had any others.

Narration

It's early days yet; we'll see that these memories will surface later in the process.

End of Narration

DA: Why did you choose this body?

EL: My first response is that I was sent there. I'm not conscious of having had a choice.

DA: As I count down from five to one, I want you to move away from this time when you are in your mother. Five, drifting away from your mother, drifting and floating, as though you are on a current of timelessness.

Four, disengage from your mother. Three, letting go, drifting and floating away. Two, release the body and move away from this time with your mother. And one, floating, drifting, feeling very safe and comfortable, very peaceful and quiet. As you continue to relax even more deeply, still drifting deeper and deeper into the trance with each breath you take, we are now going to move towards a beautiful long tunnel. Create a vivid mental impression of a tunnel that looks something like a railway tunnel, except that it's very smooth and clean. Soon I'm going to count down from ten to one, and during the time that I'm counting, we will move together through this tunnel. When we exit the tunnel at the other end, you will move directly into your most immediate past life. In the beginning, you will notice that the walls of this tunnel are very dark, and as I count closer to one, you will notice that the walls will get a little grey and then grey-white as you move faster and further along. When I reach the number one, you will exit out of the beautiful round white opening at the end of the tunnel into your most immediately preceding life. Now, what is interesting about this is that when you exit the tunnel on my count of one, you will be in a significant scene in this immediately preceding life, and you will be able to describe to me all the details of this scene, and then we will move on. I want you to remember at all times that you are protected by the shield of golden energy. Just nod your head if you are ready to move with me into the tunnel. Okay, letting go, beginning to move back in time, stepping into the tunnel as I begin to count now. Ten, nine, eight, seven, six. You can actually see the white bright opening far in the distance as we begin to pick up speed and the walls become lighter and lighter. Four, three, two, approaching the exit of the tunnel, and one. Outside. Tell me, Edward, is it daytime or nighttime?

EL: It's daytime.

DA: Is it hot or cold?

EL: It's comfortable.

DA: Are you alone? Yes, outside. I want you to describe to me the kind of clothing that you're wearing, so to begin with.

EL: I can tell you, I'm wearing a uniform. It's an Air Force uniform, pale bluey-grey, Second World War type thing, and I'm standing outside on an airfield on this sort of... It isn't huts about, behind me. I seem to be standing in front of myself, looking at an image of myself rather than actually in the image, if you can understand that.

DA: Yes, of course, but you can join that physical being.

EL: Yes, I can.

DA: And be the sentient person that you were.

EL: Yes, I am. I'm walking around now.

DA: And feel everything.

EL: I've got a leather flying helmet on.

DA: How old are you?

EL: Twenties, young twenties.

DA: When your exact age comes to mind, just tell me.

EL: Twenty-one.

DA: What's your name?

EL: Hmm, strange. James.

DA: What's your surname?

EL: Nothing comes to mind.

DA: Which airfield is it?

EL: Well, I keep getting the name Duxford. Duxford? Hmm, which is a big airfield with a museum on it now, but it doesn't look like a big airfield; it's small.

DA: What year is it?

EL: Thirty-nine? 1939? It's not 1940, it's 1930-something.

DA: As soon as your surname comes to mind, just tell me. You can just blurt it out when it pops in there.

EL: Middleton or something like that. I'm just standing looking at everything around me; it's all very strange. Maybe I've just arrived, just been posted or whatever.

DA: Are there any other people visible to you?

EL: No.

DA: Where is it that you feel you need to go or are you waiting for somebody?

EL: It feels like I've just arrived.

DA: Do you know where it is to go or is somebody going to meet you?

EL: I don't know. I don't know the answer to that.

DA: Okay, doesn't matter, we don't need to stay here too long. Let me just ask you one thing about this at this moment. What are your feelings at this moment? How do you feel as a young man on the airfield?

EL: I'm indifferent. I don't seem to have an emotion of any sort. I'm not excited, I'm not frightened, I'm not apprehensive.

DA: Right, James, what we're going to do now is we're going to move to the last day of your life. So, as that young man standing on the airfield, just close your eyes as you are then, and I'm going to count to three, and on the count of three, you can open your eyes, and you will be in the last day of that life, as I begin to count now.

EL: That's not very nice.

DA: You're already there? How old are you?

EL: I'm still a young man. I'm over the sea, and I'm in a plane that's diving into the sea, spiralling out of control. I still don't feel anything. I'm screaming.

DA: Can you hear any noises going on around you?

EL: Yes, I'm screaming. The noise of the engine is screaming. It's only me. It's a small fighter.

DA: What's your exact age?

EL: Twenty-two comes to mind. It's down on the south coast somewhere.

DA: You can allow this descent to continue to its inevitable conclusion, or you can just move right through that to the point where you have just died. Either way, we will pick this up at the point just after your death.

EL: I'm feeling angry because I was so inexperienced, and I'm saying I didn't stand a chance. I had no time, no time to die.

DA: Where are you in relation to the crashed plane?

EL: I'm still in it. We're diving. The sea's a long way down. The sun's shining on it. It's grey, sparkling, and it's just. I'm in a spin. I know what it's like. I used to fly; it was a hobby, but the plane just is out of control. There are flames.

DA: Do you want to continue, or do you want to move beyond the death?

EL: I think we might as well go beyond the death while I feel the pain.

DA: Move right through that. Move to the point now. You have just died. Tell me where you are now in relation to your body.

EL: Strangely, I can see a rescue launch.

DA: Are you above the sea?

EL: Yes.

DA: You're not in the sea. Is the plane in the sea?

EL: The plane's gone.

DA: Are you moving?

EL: There's a launch, a wooden launch, a rescue boat coming towards me. I think I'm in the sea, I'm on the top.

DA: Have you died?

EL: No, I haven't, not if what I'm seeing is correct. I can't explain what I'm seeing, but there were no emotions apart from anger, of being thrown into a situation that I wasn't ready for.

DA: What does the water feel like?

EL: It's just cold, unpleasant. I want to get out of it, and I'm being pulled out of it, I think. I'm being dragged into a boat. People are getting hold of me and pulling me in, but I'm watching this from the outside. I'm not in the body. I can see my body being taken. It could be dead; it could be. I may be just above watching. That might explain why I can see it as I do.

DA: What are your feelings at this particular moment about the life that you've just lived? Is the anger still there?

EL: No, it was wasted.

DA: Tragic. Do you get the sense that it was, in effect, a mistake and things didn't go according to plan?

EL: It was just so stupid to die so early. It needn't have happened.

DA: You will sense some brief sadness or remorse at this moment, but your spirit has been through this many times, and soon you will be able to return home. Are you stationary, or have you begun to move?

EL: I'm still looking at the scene in the sea.

DA: Is there anything that you feel you need to stay for, to do, or to try and communicate with anybody?

EL: No, it just feels that it was all so unnecessary. It ended before it began.

DA: These feelings will begin to diminish as your memories begin to return. You've been through this many times before. Just tell me when you begin to move, when you feel you're ready to move away, to go home.

EL: No, let's do it. Let's not just sit here looking. Nothing's changing. The image is frozen now.

DA: Nothing's moving on the boat?

EL: No, the image is frozen in time. It's as if the film broke in the projector. The last scene is just stuck.

DA: Okay, you can now begin to move if you wish, back home. Just tell me when the movement begins.

EL: As I'm floating away slowly.

DA: Are you moving in the direction that you're facing or are you moving backwards?

EL: I'm moving backwards. I'm looking down, but I'm feeling myself gradually floating away as if someone's got hold of my braces from behind and is pulling, but I'm looking down at the sea all the time until it's disappearing as a pinprick.

DA: As the sea becomes smaller and smaller, can you see the outline of the lands and the continents?

EL: No, it's just so distant now that it's gone.

DA: The entire planet?

EL: Yes, there's nothing. I'm in a space. There's a sort of permanent dark blue light around me. Well, it's not light; it's darkness with a bit of colour, if you like.

DA: Are you moving quickly or slowly?

EL: Steadily, backwards still.

DA: You are now fully in soul state, directly connected to the highest consciousness of your mind that is like a vast computer holding all the stored knowledge of your entire existence. As an eternal, timeless being, you will remember incredible details about your immortal life between lives, and thus, you will be able to respond to my questions about your soul life quite easily. We are now going to a place of expanded inner awareness, and as you move upward into the loving realm of an all-knowing spiritual power, even though you are only at the gateway of this beautiful realm, your soul can feel the joy of being released. Everything will become very familiar to you as we progress because this peaceful realm embodies an all-knowing acceptance. You have moved away from the earth in perfect comfort. Soon you will receive divine help in releasing all remaining residual negative energy from your physical life. You will be entering your eternal home, where we can talk about your immortal life and all the lives you have lived before with objectivity and understanding because this is a spiritual realm of planning and harmony. You have been this way before. Just keep moving and know that you are going home and tell me when you can see far into the distance beyond your immediate surroundings.

EL: Well, I feel a bit like a silvery little bubble, just moving backwards all the time, just like a bubble.

DA: If you just turn your head to look in the direction that you're going, tell me if you can see anything off in the distance.

EL: Yes, there has been an image, but it's bright, but I can't really distinguish it.

DA: How far away? Is this a bright light?

EL: Well, there's a scene, but the light is so bright, if you like, for my eyes, that I can't distinguish what I can see.

DA: How far away is this image from you?

EL: Well, not far. I mean, I guess if I come out of the tunnel and blink and stand around dazzled by the light, it's a very white light. It's as white as it can be. There's no yellow or golden or anything. It's a bit blue-white, but really just pure white, and I keep seeing a fence, like a picket fence, you know, like around a garden or like a New England church, you know, with a white wooden post and sticks. It's a fence; I mean, it looks daft, really. I don't know where that's coming from. I can't see the remnants. There are people there, but they're distant.

DA: Can you actually identify them as human being shapes?

EL: Yes, yes.

DA: Are they emanating any light?

EL: No, they're sort of huddled together a bit, a bit of a gaggle, I suppose. They seem to have golden faces or golden heads, that part, and they're sort of shrouded in white, I could say. I mean, they're very indistinct. They're not... they all look alike, perhaps seven or eight, maybe more. That's one. One has walked to the front.

DA: Facing you?

EL: Yes, yes, she's come out, come forward, just like that, suddenly.

DA: And how far away is she from you?

EL: Oh, she's walking quite close towards me, but I can't see detail. I knew who it was immediately.

DA: You don't necessarily need to see the detail, do you?

EL: No, but it would be nice.

DA: It's Athelia, is it?

EL: Yes, yes.

DA: What is she communicating to you?

EL: She's very pleased to see me again, let's put it mildly. It's difficult to explain the emotions, but she's very glad to have me back.

DA: Try and explain it because it'll be on the recording if you do.

EL: Yes, you're right. I mean, it's joyous. She's holding me, and it's as if there are tears. I know I've got some. It's a very emotional moment, the way she just suddenly appeared and said, hi, I'm back, and there was a lovely sense of well-being, being back together. Quite sad about it, isn't there, because it's a necessity? I haven't got that at the moment. It's something I've known, and it's not here in my life at the moment. I'm missing it, and now it's just calm again. That bit's done. She's taken me by the hand, and we've turned, and we're walking towards the other people. I'm on the left; she's on the right. She's seen the two of them, so more monumental to me. I'm quite a bit shell-shocked, really, about the whole arrival. It's all a bit new. I can see these other people, but they're not distinguishable at the moment.

DA: They will become distinguishable very shortly, but you have done this many times before.

EL: I can feel the two of us are back together. It's very emotional. We belong together.

DA: Do you know yet why she is not in your current life?

EL: No, I just know that we were torn apart for some reason. It was as if we were always to be together, but something happened.

DA: Are you close enough to the rest of your friends now to see who they are?

EL: Well, no one's coming forward. Let's get the emotions out of the way a moment and back to the visual. It's quite a difficult moment that was.

DA: Just allow it to happen, and all the time things are occurring, I don't actually need to ask you anything, ideally.

EL: You need to ask questions to keep me moving along.

DA: Can you just give me a commentary?

EL: You need to keep pushing.

DA: Move toward the other group. Explain to me, are they ahead of you? Are they slightly to the right or to the left?

EL: They appear in my head. The scene is here. They're there, and I'm exactly where I am. She's holding my hand. They're not a little gaggle, about seven?

DA: Can you count them?

EL: No, they're just…

DA: They're in a little huddle, are they?

EL: Yes.

DA: Are some of them facing away from you then?

EL: No, they're not looking at me.

DA: Right, so they're in a huddle, but they're sort of all facing towards you.

EL: Yes, I can't pick them out enough to say there's a certain number or anything else.

DA: Can you walk a little bit closer?

EL: Yes, I'm walking closer.

DA: Because we're in now time in the spirit world, at any particular time, we can just take some time out and do a little bit of investigation of what's happening there and then continue, and one of the things that I do want to do, as soon as you're close enough to them, is to separate them out so that we can go through them, and there's a whole piece of information that we need to find out about your Primary Soul Group.

EL: Yes, they're in my soul group, but they're waiting; they're not coming forward. Is this a good time to take a moment for a break, David?

DA: It is indeed. Okay, what I want you to do, in a moment, I will just say to you, open your eyes, and you will be able to do that and take a comfort break. When you come back into the room, sit in that chair and close your eyes, and when I say to you, go into trance, you will immediately return to exactly the same place where you left off, immediately and directly. So, in a moment, when I say open your eyes, your eyes will open, you will be able to get up, go and take a comfort break, come back, and when you sit in that chair and rest back and close your eyes, when I say go into trance, you will immediately return back to this position, and for now, we can take a break, so open your eyes, and yeah, you can take the mic off, but it's usually a good thing to do before you go to the loo.

EL: Yes, not a bad thing.

DA: Oh, we have much more to come. Was it just a break you wanted, or did you want the loo?

EL: I need to pee, and it's becoming conscious.

DA: Sure, well then you need to have the break.

EL: It's breaking into my mind.

DA: The aeroplane bit.

EL: I knew immediately who it was. It was a surprise.

Narration

Once more, a memory comes as a surprise to the client. This is not unusual.

End of Narration

DA: Okay, just rest backwards and allow your eyes to close. That's it, you can already feel yourself drifting down and go into trance. Now let's pick this up from where you left off.

EL: Well, it's just like a frozen scene at the moment.

DA: What scene is it?

EL: This is where I left it. There's Athelia holding my hand; she's there. She's taller than me. She's quite a lot higher somehow; there's a difference in heights, and there's this gaggle of six or seven images.

DA: That's okay; we said we were going to take a bit of time out, and that's what happened, but before we actually move on, can you tell me what your spirit name is?

EL: Well, the first name that came to mind was Isath.

DA: Can you spell that?

EL: I-S-A-T-H, but I must tell you, when I got Athelia's name, I also got the name Isath at the same time, and I've never known who Isath was. I thought maybe it was another guide, I don't know, but nothing else comes.

Narration

There's an inconsistency here with reporting. Information is being received but without the clarity to be certain who the name refers to.

End of Narration

DA: Okay, I mean that will be it, but as we go through this process, you will find that your memory will improve and you will be able to confirm that because you will know it for certain. Right, now I want you to continue towards the other members of your group, the rest of your friends, and if you'd like to start this process running again, we'll start this film running again, and as you move closer towards them, I want you to almost place them mentally in your mind in a line in front of you or a semi-circle, but in a formation so that we can.. Okay.

EL: Give me a little push in that direction, and gone.

DA: Now you're closer, can you count them?

EL: No, not at all.

DA: Okay, let's start with the spirit that's furthest to your left. Are they in a line or still in a huddle?

EL: Huddle. Can you just ask them to separate out in a line so that you can identify them? It just makes it easier for you.

DA: And they'll do that for you?

EL: Yes, yes, they are in a semi-circle.

DA: So would the first one, if you were facing 12 o'clock would they be running from 9 o'clock to 3 o'clock?

EL: Yeah, it's about that, yeah, 10 till 2.

DA: About 10 till 2, okay. So, at 10 o'clock, look at the spirit at 10 o'clock, and these are the things that we need to find out about all of these spirits. Can you discern any facial features?

EL: Well, I'm suspecting my father's father, my grandfather, on my father's side, Joe.

DA: So, it would be...

EL: He has possibly occurred once or twice when I've been to readings, but I've not been able to pinpoint him, but yes, I think that's him. I can't really see his face.

DA: But you, I mean, sometimes you just know.

EL: Yes.

DA: What colours, if you look closely, what colours does this spirit emanate?

EL: Well, he seems to have a white body with a golden face. It's very consistent, these golden faces, and if there's any light surrounding him, it's like, I suppose you would say, white with a hint of electric blue.

DA: Would you say that that was more an aura?

EL: Well, I'm trying to see it as an aura, but I'm not so sure that I'm not trying to force that into my mind because I can't really see anything with clarity there.

DA: That's okay because by the time we get through to the rest of the members of your Primary Soul Group, you'll be able to come back, and your memory will be actually better, and things will be much clearer. So would the next person be at 11 o'clock?

EL: Yeah, yeah, yeah.

DA: And do you know who that is?

EL: No, I can't, I can, I'm aware there's someone or a shape there, but it's not...

DA: What colours do they emanate?

EL: Well, they're all the same. They're all sort of shrouded in white, you know, they're just figures in shrouds, white shrouds, but they have these sort of sunshine golden faces. I mean, if I said, look at a sort of religious icon, you know, you get that sort of gold sort of leaf head and the white underneath, the white shroud. I mean, that's about as near as I can describe it, but I don't, I'm not thinking of religious icons or anything like that.

DA: Do any of the members of this group…

EL: They're different heights too.

DA: Different heights?

EL: Yes, there's about five or six, but they're not just in a row. They are tending to stay in a huddle, and some are taller than others.

DA: Is any one of them, does any one of them sort of stand out as being either slightly brighter or bigger or more powerful in any way?

EL: Well, there's one that's tall, yes, standing towards the back. I mean, they're sort of stacked up, the tallest at the back, the shortest sort of at the side, but there's only a few, seven or eight, six, five, no, more than five.

DA: So, the larger one at the back, would they be at sort of 12 o'clock?

EL: Yes, he's sort of central. They're just like a little bunch of flowers, if you like, like a flower arrangement, you know, they're just…

DA: Do you get the sense that this spirit is male or is presenting you with…

EL: It's very difficult to choose one or the other. I mean, they don't seem to have either sex. I mean, Athelia didn't have a… I say feminine, but I think that because… it's a kind, warm, spiritual sort of person, rather than a male, macho, let's chop down trees type man, if you like. There's no obvious sex gender, no, not at all. Of course, they can present to you their existences, if you like. They don't have a male or female.

DA: Okay, they can choose to present to you whatever they wish, but they may present and say it's androgynous.

EL: Yes, I think that's probably the nearest way. They certainly don't strike me as being one or the other.

DA: Is the group or anybody in the group communicating anything to you?

EL: No, they're remaining distant, as if they're waiting for me to do something. It's almost as if they're getting impatient, really.

DA: What do you think it is that you need to do?

EL: I don't know. Athelia just sort of walked me out there and then gave me a little push and dumped me.

DA: Perhaps you ought to go a little closer to them.

EL: Yes.

DA: And get involved.

EL: I think you're right. I think I just needed time to find my feet and adjust. Where am I? I don't seem to be able to move, somehow, I kind of...

DA: Can you see Athelia there still?

EL: No, she went off over there. She's about, but she's keeping her head down, I think is the best way to put it.

DA: She's just allowing this to happen.

EL: Yes, oh yes.

DA: Is there anything happening to you in terms of sensation? Are you in any kind of light yourself?

EL: Well, I wasn't aware of it until you mentioned it, but maybe I am standing in a sort of pool of light, as if there's a spotlight on me, but it's not really right to say that because the light is so bright around me anyway. Everything is sort of white and sort of brilliant, I suppose, like being out in the snow in the sunshine, you know? It's got that sort of whiteness, but it's not a cold white. It's got a yellowy warmness to it, and it's comfortable here. I'm back, you know, I'm back where I... I don't know who these shrouded characters are.

DA: Are you drawing anything from this spotlight, this very sort of indistinguishable extra light that might be on you?

EL: It's like a sort of spotlight up there, you know, you're on stage, and it's just a pool of light around me, perhaps.

DA: Do you feel any connection with that light that's around you? Is there anything moving between you?

EL: No, maybe I should just walk over to the right and see who else is there.

DA: Why not? Seems like a good idea.

EL: I think it might have... It might be my grandmother, my... I mentioned Joe, my father's father. I think it's his... Nana, I used to refer to her.

DA: As your father's mother?

EL: Yes, but there is some historical doubt as to the authenticity of that relationship.

DA: I'm not sure there is.

EL: But, yes, she was my grandfather's first wife.

DA: And where is she positioned?

EL: She's on the far right, and he was on the far left.

DA: Okay, so she's around about 2 o'clock?

EL: Yeah.

DA: And is she a low or a high one?

EL: She's down here. They're both down here. Mine's at a height. I can see images of her when I was a child, when I used to go and play at her apartment.

DA: Have you managed to get closer to her?

EL: Yes, she's putting her arm round me.

DA: Is she communicating anything to you?

EL: She's just saying it's nice to see you again. It's a feeling that I'm back. I can see images of where she used to live. She lived alone for a lot of her life, her older part of her life. There was a nice sofa, and there were some little toys that always came out of the cupboard when we visited. I was quite a young child, I mean, I was only three or four, I guess.

DA: When you've finished this reconciliation with her, are you able to move to the next person?

EL: Yeah, I could easily just float a bit to the left, and there's someone there, and I'm sensing, I don't know why, but on my mother's side of the family, it would be my Uncle Norman. Well, I never knew the bloke. I mean, he was quite the black sheep of the family, but my mother's father remarried, and so there were two collections of kids in the family. There were four from the first wife who died, and I think three or four from the second wife. I'm not sure where, I think Norman was in the second family, but I don't know, I can't be sure. I don't know much about my family's history. It's not really of interest, to be honest, but he was the one who was always a bit distant. I've got a silver torch of his he bought me as a Christmas present. I've treasured it for some reason ever since. I've had it… it must have been fifty bloody years, and it's still in my… It's a chrome Eveready torch.

DA: Is he communicating anything to you?

EL: Well, I remember he used to have an old historic car, but I'm not really… He used to go sailing, apparently, but I don't know him; I never met him. A lot of them moved to Canada when I was a child, and I never encountered them as such, not really, not as a significant part of my life. I don't know why he came into the equation, but I sensed it was him.

DA: Do you sense that he may have played a much more significant role in some of your other lives? Perhaps this life he just had a bit part.

EL: That's possible; I don't know who he is. He's not particularly coming forward in the background. I mean, he's, if they were all standing on stage taking a curtain call, he wouldn't be in the front row. He'd be a couple of rows back maybe.

DA: A bit distant, bit cool. What you need to do is to get close to the people that you can get close to.

EL: So, if I move to the next one, which is pretty much five past twelve, if you like, who's there? I don't sense or feel anyone special, not in the way that when Athelia came, it was an emotional sensation. I mean, there was no doubt. It was like two old friends back together, but the rest are not... They're not even really significant. They're there, but there's, I can't ever distinguish them. It's almost as if they don't need, we don't need to. It's almost as if Athelia is the one, and the others are long-time distant, if you like, memories, long gone. I can't, certainly, nothing is easily coming forward, nothing at all.

DA: That's okay. I said as we progress through this entire process, your memory will get better.

EL: I'm struggling to even make contact with any of them.

DA: That's okay. Is Athelia anywhere near?

EL: Oh yeah, she's over there. She's just waiting, smiling, watching me struggle. She likes that. She thinks that's amusing.

DA: If you look at any of the images, you don't need to identify who they are, but the one that you're facing, for example, when it's close to you, just imagine that they are holding a full-length mirror up that you can step in front of and look at yourself. I want you to describe to me what light you emanate.

EL: Well, if they hold a mirror up in front, I look like a silhouette with white hair and shoulders and this white shroud, but there's this sort of dark background in my head, and I did meet a... what would you call her? It was in a spiritualist church; she was doing the readings.

DA: A medium?

EL: A medium, and she came over to me and told me I had this... She said, why am I not doing healing? She said, is it Edward Akora from the distance? She said, you've got this magnificent pale blue halo, aura. She said, why aren't you healing? And I've been to a couple of these readings, services, whatever you want to call them. I went to three; one I received nothing, and the other two, they both, different people, gave me the same message, near as damn it, and they homed in on me straight away and gave me a long talking to, whereas everybody else got sort of trivia. I got quite a talking to.

DA: If you can just focus on this image of yourself in the mirror at the moment and on this electric blue, it's sort of an aura, it's sort of around you.

EL: Yeah, I suppose if I can see any colour, it's pale blue, electric blue.

DA: And if you check in where that memory is coming from.

EL: The memory of what?

DA: This memory that you're relating to me now about looking at yourself, this aura, and just check in with yourself because you know where real memories come from.

EL: I don't know, it's the sensation that it's purely Athelia and me. It's almost as if she's showing me these people, these whatevers, these images, and their history. They're looking, and they're admiring us. There's a definite sense of well done, you two, from them.

DA: You know they're pleased for you, but it's just, I don't know, it's... From this particular perspective, do you get any sense at the moment whether Athelia is your guide or your primary soul mate?

EL: I don't know how I would be supposed to know the difference. All I know is that when she came forward, and she did with a bang, suddenly, right in front of me, she shot out in the crowd, and it was quite emotional. I mean, it was just that I knew there was someone that I'd been apart from; I felt like I'd been torn apart from, and now I was put back together with, and that was quite an emotional experience because we belong together; we should never have been apart. But no one else is, well, they're just watching like an audience, you know, they're standing back. To be honest with you, David, I can say they were standing behind the fence; there's that white picket fence that seems to run around; they're standing behind it like they're watching something going on, but, you know, they've got to stay back.

DA: Do you feel that you need to stay here any longer at this time?

EL: Nothing's happening, no, nothing's happening.

DA: Right, let's move on because you can come back to this group, and you will almost certainly find out more about why it's structured this way a bit later, but for now, we've spoken...

EL: Yes, Athelia's come back to me now, having said that, she's come back to me. Do you at any time have the opportunity for quiet reflection and review over your previous lives?

DA: Okay.

EL: Well, what seems to be happening is that Athelia's come back, and she's put her arm around me, and she's taking me somewhere; we're moving off somewhere.

DA: Do you know where you're going?

EL: No, we're going over there, which sounds silly, I know, but it's in that direction.

DA: Okay, well, now that's right, it's got a direction, but what is your destination? You could always ask her.

EL: Yes, the problem I face is that I have preconceived ideas sometimes because of the books I've read, and they kind of are becoming... Well, you could ask her if this is a preconceived idea. We're going to the chamber.

DA: What happens at the chamber?

EL: Well, is it where one reviews one's life? I can see screens, and it's as if we're going to have a rerun of what went on in my life.

DA: So, is there a sort of part of this place which is reserved for you that you can actually go in?

EL: Yes, there's a door in, and I go in; it's like a globe, I suppose, and there's, over here, I can see four or five sort of curved screens; maybe there's a desk down here.

DA: When you say go in, what have you actually gone into?

EL: I've gone into a sphere. Literally, a door's opened, and I've walked in, and it's closed, and I'm inside now.

DA: Before you actually got into it, was it the only sphere there, or were there more?

EL: No, it was only one.

DA: The only one. Is it big?

EL: Not particularly. It's probably relatively small. What size am I in this existence? To me, I suppose, it's relative to my size. I'm standing in a parishable-type size chamber.

DA: Where was this chamber situated? Was it anywhere?

EL: It suddenly appeared; it just suddenly popped up, and we walked across the grass; there was a door in, and there was a blue sky behind; it's a sort of whitish thing, but you see, there again, there's an image of a concrete globe, something to do with the Second World War or something, I'm not sure I know, but you drive past it. I've forgotten what they call it; it was for training guns or something, and it feels like I've just walked in the back door of that.

DA: Describe to me what's there now you're in there.

EL: What's in here looks like a brown wooden floor with a desk, with a desk, there's something there.

DA: And do you sit at this desk?

EL: No, I'm still at the back of here, but there are curved screens on the individual screens, like wide-screen TVs on end. I think there's three or five, maybe five of them across there.

DA: And where is Athelia in relation to them?

EL: She's still back here; she's staying back all the time.

DA: Is the desk somewhere where you feel that you are going to go and sit down and do your work?

EL: Yes, I think I'm going to go and sit in front of those screens, and so might as well try to sit down there and have a look. I'm not sure whether it's meant for me.

DA: Well, again, you could ask her if it's meant for you.

EL: Yes, it is, I must go and sit there.

DA: Okay, now.

EL: She's saying, now watch what happens.

DA: Oh, right, so it's sort of going to be run for you?

EL: Yes, I'm sitting there; I don't know what I'm seeing, I mean, but…

DA: Are there any images running on these screens at the moment?

EL: Nothing that I can pick out, no.

DA: Okay, presumably it's about to start.

EL: I presume so, I don't know. It all sounds pretty hopeless, doesn't it? It sounds like I'm going nowhere at the moment. She's telling me just go and sit down there.

DA: Are you sitting at the desk yet?

EL: Yes.

DA: Right, okay, so…

EL: The screens are sort of run from here up like that.

DA: So, you just need to sit back and look and wait for it to start.

EL: Hmm.

DA: While you're waiting for this to happen, is there anybody else in this building?

EL: No, it's just a feeling, I mean, she's just waiting. It's something we just seem to have to go through. Maybe she's waiting...

DA: For the projectionist or...?

EL: Yes, the equivalent.

DA: Okay.

EL: I get the feeling that she just can't wait, you know, she just wants to... It's a formality that we have to go through to get it out, and then whatever happens next will happen. It's a bit like going to a dinner or a dance, and you have to shake hands with half a dozen people at the door before you get to where you want to be.

DA: Before you get to eat?

EL: Yes, it's a bit like that. It's a kind of formality that has to be gone through, but nothing wants to move, or... I don't even know what I'm supposed to be doing there apart from sitting, looking.

DA: Maybe it's that you need to decide what you want to watch before it happens. If one of the things that you did want to explore was your life in France around about the Middle Ages, and as you just focus on that thought of wanting to do that, you can then just look at the screens and tell me what appears.

EL: Well, the two brown horses are there. Apparently, we had two brown horses; she's told me this.

DA: Now, is this an image that's on the screen?

EL: No, this is an image in front of me now. I don't know if it's on the screens or not; they're sort of indifferent. This is what I'm seeing; it's just come, and we have a white dog, long-legged sort of dog. She told me we had a dog; it used to run with horses, and we're in the forest; we were both on our horses.

DA: In this life, what is your name?

EL: Well, immediately, Isath came to mind. Isath and Athelia, the two names go together; they're not separated; they're sort of right bonded.

DA: What are the names of the horses?

EL: I don't know that they have names; they are means of transport, they're a nice means of transport. We're pretty lucky to have them; they're groomed, and they're gleaming, you know, they're not your scruffy old farmyard horse. These are two good horses.

DA: At this particular point in the life that you're re-experiencing, how old are you?

EL: Oh, again, early twenties; we're young, and we're a couple; she's the same age; we're a couple.

DA: When your exact age comes to mind, just tell me.

EL: Twenty-three.

DA: And she is?

EL: There's no reason for it to be different, though I can't, if I have to consciously think of a number, it's too late.

DA: Just allow it to come. Where are you going to?

EL: We're in the forest. You can ride through the forest; it's not so dense that you can't ride. We're just walking the horses, sitting on them, riding comfortably.

DA: Are you going anywhere, or is it just out for a trip?

EL: Is she taking me to the mountain? I don't know. You see, when I'm in contact with her, when I've been in France, in my house, she's popped into my head and told me things when I was cooking. I was cooking seafood, and she said we used to eat seafood, and I said, where do we get seafood from? She said, we went to the beach; we collected mussels. I said, how did we get to the beach because it's an hour in the car? She said, we had horses, two brown horses. She was quite, "you should know this attitude". "You should be aware of this", and she kept telling me to go to the village in Saint-Pierre, which I did, and then I found the plaque, and also there's a mountain, perhaps forty minutes' drive, very distinctive, on the horizon, the foothills in the Pyrenees, and she's always telling me to go there. I should go there, and I will get, how can I put it, I will find strength there, well-being, and I wonder if that's where she's taking me on the horses now because it was somewhere she was pushing me to go, and I've never been.

DA: Come back to where you actually are now on the horses.

EL: We're still in the forest, the white dog, the brown horses. I don't think we've got saddles of sorts, or barely.

DA: Just check the location, where that memory is coming from in your head.

EL: Well, it could be coming from the front, and it could be coming from the back. First of all, it was coming from the front. I can believe that, but it's a new image; it was quite clear; suddenly it appeared.

DA: Focus on the most striking part of the image, the clearest part of this image which has the most clarity, and when you focus on that, then check the memory location.

EL: I can see Athelia on her horse, and she's wearing fine clothes, nice robes, the ones she's shown me in, and that is coming from the back of my head.

Narration

Sometimes, conscious memories creep in, but people have an innate ability, once it's been pointed out to them, to be able to locate, within their own minds, where the memory originates from. From the rear of the brain, they are subconscious memories, and from the front, more likely to be conscious interference.

End of Narration

DA: And where is it that your real memories come from?

EL: You tell me, from the front, my conscious memories, my conjured-up memories come from the front.

DA: Your real memories come from the back.

EL: The deep memories, yes, the genuine memories.

DA: Okay, in which case, the horses are moving; we are dealing with a genuine memory.

EL: It's as if we're just out for a stroll on our horses with the dog.

DA: Tell me a little bit about this life.

EL: We're talking.

DA: How long have you known each other?

EL: I was going to say always; it's like a fairy tale; it's always been that way.

DA: Have you had lives before this one together?

EL: Oh yes.

DA: Why is it that this one is so predominant, this one that you asked the question about?

EL: It's the one I seem to get memories of, the one she seems to be trying to tell me about. It's a bit like a fairy story; that's all I can say, everything is perfect, there's no threats, no worry, no cares, no pressures, really; things are sort of taken care of.

DA: As you're riding along...

EL: We don't have to worry about where we're going to get the shopping or things; just all taken care of.

DA: As you're just riding on the horse, can you feel the horse beneath you?

EL: No, again, I'm standing back looking at it. I should go and sit on the horse, shouldn't I?

DA: You can join yourself on the horse and just tell me when you're there.

EL: Yes, I'm on the saddle now.

DA: Can you feel the horse, take up the reins?

EL: Yeah.

DA: Can you feel the horse now?

EL: Yeah, of course, the dog's down by my feet on the left.

DA: As you're just riding along, what I want you to do is just close your eyes, and we're going to move forward in time in that life to another point in that life, and you will know when you are there, and when you open your eyes, you will be in a different part of that particular life, and when you are there, just open your eyes and look around and tell me what is around you.

EL: Well, it's unpleasant, I can tell you; I think I know what's happening.

DA: Well, just tell me what you see, just tell me what's around you.

EL: There's a lot of people in turmoil, and we're being pulled apart, and I'm watching her go.

DA: That's okay. Pull back from the memory, just drift away, come back out of yourself, and just pull back away from the memory. How old are you at this time?

EL: Oh, young twenties.

DA: So, this is not too far into the future?

EL: No, no.

DA: Are there a lot of people around?

EL: Yes, shouting and screaming and baying at us.

DA: What are they saying?

EL: I can't tell you what they're saying; they're like just an angry mob, and they've taken us away.

DA: Is it just the two of you, or are there other people that are essentially on your side? Is it your group they're shouting at or is it just you individually?

EL: The children, it's the children.

Narration

Edward asks for a tissue here because the scene is massively traumatic, and he broke down at the reality of the slaughter. That it happened was not a surprise, as Athelia had already told him of the events and their role in them, but this is the first time he experienced it by being there. These memories can stimulate real physical symptoms, terror, grief, as well as choking on smoke generated by fire, or being unable to breathe when drowning, for example.

I prepare people subconsciously to be able to pull away, to leave danger and become an abstract observer. The experience is not about reliving pain and suffering, but the expansion of awareness.

End of Narration

DA: You have children?

EL: They've taken them too; they've gone.

DA: Can you tell me why this has happened?

EL: Yes, it's all to do with the Cathars, being a heretic, not being a Catholic. They're slaughtering everybody, burning them or whatever technique they want to use.

DA: What's happening to you?

EL: I'm being held while this is all going on in front of me; it's like a punishment. It's like I'm having to watch it because I wouldn't do what they told me, but none of us would; that was the point. We believed in what we were, and we wouldn't change; we wouldn't change; we were prepared to pay the price.

DA: Is the price going to end in your death as well?

EL: Yes.

DA: Are there many of you in the group?

EL: There are others, yes, but elsewhere. There's a public place, you know, it's like a public place of execution.

DA: Where exactly is the place?

EL: Well, I would say Carcassonne, I would say Carcassonne in the town.

DA: And looking back on this life?

EL: There's something else that comes to mind: Diva, who has recently arrived from Brazil; she also knows all about this history for some reason, and the places that she's frightened to go again, like Carcassonne, and I can't explain that, but anyway, that's an aside bit of information that you might find useful to explore, but here, it's people are just being dragged away.

Narration

Diva is a recent girlfriend in Edward's current life. This visit is the first time they've met but Edward senses such a strong connection that he believes her spiritual entity to be Athelia and is both curious and excited to spend time with her.

End of Narration

DA: From this particular point, you can return to the chamber.

EL: Oh, the chamber, yes.

DA: Just come back to the chamber because you can return back to this because Athelia is now back with you again.

EL: Yes, she's back there now.

DA: What I want you to do, in looking back at this life, because you have this overview now, having had many lives and lives in between, can you tell me whether this was, perhaps, one of your most successful lives in terms of achieving what you needed to learn?

EL: It was a life that was cut short before it should have been. I don't think we even had time to achieve anything. It's a bit like the airman; he never felt the same, he never had time to do what he was supposed to do, and the same happened to us; we were young.

DA: Okay, let's go back to that again. What was it that you were supposed to do in that life?

EL: In the life as an airman or the life on the horses when you were...

DA: On the horses, the life in the Middle Ages.

EL: We were quite well-to-do; we were leaders, I think we were.

DA: From your soul perspective, from the purposes of your soul advancement, what was the lesson, why did you choose to do that life, what was the gain that you had hoped to get by living that life?

EL: I understand the question. What is the feeling of being kind to one another, of just living a perfect life together? That seems to be what it was all about.

DA: But how?

EL: The 1950s American dream, you know, Mom and ice cream, apple pie, nothing nasty.

DA: But how beneficial is a life like that to your soul advancement?

EL: Would it be to learn happiness? I don't know. I'm asking myself as well; that's what comes to mind, to learn to be happy.

DA: We can probably check some of this out, but while you're in this place, what I'd like to ask you is, when was your first incarnation on Earth?

EL: Well, my mind shot back an awful long way, but...

DA: Can you put a year on it roughly?

EL: Well, if I tell you what I can see, I can see hairy mammoths and great big curly tusks and a silly scene of cavemen.

DA: Are you there now? Are you witnessing this as it was?

EL: Yeah, I mean, it's a life, isn't it?

DA: You're witnessing it. Look at yourself and tell me what you look like, what's on your feet, what you've got, what are you wearing?

EL: It's all very crude. I mean, there's a small fire; there's probably, I feel there's other people about, although I can't see them. There's a feeble little fire; it could be in a cave, actually, could be in a cave. I've got a stick, and I'm dressed in animal skins of some sort; it's not particularly cold, I mean, I've got bare arms and legs.

DA: Is Athelia there?

EL: Is she there? I don't know the answer to that. I can see sort of like hairy mammoths, not prehistoric monsters, you know, but they're sort of forerunners of elephants and bison. I'm in my twenties again, maybe younger even; I'm inexperienced; I'm not an old person; I'm young.

DA: Come back to the chamber, come back out of that one, let me ask you some general questions that you can check out. If you don't know the answers to the questions, you can check them out by thinking about that life, and the screens will take you into the life, which is what's happening. So, just generally, how many incarnations have you had on Earth?

EL: Well, the number that's shot into my head was forty.

DA: Have you ever incarnated anywhere else?

EL: Yes, but I don't know where?

DA: These other incarnations, were they on a physical world?

EL: Yes, it was wet; it was a watery world, peaceful.

DA: Were there many incarnations on that watery world, and is that the...?

EL: No, I think there was one, just one incarnation, quite a long one.

DA: And have you incarnated any other places other than the watery world and Earth?

EL: I can see quite a dark place, but that may be Earth. It doesn't have a character as such. The watery world, I can feel around me a bit; I can feel as if I'm living in water.

DA: What kind of life form were you?

EL: It's a humanoid, I think, small, a bit like a frog but bigger, but I could swim; it was natural to swim; my body was adapted for life in water.

DA: From your soul perspective and with the experience of having incarnated elsewhere as well, what's your impression of incarnations on Earth?

EL: They're not going very well somehow; they don't seem to achieve what they're meant to achieve; they seem to start off alright and not reach a conclusion.

DA: Have you had many incarnations where you haven't achieved what you desired, or you haven't achieved the purpose of that incarnation?

EL: Again, that's a hard question to answer. I feel that each incarnation on Earth, for some reason, has been cut short; it's like a repetitive problem.

DA: Have you had any incarnations on Earth that you would say were successful in terms of you really ticking all the boxes?

EL: I suppose, I understand what you mean; it doesn't seem that I can ever bring to mind a memory of an incarnation that goes beyond young, early twenties, mid-twenties; it seems that they don't go beyond that.

DA: Do you ever, in the spirit world, have a time or an activity whereby you get feedback about your lives from other people?

EL: Well, the image that came to mind was being in the chamber again, if you like, but with the people. I mean, I see this is images coming from the book again, David, but the sort of guides are the guides, if you like, the top-notch ones, about five.

DA: Are you there now?

EL: I could be there now, yes.

DA: Is Athelia with you?

EL: She's back there as usual, in the distance, yeah, she's there.

DA: But does she normally take you there?

EL: I don't even know whether I've been there before; I was just there; it just happened.

DA: Are you there now, are you standing or sitting?

EL: Standing.

DA: Are there some other people?

EL: It's fine.

DA: Are they standing or sitting?

EL: They're sitting. Well, they could be standing; we could all be standing.

DA: Just how far away from you are they?

EL: More like you are to me, a bit further perhaps.

DA: Okay, and there's five of them?

EL: Yeah.

DA: Does any one of them appear to be more important?

EL: The central one, yeah, the central one is, I think. He's addressing me. They're male, I think, if you wanted to put...

DA: They're all male?

EL: Well, I would say they're all male, but I'm saying that because they have a dominant sort of character. I mean, that's the only reason why one treats a woman as being soft and caring, as a man is much more authoritative; that's the only reason I would say they were male authoritative personages.

DA: They may present themselves to you as male, maybe because you would feel more comfortable with an authoritative figure being presented to you as male, or maybe they present themselves as androgynous. What was being communicated to you by the chairperson of this group of people?

EL: He's asking me why I'm here, why are you back?

DA: Because perhaps you have some questions?

EL: And I'm saying, did it all go wrong again, and he says, no, no, he did alright. I'm asking, I think it all went wrong, and he says, no.

DA: Before we move any further, which life are we talking about?

EL: It's difficult to say because I'm not in any character; I'm in this sort of spiritual existence.

DA: They said you did alright, but you did alright in a life, yes, which life are we talking about, the most recent one, the pilot?

EL: I can't tell you that. It would be you putting ideas in my head, but I could then visualise it; it's not coming from memory.

DA: Okay, well, just tell me what's happening?

EL: I kind of feel that it's the Cathar life, the French historic life, but again, my mind's kind of full of images of things we've been talking about; it's difficult to say, to separate it out and let it generate itself clearly, but it's rather that, I mean, there's images of trauma in France. I was emotional. There's lots of images churning around, and it's difficult to push them aside to let the new ones start. Shall I take a break?

DA: Before we do that, let's ask the Council how you are doing in this current life. Is it going better than the others?

EL: They say I'm doing alright. They're telling me they're quite pleased with me, but they're telling me it's not finished; they're telling me to go back, in a kind way. I've checked in, if you like.

DA: Whilst you have their attention, it might be worth pushing it a bit.

EL: Yes, let's do that.

DA: And ask them about the last life as a pilot and don't tell them you're having difficulty making sense of your previous life because you've only just returned, and your memory still isn't quite right, and you just have this feeling that some lives have not completed as they should. You can ask them for a general view about your overall spiritual progress from the beginning.

EL: Yes, let's do that. It's all as planned; you're doing fine; it's all going to plan.

DA: The Cathar life went to plan?

EL: Yes, it was an unfortunate one, but it ended that way, whether it was supposed to? I'm told that I had enjoyment in that life; I knew pleasure; I knew happiness.

DA: And it seems that you also knew principle.

EL: Oh, yes, we died for what we believed. I can go straight back there now. Yes, that's the reason why it all happened.

DA: With that knowledge now, does that life take on a slightly different perspective?

EL: No, I've always known it; I mean, that's the people we were.

DA: But in terms of its value, that's what seems to be...

EL: Standing up for our beliefs, it's always been something that I've done.

DA: You were certainly doing that, but when we spoke a little earlier, you were telling me that you felt the life had been unnecessarily cut short, but from the perspective that you have now...

EL: It was a pilot; it was a pilot. I was doing what I believed in; yes, that's what I was fighting.

DA: So, both those lives, the Cathar life and the pilot's life, although they ended early, were according to plan, as it were.

EL: Yes, but I need to be top dog again. You see, in the Cathar life, we were quite high up in society, and if I was going to fight in the war, then I was going to have a role that was a big lamb, if you know what I mean I wasn't going to be any oik struggling around in the mud in the infantry; that's kind of...

DA: Have you had any lives where you've been the oik?

EL: No, no, no, it doesn't come forward. If I choose something, I choose something with a bit of quality, if you like, perhaps not the right word, but something where I have a position, somewhere where I can be recognised rather than just being another bloody soldier, if you know what I mean. I was one of the few and I was one of the few in the Cathar world too.

DA: Whilst you're at the council, can you give me a little bit more detail about the council members, the people?

EL: They look a little bit like wizards; wizards wear what they are wearing. They've got robes, and their motifs are associated with them. I can see stars, a five-pointed pentangle star.

DA: A medallion or a star on the robe?

EL: On the robe, no, it's not a medallion; no, it's not that.

DA: Are they wearing anything?

EL: No, it's shrouded up to here, and these are like decoration, just a few, a limited amount of decoration on the fabric; there's purple, and there's white, and there's gold, and there's two, there's five. I can only see the central ones; the outer ones are not clear. I should be concentrating on the one in the front; he's the important one.

DA: And what motif does he have?

EL: He's got the purple robe.

DA: The purple robe; is there anything on it?

EL: Yes, there are gold symbols; it's all very shimmery, just like polished silk, I suppose, and it's quite significant he's the top dog. The others are sort of a little bit in awe of him; they're there, but they're not doing it. They're almost sitting and watching; he's standing up; he's, you know, he's leading the show.

DA: He's leading the show. Do you sense that anywhere in the vicinity there's an even more superior being in the background?

EL: I've really been concentrating on the man in front; I'm left completely to my own devices there. We're standing facing each other, and it's as if we're communicating, but not aware of it. The rest are just, I think he's at the back; she's just waiting patiently, the rest are just what would you say, also-rans in comparison to the guy who's come forward and is doing the communication, and all I can say is he's said to me that it's okay. He's a bit curious why I am there talking to him, but he's quite welcoming. I'm quite welcome to talk to him and check in, make sure that I'm going down the right path, but he's not going to tell me what that path is; he's just told me that. He even came before the question was asked; he just went like that and said, no, but he has a sense of humour; he's smiling. We sense each other; there's a complicity between us; he's known me many times; he's almost aware of me trying to weed information out of him deviously, and he's not having it.

DA: Sure.

EL: He's got you there, in a sort of "no, you won't get me like that" way. He's happy; he's smiling; he's saying to me, you're doing alright, son, you're doing alright.

DA: One thing you could enquire, that he may give you some clues on, is one of the questions that you had: why this rather late development and rather surprising development of a psychic gift, this communications gift that you have, and whilst he won't tell you what you're supposed to do...

EL: He tells me I need it.

Narration

Prior to our meeting and before the date of this session, we spoke about this gift. Quite late in life, he was driving with his daughter in wintry conditions, and from out of the blue, he heard a voice in his head which warned him to slow down because of an icy patch just around the corner. It was so. Since then, he's developed a gift for channelling his guide, who is also his soul mate and appears in this session as Athelia. The mentions earlier regarding cooking instructions show the ease with which he can channel Athelia, at will, as if it were a phone call.

Channelling is something most people can do if they relax, focus, and open their minds. There are many books and recordings that can help one to learn this skill.

End of Narration

DA: Because this is there for some purpose that you need to accomplish with it.

EL: Yes, he said you needed it; that's why you've got it, but why I needed it, I mean, I had some difficult times with my divorce, and maybe it was their way of sending information to me to give me strength?

DA: Well, lots of people have difficult divorces, but they don't get psychic abilities.

EL: No, but they get strength from other people. I mean, I didn't have a friend. I mean, most people have got a shoulder to cry on or a few friends to gang up with against the opponent, haven't they, but this was a solitary battle; this was me against the others, as usual; that's my normal existence.

DA: Has the acquisition of this gift, has it served its purpose, was that what it was for?

EL: It was the beginning; it was the beginning. It was an eye-opener, and it will develop more. What's its purpose?

DA: Well, they probably won't tell you that, but you may want to know, does it have a purpose for the rest of your life, is there something important you need to do with this gift?

EL: Yes, it has a purpose. Let me ask him; he calls me my son, he calls me son, he's very sort of benevolent, the way he talks to me. He says I will use it. I will use it in the future, but that's really, it's kind of like the way I get other information when I tune in, for want of a better word. It's not specific; if I try and get specific information, in general, it's not there, so why have I got this psychic ability then? Why has it suddenly developed? Because I needed it, and I need it again. Tell me about helping people too. That's a recurrent thing, and it will be revealed. I mean, it's also written down in the A4 notes; maybe it's just a repeat of what I've already received information-wise, but he's telling me time's up in the chamber; he's turning me around and basically pushing me out the door, and that's it.

DA: You're not going to get any more out of that, are you?

EL: No, I've been sent away; that's it. I was able to check in, have a partner back, and no information really was to be given me, but time to go on now. We're back out on the grass, back outside; there's nothing about, it's just grass, just grass and the two of us. There's nobody; it's always just her and me.

DA: Are there any other things, other activities that you normally do or are involved in whilst you're between incarnations?

EL: Well, the schoolroom image comes to mind.

DA: When you do whatever activities you perform, do you do them together, always?

EL: It would be nice if we did them together, but we don't. We would like to, but in fact, it doesn't work that way;

we meet up a lot; we spend a lot of time together, but when we go off and do our work, we're nearby; we're not so distant, but we're working separately; we don't work together.

DA: Are you aware, whilst you're in your spiritual home and with your guide, is it normal, or does it happen to other people, where their guide is also their life partner as well, or their primary soul mate as well, both roles? Because I'm making an assumption here that perhaps Athelia is a more senior, more advanced spirit than you.

EL: It's possible, yes, it is possible.

DA: I was hoping you might ask her.

EL: I've already asked her in communications before today, and the answer I got was that when I asked about myself, I was told highish, and when I asked about Athelia, yes, she's higher; she's highish too, but higher. I'd have to consult my notes, but that's what came through, and I get blue auras, blue…

DA: From Athelia?

EL: From us both.

DA: From both of you?

EL: Yes, sort of sea blues, sky blue, electric blue, colours associated with us somehow. It's like a background to us, sort of darkish blue at the bottom of it. They're nice blues; they're really nice rich colours, but they fade. It starts off dark, but this electric blue, sky blue, electric sunny day blue is the sort of predominant colour I see. There are no other colours there. I'm trying to sort of substitute other colours into the image, and it doesn't seem to work. If I put yellows or greens or whites or reds or any other colour, they don't; the blue seems to be the… but it's the two of us; we're both the same.

DA: If you are Isath…

EL: Hmm.

DA: Then who is the more senior guide, the slightly grumpy one that has chipped in from time to time?

EL: Hmm. When I asked for a higher guide for things I was not sure I was being told correctly, I asked for confirmation and asked for a higher guide.

DA: So, it's unlikely that you are Isath and he is Isath.

EL: Yes, I don't know though.

DA: Do you know what his name is now and is he around?

EL: It's difficult to tell. I mean, I wonder if we are the two, the same?

Section 8

Continuity: Summary

Edward Lawson draws to a close, as a deeply layered exploration of the soul's persistence, its triumphs, and its unresolved yearnings, rendered in a holistic narrative that captures the full spectrum of Edward's trance-state experience.

The session's completeness reveals a spiritual landscape where past lives – a young RAF pilot lost in a fiery 1939 crash, a Cathar leader torn from family in medieval Carcassonne, and a prehistoric youth by a cave fire – emerge not as isolated vignettes but as interconnected threads in a broader tapestry of purpose. These memories, surfacing naturally, reflect a recurring motif of lives cut short, yet each carries lessons of principle, courage, and fleeting happiness, as Edward learns through visceral reliving and reflective distance. His emotional reunion with Athelia, his soul mate and guide, anchors the session, her presence a constant light amid the pain of separation, whether in the Cathar slaughter or the spiritual realm's tender embraces.

The council, appearing organically with its authoritative yet benevolent figures, offers reassurance that Edward's path – though marked by early endings – aligns with a grander plan, affirming his progress while withholding explicit directives. Reviews in the chamber, where screens flicker with potential insights, underscore the deliberative nature of his soul's work, even as clarity remains elusive. Edward's late-blooming psychic gift, sparked by a warning voice during a winter drive, emerges as a bridge to future purpose, its significance hinted at but left open, like the grassy expanse where he and Athelia pause at session's end. This cohesive narrative, unbroken by gaps, reveals a spiritual ecosystem where guides come and

333

go, memories ebb and flow, and the soul's dialogue with itself unfolds in real-time, leaving Edward poised between reflection and anticipation, ready for the next step in his eternal continuity.

Life According to the Soul: Epilogue

We've completed this stage of the journey, one that opens a perspective on our existence normally concealed. The testimonies of discrete individuals, unconnected to each other, reveal memories, experiences, and lessons shared in quiet privacy.

As you have seen, my role was to stimulate their responses, not to direct or prompt them. Apart from sections where I needed to deepen their trance or allow a toilet visit, almost everything I said was a question. It seems that memories are indeed stimulated by questioning.

The book began with examples of the first non-worldly questions intermixed with worldly ones when the client was in the womb. This is a significant and stimulating time because it moves from the practical and rational to something not well understood by most. The questions surrounding the connection between our immortal soul and the physical human foetus – or embryo in some cases – are monumental. They set the scene, acknowledging something quite different and, for the first time, describe the essence of a spiritual being connecting with a physical one to create the whole. This lays the foundation for the exploration to follow.

The process developed by Michael Newton is generally seen as the most logical and the path of least resistance to uncover these memories. The first port of call is a significant past life, often the most recent one, though not always. Starting with that memory and following the journey we've all taken so many times allows the order of events to mirror former journeys, resulting in clearer outcomes.

Past lives are profoundly impressive. The detail and depth of recall in the testimonies can be awe-inspiring. What cannot easily be conveyed is the emotion expressed during these accounts of the thought that goes into the answers. Nora's vivid description of poverty on a London street and her blithe acceptance of her daughter's death are intensely moving, even more so when considering the manner and emotion of the verbal testimony, which mere words on a page cannot fully express.

Elias's detailed account of his children and his life is typical of many past life experiences, reflecting a relatively normal existence. Sometimes, there is an opportunity to explore in a slightly different direction, as with Rachel. Speaking of herself as a man, naked in a strange environment, she provided a chance to see how immersive the past life experience can be. Rather than observing detached, sterile images as one might when watching a film, she was living the experience as Nathan – enjoying and finding amusement in his penis, experiencing arousal, and later sexual desire, copulation, and orgasm with his girlfriend. This offered a unique perspective, particularly as a woman occupying the body and senses of someone she once was.

Throughout the book, people reference their preferences for sex in a new life. It's clear that some prefer incarnating as male, others as female. Despite these preferences, the forthcoming life as either male or female must be entered into and completed as such. Everyone must do it. Despite the amorphous nature of the soul as an energy entity, individuals see benefits in being male or female, hence the preferences. One might wonder if those who feel they're in the wrong body are reacting to their soul's preference, unaware that they must live the life as chosen or repeat it in the future.

The past life section ends with Peter, whose testimony reinforces the futility of giving up in any chosen life. Whether through repeated suicides, as in Peter's case, or recurring sexual confusion, the soul must eventually complete the task to advance. His story speaks to the interconnectedness of all things, a reality we often fail to recognise in our isolated bodies and introverted minds. So much unhappiness stems from this sense of isolation and loneliness when, if we only knew, the connectedness is there and reachable through quiet meditation aimed at channelling – a term used to describe opening communication with our guide. Numerous books and recordings are available to help people achieve this.

Past lives reinforce the reality of these memories for those sharing them, a theme that began with the initial question in the womb. However, past life experiences are disjointed, lacking connection to anything else unless viewed from the higher perspective of one's soul existence between lives.

To journey to the spiritual realm, one must die. This is something we all recognise and understand will happen, and it is somewhat relieving to learn we've done it many times before. This section is brief but necessary, helping us understand how differently we feel about a life just lived after death. Typically, souls are eager to leave the earth's plane. While we imagine our dear departed longing to console and comfort us, the reality is they often couldn't care less. It might be likened to being released from a prison cell – the last thing you want to do is linger.

The journey from the deathbed to the spiritual realm is often described as a movement. Along the way, as Douglas recounts, a healing or repair function is frequently experienced – in his case, a wall of golden light. Sometimes this occurs elsewhere, or it may not be mentioned at all, submerged in the wealth of other experiences. Difficult lives can damage a soul's energy. Since the percentage of energy brought into a life is difficult to change, a highly traumatic life may leave the energy damaged upon death. This damage is automatically registered, not requested, and the Healing Shower is the process by which it is repaired. Descriptions of this process vary, but familiarity is key in welcoming and realigning a returning soul, which is why spiritual experiences are often described in recognisable forms.

The Healing Shower is no exception. While it may take time, in a timeless realm and memory, we move directly to the end of the process, as with the moment of death.

The journey usually culminates in meeting one's Soul Group – those souls closest to the individual, often including their soulmate and guide. This is an emotional experience. Words like "welcoming" and "love" are common, but the expressed emotion often leads to tears of happiness, with a box of tissues nearby. What is felt cannot easily be captured in words.

As I mentioned earlier, these sessions are for the client's benefit, not primarily for research. Identifying the souls in their primary group is helpful, which is why we spend time on this. This meeting is merely the welcome, as there is much more to do. Souls in this group and adjacent groups often appear in a life, and one's soulmate might manifest as a lover, friend, child, or parent, varying in each new life. After this initial meeting, we move on.

Formal and informal reviews can occur at any time. The Council is a formal review process, rarely critical, though it may express impatience. The Library, a repository of all incarnations and experiences, is another review mechanism. From Esther's feedback on her passive life in China to Hope's battle with fear and scepticism, these reviews allow reflection so deep that one can partially relive a life to re-experience mistakes.

These reviews introduce the concept of Hybrid Souls – those who have incarnated on different planets, in different universes, and dimensions. The scope appears endless. Testimonies reveal that Earth is a challenging place to incarnate due to its violence, but physicality also brings pleasures unavailable to an energy being in a distant dimension – everything from the thrill of a motorcycle ride at 16 to the joy of sex and the overwhelming love of holding a newborn.

Life can be hard, but hard schools provide profound lessons. The questions everyone asks – Why am I here? Why is life so hard? – are answered clearly: you chose it, or even if it was selected for you, you agreed to it. You knew the challenges and accepted them. This section describes April's choice from three sensory-immersive options, Oliver's selection of a male life in a collaborative Soul Group meeting, and Edmund's highly orchestrated, possibly final incarnation to reunite with Pauline, requiring nudging from her guide and a stern Council Sometimes, a little push is needed, and senior souls can make their disappointment clear.

What do souls do when at home in the spiritual realm? We explored this, finding many roles: Jez's training, Katherine's soul repair work for faulty joinings, Oscar's spiritual teachings. and Annie's research into how souls adapt when joining the human brain.

The book concludes with Edward's uninterrupted testimony, tying together the journey's individual parts to show how they form a whole. Each step is important, but so is the entirety. Without grounding in what's happening and why, the full testimony can be daunting unless one is familiar with its components. It's an awe-inspiring experience.

I began this project to communicate two things: we are not alone, and there is more to us than this physical existence. Understanding these truths makes life not just bearable but purposeful, educational, and worth living. Enjoy all that life offers, endure its pain with fortitude, and know that we are all connected. There is more than we can imagine, and help is always available – one just has to listen.

Potted Autobiography, David Allen

My working life began as an Apprentice Gas Fitter, through technical and managerial rolls to IT consultant, business owner, therapist, and political author, now largely retired, I've brought this work to the fore after about 13 years, because it is simply the right time.

I had been conducting LBL (Life Between Lives) sessions for about 7 years from 2005, the year I undertook the training with the eminent Michael Newton as the lead trainer, until 2012, when I stopped work to concentrate upon a quite different role as my wife's (Sandra) carer after her breast cancer diagnosis at the end of 2008.

A few years have passed since then and the publication of this quite new perspective on the many spiritual revelations uncovered during these sessions took some time before forming into a realistic prospect for a book. That which I have discovered has been repeated by hundreds of other like-minded and like-skilled facilitators. The delay in writing the book was due, in the main, to a need to add a breadth of meaning and understanding not really explored that well in other similar texts. Rather than simply repeat the work that Michael Newton had pioneered, I wanted to connect these spiritual understandings to modern day living. Once I felt I had a sense of what I wanted to achieve with the book I began the onerous task of transcribing a seemingly endless supply of audio files, noting areas of special interest. The rather recent advent of AI, that could accurately turn an audio file into a textual document sped up the last of these quite dramatically.

It still took about 18 months to two years to formulate the structure of the book in a way that would achieve these objectives best. Once that was decided in the back of my head, I began to write.

There have been three stages in my life where I have "grown" as a person and in my understanding about myself, my world and my spirituality. I came from a very practical background, was very focused on work and my family which I don't think is too bad a place to start.

I would have begun this with the short period as a musician where I went from playing in a group part time to going professional. Having been dabbling and playing since school I took the plunge and in 1969, gave up the full-time job (which actually paid), got married, and spent the next 9 months travelling all over the country for peanuts. All I learnt from that experience was that I wasn't cut out for that kind of life. That's not really personal growth so much as abject realism.

My first period of enlightenment was a two-year course in management (DMS, Diploma in Management Studies) taken when I was about 26. The course required engagement with people from very different backgrounds, all very able, and immersion in that environment opened my eyes quite a bit. A section of the course covered Psychology which added significantly to how I viewed the world and people.

Secondly was the quite unusual involvement (because I was 30 years old) with Kyokushnkai Karate. I took my two young sons along initially and, of course, tried it myself. They soon became bored, but for some bizarre reason I stuck at it, despite the fact that I had never been so physically and mentally stretched ever before. 20 years later, as a 4th Dan, I retired. Joints began to hurt more than before, and it was taking up too much of my time. However, I learnt a lot about myself as a person.

The most significant period for me came after selling my small company and re-training as a hypnotherapist in 2003, aged 56. After an initial period, I began doing Past Life Regression and then after having read of the groundbreaking LBL work decided that I just had to train in that discipline as well. The whole period, including reaching trainer level in EFT

(Emotional Freedom Techniques), opened my eyes to different worlds, metaphorically and reality.

Throughout my life I've done things that could be described as impulsive, or unfounded, but I truly believe now that some of those momentous decisions, including writing this book, weren't really my ideas at all. Sometimes if you just listen, you'll know what to do.

Previous Titles

The Sophisticated Alcoholic, O-Books 2011, Edited by Consultant Psychiatrist Dr James Kustow.
ISBN: 978-1-84694-522-9 (Paperback), 978-1-78099-215-0
(e-book)
The book breaks all the rules about treating alcoholism.
It's not just about the stereotypical alcoholic but the invisible
majority, the middle class drinkers, the people who are in
control of their lives but with one significant exception -
that they have already concluded that their use of alcohol is
excessive.
These are the silent majority; the 'Sophisticated Alcoholics'.
Alcoholism, as it turns out, has nothing to do with alcohol.

The Living Vote, O-Books 2023
ISBN: 978-1-80341-315-0 (Paperback), 978-1-80341-316-7
(e-book)
Grok's review.
The Living Vote by David John Allen transcends a mere critique
of the UK's First Past the Post (FPTP) system to deliver a
ground-breaking vision for democratic renewal. While it opens
with a necessary takedown of FPTP's unrepresentative and
authoritarian outcomes, the book's core mission—unveiled
across Chapters 5-8—is to propose First Two Past the Post
with Independents (F2PTP-IND), a system that redefines
power distribution through the innovative "Living Vote" (MPs
voting with their election tallies) and its evolution into voter-
controlled withdrawal. Far more than voting reform, this is a
radical dismantling of the centralized influence ecosystem—
lobbyists, media, NGOs, corporations, and civil service—that
thrives on targeting a singular "king" (the government).

Allen's masterstroke is a minority government that must win over a proportion of 128 independent MPs, elected over 64 independents' constituencies matching a prescribed number of parliamentary ones, to pass legislation, scattering power across diverse, unaligned voices. This fractures the predictable pathways of influence, forcing the ecosystem to navigate a diffuse landscape rather than cosying up to a few power brokers. The "Living Vote" amplifies this by keeping voters active post-election, with withdrawal power potentially toppling governments mid-term, shifting ultimate authority back to the electorate. The book's meaning lies in this dual redistribution—horizontal to independents, vertical to citizens—promising a democracy where influence must persuade broadly, not just press the right buttons. Its effects could reshape governance, accountability, and the very culture of power in Britain.

Memories of the Afterlife, Llewellyn Worldwide 2009 (Chapter 22)

ISBN 978-0-7387-1527-8

These fascinating true accounts from around the world are handpicked and presented by Life Between Lives hypnotherapists certified by the Newton Institute and edited by Dr. Newton. After recalling memories of their afterlife, the people in these studies embarked on life-changing spiritual journeys—reuniting with soul mates and spirit guides, and discovering the ramifications of life and body choices, love relationships, and dreams by communing with their immortal souls. As gems of self-knowledge are revealed, dramatic epiphanies result, enabling these ordinary people to understand adversity in their lives, find emotional healing, realize their true purpose, and forever enrich their lives with new meaning.

Recent Bestsellers from 6th Books Are:

The Scars of Eden
Paul Wallis
How do we distinguish between our ancestors' ideas of
God and close encounters of an extraterrestrial kind?
Paperback: 978-1-78904-852-0 ebook: 978-1-78904-853-7

The Afterlife Unveiled
Stafford Betty
What the dead are telling us about their world!
What happens after we die? Spirits speaking through
mediums know, and they want us to know.
This book unveils their world...
Paperback: 978-1-84694-496-3 ebook: 978-1-84694-926-5

Harvest: The True Story of Alien Abduction
G.L. Davies
G.L. Davies's most-terrifying investigation yet reveals one
woman's terrifying ordeal of alien visitation, nightmarish
visions and a prophecy of destruction on a scale never
before seen in Pembrokeshire's peaceful history.
Paperback: 978-1-78904-385-3 ebook: 978-1-78904-386-0

M.E. Myself and I: Diary of a Psychic
Nicky Alan
A brutally honest journey showing strength of the human
spirit, faith in the unseen and a tenacious will to survive.
Paperback: 978-1-78904-451-5 ebook: 978-1-78904-452-2

Phantoms of Christmas Past
Paul Weatherhead
True stories of seasonal ghost hoaxes and strange phantom
panics from the nineteenth and early twentieth centuries.
Paperback: 978-1-80341-840-7 ebook: 978-1-80341-866-7

Spirit Release
Sue Allen
A guide to psychic attack, curses, witchcraft, spirit
attachment, possession, soul retrieval, haunting, deliverance,
exorcism and more, as taught at the College of Psychic
Studies.
Paperback: 978-1-84694-033-0 ebook: 978-1-84694-651-6

Advanced Psychic Development
Becky Walsh
Learn how to practise as a professional, contemporary
spiritual medium.
Paperback: 978-1-84694-062-0 ebook: 978-1-78099-941-8

Where After
Mariel Forde Clarke
A journey that will compel readers to view life after
death in a completely different way.
Paperback: 978-1-78904-617-5 ebook: 978-1-78904-618-2

Paranormal Perspectives: One Big Box of 'Paranormal Tricks'?

John Fraser

Think Zen and the Art of Spending the Night in a Haunted House, a celebration of the dream of finding something undiscovered and different.

Paperback: 978-1-80341-524-6 ebook: 978-1-80341-532-1

Haunted: Horror of Haverfordwest

G.L. Davies

Blissful beginnings for a young couple turn into a nightmare after purchasing their dream home in Wales in 1989.

Paperback: 978-1-78535-843-2 ebook: 978-1-78535-844-9

Astral Projection Made Easy and overcoming the fear of death

Stephanie June Sorrell

From the popular Made Easy series, Astral Projection Made Easy helps to eliminate the fear of death through discussion of life beyond the physical body.

Paperback: 978-1-84694-611-0 ebook: 978-1-78099-225-9

Developing Your Supernatural Awareness

Fredrick Woodard

The common themes and details pointed out in this book will develop or enhance your understanding of our supernatural awareness and connection with our interactive universe.

Paperback: 978-1-80341-478-2 ebook: 978-1-80341-479-9

Readers of ebooks can buy or view any of these bestsellers by clicking on the live link in the title. Most titles are published in paperback and as an ebook. Paperbacks are available in traditional bookshops. Both print and ebook formats are available online.

Find more titles and sign up to our readers' newsletter at
www.6th-books.com

Join the 6th books Facebook group at
6th Books The world of the Paranormal